Merriam-Webster's Spanish-English VISUAL Dictionary

Under the direction of
Jean-Claude Corbeil

Merriam-Webster, Incorporated

Springfield, Massachusetts

USA

Merriam-Webster Inc.

www.Merriam-Webster.com
www.VisualDictionaryOnline.com

Merriam-Webster's Spanish-English Visual Dictionary

was created and produced by

QA International, a division of
Les Éditions Québec Amérique Inc.
7240, Saint-Hubert Street
Montreal, Quebec, Canada H2R 2N1
T +1 514.499.3000 F +1 514.499.3010
www.ikonet.com
www.qa-international.com

Published by Merriam-Webster Inc. 2011
© 2011 QA International.
All rights reserved.

ISBN: 978-0-87779-292-5

Original French terminology developed
by Jean-Claude Corbeil
and Ariane Archambault

Printed in India.
14 13 12 11 10 9 8 7 6   25 24 23 22
847 version 4.0.0

ACKNOWLEDGEMENTS

Our deepest gratitude to the individuals, institutions, companies, and businesses that have provided us with the latest technical documentation for use in preparing this edition of the *Visual*.

Canadian Space Agency (Réjean Lemieux, Danièle Laroque, Antoinette Cickello); Claude Arsenault (president, Association des moulins du Québec); Michel Ballarin (soccer coach); Pierre Boulé (president, Confort Expert); Centre de formation professionnelle de Sorel-Tracy (Alain Boucher, Jacques Doyon, Andrée-Anne Martin); Pierre Chastenay (Montréal Planetarium); Ève Christian (meteorologist); Luc Cockenpot (Institut du tourisme et de l'hôtellerie du Québec); Jacques Dancosse (Montréal Biodome); Patrice Desbiens (nuclear engineer); Laval Dupuis (École des métiers de l'équipement motorisé de Montréal); Entreprise Garant (Julie Nolet, Stéphanie Lacroix); Fédération de basketball de France (Julien Guérineau); Quebec Basketball Federation (Daniel Grimard, Isabelle Watier); Fédération d'haltérophilie du Québec (Augustin Brassard); Caroline Gagné (Studio du Verre); Jacqueline Goy (Institut océanographique de Paris); Christian Guibourt (technical director, Badminton Québec); Michel J. Houle (Hewitt); Hydro-Québec (terminology); Robert Lacerte (sports commentator, Radio-Canada); Robert Lamontagne (Université de Montréal); Lozeau (Alexandre Gagné, Frédéric Montpetit); Olivier-Louis Robert (science journalist); Iris Sautier (silk screen printing); Société Radio-Canada, Service linguistique et Direction générale des communications et images de marque (Annie Nociti Dubois, assistant, internal and institutional communications); Gilles Taillon (executive director, Baseball Québec); Pierre Turcotte (agronomist-phytogenetics specialist).

PUBLISHER

QA International, a division of
Les Éditions Québec Amérique Inc.
President and CEO: Jacques Fortin
Vice-president: Caroline Fortin

Editorial Director: Martine Podesto
Artistic Director: Johanne Plante

EDITORIAL STAFF

Editor-in-Chief: Anne Rouleau
Editorial Assistants:
Myriam Caron Belzile
Jeanne Dompierre
Catherine Gendreau

TERMINOLOGICAL RESEARCH

Terminology Advisor: Jean-Claude Corbeil
Sophie Ballarin
Carole Brunet
Hélène Mainville
Kathe Roth
Locordia Communications

ILLUSTRATIONS

Senior Illustrator: Anouk Noël
Manuela Bertoni
Marthe Boisjoly
Érica Charest
Jocelyn Gardner
Guillaume Grégoire
Anik Lafrenière
Alain Lemire
Raymond Martin
Jordi Vinals

PRODUCTION

Production Director: Claude Laporte
Print Manager: Salvatore Parisi

LAYOUT

Senior Graphic Artist: Pascal Goyette
Edgar Abarquez
Karine Lévesque
Fernando Salvador Marroquín
Julie Villemaire

PROGRAMMING

Senior Programmer: Gabriel Trudeau-St-Hilaire
Alex Gagnon
Ronald Santiago

DATA MANAGEMENT

Patrick Mercurc

LINGUISTIC REVISION

Liliane Michaud
Veronica Schami Editorial Services Inc.

PREPRESS

Benjamin Dubé
François Hénault

MERRIAM-WEBSTER EDITORS

Susan L. Brady
Daniel B. Brandon
Rebecca R. Bryer-
 Charette
Christopher C. Connor
Daniel J. Hopkins
Benjamin T. Korzec Joan

Joan I. Narmontas
Madeline L. Novak
Adrienne M. Scholz
Neil S. Serven
Kory L. Stamper
Mark A. Stevens
Linda P. Wood

CONTRIBUTIONS

QA International would like to extend a special thank you to the following people for their contribution to this work:
Jean-Yves Ahern, Danielle Bader, Stéphane Batigne, Jean Beaumont, Sylvain Bélanger, Pascal Bilodeau, Yan Bohler, Mélanie Boivin, Guy Bonin, Catherine Briand, Julie Cailliau, Jessie Daigle, Serge D'Amico, François Fortin, Éric Gagnon, Hélène Gauthier, Mélanie Giguère-Gilbert, Benoît Grégoire, Nathalie Guillo, Martin Lemieux, Rielle Lévesque, Véronique Loranger, Émilie McMahon, Philippe Mendes Campeau, Tony O'Riley, Carl Pelletier, Sylvain Robichaud, Michel Rouleau, Claude Thivierge, François Turcotte-Goulet, Gilles Vézina, Kathleen Wynd.

Québec Amérique would also like to acknowledge the contribution of Jean-Claude Corbeil and Ariane Archambault, authors of the original French terminology of the *Visual*, who were also played a key role in defining the table of contents and overseeing the development and evolution of the three first editions of the publication.

Introduction

Merriam-Webster's Spanish-English Visual Dictionary is designed to meet the needs of users who speak, are learning, or need to understand words in Spanish or English. Every image in the dictionary is named in both languages to help users identify and understand a particular object and words associated with that object or its parts. In addition, the dictionary can serve as a vocabulary-building resource for both of the languages, as users will find vocabulary they need to master in regard to many aspects of life, such as food, clothing, transportation, science, and sports. The title of every section is also given in both English and Spanish, and the Index includes both English and Spanish terms to make it useful to speakers of both English and Spanish.

The aim of this dictionary has been to bring together in one volume the technical and everyday terms required to understand the contemporary world and the specialized fields that shape our daily experience. In effect, it provides an inventory of our physical environment for users who need to know and understand general and specialized terms in a wide variety of fields.

The history of the _Visual Dictionary_

Merriam-Webster's Spanish-English Visual Dictionary is based on the new fourth edition of QA International's _Visual Dictionary_, published on the 25th anniversary of the publication of the first edition of this reference work in 1986. The idea for this dictionary began with a fortuitous meeting between editor Jacques Fortin and linguist Jean-Claude Corbeil in 1982 in Paris. The meeting spawned the development of an original project that brought together a team of terminologists, linguists, researchers, translators, and illustrators, and culminated in the release of the first _Visual Thematic Dictionary_.

From the beginning, illustration was chosen over photography because of its ability to "bring out the most significant details of an object, purging the image of everything that is ancillary or accidental. ... The image appears simpler and more stripped down, gaining conceptual clarity for a better definition."

The growth of knowledge and technology over the past 25 years has also ushered in changes to the dictionary's contents. For example, the section on photography was entirely redesigned to take into account the growth of digital photography, and the section on the solar system was updated to present the new classification of celestial bodies.

Many subjects have also been expanded, often by illustrating previously little-known or non-existent objects (the touch screen smartphone, the tablet computer, etc.), or by introducing diagrams that explain phenomena or processes. And new subjects, such as the global positioning system (GPS), alternative fuels, and modern medical equipment, have also made an appearance.

To accomplish this, the number of illustrations has been increased,

1986

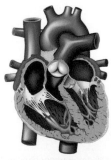

1992

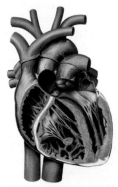

2011

bringing the total number to more than 8,000. Many other illustrations have been entirely redrawn or retouched to give them a more modern look. Another indication of the expanding wealth of information in the dictionary is the growth in the number of terms covered, with more than 4,000 new entries, bringing the total to nearly 25,000 in each language.

Structure of the Visual

This book has three sections: the front-matter pages, including the list of themes and the table of contents; the body of the text, that is, the detailed treatment of each theme; and the alphabetical index. Information is presented in hierarchical form, moving from the most abstract to the most concrete: theme, subtheme, title, subtitle, illustration, terminology.

The content of this book is divided into 18 THEMES, which are then divided into SUBTHEMES. For example, the theme *Astronomy* is divided into three subthemes: *Celestial bodies, Astronomical observation* and *Astronautics.* The TITLE has a variety of functions: to name the illustration of a unique object, of which the principal parts are identified (e.g. *exterior door*); and to bring together under one designation illustrations that belong to the same conceptual sphere but that represent a variety of elements, each with its own designations and terminology (e.g. the title *household appliances* brings together illustrations of a refrigerator, freezer, etc.). At times, the chief members of a class of objects are brought together under the same SUBTITLE, each with its own name but without a

detailed terminological analysis (e.g. the subtitle *armchair* brings together various types of armchairs).

Finally, the ILLUSTRATION shows realistically and precisely an object, a process, or a phenomenon, and the most significant details from which they are constructed. It serves as a visual definition of the term.

Terminology

Each word in the *Spanish-English Visual Dictionary* has been carefully selected after consulting authoritative sources reflecting the appropriate level of specialization. There may be cases where documented usage indicates that different terms are used to name the same item. In such instances, the word most frequently used by the most highly regarded authors has been chosen.

The INDEX lists all significant words in the dictionary in alphabetical order. Many terms have been grouped to make it easy to search for precise illustrations or words. For example, the terms *morphology of a bird* and *skeleton of a bird* have been grouped under *bird*, with a referral back to the corresponding pages in the book.

Methods of consultation

One may gain access to the contents of the *Spanish-English Visual Dictionary* in a variety of ways:

- Users can start from the list of THEMES at the end of the front-matter pages, or by using the detailed TABLE OF CONTENTS in the front matter and at the start of each theme.

- With the INDEX, users can find a word, so as to see what it corresponds to, or to examine the illustration that depicts it.

- Users can take advantage of the illustrations and hierarchical structure to enable them to find a word even if they have only a vague idea of what it is— a valuable feature when you don't know what word you are looking for.

6

Explanatory Chart

Subtheme
Themes are divided into subthemes.

Title
The title appears first in English and then in Spanish. If the title runs over a number of pages, it is printed in gray on subsequent pages and in English only.

Color reference
Each theme is identified by a color which appears on the edge of the page to facilitate quick access to each section in the book.

Theme
The name of the theme appears in English on each page. It appears in both Spanish and English on the opening page at the beginning of each theme.

Narrow lines
Narrow lines link the term to the item indicated. Where too many lines would make reading difficult, they have been replaced by color codes with captions or, in rare cases, by numbers.

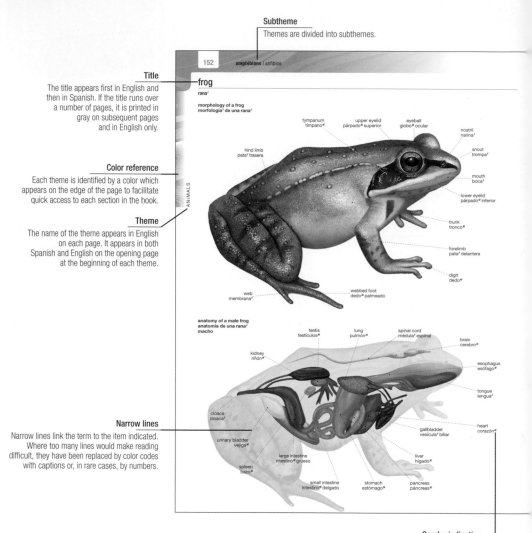

frog
rana*f*

morphology of a frog
morfología*f* de una rana*f*

tympanum / tímpano*m*
upper eyelid / párpado*m* superior
eyeball / globo*m* ocular
nostril / narina*f*
hind limb / pata*f* trasera
snout / trompa*f*
mouth / boca*f*
lower eyelid / párpado*m* inferior
trunk / tronco*m*
forelimb / pata*f* delantera
digit / dedo*m*
web / membrana*f*
webbed foot / dedo*m* palmeado

ANIMALS

anatomy of a male frog
anatomía*f* de una rana*f* macho

testis / testículos*m*
lung / pulmón*m*
spinal cord / médula*f* espinal
brain / cerebro*m*
kidney / riñón*m*
esophagus / esófago*m*
tongue / lengua*f*
cloaca / cloaca*f*
heart / corazón*m*
gallbladder / vesícula*f* biliar
urinary bladder / vejiga*f*
liver / hígado*m*
spleen / bazo*m*
large intestine / intestino*m* grueso
small intestine / intestino*m* delgado
stomach / estómago*m*
pancreas / páncreas*m*

Gender indication
F: feminine
M: masculine
The gender is indicated for each word in Spanish. Names for functions that can be fulfilled equally by a man or a woman can often be of either gender. In these cases, the gender assigned to the word depends on the gender of the character depicted in the illustration.

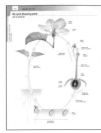

Diagram

More abstract natural phenomena or processes are represented by descriptive diagrams. Colored arrows indicate links between the various elements of the diagram.

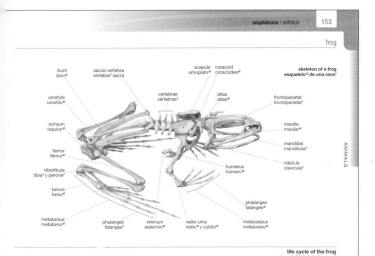

frog

skeleton of a frog
esqueleto*M* de una rana*F*

ilium
ilion*M*

sacral vertebra
vértebra*F* sacra

scapula
omoplato*M*

coracoid
coracoides*M*

urostyle
urostilo*M*

vertebrae
vértebras*F*

atlas
atlas*M*

frontoparietal
frontoparietal*F*

ischium
isquion*M*

maxilla
maxilar*M*

mandible
mandíbula*F*

femur
fémur*M*

clavicle
clavícula*F*

tibiofibula
tibia*F* y peroné*F*

humerus
húmero*M*

tarsus
tarso*M*

phalanges
falanges*M*

metatarsus
metatarso*M*

phalanges
falanges*F*

sternum
esternón*M*

radio-ulna
radio*M* y cúbito*M*

metacarpus
metacarpo*M*

ANIMALS

life cycle of the frog
metamórfosis*F* de la rana*F*

eggs
huevos*M*

tadpole
renacuajo*M*

hind limb
extremidad*F* posterior

external gills
branquias*F* externas

operculum
opérculo*M*

forelimb
extremidad*F* delantera

examples of amphibians
ejemplos*M* de anfibios*M*

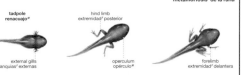

salamander
salamandra*F*

wood frog
rana*F* de bosque*M*

common toad
sapo*M* común

common frog
rana*F* bermeja

tree frog
rana*F* arborícola

newt
tritón*M*

bullfrog
rana*F* toro*M*

Northern leopard frog
rana*F* leopardo*M*

adhesive disk
ventosa*F*

Illustration

The illustration serves as the visual identification for the terms associated with it.

Subtitle

The subtitle groups together illustrations representing members of the same class of objects.

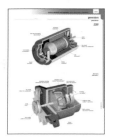

Section

In certain cases, where highlighting a portion of the inner parts of the illustrated object has been deemed relevant, blue lines have been traced over the cut lines to avoid any confusion about the true appearance of the object.

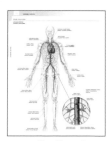

Magnifier and zoom

The magnifier and zoom feature enlarges certain areas of a complex illustration to facilitate viewing of its major parts.

Contents

ASTRONOMY 12

Celestial bodies..........14
solar system, planets, satellites and dwarf planets, Sun, Moon, meteorite, comet, star, galaxy

Astronomical observation..........20
planetarium, constellations of the Southern Hemisphere, constellations of the Northern Hemisphere, celestial coordinate system, refracting telescope, reflecting telescope, radio telescope, space telescope, astronomical observatory

Astronautics..........30
space probe, spacesuit, international space station, spaceship, space launcher

EARTH 40

Geography..........42
Earth coordinate system, azimuthal projection, configuration of the continents, physical cartography, political cartography, remote sensing

Geology..........66
structure of the Earth, Earth features, geological phenomena, minerals

Meteorology..........79
profile of the Earth's atmosphere, seasons of the year, meteorological forecast, weather map, station model, international weather symbols, meteorological station, meteorological measuring instruments, weather satellites, climates of the world, clouds, tornado and waterspout, tropical cyclone, precipitation

Environment..........92
vegetation regions, types of vegetation, food chain, structure of the biosphere, hydrologic cycle, carbon-oxygen cycle, natural greenhouse effect, enhanced greenhouse effect, air pollution, land pollution, water pollution, acid rain, selective sorting of waste

PLANTS AND PLANTLIKE ORGANISMS 100

Plant life..........102
plant cell, photosynthesis, unusual plants, life cycle (flowering plant), plant growth

Plants & plantlike organisms..........106
lichen, moss, plants & plantlike organisms, fern, mushroom

Plant..........109
parts of a plant, root, stem, leaf, flower, fruit, grape, tree, conifer

Industrial use..........122
grain industry, textile industry, rubber industry, paper industry

ANIMALS 126

Evolution of life..........128
origin and evolution of species, biological taxonomy

Simple organisms..........133
animal cell, unicellular organisms, sponge, jellyfish, starfish, examples of simple organisms

Mollusks..........136
univalve shell, bivalve shell, snail, octopus

Crustaceans..........139
lobster

Insects and arachnids..........140
butterfly, honeybee, spider, examples of insects, examples of arachnids

Cartilaginous fishes..........148
shark, examples of cartilaginous fishes

Bony fishes..........149
perch, examples of bony fishes

Amphibians..........152
frog, examples of amphibians

Reptiles..........154
snake, turtle, examples of reptiles

Birds..........158
bird, examples of aquatic birds and shorebirds, examples of land birds

Insectivorous mammals..........164
mole, examples of insectivorous mammals

Rodents..........165
rat, examples of rodents

Lagomorphs..........167
rabbit, examples of lagomorphs

Ungulate mammals..........168
horse, examples of hooves, examples of ungulate mammals

Carnivorous mammals..........174
dog, examples of dog breeds, cat, examples of cat breeds, examples of carnivorous mammals

Marine mammals..........182
dolphin, examples of marine mammals

Primates..........184
gorilla, examples of primates

Flying mammals..........186
bat, examples of flying mammals

Marsupials..........188
kangaroo, examples of marsupials

HUMAN BEING 190

Human body..........192
man, woman

Anatomy..........196
muscles, skeleton, teeth, joints, blood circulation, respiratory system, digestive system, urinary system, nervous system, reproductive system, endocrine system, lymphatic system

Sense organs..........231
smell and taste, hearing, touch, sight

FOOD AND KITCHEN 240

Supply..........242
origin of food, farmstead

Plant-derived food..........244
mushrooms, seaweed, bulb vegetables, tuber vegetables, leaf vegetables, fruit vegetables, stalk vegetables, root vegetables, inflorescence vegetables, legumes, fruits, spices, herbs, cereals, coffee and infusions

Animal-derived food..........265
mollusks, crustaceans, marine fishes, freshwater fishes, fish presentation, eggs, meat

Processed food 277
delicatessen, cereal products, dairy products, pasta, Asian noodles, rice,
soybean products, fats and oils, sugar, chocolate, condiments

Food business 288
supermarket, restaurant, self-service restaurant, food presentation

Kitchen 296
kitchen: general view

Tableware 297
glassware, knife, spoon, fork, silverware accessories, dinnerware, place
setting

Kitchen equipment 306
kitchen utensils, cooking utensils, small domestic appliances

HOUSE   320

Location 322
exterior of a house, pool

Elements of a house 325
exterior door, lock, window

Structure of a house 328
site plan, main rooms, frame, roof truss, foundation, wood flooring, textile
floor coverings, stairs

Heating 336
wood firing, forced warm-air system, forced hot-water system, auxiliary
heating, heat pump

Air conditioning 342
control devices, air-conditioning appliances

Plumbing 344
plumbing system, pedestal-type sump pump, septic tank, bathroom,
toilet, water-heater tank, faucets, fittings, examples of branching

Electricity 354
distribution panel, electricity meter, network connection, contact devices,
lighting

House furnishings 360
armchair, side chair, seats, table, bed, storage furniture, children's
furniture, window accessories, lights, home appliances, household
equipment

DO-IT-YOURSELF AND GARDENING   382

Materials 384
basic building materials, covering materials, insulating materials, wood

Carpentry 387
accessories, measuring and marking tools, nailing tools, screwdriving
tools, sawing tools, drilling tools, shaping tools, gripping and tightening
tools

Plumbing and masonry 402
plumbing tools, masonry tools

Electricity 404
electrical tools

Soldering 406
soldering tools

Painting upkeep 408
painting material

Ladders and stepladders 409
ladders, stepladders

Pleasure garden 410
garden

Yard and garden equipment 411
miscellaneous equipment, tools for loosening the earth, watering tools,
pruning and cutting tools, hand tools, seeding and planting tools, lawn
care

Snow removal 421
snow removal tools

CLOTHING   422

Textiles 424
fibers, woven goods, fabric care symbols

Historical clothes 426
examples of ancient costumes, examples of traditional clothing

Men's clothing 430
jackets, shirt, pants, sock, underwear, coats

Unisex clothing 437
sweaters

Women's clothing 438
dresses, skirts, tops, pants, jackets, vest and sweaters, coats, underwear,
hose, nightclothes

Specialty clothing 448
children's clothing, sportswear

Design and finishing 452
pockets, sleeves, pleats, collars, necks, necklines

Headgear 457
men's headgear, women's headgear, unisex headgear

Shoes 459
men's shoes, women's shoes, unisex shoes, accessories

Dress accessories 464
gloves, miscellaneous accessories

PERSONAL ACCESSORIES AND ARTICLES   466

Personal accessories 468
jewelry, nail care, makeup, body care, hairdressing

Personal articles 479
shaving, eyeglasses, contact lenses, dental care, smoking accessories,
leather goods, handbags, luggage, umbrella and stick, child care, pet care

ARTS AND ARCHITECTURE   496

Ancient architecture 498
pyramid, Greek theater, Greek temple, architectural styles, Roman house,
Roman amphitheater

Military architecture 504
castle, Vauban fortification

Western architecture 506
Gothic cathedral, Romanesque church, Renaissance villa, Baroque
church, art deco building, international style skyscraper

Asian and pre-Columbian architecture 513
pagoda, Aztec temple

Elements of architecture 514
examples of arches, examples of doors, examples of roofs, examples of
windows, escalator, elevator

Housing 520
traditional houses, city houses

Fine arts 522
museum, painting and drawing, wood carving

Graphic arts 532
printing, relief printing process, intaglio printing process, lithography, screen printing, fine bookbinding

Performing arts 540
theater, movie set, movie theater

Music 545
symphony orchestra, examples of instrumental groups, stringed instruments, wind instruments, keyboard instruments, percussion instruments, electronic music, traditional musical instruments, musical notation, musical accessories

Crafts 565
embroidery, sewing, knitting, weaving, pottery, bobbin lace, stained glass

COMMUNICATIONS   580

Languages of the world 582
major language families

Written communication 584
writing, typography, symbols, postal service network, newspaper

Photography 591
film cameras, films, film reflex camera, digital non-reflex cameras, digital reflex camera, memory cards, batteries, photographic accessories, lenses, digital photo management, film processing, transparency viewing

Telecommunications 602
broadcast satellite communication, telecommunication satellites, telecommunications by satellite

Radio 604
studio and control room, microphones and accessories

Television 605
program production, television reception, camcorders

Sound reproducing system 614
elements of a sound reproducing system, mini stereo sound system, portable sound systems

Wireless communication 621
walkie-talkie, numeric pager, CB radio

Telephony 622
cellular telephone, examples of telephones

OFFICE AUTOMATION   626

Computing equipment 628
all-in-one computer, tower case computer, laptop computer, connection devices, connecting cables, input devices, output devices, data storage devices, protection devices, miscellaneous computer tools

Networking 640
examples of networks, Internet, Internet uses

Office 644
office organization, office furniture, photocopier, stationery

TRANSPORT AND MACHINERY   656

Road transport 658
road system, fixed bridges, movable bridges, road tunnel, road signs

Automotive road transport 668
service station, automobile, electric automobile, hybrid automobile, brakes, types of engines, radiator, spark plug, tire, battery, accessories, campers, bus, trucking, motorcycle, 4x4 all-terrain vehicle

Cycling road transport 698
bicycle

Rail transport 703
railroad station, passenger station, types of passenger cars, diesel-electric locomotive, high-speed train, yard, freight car, railroad track, crossing gate

Urban rail transport 714
subway, streetcar

Maritime transport 718
harbor, canal lock, ancient ships, traditional ships, examples of sails, examples of rigs, four-masted bark, examples of boats and ships, anchor, life-saving equipment, navigation devices, maritime signals, maritime buoyage system

Air transport 740
airport, long-range jet, examples of airplanes, examples of tail shapes, examples of wing shapes, movements of an airplane, forces acting on an airplane, helicopter, examples of helicopters

Material handling 754
typical devices, cranes, container

Heavy machinery 758
bulldozer, backhoe loader, scraper, power shovel, grader, dump truck, asphalt paver, road roller, snowblower, street sweeper, tractor, agricultural machinery

ENERGY   768

Geothermal energy 770
production of electricity from geothermal energy, geothermal house

Fossil energy 771
coal mine, thermal energy, oil, natural gas, alternative fuel

Hydroelectricity 785
hydroelectric complex, steps in production of electricity, examples of dams, electricity transmission, tidal power plant

Nuclear energy 795
production of electricity from nuclear energy, nuclear generating station, fuel handling sequence, fuel bundle, nuclear reactor, types of reactors

Solar energy 802
solar cell, flat-plate solar collector, solar cell system, solar furnace, production of electricity from solar energy, solar house

Wind energy 806
windmills, wind turbines and electricity production

SCIENCE   808

Chemistry 810
matter, chemical elements, laboratory equipment

Physics: mechanics 816
gearing systems, double pulley system, lever

Physics: electricity and magnetism 817
magnetism, electrical circuit, generators, dry cells, electronics

Physics: optics 821
electromagnetic spectrum, wave, color synthesis, light waves trajectory, lenses, mirror, optical devices

Measuring devices 827
measure of temperature, measure of time, measure of weight, measure of distance, measure of thickness, measure of length, measure of angles

Scientific symbols 834
chemistry, biology, International System of Units (SI), Roman numerals, geometry, mathematics, graphic representations

SOCIETY 840

City 842
metropolitan area, downtown, street, office building, shopping mall,
department store, convention center, hotel, common symbols

Economy and finance 858
bank branch, examples of currency abbreviations, money and modes of
payment

Justice 862
court, prison

Education 866
library, school

SPORTS AND GAMES 930

Sports facilities 932
sports complex, scoreboard, competition

Track and field 934
track and field, jumping, throwing

Ball sports 938
baseball, softball, cricket, field hockey, soccer, lacrosse, rugby, football,
Canadian football, netball, basketball, volleyball, team handball

Racket sports 961
table tennis, badminton, racquetball, squash, tennis

Gymnastics 969
gymnastics, rhythmic gymnastics, trampoline

Aquatic and nautical sports 974
water polo, swimming, diving, sailing, sailboard, rowing and sculling,
canoe, canoe-kayak: flatwater racing, kayak, waterskiing, surfing, scuba
diving

Combat sports 990
boxing, wrestling, judo, karate, taekwondo, kendo, sumo, kung fu, jujitsu,
aikido, fencing

Strength sports 999
weightlifting, fitness equipment

Equestrian sports 1002
show jumping, riding, dressage, horse racing, polo

Precision and accuracy sports 1009
archery, shotgun shooting, rifle shooting, pistol shooting, billiards, lawn
bowling, pétanque, bowling, golf

Cycling 1020
road racing, mountain biking, track cycling, BMX

Motor sports 1022
auto racing, motorcycling, personal watercraft, snowmobile

Winter sports 1027
curling, ice hockey, figure skating, speed skating, bobsled, luge, skeleton,
sliding track, ski resort, snowboarding, alpine skiing, freestyle skiing, ski
jumping, speed skiing, cross-country skiing, biathlon, snowshoeing

Sports on wheels 1044
skateboarding, in-line skating

Aerial sports 1046
parachuting, hang gliding, glider, ballooning

Mountain sports 1050
mountaineering

Outdoor leisure 1052
camping, knots, fishing

Games 1062
dice and dominoes, playing cards, board games, jigsaw puzzle, mah-
jongg, video games, roulette, darts, soccer table, slot machine, Ultimate,
pinball machine, kite

ASTRONOMY	12
EARTH	40
PLANTS AND PLANTLIKE ORGANISMS	100
ANIMALS	126
HUMAN BEING	190
FOOD AND KITCHEN	240
HOUSE	320
DO-IT-YOURSELF AND GARDENING	382
CLOTHING	422
PERSONAL ACCESSORIES AND ARTICLES	466
ARTS AND ARCHITECTURE	496
COMMUNICATIONS	580
OFFICE AUTOMATION	626
TRANSPORT AND MACHINERY	656
ENERGY	768
SCIENCE	808
SOCIETY	840
SPORTS AND GAMES	930
INDEX	1072

ASTRONOMY

astronomía

CELESTIAL BODIES — 14

solar system	14
planets, satellites and dwarf planets	14
Sun	16
Moon	17
meteorite	18
comet	18
star	18
galaxy	19

ASTRONOMICAL OBSERVATION — 20

planetarium	20
constellations of the Southern Hemisphere	20
constellations of the Northern Hemisphere	22
celestial coordinate system	23
refracting telescope	24
reflecting telescope	25
radio telescope	26
space telescope	27
astronomical observatory	28

ASTRONAUTICS — 30

space probe	30
spacesuit	33
international space station	34
spaceship	36
space launcher	39

solar system

sistema^M solar

outer planets
planetas^M externos

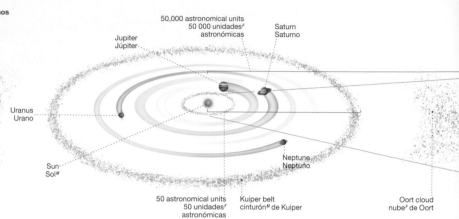

50,000 astronomical units
50 000 unidades^F
astronómicas

Saturn
Saturno

Jupiter
Júpiter

Uranus
Urano

Sun
Sol^M

Neptune
Neptuno

50 astronomical units
50 unidades^F
astronómicas

Kuiper belt
cinturón^M de Kuiper

Oort cloud
nube^F de Oort

planets, satellites and dwarf planets

planetas^M, satélites^M y plutoides^M

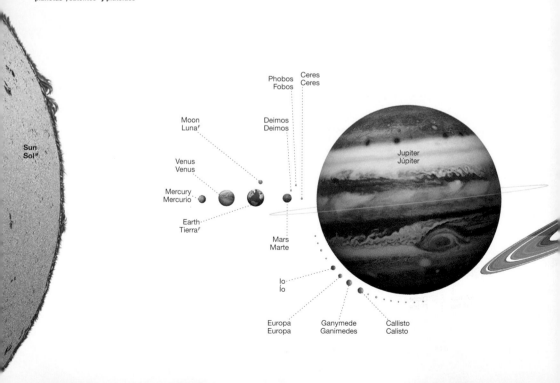

Sun
Sol^M

Phobos
Fobos

Ceres
Ceres

Moon
Luna^F

Deimos
Deimos

Venus
Venus

Jupiter
Júpiter

Mercury
Mercurio

Earth
Tierra^F

Mars
Marte

Io
Ío

Europa
Europa

Ganymede
Ganimedes

Callisto
Calisto

solar system

inner planets
planetasᴹ internos

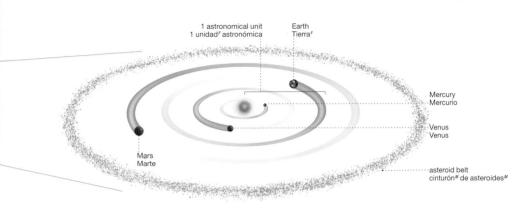

1 astronomical unit
1 unidadᶠ astronómica

Earth
Tierraᶠ

Mercury
Mercurio

Venus
Venus

Mars
Marte

asteroid belt
cinturónᴹ de asteroidesᴹ

planets, satellites and dwarf planets

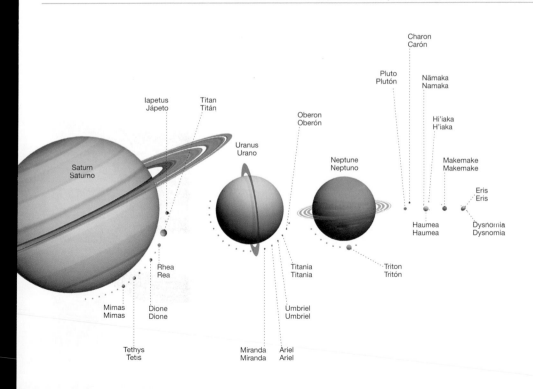

Charon
Carón

Pluto
Plutón

Nāmaka
Namaka

Iapetus
Jápeto

Titan
Titán

Oberon
Oberón

Hi'iaka
H'iaka

Uranus
Urano

Neptune
Neptuno

Makemake
Makemake

Saturn
Saturno

Eris
Eris

Haumea
Haumea

Dysnomia
Dysnomia

Rhea
Rea

Titania
Titania

Triton
Tritón

Mimas
Mimas

Dione
Dione

Umbriel
Umbriel

Tethys
Tetis

Miranda
Miranda

Ariel
Ariel

Sun

Sol[M]

structure of the Sun
estructura[F] del Sol[M]

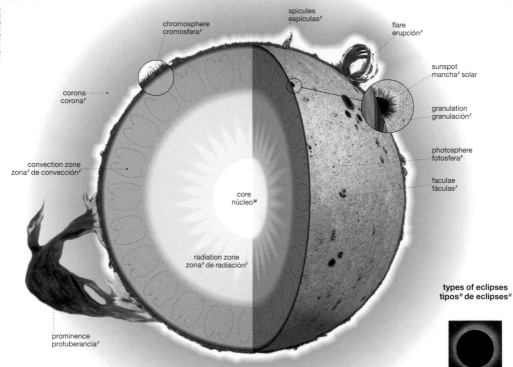

chromosphere
cromosfera[F]

spicules
espículas[F]

flare
erupción[F]

sunspot
mancha[F] solar

granulation
granulación[F]

corona
corona[F]

photosphere
fotosfera[F]

faculae
fáculas[F]

convection zone
zona[F] de convección[F]

core
núcleo[M]

radiation zone
zona[F] de radiación[F]

prominence
protuberancia[F]

types of eclipses
tipos[M] de eclipses[M]

annular eclipse
eclipse[M] anular

solar eclipse
eclipse[M] solar

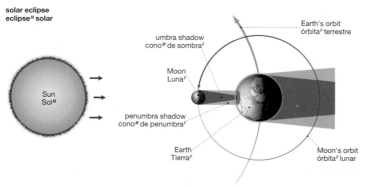

umbra shadow
cono[M] de sombra[F]

Moon
Luna[F]

Earth's orbit
órbita[F] terrestre

Sun
Sol[M]

penumbra shadow
cono[M] de penumbra[F]

Earth
Tierra[F]

Moon's orbit
órbita[F] lunar

partial eclipse
eclipse[M] parcial

total eclipse
eclipse[M] total

Moon
Luna[F]

ASTRONOMY

types of eclipses
tipos[M] de eclipses[M]

partial eclipse
eclipse[M] parcial

total eclipse
eclipse[M] total

lunar features
superficie[F] lunar

cliff
risco[M]

bay
bahía[F]

crater
cráter[M]

ocean
océano[M]

cirque
circo[M]

crater ray
estela[F] luminosa del
cráter[M]

lake
lago[M]

highland
continente[M]

sea
mar[M]

mountain range
cordillera[F]

wall
muro[M]

lunar eclipse
eclipse[M] de Luna[F]

Earth's orbit
órbita[F] terrestre

Sun
Sol[M]

Earth
Tierra[F]

Moon's orbit
órbita[F] lunar

Moon
Luna[F]

umbra shadow
cono[M] de sombra[F]

penumbra shadow
cono[M] de penumbra[F]

phases of the Moon
fases[F] de la Luna[F]

new moon
Luna[F] nueva

new crescent
Luna[F] creciente

first quarter
cuarto[M] creciente

waxing gibbous
quinto octante[M]

full moon
Luna[F] llena

waning gibbous
tercer octante[M]

last quarter
cuarto[M] menguante

old crescent
Luna[F] menguante

ASTRONOMY

meteorite
meteorito[M]

**stony meteorites
meteoritos[M] pétreos**

**iron meteorite
meteorito[M] ferroso**

**stony-iron meteorite
meteorito[M] pétreo-
ferroso**

**chondrite
condrito[M]**

**achondrite
acondrito[M]**

comet
cometa[M]

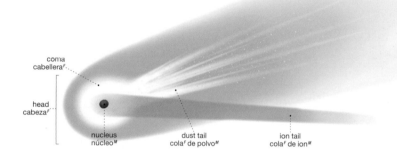

coma
cabellera[F]

head
cabeza[F]

nucleus
núcleo[M]

dust tail
cola[F] de polvo[M]

ion tail
cola[F] de ion[M]

star
estrella[F]

**low-mass stars
estrellas[F] de baja
magnitud[F]**

**massive stars
estrellas[F] de alta
magnitud[F]**

**supernova
supernova[F]**

**black hole
agujero[M] negro**

**red giant
gigante[F] roja**

**brown dwarf
enana[F] parda**

**black dwarf
enana[F] negra**

**white dwarf
enana[F] blanca**

**pulsar
pulsar[M]**

**planetary nebula
nebulosa[F] planetaria**

**nova
nova[F]**

**main-sequence star
estrella[F] de secuencia[F]
principal**

**neutron star
estrella[F] de neutrones[M]**

**supergiant
supergigante[M]**

galaxy
galaxia^f

Hubble's classification
clasificación^f de Hubble

Milky Way
Vía^f Láctea

elliptical galaxy
galaxia^f elíptica

lenticular galaxy
galaxia^f lenticular

normal spiral galaxy
galaxia^f espiral normal

barred spiral galaxy
galaxia^f espiral barrada

type I irregular galaxy **type II irregular galaxy**
galaxia^f irregular de tipo^M I **galaxia^f irregular de tipo^M II**

Milky Way: seen from above
Vía^f Láctea: vista^f desde arriba^f

nucleus
núcleo^M

spiral arm
brazo^M espiral

Milky Way: side view
Vía^f Láctea : vista^f lateral

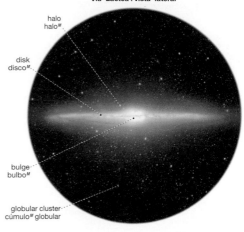

halo
halo^M

disk
disco^M

bulge
bulbo^M

globular cluster
cúmulo^M globular

ASTRONOMY

planetarium

planetario^M

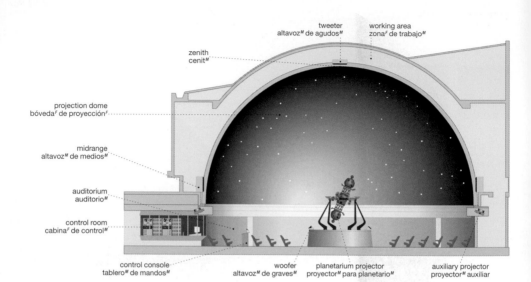

tweeter	working area
altavoz^M de agudos^M	zona^F de trabajo^M

zenith
cenit^M

projection dome
bóveda^F de proyección^F

midrange
altavoz^M de medios^M

auditorium
auditorio^M

control room
cabina^F de control^M

control console
tablero^M de mandos^M

woofer
altavoz^M de graves^M

planetarium projector
proyector^M para planetario^M

auxiliary projector
proyector^M auxiliar

constellations of the Southern Hemisphere

constelaciones^F del hemisferio^M austral

1	Cetus Ballena^F	8	Sculptor Taller^M de Escultor^M	15	Indus Indio^M	22	Ara Altar^M
2	Aquarius Acuario^M	9	Eridanus Erídano^M	16	Telescopium Telescopio^M	23	Triangulum Australe Triángulo^M Austral
3	Aquila Águila^F	10	Fornax Horno^M	17	Corona Australis Corona^F Austral	24	Apus Ave^F del Paraíso^M
4	Capricornus Capricornio^M	11	Horologium Reloj^M	18	Sagittarius Sagitario^M	25	Octans Octante^M
5	Microscopium Microscopio^M	12	Phoenix Fénix^M	19	Scutum Escudo^M	26	Hydrus Hidra^F macho
6	Pisces Austrinus Pez^M Austral	13	Tucana Tucán^M	20	Scorpius Escorpión^M	27	Mensa Mesa^F
7	Grus Grulla^M	14	Pavo Pavo^M	21	Norma Regla^F	28	Reticulum Retículo^M

constellations of the Southern Hemisphere

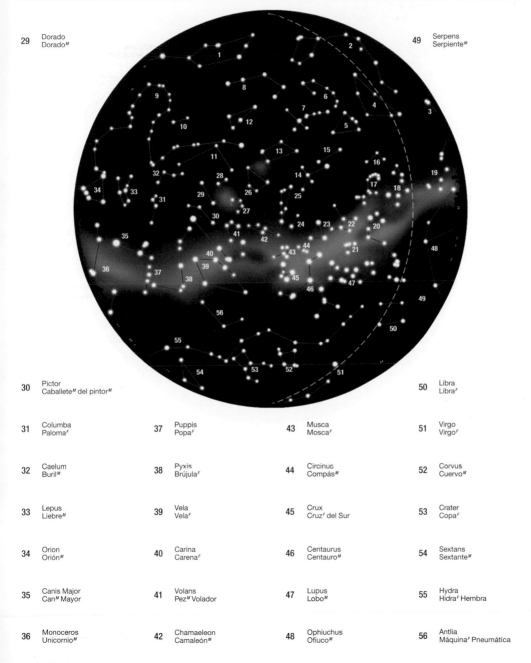

29 Dorado
Dorado^M

49 Serpens
Serpiente^M

30 Pictor
Caballete^M del pintor^M

50 Libra
Libra^F

31 Columba
Paloma^F

37 Puppis
Popa^F

43 Musca
Mosca^F

51 Virgo
Virgo^F

32 Caelum
Buril^M

38 Pyxis
Brújula^F

44 Circinus
Compás^M

52 Corvus
Cuervo^M

33 Lepus
Liebre^M

39 Vela
Vela^F

45 Crux
Cruz^F del Sur

53 Crater
Copa^F

34 Orion
Orión^M

40 Carina
Carena^F

46 Centaurus
Centauro^M

54 Sextans
Sextante^M

35 Canis Major
Can^M Mayor

41 Volans
Pez^M Volador

47 Lupus
Lobo^M

55 Hydra
Hidra^F Hembra

36 Monoceros
Unicornio^M

42 Chamaeleon
Camaleón^M

48 Ophiuchus
Ofiuco^M

56 Antlia
Máquina^F Pneumática

constellations of the Southern Hemisphere

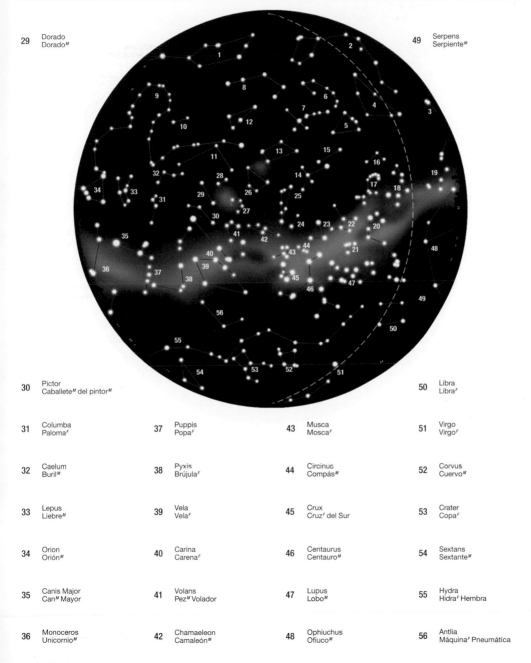

29 Dorado
Dorado[M]

49 Serpens
Serpiente[M]

30 Pictor
Caballete[M] del pintor[M]

50 Libra
Libra[F]

31 Columba
Paloma[F]

37 Puppis
Popa[F]

43 Musca
Mosca[F]

51 Virgo
Virgo[F]

32 Caelum
Buril[M]

38 Pyxis
Brújula[F]

44 Circinus
Compás[M]

52 Corvus
Cuervo[M]

33 Lepus
Liebre[M]

39 Vela
Vela[F]

45 Crux
Cruz[F] del Sur

53 Crater
Copa[F]

34 Orion
Orión[M]

40 Carina
Carena[F]

46 Centaurus
Centauro[M]

54 Sextans
Sextante[M]

35 Canis Major
Can[M] Mayor

41 Volans
Pez[M] Volador

47 Lupus
Lobo[M]

55 Hydra
Hidra[F] Hembra

36 Monoceros
Unicornio[M]

42 Chamaeleon
Camaleón[M]

48 Ophiuchus
Ofiuco[M]

56 Antlia
Máquina[F] Pneumática

constellations of the Northern Hemisphere

constelacionesʳ **del hemisferio**ᴹ **boreal**

1	Pisces Piscisᴹ						
2	Cetus Ballenaʳ	7	Equuleus Caballoᴹ Menor	12	Lacerta Lagartoᴹ	17	Orion Oriónᴹ
3	Aries Ariesᴹ	8	Delphinus Delfínᴹ	13	Cepheus Cefeoᴹ	18	Auriga Cocheroᴹ
4	Triangulum Triánguloᴹ	9	Aquila Águilaʳ	14	Cassiopeia Casiopeaʳ	19	Camelopardalis Jirafaʳ
5	Andromeda Andrómedaʳ	10	Sagitta Flechaʳ	15	Perseus Perseoᴹ	20	Lynx Linceᴹ
6	Pegasus Pegasoᴹ	11	Cygnus Cisneᴹ	16	Taurus Tauroᴹ	21	Ursa Minor Osaʳ Menor

constellations of the Northern hemisphere

22	Draco Dragón[M]	27	Corona Borealis Corona[F] Boreal	32	Ursa Major Osa[F] Mayor	37	Canis Minor Can[M] Menor
23	Lyra Lira[F]	28	Boötes Boyero[M]	33	Leo Minor León[M] Menor	38	Gemini Géminis[F]
24	Ophiuchus Ofiuco[M]	29	Virgo Virgo[F]	34	Leo León[M]	39	Vulpecula Zorra[F]
25	Hercules Hércules[M]	30	Coma Berenices Cabellera[F] de Berenice	35	Hydra Hidra[F] Hembra	40	Milky Way Vía[F] Láctea
26	Serpens Serpiente[F]	31	Canes Venatici Lebreles[M]	36	Cancer Cáncer[M]	41	North Star Estrella[F] Polar

celestial coordinate system

sistema[M] de coordenadas[F] astronómicas

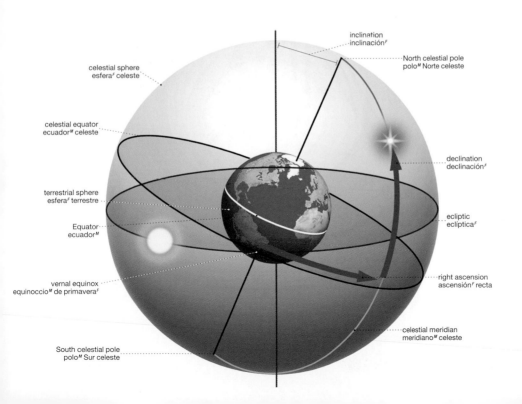

inclination
inclinación[F]

North celestial pole
polo[M] Norte celeste

celestial sphere
esfera[F] celeste

celestial equator
ecuador[M] celeste

declination
declinación[F]

terrestrial sphere
esfera[F] terrestre

ecliptic
eclíptica[F]

Equator
ecuador[M]

vernal equinox
equinoccio[M] de primavera[F]

right ascension
ascensión[F] recta

celestial meridian
meridiano[M] celeste

South celestial pole
polo[M] Sur celeste

ASTRONOMY

refracting telescope
telescopio*M* refractor

general view
vista*F* general

finderscope
anteojo*M* buscador

cradle
abrazadera*F*

main tube
tubo*M* principal

dew shield
parasol*M*

eyepiece
ocular*M*

eyepiece holder
portaocular*M*

star diagonal
ocular*M* acodado

focusing knob
botón*M* de enfoque*M*

declination setting scale
círculo*M* graduado de declinación*F*

azimuth clamp
palanca*F* de bloqueo*M* del acimut*M*

altitude clamp
palanca*F* de bloqueo*M* de la altura*F*

azimuth fine adjustment
ajuste*M* fino del acimut*M*

altitude fine adjustment
ajuste*M* fino de la altura*F*

right ascension setting scale
anillo*M* graduado de ascensión*F*
recta

fork
horquilla*F*

counterweight
contrapeso*M*

tripod accessories shelf
repisa*F* para accesorios*M*

tripod
trípode*M*

cross section of a refracting
telescope
sección*F* transversal de un
telescopio*M* refractor

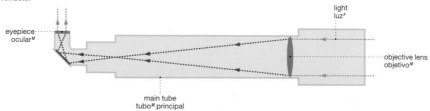

eyepiece
ocular*M*

light
luz*F*

objective lens
objetivo*M*

main tube
tubo*M* principal

reflecting telescope
telescopio^M reflector

general view
vista^F general

support
soporte^M

finderscope
anteojo^M buscador

eyepiece
ocular^M

cradle
abrazadera^F

main tube
tubo^M principal

focusing knob
botón^M de enfoque^M

declination setting scale
anillo^M graduado de declinación^F

azimuth clamp
palanca^F de bloqueo^M del acimut^M

altitude clamp
palanca^F de bloqueo^M de la altura^F

right ascension setting scale
anillo^M graduado de ascensión^F
recta

azimuth fine adjustment
ajuste^M fino del acimut^M

altitude fine adjustment
ajuste^M fino de la altura^F

cross section of a reflecting telescope
sección^F transversal de un telescopio^M reflector

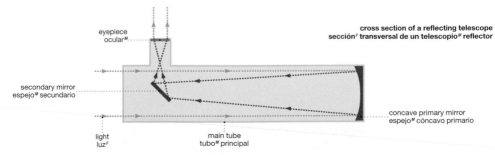

eyepiece
ocular^M

secondary mirror
espejo^M secundario

concave primary mirror
espejo^M cóncavo primario

light
luz^F

main tube
tubo^M principal

radio telescope

radiotelescopio[M]

steerable parabolic reflector
reflector[M] **parabólico móvil**

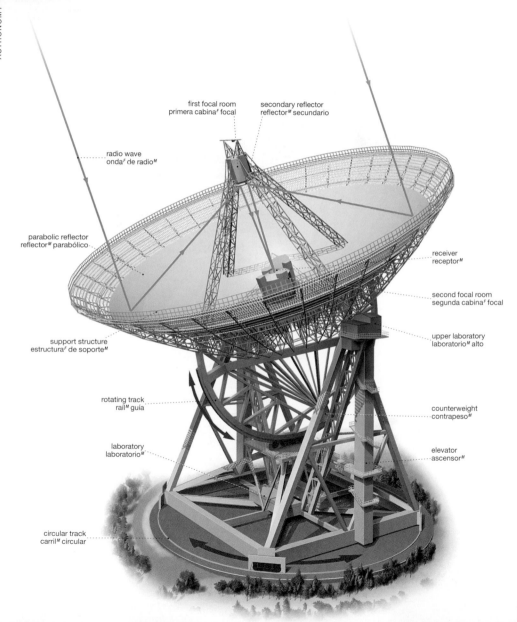

first focal room
primera cabina[F] focal

secondary reflector
reflector[M] secundario

radio wave
onda[F] de radio[M]

parabolic reflector
reflector[M] parabólico

receiver
receptor[M]

second focal room
segunda cabina[F] focal

support structure
estructura[F] de soporte[M]

upper laboratory
laboratorio[M] alto

rotating track
rail[M] guía

counterweight
contrapeso[M]

laboratory
laboratorio[M]

elevator
ascensor[M]

circular track
carril[M] circular

space telescope

telescopio^M espacial

**Hubble Space
Telescope
telescopio^M espacial
Hubble**

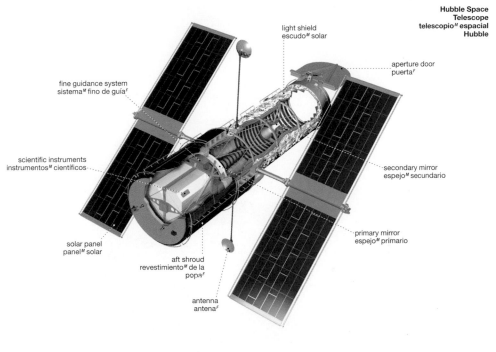

light shield
escudo^M solar

aperture door
puerta^F

fine guidance system
sistema^M fino de guía^F

scientific instruments
instrumentos^M científicos

secondary mirror
espejo^M secundario

solar panel
panel^M solar

primary mirror
espejo^M primario

aft shroud
revestimiento^M de la
popa^F

antenna
antena^F

**James Webb Space
Telescope
telescopio^M espacial James
Webb**

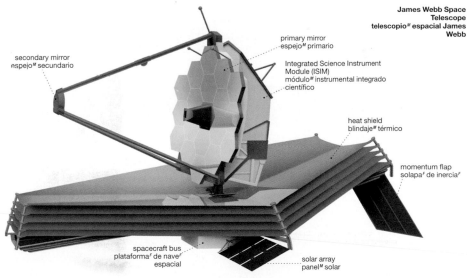

secondary mirror
espejo^M secundario

primary mirror
espejo^M primario

Integrated Science Instrument
Module (ISIM)
módulo^M instrumental integrado
científico

heat shield
blindaje^M térmico

momentum flap
solapa^F de inercia^F

spacecraft bus
plataforma^F de nave^F
espacial

solar array
panel^M solar

astronomical observatory

observatorio^M astronómico

cross section of an astronomical
observatory
corte^M de un observatorio^M astronómico

external view
vista^F externa

dome shutter
obturador^M de la cúpula^F

rotating dome
cúpula^F giratoria

prime focus observing capsule
cabina^F en el foco^M primario

horseshoe mount
montura^F en herradura^F

telescope
telescopio^M

secondary mirror
espejo^M secundario

hour angle gear
ángulo^M horario

prime focus
foco^M primario

light
luz^F

exterior dome shell
cubierta^F exterior de la cúpula^F

telescope base
base^F del telescopio^M

flat mirror
espejo^M plano

polar axis
eje^M polar

primary mirror
espejo^M primario

coudé focus
foco^M coudé

laboratory
laboratorio^M

observation post
puesto^M de observación^F

Cassegrain focus
foco^M Cassegrain

interior dome shell
cubierta^F interior de la cúpula^F

astronomical observatory

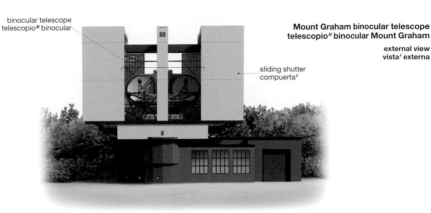

binocular telescope
telescopio^M binocular

Mount Graham binocular telescope
telescopio^M binocular Mount Graham

external view
vista^F externa

sliding shutter
compuerta^F

binocular telescope
telescopio^M binocular

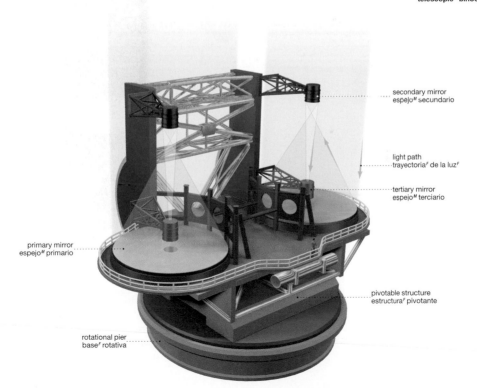

secondary mirror
espejo^M secundario

light path
trayectoria^F de la luz^F

tertiary mirror
espejo^M terciario

primary mirror
espejo^M primario

pivotable structure
estructura^F pivotante

rotational pier
base^F rotativa

ASTRONOMY

space probe

sonda*f* espacial

**examples of space probes
ejemplos*M* de sondas*f* espaciales**

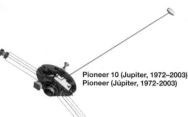

Pioneer 10 (Jupiter, 1972–2003)
Pioneer (Júpiter, 1972-2003)

Mariner 10 (Mercury, 1973–1975)
Mariner (Mercurio, 1973-1975)

Luna 1 (Moon, 1959)
Luna 1 (Luna*f*, 1959)

Voyager (gas planets, 1977–)
Voyager (planetas*M* gaseosos, 1977-)

Giotto (Halley's comet, 1985–1992)
Giotto (cometa*M* Halley, 1985-1992)

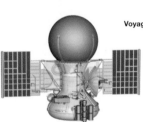

Venera 9 (Venus, 1975)
Venera (Venus, 1975)

Magellan (Venus, 1989–1994)
Magallanes (Venus, 1989-1994)

Galileo (Jupiter, 1989–2003)
Galileo (Júpiter, 1989-2003)

Ulysses (Sun, 1990–2009)
Ulises (Sol, 1990-2009)

ASTRONOMY

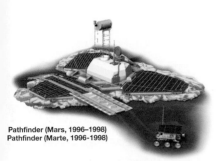

Pathfinder (Mars, 1996–1998)
Pathfinder (Marte, 1996-1998)

Huygens (Titan, 1997–2005)
Huygens (Titán, 1997-2005)

Cassini (Saturn, 1997–)
Cassini (Saturno, 1997-)

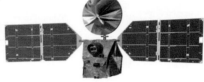

Mars Reconnaissance Orbiter (Mars, 2005–)
Mars Reconnaissance Orbiter (Marte, 2005-)

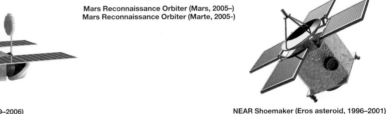

Stardust (Wild-2 comet, 1999–2006)
Stardust (cometa^M Wild-2, 1999-2006)

NEAR Shoemaker (Eros asteroid, 1996–2001)
NEAR Shoemaker (asteroide^M Eros, 1996-2001)

2001 Mars Odyssey (Mars, 2001–)
Mars Odyssey (Marte, 2001-)

Phoenix (Mars, 2007–2008)
Phoenix (Marte, 2007-2008)

impactor
impactador^M

Deep Impact (Tempel 1 comet, 2005)
Deep Impact (cometa^M Tempel-1, 2005)

New Horizons (Pluto, 2006–)
New Horizons (Plutón, 2006-)

ASTRONOMY

space probe

orbiter (Viking, 1976–1980)
módulo^M orbital (Viking, 1976-1980)

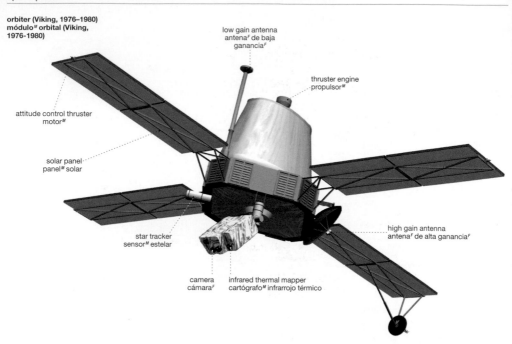

low gain antenna
antena^F de baja ganancia^F

thruster engine
propulsor^M

attitude control thruster
motor^M

solar panel
panel^M solar

star tracker
sensor^M estelar

high gain antenna
antena^F de alta ganancia^F

camera
cámara^F

infrared thermal mapper
cartógrafo^M infrarrojo térmico

lander (Viking)
módulo^M de aterrizaje^M
(Viking)

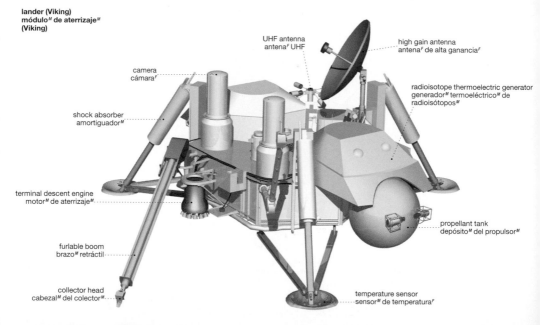

UHF antenna
antena^F UHF

high gain antenna
antena^F de alta ganancia^F

camera
cámara^F

radioisotope thermoelectric generator
generador^M termoeléctrico^M de
radioisótopos^M

shock absorber
amortiguador^M

terminal descent engine
motor^M de aterrizaje^M

propellant tank
depósito^M del propulsor^M

furlable boom
brazo^M retráctil

collector head
cabezal^M del colector^M

temperature sensor
sensor^M de temperatura^F

spacesuit
traje^M espacial

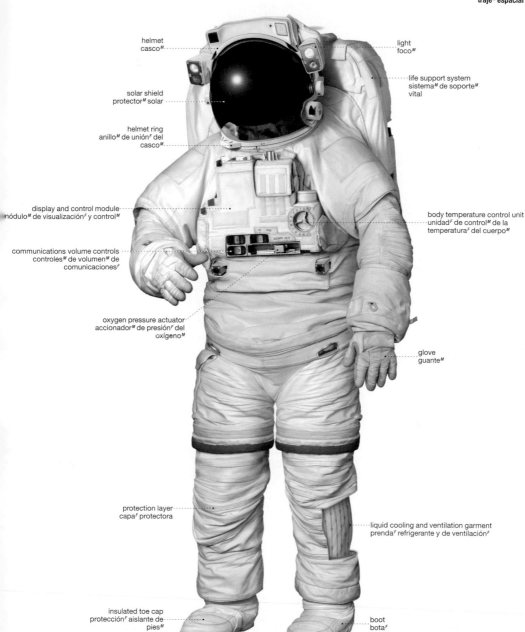

helmet
casco^M

light
foco^M

life support system
sistema^M de soporte^M
vital

solar shield
protector^M solar

helmet ring
anillo^M de unión^F del
casco^M

display and control module
módulo^M de visualización^F y control^M

body temperature control unit
unidad^F de control^M de la
temperatura^F del cuerpo^M

communications volume controls
controles^M de volumen^M de
comunicaciones^F

oxygen pressure actuator
accionador^M de presión^F del
oxígeno^M

glove
guante^M

protection layer
capa^F protectora

liquid cooling and ventilation garment
prenda^F refrigerante y de ventilación^F

insulated toe cap
protección^F aislante de
pies^M

boot
bota^F

international space station
estación^f espacial internacional

general view
vista^f general

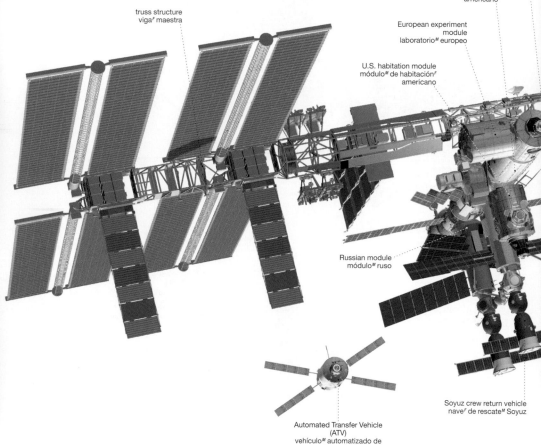

mating adaptor
adaptador^M de acoplamiento^M

U.S. experiment module
módulo^M experimental
americano

European experiment
module
laboratorio^M europeo

truss structure
viga^F maestra

U.S. habitation module
módulo^M de habitación^F
americano

Russian module
módulo^M ruso

Soyuz crew return vehicle
nave^F de rescate^M Soyuz

Automated Transfer Vehicle
(ATV)
vehículo^M automatizado de
transferencia^F (VAT)

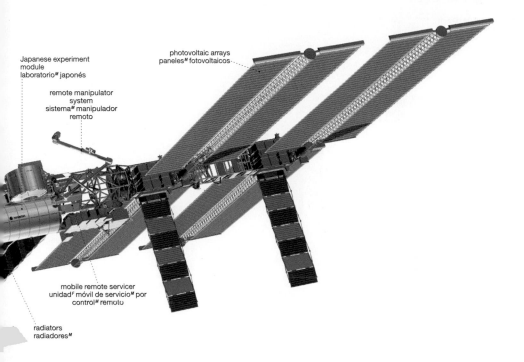

Japanese experiment
module
laboratorio^M japonés

photovoltaic arrays
paneles^M fotovoltaicos

remote manipulator
system
sistema^M manipulador
remoto

mobile remote servicer
unidad^F móvil de servicio^M por
control^M remoto

radiators
radiadores^M

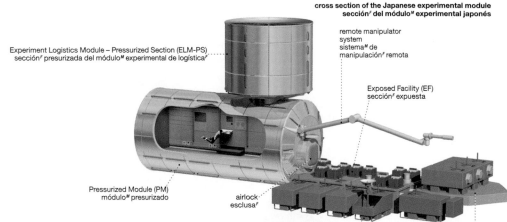

cross section of the Japanese experimental module
sección^F del módulo^M experimental japonés

Experiment Logistics Module – Pressurized Section (ELM-PS)
sección^F presurizada del módulo^M experimental de logística^F

remote manipulator
system
sistema^M de
manipulación^F remota

Exposed Facility (EF)
sección^F expuesta

Pressurized Module (PM)
módulo^M presurizado

airlock
esclusa^F

Inter-Orbit Communication System (ICS)
sistema^M de comunicación^F inter-orbital

Experiment Logistics Module –
Exposed Facility (ELM-EF)
módulo^M experimental de logística^F

spaceship

nave^F espacial

space shuttle at takeoff
transbordador^M espacial en
posición^F de lanzamiento^M

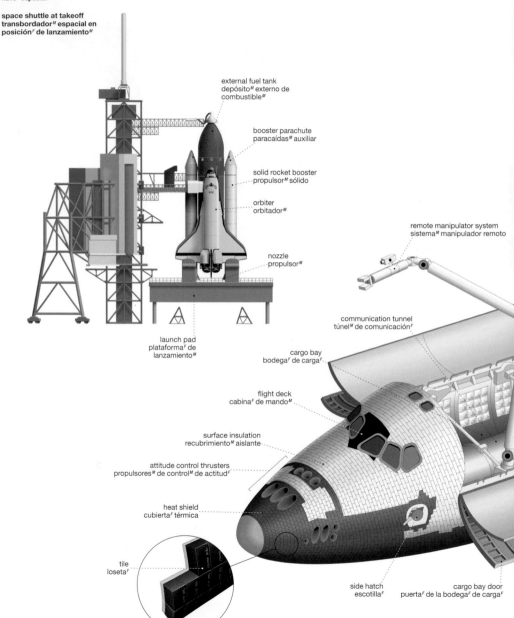

external fuel tank
depósito^M externo de
combustible^M

booster parachute
paracaídas^M auxiliar

solid rocket booster
propulsor^M sólido

orbiter
orbitador^M

nozzle
propulsor^M

launch pad
plataforma^F de
lanzamiento^M

remote manipulator system
sistema^M manipulador remoto

communication tunnel
túnel^M de comunicación^F

cargo bay
bodega^F de carga^F

flight deck
cabina^F de mando^M

surface insulation
recubrimiento^M aislante

attitude control thrusters
propulsores^M de control^M de actitud^F

heat shield
cubierta^F térmica

tile
loseta^F

side hatch
escotilla^F

cargo bay door
puerta^F de la bodega^F de carga^F

spaceship

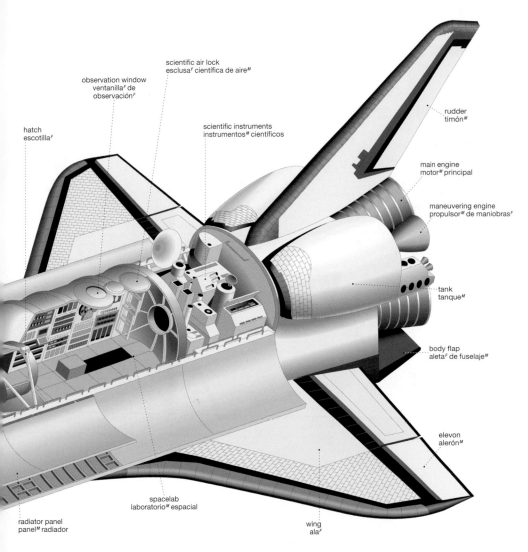

orbiter
orbitador^M

ASTRONOMY

scientific air lock
esclusa^F científica de aire^M

observation window
ventanilla^F de
observación^F

rudder
timón^M

hatch
escotilla^F

scientific instruments
instrumentos^M científicos

main engine
motor^M principal

maneuvering engine
propulsor^M de maniobras^F

tank
tanque^M

body flap
aleta^F de fuselaje^M

elevon
alerón^M

spacelab
laboratorio^M espacial

radiator panel
panel^M radiador

wing
ala^F

spaceship

examples of spaceships
ejemplos^M de transbordadores^M espaciales

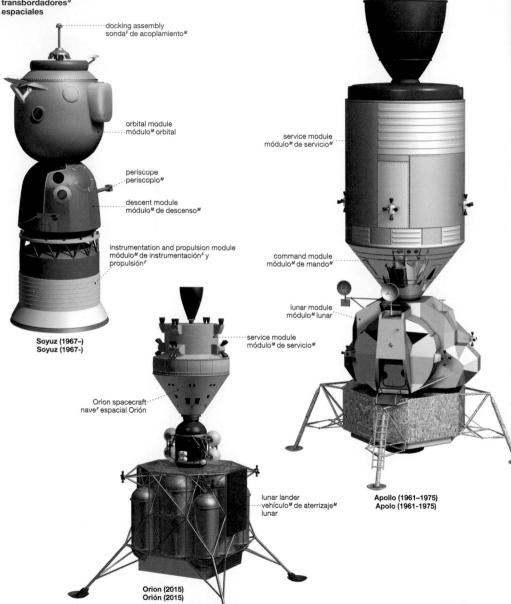

docking assembly
sonda^F de acoplamiento^M

orbital module
módulo^M orbital

periscope
periscopio^M

descent module
módulo^M de descenso^M

instrumentation and propulsion module
módulo^M de instrumentación^F y propulsión^F

Soyuz (1967–)
Soyuz (1967-)

service module
módulo^M de servicio^M

command module
módulo^M de mando^M

lunar module
módulo^M lunar

Apollo (1961–1975)
Apolo (1961-1975)

service module
módulo^M de servicio^M

Orion spacecraft
nave^F espacial Orión

lunar lander
vehículo^M de aterrizaje^M lunar

Orion (2015)
Orión (2015)

space launcher
cohete^M espacial

examples of space launchers
ejemplos^M de lanzadores^M
espaciales

cross section of a space launcher (Ariane V)
sección^M transversal de un lanzador^M espacial (Ariane V, 1996-)

Ariane IV (1988–2003)
Ariane IV (1988-2003)

Soyuz (1966–)
Soyuz (1966-)

Saturn V (1967–1973)
Saturno V (1967-1973)

Titan IV (1989–2005)
Titan IV (1989-2005)

Delta II (1990–)
Delta II (1990-)

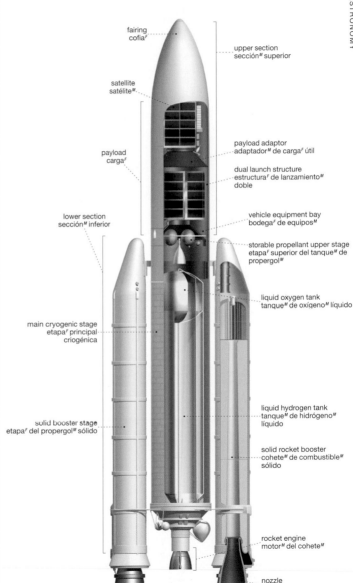

fairing
cofia^F

upper section
sección^M superior

satellite
satélite^M

payload adaptor
adaptador^M de carga^F útil

payload
carga^F

dual launch structure
estructura^F de lanzamiento^M
doble

lower section
sección^M inferior

vehicle equipment bay
bodega^F de equipos^M

storable propellant upper stage
etapa^F superior del tanque^M de
propergol^M

liquid oxygen tank
tanque^M de oxígeno^M líquido

main cryogenic stage
etapa^F principal
criogénica

liquid hydrogen tank
tanque^M de hidrógeno^M
líquido

solid rocket booster
cohete^M de combustible^M
sólido

solid booster stage
etapa^F del propergol^M sólido

rocket engine
motor^M del cohete^M

nozzle
tobera^F

EARTH

Tierra

GEOGRAPHY   42

Earth coordinate system   42
azimuthal projection   43
configuration of the continents   44
physical cartography   45
political cartography   53
remote sensing   63

GEOLOGY   66

structure of the Earth   66
Earth features   70
geological phenomena   75
minerals   78

METEOROLOGY   79

profile of the Earth's atmosphere   79
seasons of the year   80
meteorological forecast   80
weather map   81
station model   81
international weather symbols   82
meteorological station   84
meteorological measuring instruments   84
weather satellites   86
climates of the world   87
clouds   88
tornado and waterspout   89
tropical cyclone   89
precipitation   90

ENVIRONMENT   92

vegetation regions   92
types of vegetation   93
food chain   94
structure of the biosphere   94
hydrologic cycle   95
carbon-oxygen cycle   95
natural greenhouse effect   96
enhanced greenhouse effect   96
air pollution   97
land pollution   97
water pollution   98
acid rain   98
selective sorting of waste   99

EARTH

Earth coordinate system
sistema^M de coordenadas^F terrestres

grid system
sistema^M de retícula^F

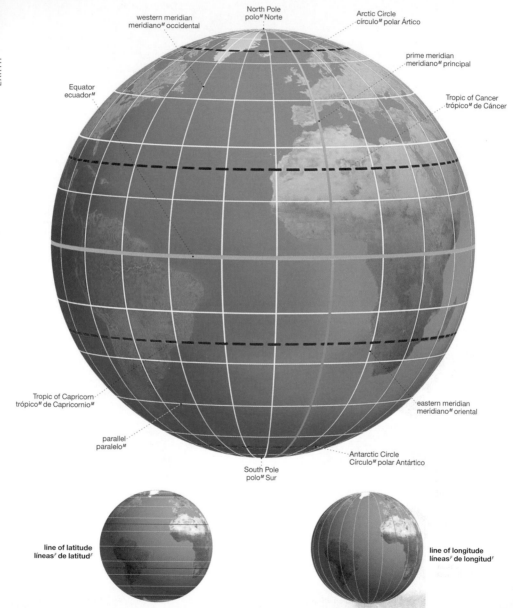

western meridian
meridiano^M occidental

North Pole
polo^M Norte

Arctic Circle
círculo^M polar Ártico

prime meridian
meridiano^M principal

Equator
ecuador^M

Tropic of Cancer
trópico^M de Cáncer

Tropic of Capricorn
trópico^M de Capricornio^M

eastern meridian
meridiano^M oriental

parallel
paralelo^M

Antarctic Circle
Círculo^M polar Antártico

South Pole
polo^M Sur

line of latitude
líneas^F de latitud^F

line of longitude
líneas^F de longitud^F

Earth coordinate system

hemispheres
hemisferios^M

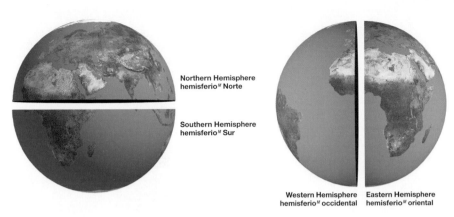

Northern Hemisphere
hemisferio^M Norte

Southern Hemisphere
hemisferio^M Sur

Western Hemisphere
hemisferio^M occidental

Eastern Hemisphere
hemisferio^M oriental

azimuthal projection

proyecciones^F cartográficas

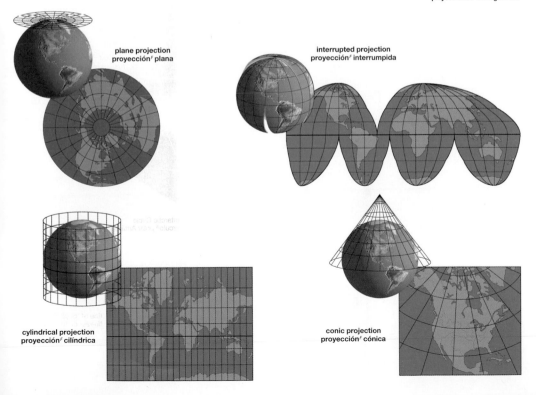

plane projection
proyección^F plana

interrupted projection
proyección^F interrumpida

cylindrical projection
proyección^F cilíndrica

conic projection
proyección^F cónica

EARTH

configuration of the continents

configuración^F de los continentes^M

planisphere
planisferio^M

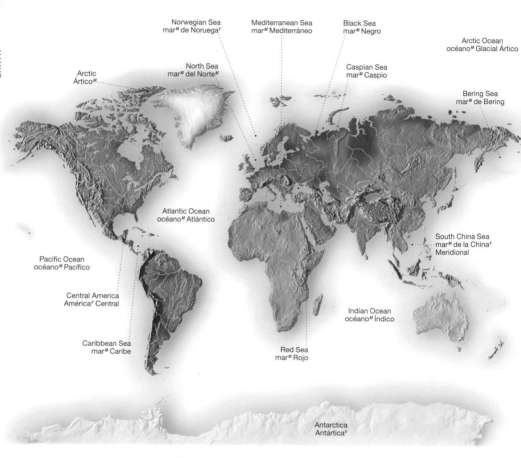

Norwegian Sea
mar^M de Noruega^F

Mediterranean Sea
mar^M Mediterráneo

Black Sea
mar^M Negro

Arctic Ocean
océano^M Glacial Ártico

Arctic
Ártico^M

North Sea
mar^M del Norte^M

Caspian Sea
mar^M Caspio

Bering Sea
mar^M de Bering

Atlantic Ocean
océano^M Atlántico

South China Sea
mar^M de la China^F
Meridional

Pacific Ocean
océano^M Pacífico

Central America
América^F Central

Indian Ocean
océano^M Índico

Caribbean Sea
mar^M Caribe

Red Sea
mar^M Rojo

Antarctica
Antártica^F

North America
América^F del Norte^M

Europe
Europa^F

Eurasia
Eurasia^F

South America
América^F del Sur

Asia
Asia^F

Oceania
Oceanía^F

Africa
África^F

physical cartography

cartografía^F física

physical map legends
letreros^M de mapas^M físicos

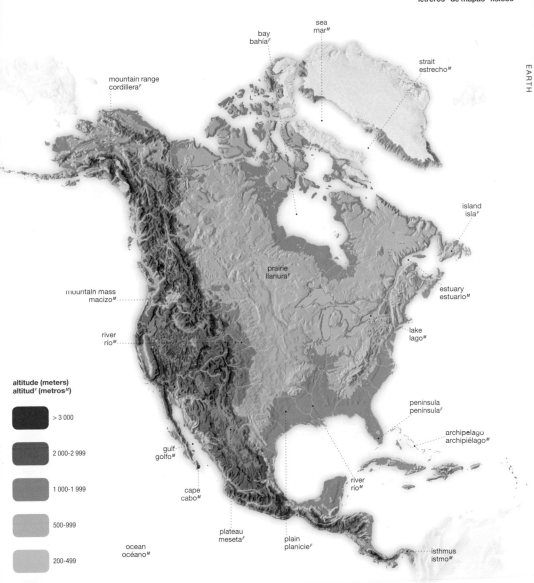

sea
mar^M

bay
bahía^F

strait
estrecho^M

mountain range
cordillera^F

island
isla^F

prairie
llanura^F

mountain mass
macizo^M

estuary
estuario^M

river
río^M

lake
lago^M

peninsula
península^F

altitude (meters)
altitud^F (metros^M)

archipelago
archipiélago^M

> 3 000

gulf
golfo^M

river
río^M

2 000-2 999

cape
cabo^M

1 000-1 999

500-999

ocean
océano^M

plateau
meseta^F

plain
planicie^F

isthmus
istmo^M

200-499

0-199

EARTH

physical cartography

Arctic
Ártico^M

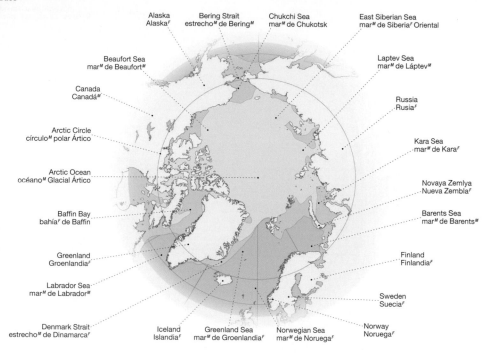

Alaska
Alaska^F

Bering Strait
estrecho^M de Bering^M

Chukchi Sea
mar^M de Chukotsk

East Siberian Sea
mar^M de Siberia^F Oriental

Beaufort Sea
mar^M de Beaufort^M

Laptev Sea
mar^M de Láptev^M

Canada
Canadá^M

Russia
Rusia^F

Arctic Circle
círculo^M polar Ártico

Kara Sea
mar^M de Kara^F

Arctic Ocean
océano^M Glacial Ártico

Novaya Zemlya
Nueva Zembla^F

Baffin Bay
bahía^F de Baffin

Barents Sea
mar^M de Barents^M

Greenland
Groenlandia^F

Finland
Finlandia^F

Labrador Sea
mar^M de Labrador^M

Sweden
Suecia^F

Denmark Strait
estrecho^M de Dinamarca^F

Iceland
Islandia^F

Greenland Sea
mar^M de Groenlandia^F

Norwegian Sea
mar^M de Noruega^F

Norway
Noruega^F

Antarctica
Antártica^F

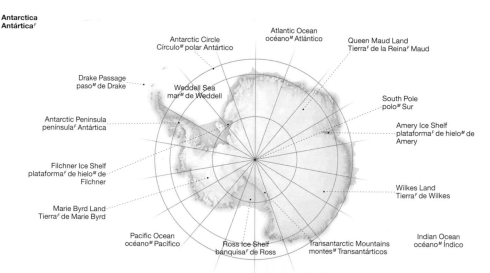

Antarctic Circle
Círculo^M polar Antártico

Atlantic Ocean
océano^M Atlántico

Queen Maud Land
Tierra^F de la Reina^F Maud

Drake Passage
paso^M de Drake

Weddell Sea
mar^M de Weddell

South Pole
polo^M Sur

Antarctic Peninsula
península^F Antártica

Amery Ice Shelf
plataforma^F de hielo^M de
Amery

Filchner Ice Shelf
plataforma^F de hielo^M de
Filchner

Wilkes Land
Tierra^F de Wilkes

Marie Byrd Land
Tierra^F de Marie Byrd

Pacific Ocean
océano^M Pacífico

Ross Ice Shelf
banquisa^F de Ross

Transantarctic Mountains
montes^M Transantárticos

Indian Ocean
océano^M Índico

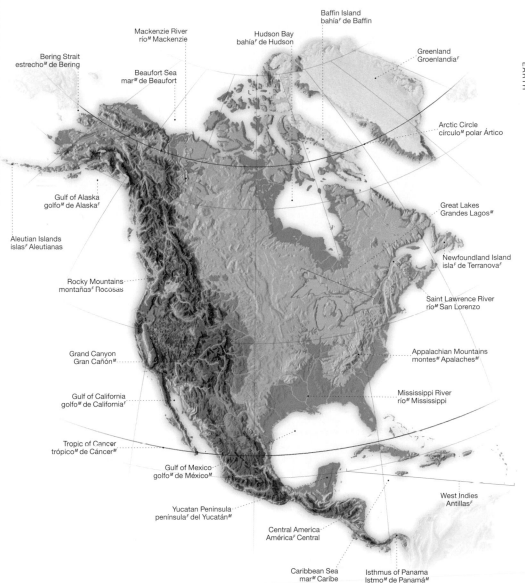

Baffin Island
bahía^F de Baffin

Mackenzie River
río^M Mackenzie

Hudson Bay
bahía^F de Hudson

Greenland
Groenlandia^F

Bering Strait
estrecho^M de Bering

Beaufort Sea
mar^M de Beaufort

Arctic Circle
círculo^M polar Ártico

Gulf of Alaska
golfo^M de Alaska^F

Great Lakes
Grandes Lagos^M

Aleutian Islands
islas^F Aleutianas

Newfoundland Island
isla^F de Terranova^F

Rocky Mountains
montañas^F Rocosas

Saint Lawrence River
río^M San Lorenzo

Grand Canyon
Gran Cañón^M

Appalachian Mountains
montes^M Apalaches^M

Gulf of California
golfo^M de California^F

Mississippi River
río^M Mississippi

Tropic of Cancer
trópico^M de Cáncer^M

Gulf of Mexico
golfo^M de México^F

West Indies
Antillas^F

Yucatan Peninsula
península^F del Yucatán^M

Central America
América^F Central

Caribbean Sea
mar^M Caribe

Isthmus of Panama
Istmo^M de Panamá^M

physical cartography

South America
América^F del Sur

Orinoco River
río^M Orinoco

Amazon River
río^M Amazonas

Gulf of Panama
golfo^M de Panamá^M

Equator
ecuador^M

Andes Cordillera
cordillera^F de los Andes^M

Lake Titicaca
lago^M Titicaca

Atacama Desert
desierto^M de Atacama

Tropic of Capricorn
trópico^M de Capricornio^M

Paraná River
río^M Paraná

Patagonia
Patagonia^F

Falkland Islands
islas^F Malvinas

South Georgia
Georgia^F del Sur^M

Tierra del Fuego
Tierra^F del Fuego^M

Cape Horn
cabo^M de Hornos

Drake Passage
paso^M de Drake

physical cartography

Europe
Europa[F]

EARTH

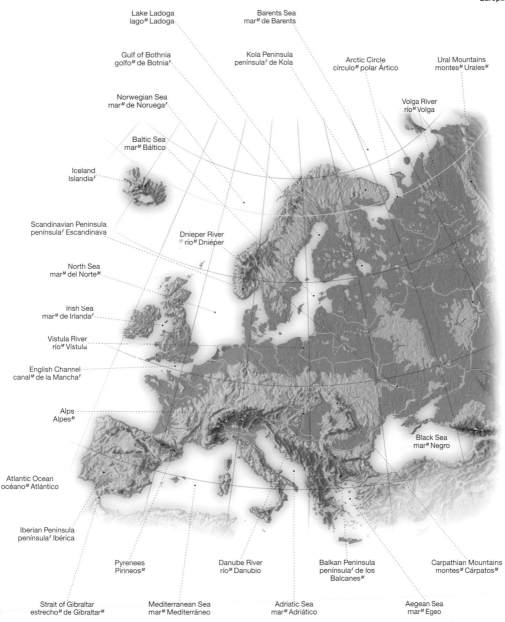

Lake Ladoga
lago[M] Ladoga

Barents Sea
mar[M] de Barents

Gulf of Bothnia
golfo[M] de Botnia[F]

Kola Peninsula
península[F] de Kola

Arctic Circle
círculo[M] polar Ártico

Ural Mountains
montes[M] Urales[M]

Norwegian Sea
mar[M] de Noruega[F]

Volga River
río[M] Volga

Baltic Sea
mar[M] Báltico

Iceland
Islandia[F]

Scandinavian Peninsula
península[F] Escandinava

Dnieper River
río[M] Dniéper

North Sea
mar[M] del Norte[M]

Irish Sea
mar[M] de Irlanda[F]

Vistula River
río[M] Vístula

English Channel
canal[M] de la Mancha[F]

Alps
Alpes[M]

Black Sea
mar[M] Negro

Atlantic Ocean
océano[M] Atlántico

Iberian Peninsula
península[F] Ibérica

Pyrenees
Pirineos[M]

Danube River
río[M] Danubio

Balkan Peninsula
península[F] de los
Balcanes[M]

Carpathian Mountains
montes[M] Cárpatos[M]

Strait of Gibraltar
estrecho[M] de Gibraltar[M]

Mediterranean Sea
mar[M] Mediterráneo

Adriatic Sea
mar[M] Adriático

Aegean Sea
mar[M] Egeo

physical cartography

Africa
África[F]

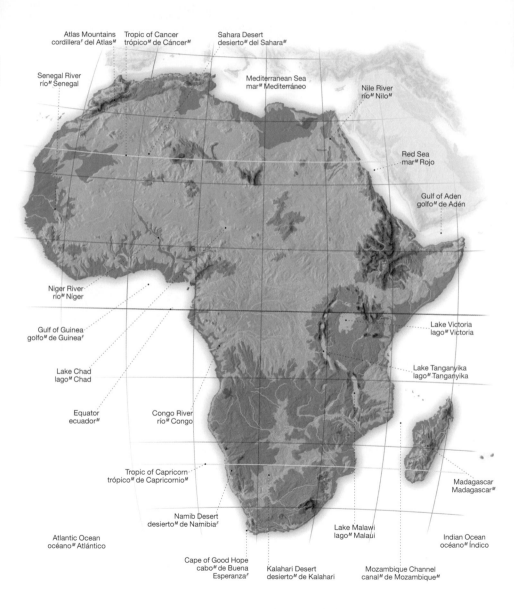

Atlas Mountains
cordillera[F] del Atlas[M]

Tropic of Cancer
trópico[M] de Cáncer[M]

Sahara Desert
desierto[M] del Sahara[M]

Senegal River
río[M] Senegal

Mediterranean Sea
mar[M] Mediterráneo

Nile River
río[M] Nilo[M]

Red Sea
mar[M] Rojo

Gulf of Aden
golfo[M] de Adén

Niger River
río[M] Níger

Lake Victoria
lago[M] Victoria

Gulf of Guinea
golfo[M] de Guinea[F]

Lake Tanganyika
lago[M] Tanganyika

Lake Chad
lago[M] Chad

Equator
ecuador[M]

Congo River
río[M] Congo

Tropic of Capricorn
trópico[M] de Capricornio[M]

Madagascar
Madagascar[M]

Namib Desert
desierto[M] de Namibia[F]

Lake Malawi
lago[M] Malaui

Atlantic Ocean
océano[M] Atlántico

Indian Ocean
océano[M] Índico

Cape of Good Hope
cabo[M] de Buena
Esperanza[F]

Kalahari Desert
desierto[M] de Kalahari

Mozambique Channel
canal[M] de Mozambique[M]

physical cartography

Asia
Asiaᶠ

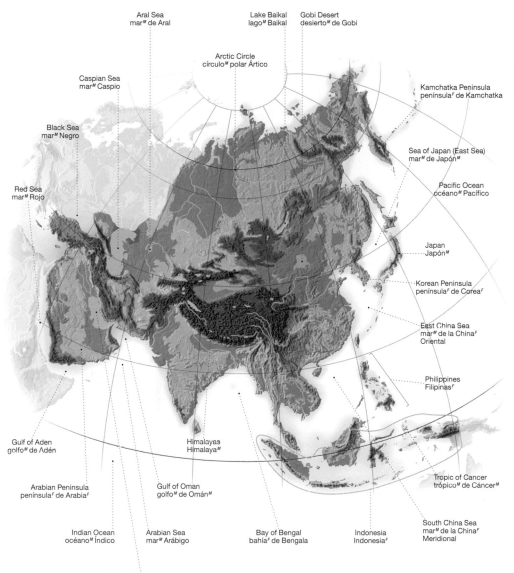

Aral Sea
marᴹ de Aral

Lake Baikal
lagoᴹ Baikal

Gobi Desert
desiertoᴹ de Gobi

Arctic Circle
círculoᴹ polar Ártico

Kamchatka Peninsula
penínsulaᶠ de Kamchatka

Caspian Sea
marᴹ Caspio

Black Sea
marᴹ Negro

Sea of Japan (East Sea)
marᴹ de Japónᴹ

Pacific Ocean
océanoᴹ Pacífico

Red Sea
marᴹ Rojo

Japan
Japónᴹ

Korean Peninsula
penínsulaᶠ de Coreaᶠ

East China Sea
marᴹ de la Chinaᶠ
Oriental

Philippines
Filipinasᶠ

Gulf of Aden
golfoᴹ de Adén

Himalayas
Himalayaᴹ

Tropic of Cancer
trópicoᴹ de Cáncerᴹ

Arabian Peninsula
penínsulaᶠ de Arabiaᶠ

Gulf of Oman
golfoᴹ de Ománᴹ

South China Sea
marᴹ de la Chinaᶠ
Meridional

Indian Ocean
océanoᴹ Índico

Arabian Sea
marᴹ Arábigo

Bay of Bengal
bahíaᶠ de Bengala

Indonesia
Indonesiaᶠ

Persian Gulf
golfoᴹ Pérsico

EARTH

physical cartography

Oceania
Oceanía*F*

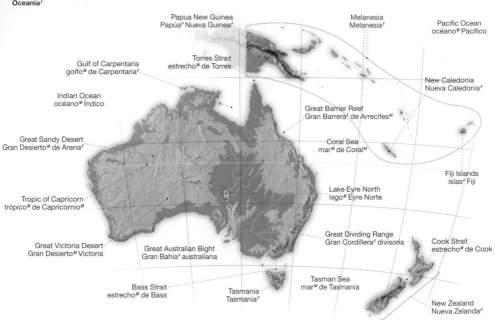

Papua New Guinea
Papúa*F* Nueva Guinea*F*

Melanesia
Melanesia*F*

Pacific Ocean
océano*M* Pacífico

Gulf of Carpentaria
golfo*M* de Carpentaria*F*

Torres Strait
estrecho*M* de Torres

New Caledonia
Nueva Caledonia*F*

Indian Ocean
océano*M* Índico

Great Barrier Reef
Gran Barrera*F* de Arrecifes*M*

Great Sandy Desert
Gran Desierto*M* de Arena*F*

Coral Sea
mar*M* de Coral*M*

Fiji Islands
islas*F* Fiji

Tropic of Capricorn
trópico*M* de Capricornio*M*

Lake Eyre North
lago*M* Eyre Norte

Great Victoria Desert
Gran Desierto*M* Victoria

Great Australian Bight
Gran Bahía*F* australiana

Great Dividing Range
Gran Cordillera*F* divisoria

Cook Strait
estrecho*M* de Cook

Bass Strait
estrecho*M* de Bass

Tasmania
Tasmania*F*

Tasman Sea
mar*M* de Tasmania

New Zealand
Nueva Zelanda*F*

urban map legends
letreros*M* de mapas*M*
urbanos

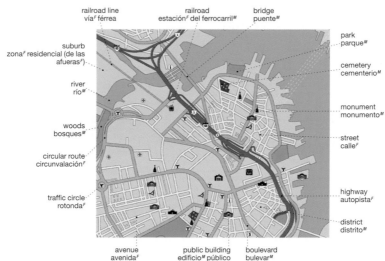

railroad line
vía*F* férrea

railroad
estación*F* del ferrocarril*M*

bridge
puente*M*

park
parque*M*

suburb
zona*F* residencial (de las
afueras*F*)

cemetery
cementerio*M*

river
río*M*

monument
monumento*M*

woods
bosques*M*

street
calle*F*

circular route
circunvalación*F*

traffic circle
rotonda*F*

highway
autopista*F*

district
distrito*M*

avenue
avenida*F*

public building
edificio*M* público

boulevard
bulevar*M*

EARTH

physical cartography

road map legends
letreros^M de mapas^M de
carreteras^F

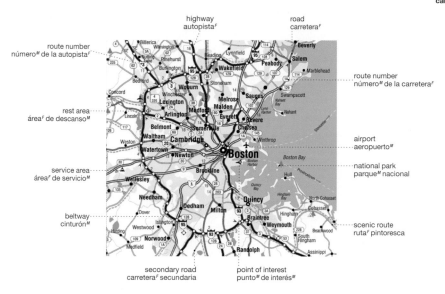

highway
autopista^F

road
carretera^F

route number
número^M de la autopista^F

route number
número^M de la carretera^F

rest area
área^F de descanso^M

airport
aeropuerto^M

service area
área^F de servicio^M

national park
parque^M nacional

beltway
cinturón^M

scenic route
ruta^F pintoresca

secondary road
carretera^F secundaria

point of interest
punto^M de interés^M

political cartography

cartografía^F política

political map legends
letreros^M de mapas^M políticos^M

province
provincia^F

internal boundary
frontera^F interna

city
ciudad^F

international boundary
frontera^F internacional

capital
capital^F

state
estado^M

country
país^M

political cartography

North America and Central America
América^F del Norte^M y América^F
Central

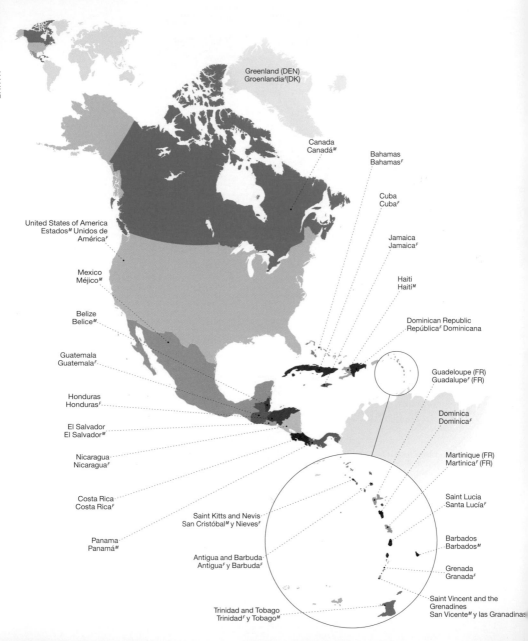

Greenland (DEN)
Groenlandia*(DK)

Canada
Canadá*

Bahamas
Bahamas*

Cuba
Cuba*

United States of America
Estados* Unidos de
América*

Jamaica
Jamaica*

Haiti
Haití*

Mexico
Méjico*

Belize
Belice*

Dominican Republic
República* Dominicana

Guatemala
Guatemala*

Guadeloupe (FR)
Guadalupe* (FR)

Honduras
Honduras*

Dominica
Dominica*

El Salvador
El Salvador*

Martinique (FR)
Martinica* (FR)

Nicaragua
Nicaragua*

Saint Lucia
Santa Lucía*

Costa Rica
Costa Rica*

Barbados
Barbados*

Saint Kitts and Nevis
San Cristóbal* y Nieves*

Panama
Panamá*

Grenada
Granada*

Antigua and Barbuda
Antigua* y Barbuda*

Saint Vincent and the
Grenadines
San Vicente* y las Granadinas

Trinidad and Tobago
Trinidad* y Tobago*

EARTH

Venezuela
Venezuela^r

Guyana
Guyana^r

Suriname
Surinam^M

Colombia
Colombia^r

French Guiana (FR)
Guyana^r Francesa (FR)

Ecuador
Ecuador^M

Peru
Perú^M

Brazil
Brasil^M

Bolivia
Bolivia^r

Paraguay
Paraguay^M

Uruguay
Uruguay^M

Chile
Chile^M

Argentina
Argentina^r

political cartography

Europe
Europa[F]

Iceland
Islandia[F]

Sweden
Suecia[F]

Finland
Finlandia[F]

Norway
Noruega[F]

Denmark
Dinamarca[F]

Belgium
Bélgica[F]

Netherlands
Países Bajos[M]

United Kingdom
Reino Unido[M]

Russia
Rusia[F]

Luxembourg
Luxemburgo[M]

Poland
Polonia[F]

Ireland
Irlanda[F]

Germany
Alemania[F]

Switzerland
Suiza[F]

Slovakia
Eslovaquia[F]

France
Francia[F]

Czech Republic
República[F] Checa

Andorra
Andorra[F]

Austria
Austria[F]

Hungary
Hungría[F]

Portugal
Portugal[M]

Vatican City State
Ciudad[F] de Vaticano[M]

Slovenia
Eslovenia[F]

Spain
España[F]

Liechtenstein
Liechtenstein[M]

Italy
Italia[F]

Malta
Malta[F]

Monaco
Mónaco[M]

San Marino
San Marino[M]

Russia
Rusia*F*

Estonia
Estonia*F*

Latvia
Letonia*F*

Belarus
Bielorrusia*F*

Lithuania
Lituania*F*

Ukraine
Ucrania*F*

Bosnia and Herzegovina
Bosnia*F* y Herzegovina*F*

Croatia
Croacia*F*

Serbia
Serbia*F*

Montenegro
Montenegro*M*

Albania
Albania*F*

Greece
Grecia*F*

Cyprus
Chipre*M*

Kosovo
Kósovo*M*

Macedonia
Macedonia*F*

Moldova
Moldavia*F*

Romania
Rumanía*F*

Georgia
Georgia*F*

Bulgaria
Bulgaria*F*

Turkey
Turquía*F*

political cartography

Asia
Asia[F]

EARTH

Russia
Rusia[F]

Turkmenistan
Turkmenistán[M]

Kazakhstan
Kazajistán[M]

Iran
Irán[M]

Uzbekistan
Uzbekistán[M]

Azerbaijan
Azerbaiyán[M]

Kyrgyzstan
Kirguizistán[M]

Kuwait
Kuwait[M]

Tajikistan
Tayikistán[M]

Iraq
Iraq[M]

Armenia
Armenia[F]

Syria
Siria[F]

Nepal
Nepal[M]

Lebanon
Líbano[M]

Bhutan
Bután[M]

Gaza Strip
Franja[F] de Gaza[F]

Afghanistan
Afganistán[M]

Bangladesh
Bangladesh[M]

Jordan
Jordania[F]

Pakistan
Pakistán[M]

India
India[F]

Israel
Israel[M]

United Arab Emirates
Emiratos[M] Árabes Unidos

Sri Lanka
Sri Lanka[F]

West Bank
Cisjordania[F]

Saudi Arabia
Arabia[F] Saudí

Oman
Omán[M]

Yemen
Yemen[M]

Maldives
Maldivas[F]

Qatar
Qatar[M]

Bahrain
Bahrein[M]

Russia
Rusia[F]

Mongolia
Mongolia[F]

North Korea
Corea[F] del Norte[M]

China
China[F]

Japan
Japón[M]

South Korea
Corea[F] del Sur[M]

Myanmar
Birmania[F]

Laos
Laos[M]

Vietnam
Vietnam[M]

Thailand
Tailandia[F]

Philippines
Filipinas[F]

Cambodia
Camboya[F]

Brunei Darussalam
Brunei[M]

Malaysia
Malasia[F]

Indonesia
Indonesia[F]

East Timor
Timor[M] Oriental

Singapore
Singapur[M]

political cartography

Africa
África^F

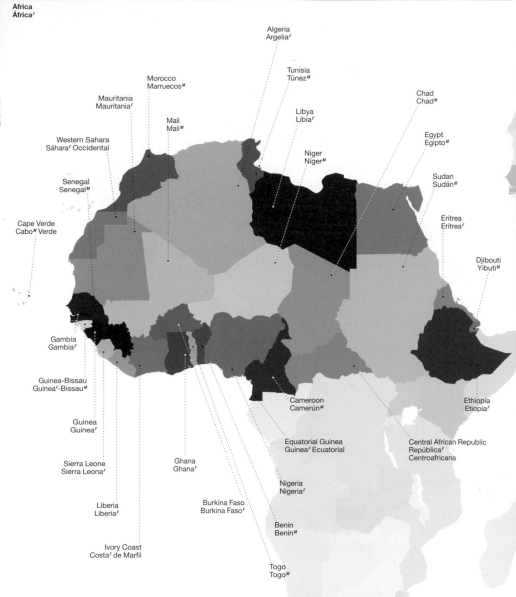

Algeria
Argelia^F

Tunisia
Túnez^M

Chad
Chad^M

Morocco
Marruecos^M

Libya
Libia^F

Egypt
Egipto^M

Mauritania
Mauritania^F

Mali
Mali^M

Niger
Níger^M

Sudan
Sudán^M

Western Sahara
Sáhara^F Occidental

Eritrea
Eritrea^F

Senegal
Senegal^M

Djibouti
Yibuti^M

Cape Verde
Cabo^M Verde

Gambia
Gambia^F

Ethiopia
Etiopía^F

Guinea-Bissau
Guinea^F-Bissau^M

Cameroon
Camerún^M

Guinea
Guinea^F

Equatorial Guinea
Guinea^F Ecuatorial

Central African Republic
República^F
Centroafricana

Sierra Leone
Sierra Leona^F

Ghana
Ghana^F

Nigeria
Nigeria^F

Liberia
Liberia^F

Burkina Faso
Burkina Faso^F

Benin
Benín^M

Ivory Coast
Costa^F de Marfil

Togo
Togo^M

political cartography

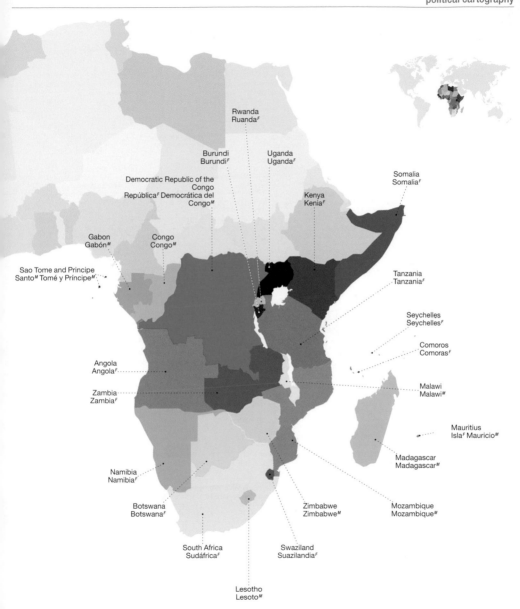

Rwanda
Ruanda[F]

Burundi
Burundi[F]

Uganda
Uganda[F]

Democratic Republic of the
Congo
República[F] Democrática del
Congo[M]

Kenya
Kenia[F]

Somalia
Somalia[F]

Gabon
Gabón[M]

Congo
Congo[M]

Sao Tome and Principe
Santo[M] Tomé y Príncipe[M]

Tanzania
Tanzania[F]

Seychelles
Seychelles[F]

Angola
Angola[F]

Comoros
Comoras[F]

Zambia
Zambia[F]

Malawi
Malawi[M]

Mauritius
Isla[F] Mauricio[M]

Madagascar
Madagascar[M]

Namibia
Namibia[F]

Zimbabwe
Zimbabwe[M]

Mozambique
Mozambique[M]

Botswana
Botswana[F]

South Africa
Sudáfrica[F]

Swaziland
Suazilandia[F]

Lesotho
Lesoto[M]

political cartography

Oceania
Oceanía[F]

Northern Mariana Islands
(US)
Islas[F] Marianas[F] del
Norte[M] (US)

Nauru
Nauru[M]

Micronesia
Micronesia[F]

Marshall Islands
Islas[F] Marshall[M]

Guam (US)
Guam[M] (US)

Kiribati
Kiribati[M]

Solomon Islands
Islas[F] Salomón[M]

Tuvalu
Tuvalu[M]

Palau
Palau[M]

Samoa
Samoa[F]

Papua New Guinea
Papúa[F] Nueva Guinea[F]

Wallis and Futuna Island
(FR)
Islas[F] Wallis[F] y Futuna[F]
(FR)

Vanuatu
.Vanuatu[M]

Tonga
Tonga[F]

New Caledonia (FR)
Nueva Caledonia[F] (FR)

Fiji
Fiyi[F]

Australia
Australia[F]

New Zealand
Nueva Zelanda[F]

remote sensing

teledetección^M

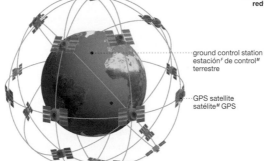

GPS navigation satellite network
red^F **GPS de navegación**^F **por**
satélite^M

ground control station
estación^F de control^M
terrestre

GPS satellite
satélite^M GPS

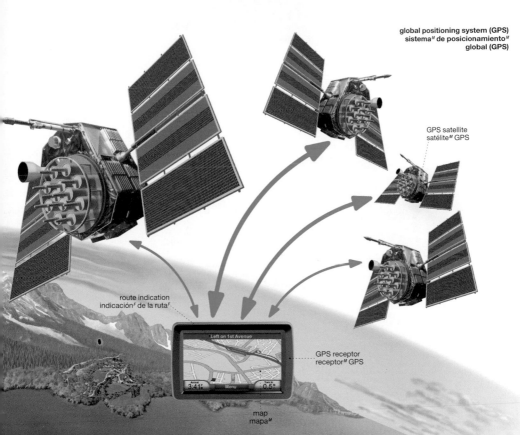

global positioning system (GPS)
sistema^M **de posicionamiento**^M
global (GPS)

GPS satellite
satélite^M GPS

route indication
indicación^F de la ruta^F

Left on 1st Avenue

Arrival
3:41

Menu

Turn in
0.5

GPS receptor
receptor^M GPS

map
mapa^M

EARTH

remote sensing

radar
radar[M]

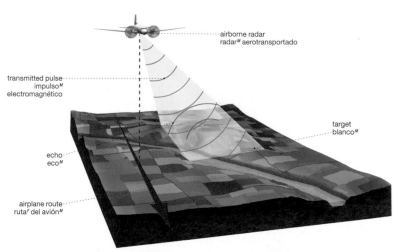

airborne radar
radar[M] aerotransportado

transmitted pulse
impulso[M]
electromagnético

target
blanco[M]

echo
eco[M]

airplane route
ruta[F] del avión[M]

Radarsat satellite
satélite[M] Radarsat

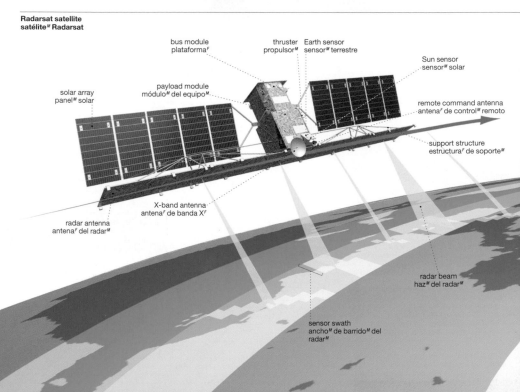

bus module
plataforma[F]

thruster
propulsor[M]

Earth sensor
sensor[M] terrestre

Sun sensor
sensor[M] solar

solar array
panel[M] solar

payload module
módulo[M] del equipo[M]

remote command antenna
antena[F] de control[M] remoto

support structure
estructura[F] de soporte[M]

X-band antenna
antena[F] de banda X[F]

radar antenna
antena[F] del radar[M]

radar beam
haz[M] del radar[M]

sensor swath
ancho[M] de barrido[M] del
radar[M]

remote sensing

sonar
sonar[M]

ship
nave[F]

ultrasound waves
emission
emisión[F] de ondas[F]
ultrasónicas

echo
eco[M]

target
blanco[M]

**satellite remote
sensing
teledetección**[M] **por
satélite**[M]

energy source
fuente[F] de energía[F]

passive sensor
sensor[M] pasivo

data recording
registro[M] de datos[M]

active sensor
sensor[M] activo

data recording
registro[M] de datos[M]

data processing
tratamiento[M] de datos[M]

data reception
recepción[F] de datos[M]

natural radiation
radiación[F] natural

reflection
reflexión[F]

artificial radiation
radiación[F] artificial

data transmission
transmisión[F] de datos[M]

target
blanco[M]

target
blanco[M]

structure of the Earth

estructura^F de la Tierra^F

cross section of the Earth
corte^M de la Tierra^F

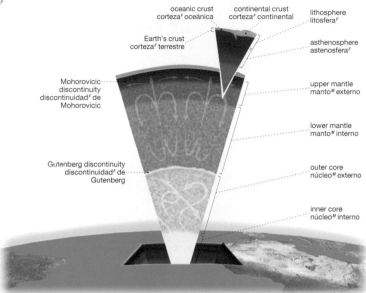

oceanic crust
corteza^F oceánica

continental crust
corteza^F continental

lithosphere
litosfera^F

Earth's crust
corteza^F terrestre

asthenosphere
astenosfera^F

Mohorovicic
discontinuity
discontinuidad^F de
Mohorovicic

upper mantle
manto^M externo

lower mantle
manto^M interno

Gutenberg discontinuity
discontinuidad^F de
Gutenberg

outer core
núcleo^M externo

inner core
núcleo^M interno

section of the Earth's crust
corte^M de la corteza^F
terrestre

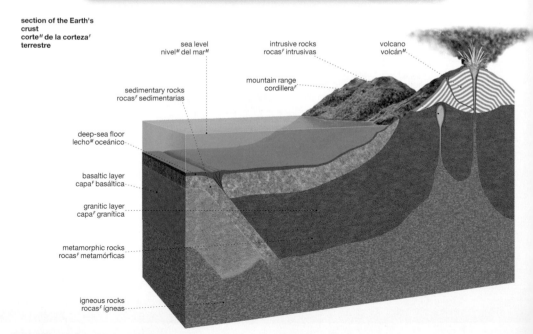

sea level
nivel^M del mar^M

intrusive rocks
rocas^F intrusivas

volcano
volcán^M

sedimentary rocks
rocas^F sedimentarias

mountain range
cordillera^F

deep-sea floor
lecho^M oceánico

basaltic layer
capa^F basáltica

granitic layer
capa^F granítica

metamorphic rocks
rocas^F metamórficas

igneous rocks
rocas^F ígneas

structure of the Earth

ocean floor
fondo^M **oceánico**

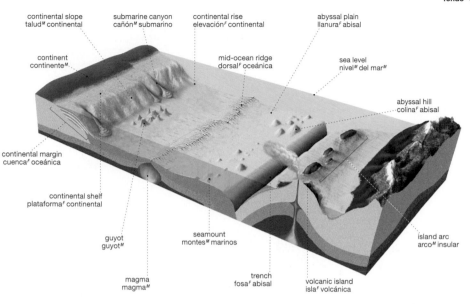

continental slope
talud^M continental

submarine canyon
cañón^M submarino

continental rise
elevación^F continental

abyssal plain
llanura^F abisal

continent
continente^M

mid-ocean ridge
dorsal^F oceánica

sea level
nivel^M del mar^M

abyssal hill
colina^F abisal

continental margin
cuenca^F oceánica

continental shelf
plataforma^F continental

guyot
guyot^M

seamount
montes^M marinos

island arc
arco^M insular

magma
magma^M

trench
fosa^F abisal

volcanic island
isla^F volcánica

cave
gruta^F

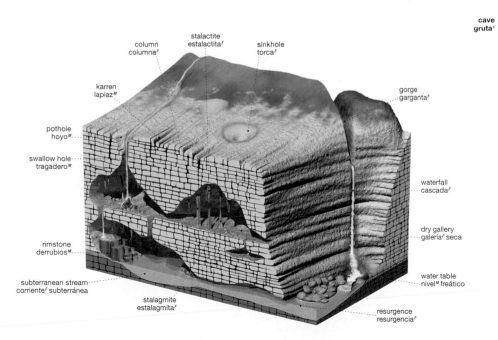

column
columna^F

stalactite
estalactita^F

sinkhole
torca^F

karren
lapiaz^M

gorge
garganta^F

pothole
hoyo^M

swallow hole
tragadero^M

waterfall
cascada^F

dry gallery
galería^F seca

rimstone
derrubios^M

subterranean stream
corriente^F subterránea

stalagmite
estalagmita^F

water table
nivel^M freático

resurgence
resurgencia^F

structure of the Earth

tectonic plates
placas^f **tectónicas**

EARTH

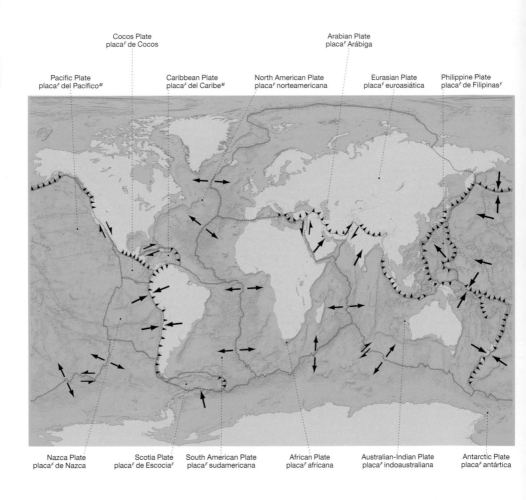

Cocos Plate
placa^f de Cocos

Arabian Plate
placa^f Arábiga

Pacific Plate
placa^f del Pacífico^M

Caribbean Plate
placa^f del Caribe^M

North American Plate
placa^f norteamericana

Eurasian Plate
placa^f euroasiática

Philippine Plate
placa^f de Filipinas^f

Nazca Plate
placa^f de Nazca

Scotia Plate
placa^f de Escocia^f

South American Plate
placa^f sudamericana

African Plate
placa^f africana

Australian-Indian Plate
placa^f indoaustraliana

Antarctic Plate
placa^f antártica

subduction
subducción^f

transform plate
boundaries
fallas^f **transformantes**

convergent plate boundaries
placas^f **convergentes**

divergent plate boundaries
placas^f **divergentes**

ocean trenches and ridges
fosas[F] y dorsales[F] oceánicas

Puerto Rico Trench
fosa[F] de Puerto[M] Rico

Mariana Trench
fosa[F] de las Marianas[F]

Aleutian Trench
fosa[F] de las Aleutianas[F]

Europe
Europa[F]

Ryukyu Trench
fosa[F] Ryukyu

Japan Trench
fosa[F] de Japón[M]

North America
América[F] del Norte[M]

Mid-Atlantic Ridge
dorsal[F] del Atlántico[M]
medio

Asia
Asia[F]

Kuril Trench
fosa[F] de las Kuriles

East Pacific Ridge
dorsal[F] del Pacífico[M]
oriental

Africa
África[F]

Java Trench
fosa[F] de Java[F]

Kermadec-Tonga Trench
fosa[F] de Kermadec-Tonga[M]

Pacific-Antarctic Ridge
dorsal[F] del
Pacífico[M]-Antártico[M]

Southwest Indian Ridge
dorsal[F] del Índico[M]
suroeste

Southeast Indian Ridge
dorsal[F] del Índico[M] sureste

Australia
Australia[F]

Peru-Chile Trench
fosa[M] Perú[M]-Chile[M]

Mid-Indian Ridge
dorsal[F] del Índico[M] medio

Philippine Trench
fosa[F] de las Filipinas[F]

South America
América[F] del Sur[M]

EARTH

Earth features

caracteristicas^F de la Tierra^F

**common coastal
features
configuración^F del
litoral^M**

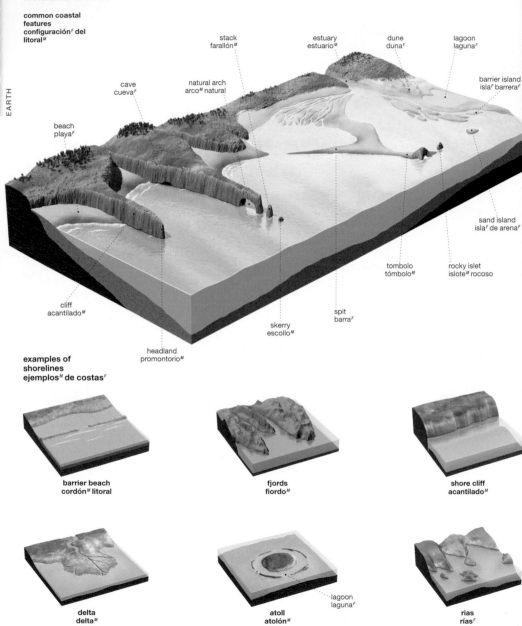

stack
farallón^M

estuary
estuario^M

dune
duna^F

lagoon
laguna^F

cave
cueva^F

natural arch
arco^M natural

barrier island
isla^F barrera^F

beach
playa^F

sand island
isla^F de arena^F

tombolo
tómbolo^M

rocky islet
islote^M rocoso

cliff
acantilado^M

spit
barra^F

skerry
escollo^M

**examples of
shorelines
ejemplos^M de costas^F**

headland
promontorio^M

**barrier beach
cordón^M litoral**

**fjords
fiordo^M**

**shore cliff
acantilado^M**

**delta
delta^M**

**atoll
atolón^M**

lagoon
laguna^F

**rias
rías^F**

Earth features

mountain
montaña^F

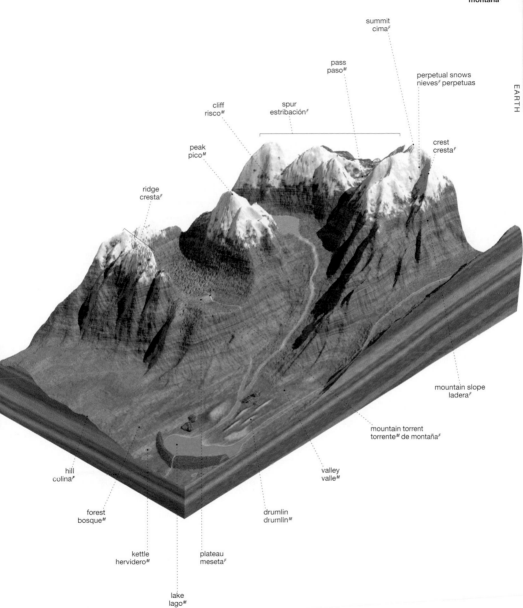

summit
cima^F

pass
paso^M

perpetual snows
nieves^F perpetuas

cliff
risco^M

spur
estribación^F

crest
cresta^F

peak
pico^M

ridge
cresta^F

mountain slope
ladera^F

mountain torrent
torrente^M de montaña^F

hill
colina^F

valley
valle^M

forest
bosque^M

drumlin
drumlin^M

kettle
hervidero^M

plateau
meseta^F

lake
lago^M

Earth features

glacier
glaciar[M]

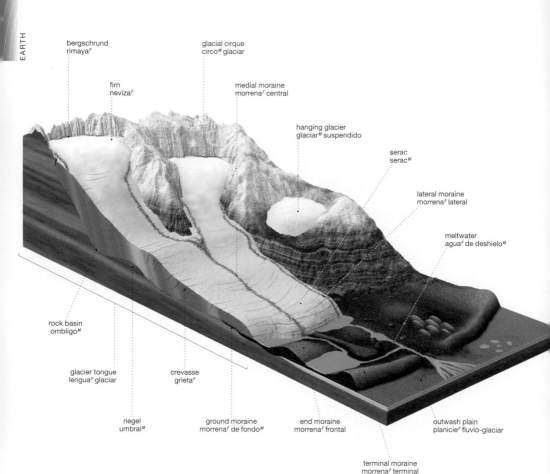

bergschrund
rimaya[F]

glacial cirque
circo[M] glaciar

firn
neviza[F]

medial moraine
morrena[F] central

hanging glacier
glaciar[M] suspendido

serac
serac[M]

lateral moraine
morrena[F] lateral

meltwater
agua[F] de deshielo[M]

rock basin
ombligo[M]

glacier tongue
lengua[F] glaciar

crevasse
grieta[F]

riegel
umbral[M]

ground moraine
morrena[F] de fondo[M]

end moraine
morrena[F] frontal

outwash plain
planicie[F] fluvio-glaciar

terminal moraine
morrena[F] terminal

watercourse
corriente^F de agua^F

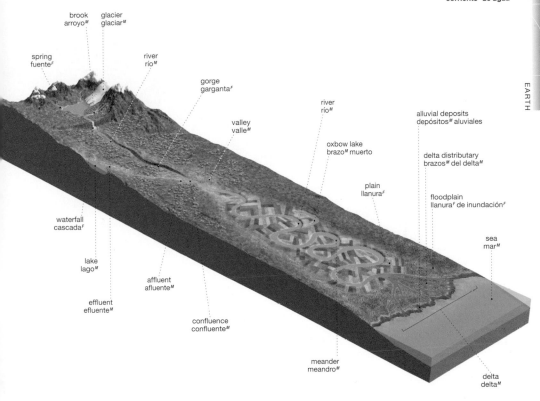

brook
arroyo^M

glacier
glaciar^M

spring
fuente^F

river
río^M

gorge
garganta^F

valley
valle^M

river
río^M

oxbow lake
brazo^M muerto

alluvial deposits
depósitos^M aluviales

delta distributary
brazos^M del delta^M

plain
llanura^F

floodplain
llanura^F de inundación^F

waterfall
cascada^F

sea
mar^M

lake
lago^M

affluent
afluente^M

effluent
efluente^M

confluence
confluente^M

meander
meandro^M

delta
delta^M

examples of lakes
ejemplos^M de lagos^F

glacial lake
lago^M glaciar

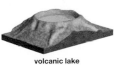

volcanic lake
lago^M volcánico

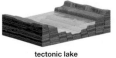

tectonic lake
lago^M tectónico

oxbow lake
lago^M de brazo^M muerto

oasis
oasis^M

artificial lake
embalse^M

EARTH

Earth features

desert
desierto[M]

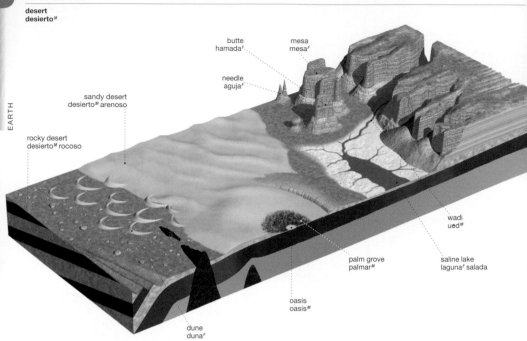

butte
hamada[F]

mesa
mesa[F]

needle
aguja[F]

sandy desert
desierto[M] arenoso

rocky desert
desierto[M] rocoso

wadi
ued[M]

palm grove
palmar[M]

saline lake
laguna[F] salada

oasis
oasis[M]

dune
duna[F]

examples of dunes
ejemplos[M] de dunas[F]

crescentic dune
barján[M]

star dune
duna[F] **en estrella**[F]

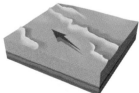

wind direction
dirección[F] del viento[M]

parabolic dune
duna[F] **parabólica**

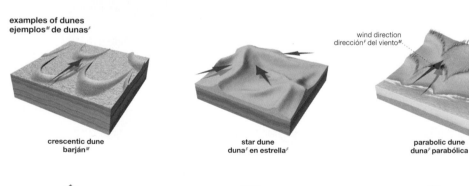

longitudinal dunes
dunas[F] **longitudinales**

transverse dunes
dunas[F] **transversales**

chain of dunes
cadena[F] **de dunas**[F]

EARTH

geological phenomena

fenómenos^M geológicos

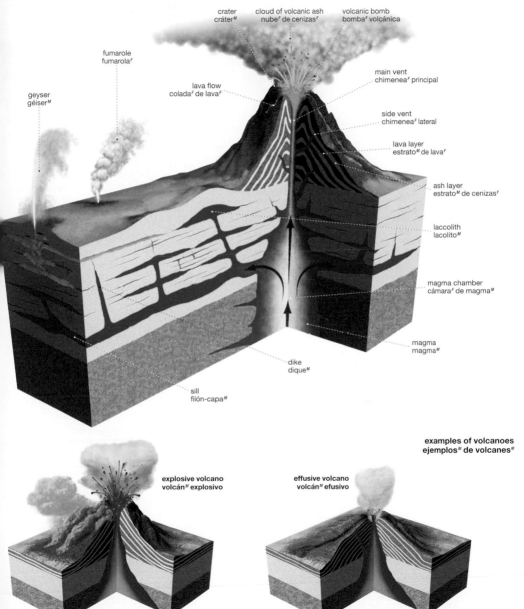

volcano
volcán^M

crater
cráter^M

cloud of volcanic ash
nube^F de cenizas^F

volcanic bomb
bomba^F volcánica

fumarole
fumarola^F

main vent
chimenea^F principal

geyser
géiser^M

lava flow
colada^F de lava^F

side vent
chimenea^F lateral

lava layer
estrato^M de lava^F

ash layer
estrato^M de cenizas^F

laccolith
lacolito^M

magma chamber
cámara^F de magma^M

magma
magma^M

dike
dique^M

sill
filón-capa^M

examples of volcanoes
ejemplos^M de volcanes^M

explosive volcano
volcán^M explosivo

effusive volcano
volcán^M efusivo

EARTH

geological phenomena

earthquake
terremoto^M

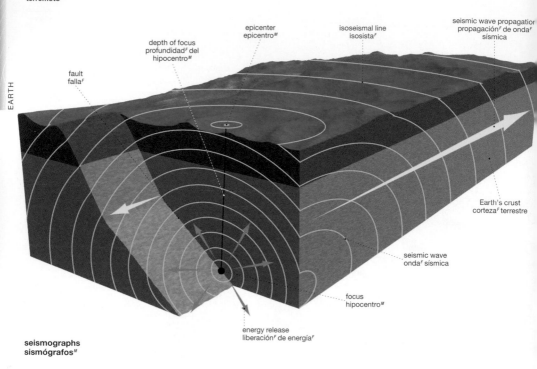

epicenter
epicentro^M

isoseismal line
isosista^F

seismic wave propagation
propagación^F de onda^F
sísmica

depth of focus
profundidad^F del
hipocentro^M

fault
falla^F

Earth's crust
corteza^F terrestre

seismic wave
onda^F sísmica

focus
hipocentro^M

energy release
liberación^F de energía^F

seismographs
sismógrafos^M

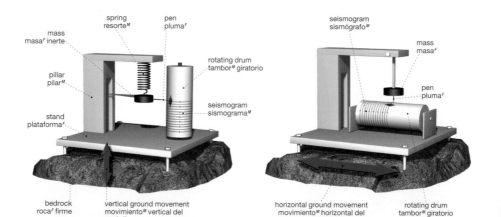

vertical seismograph
sismógrafo^M vertical

spring
resorte^M

pen
pluma^F

mass
masa^F inerte

rotating drum
tambor^M giratorio

pillar
pilar^M

seismogram
sismograma^M

stand
plataforma^F

bedrock
roca^F firme

vertical ground movement
movimiento^M vertical del
suelo^M

horizontal seismograph
sismógrafo^M horizontal

seismogram
sismógrafo^M

mass
masa^F

pen
pluma^F

horizontal ground movement
movimiento^M horizontal del
suelo^M

rotating drum
tambor^M giratorio

geological phenomena

tsunami
tsunami[M]

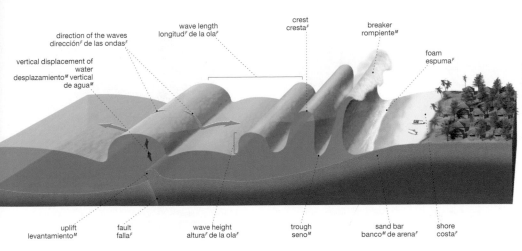

direction of the waves
dirección[F] de las ondas[F]

vertical displacement of
water
desplazamiento[M] vertical
de agua[M]

wave length
longitud[F] de la ola[F]

crest
cresta[F]

breaker
rompiente[M]

foam
espuma[F]

EARTH

uplift
levantamiento[M]

fault
falla[F]

wave height
altura[F] de la ola[F]

trough
seno[M]

sand bar
banco[M] de arena[F]

shore
costa[F]

landslides
desprendimientos[M]
de tierras[F]

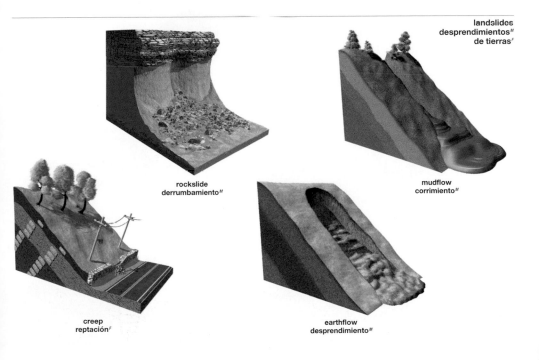

rockslide
derrumbamiento[M]

mudflow
corrimiento[M]

creep
reptación[F]

earthflow
desprendimiento[M]

minerals

mineralesᴹ

examples of common metals and
minerals
ejemplosᴹ de metalesᴹ y mineralesᴹ
comunes

mercury
mercurioᴹ

chromium
cromoᴹ

platinum
platinoᴹ

silver
plataᶠ

asbestos
asbestoᴹ

aluminum
aluminioᴹ

lead
plomoᴹ

uranium
uranioᴹ

gold
oroᴹ

nickel
níquelᴹ

iron
hierroᴹ

copper
cobreᴹ

tin
estañoᴹ

zinc
zincᴹ

titanium
titanioᴹ

examples of metal alloys
ejemplosᴹ de aleacionesᶠ de
metalesᴹ

steel = iron + carbon
aceroᴹ = hierroᴹ +
carbonoᴹ

bronze = copper + tin
bronceᴹ = cobreᴹ +
estañoᴹ

brass = copper + zinc
latónᴹ = cobreᴹ + zincᴹ

EARTH

profile of the Earth's atmosphere

corte^M de la atmósfera^F terrestre

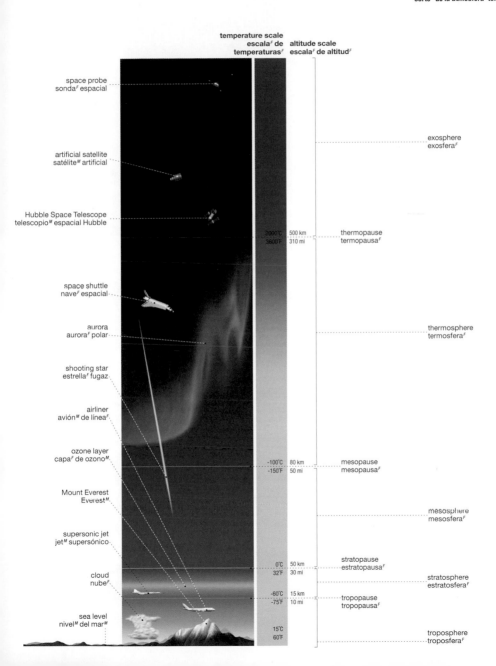

temperature scale
escala^F de
temperaturas^F

altitude scale
escala^F de altitud^F

space probe
sonda^F espacial

artificial satellite
satélite^M artificial

Hubble Space Telescope
telescopio^M espacial Hubble

space shuttle
nave^F espacial

aurora
aurora^F polar

shooting star
estrella^F fugaz

airliner
avión^M de línea^F

ozone layer
capa^F de ozono^M

Mount Everest
Everest^M

supersonic jet
jet^M supersónico

cloud
nube^F

sea level
nivel^M del mar^M

exosphere
exosfera^F

2000°C 500 km
3600°F 310 mi

thermopause
termopausa^F

thermosphere
termosfera^F

-100°C 80 km
-150°F 50 mi

mesopause
mesopausa^F

mesosphere
mesosfera^F

0°C 50 km
32°F 30 mi

stratopause
estratopausa^F

stratosphere
estratosfera^F

-60°C 15 km
-75°F 10 mi

tropopause
tropopausa^F

15°C
60°F

troposphere
troposfera^F

seasons of the year

estaciones^F del año^M

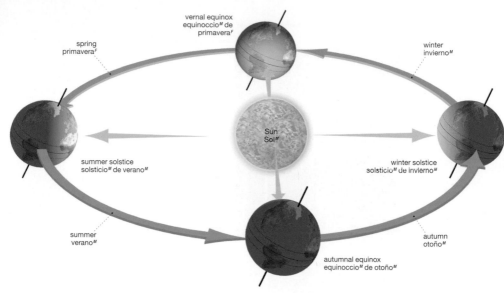

spring
primavera^F

vernal equinox
equinoccio^M de
primavera^F

winter
invierno^M

Sun
Sol^M

summer solstice
solsticio^M de verano^M

winter solstice
solsticio^M de invierno^M

summer
verano^M

autumn
otoño^M

autumnal equinox
equinoccio^M de otoño^M

meteorological forecast

previsión^F meteorológica

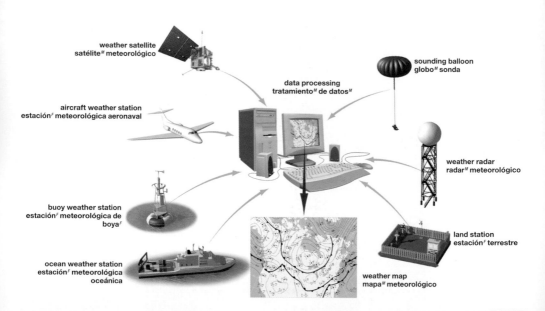

weather satellite
satélite^M meteorológico

sounding balloon
globo^M sonda

data processing
tratamiento^M de datos^M

aircraft weather station
estación^F meteorológica aeronaval

buoy weather station
estación^F meteorológica de
boya^F

weather radar
radar^M meteorológico

land station
estación^F terrestre

ocean weather station
estación^F meteorológica
oceánica

weather map
mapa^M meteorológico

weather map

mapa[M] **meteorológico**

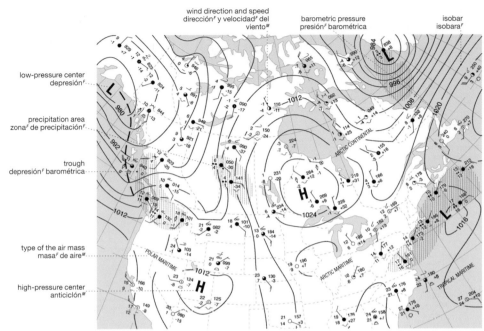

wind direction and speed
dirección[F] y velocidad[F] del
viento[M]

barometric pressure
presión[F] barométrica

isobar
isobara[F]

low-pressure center
depresión[F]

precipitation area
zona[F] de precipitación[F]

trough
depresión[F] barométrica

type of the air mass
masa[F] de aire[M]

high-pressure center
anticiclón[M]

ARCTIC CONTINENTAL

POLAR MARITIME

ARCTIC MARITIME

TROPICAL MARITIME

station model

modelo[M] **de estación**[F]

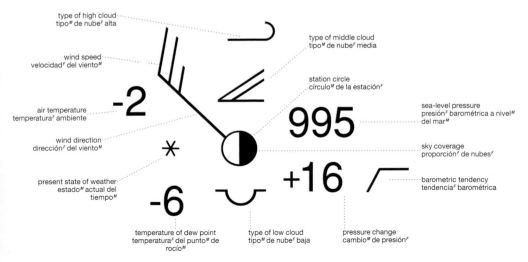

type of high cloud
tipo[M] de nube[F] alta

type of middle cloud
tipo[M] de nube[F] media

wind speed
velocidad[F] del viento[M]

station circle
círculo[M] de la estación[F]

air temperature
temperatura[F] ambiente

sea-level pressure
presión[F] barométrica a nivel[M]
del mar[M]

wind direction
dirección[F] del viento[M]

sky coverage
proporción[F] de nubes[F]

present state of weather
estado[M] actual del
tiempo[M]

barometric tendency
tendencia[F] barométrica

temperature of dew point
temperatura[F] del punto[M] de
rocío[M]

type of low cloud
tipo[M] de nube[F] baja

pressure change
cambio[M] de presión[F]

EARTH

international weather symbols
símbolos[M] meteorológicos internacionales

wind
viento[M]

 calm
sosegado[M]

 wind arrow
flecha[F] indicadora de la dirección[F] del viento[M]

 shaft
brisa[F] leve

 half barb
viento[M] suave

 barb
viento[M] moderado

 pennant
tempestad[F]

fronts
frentes[M]

 surface cold front
frente[M] frío de superficie[F]

 upper cold front
frente[M] frío en las alturas[F]

 surface warm front
frente[M] cálido de superficie[F]

 upper warm front
frente[M] cálido en las alturas[F]

 occluded front
frente[M] ocluido

 stationary front
frente[M] estacionario

sky coverage
nubosidad[F]

 very cloudy sky
cielo[M] muy nuboso

 cloudless sky
cielo[M] despejado

 clear sky
cielo[M] sereno

 slightly covered sky
cielo[M] ligeramente nuboso

 cloudy sky
cielo[M] medio nuboso

overcast sky
cielo[M] completamente nuboso

obscured sky
cielo[M] no observable

clouds
nubes[M]

stratus
estrato[M]

 altostratus
altostrato[M]

 cirrus
cirro[M]

 cumulonimbus
cumulonimbo[M]

 nimbostratus
nimbostrato[M]

 cirrostratus
cirrostrato[M]

 cumulus
cúmulo[M]

 altocumulus
altocúmulo[M]

 cirrocumulus
cirrocúmulo[M]

 stratocumulus
estratocúmulo[M]

international weather symbols

EARTH

sandstorm or dust storm
tormenta[F] de polvo[M] y arena[F]

smoke
humo[M]

thunderstorm
tormenta[F]

heavy thunderstorm
tormenta[F] eléctrica

lightning
relámpago[M]

tropical storm
tormenta[F] tropical

hurricane
huracán[M]

tornado
tornado[M]

light intermittent rain
lluvia[F] ligera
intermitente

light intermittent drizzle
llovizna[F] ligera intermitente

light intermittent snow
nieve[F] ligera intermitente

moderate intermittent
rain
lluvia[F] moderada
intermitente

moderate intermittent
drizzle
llovizna[F] moderada
intermitente

moderate intermittent
snow
nieve[F] moderada
intermitente

heavy intermittent rain
lluvia[F] intensa
intermitente

thick intermittent
drizzle
llovizna[F] fuerte
intermitente

heavy intermittent
snow
nieve[F] fuerte
intermitente

light continuous rain
lluvia[F] ligera continua

light continuous drizzle
llovizna[F] ligera continua

light continuous snow
nieve[F] ligera continua

moderate continuous
rain
lluvia[F] moderada
continua

moderate continuous
drizzle
llovizna[F] moderada
continua

moderate continuous
snow
nieve[F] moderada
continua

heavy continuous rain
lluvia[F] fuerte continua

thick continuous drizzle
llovizna[F] fuerte
continua

heavy continuous snow
nieve[F] fuerte continua

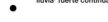
sleet
aguanieve[F]

mist
neblina[F]

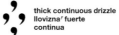
snow shower
chubasco[M] de nieve[F]

drifting snow low
viento[M] fuerte invernal alto

fog
niebla[F]

rain shower
chubasco[M]

drifting snow high
viento[M] fuerte invernal bajo

haze
neblina[F]

hail shower
granizada[F]

freezing rain
lluvia[F] helada

freezing drizzle
llovizna[F] helada

squall
chaparrón[M F]

EARTH

meteorological station

estación^F meteorológica

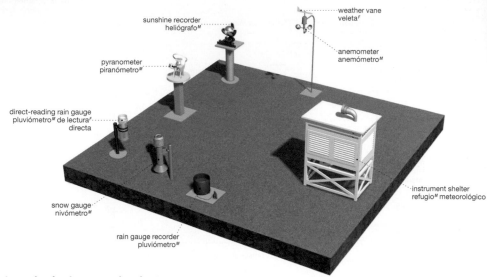

sunshine recorder
heliógrafo^M

weather vane
veleta^F

pyranometer
piranómetro^M

anemometer
anemómetro^M

direct-reading rain gauge
pluviómetro^M de lectura^F
directa

instrument shelter
refugio^M meteorológico

snow gauge
nivómetro^M

rain gauge recorder
pluviómetro^M

meteorological measuring instruments

instrumentos^M de medición^F meteorológica

measure of sunshine
medición^F de la insolación^F

measure of sky radiation
medida^F de radiación^F del
cielo^M

sunshine recorder
heliógrafo^M

pyranometer
piranómetro^M

sphere support
soporte^M de la esfera^F

lower sphere clamp
abrazadera^F inferior

glass sphere
esfera^F de vidrio^M

lower support screw
tornillo^M de soporte^M
inferior

card support
caja^F

check nut
tuerca^F de seguridad^F

sunshine card
banda^F fotosensible

leveling screw
tornillo^M nivelador

base plate
placa^F base^F

lock nut
tuerca^F de fijación^F

sub-base
base^M

sensor
sensor^M

shadow band
banda^F parasol

data logger
registrador^M de datos^M

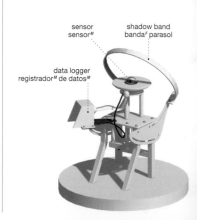

meteorological measuring instruments

direct-reading rain gauge
pluviómetro^M de lectura^F directa

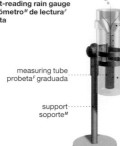

collecting funnel
embudo^M colector

tightening band
banda^F de tensión^F

measuring tube
probeta^F graduada

container
recipiente^M de vertido^M

support
soporte^M

measure of rainfall
medición^F de la lluvia^F

rain gauge recorder
pluviómetro^M

recording unit
unidad^F de registro^M

collecting vessel
recipiente^M de acumulación^F

EARTH

upper-air sounding
sondeo^M en altitud^F

sounding balloon
globo^M sonda

radiosonde
radiosonda^F

measure of air pressure
medición^F de la presión^F del aire^M

barograph
barógrafo^M

mercury barometer
barómetro^M de mercurio^M

measure of snowfall
medición^F de nevadas^F

snow gauge
nivómetro^M

measure of humidity
medición^F de la humedad^F

hygrograph
higrógrafo^M

psychrometer
psicrómetro^M

measure of temperature
medición^F de la temperatura^F

maximum and minimum thermometer
termómetro^M al máximo^M y mínimo^M

measure of wind direction
medición^F de la dirección^F del viento^M

weather vane
veleta^F

measure of cloud ceiling
medición^F de la altura^F de las nubes^F

measure of wind strength
medición^F de la fuerza^F del viento^M

anemometer
anemómetro^M

theodolite
teodolito^M

alidade
alidada^F

ceiling projector
proyector^M de altura^F máxima

EARTH

weather satellites

satélite^M meteorológico

polar-orbiting satellite
satélite^M de órbita^F polar

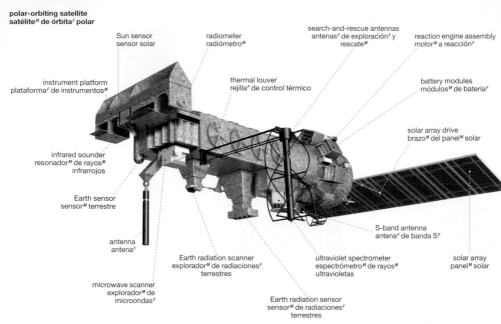

Sun sensor
sensor solar

radiometer
radiómetro^M

search-and-rescue antennas
antenas^F de exploración^F y
rescate^M

reaction engine assembly
motor^M a reacción^F

instrument platform
plataforma^F de instrumentos^M

thermal louver
rejilla^F de control térmico

battery modules
módulos^M de batería^F

solar array drive
brazo^M del panel^M solar

infrared sounder
resonador^M de rayos^M
infrarrojos

Earth sensor
sensor^M terrestre

antenna
antena^F

Earth radiation scanner
explorador^M de radiaciones^F
terrestres

ultraviolet spectrometer
espectrómetro^M de rayos^M
ultravioletas

S-band antenna
antena^F de banda S^F

solar array
panel^M solar

microwave scanner
explorador^M de
microondas^F

Earth radiation sensor
sensor^M de radiaciones^F
terrestres

geostationary satellite
satélite^M geoestacionario

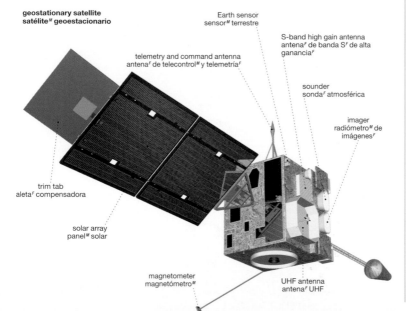

Earth sensor
sensor^M terrestre

telemetry and command antenna
antena^F de telecontrol^M y telemetría^F

S-band high gain antenna
antena^F de banda S^F de alta
ganancia^F

sounder
sonda^F atmosférica

imager
radiómetro^M de
imágenes^F

trim tab
aleta^F compensadora

solar array
panel^M solar

magnetometer
magnetómetro^M

UHF antenna
antena^F UHF

orbit of the satellites
órbita^F de los satélites^M

polar orbit
órbita^F polar

geostationary orbit
órbita^F geoestacionaria

climates of the world
climas^M del mundo^M

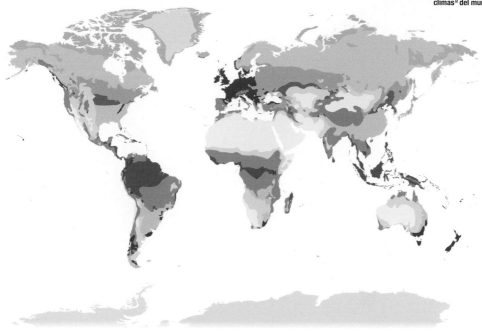

tropical climates
climas^M tropicales

 tropical rain forest
tropical^M lluvioso

 tropical wet-and-dry (savanna)
tropical^M húmedo y seco (sabana^F)

cold temperate climates
climas^M templados fríos

 humid continental-hot summer
continental^M húmedo - verano^M tórrido

 humid continental-warm summer
continental^M húmedo - verano^M fresco

 subarctic
subártico

warm temperate climates
climas^M templados cálidos

 humid subtropical
subtropical húmedo

 Mediterranean subtropical
subtropical mediterráneo

 marine
marítimo

dry climates
climas^M áridos

 steppe
estepario

 desert
desértico

polar climates
climas^M polares

 polar tundra
tundra^F

 polar ice cap
hielos^M perpetuos

highland climates
climas^M de alta montaña^F

 highland
climas^M de montaña^F

clouds
nubes[F]

high clouds
nubes[F] altas

cirrostratus
cirrostrato[M]

cirrocumulus
cirrocúmulo[M]

cirrus
cirros[M]

middle clouds
nubes[F] medias

altostratus
altostrato[M]

altocumulus
altocúmulo[M]

low clouds
nubes[F] bajas

stratocumulus
estratocúmulo[M]

nimbostratus
nimbostrato[M]

stratus
estratos[M]

clouds of vertical development
nubes[F] de desarrollo[M] vertical

cumulus
cúmulos[M]

cumulonimbus
cumulonimbo[M]

tornado and waterspout

tornado^M y tromba^F marina

waterspout
tromba^F marina

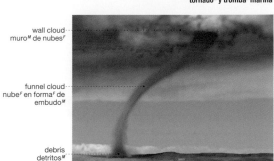

wall cloud
muro^M de nubes^F

funnel cloud
nube^F en forma^F de
embudo^M

debris
detritos^M

tornado
tornado^M

tropical cyclone

ciclón^M tropical

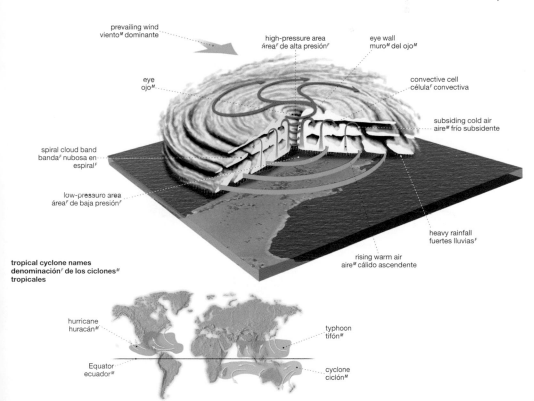

prevailing wind
viento^M dominante

high-pressure area
área^F de alta presión^F

eye wall
muro^M del ojo^M

eye
ojo^M

convective cell
célula^F convectiva

subsiding cold air
aire^M frío subsidente

spiral cloud band
banda^F nubosa en
espiral^F

low-pressure area
área^F de baja presión^F

heavy rainfall
fuertes lluvias^F

rising warm air
aire^M cálido ascendente

tropical cyclone names
denominación^F de los ciclones^M
tropicales

hurricane
huracán^M

typhoon
tifón^M

Equator
ecuador^M

cyclone
ciclón^M

precipitation

precipitación[F]

rain forms
formas[F] de lluvia[F]

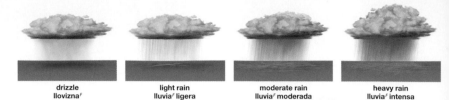

drizzle
llovizna[F]

light rain
lluvia[F] ligera

moderate rain
lluvia[F] moderada

heavy rain
lluvia[F] intensa

winter precipitation forms
formas[F] de precipitaciones[F] invernales

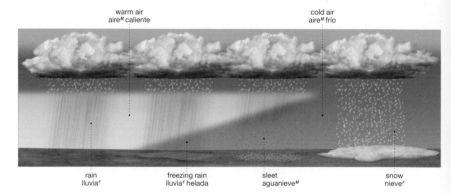

warm air
aire[M] caliente

cold air
aire[M] frío

rain
lluvia[F]

freezing rain
lluvia[F] helada

sleet
aguanieve[M]

snow
nieve[F]

snow crystals
cristales[M] de nieve[F]

needle
aguja[F]

capped column
columna[F] con capuchón[M]

sleet
cellisca[F]

snow pellet
copo[M] de nieve[F]

hail
granizo[M]

column
columna[F]

plate crystal
placa[F] de hielo[M]

spatial dendrite
dendrita[F] espacial

irregular crystal
cristales[M] irregulares

stellar crystal
estrella[F]

precipitation

stormy sky
cielo^M **turbulento**

cloud
nube^F

lightning
rayo^M

rainbow
arco^M iris

rain
lluvia^F

dew
rocío^M

rime
escarcha^F

mist
neblina^F

fog
niebla^F

frost
hielo^M

vegetation regions
distribución^F de la vegetación^F

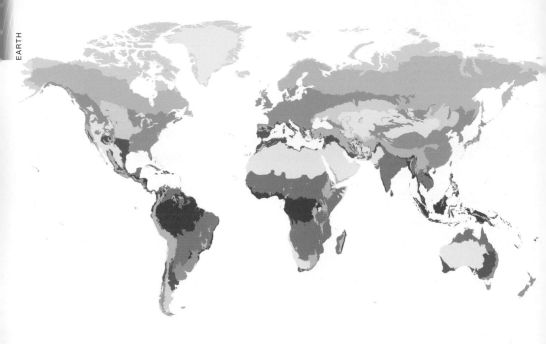

tundra
tundra^F

tropical rain forest
bosque^M tropical
húmedo

scrub
monte^M bajo

boreal forest
bosque^M boreal

temperate grassland
praderas^F templadas

desert
desierto^M

temperate forest
bosque^M templado

savanna
sabana^F

rock and ice
roca^F y hielo^M

types of vegetation
tipos*M* de vegetación*F*

boreal forest
bosque*M* boreal

temperate forest
bosque*M* templado

tropical rain forest
bosque*M* tropical

savanna
sabana*F*

scrub
monte*M* bajo

temperate grassland
praderas*F* templadas

desert
desierto*M*

tundra
tundra*F*

EARTH

food chain
cadena^F alimentaria

ecological pyramid
pirámide^F ecológica

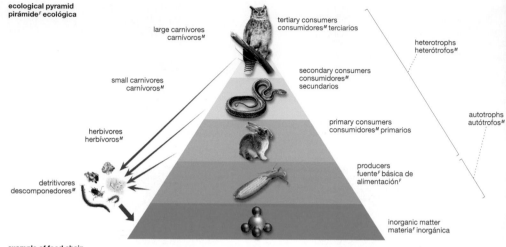

large carnivores
carnívoros^M

tertiary consumers
consumidores^M terciarios

heterotrophs
heterótrofos^M

small carnivores
carnívoros^M

secondary consumers
consumidores^M
secundarios

herbivores
herbívoros^M

primary consumers
consumidores^M primarios

autotrophs
autótrofos^M

detritivores
descomponedores^M

producers
fuente^F básica de
alimentación^F

inorganic matter
materia^F inorgánica

example of food chain
ejemplo^M de cadena^F
alimentaria

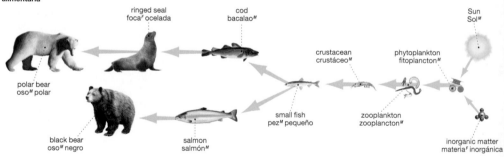

ringed seal
foca^F ocelada

cod
bacalao^M

Sun
Sol

crustacean
crustáceo^M

phytoplankton
fitoplancton^M

polar bear
oso^M polar

small fish
pez^M pequeño

zooplankton
zooplancton^M

black bear
oso^M negro

salmon
salmón^M

inorganic matter
materia^F inorgánica

structure of the biosphere
estructura^F de la biosfera^F

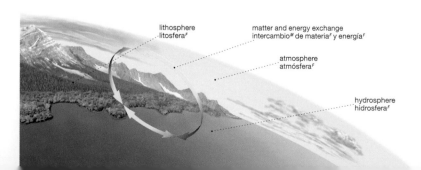

lithosphere
litosfera^F

matter and energy exchange
intercambio^M de materia^F y energía^F

atmosphere
atmósfera^F

hydrosphere
hidrosfera^F

hydrologic cycle

ciclo^M hidrológico

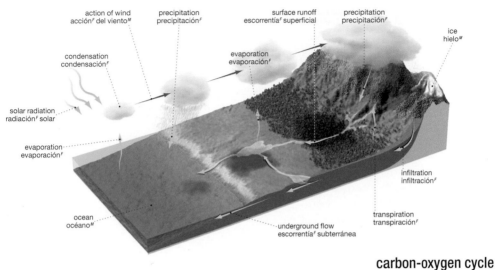

action of wind
acción^F del viento^M

precipitation
precipitación^F

surface runoff
escorrentía^F superficial

precipitation
precipitación^F

ice
hielo^M

condensation
condensación^F

evaporation
evaporación^F

solar radiation
radiación^F solar

evaporation
evaporación^F

infiltration
infiltración^F

ocean
océano^M

transpiration
transpiración^F

underground flow
escorrentía^F subterránea

carbon-oxygen cycle

ciclo^M del carbono^M-oxígeno^M

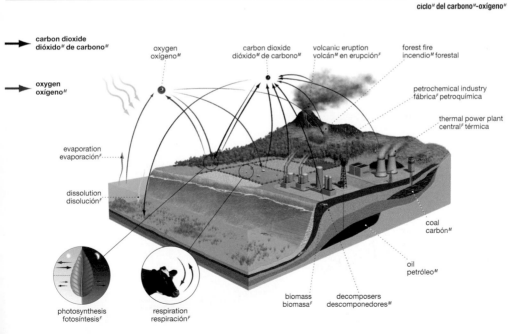

carbon dioxide
dióxido^M de carbono^M

oxygen
oxígeno^M

oxygen
oxígeno^M

oxygen
oxígeno^M

carbon dioxide
dióxido^M de carbono^M

volcanic eruption
volcán^M en erupción^F

forest fire
incendio^M forestal

petrochemical industry
fábrica^F petroquímica

thermal power plant
central^F térmica

evaporation
evaporación^F

dissolution
disolución^F

coal
carbón^M

oil
petróleo^M

photosynthesis
fotosíntesis^F

respiration
respiración^F

biomass
biomasa^F

decomposers
descomponedores^M

EARTH

natural greenhouse effect

efectoᴹ **invernadero**ᴹ **natural**

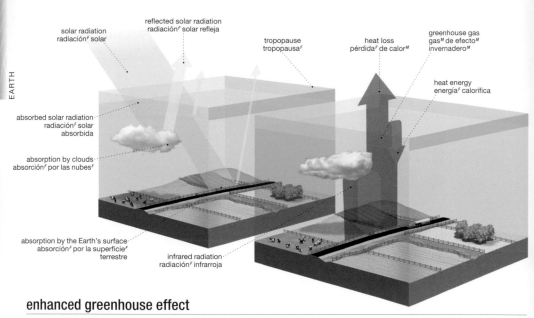

solar radiation
radiación^F solar

reflected solar radiation
radiación^F solar refleja

tropopause
tropopausa^F

heat loss
pérdida^F de calor^M

greenhouse gas
gas^M de efecto^M
invernadero^M

heat energy
energía^F calorífica

absorbed solar radiation
radiación^F solar
absorbida

absorption by clouds
absorción^F por las nubes^F

absorption by the Earth's surface
absorción^F por la superficie^F
terrestre

infrared radiation
radiación^F infrarroja

enhanced greenhouse effect

aumentoᴹ **del efecto**ᴹ **invernadero**ᴹ

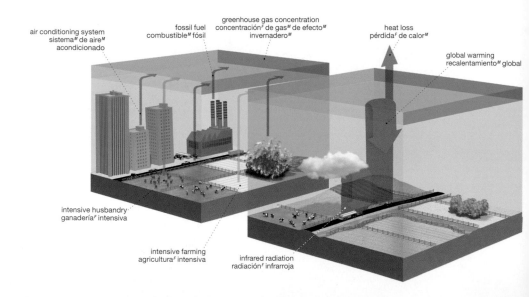

air conditioning system
sistema^M de aire^M
acondicionado

fossil fuel
combustible^M fósil

greenhouse gas concentration
concentración^F de gas^M de efecto^M
invernadero^M

heat loss
pérdida^F de calor^M

global warming
recalentamiento^M global

intensive husbandry
ganadería^F intensiva

intensive farming
agricultura^F intensiva

infrared radiation
radiación^F infrarroja

air pollution
contaminación^F del aire^M

EARTH

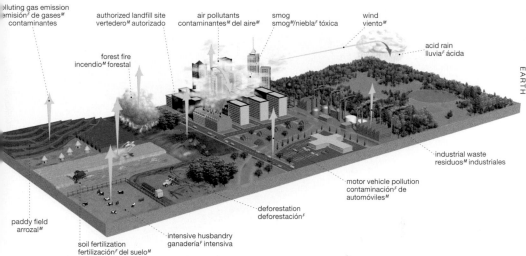

polluting gas emission
emisión^F de gases^M
contaminantes

authorized landfill site
vertedero^M autorizado

air pollutants
contaminantes^M del aire^M

smog
smog^M/niebla^F tóxica

wind
viento^M

acid rain
lluvia^F ácida

forest fire
incendio^M forestal

industrial waste
residuos^M industriales

motor vehicle pollution
contaminación^F de
automóviles^M

deforestation
deforestación^F

paddy field
arrozal^M

intensive husbandry
ganadería^F intensiva

soil fertilization
fertilización^F del suelo^M

land pollution
contaminación^F del suelo^M

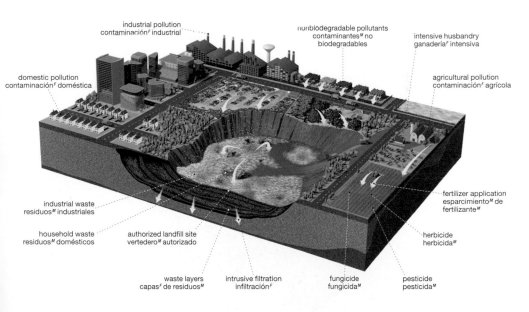

industrial pollution
contaminación^F industrial

nonbiodegradable pollutants
contaminantes^M no
biodegradables

intensive husbandry
ganadería^F intensiva

domestic pollution
contaminación^F doméstica

agricultural pollution
contaminación^F agrícola

industrial waste
residuos^M industriales

household waste
residuos^M domésticos

authorized landfill site
vertedero^M autorizado

fertilizer application
esparcimiento^M de
fertilizante^M

herbicide
herbicida^M

waste layers
capas^F de residuos^M

intrusive filtration
infiltración^F

fungicide
fungicida^M

pesticide
pesticida^M

EARTH

water pollution

contaminación^f del agua^f

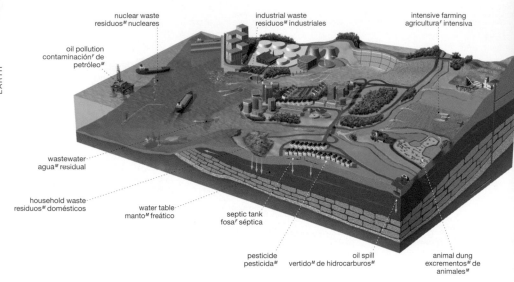

nuclear waste
residuos^M nucleares

industrial waste
residuos^M industriales

intensive farming
agricultura^f intensiva

oil pollution
contaminación^f de
petróleo^M

wastewater
agua^M residual

household waste
residuos^M domésticos

water table
manto^M freático

septic tank
fosa^f séptica

pesticide
pesticida^M

oil spill
vertido^M de hidrocarburos^M

animal dung
excrementos^M de
animales^M

acid rain

lluvia^f ácida

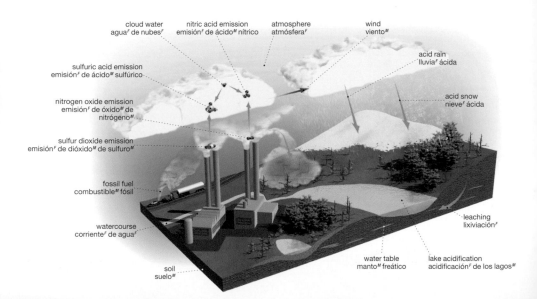

cloud water
agua^f de nubes^f

nitric acid emission
emisión^f de ácido^M nítrico

atmosphere
atmósfera^f

wind
viento^M

acid rain
lluvia^f ácida

sulfuric acid emission
emisión^f de ácido^M sulfúrico

acid snow
nieve^f ácida

nitrogen oxide emission
emisión^f de óxido^M de
nitrógeno^M

sulfur dioxide emission
emisión^f de dióxido^M de sulfuro^M

fossil fuel
combustible^M fósil

watercourse
corriente^f de agua^f

soil
suelo^M

water table
manto^M freático

leaching
lixiviación^f

lake acidification
acidificación^f de los lagos^M

EARTH

selective sorting of waste
separaciónᶠ **selectiva de residuos**ᴹ

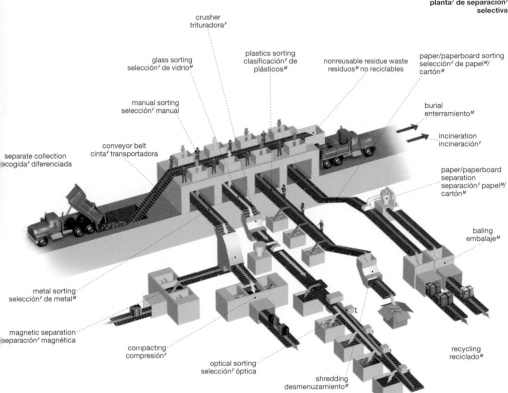

sorting plant
planta ᶠ de separación ᶠ
selectiva

crusher
trituradora ᶠ

glass sorting
selección ᶠ de vidrio ᴹ

plastics sorting
clasificación ᶠ de
plásticos ᴹ

nonreusable residue waste
residuos ᴹ no reciclables

paper/paperboard sorting
selección ᶠ de papel ᴹ/
cartón ᴹ

manual sorting
selección ᶠ manual

burial
enterramiento ᴹ

incineration
incineración ᶠ

conveyor belt
cinta ᶠ transportadora

separate collection
recogida ᶠ diferenciada

paper/paperboard
separation
separación ᶠ papel ᴹ/
cartón ᴹ

baling
embalaje ᴹ

metal sorting
selección ᶠ de metal ᴹ

magnetic separation
separación ᶠ magnética

compacting
compresión ᶠ

optical sorting
selección ᶠ óptica

shredding
desmenuzamiento ᴹ

recycling
reciclado ᴹ

---

recycling containers
contenedores ᴹ de reciclaje ᴹ

paper recycling container
contenedor ᴹ de reciclado ᴹ
de papel ᴹ

aluminum recycling container
contenedor ᴹ de reciclado ᴹ de
aluminio ᴹ

recycling bin
cubo ᴹ de basura ᶠ
reciclable

glass recycling container
contenedor ᴹ de reciclado ᴹ de vidrio ᴹ

paper collection unit
contenedor ᴹ de recogida ᶠ de
papel ᴹ

glass collection unit
contenedor ᴹ de recogida ᶠ
de vidrio ᴹ

PLANTS AND PLANTLIKE ORGANISMS

reino vegetal

PLANT LIFE   102

plant cell   102
photosynthesis   102
unusual plants   103
life cycle (flowering plant)   104
plant growth   105

PLANTS & PLANTLIKE ORGANISMS   106

lichen   106
moss   106
plants & plantlike organisms   107
fern   107
mushroom   108

PLANT   109

parts of a plant   109
root   110
stem   110
leaf   111
flower   112
fruit   114
grape   117
tree   118
conifer   120

INDUSTRIAL USE   122

grain industry   122
textile industry   123
rubber industry   124
paper industry   124

plant cell

célula^F vegetal

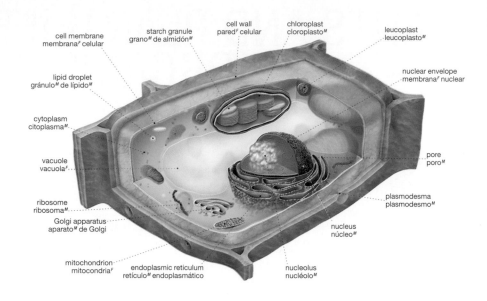

cell membrane
membrana^F celular

starch granule
grano^M de almidón^M

cell wall
pared^F celular

chloroplast
cloroplasto^M

leucoplast
leucoplasto^M

lipid droplet
gránulo^M de lípido^M

nuclear envelope
membrana^F nuclear

cytoplasm
citoplasma^M

vacuole
vacuola^F

pore
poro^M

ribosome
ribosoma^M

plasmodesma
plasmodesmo^M

Golgi apparatus
aparato^M de Golgi

nucleus
núcleo^M

mitochondrion
mitocondria^F

endoplasmic reticulum
retículo^M endoplasmático

nucleolus
nucléolo^M

photosynthesis

fotosíntesis^F

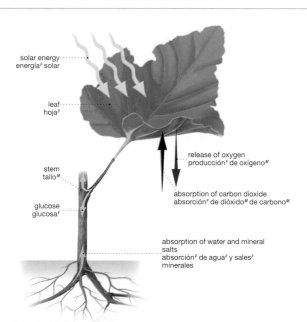

solar energy
energía^F solar

leaf
hoja^F

stem
tallo^M

glucose
glucosa^F

release of oxygen
producción^F de oxígeno^M

absorption of carbon dioxide
absorción^F de dióxido^M de carbono^M

absorption of water and mineral salts
absorción^F de agua^F y sales^F minerales

unusual plants

plantas*r* poco comunes

examples of parasitic plants
ejemplos*M* de plantas*r* parásitas

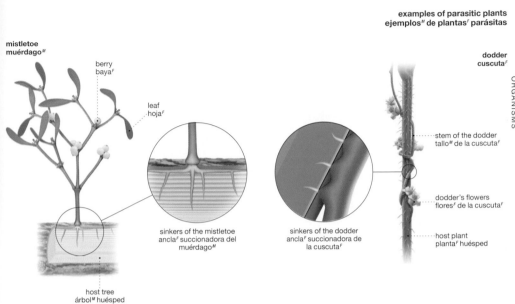

mistletoe
muérdago*M*

berry
baya*F*

leaf
hoja*F*

dodder
cuscuta*F*

stem of the dodder
tallo*M* de la cuscuta*F*

dodder's flowers
flores*F* de la cuscuta*F*

host plant
planta*F* huésped

sinkers of the mistletoe
ancla*F* succionadora del
muérdago*M*

sinkers of the dodder
ancla*F* succionadora de
la cuscuta*F*

host tree
árbol*M* huésped

examples of carnivorous plants
ejemplos*M* de plantas*r* carnívoras

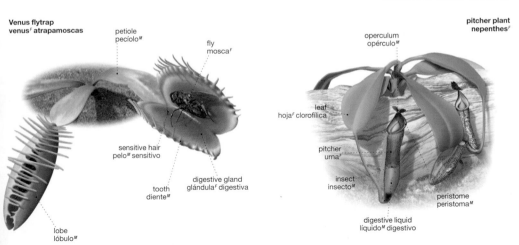

Venus flytrap
venus*F* atrapamoscas

petiole
pecíolo*M*

fly
mosca*F*

pitcher plant
nepenthes*F*

operculum
opérculo*M*

leaf
hoja*F* clorofílica

sensitive hair
pelo*M* sensitivo

pitcher
urna*F*

tooth
diente*M*

digestive gland
glándula*F* digestiva

insect
insecto*M*

peristome
peristoma*M*

lobe
lóbulo*M*

digestive liquid
líquido*M* digestivo

life cycle (flowering plant)

ciclo^M **de reproducción**^F

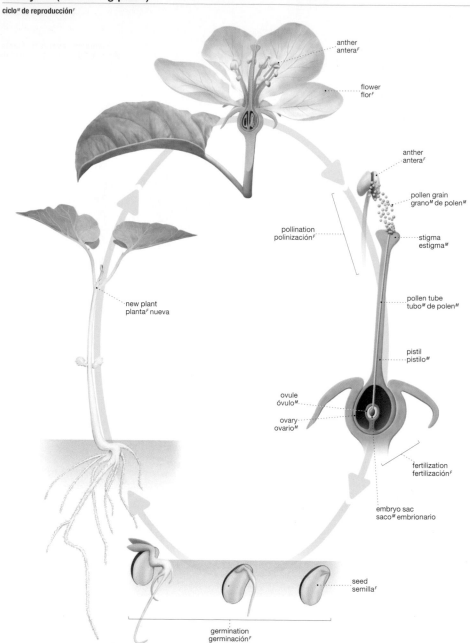

anther
antera^F

flower
flor^F

anther
antera^F

pollen grain
grano^M de polen^M

pollination
polinización^F

stigma
estigma^M

pollen tube
tubo^M de polen^M

new plant
planta^F nueva

pistil
pistilo^M

ovule
óvulo^M

ovary
ovario^M

fertilization
fertilización^F

embryo sac
saco^M embrionario

seed
semilla^F

germination
germinación^F

plant growth

crecimiento^M de una planta^F

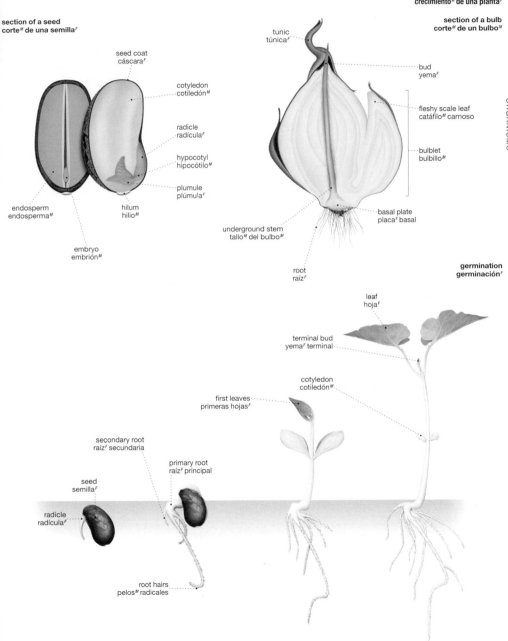

section of a seed
corte^M de una semilla^F

seed coat
cáscara^F

cotyledon
cotiledón^M

radicle
radícula^F

hypocotyl
hipocótilo^M

plumule
plúmula^F

endosperm
endosperma^M

hilum
hilio^M

embryo
embrión^M

section of a bulb
corte^M de un bulbo^M

tunic
túnica^F

bud
yema^F

fleshy scale leaf
catáfilo^M carnoso

bulblet
bulbillo^M

basal plate
placa^F basal

underground stem
tallo^M del bulbo^M

root
raíz^F

germination
germinación^F

leaf
hoja^F

terminal bud
yema^F terminal

cotyledon
cotiledón^M

first leaves
primeras hojas^F

secondary root
raíz^F secundaria

primary root
raíz^F principal

seed
semilla^F

radicle
radícula^F

root hairs
pelos^M radicales

lichen

liquen^M

structure of a lichen
estructura^F **de un**
liquen^M

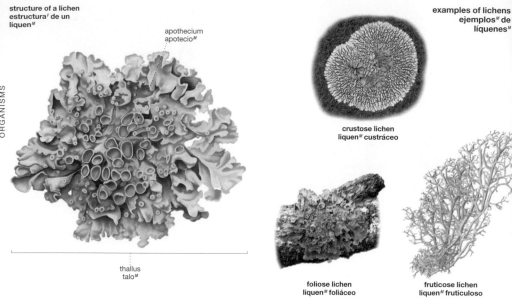

apothecium
apotecio^M

thallus
talo^M

examples of lichens
ejemplos^M **de**
líquenes^M

crustose lichen
liquen^M custráceo

foliose lichen
liquen^M foliáceo

fruticose lichen
liquen^M fruticuloso

moss

musgo^M

structure of a moss
estructura^F **de un**
musgo^M

stalk
pedúnculo^M

capsule
cápsula^F

leaf
hoja^F

stem
tallo^M

rhizoid
rizoide^M

examples of mosses
ejemplos^M **de**
musgos^M

common hair cap moss
polítrico^M

sphagnum
musgo^M esfagnáceo

plants & plantlike organisms

alga[F]

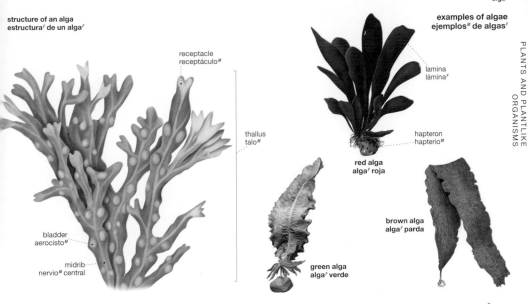

structure of an alga
estructura[F] de un alga[F]

receptacle
receptáculo[M]

thallus
talo[M]

bladder
aerocisto[M]

midrib
nervio[M] central

examples of algae
ejemplos[M] de algas[F]

lamina
lámina[F]

hapteron
hapterio[M]

red alga
alga[F] roja

brown alga
alga[F] parda

green alga
alga[F] verde

fern

helecho[M]

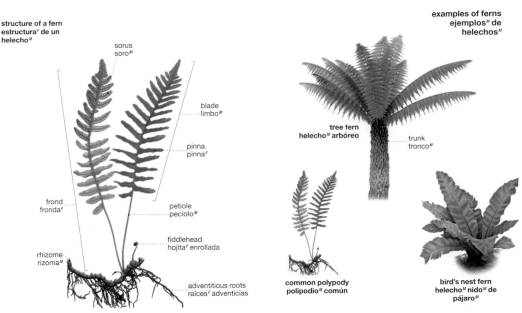

structure of a fern
estructura[F] de un
helecho[M]

sorus
soro[M]

blade
limbo[M]

pinna
pinna[F]

frond
fronda[F]

petiole
pecíolo[M]

fiddlehead
hojita[F] enrollada

rhizome
rizoma[M]

adventitious roots
raíces[F] adventicias

examples of ferns
ejemplos[M] de
helechos[M]

tree fern
helecho[M] arbóreo

trunk
tronco[M]

common polypody
polipodio[M] común

bird's nest fern
helecho[M] nido[M] de
pájaro[M]

PLANTS AND PLANTLIKE ORGANISMS

mushroom

hongo[M]

structure of a mushroom
anatomía[F] de un hongo[M]

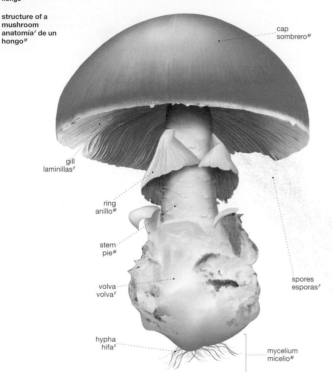

cap
sombrero[M]

gill
laminillas[F]

ring
anillo[M]

stem
pie[M]

volva
volva[F]

hypha
hifa[F]

spores
esporas[F]

mycelium
micelio[M]

examples of edible mushrooms
ejemplos[M] de setas[F] comestibles

common morel
morel[M]

king boletus
cep[M]

examples of poisonous mushrooms
ejemplos[M] de setas[F] venenosas

Satan's boletus
boletus[M] satanás[M]

fly agaric
amanita[F] muscaria

examples of deadly poisonous mushrooms
ejemplos[M] de setas[F] venenosas mortales

deadly lepiota
lepiota[F] cristata

destroying angel
amanita[F] virosa

parts of a plant
partes^F **de una planta**^F

structure of a plant
anatomía^F **de una planta**^F

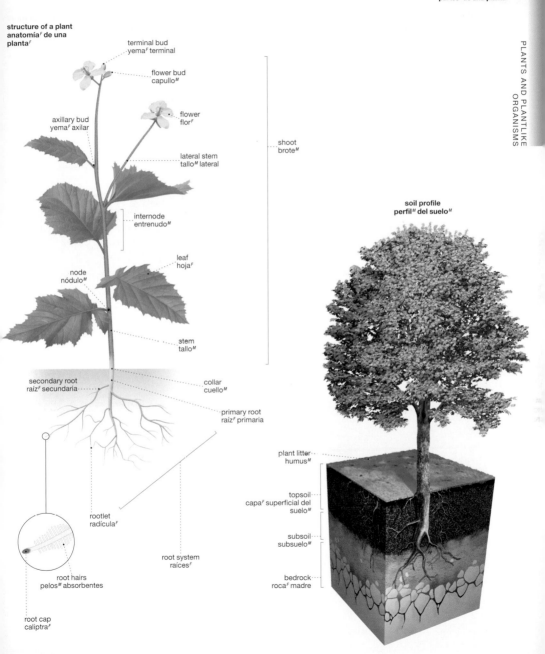

terminal bud
yema^F terminal

flower bud
capullo^M

flower
flor^F

axillary bud
yema^F axilar

lateral stem
tallo^M lateral

shoot
brote^M

internode
entrenudo^M

leaf
hoja^F

node
nódulo^M

stem
tallo^M

secondary root
raíz^F secundaria

collar
cuello^M

primary root
raíz^F primaria

rootlet
radícula^F

root system
raíces^F

root hairs
pelos^M absorbentes

root cap
caliptra^F

soil profile
perfil^M **del suelo**^M

plant litter
humus^M

topsoil
capa^F superficial del suelo^M

subsoil
subsuelo^M

bedrock
roca^F madre

root

raíz^F

structure of a root
estructura^F de una raíz^F

examples of roots
ejemplos^M de raíces^F

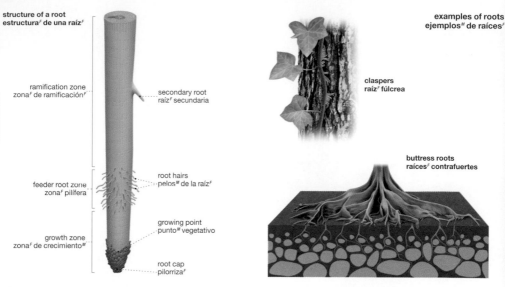

ramification zone
zona^F de ramificación^F

secondary root
raíz^F secundaria

claspers
raíz^F fúlcrea

feeder root zone
zona^F pilífera

root hairs
pelos^M de la raíz^F

buttress roots
raíces^F contrafuertes

growing point
punto^M vegetativo

growth zone
zona^F de crecimiento^M

root cap
pilorriza^F

stem

tallo^M

section of a stem
corte^M de un tallo^M

**examples of atypical
stems
ejemplos^M de tallos^M
raros**

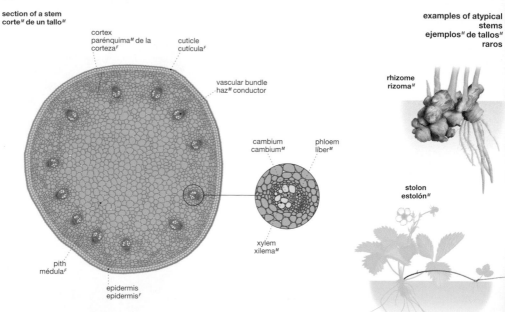

cortex
parénquima^M de la
corteza^F

cuticle
cutícula^F

vascular bundle
haz^M conductor

rhizome
rizoma^M

cambium
cambium^M

phloem
líber^M

stolon
estolón^M

xylem
xilema^M

pith
médula^F

epidermis
epidermis^F

leaf
hoja[f]

simple leaves
hojas[f] simples

reniform
reniforme

cordate
acorazonada

orbiculate
orbicular

spatulate
espatulada

linear
acicular

hastate
astada

ovate
aovada

lanceolate
lanceolada

peltate
peltada

structure of a leaf
estructura[f] de una hoja[f]

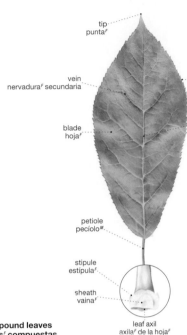

tip
punta[f]

vein
nervadura[f] secundaria

blade
hoja[f]

margin
borde[M]

midrib
nervadura[f] principal

petiole
pecíolo[M]

stipule
estípula[f]

sheath
vaina[f]

leaf axil
axila[f] de la hoja[f]

compound leaves
hojas[f] compuestas

trifoliolate
trifoliada

pinnatifid
pinatífida

palmate
palmeada

abruptly pinnate
paripinnada

odd pinnate
imparipinnada

leaf margins
bordes[M] de hojas[f]

serrate
dentada

doubly serrate
doble dentada

crenate
festoneada

ciliate
ciliada

entire
entera

lobate
lobulada

flower

flor*F*

structure of a flower
estructura*F* de una flor*F*

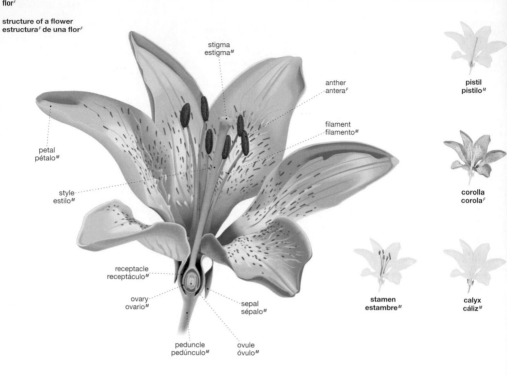

stigma
estigma*M*

anther
antera*F*

filament
filamento*M*

petal
pétalo*M*

style
estilo*M*

receptacle
receptáculo*M*

ovary
ovario*M*

sepal
sépalo*M*

peduncle
pedúnculo*M*

ovule
óvulo*M*

pistil
pistilo*M*

corolla
corola*F*

stamen
estambre*M*

calyx
cáliz*M*

types of inflorescences
variedades*F* de inflorescencias*F*

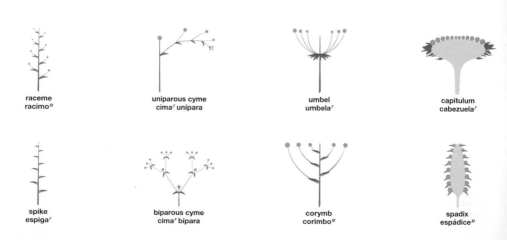

raceme
racimo*M*

uniparous cyme
cima*F* unípara

umbel
umbela*F*

capitulum
cabezuela*F*

spike
espiga*F*

biparous cyme
cima*F* bípara

corymb
corimbo*M*

spadix
espádice*M*

flower

examples of flowers
ejemplos^M de flores^F

PLANTS AND PLANTLIKE
ORGANISMS

tulip
tulipán^M

lily of the valley
muguete^M

carnation
clavel^M

rose
rosa^F

orchid
orquídea^F

begonia
begonia^F

lily
azucena^F

violet
violeta^F

crocus
croco^M

daffodil
narciso^M

poppy
amapola^F

thistle
cardo^M

pansy
pensamiento^M

buttercup
botón^M de oro^M

daisy
margarita^F

primrose
prímula^F

geranium
geranio^M

dandelion
diente^M de león^M

sunflower
girasol^M

fruit

fruta*F*

fleshy berry fruit
fruto*M* carnoso: baya*F*

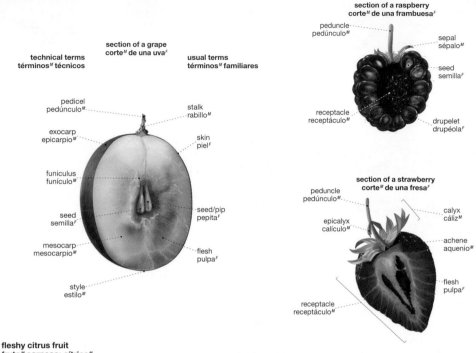

section of a grape
corte*M* de una uva*F*

technical terms
términos*M* técnicos

usual terms
términos*M* familiares

pedicel
pedúnculo*M*.

exocarp
epicarpio*M*

funiculus
funículo*M*

seed
semilla*F*

mesocarp
mesocarpio*M*

style
estilo*M*

stalk
rabillo*M*

skin
piel*F*

seed/pip
pepita*F*

flesh
pulpa*F*

section of a raspberry
corte*M* de una frambuesa*F*

peduncle
pedúnculo*M*

receptacle
receptáculo*M*

sepal
sépalo*M*

seed
semilla*F*

drupelet
drupéola*F*

section of a strawberry
corte*M* de una fresa*F*

peduncle
pedúnculo*M*.

epicalyx
calículo*M*

receptacle
receptáculo*M*

calyx
cáliz*M*

achene
aquenio*M*

flesh
pulpa*F*

fleshy citrus fruit
fruto*M* carnoso: cítrico*M*

section of an orange
corte*M* de una naranja*F*

technical terms
términos*M* técnicos

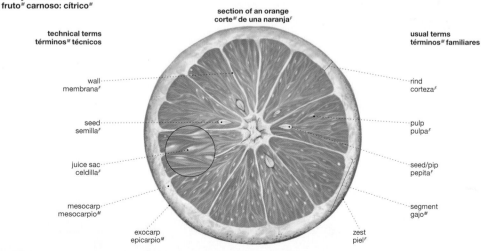

wall
membrana*F*

seed
semilla*F*

juice sac
celdilla*F*

mesocarp
mesocarpio*M*

exocarp
epicarpio*M*

usual terms
términos*M* familiares

rind
corteza*F*

pulp
pulpa*F*

seed/pip
pepita*F*

segment
gajo*M*

zest
piel*F*

fleshy pome fruit
pomo^M **carnoso**

section of an apple
corte^M de una manzana^F

technical terms
términos^M técnicos

usual terms
términos^M familiares

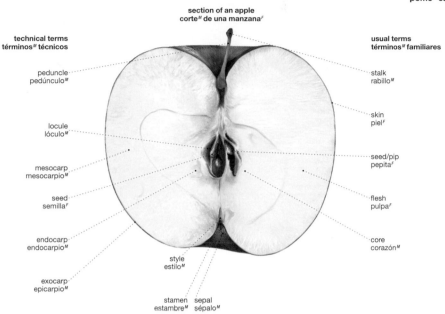

peduncle
pedúnculo^M

locule
lóculo^M

mesocarp
mesocarpio^M

seed
semilla^F

endocarp
endocarpio^M

exocarp
epicarpio^M

style
estilo^M

stamen   sepal
estambre^M sépalo^M

stalk
rabillo^M

skin
piel^F

seed/pip
pepita^F

flesh
pulpa^F

core
corazón^M

fleshy stone fruit
drupa^F

technical terms
términos^M técnicos

section of a peach
corte^M de un durazno^M

usual terms
términos^M familiares

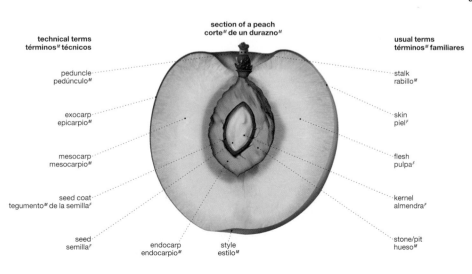

peduncle
pedúnculo^M

exocarp
epicarpio^M

mesocarp
mesocarpio^M

seed coat
tegumento^M de la semilla^F

seed
semilla^F

endocarp
endocarpio^M

style
estilo^M

stalk
rabillo^M

skin
piel^F

flesh
pulpa^F

kernel
almendra^F

stone/pit
hueso^M

PLANTS AND PLANTLIKE ORGANISMS

fruit

**examples of dry
fruits
ejemplos**^M **de frutos**^M
secos

section of a silique (mustard)
corte^M de una vaina^F
(mostaza^F)

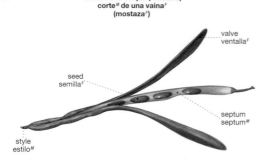

valve
ventalla^F

seed
semilla^F

septum
septum^M

style
estilo^M

section of a capsule (poppy)
corte^M de una cápsula^F
(amapola^F)

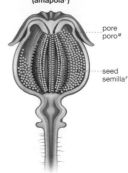

pore
poro^M

seed
semilla^F

section of a legume (pea)
corte^M de una legumbre^F
(guisante^M)

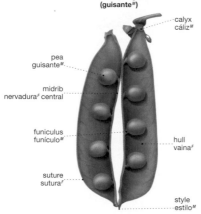

calyx
cáliz^M

pea
guisante^M

midrib
nervadura^F central

funiculus
funículo^M

hull
vaina^F

suture
sutura^F

style
estilo^M

section of a follicle (star anise)
corte^M de un folículo^M (anís^M estrellado)

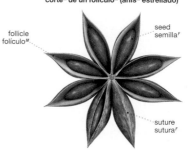

follicle
folículo^M

seed
semilla^F

suture
sutura^F

section of a nut (hazelnut)
corte^M de una avellana^F

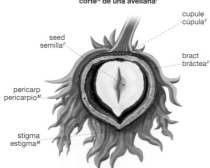

cupule
cúpula^F

seed
semilla^F

bract
bráctea^F

pericarp
pericarpio^M

stigma
estigma^M

section of a nut (walnut)
corte^M de una nuez^F

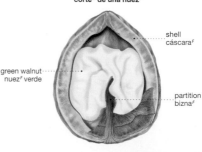

shell
cáscara^F

green walnut
nuez^F verde

partition
bizna^F

grape
uva[F]

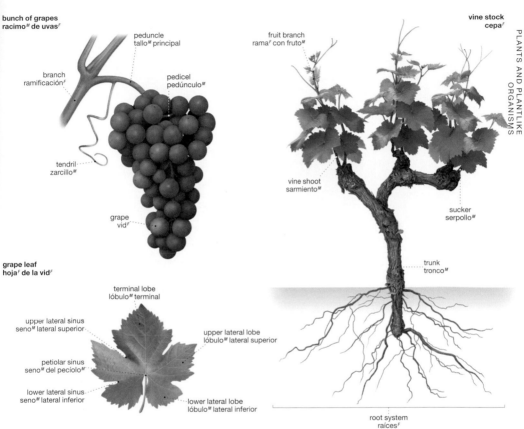

bunch of grapes
racimo[M] de uvas[F]

peduncle
tallo[M] principal

branch
ramificación[F]

pedicel
pedúnculo[M]

tendril
zarcillo[M]

grape
vid[F]

vine stock
cepa[F]

fruit branch
rama[F] con fruto[M]

vine shoot
sarmiento[M]

sucker
serpollo[M]

trunk
tronco[M]

grape leaf
hoja[F] de la vid[F]

terminal lobe
lóbulo[M] terminal

upper lateral sinus
seno[M] lateral superior

upper lateral lobe
lóbulo[M] lateral superior

petiolar sinus
seno[M] del pecíolo[M]

lower lateral sinus
seno[M] lateral inferior

lower lateral lobe
lóbulo[M] lateral inferior

root system
raíces[F]

maturing steps
etapas[F] de la
maduración[F]

flowering
floración[F]

fruition
fructificación[F]

ripening
envero[M]

ripeness
madurez[F]

tree

árbolᴹ

structure of a tree
anatomíaᶠ **de un árbol**ᴹ

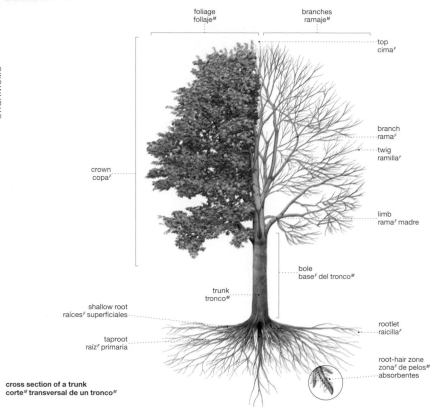

foliage
follaje**ᴹ**

branches
ramaje**ᴹ**

top
cima**ᶠ**

branch
rama**ᶠ**

twig
ramilla**ᶠ**

limb
rama**ᶠ** madre

crown
copa**ᶠ**

bole
base**ᶠ** del tronco**ᴹ**

trunk
tronco**ᴹ**

shallow root
raíces**ᶠ** superficiales

taproot
raíz**ᶠ** primaria

rootlet
raicilla**ᶠ**

root-hair zone
zona**ᶠ** de pelos**ᴹ**
absorbentes

cross section of a trunk
corteᴹ **transversal de un tronco**ᴹ

wood ray
radio**ᴹ** medular

pith
médula**ᶠ**

annual ring
anillo**ᴹ** de crecimiento**ᴹ**

cambium
cambium**ᴹ**

heartwood
duramen**ᴹ**

phloem
líber**ᴹ**

sapwood
albura**ᶠ**

bark
corteza**ᶠ**

stump
tocónᴹ

shoot
retoño**ᴹ**

tree

examples of broadleaved trees
ejemplos^M de latifolios^M

oak
roble^M

birch
abedul^M

weeping willow
sauce^M llorón

poplar
álamo^M

palm tree
palmera^F

maple
arce^M

beech
haya^F

walnut
nogal^M

tree

examples of broadleaved trees

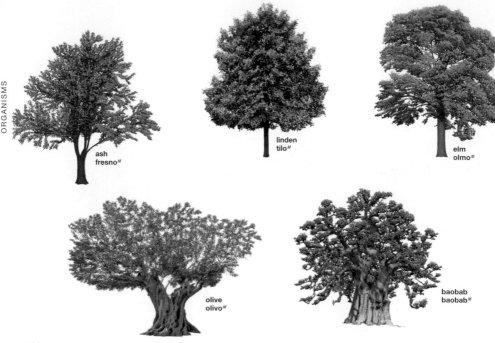

ash
fresno^M

linden
tilo^M

elm
olmo^M

olive
olivo^M

baobab
baobab^M

conifer

conífera^F

reproductive
structures
estructuras^F de
reproducción^F

pine seed
piñón^M

cone
piña^F

examples of leaves
ejemplos^M de hojas^F

pine needles
agujas^F del pino^M

spruce needles
agujas^F de pícea^F

branch
rama^F

female cone
cono^M femenino

male cone
cono^M masculino

fir needles
agujas^F del abeto^M

cypress scalelike leaves
hojas^F escamadas del
ciprés^M

conifer

examples of conifers
ejemplos^M de coníferas^F

umbrella pine
pino^M piñonero

cedar of Lebanon
cedro^M del Líbano^M

cypress
ciprés^M

spruce
picea^F

larch
alerce^M

eastern white pine
pino^M blanco

fir
abeto^M

redwood
secuoya^F

grain industry

industria^F de cereales^M

**main grain plants
principales plantas^F de
cereales^M**

buckwheat
trigo^M sarraceno

buckwheat: raceme
trigo^M sarraceno:
racimo^M

wheat
trigo^M

wheat: spike
trigo^M: espiga^F

**section of a grain of wheat
corte^M de un grano^M de trigo^M**

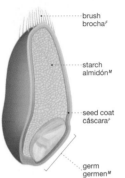

brush
brocha^F

starch
almidón^M

seed coat
cáscara^F

germ
germen^M

rice
arroz^M

rice: panicle
arroz^M: panícula^F

barley
cebada^F

barley: spike
cebada^F: espiga^F

rye
centeno^M

rye: spike
centeno^M: espiga^F

oats
avena^F

oats: panicle
avena^F: panícula

sorghum
sorgo^M

sorghum: panicle
sorgo^M: panícula^F

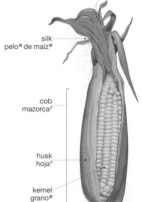

silk
pelo^M de maíz^M

cob
mazorca^F

husk
hoja^F

kernel
grano^M

millet
mijo^M

millet: spikelike panicle
mijo^M: espiga^F

corn
maíz^M

corn: ear
maíz^M: mazorca^F

grain industry

examples of products
ejemplos^M de productos^M

bread
pan^M

pasta
pasta^F

pastries
pasteles^M

cornmeal
harina^F de maíz^M

breakfast cereal
cereales^M

flour
harina^F

couscous
cuscús^M

corn oil
aceite^M vegetal

textile industry

fábrica^F textil

fiber plants
ejemplos^M de fibras^F
vegetales

examples of products
ejemplos^M de productos^M

flax
lino^M

hemp
cáñamo^M

cloth
ropa^F

rope
cuerda^F

cotton plant
algodón^M

cotton swab
bastoncillo^M de algodón^M

rubber industry

industria^F del caucho^M

natural rubber source
fuente^F de caucho^M natural

examples of products
ejemplos^M de productos^M

ball
pelota^F

rubber tree
árbol^M de caucho^M

latex harvest
recogida^F de látex^M

tire
neumático^M

boot
bota^F

paper industry

industria^F papelera^F

pulp fiber sources
fuentes^M de fibra^F

examples of products
ejemplos^M de productos^M

stationery
papelería^F

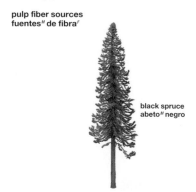

black spruce
abeto^M negro

newsprint
papel^M de periódico^M

rags
trapos^M

carton
cartón^M

paper industry

**papermaking
fabricación^F de
papel^M**

PLANTS AND PLANTLIKE ORGANISMS

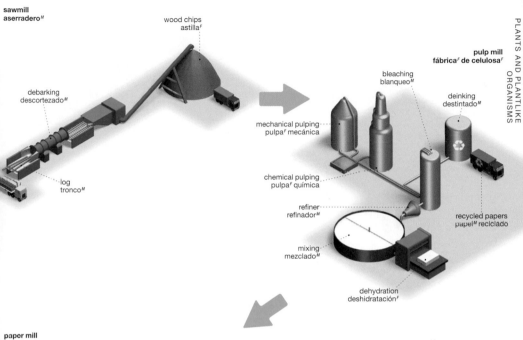

**sawmill
aserradero**^M

wood chips
astilla^F

**pulp mill
fábrica^F de celulosa^F**

bleaching
blanqueo^M

deinking
destintado^M

debarking
descortezado^M

mechanical pulping
pulpa^F mecánica

log
tronco^M

chemical pulping
pulpa^F química

refiner
refinador^M

recycled papers
papel^M reciclado

mixing
mezclado^M

dehydration
deshidratación^F

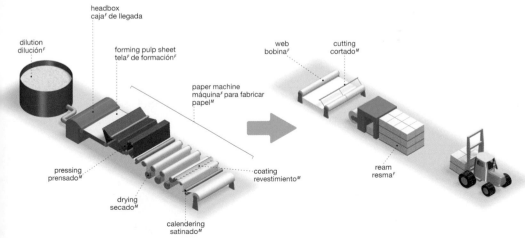

**paper mill
papelera^F**

headbox
caja^F de llegada

dilution
dilución^F

forming pulp sheet
tela^F de formación^F

web
bobina^F

cutting
cortado^M

paper machine
máquina^F para fabricar
papel^M

pressing
prensado^M

coating
revestimiento^M

ream
resma^F

drying
secado^M

calendering
satinado^M

EVOLUTION OF LIFE 128

origin and evolution of species 128
biological taxonomy 132

SIMPLE ORGANISMS 133

animal cell 133
unicellular organisms 133
sponge 134
jellyfish 134
starfish 135
examples of simple organisms 135

MOLLUSKS 136

univalve shell 136
bivalve shell 136
snail 137
octopus 138

CRUSTACEANS 139

lobster 139

INSECTS AND ARACHNIDS 140

butterfly 140
honeybee 142
spider 145
examples of insects 146
examples of arachnids 147

CARTILAGINOUS FISHES 148

shark 148
examples of cartilaginous fishes 148

BONY FISHES 149

perch 149
examples of bony fishes 150

ANIMALS
reino animal

AMPHIBIANS 152

frog 152
examples of amphibians 153

REPTILES 154

snake 154
turtle 155
examples of reptiles 156

BIRDS 158

bird 158
examples of aquatic birds and shorebirds 161
examples of land birds 162

INSECTIVOROUS MAMMALS 164

mole 164
examples of insectivorous mammals 164

RODENTS 165

rat 165
examples of rodents 166

LAGOMORPHS 167

rabbit 167
examples of lagomorphs 167

UNGULATE MAMMALS 168

horse 168
examples of hooves 171
examples of ungulate mammals 172

CARNIVOROUS MAMMALS 174

dog 174
examples of dog breeds 176
cat 178
examples of cat breeds 179
examples of carnivorous mammals 180

MARINE MAMMALS 182

dolphin 182
examples of marine mammals 183

PRIMATES 184

gorilla 184
examples of primates 185

FLYING MAMMALS 186

bat 186
examples of flying mammals 187

MARSUPIALS 188

kangaroo 188
examples of marsupials 189

origin and evolution of species

origen[M] y evolución[F] de las especies[F]

ANIMALS

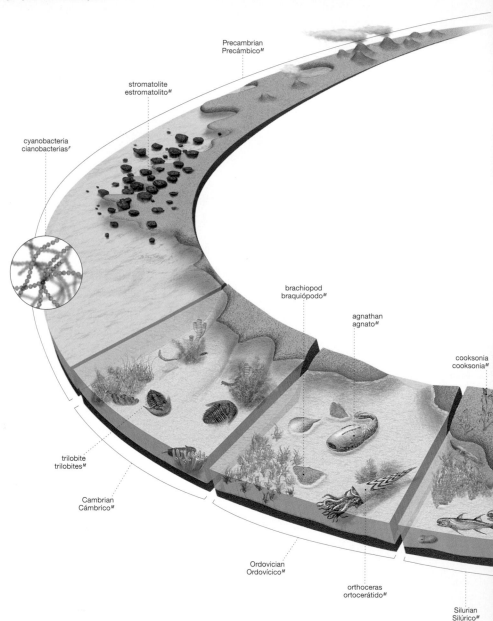

Precambrian
Precámbrico[M]

stromatolite
estromatolito[M]

cyanobacteria
cianobacterias[F]

brachiopod
braquiópodo[M]

agnathan
agnato[M]

cooksonia
cooksonia[M]

trilobite
trilobites[M]

Cambrian
Cámbrico[M]

Ordovician
Ordovícico[M]

orthoceras
ortocerátido[M]

Silurian
Silúrico[M]

ANIMALS

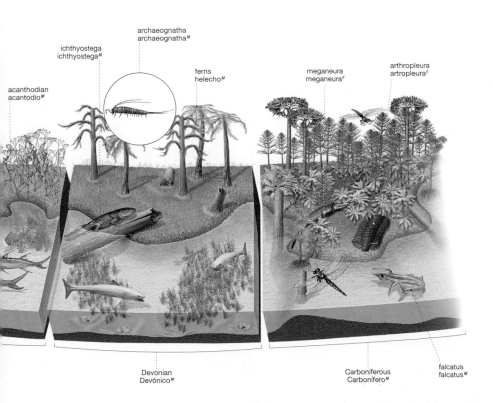

acanthodian
acantodio^M

ichthyostega
ichthyostega^M

archaeognatha
archaeognatha^M

ferns
helecho^M

meganeura
meganeura^F

arthropleura
artropleura^F

Devonian
Devónico^M

Carboniferous
Carbonífero^M

falcatus
falcatus^M

origin and evolution of species

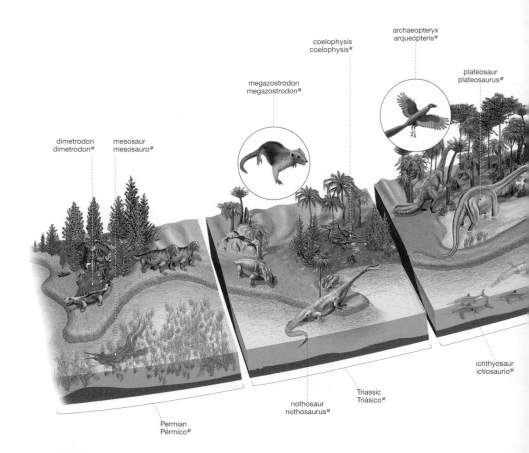

dimetrodon
dimetrodon*M*

mesosaur
mesosauro*M*

megazostrodon
megazostrodon*M*

coelophysis
coelophysis*M*

archaeopteryx
arqueópteris*M*

plateosaur
plateosaurus*M*

ichthyosaur
ictiosaurio*M*

Permian
Pérmico*M*

nothosaur
nothosaurus*M*

Triassic
Triásico*M*

ANIMALS

origin and evolution of species

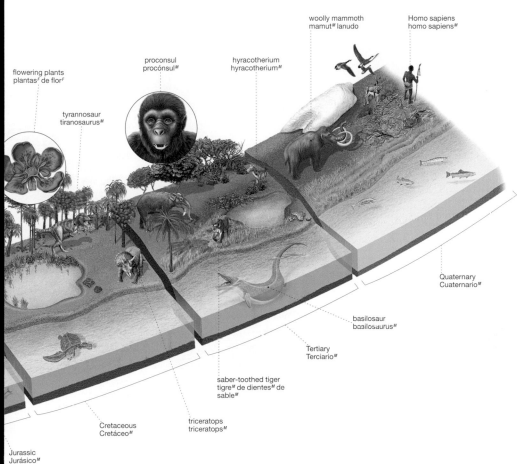

flowering plants
plantas^F de flor^F

proconsul
procónsul^M

hyracotherium
hyracotherium^M

woolly mammoth
mamut^M lanudo

Homo sapiens
homo sapiens^M

tyrannosaur
tiranosaurus^M

Quaternary
Cuaternario^M

basilosaur
basilosaurus^M

Tertiary
Terciario^M

saber-toothed tiger
tigre^M de dientes^M de
sable^M

Cretaceous
Cretáceo^M

triceratops
triceratops^M

Jurassic
Jurásico^M

biological taxonomy
clasificación^M biológica

example of classification: cat
ejemplos^M de clasificación ^F: gato^M

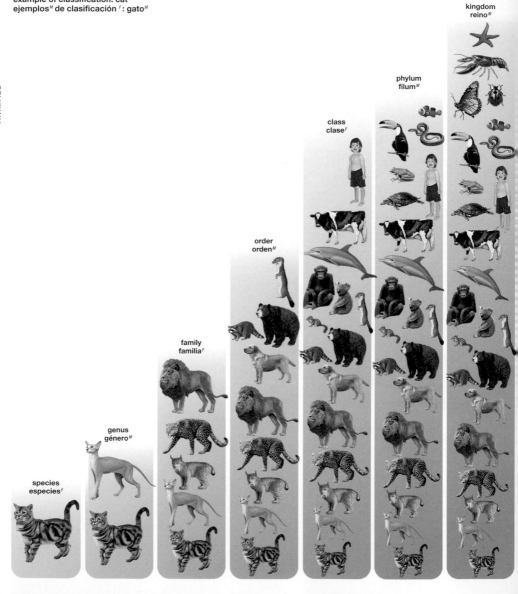

kingdom
reino^M

phylum
filum^M

class
clase^F

order
orden^M

family
familia^F

genus
género^M

species
especies^F

animal cell

célula^F animal

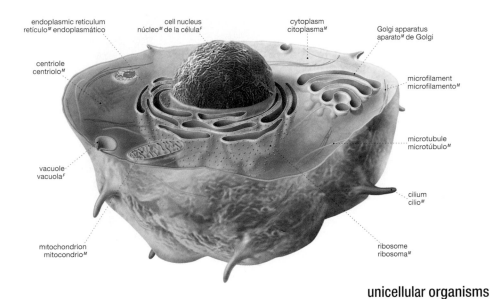

endoplasmic reticulum
retículo^M endoplasmático

cell nucleus
núcleo^M de la célula^F

cytoplasm
citoplasma^M

Golgi apparatus
aparato^M de Golgi

centriole
centriolo^M

microfilament
microfilamento^M

microtubule
microtúbulo^M

vacuole
vacuola^F

cilium
cilio^M

mitochondrion
mitocondrio^M

ribosome
ribosoma^M

ANIMALS

unicellular organisms

organismos^M unicelulares

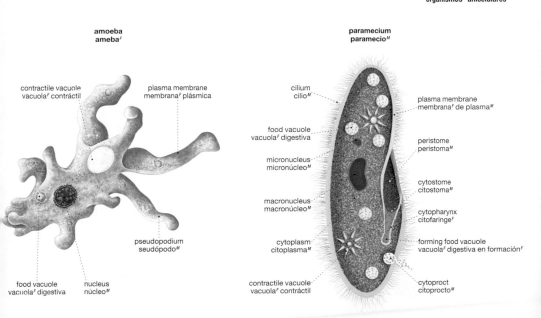

amoeba
ameba^F

paramecium
paramecio^M

contractile vacuole
vacuola^F contráctil

plasma membrane
membrana^F plásmica

cilium
cilio^M

plasma membrane
membrana^F de plasma^M

food vacuole
vacuola^F digestiva

peristome
peristoma^M

micronucleus
micronúcleo^M

cytostome
citostoma^M

macronucleus
macronúcleo^M

cytopharynx
citofaringe^F

pseudopodium
seudópodo^M

cytoplasm
citoplasma^M

forming food vacuole
vacuola^F digestiva en formación^F

food vacuole
vacuola^F digestiva

nucleus
núcleo^M

contractile vacuole
vacuola^F contráctil

cytoproct
citoprocto^M

ANIMALS

sponge
esponja[F]

morphology of a sponge
morfología[F] de una esponja[F]

spicule
espícula[F]

anatomy of a sponge
anatomía[F] de una esponja[F]

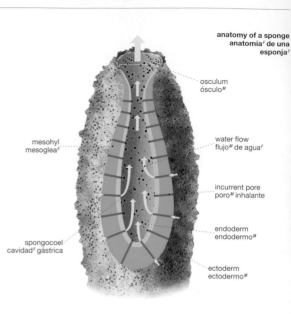

osculum
ósculo[M]

mesohyl
mesoglea[F]

water flow
flujo[M] de agua[F]

incurrent pore
poro[M] inhalante

endoderm
endodermo[M]

spongocoel
cavidad[F] gástrica

ectoderm
ectodermo[M]

jellyfish
medusa[F]

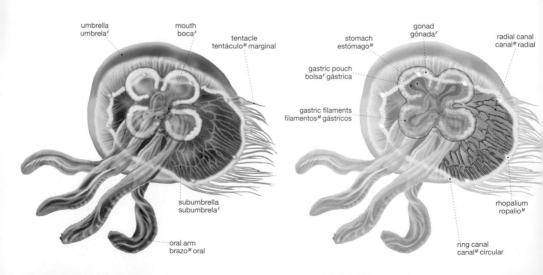

morphology of a jellyfish
morfología[F] de una medusa[F]

umbrella
umbrela[F]

mouth
boca[F]

tentacle
tentáculo[M] marginal

subumbrella
subumbrela[F]

oral arm
brazo[M] oral

anatomy of a jellyfish
anatomía[F] de una medusa[F]

stomach
estómago[M]

gonad
gónada[F]

radial canal
canal[M] radial

gastric pouch
bolsa[F] gástrica

gastric filaments
filamentos[M] gástricos

rhopalium
ropalio[M]

ring canal
canal[M] circular

starfish
estrella^F de mar^M

morphology of a starfish
morfología^F de una estrella^F
de mar^M

arm
brazo^M

spine
espina^F

central disk
disco^M central

anatomy of a starfish
anatomía^F de una estrella^F de
mar^M

madreporite
placa^F madrepórica

gonopore
gónada^F

anus
ano^M

intestine
intestino^M

eyespot
mancha^F ocular

tube foot
pie^M ambulacral

ring canal
canal^M anular

pyloric cecum
ciego^M pilórico

radial canal
canal^M radial

gonad
gónada^F

rectal cecum
ciego^M rectal

ampulla
ampolla^F

esophagus
esófago^M

mouth
boca^F

stomach
estómago^M

examples of simple organisms
ejemplos^M de animales^M primitivos

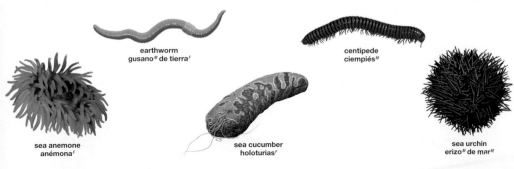

earthworm
gusano^M de tierra^F

centipede
ciempiés^M

sea anemone
anémona^F

sea cucumber
holoturias^F

sea urchin
erizo^M de mar^M

ANIMALS

univalve shell
concha^F univalva

morphology of a univalve shell
morfología^F de una concha^F univalva

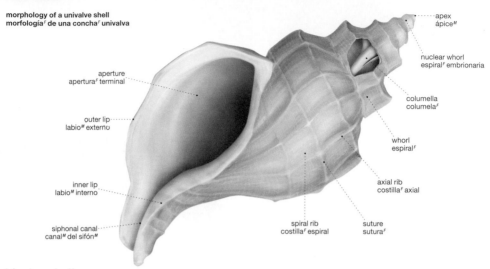

apex
ápice^M

nuclear whorl
espiral^F embrionaria

aperture
apertura^F terminal

columella
columela^F

outer lip
labio^M externo

whorl
espiral^F

inner lip
labio^M interno

axial rib
costilla^F axial

siphonal canal
canal^M del sifón^M

spiral rib
costilla^F espiral

suture
sutura^F

bivalve shell
concha^F bivalva

anatomy of a bivalve shell
anatomía^F de una concha^F bivalva

morphology of a bivalve shell
morfología^F de una concha^F
bivalva

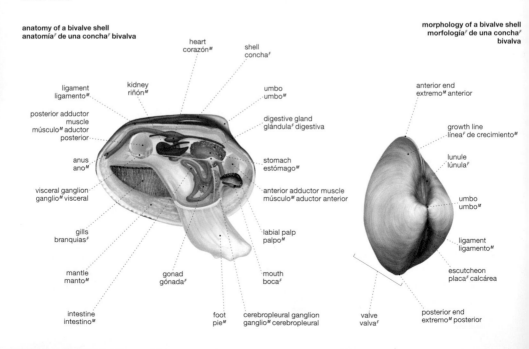

heart
corazón^M

shell
concha^F

ligament
ligamento^M

kidney
riñón^M

umbo
umbo^M

anterior end
extremo^M anterior

posterior adductor
muscle
músculo^M aductor
posterior

digestive gland
glándula^F digestiva

growth line
línea^F de crecimiento^M

anus
ano^M

stomach
estómago^M

lunule
lúnula^F

visceral ganglion
ganglio^M visceral

anterior adductor muscle
músculo^M aductor anterior

umbo
umbo^M

gills
branquias^F

labial palp
palpo^M

ligament
ligamento^M

mantle
manto^M

gonad
gónada^F

mouth
boca^F

escutcheon
placa^F calcárea

intestine
intestino^M

foot
pie^M

cerebropleural ganglion
ganglio^M cerebropleural

valve
valva^F

posterior end
extremo^M posterior

snail

caracol^M

morphology of a snail
morfología^F de un caracol^M

whorl
espira^F

shell
concha^F

apex
ápice^M

growth line
línea^F de crecimiento^M

eye
ojo^M

head
cabeza^F

ANIMALS

tentacle
tentáculo^M táctil

foot
pie^M

mouth
boca^F

eyestalk
tentáculo^M ocular

anatomy of a snail
anatomía^F de un caracol^M

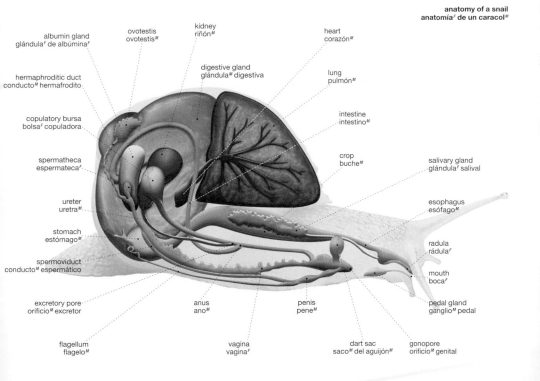

albumin gland
glándula^F de albúmina^F

ovotestis
ovotestis^M

kidney
riñón^M

heart
corazón^M

hermaphroditic duct
conducto^M hermafrodito

digestive gland
glándula^M digestiva

lung
pulmón^M

copulatory bursa
bolsa^F copuladora

intestine
intestino^M

spermatheca
espermateca^F

crop
buche^M

salivary gland
glándula^F salival

ureter
uretra^M

esophagus
esófago^M

stomach
estómago^M

radula
rádula^F

spermoviduct
conducto^M espermático

mouth
boca^F

excretory pore
orificio^M excretor

anus
ano^M

penis
pene^M

pedal gland
ganglio^M pedal

flagellum
flagelo^M

vagina
vagina^F

dart sac
saco^M del aguijón^M

gonopore
orificio^M genital

octopus

pulpo^M

morphology of an octopus
morfología^F **de un pulpo**^M

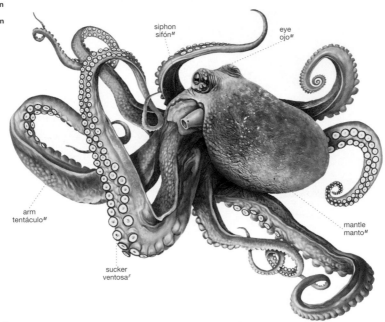

siphon
sifón^M

eye
ojo^M

arm
tentáculo^M

mantle
manto^M

sucker
ventosa^F

anatomy of an octopus
anatomía^F **de un pulpo**^M

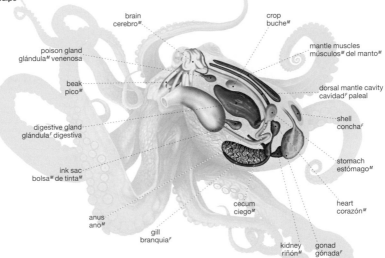

brain
cerebro^M

crop
buche^M

poison gland
glándula^M venenosa

mantle muscles
músculos^M del manto^M

beak
pico^M

dorsal mantle cavity
cavidad^F paleal

digestive gland
glándula^F digestiva

shell
concha^F

ink sac
bolsa^M de tinta^M

stomach
estómago^M

anus
ano^M

cecum
ciego^M

heart
corazón^M

gill
branquia^F

kidney
riñón^M

gonad
gónada^F

lobster

bogavante[M]

morphology of a lobster
morfología[F] de un
bogavante[M]

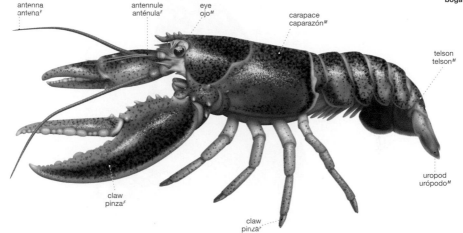

antenna
antena[F]

antennule
anténula[F]

eye
ojo[M]

carapace
caparazón[M]

telson
telson[M]

uropod
urópodo[M]

claw
pinza[F]

claw
pinza[F]

ANIMALS

thoracic legs
apéndices[M] torácicos

cephalothorax
cefalotórax[M]

abdomen
abdomen[M]

tail
cola[F]

anatomy of a lobster
anatomía[F] de un
bogavante[M]

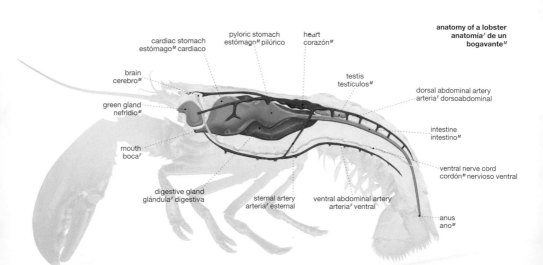

cardiac stomach
estómago[M] cardiaco

pyloric stomach
estómago[M] pilórico

heart
corazón[M]

brain
cerebro[M]

testis
testículos[M]

dorsal abdominal artery
arteria[F] dorsoabdominal

green gland
nefridio[M]

intestine
intestino[M]

mouth
boca[F]

ventral nerve cord
cordón[M] nervioso ventral

digestive gland
glándula[F] digestiva

sternal artery
arteria[F] esternal

ventral abdominal artery
arteria[F] ventral

anus
ano[M]

butterfly

mariposa[F]

morphology of a butterfly
morfología[F] de una mariposa[F]

ANIMALS

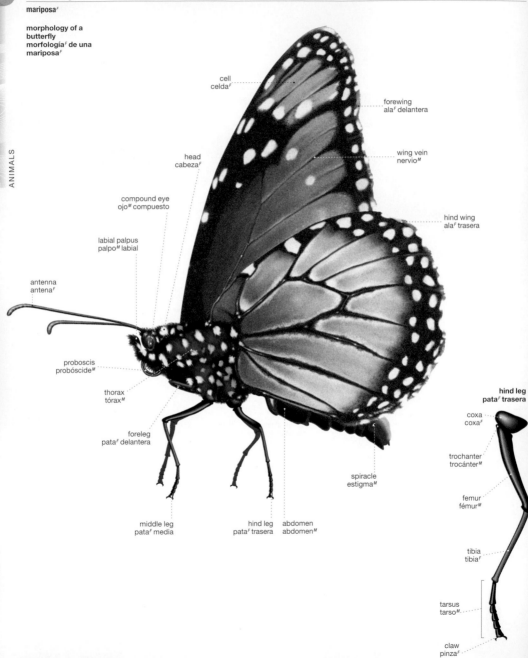

cell
celda[F]

forewing
ala[F] delantera

head
cabeza[F]

wing vein
nervio[M]

compound eye
ojo[M] compuesto

hind wing
ala[F] trasera

labial palpus
palpo[M] labial

antenna
antena[F]

proboscis
probóscide[M]

thorax
tórax[M]

foreleg
pata[F] delantera

spiracle
estigma[M]

middle leg
pata[F] media

hind leg
pata[F] trasera

abdomen
abdomen[M]

hind leg
pata[F] trasera

coxa
coxa[F]

trochanter
trocánter[M]

femur
fémur[M]

tibia
tibia[F]

tarsus
tarso[M]

claw
pinza[F]

butterfly

anatomy of a female butterfly
anatomía^M de una mariposa^F hembra^F

ANIMALS

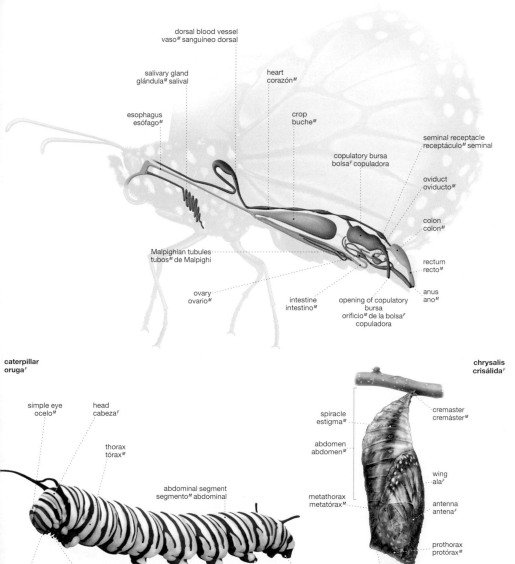

dorsal blood vessel
vaso^M sanguíneo dorsal

salivary gland
glándula^M salival

heart
corazón^M

esophagus
esófago^M

crop
buche^M

seminal receptacle
receptáculo^M seminal

copulatory bursa
bolsa^F copuladora

oviduct
oviducto^M

colon
colon^M

Malpighian tubules
tubos^M de Malpighi

rectum
recto^M

ovary
ovario^M

intestine
intestino^M

opening of copulatory
bursa
orificio^M de la bolsa^F
copuladora

anus
ano^M

caterpillar
oruga^F

chrysalis
crisálida^F

simple eye
ocelo^M

head
cabeza^F

thorax
tórax^M

spiracle
estigma^M

cremaster
cremáster^M

abdomen
abdomen^M

abdominal segment
segmento^M abdominal

wing
ala^F

metathorax
metatórax^M

antenna
antena^F

prothorax
protórax^M

mandible
mandíbula^F

walking leg
pata^F torácica

proleg
pata^F ventosa

anal clasper
pata^F anal

mesothorax
mesotórax^M

honeybee

abeja^F

morphology of a honeybee: worker
morfología^F de una abeja^F trabajadora

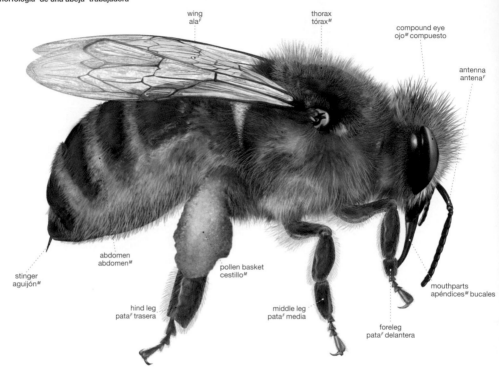

wing
ala^F

thorax
tórax^M

compound eye
ojo^M compuesto

antenna
antena^F

abdomen
abdomen^M

pollen basket
cestillo^M

mouthparts
apéndices^M bucales

stinger
aguijón^M

hind leg
pata^F trasera

middle leg
pata^F media

foreleg
pata^F delantera

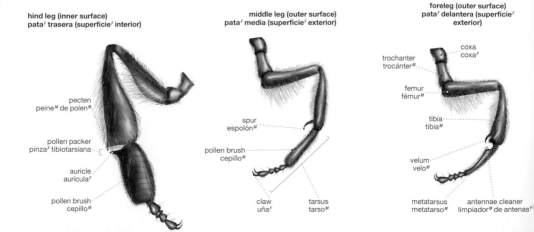

hind leg (inner surface)
pata^F trasera (superficie^F interior)

middle leg (outer surface)
pata^F media (superficie^F exterior)

foreleg (outer surface)
pata^F delantera (superficie^F exterior)

pecten
peine^M de polen^M

pollen packer
pinza^F tibiotarsiana

auricle
aurícula^F

pollen brush
cepillo^M

spur
espolón^M

pollen brush
cepillo^M

claw
uña^F

tarsus
tarso^M

coxa
coxa^F

trochanter
trocánter^M

femur
fémur^M

tibia
tibia^M

velum
velo^M

metatarsus
metatarso^M

antennae cleaner
limpiador^M de antenas^F

ANIMALS

anatomy of a honeybee
anatomía^F de una
abeja^F

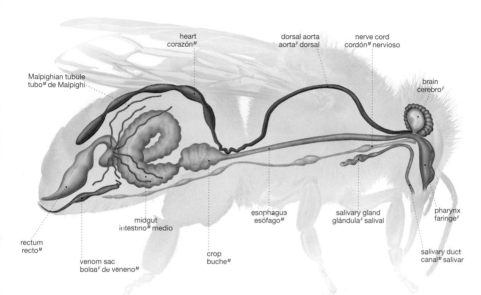

heart
corazón^M

dorsal aorta
aorta^F dorsal

nerve cord
cordón^M nervioso

brain
cerebro^F

Malpighian tubule
tubo^M de Malpighi

esophagus
esófago^M

salivary gland
glándula^F salival

pharynx
faringe^F

midgut
intestino^M medio

crop
buche^M

salivary duct
canal^M salivar

rectum
recto^M

venom sac
bolsa^F de veneno^M

head
cabeza^F

castes
castas^F

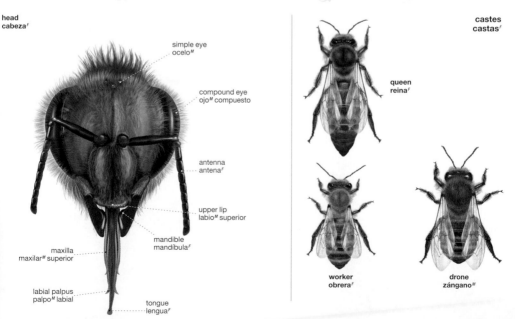

simple eye
ocelo^M

compound eye
ojo^M compuesto

queen
reina^F

antenna
antena^F

upper lip
labio^M superior

mandible
mandíbula^F

maxilla
maxilar^M superior

labial palpus
palpo^M labial

tongue
lengua^F

worker
obrera^F

drone
zángano^M

ANIMALS

honeybee

hive
colmena^F

exit cone
respiradero^M

outer cover
techo^M

super
alza^F

frame
bastidor^M

alighting board
estribo^M

entrance
entrada^F

roof
techo^M

honeycomb
panal^M

cell
celdilla^F

queen excluder
separador^M de reinas^F

brood chamber
cámara^F de incubación^F

hive body
cuerpo^M de la colmena^F

entrance slide
reductor^M de entrada^F

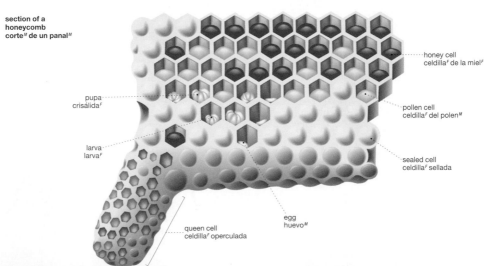

section of a
honeycomb
corte^M **de un panal**^{M}

pupa
crisálida^F

larva
larva^F

queen cell
celdilla^F operculada

egg
huevo^M

honey cell
celdilla^F de la miel^F

pollen cell
celdilla^F del polen^M

sealed cell
celdilla^F sellada

spider
araña^F

ANIMALS

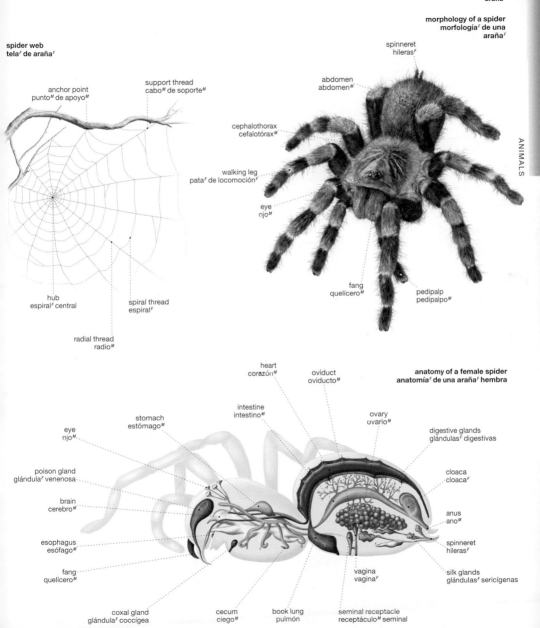

morphology of a spider
morfología^F de una
araña^F

spinneret
hileras^F

abdomen
abdomen^M

cephalothorax
cefalotórax^M

walking leg
pata^F de locomoción^F

eye
ojo^M

fang
quelícero^M

pedipalp
pedipalpo^M

spider web
tela^F de araña^F

anchor point
punto^M de apoyo^M

support thread
cabo^M de soporte^M

hub
espiral^F central

spiral thread
espiral^F

radial thread
radio^M

heart
corazón^M

oviduct
oviducto^M

anatomy of a female spider
anatomía^F de una araña^F hembra

intestine
intestino^M

ovary
ovario^M

stomach
estómago^M

digestive glands
glándulas^F digestivas

eye
ojo^M

cloaca
cloaca^F

poison gland
glándula^F venenosa

anus
ano^M

brain
cerebro^M

spinneret
hileras^F

esophagus
esófago^M

silk glands
glándulas^F sericígenas

fang
quelícero^M

vagina
vagina^F

coxal gland
glándula^F coccígea

cecum
ciego^M

book lung
pulmón^M

seminal receptacle
receptáculo^M seminal

ANIMALS

examples of insects
ejemplos^M de insectos^M

flea
pulga^F

louse
piojo^M

termite
termita^F

mosquito
mosquito^M

tsetse fly
mosca^F tsetsé

furniture beetle
carcoma^F

ladybug
mariquita^F

fly
mosca^F

ant
hormiga^F

burying beetle
escarabajo^M necróforo

yellow jacket
avispa^F

hornet
avispón^M

horsefly
tábano^M

oriental cockroach
cucaracha^F oriental

earwig
tijereta^F

stinkbug
chinche^F

water bug
chinche^F acuática

clothes moth
polilla^F

cockchafer
escarabajo^M

bumblebee
abejorro^M

scarab beetle
escarabajo^M

examples of insects

ANIMALS

atlas moth
oruga^F de polilla^F

monarch butterfly
mariposa^F monarca^M

cicada
cigarra^F

mantis
mantis^F religiosa

dragonfly
libélula^F

peppered moth
polilla^F de abedul^M

bow-winged grasshopper
grillo^M campestre

water strider
opilión^M

great green bush-cricket
saltamontes^M verde

examples of arachnids

ejemplos^M de arácnidos^M

crab spider
araña^F cangrejo

black widow
viuda^F negra

scorpion
escorpión^M

garden spider
epeira^F

tick
garrapata^F

water spider
araña^F de agua^F

Mexican red-kneed
tarantula
migala^F

ANIMALS

shark

tiburón[M]

morphology of a shark
morfología[F] de un
tiburón[M]

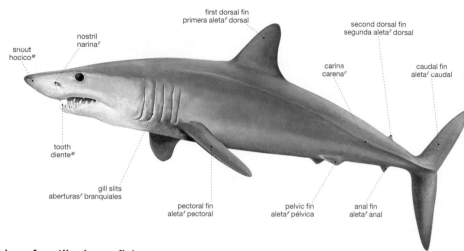

first dorsal fin
primera aleta[F] dorsal

second dorsal fin
segunda aleta[F] dorsal

nostril
narina[F]

snout
hocico[M]

carina
carena[F]

caudal fin
aleta[F] caudal

tooth
diente[M]

gill slits
aberturas[F] branquiales

pectoral fin
aleta[F] pectoral

pelvic fin
aleta[F] pélvica

anal fin
aleta[F] anal

examples of cartilaginous fishes

ejemplos[M] de peces[M] cartilaginosos

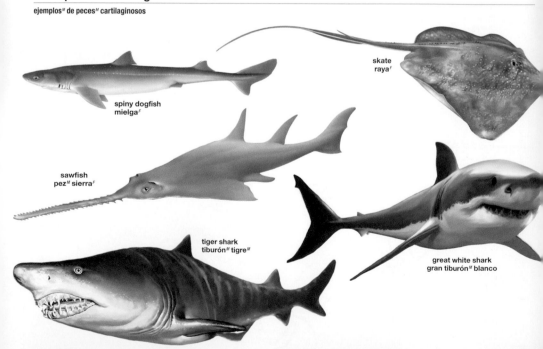

spiny dogfish
mielga[F]

skate
raya[F]

sawfish
pez[M] sierra[F]

tiger shark
tiburón[M] tigre[M]

great white shark
gran tiburón[M] blanco

ANIMALS

perch

perca^F

anatomy of a perch
anatomía^M **de una perca**^F

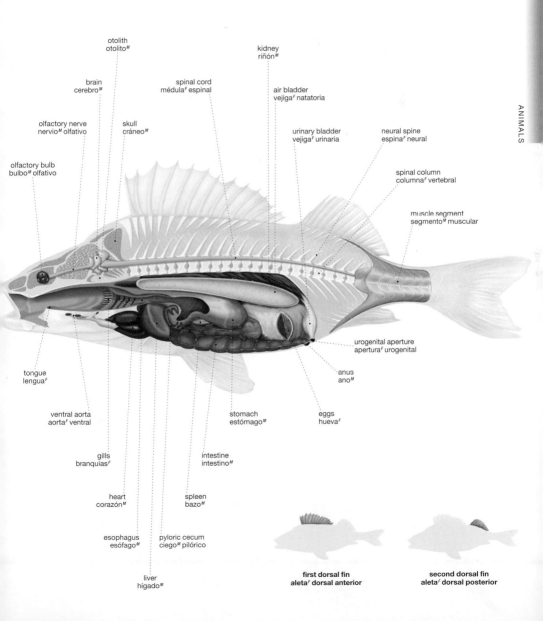

otolith
otolito^M

kidney
riñón^M

brain
cerebro^M

spinal cord
médula^F espinal

air bladder
vejiga^F natatoria

olfactory nerve
nervio^M olfativo

skull
cráneo^M

urinary bladder
vejiga^F urinaria

neural spine
espina^F neural

olfactory bulb
bulbo^M olfativo

spinal column
columna^F vertebral

muscle segment
segmento^M muscular

tongue
lengua^F

urogenital aperture
apertura^F urogenital

anus
ano^M

ventral aorta
aorta^F ventral

stomach
estómago^M

eggs
hueva^F

gills
branquias^F

intestine
intestino^M

heart
corazón^M

spleen
bazo^M

esophagus
esófago^M

pyloric cecum
ciego^M pilórico

liver
hígado^M

first dorsal fin
aleta^F **dorsal anterior**

second dorsal fin
aleta^F **dorsal posterior**

ANIMALS

perch

morphology of a perch
morfología^F de una perca^F

spiny ray
radio^M espinoso

operculum
opérculo^M

soft ray
radio^M blando

caudal fin
aleta^F caudal

premaxilla
premaxilar^M

nostril
narina^F

lateral line
línea^F lateral

anal fin
aleta^F anal

scale
escama^F

maxilla
maxilar^M

pectoral fin
aleta^F pectoral

pelvic fin
aleta^F abdominal

mandible
mandíbula^F

examples of bony fishes

ejemplos^M de peces^M óseos

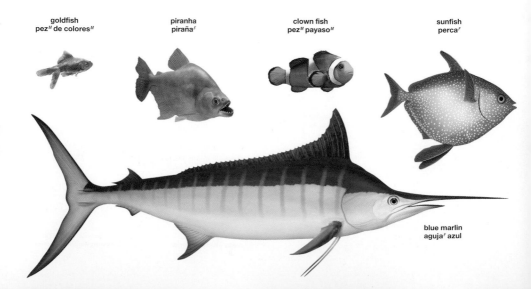

goldfish
pez^M de colores^M

piranha
piraña^F

clown fish
pez^M payaso^M

sunfish
perca^F

blue marlin
aguja^F azul

examples of bony fishes

flying fish
pez^M volador^M

discus
discus^M

deep sea anglerfish
rape^M abisal

porcupine fish
pez^M globo^M

lungfish
pez^M pulmonado

catfish
pez^M gato^M

lantern fish
pez^M linterna^F

sea horse
caballito^M de mar^M

bluestreak cleaner wrasse
pez^M limpiador

parrot fish
pez^M loro^M

electric eel
anguila^F eléctrica

ANIMALS

frog
rana^F

morphology of a frog
morfología^F de una rana^F

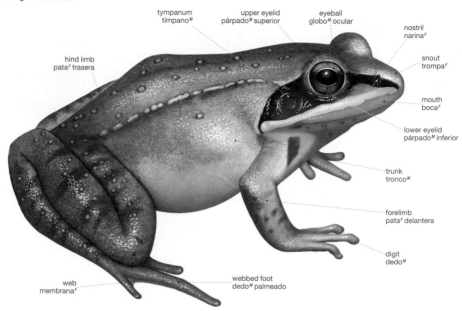

tympanum
tímpano^M

upper eyelid
párpado^M superior

eyeball
globo^M ocular

nostril
narina^F

hind limb
pata^F trasera

snout
trompa^F

mouth
boca^F

lower eyelid
párpado^M inferior

trunk
tronco^M

forelimb
pata^F delantera

digit
dedo^M

web
membrana^F

webbed foot
dedo^M palmeado

anatomy of a male frog
anatomía de una rana^F
macho

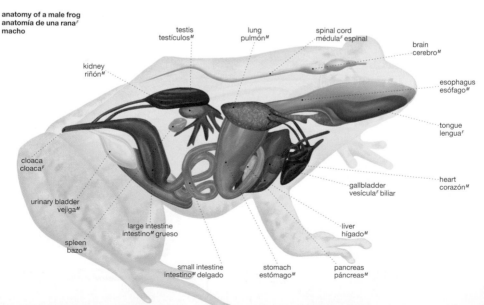

testis
testículos^M

lung
pulmón^M

spinal cord
médula^F espinal

brain
cerebro^M

kidney
riñón^M

esophagus
esófago^M

tongue
lengua^F

cloaca
cloaca^F

heart
corazón^M

urinary bladder
vejiga^M

gallbladder
vesícula^F biliar

large intestine
intestino^M grueso

liver
hígado^M

spleen
bazo^M

small intestine
intestino^M delgado

stomach
estómago^M

pancreas
páncreas^M

frog

skeleton of a frog
esqueleto^M de una rana^F

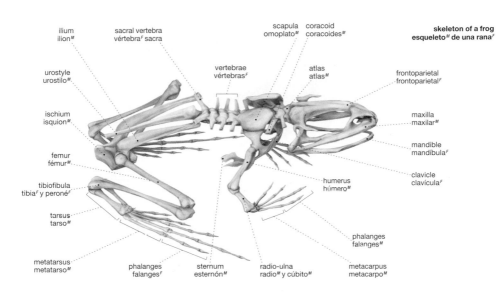

ilium
ilion^M

sacral vertebra
vértebra^F sacra

scapula
omoplato^M

coracoid
coracoides^M

vertebrae
vértebras^F

atlas
atlas^M

frontoparietal
frontoparietal^F

urostyle
urostilo^M

maxilla
maxilar^M

ischium
isquion^M

mandible
mandíbula^F

clavicle
clavícula^F

femur
fémur^M

humerus
húmero^M

tibiofibula
tibia^F y peroné^F

tarsus
tarso^M

phalanges
falanges^M

metatarsus
metatarso^M

phalanges
falanges^F

sternum
esternón^M

radio-ulna
radio^M y cúbito^M

metacarpus
metacarpo^M

life cycle of the frog
metamórfosis^F de la rana^F

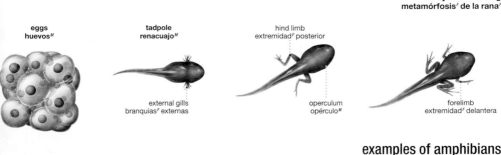

eggs
huevos^M

tadpole
renacuajo^M

hind limb
extremidad^F posterior

external gills
branquias^F externas

operculum
opérculo^M

forelimb
extremidad^F delantera

examples of amphibians
ejemplos^M de anfibios^M

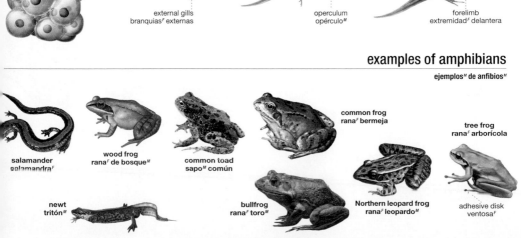

salamander
salamandra^F

wood frog
rana^F de bosque^M

common toad
sapo^M común

common frog
rana^F bermeja

tree frog
rana^F arborícola

newt
tritón^M

bullfrog
rana^F toro^M

Northern leopard frog
rana^F leopardo^M

adhesive disk
ventosa^F

ANIMALS

snake

serpiente^F

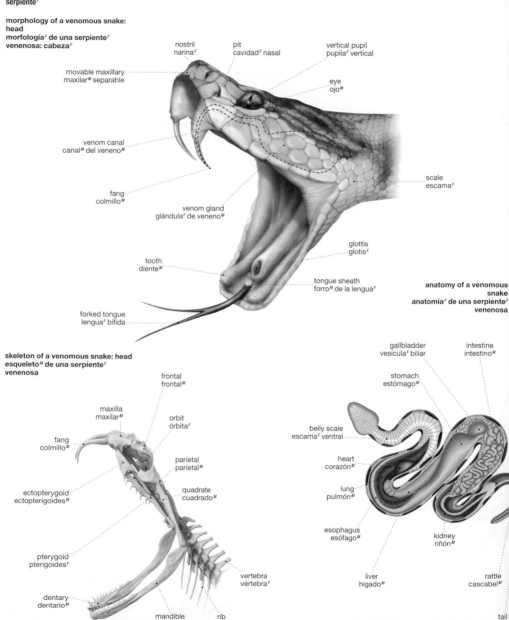

morphology of a venomous snake: head
morfología^F de una serpiente^F venenosa: cabeza^F

nostril
narina^F

pit
cavidad^F nasal

vertical pupil
pupila^F vertical

movable maxillary
maxilar^M separable

eye
ojo^M

venom canal
canal^M del veneno^M

scale
escama^F

fang
colmillo^M

venom gland
glándula^F de veneno^M

glottis
glotis^F

tooth
diente^M

tongue sheath
forro^M de la lengua^F

anatomy of a venomous snake
anatomía^F de una serpiente^F venenosa

forked tongue
lengua^F bífida

skeleton of a venomous snake: head
esqueleto^M de una serpiente^F venenosa

frontal
frontal^M

gallbladder
vesícula^F biliar

intestine
intestino^M

maxilla
maxilar^M

orbit
órbita^F

stomach
estómago^M

fang
colmillo^M

belly scale
escama^F ventral

ectopterygoid
ectopterigoides^M

parietal
parietal^M

heart
corazón^M

quadrate
cuadrado^M

lung
pulmón^M

pterygoid
pterigoides^F

esophagus
esófago^M

kidney
riñón^M

vertebra
vértebra^F

dentary
dentario^M

liver
hígado^M

rattle
cascabel^F

mandible
mandíbula^F

rib
costilla^F

tail
cola^F

turtle

tortuga^F

morphology of a turtle
morfología^F de una
tortuga^F

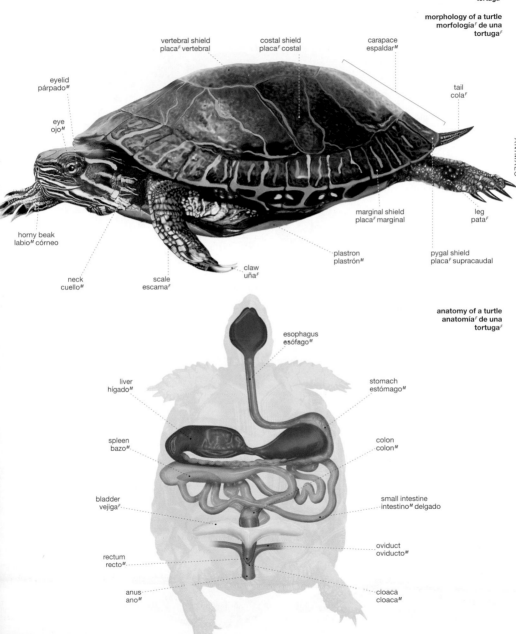

vertebral shield
placa^F vertebral

costal shield
placa^F costal

carapace
espaldar^M

eyelid
párpado^M

tail
cola^F

eye
ojo^M

ANIMALS

horny beak
labio^M córneo

neck
cuello^M

scale
escama^F

claw
uña^F

plastron
plastrón^M

marginal shield
placa^F marginal

leg
pata^F

pygal shield
placa^F supracaudal

anatomy of a turtle
anatomía^F de una
tortuga^F

esophagus
esófago^M

liver
hígado^M

stomach
estómago^M

spleen
bazo^M

colon
colon^M

bladder
vejiga^F

small intestine
intestino^M delgado

oviduct
oviducto^M

rectum
recto^M

anus
ano^M

cloaca
cloaca^M

ANIMALS

examples of reptiles
ejemplos^M de reptiles^M

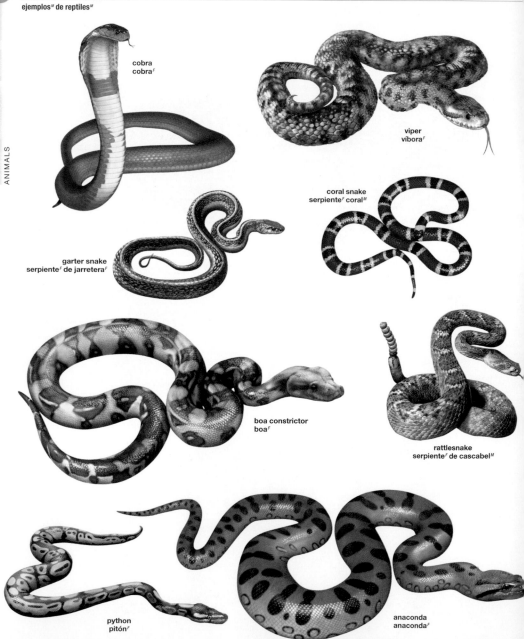

cobra
cobra^F

viper
víbora^F

coral snake
serpiente^F coral^M

garter snake
serpiente^F de jarretera^F

boa constrictor
boa^F

rattlesnake
serpiente^F de cascabel^M

python
pitón^F

anaconda
anaconda^F

ANIMALS

gecko
geco^M

green lizard
lagarto^M

chameleon
camaleón^M

monitor lizard
varano^M

iguana
iguana^F

caiman
caimán^M

alligator
aligátor^M

crocodile
cocodrilo^M

ANIMALS

bird
ave^F

morphology of a bird
morfología^F de un pájaro^M

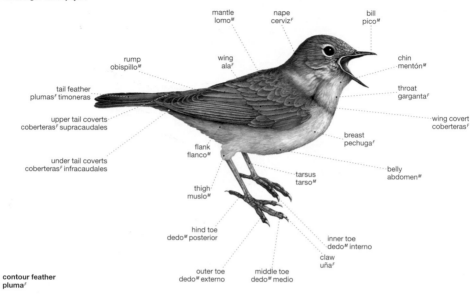

mantle
lomo^M

nape
cerviz^F

bill
pico^M

rump
obispillo^M

wing
ala^F

chin
mentón^M

tail feather
plumas^F timoneras

throat
garganta^F

upper tail coverts
coberteras^F supracaudales

wing covert
coberteras^F

under tail coverts
coberteras^F infracaudales

flank
flanco^M

breast
pechuga^F

belly
abdomen^M

thigh
muslo^M

tarsus
tarso^M

hind toe
dedo^M posterior

inner toe
dedo^M interno

claw
uña^F

outer toe
dedo^M externo

middle toe
dedo^M medio

contour feather
pluma^F

head
cabeza^F

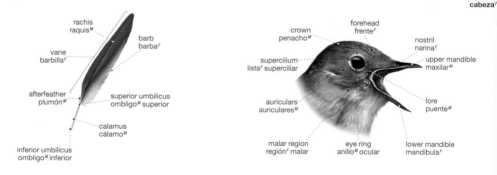

rachis
raquis^M

barb
barba^F

vane
barbilla^F

afterfeather
plumón^M

superior umbilicus
ombligo^M superior

calamus
cálamo^M

inferior umbilicus
ombligo^M inferior

crown
penacho^M

forehead
frente^F

nostril
narina^F

supercilium
lista^F superciliar

upper mandible
maxilar^M

auriculars
auriculares^M

lore
puente^M

malar region
región^F malar

eye ring
anillo^M ocular

lower mandible
mandíbula^F

wing
ala^F

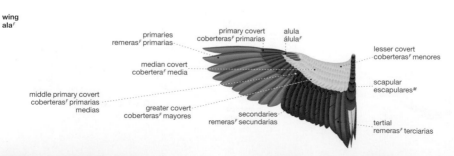

primaries
remeras^F primarias

primary covert
coberteras^F primarias

alula
álula^F

lesser covert
coberteras^F menores

median covert
cobertera^F media

middle primary covert
coberteras^F primarias
medias

greater covert
coberteras^F mayores

secondaries
remeras^F secundarias

scapular
escapulares^M

tertial
remeras^F terciarias

bird

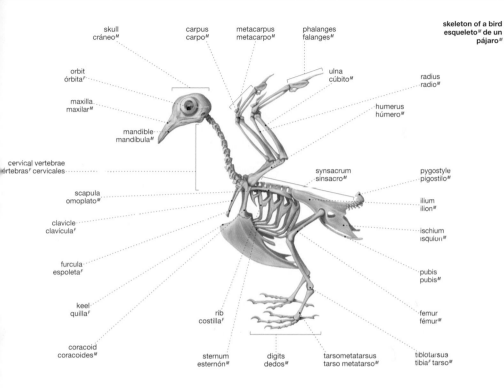

skeleton of a bird
esqueletoᴹ **de un**
pájaroᴹ

skull
cráneoᴹ

carpus
carpoᴹ

metacarpus
metacarpoᴹ

phalanges
falangesᴹ

ulna
cúbitoᴹ

radius
radioᴹ

orbit
órbitaᶠ

maxilla
maxilarᴹ

humerus
húmeroᴹ

mandible
mandíbulaᴹ

cervical vertebrae
értebrasᶠ cervicales

synsacrum
sinsacroᴹ

pygostyle
pigostiloᴹ

scapula
omoplatoᴹ

ilium
ilionᴹ

clavicle
clavículaᶠ

ischium
isquionᴹ

furcula
espoletaᶠ

pubis
pubisᴹ

keel
quillaᶠ

rib
costillaᶠ

femur
fémurᴹ

coracoid
coracoidesᴹ

sternum
esternónᴹ

digits
dedosᴹ

tarsometatarsus
tarso metatarsoᴹ

tibiotarsus
tibiaᶠ tarsoᴹ

ANIMALS

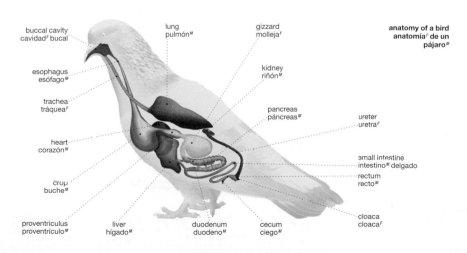

anatomy of a bird
anatomíaᶠ **de un**
pájaroᴹ

buccal cavity
cavidadᶠ bucal

lung
pulmónᴹ

gizzard
mollejaᶠ

esophagus
esófagoᴹ

kidney
riñónᴹ

trachea
tráqueaᶠ

pancreas
páncreasᴹ

ureter
uretraᶠ

heart
corazónᴹ

small intestine
intestinoᴹ delgado

rectum
rectoᴹ

crop
bucheᴹ

proventriculus
proventrículoᴹ

liver
hígadoᴹ

duodenum
duodenoᴹ

cecum
ciegoᴹ

cloaca
cloacaᶠ

ANIMALS

bird

egg
huevo^M

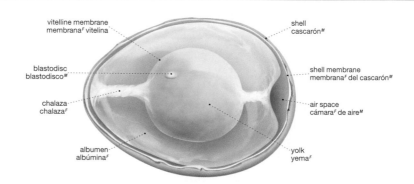

vitelline membrane
membrana^F vitelina

shell
cascarón^M

blastodisc
blastodisco^M

shell membrane
membrana^F del cascarón^M

chalaza
chalaza^F

air space
cámara^F de aire^M

albumen
albúmina^F

yolk
yema^F

examples of bills
ejemplos^M de picos^M

aquatic bird
ave^F acuática

granivorous bird
ave^F granívora

insectivorous bird
ave^F insectívora

bird of prey
ave^F de rapiña^F

wading bird
ave^F zancuda

examples of feet
ejemplos^M de patas^F

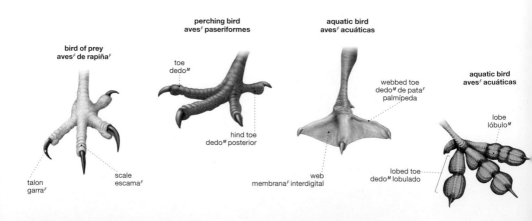

perching bird
aves^F paseriformes

aquatic bird
aves^F acuáticas

bird of prey
aves^F de rapiña^F

toe
dedo^M

aquatic bird
aves^F acuáticas

webbed toe
dedo^M de pata^F
palmípeda

lobe
lóbulo^M

hind toe
dedo^M posterior

talon
garra^F

scale
escama^F

web
membrana^F interdigital

lobed toe
dedo^M lobulado

examples of aquatic birds and shorebirds

ejemplos*M* de aves*F* acuáticas y costeras

tern
golondrina*F* de mar*M*

duck
pato*M*

auk
alca*F*

gull
gaviota*F*

kingfisher
martín*M* pescador

ANIMALS

oystercatcher
ostrero*M*

pelican
pelícano*M*

albatross
albatros*M*

swan
cisne*M*

heron
garza*F*

penguin
pingüino*M*

stork
cigüeña*F*

flamingo
flamenco*M*

examples of land birds

ejemplos^M de pájaros^M terrestres

bullfinch
pardillo^M

goldfinch
jilguero^M

swift
vencejo^M

hummingbird
colibrí^M

sparrow
gorrión^M

jay
arrendajo^M

nightingale
ruiseñor^M

lapwing
avefría^F

European robin
petirrojo^M

chaffinch
pinzón^M

toucan
tucán^M

swallow
golondrina^F

cardinal
cardenal^M

turkey
pavo^M

ostrich
avestruz^M

peacock
pavo^M real

guinea fowl
pintada^F

examples of land birds

macaw
guacamayo^M

quail
codorniz^F

starling
estornino^M

pigeon
paloma^F

shrike
alcaudón^M

ANIMALS

northern saw-whet owl
lechuza^F norteña

woodpecker
pájaro^M carpintero

cockatoo
cacatúa^F

falcon
halcón^M

vulture
buitre^M

partridge
perdiz^F

pheasant
faisán^M

raven
cuervo^M

great horned owl
búho^M real

condor
cóndor^M

domestic goose
oca^F

chick
polluelo^M

eagle
águila^F

hen
gallina^F

rooster
gallo^M

mole

topo^M

morphology of a mole
morfología^F de un topo^M

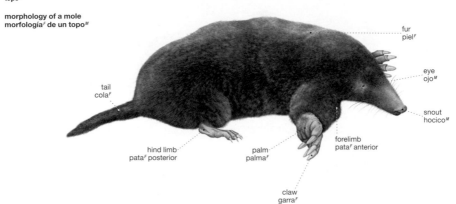

fur
piel^F

eye
ojo^M

tail
cola^F

snout
hocico^M

hind limb
pata^F posterior

palm
palma^F

forelimb
pata^F anterior

claw
garra^F

skeleton of a mole
esqueleto^M de un topo^M

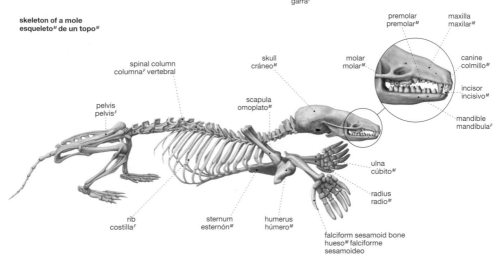

premolar
premolar^M

maxilla
maxilar^M

spinal column
columna^F vertebral

skull
cráneo^M

molar
molar^M

canine
colmillo^M

scapula
omoplato^M

incisor
incisivo^M

pelvis
pelvis^F

mandible
mandíbula^F

ulna
cúbito^M

radius
radio^M

rib
costilla^F

sternum
esternón^M

humerus
húmero^M

falciform sesamoid bone
hueso^M falciforme
sesamoideo

examples of insectivorous mammals

ejemplos^M de mamíferos^M insectívoros

shrew
musaraña^F

hedgehog
erizo^M

pangolin
pangolín^M

anteater
oso^M hormiguero

rat

rata^F

ANIMALS

morphology of a rat
morfología^F de una
rata^F

pinna
pabellón^M de la oreja^F

vibrissa
vibrisas^F

nose
nariz^F

digit
dedo^M

claw
garra^F

fur
pelaje^M

tail
cola^F

skeleton of a rat
esqueleto^M de una rata^F

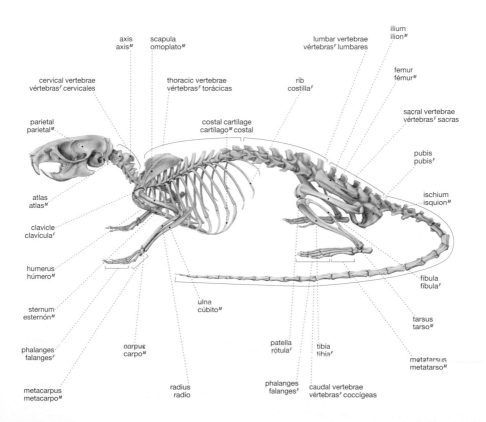

axis
axis^M

scapula
omoplato^M

lumbar vertebrae
vértebras^F lumbares

ilium
ilion^M

cervical vertebrae
vértebras^F cervicales

thoracic vertebrae
vértebras^F torácicas

rib
costilla^F

femur
fémur^M

parietal
parietal^M

costal cartilage
cartílago^M costal

sacral vertebrae
vértebras^F sacras

atlas
atlas^M

pubis
pubis^F

clavicle
clavícula^F

ischium
isquion^M

humerus
húmero^M

fibula
fíbula^F

sternum
esternón^M

ulna
cúbito^M

tarsus
tarso^M

phalanges
falanges^F

carpus
carpo^M

patella
rótula^F

tibia
tibia^F

metatarsus
metatarso^M

metacarpus
metacarpo^M

radius
radio

phalanges
falanges^F

caudal vertebrae
vértebras^F coccígeas

ANIMALS

rat

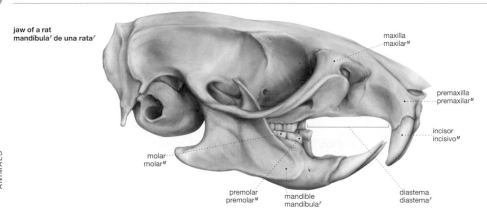

jaw of a rat
mandíbula^F **de una rata**^{F}

maxilla
maxilar^M

premaxilla
premaxilar^M

incisor
incisivo^M

diastema
diastema^F

mandible
mandíbula^F

premolar
premolar^M

molar
molar^M

examples of rodents

ejemplos^M de roedores^M

field mouse
ratón^M **de campo**^{M}

chipmunk
ardilla^F **listada**

hamster
hámster^M

woodchuck
marmota^F

rat
rata^F

jerboa
jerbo^M

squirrel
ardilla^F

beaver
castor^M

guinea pig
cobaya^F

porcupine
puerco^M **espín**

rabbit

conejo^M

morphology of a rabbit
morfología^F de un conejo^M

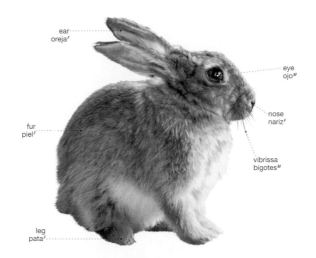

ear
oreja^F

eye
ojo^M

nose
nariz^F

fur
piel^F

vibrissa
bigotes^M

leg
pata^F

jaw of a rabbit
mandíbula^F de un conejo^M

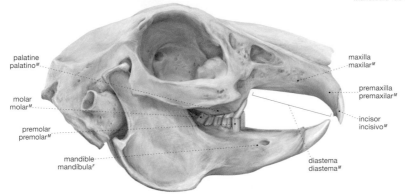

palatine
palatino^M

maxilla
maxilar^M

molar
molar^M

premaxilla
premaxilar^M

premolar
premolar^M

incisor
incisivo^M

mandible
mandíbula^F

diastema
diastema^M

examples of lagomorphs

ejemplos^M de lagomorfos^M

hare
liebre^F

rabbit
conejo^M

pika
pica^F

ANIMALS

horse

caballo[M]

morphology of a horse
morfología[F] de un
caballo[M]

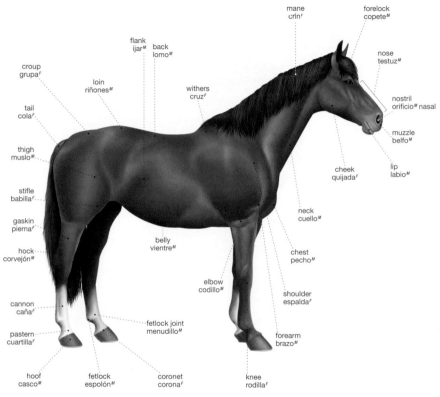

mane
crln[F]

forelock
copete[M]

nose
testuz[M]

nostril
orificio[M] nasal

muzzle
belfo[M]

lip
labio[M]

cheek
quijada[F]

flank
ijar[M]

back
lomo[M]

croup
grupa[F]

loin
riñones[M]

withers
cruz[F]

tail
cola[F]

thigh
muslo[M]

stifle
babilla[F]

neck
cuello[M]

gaskin
pierna[F]

belly
vientre[M]

hock
corvejón[M]

chest
pecho[M]

elbow
codillo[M]

cannon
caña[F]

shoulder
espalda[F]

pastern
cuartilla[F]

fetlock joint
menudillo[M]

forearm
brazo[M]

hoof
casco[M]

fetlock
espolón[M]

coronet
corona[F]

knee
rodilla[F]

gaits
andaduras[F]

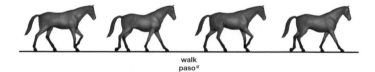

walk
paso[M]

trot
trote[M]

anatomy of a horse
anatomía^F de un
caballo^M

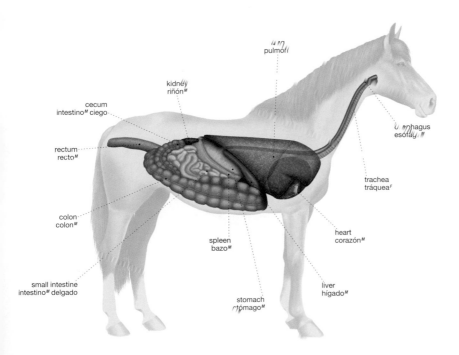

lung
pulmón^M

kidney
riñón^M

cecum
intestino^M ciego

rectum
recto^M

colon
colon^M

small intestine
intestino^M delgado

spleen
bazo^M

stomach
estómago^M

esophagus
esófago^M

trachea
tráquea^F

heart
corazón^M

liver
hígado^M

gaits

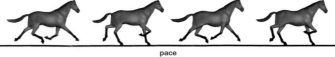

pace
portante^M

canter
galope^M

ANIMALS

horse

skeleton of a horse
esqueleto^M **de un**
caballo^M

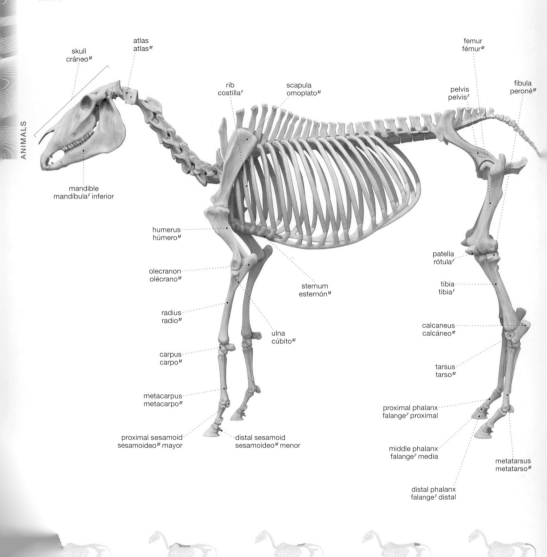

skull
cráneo^M

atlas
atlas^M

rib
costilla^F

scapula
omoplato^M

femur
fémur^M

fibula
peroné^M

pelvis
pelvis^F

mandible
mandíbula^F inferior

humerus
húmero^M

olecranon
olécrano^M

radius
radio^M

carpus
carpo^M

metacarpus
metacarpo^M

proximal sesamoid
sesamoideo^M mayor

sternum
esternón^M

ulna
cúbito^M

distal sesamoid
sesamoideo^M menor

patella
rótula^F

tibia
tibia^F

calcaneus
calcáneo^M

tarsus
tarso^M

proximal phalanx
falange^F proximal

middle phalanx
falange^F media

distal phalanx
falange^F distal

metatarsus
metatarso^M

vertebrae
cervicales

thoracic vertebrae
vértebras^F torácicas

lumbar vertebrae
vértebras^F lumbares

sacral vertebrae
vértebras^F sacras

caudal vertebrae
vértebras^F caudales

horse

hoof: plantar surface
casco^M : superficie^F plantar

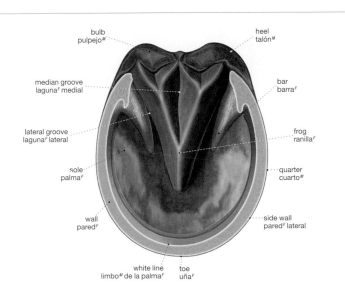

bulb
pulpejo^M

heel
talón^M

median groove
laguna^F medial

bar
barra^F

lateral groove
laguna^F lateral

frog
ranilla^F

sole
palma^F

quarter
cuarto^M

wall
pared^F

side wall
pared^F lateral

white line
limbo^M de la palma^F

toe
uña^F

ANIMALS

horseshoe
herradura^F

hoof
casco^M

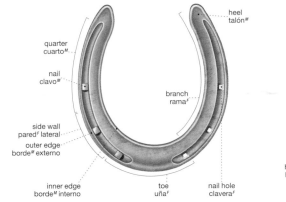

heel
talón^M

quarter
cuarto^M

nail
clavo^M

branch
rama^F

side wall
pared^F lateral

outer edge
borde^M externo

inner edge
borde^M interno

toe
uña^F

nail hole
clavera^F

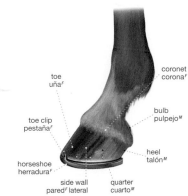

coronet
corona^F

toe
uña^F

bulb
pulpejo^M

toe clip
pestaña^F

heel
talón^M

horseshoe
herradura^F

side wall
pared^F lateral

quarter
cuarto^M

examples of hooves

ejemplos^M de pezuñas^F

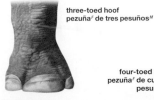

two-toed hoof
pezuña^F de dos pesuños^M

three-toed hoof
pezuña^F de tres pesuños^M

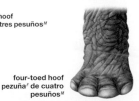

one-toed hoof
pezuña^F de un pesuño^M

four-toed hoof
pezuña^F de cuatro pesuños^M

examples of ungulate mammals

ejemplos^M de mamíferos^M ungulados

ANIMALS

peccary
pécari^M

wild boar
jabalí^M

pig
cerdo^M

sheep
oveja^F

okapi
okapi^M

antelope
antílope^M

goat
cabra^F

white-tailed deer
ciervo^M de Virginia^F

llama
llama^F

moose
alce^M

mouflon
muflón^M

caribou
reno^M

elk
uapití^M

ass
asno^M

mule
mula^F

horse
caballo^M

zebra
cebra^F

examples of ungulate mammals

ANIMALS

cow
vaca^F

ox
buey^M

calf
ternero^M

yak
yak^M

hippopotamus
hipopótamo^M

rhinoceros
rinoceronte^M

dromedary camel
dromedario^M

Bactrian camel
camello^M Bactriano

Cape buffalo
búfalo^M africano

giraffe
jirafa^F

elephant
elefante^M

bison
bisonte^M

ANIMALS

dog
perro^M

morphology of a dog
morfología^F **de un perro**^M

withers
cruz^F

thigh
muslo^M

back
lomo^M

tail
cola^F

shoulder
paletilla^F

elbow
codo^M

forearm
antebrazo^M

knee
rodilla^F

wrist
codillo^M

hock
corvejón^M

toe
garra^F

head of a dog
cabeza^F **de un perro**^M

eye
ojo^M

stop
entrecejo^M

cheek
quijada^F

nose
nariz^F

ear
oreja^F

muzzle
hocico^M

flews
belfos^M

dog's forepaw
pata^F **delantera del**
perro^M

claw
uña^F

digital pad
almohadilla^F digital

toe
garra^F

metacarpal pad
almohadilla^F metacarpia

dewclaw
espolón^M

dew pad
almohadilla^F del espolón^M

carpal pad
almohadilla^F carpal

ANIMALS

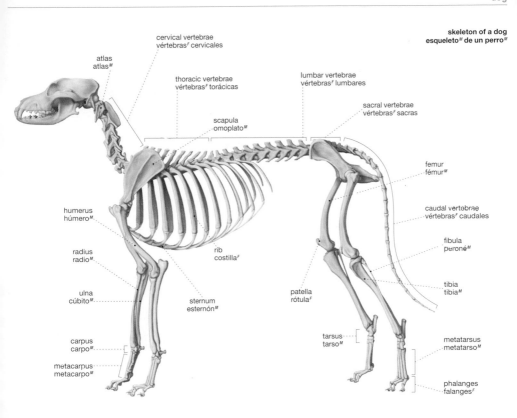

skeleton of a dog
esqueletoM **de un perro**M

cervical vertebrae
vértebrasF cervicales

atlas
atlasM

thoracic vertebrae
vértebrasF torácicas

lumbar vertebrae
vértebrasF lumbares

sacral vertebrae
vértebrasF sacras

scapula
omoplatoM

femur
fémurM

caudal vertebrae
vértebrasF caudales

humerus
húmeroM

fibula
peronéM

radius
radioM

rib
costillaF

ulna
cúbitoM

sternum
esternónM

tibia
tibiaM

patella
rótulaF

carpus
carpoM

tarsus
tarsoM

metatarsus
metatarsoM

metacarpus
metacarpoM

phalanges
falangesF

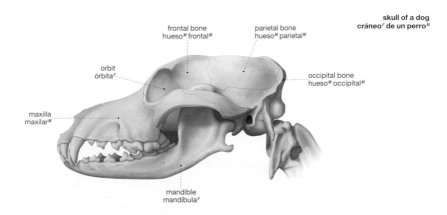

skull of a dog
cráneoF **de un perro**M

frontal bone
huesoM frontalM

parietal bone
huesoM parietalM

orbit
órbitaF

occipital bone
huesoM occipitalM

maxilla
maxilarM

mandible
mandíbulaF

examples of dog breeds

ejemplos*M* de perros*M*

ANIMALS

Brittany spaniel
spaniel*M*

poodle
caniche*M*

fox terrier
fox terrier*M*

schnauzer
schnauzer*M*

chowchow
chow chow*M*

collie
collie*M*

dalmatian
dálmata*M*

Yorkshire terrier
yorkshire terrier*M*

Pomeranian
pomerania*M*

bulldog
buldog*M*

examples of dog breeds

greyhound
lebrero[M]

German shepherd
pastor[M] alemán

Labrador retriever
labrador retriever[M]

golden retriever
golden retriever[M]

Saint Bernard
San Bernardo[M]

Great Dane
Gran Danés[M]

ANIMALS

cat
gato^M **doméstico**

head of a cat
cabeza^F **de un gato**^M

whiskers
bigotes^M

upper eyelid
párpado^M superior

lower eyelid
párpado^M inferior

nictitating membrane
párpado^M interno

whiskers
bigotes^M

eyelashes
pestañas^F

pupil
pupila^F

nose leather
ala^F de la nariz^F

muzzle
hocico^M

lip
labio^M

morphology of a cat
morfología^F **de un gato**^M

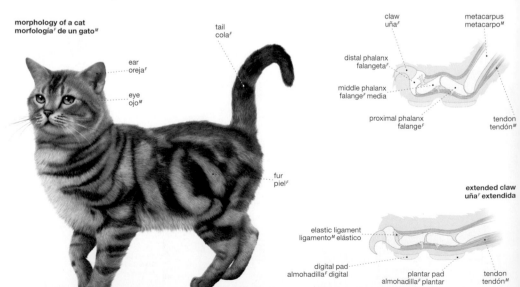

tail
cola^F

ear
oreja^F

eye
ojo^M

fur
piel^F

retracted claw
uña^F **retraída**

claw
uña^F

metacarpus
metacarpo^M

distal phalanx
falangeta^F

middle phalanx
falange^F media

proximal phalanx
falange^F

tendon
tendón^M

extended claw
uña^F **extendida**

elastic ligament
ligamento^M elástico

digital pad
almohadilla^F digital

plantar pad
almohadilla^F plantar

tendon
tendón^M

examples of cat breeds
ejemplos*ᴹ* de gatos*ᴹ*

sphynx
esfinge*ᶠ*

Abyssinian
abisinio*ᴹ*

Siamese
siamés*ᴹ*

Norwegian forest cat
gato*ᴹ* bosque*ᴹ* de Noruega*ᶠ*

Russian blue
azul ruso*ᴹ*

Manx
Manx*ᴹ*

Persian
persa*ᴹ*

American shorthair
American*ᴹ* shorthair

Maine coon
Maine Coon*ᴹ*

Bengal
gato*ᴹ* de Bengala*ᶠ*

examples of carnivorous mammals

ejemplos^M de mamíferos^M carnívoros

ANIMALS

weasel
comadreja^F

stone marten
garduña^F

mink
visón^M

mongoose
mangosta^F

ferret
hurón^M

skunk
mofeta^F

marten
marta^F

river otter
nutria^F de río^M

badger
tejón^M

fennec
fenec^M

hyena
hiena^F

fox
zorro^M

raccoon
mapache^M

cougar
puma^M

lynx
lince^M

wolverine
glotón^M

examples of carnivorous mammals

ANIMALS

leopard
leopardo*M*

tiger
tigre*M*

jaguar
jaguar*M*

wolf
lobo*M*

cheetah
guepardo*M*

lion
león*M*

black bear
oso*M* negro

polar bear
oso*M* polar

dolphin
delfín[M]

morphology of a dolphin
morfología[F] de un delfín[M]

ANIMALS

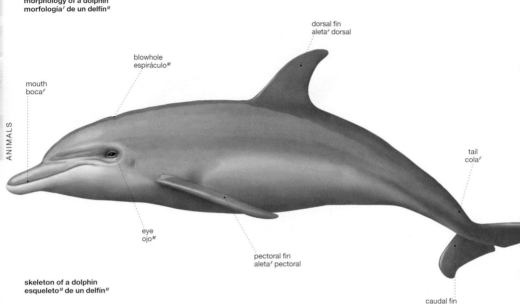

dorsal fin
aleta[F] dorsal

blowhole
espiráculo[M]

mouth
boca[F]

tail
cola[F]

eye
ojo[M]

pectoral fin
aleta[F] pectoral

caudal fin
aleta[F] caudal

skeleton of a dolphin
esqueleto[M] de un delfín[M]

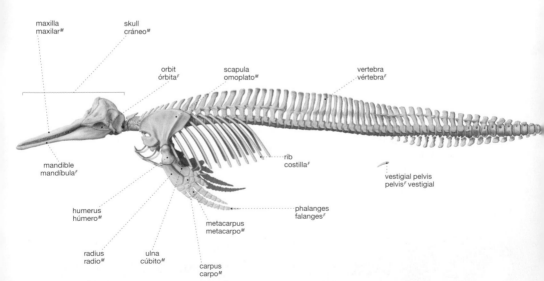

maxilla
maxilar[M]

skull
cráneo[M]

orbit
órbita[F]

scapula
omoplato[M]

vertebra
vértebra[F]

mandible
mandíbula[F]

rib
costilla[F]

vestigial pelvis
pelvis[F] vestigial

humerus
húmero[M]

phalanges
falanges[F]

metacarpus
metacarpo[M]

radius
radio[M]

ulna
cúbito[M]

carpus
carpo[M]

examples of marine mammals
ejemplos^M de mamíferos^M acuáticos

walrus
morsa^F

sea lion
león^M marino

seal
foca^F

ANIMALS

narwhal
narval^M

dolphin
delfín^M

porpoise
marsopa^F

beluga whale
ballena^F blanca

killer whale
orca^F

humpback whale
ballena^F jorobada

northern right whale
ballena^F franca del
norte^M

sperm whale
cachalote^M

ANIMALS

gorilla
gorila^M

skeleton of a gorilla
esqueleto^M de un
gorila^M

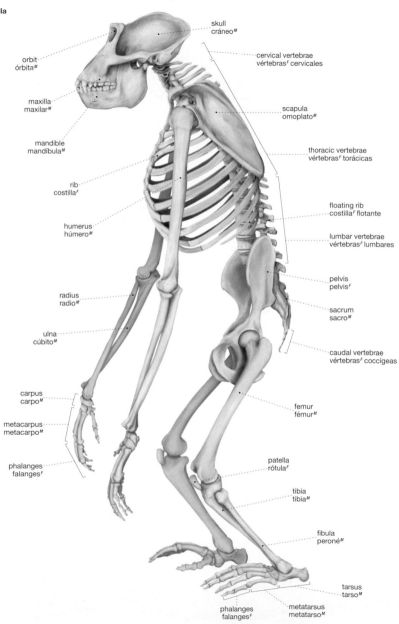

skull
cráneo^M

orbit
órbita^M

cervical vertebrae
vértebras^F cervicales

maxilla
maxilar^M

scapula
omoplato^M

mandible
mandíbula^M

thoracic vertebrae
vértebras^F torácicas

rib
costilla^F

floating rib
costilla^F flotante

humerus
húmero^M

lumbar vertebrae
vértebras^F lumbares

radius
radio^M

pelvis
pelvis^F

sacrum
sacro^M

ulna
cúbito^M

caudal vertebrae
vértebras^F coccígeas

carpus
carpo^M

femur
fémur^M

metacarpus
metacarpo^M

phalanges
falanges^F

patella
rótula^F

tibia
tibia^M

fibula
peroné^M

tarsus
tarso^M

phalanges
falanges^F

metatarsus
metatarso^M

ANIMALS

gorilla

morphology of a gorilla
morfología^F de un
gorila^M

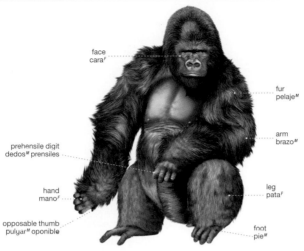

face
cara^F

fur
pelaje^M

arm
brazo^M

prehensile digit
dedos^M prensiles

hand
mano^F

leg
pata^F

opposable thumb
pulgar^M oponible

foot
pie^M

examples of primates

ejemplos^M de primates^M

tamarin
tamarino^M

gibbon
gibón^M

chimpanzee
chimpancé^M

capuchin
capuchino^M

marmoset
tití^M

orangutan
orangután^M

lemur
lémur^M

baboon
babuino^M

macaque
macaco^M

ANIMALS

bat

murciélago^M

morphology of a bat
morfología^F **de un murciélago**^M

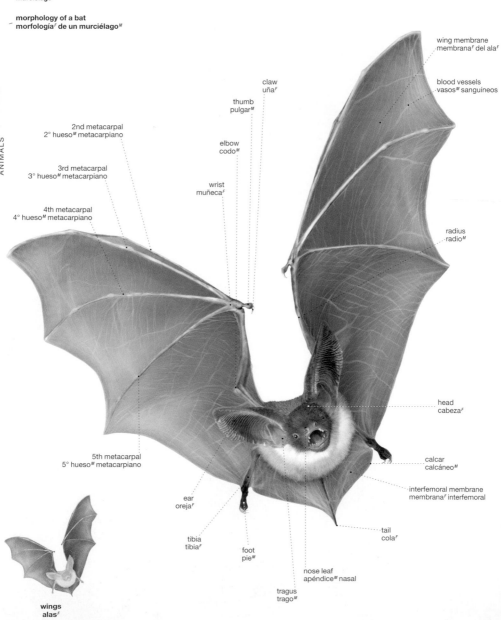

wing membrane
membrana^F del ala^F

blood vessels
vasos^M sanguíneos

claw
uña^F

thumb
pulgar^M

2nd metacarpal
2° hueso^M metacarpiano

elbow
codo^M

3rd metacarpal
3° hueso^M metacarpiano

wrist
muñeca^F

4th metacarpal
4° hueso^M metacarpiano

radius
radio^M

head
cabeza^F

5th metacarpal
5° hueso^M metacarpiano

calcar
calcáneo^M

interfemoral membrane
membrana^F interfemoral

ear
oreja^F

tail
cola^F

tibia
tibia^F

foot
pie^M

nose leaf
apéndice^M nasal

tragus
trago^M

wings
alas^F

bat

ANIMALS

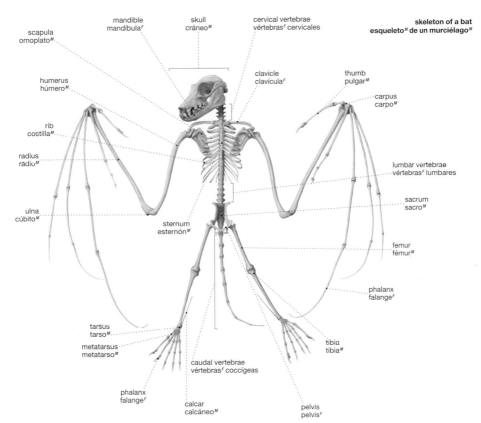

skeleton of a bat
esqueleto de un murciélago**

scapula
omoplato**

mandible
mandíbula**

skull
cráneo**

cervical vertebrae
vértebras** cervicales

humerus
húmero**

clavicle
clavícula**

thumb
pulgar**

carpus
carpo**

rib
costilla**

radius
radio**

lumbar vertebrae
vértebras** lumbares

sacrum
sacro**

ulna
cúbito**

femur
fémur**

sternum
esternón**

phalanx
falange**

tarsus
tarso**

metatarsus
metatarso**

caudal vertebrae
vértebras** coccígeas

tibia
tibia**

phalanx
falange**

calcar
calcáneo**

pelvis
pelvis**

examples of flying mammals

ejemplos** de mamíferos** voladores

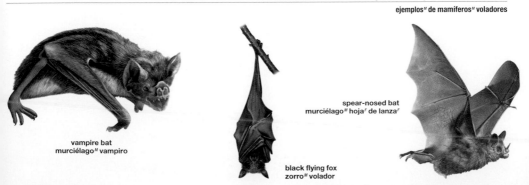

vampire bat
murciélago vampiro**

black flying fox
zorro volador**

spear-nosed bat
murciélago hoja** de lanza**

kangaroo

canguro^M

skeleton of a kangaroo
esqueleto^M **de un**
canguro^M

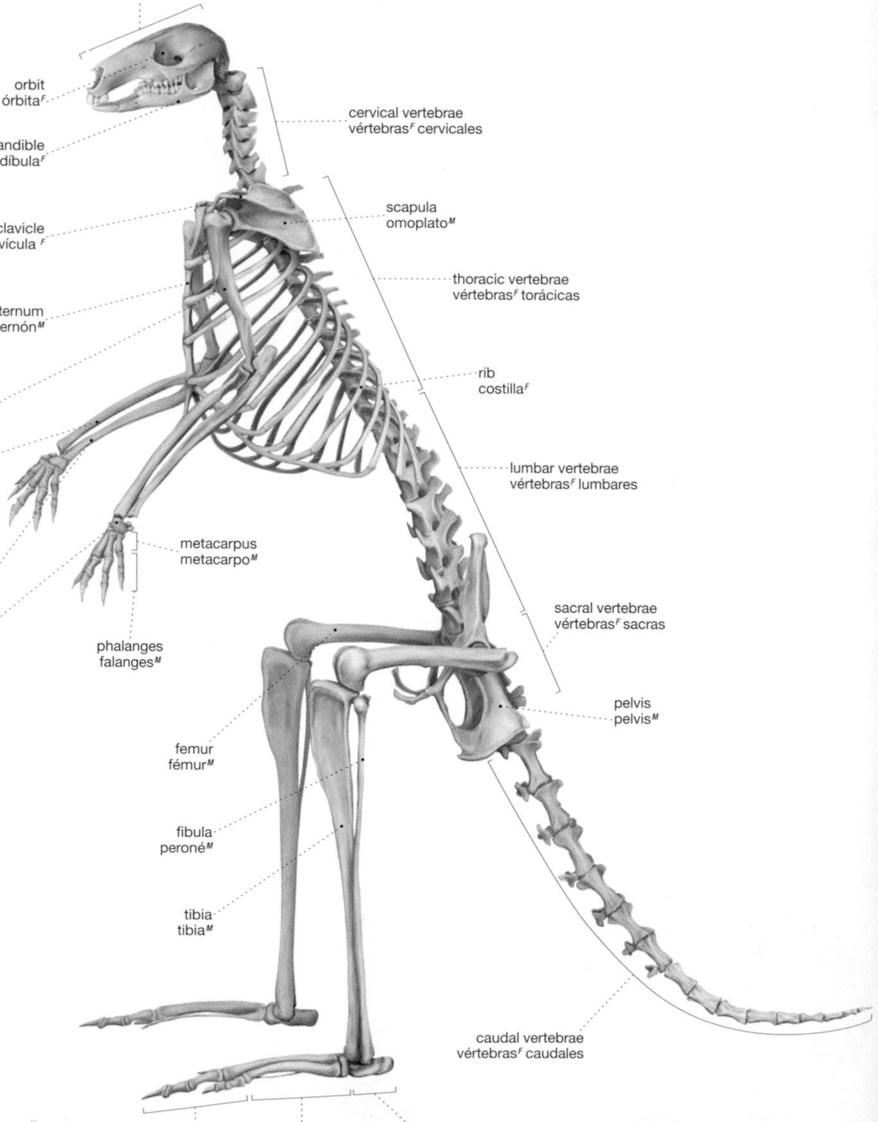

skull
cráneo^M

orbit
órbita^F

cervical vertebrae
vértebras^F cervicales

mandible
mandíbula^F

clavicle
clavícula ^{F}

scapula
omoplato^M

thoracic vertebrae
vértebras^F torácicas

sternum
esternón^M

humerus
húmero^M

rib
costilla^F

radius
radio^M

lumbar vertebrae
vértebras^F lumbares

metacarpus
metacarpo^M

ulna
cúbito^M

carpus
carpo^M

sacral vertebrae
vértebras^F sacras

phalanges
falanges^M

pelvis
pelvis^M

femur
fémur^M

fibula
peroné^M

tibia
tibia^M

caudal vertebrae
vértebras^F caudales

phalanges
falanges^M

metatarsus
metatarso^M

tarsus
tarso^M

morphology of a
kangaroo
morfología^F de un
canguro^M

pinna
pabellón^M de la oreja^F

fur
pelaje^M

snout
hocico^M

thigh
pata^F

forelimb
pata^F delantera

pouch
bolsa^F

claw
garra^F

tail
cola^F

hind limb
pata^F posterior

digit
dedo^M

foot
pie^M

ANIMALS

examples of marsupials

ejemplos^M de mamíferos^M marsupiales

opossum
oposum^M

Tasmanian devil
diablo^M de Tasmania^F

koala
koala^M

wallaby
walaby^M

kangaroo
canguro^M

HUMAN BEING

ser humano

HUMAN BODY   **192**

man   192
woman   194

ANATOMY   **196**

muscles   196
skeleton   199
teeth   206
joints   207
blood circulation   209
respiratory system   214
digestive system   216
urinary system   218
nervous system   220
reproductive system   226
endocrine system   229
lymphatic system   230

SENSE ORGANS   **231**

smell and taste   231
hearing   234
touch   236
sight   238

man

hombre^M

anterior view
vista^F **anterior**

HUMAN BEING

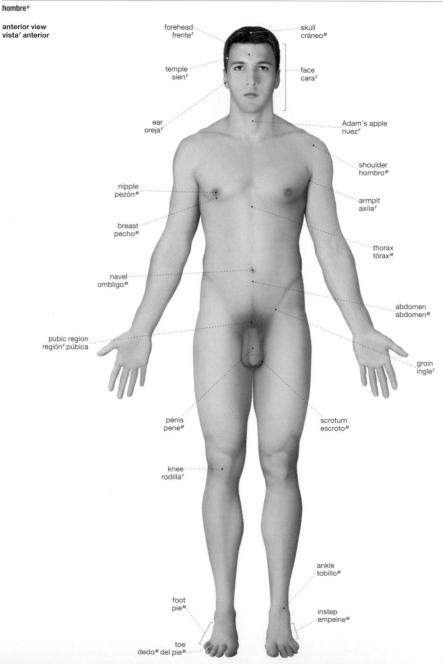

forehead
frente^F

skull
cráneo^M

temple
sien^F

face
cara^F

ear
oreja^F

Adam's apple
nuez^F

shoulder
hombro^M

nipple
pezón^M

armpit
axila^F

breast
pecho^M

thorax
tórax^M

navel
ombligo^M

abdomen
abdomen^M

pubic region
región^F púbica

groin
ingle^F

penis
pene^M

scrotum
escroto^M

knee
rodilla^F

ankle
tobillo^M

foot
pie^M

instep
empeine^M

toe
dedo^M del pie^M

HUMAN BEING

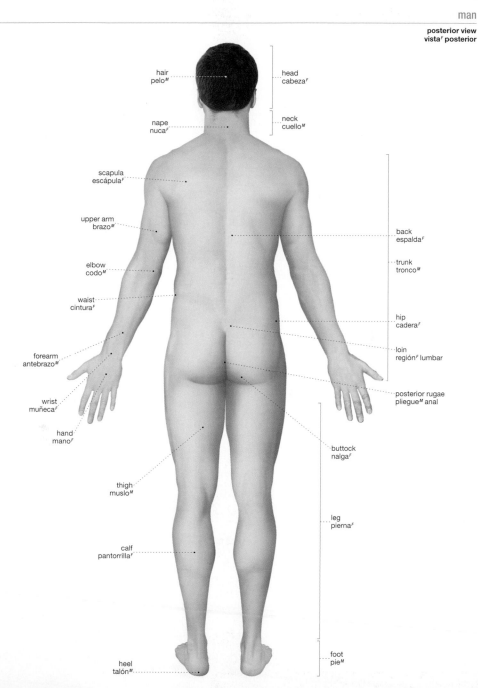

hair
pelo^M

head
cabeza^F

nape
nuca^F

neck
cuello^M

scapula
escápula^F

upper arm
brazo^M

back
espalda^F

elbow
codo^M

trunk
tronco^M

waist
cintura^F

hip
cadera^F

forearm
antebrazo^M

loin
región^F lumbar

wrist
muñeca^F

posterior rugae
pliegue^M anal

hand
mano^F

buttock
nalga^F

thigh
muslo^M

leg
pierna^F

calf
pantorrilla^F

foot
pie^M

heel
talón^M

woman

mujer^F

anterior view
vista^F **anterior**

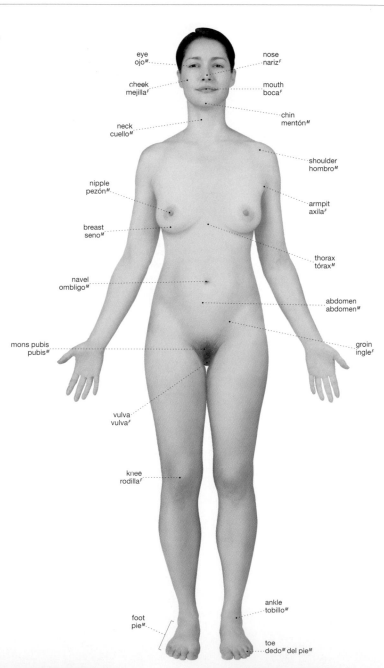

eye
ojo^M

nose
nariz^F

cheek
mejilla^F

mouth
boca^F

chin
mentón^M

neck
cuello^M

shoulder
hombro^M

nipple
pezón^M

armpit
axila^F

breast
seno^M

thorax
tórax^M

navel
ombligo^M

abdomen
abdomen^M

mons pubis
pubis^M

groin
ingle^F

vulva
vulva^F

knee
rodilla^F

ankle
tobillo^M

foot
pie^M

toe
dedo^M del pie^M

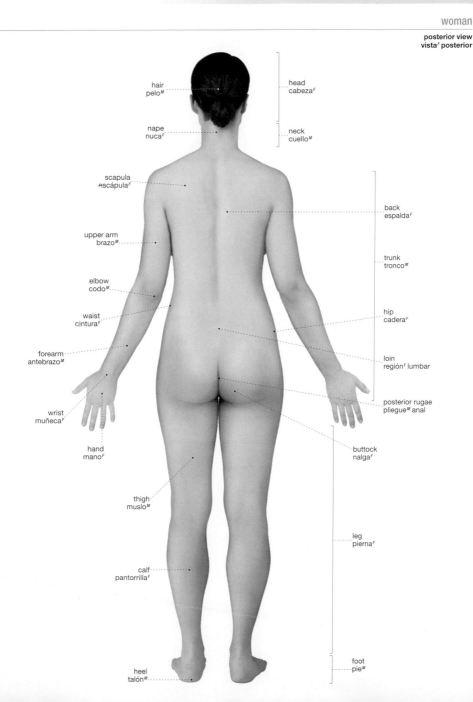

hair
pelo^M

head
cabeza^F

nape
nuca^F

neck
cuello^M

scapula
escápula^F

back
espalda^F

upper arm
brazo^M

trunk
tronco^M

elbow
codo^M

hip
cadera^F

waist
cintura^F

forearm
antebrazo^M

loin
región^F lumbar

wrist
muñeca^F

posterior rugae
pliegue^M anal

hand
mano^F

buttock
nalga^F

thigh
muslo^M

leg
pierna^F

calf
pantorrilla^F

heel
talón^M

foot
pie^M

muscles

músculos^M

anterior view
vista^F anterior

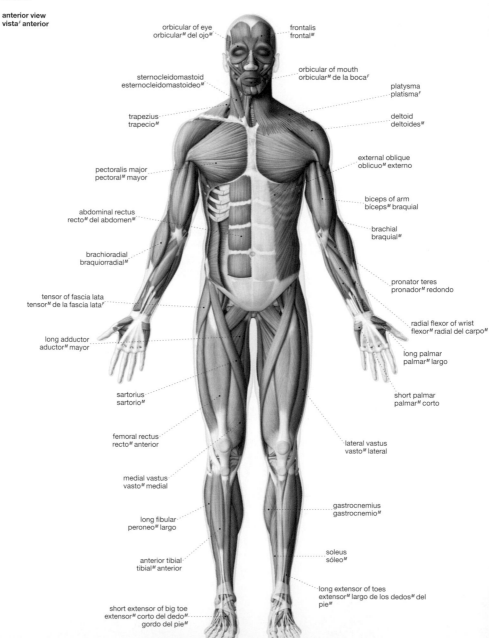

orbicular of eye
orbicular^M del ojo^M

frontalis
frontal^M

sternocleidomastoid
esternocleidomastoideo^M

orbicular of mouth
orbicular^M de la boca^F

platysma
platisma^F

trapezius
trapecio^M

deltoid
deltoides^M

external oblique
oblicuo^M externo

pectoralis major
pectoral^M mayor

biceps of arm
bíceps^M braquial

abdominal rectus
recto^M del abdomen^M

brachial
braquial^M

brachioradial
braquiorradial^M

pronator teres
pronador^M redondo

tensor of fascia lata
tensor^M de la fascia lata^F

radial flexor of wrist
flexor^M radial del carpo^M

long adductor
aductor^M mayor

long palmar
palmar^M largo

sartorius
sartorio^M

short palmar
palmar^M corto

femoral rectus
recto^M anterior

lateral vastus
vasto^M lateral

medial vastus
vasto^M medial

gastrocnemius
gastrocnemio^M

long fibular
peroneo^M largo

soleus
sóleo^M

anterior tibial
tibial^M anterior

long extensor of toes
extensor^M largo de los dedos^M del
pie^M

short extensor of big toe
extensor^M corto del dedo^M
gordo del pie^M

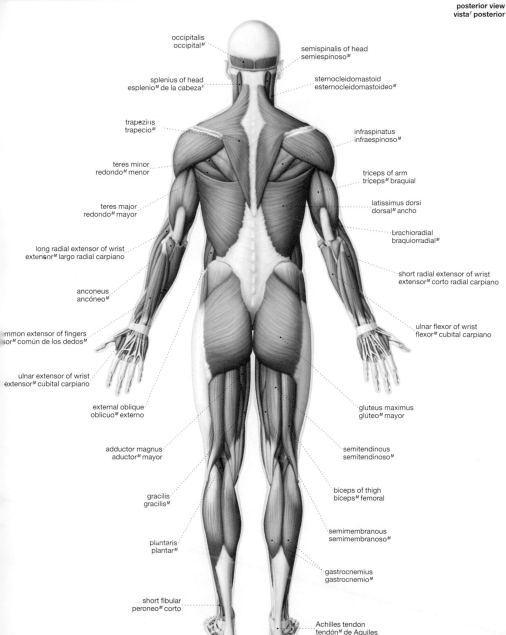

occipitalis
occipital^M

semispinalis of head
semiespinoso^M

splenius of head
esplenio^M de la cabeza^F

sternocleidomastoid
esternocleidomastoideo^M

trapezius
trapecio^M

infraspinatus
infraespinoso^M

teres minor
redondo^M menor

triceps of arm
tríceps^M braquial

teres major
redondo^M mayor

latissimus dorsi
dorsal^M ancho

brachioradial
braquiorradial^M

long radial extensor of wrist
extensor^M largo radial carpiano

short radial extensor of wrist
extensor^M corto radial carpiano

anconeus
ancóneo^M

common extensor of fingers
extensor^M común de los dedos^M

ulnar flexor of wrist
flexor^M cubital carpiano

ulnar extensor of wrist
extensor^M cubital carpiano

external oblique
oblicuo^M externo

gluteus maximus
glúteo^M mayor

adductor magnus
aductor^M mayor

semitendinous
semitendinoso^M

biceps of thigh
bíceps^M femoral

gracilis
gracilis^M

semimembranous
semimembranoso^M

plantaris
plantar^M

gastrocnemius
gastrocnemio^M

short fibular
peroneo^M corto

Achilles tendon
tendón^M de Aquiles

HUMAN BEING

muscles

muscle tissue
tejido^M **muscular**

striated muscle
(sartorius
músculo^M **estriado**

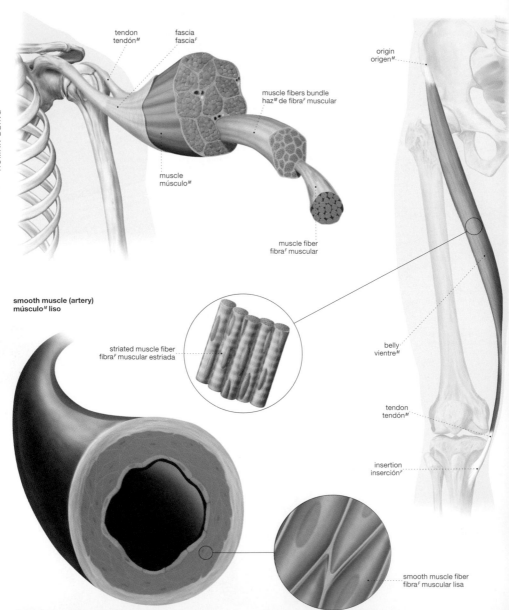

tendon
tendón^M

fascia
fascia^F

muscle fibers bundle
haz^M de fibra^F muscular

muscle
músculo^M

muscle fiber
fibra^F muscular

origin
origen^M

smooth muscle (artery)
músculo^M **liso**

striated muscle fiber
fibra^F muscular estriada

belly
vientre^M

tendon
tendón^M

insertion
inserción^F

smooth muscle fiber
fibra^F muscular lisa

skeleton
esqueleto^M

types of bones
tipos^M de huesos^M

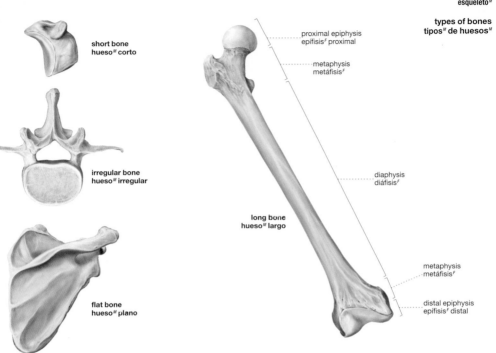

short bone
hueso^M corto

irregular bone
hueso^M irregular

flat bone
hueso^M plano

long bone
hueso^M largo

proximal epiphysis
epífisis^F proximal

metaphysis
metáfisis^F

diaphysis
diáfisis^F

metaphysis
metáfisis^F

distal epiphysis
epífisis^F distal

structure of a long bone
estructura^M de un hueso^M largo

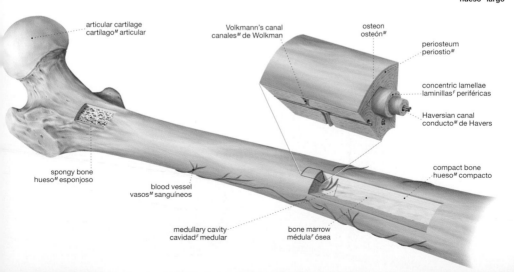

articular cartilage
cartílago^M articular

Volkmann's canal
canales^M de Wolkman

osteon
osteón^M

periosteum
periostio^M

concentric lamellae
laminillas^F periféricas

Haversian canal
conducto^M de Havers

compact bone
hueso^M compacto

spongy bone
hueso^M esponjoso

blood vessel
vasos^M sanguíneos

medullary cavity
cavidad^F medular

bone marrow
médula^F ósea

skeleton

anterior view
vista^F **anterior**

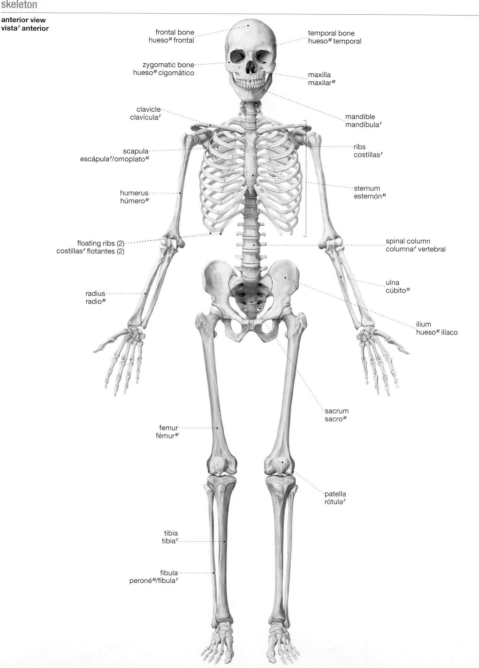

frontal bone
hueso^M frontal

temporal bone
hueso^M temporal

zygomatic bone
hueso^M cigomático

maxilla
maxilar^M

clavicle
clavícula^F

mandible
mandíbula^F

scapula
escápula^F/omoplato^M

ribs
costillas^F

humerus
húmero^M

sternum
esternón^M

floating ribs (2)
costillas^F flotantes (2)

spinal column
columna^F vertebral

radius
radio^M

ulna
cúbito^M

ilium
hueso^M ilíaco

sacrum
sacro^M

femur
fémur^M

patella
rótula^F

tibia
tibia^F

fibula
peroné^M/fíbula^F

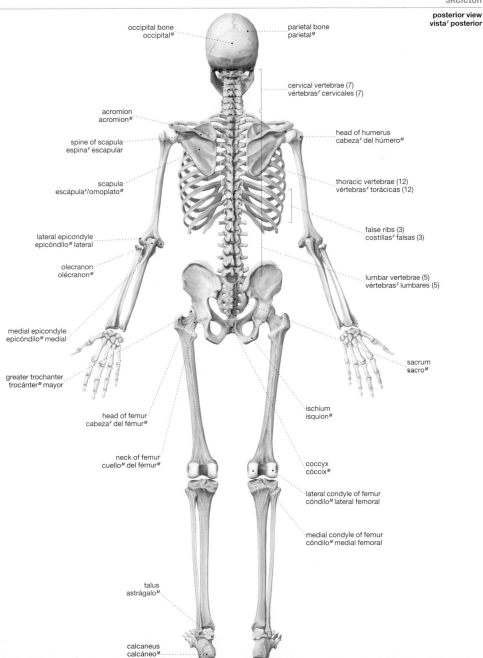

occipital bone
occipital^M

parietal bone
parietal^M

cervical vertebrae (7)
vértebras^F cervicales (7)

acromion
acromion^M

head of humerus
cabeza^F del húmero^M

spine of scapula
espina^F escapular

scapula
escápula^F/omoplato^M

thoracic vertebrae (12)
vértebras^F torácicas (12)

lateral epicondyle
epicóndilo^M lateral

false ribs (3)
costillas^F falsas (3)

olecranon
olécranon^M

lumbar vertebrae (5)
vértebras^F lumbares (5)

medial epicondyle
epicóndilo^M medial

greater trochanter
trocánter^M mayor

sacrum
sacro^M

head of femur
cabeza^F del fémur^M

ischium
isquion^M

neck of femur
cuello^M del fémur^M

coccyx
cóccix^M

lateral condyle of femur
cóndilo^M lateral femoral

medial condyle of femur
cóndilo^M medial femoral

talus
astrágalo^M

calcaneus
calcáneo^M

HUMAN BEING

skeleton

hand
huesos^M **de la mano**^F

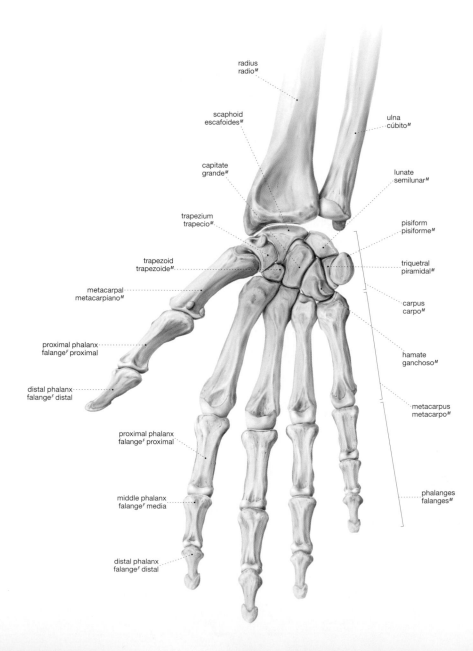

radius
radio^M

scaphoid
escafoides^M

ulna
cúbito^M

capitate
grande^M

lunate
semilunar^M

trapezium
trapecio^M

pisiform
pisiforme^M

trapezoid
trapezoide^M

triquetral
piramidal^M

metacarpal
metacarpiano^M

carpus
carpo^M

proximal phalanx
falange^F proximal

hamate
ganchoso^M

distal phalanx
falange^F distal

metacarpus
metacarpo^M

proximal phalanx
falange^F proximal

middle phalanx
falange^F media

phalanges
falanges^M

distal phalanx
falange^F distal

foot: anterior view
pie^M : vista^F frontal

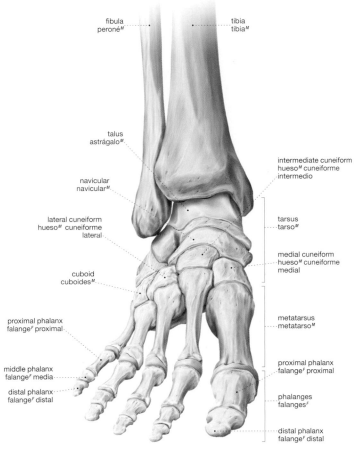

fibula
peroné^M

tibia
tibia^M

talus
astrágalo^M

intermediate cuneiform
hueso^M cuneiforme
intermedio

navicular
navicular^M

lateral cuneiform
hueso^M cuneiforme
lateral

tarsus
tarso^M

medial cuneiform
hueso^M cuneiforme
medial

cuboid
cuboides^M

proximal phalanx
falange^F proximal

metatarsus
metatarso^M

middle phalanx
falange^F media

proximal phalanx
falange^F proximal

distal phalanx
falange^F distal

phalanges
falanges^F

distal phalanx
falange^F distal

foot: lateral view
pie^M : vista^F lateral

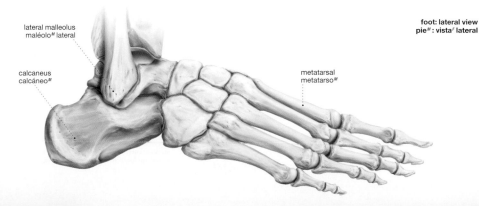

lateral malleolus
maléolo^M lateral

calcaneus
calcáneo^M

metatarsal
metatarso^M

skeleton

spinal column
columna^f vertebral

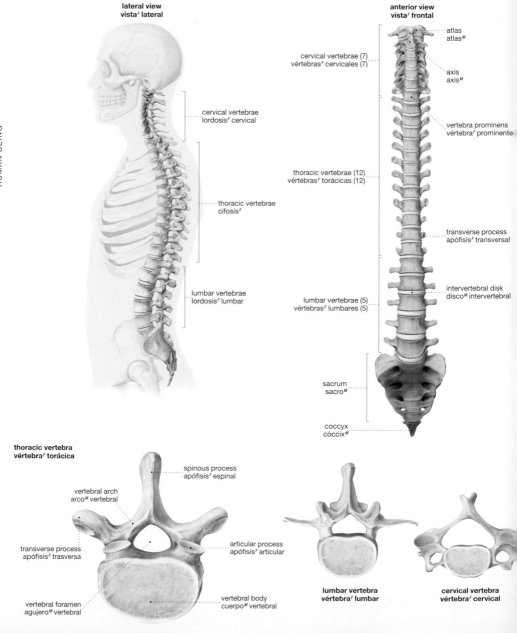

lateral view
vista^f lateral

anterior view
vista^f frontal

atlas
atlas^M

cervical vertebrae (7)
vértebras^f cervicales (7)

axis
axis^M

cervical vertebrae
lordosis^f cervical

vertebra prominens
vértebra^f prominente

thoracic vertebrae (12)
vértebras^f torácicas (12)

thoracic vertebrae
cifosis^f

transverse process
apófisis^f transversal

intervertebral disk
disco^M intervertebral

lumbar vertebrae
lordosis^f lumbar

lumbar vertebrae (5)
vértebras^f lumbares (5)

sacrum
sacro^M

coccyx
cóccix^M

thoracic vertebra
vértebra^f torácica

spinous process
apófisis^f espinal

vertebral arch
arco^M vertebral

transverse process
apófisis^f trasversa

articular process
apófisis^f articular

vertebral foramen
agujero^M vertebral

vertebral body
cuerpo^M vertebral

lumbar vertebra
vértebra^f lumbar

cervical vertebra
vértebra^f cervical

adult's skull: lateral view
cráneo^M: vista^F lateral

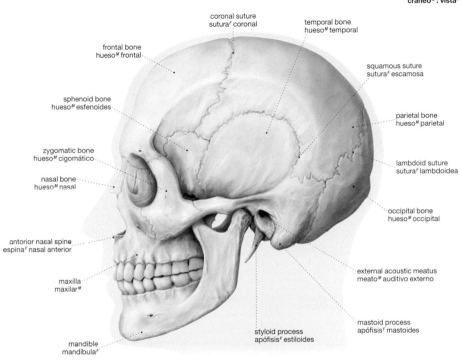

coronal suture
sutura^F coronal

temporal bone
hueso^M temporal

frontal bone
hueso^M frontal

squamous suture
sutura^F escamosa

sphenoid bone
hueso^M esfenoides

parietal bone
hueso^M parietal

zygomatic bone
hueso^M cigomático

lambdoid suture
sutura^F lambdoidea

nasal bone
hueso^M nasal

occipital bone
hueso^M occipital

anterior nasal spine
espina^F nasal anterior

maxilla
maxilar^M

external acoustic meatus
meato^M auditivo externo

mandible
mandíbula^F

styloid process
apófisis^F estiloides

mastoid process
apófisis^F mastoides

child's skull: lateral view
cráneo^M de un niño^M: vista^F lateral

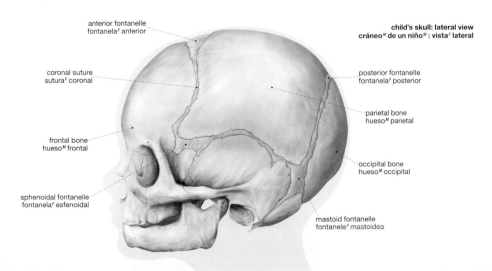

anterior fontanelle
fontanela^F anterior

coronal suture
sutura^F coronal

posterior fontanelle
fontanela^F posterior

parietal bone
hueso^M parietal

frontal bone
hueso^M frontal

occipital bone
hueso^M occipital

sphenoidal fontanelle
fontanela^F esfenoidal

mastoid fontanelle
fontanela^F mastoidea

teeth

dientes^M

human denture
dentadura^F humana

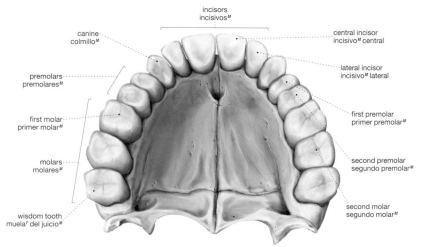

incisors
incisivos^M

canine
colmillo^M

central incisor
incisivo^M central

lateral incisor
incisivo^M lateral

premolars
premolares^M

first molar
primer molar^M

first premolar
primer premolar^M

second premolar
segundo premolar^M

molars
molares^M

second molar
segundo molar^M

wisdom tooth
muela^F del juicio^M

section of a molar
corte^M de un molar^M

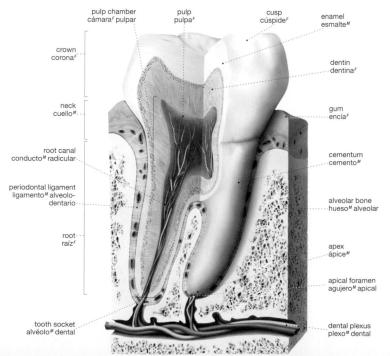

pulp chamber
cámara^F pulpar

pulp
pulpa^F

cusp
cúspide^F

enamel
esmalte^M

crown
corona^F

dentin
dentina^F

neck
cuello^M

gum
encía^F

root canal
conducto^M radicular

cementum
cemento^M

periodontal ligament
ligamento^M alveolo-
dentario

alveolar bone
hueso^M alveolar

root
raíz^F

apex
ápice^M

apical foramen
agujero^M apical

tooth socket
alvéolo^M dental

dental plexus
plexo^M dental

joints

articulaciones[F]

section of a synovial joint
corte[M] **de una articulación**[F] **sinovial**

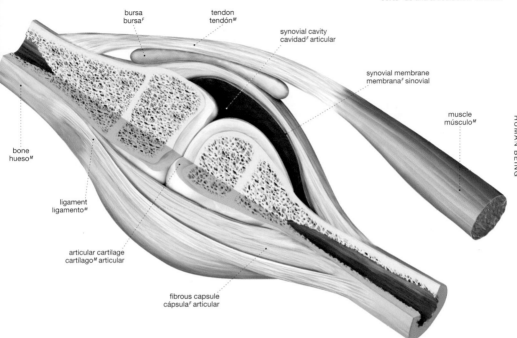

bursa
bursa[F]

tendon
tendón[M]

synovial cavity
cavidad[F] articular

synovial membrane
membrana[F] sinovial

muscle
músculo[M]

bone
hueso[M]

ligament
ligamento[M]

articular cartilage
cartílago[M] articular

fibrous capsule
cápsula[F] articular

HUMAN BEING

examples of synovial joints
ejemplos[M] **de articulaciones**[F]
sinoviales

hinge joint
articulación[F] **en bisagra**[F]

ball-and-socket joint
articulación[F] **esferoidea**

pivot joint
articulación[F] **en pivote**[M]

elbow
codo[M]

shoulder
hombro[M]

leg
pierna

humerus
húmero[M]

ulna
cúbito[M]

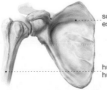

scapula
escápula[F]

humerus
húmero[M]

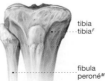

tibia
tibia[F]

fibula
peroné[M]

joints

examples of synovial joints

gliding joint
articulación^F plana/
artrodial

saddle joint
articulación^F en silla^F de
montar

condyloid joint
articulación^F condilar

HUMAN BEING

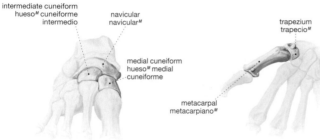

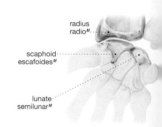

intermediate cuneiform
hueso^M cuneiforme
intermedio

navicular
navicular^M

medial cuneiform
hueso^M medial
cuneiforme

trapezium
trapecio^M

metacarpal
metacarpiano^M

radius
radio^M

scaphoid
escafoides^M

lunate
semilunar^M

tarsus
tarso^M

thumb
pulgar^M

wrist
muñeca^F

example of fibrous joint
ejemplos^M de articulaciones^F
fibrosas

examples of cartilaginous joints
ejemplos^M de articulaciones^F cartilaginosas

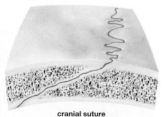

cranial suture
sutura^F craneal

pubic symphysis
sínfisis^F púbica

intervertebral disk
disco^M intervertebral

blood circulation
circulación^F sanguínea

composition of the blood
composición^F de la sangre^F

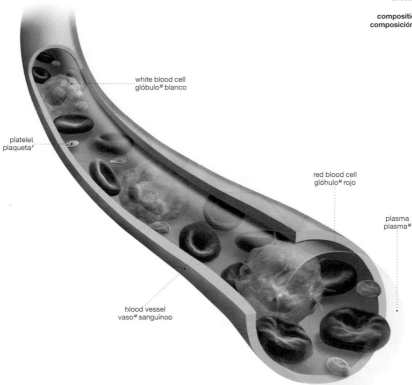

white blood cell
glóbulo^M blanco

platelet
plaqueta^F

red blood cell
glóbulo^M rojo

plasma
plasma^M

blood vessel
vaso^M sanguíneo

section of a vein
corte^M de una vena^F

section of an artery
corte^M de una arteria^F

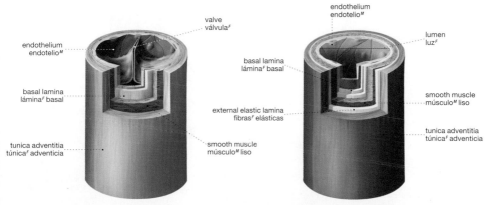

endothelium
endotelio^M

valve
válvula^F

basal lamina
lámina^F basal

tunica adventitia
túnica^F adventicia

smooth muscle
músculo^M liso

endothelium
endotelio^M

lumen
luz^F

basal lamina
lámina^F basal

external elastic lamina
fibras^F elásticas

smooth muscle
músculo^M liso

tunica adventitia
túnica^F adventicia

blood circulation

principal arteries
arterias^f principales

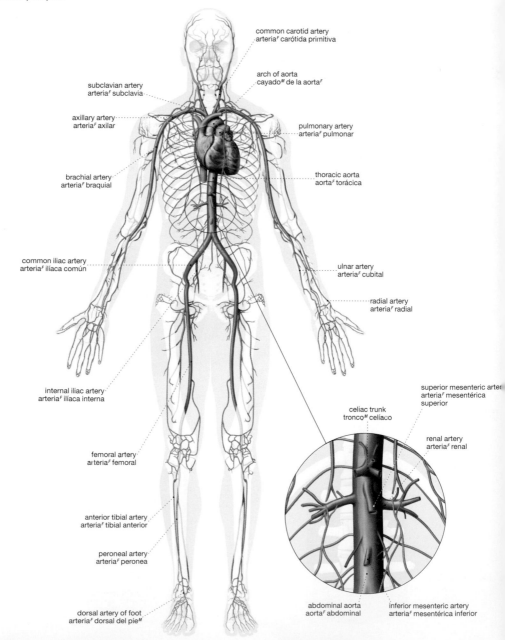

common carotid artery
arteria^f carótida primitiva

arch of aorta
cayado^M de la aorta^f

subclavian artery
arteria^f subclavia

axillary artery
arteria^f axilar

pulmonary artery
arteria^f pulmonar

brachial artery
arteria^f braquial

thoracic aorta
aorta^f torácica

common iliac artery
arteria^f ilíaca común

ulnar artery
arteria^f cubital

radial artery
arteria^f radial

internal iliac artery
arteria^f ilíaca interna

superior mesenteric arter
arteria^f mesentérica
superior

celiac trunk
tronco^M celíaco

renal artery
arteria^f renal

femoral artery
arteria^f femoral

anterior tibial artery
arteria^f tibial anterior

peroneal artery
arteria^f peronea

dorsal artery of foot
arteria^f dorsal del pie^M

abdominal aorta
aorta^f abdominal

inferior mesenteric artery
arteria^f mesentérica inferior

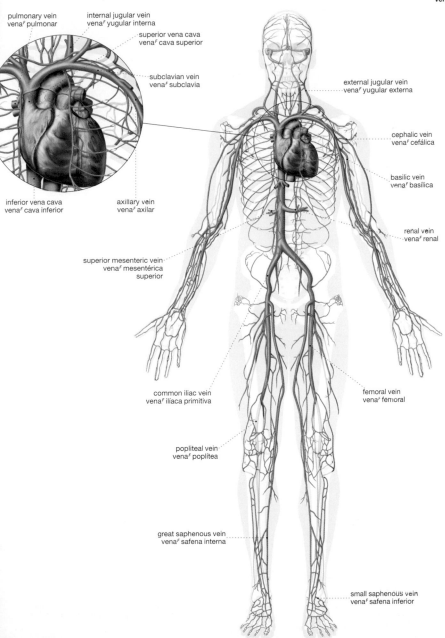

pulmonary vein
vena^f pulmonar

internal jugular vein
vena^f yugular interna

superior vena cava
vena^f cava superior

subclavian vein
vena^f subclavia

external jugular vein
vena^f yugular externa

cephalic vein
vena^f cefálica

basilic vein
vena^f basílica

inferior vena cava
vena^f cava inferior

axillary vein
vena^f axilar

renal vein
vena^f renal

superior mesenteric vein
vena^f mesentérica
superior

common iliac vein
vena^f ilíaca primitiva

femoral vein
vena^f femoral

popliteal vein
vena^f poplítea

great saphenous vein
vena^f safena interna

small saphenous vein
vena^f safena inferior

HUMAN BEING

anatomy | anatomía

blood circulation

systemic circulation
circulación^F **sistémica**

HUMAN BEING

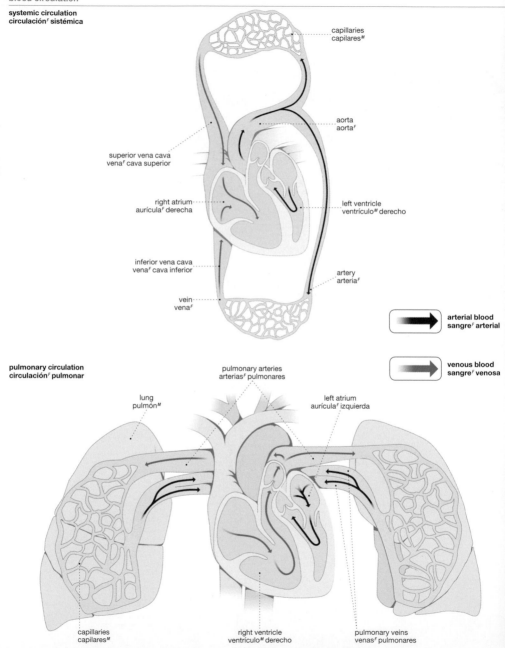

capillaries
capilares^M

aorta
aorta^F

superior vena cava
vena^F cava superior

right atrium
aurícula^F derecha

left ventricle
ventrículo^M derecho

inferior vena cava
vena^F cava inferior

artery
arteria^F

vein
vena^F

arterial blood
sangre^F arterial

venous blood
sangre^F venosa

pulmonary circulation
circulación^F **pulmonar**

pulmonary arteries
arterias^F pulmonares

lung
pulmón^M

left atrium
aurícula^F izquierda

capillaries
capilares^M

right ventricle
ventrículo^M derecho

pulmonary veins
venas^F pulmonares

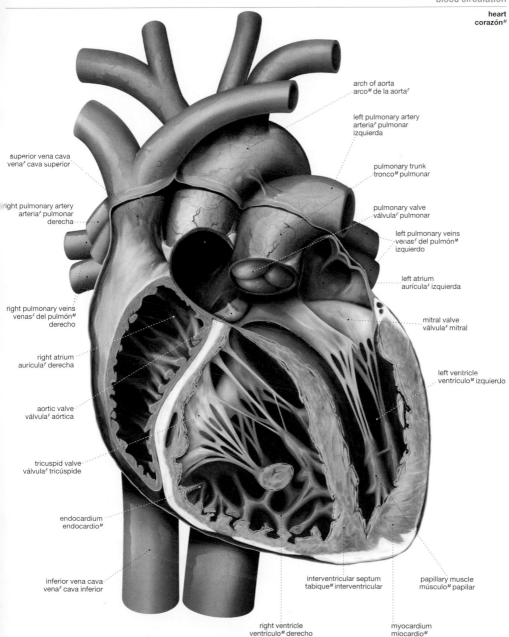

arch of aorta
arco^M de la aorta^F

left pulmonary artery
arteria^F pulmonar
izquierda

superior vena cava
vena^F cava superior

pulmonary trunk
tronco^M pulmonar

right pulmonary artery
arteria^F pulmonar
derecha

pulmonary valve
válvula^F pulmonar

left pulmonary veins
venas^F del pulmón^M
izquierdo

left atrium
aurícula^F izquierda

right pulmonary veins
venas^F del pulmón^M
derecho

mitral valve
válvula^F mitral

right atrium
aurícula^F derecha

left ventricle
ventrículo^M izquierdo

aortic valve
válvula^F aórtica

tricuspid valve
válvula^F tricúspide

endocardium
endocardio^M

inferior vena cava
vena^F cava inferior

interventricular septum
tabique^M interventricular

papillary muscle
músculo^M papilar

right ventricle
ventrículo^M derecho

myocardium
miocardio^M

HUMAN BEING

respiratory system

aparato^M respiratorio

main organs
órganos^M principales

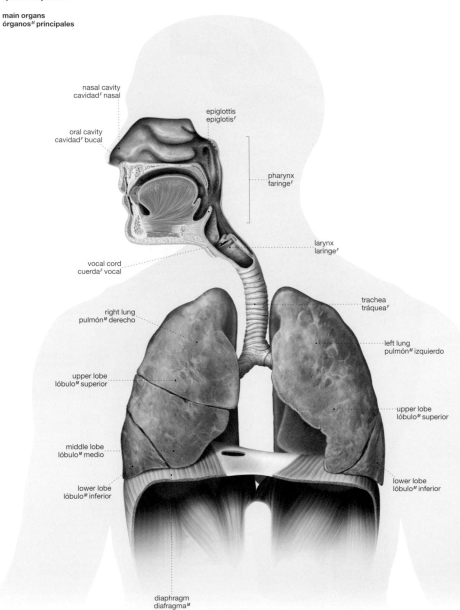

nasal cavity
cavidad^F nasal

epiglottis
epiglotis^F

oral cavity
cavidad^F bucal

pharynx
faringe^F

larynx
laringe^F

vocal cord
cuerda^F vocal

trachea
tráquea^F

right lung
pulmón^M derecho

left lung
pulmón^M izquierdo

upper lobe
lóbulo^M superior

upper lobe
lóbulo^M superior

middle lobe
lóbulo^M medio

lower lobe
lóbulo^M inferior

lower lobe
lóbulo^M inferior

diaphragm
diafragma^M

lungs
pulmones^M

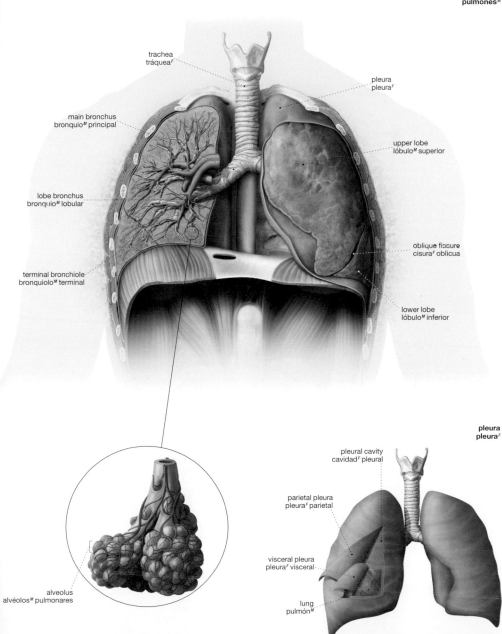

trachea
tráquea^F

pleura
pleura^F

main bronchus
bronquio^M principal

upper lobe
lóbulo^M superior

lobe bronchus
bronquio^M lobular

oblique fissure
cisura^F oblicua

terminal bronchiole
bronquiolo^M terminal

lower lobe
lóbulo^M inferior

alveolus
alvéolos^M pulmonares

pleura
pleura^F

pleural cavity
cavidad^F pleural

parietal pleura
pleura^F parietal

visceral pleura
pleura^F visceral

lung
pulmón^M

HUMAN BEING

digestive system

aparato^M **digestivo**

main organs
órganos^M **principales**

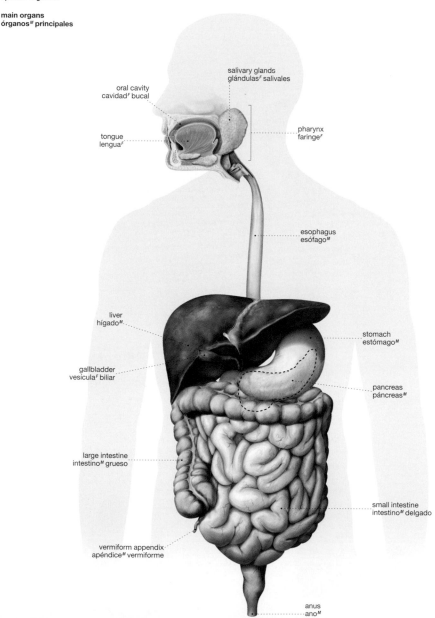

salivary glands
glándulas^F salivales

oral cavity
cavidad^F bucal

tongue
lengua^F

pharynx
faringe^F

esophagus
esófago^M

liver
hígado^M

stomach
estómago^M

gallbladder
vesícula^F biliar

pancreas
páncreas^M

large intestine
intestino^M grueso

small intestine
intestino^M delgado

vermiform appendix
apéndice^M vermiforme

anus
ano^M

large intestine
intestino grueso

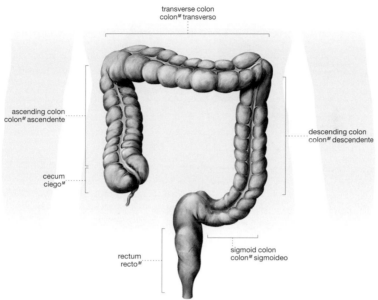

transverse colon
colon transverso

ascending colon
colon ascendente

descending colon
colon descendente

cecum
ciego

rectum
recto

sigmoid colon
colon sigmoideo

small intestine
intestino delgado

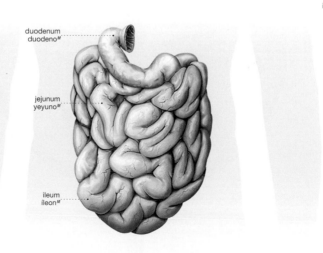

duodenum
duodeno

jejunum
yeyuno

ileum
íleon

urinary system

aparato^M **urinario**

main organs
órganos^M **principales**

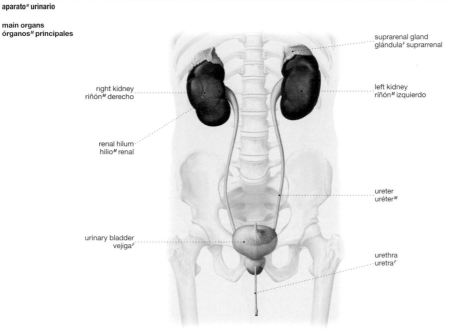

suprarenal gland
glándula^F suprarrenal

right kidney
riñón^M derecho

left kidney
riñón^M izquierdo

renal hilum
hilio^M renal

ureter
uréter^M

urinary bladder
vejiga^F

urethra
uretra^F

urinary bladder: frontal section
vejiga^F **: corte**^M **frontal**

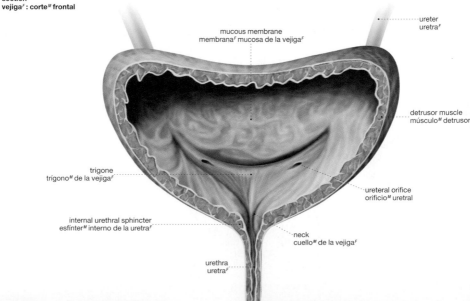

mucous membrane
membrana^F mucosa de la vejiga^F

ureter
uretra^F

detrusor muscle
músculo^M detrusor

trigone
trígono^M de la vejiga^F

ureteral orifice
orificio^M uretral

internal urethral sphincter
esfínter^M interno de la uretra^F

neck
cuello^M de la vejiga^F

urethra
uretra^F

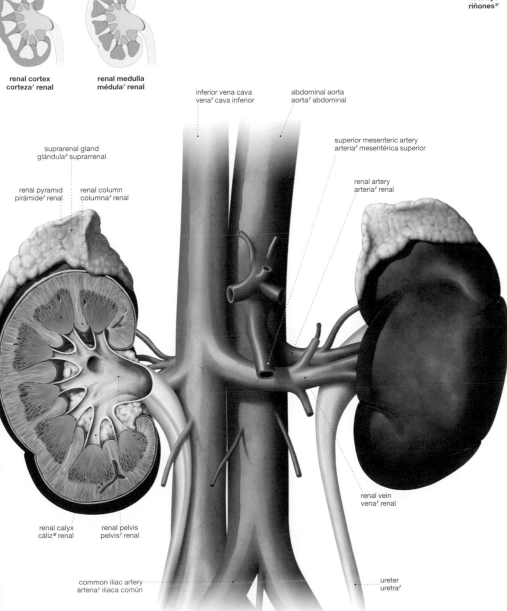

kidneys
riñonesᴹ

renal cortex
corteza*ᶠ* renal

renal medulla
médula*ᶠ* renal

inferior vena cava
vena*ᶠ* cava inferior

abdominal aorta
aorta*ᶠ* abdominal

superior mesenteric artery
arteria*ᶠ* mesentérica superior

suprarenal gland
glándula*ᶠ* suprarrenal

renal artery
arteria*ᶠ* renal

renal pyramid
pirámide*ᶠ* renal

renal column
columna*ᶠ* renal

renal vein
vena*ᶠ* renal

renal calyx
cáliz*ᴹ* renal

renal pelvis
pelvis*ᶠ* renal

common iliac artery
arteria*ᶠ* ilíaca común

ureter
uretra*ᶠ*

nervous system

sistema^M nervioso

**structure of nervous
system**
estructura^F del sistema^M
nervioso

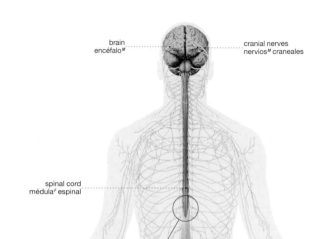

brain
encéfalo^M

cranial nerves
nervios^M craneales

central nervous system
sistema^M nervioso central

peripheral nervous system
sistema^M nervioso periférico

spinal cord
médula^F espinal

spinal nerves
nervios^M raquídeos

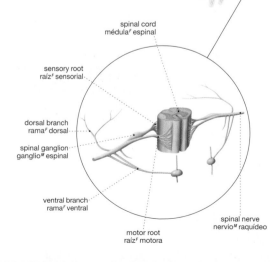

spinal cord
médula^F espinal

sensory root
raíz^F sensorial

dorsal branch
rama^F dorsal

spinal ganglion
ganglio^M espinal

ventral branch
rama^F ventral

motor root
raíz^F motora

spinal nerve
nervio^M raquídeo

nervous system

neuron
neurona*F*

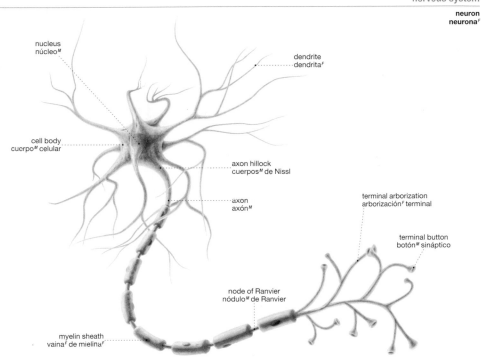

nucleus
núcleo*M*

dendrite
dendrita*F*

cell body
cuerpo*M* celular

axon hillock
cuerpos*M* de Nissl

axon
axón*M*

terminal arborization
arborización*F* terminal

terminal button
botón*M* sináptico

node of Ranvier
nódulo*M* de Ranvier

myelin sheath
vaina*F* de mielina*F*

reflex arc
impulso*M* nervioso

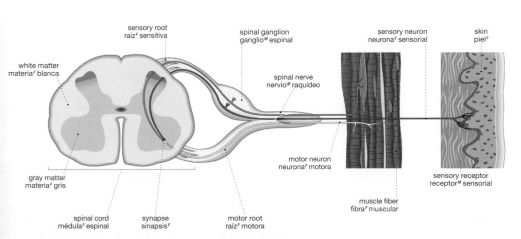

sensory root
raíz*F* sensitiva

spinal ganglion
ganglio*M* espinal

sensory neuron
neurona*F* sensorial

skin
piel*F*

white matter
materia*F* blanca

spinal nerve
nervio*M* raquídeo

motor neuron
neurona*F* motora

gray matter
materia*F* gris

sensory receptor
receptor*M* sensorial

spinal cord
médula*F* espinal

synapse
sinapsis*F*

motor root
raíz*F* motora

muscle fiber
fibra*F* muscular

nervous system

brain
encéfalo^M

frontal section
corte^M **frontal**

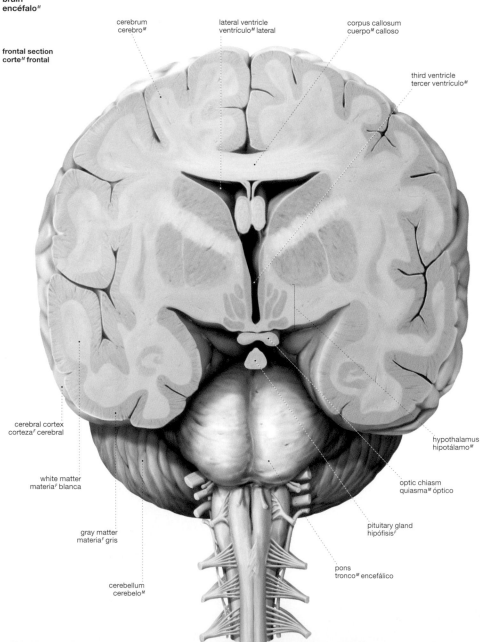

cerebrum
cerebro^M

lateral ventricle
ventrículo^M lateral

corpus callosum
cuerpo^M calloso

third ventricle
tercer ventrículo^M

cerebral cortex
corteza^F cerebral

white matter
materia^F blanca

gray matter
materia^F gris

cerebellum
cerebelo^M

hypothalamus
hipotálamo^M

optic chiasm
quiasma^M óptico

pituitary gland
hipófisis^F

pons
tronco^M encefálico

nervous system

cerebrum: superior view
cerebro^M: vista^F superior

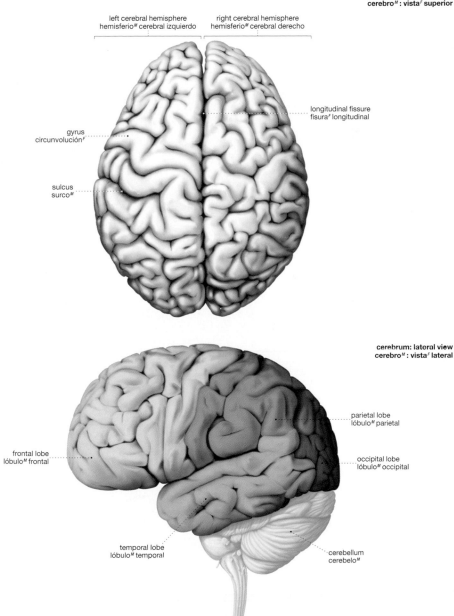

left cerebral hemisphere
hemisferio^M cerebral izquierdo

right cerebral hemisphere
hemisferio^M cerebral derecho

longitudinal fissure
fisura^F longitudinal

gyrus
circunvolución^F

sulcus
surco^M

HUMAN BEING

cerebrum: lateral view
cerebro^M: vista^F lateral

parietal lobe
lóbulo^M parietal

frontal lobe
lóbulo^M frontal

occipital lobe
lóbulo^M occipital

temporal lobe
lóbulo^M temporal

cerebellum
cerebelo^M

nervous system

spinal cord
médula^F espinal

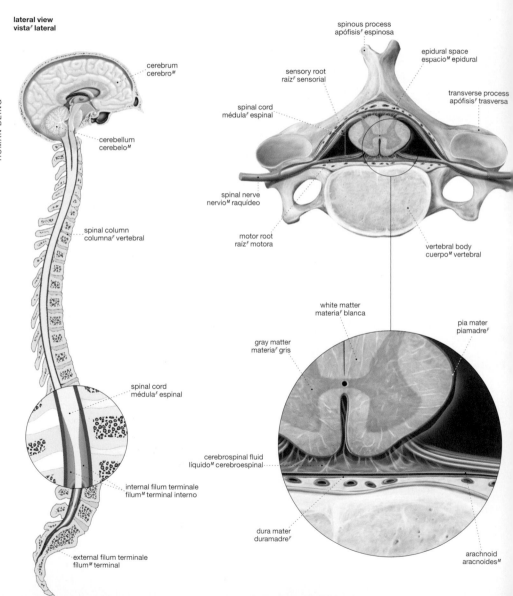

spinal column: cross section
columna^F vertebral : corte

lateral view
vista^F lateral

cerebrum
cerebro^M

cerebellum
cerebelo^M

spinal column
columna^F vertebral

spinal cord
médula^F espinal

internal filum terminale
filum^M terminal interno

external filum terminale
filum^M terminal

spinous process
apófisis^F espinosa

sensory root
raíz^F sensorial

spinal cord
médula^F espinal

epidural space
espacio^M epidural

transverse process
apófisis^F trasversa

spinal nerve
nervio^M raquídeo

motor root
raíz^F motora

vertebral body
cuerpo^M vertebral

white matter
materia^F blanca

pia mater
piamadre^F

gray matter
materia^F gris

cerebrospinal fluid
líquido^M cerebroespinal

dura mater
duramadre^F

arachnoid
aracnoides^M

nervous system

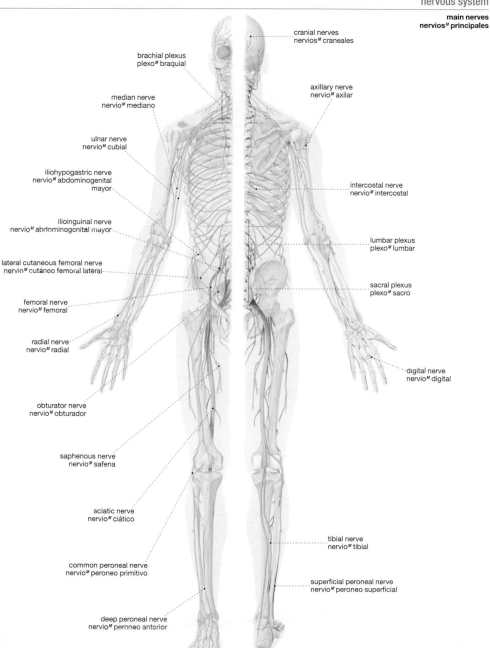

cranial nerves
nervios*M* craneales

brachial plexus
plexo*M* braquial

axillary nerve
nervio*M* axilar

median nerve
nervio*M* mediano

ulnar nerve
nervio*M* cubial

iliohypogastric nerve
nervio*M* abdominogenital
mayor

intercostal nerve
nervio*M* intercostal

ilioinguinal nerve
nervio*M* abdominogenital mayor

lumbar plexus
plexo*M* lumbar

lateral cutaneous femoral nerve
nervio*M* cutáneo femoral lateral

sacral plexus
plexo*M* sacro

femoral nerve
nervio*M* femoral

radial nerve
nervio*M* radial

digital nerve
nervio*M* digital

obturator nerve
nervio*M* obturador

saphenous nerve
nervio*M* safena

sciatic nerve
nervio*M* ciático

tibial nerve
nervio*M* tibial

common peroneal nerve
nervio*M* peroneo primitivo

superficial peroneal nerve
nervio*M* peroneo superficial

deep peroneal nerve
nervio*M* peroneo anterior

reproductive system

sistema^M reproductivo

female reproductive organs
órganos^M genitales femeninos

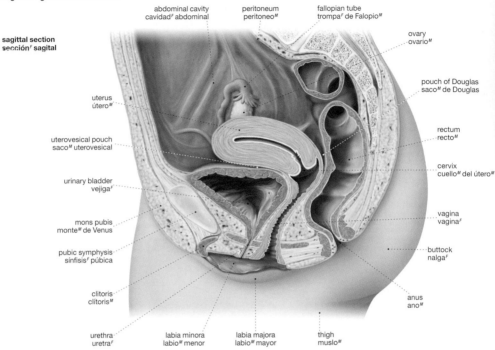

sagittal section
sección^F sagital

abdominal cavity
cavidad^F abdominal

peritoneum
peritoneo^M

fallopian tube
trompa^F de Falopio^M

ovary
ovario^M

pouch of Douglas
saco^M de Douglas

rectum
recto^M

cervix
cuello^M del útero^M

vagina
vagina^F

buttock
nalga^F

anus
ano^M

thigh
muslo^M

labia majora
labio^M mayor

labia minora
labio^M menor

urethra
uretra^F

clitoris
clítoris^M

pubic symphysis
sínfisis^F púbica

mons pubis
monte^M de Venus

urinary bladder
vejiga^F

uterovesical pouch
saco^M uterovesical

uterus
útero^M

egg
óvulo^M

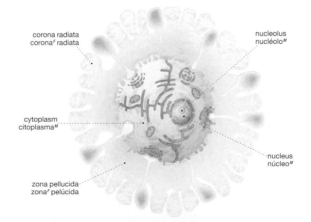

corona radiata
corona^F radiata

nucleolus
nucléolo^M

cytoplasm
citoplasma^M

nucleus
núcleo^M

zona pellucida
zona^F pelúcida

frontal section
corteᴹ **frontal**

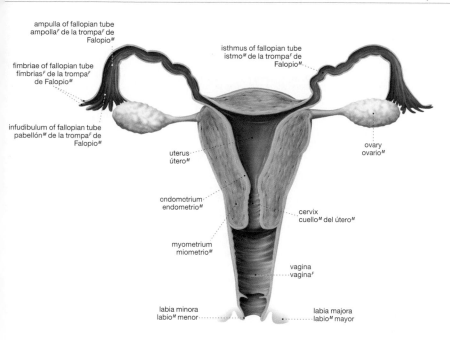

ampulla of fallopian tube
ampolla^F de la trompa^F de
Falopio^M

isthmus of fallopian tube
istmo^M de la trompa^F de
Falopio^M.

fimbriae of fallopian tube
fímbrias^F de la trompa^F
de Falopio^M

infudibulum of fallopian tube
pabellón^M de la trompa^F de
Falopio^M

ovary
ovario^M

uterus
útero^M

cervix
cuello^M del útero^M

ondomotrium
endometrio^M

myometrium
miometrio^M

vagina
vagina^F

labia minora
labio^M menor

labia majora
labio^M mayor

HUMAN BEING

breast
senoᴹ

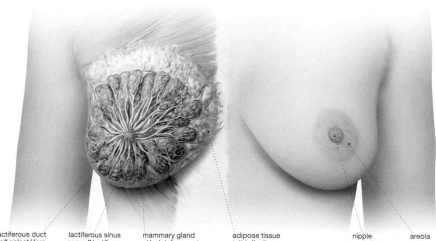

lactiferous duct
onducto^M galactóforo

lactiferous sinus
senos^M lactíferos

mammary gland
glándula^F mamaria

adipose tissue
tejido^M adiposo

nipple
pezón^M

areola
aréola^F

reproductive system

male reproductive organs
órganos^M **genitales**
masculinos

sagittal section
sección^F **sagital**

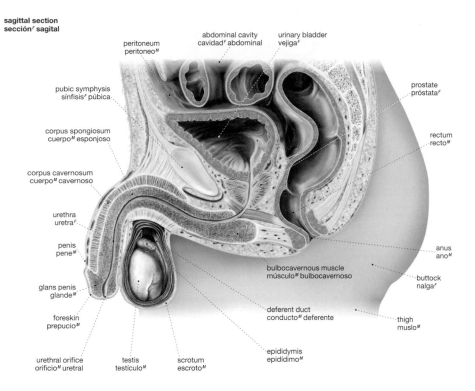

peritoneum
peritoneo^M

abdominal cavity
cavidad^F abdominal

urinary bladder
vejiga^F

pubic symphysis
sínfisis^F púbica

prostate
próstata^F

corpus spongiosum
cuerpo^M esponjoso

rectum
recto^M

corpus cavernosum
cuerpo^M cavernoso

urethra
uretra^F

penis
pene^M

anus
ano^M

bulbocavernous muscle
músculo^M bulbocavernoso

glans penis
glande^M

buttock
nalga^F

foreskin
prepucio^M

deferent duct
conducto^M deferente

thigh
muslo^M

urethral orifice
orificio^M uretral

testis
testículo^M

scrotum
escroto^M

epididymis
epidídimo^M

sperm cell
espermatozoide^M

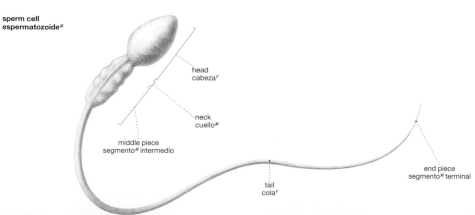

head
cabeza^F

neck
cuello^M

middle piece
segmento^M intermedio

tail
cola^F

end piece
segmento^M terminal

endocrine system

sistema *M* **endocrino**

endocrine glands
glándulas *F* **endocrinas**

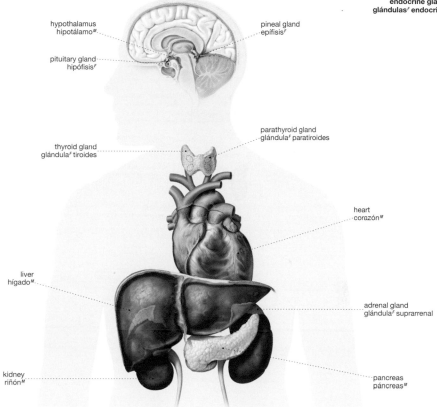

hypothalamus
hipotálamo *M*

pituitary gland
hipófisis *F*

pineal gland
epífisis *F*

parathyroid gland
glándula *F* paratiroides

thyroid gland
glándula *F* tiroides

heart
corazón *M*

liver
hígado *M*

adrenal gland
glándula *F* suprarrenal

kidney
riñón *M*

pancreas
páncreas *M*

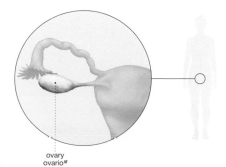

ovary
ovario *M*

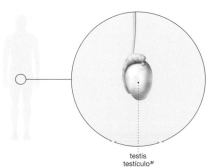

testis
testículo *M*

lymphatic system

sistema^M linfático

main organs
órganos^M principales

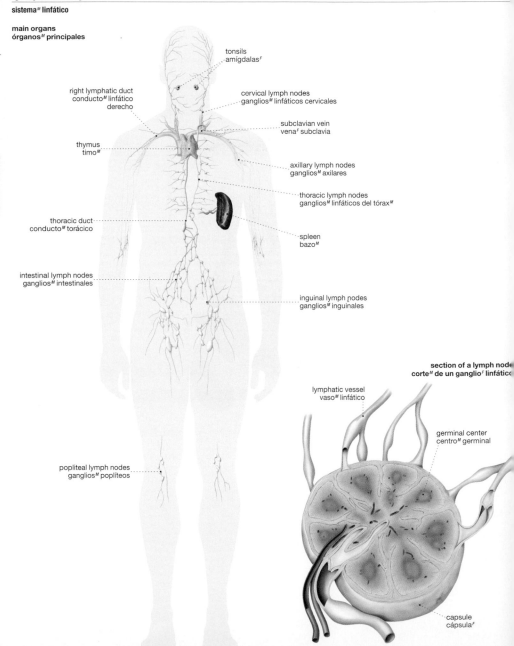

tonsils
amígdalas^F

right lymphatic duct
conducto^M linfático
derecho

cervical lymph nodes
ganglios^M linfáticos cervicales

subclavian vein
vena^F subclavia

thymus
timo^M

axillary lymph nodes
ganglios^M axilares

thoracic lymph nodes
ganglios^M linfáticos del tórax^M

thoracic duct
conducto^M torácico

spleen
bazo^M

intestinal lymph nodes
ganglios^M intestinales

inguinal lymph nodes
ganglios^M inguinales

popliteal lymph nodes
ganglios^M poplíteos

section of a lymph node
corte^M de un ganglio^F linfático

lymphatic vessel
vaso^M linfático

germinal center
centro^M germinal

capsule
cápsula^F

HUMAN BEING

smell and taste

olfato^M y gusto^M

mouth
boca^F

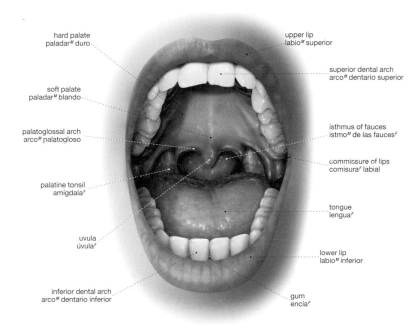

hard palate
paladar^M duro

soft palate
paladar^M blando

palatoglossal arch
arco^M palatogloso

palatine tonsil
amígdala^F

uvula
úvula^F

inferior dental arch
arco^M dentario inferior

upper lip
labio^M superior

superior dental arch
arco^M dentario superior

isthmus of fauces
istmo^M de las fauces^F

commissure of lips
comisura^F labial

tongue
lengua^F

lower lip
labio^M inferior

gum
encía^F

HUMAN BEING

nose
nariz^F

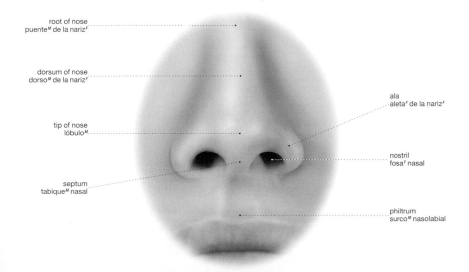

root of nose
puente^M de la nariz^F

dorsum of nose
dorso^M de la nariz^F

tip of nose
lóbulo^M

septum
tabique^M nasal

ala
aleta^F de la nariz^F

nostril
fosa^F nasal

philtrum
surco^M nasolabial

smell and taste

nasal cavity
cavidad^F nasal

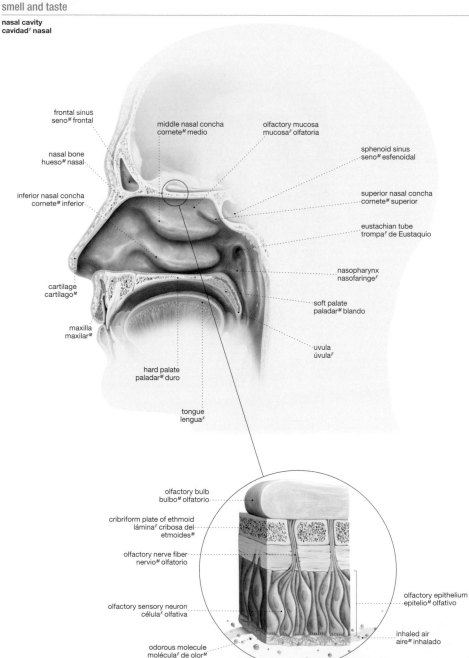

frontal sinus
seno^M frontal

middle nasal concha
cornete^M medio

olfactory mucosa
mucosa^F olfatoria

sphenoid sinus
seno^M esfenoidal

nasal bone
hueso^M nasal

inferior nasal concha
cornete^M inferior

superior nasal concha
cornete^M superior

eustachian tube
trompa^F de Eustaquio

cartilage
cartílago^M

nasopharynx
nasofaringe^F

soft palate
paladar^M blando

maxilla
maxilar^M

uvula
úvula^F

hard palate
paladar^M duro

tongue
lengua^F

olfactory bulb
bulbo^M olfatorio

cribriform plate of ethmoid
lámina^F cribosa del
etmoides^M

olfactory nerve fiber
nervio^M olfatorio

olfactory sensory neuron
célula^F olfativa

olfactory epithelium
epitelio^M olfativo

inhaled air
aire^M inhalado

odorous molecule
molécula^F de olor^M

HUMAN BEING

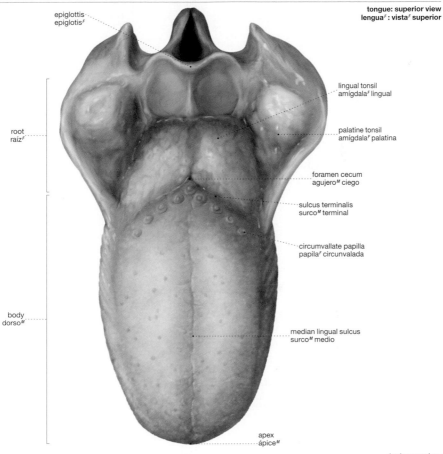

tongue: superior view
lengua^F : vista^F superior

epiglottis
epiglotis^F

lingual tonsil
amígdala^F lingual

palatine tonsil
amígdala^F palatina

root
raíz^F

foramen cecum
agujero^M ciego

sulcus terminalis
surco^M terminal

circumvallate papilla
papila^F circunvalada

body
dorso^M

median lingual sulcus
surco^M medio

apex
ápice^M

HUMAN BEING

taste receptors
receptores^M gustativos

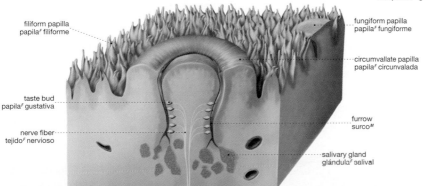

filiform papilla
papila^F filiforme

fungiform papilla
papila^F fungiforme

circumvallate papilla
papila^F circunvalada

taste bud
papila^F gustativa

nerve fiber
tejido^F nervioso

furrow
surco^M

salivary gland
glándula^F salival

hearing

oído^M

pinna
pabellón^M **auricular**

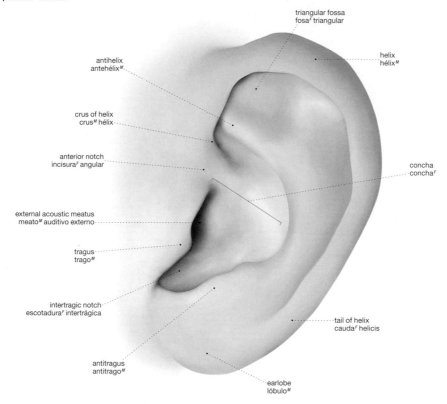

triangular fossa
fosa^F triangular

helix
hélix^M

antihelix
antehélix^M

crus of helix
crus^M hélix

anterior notch
incisura^F angular

concha
concha^F

external acoustic meatus
meato^M auditivo externo

tragus
trago^M

intertragic notch
escotadura^F intertrágica

tail of helix
cauda^F helicis

antitragus
antitrago^M

earlobe
lóbulo^M

HUMAN BEING

external ear
oreja^F

middle ear
oído^M **medio**

inner ear
oído^M **interno**

structure of the ear
estructura^F **del oído**^M

superior semicircular canal
conducto^M semicircular superior

posterior semicircular canal
conducto^M semicircular posterior

lateral semicircular canal
conducto^M semicircular lateral

vestibular nerve
nervio^M vestibular

cochlear nerve
nervio^M auditivo

vestibule
vestíbulo^M

cochlea
cóclea^F

Eustachian tube
trompa^F de Eustaquio

pinna
pabellón^M auricular

eardrum
tímpano^M

external acoustic meatus
meato^M auditivo externo

HUMAN BEING

incus
yunque^M

malleus
martillo^M

stapes
estribo^M

auditory ossicles
huesillos^M **auditivos**

mechanism of hearing
mecanismo^M **auditivo**

oval window
ventana^F oval

cochlear nerve
nervio^M coclear

auditory ossicles
huesillos^M auditivos

cochlea
cóclea^F

sound waves
vibraciones^F sonoras

external acoustic meatus
meato^M auditivo externo

round window
membrana^F secundaria
del tímpano^M

eardrum
tímpano^M

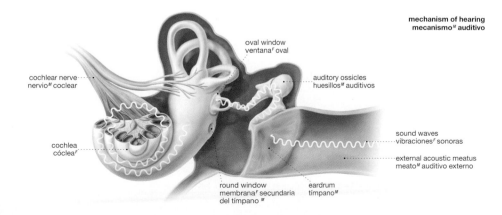

touch

tacto^M

skin
piel^F

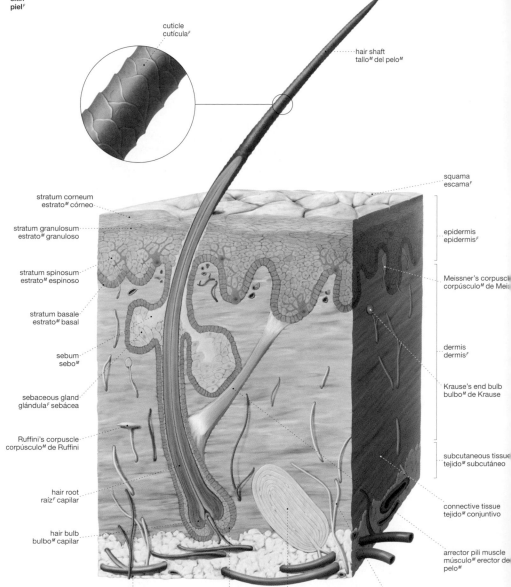

cuticle
cutícula^F

hair shaft
tallo^M del pelo^M

squama
escama^F

stratum corneum
estrato^M córneo

stratum granulosum
estrato^M granuloso

epidermis
epidermis^F

stratum spinosum
estrato^M espinoso

Meissner's corpuscle
corpúsculo^M de Meis

stratum basale
estrato^M basal

sebum
sebo^M

dermis
dermis^F

sebaceous gland
glándula^F sebácea

Krause's end bulb
bulbo^M de Krause

Ruffini's corpuscle
corpúsculo^M de Ruffini

subcutaneous tissue
tejido^M subcutáneo

hair root
raíz^F capilar

connective tissue
tejido^M conjuntivo

hair bulb
bulbo^M capilar

arrector pili muscle
músculo^M erector de
pelo^M

adipose tissue
tejido^M adiposo

hair follicle
folículo^M capilar

Pacinian corpuscle
corpúsculo^M de Pacini

nerve fiber
tejido^F nervioso

touch

hand
mano^F

palm
palma^F

middle finger
dedo^M del corazón^M

ring finger
dedo^M anular

index finger
dedo^M índice

little finger
dedo^M meñique

thumb
pulgar^M

back
dorso^M

lunula
lúnula^F

finger
dedo^M

fingernail
uña^F

wrist
muñeca^F

HUMAN BEING

section of a finger
corte^M **de un dedo**^M

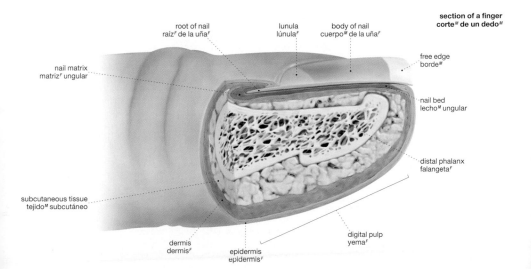

root of nail
raíz^F de la uña^F

lunula
lúnula^F

body of nail
cuerpo^M de la uña^F

free edge
borde^M

nail matrix
matriz^F ungular

nail bed
lecho^M ungular

distal phalanx
falangeta^F

subcutaneous tissue
tejido^M subcutáneo

dermis
dermis^F

epidermis
epidermis^F

digital pulp
yema^F

sight

vista^F

eye
ojo^M

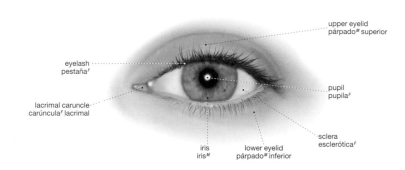

upper eyelid
párpado^M superior

eyelash
pestaña^F

pupil
pupila^F

lacrimal caruncle
carúncula^F lacrimal

sclera
esclerótica^F

iris
iris^M

lower eyelid
párpado^M inferior

HUMAN BEING

eyeball
globo^M **ocular**

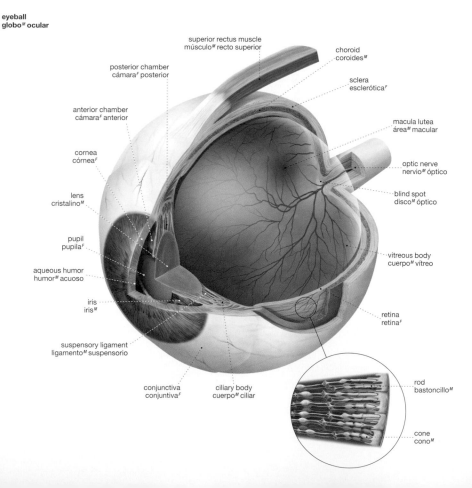

superior rectus muscle
músculo^M recto superior

choroid
coroides^M

posterior chamber
cámara^F posterior

sclera
esclerótica^F

anterior chamber
cámara^F anterior

macula lutea
área^M macular

cornea
córnea^F

optic nerve
nervio^M óptico

lens
cristalino^M

blind spot
disco^M óptico

pupil
pupila^F

aqueous humor
humor^M acuoso

vitreous body
cuerpo^M vítreo

iris
iris^M

retina
retina^F

suspensory ligament
ligamento^M suspensorio

conjunctiva
conjuntiva^F

ciliary body
cuerpo^M ciliar

rod
bastoncillo^M

cone
cono^M

normal vision
visión^F normal

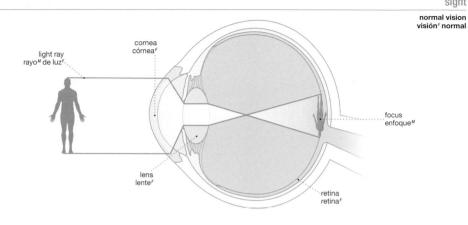

cornea
córnea^F

light ray
rayo^M de luz^F

focus
enfoque^M

lens
lente^F

retina
retina^F

HUMAN BEING

vision defects
defectos^M de la
visión^F

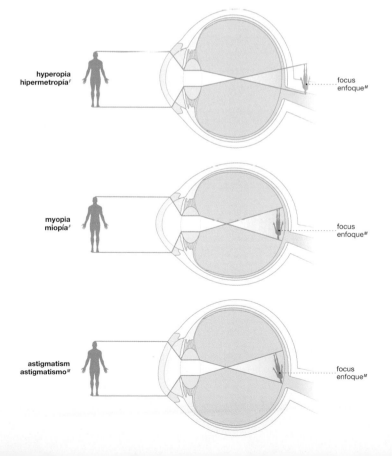

hyperopia
hipermetropía^F

focus
enfoque^M

myopia
miopía^F

focus
enfoque^M

astigmatism
astigmatismo^M

focus
enfoque^M

FOOD AND KITCHEN

productos alimenticios y de cocina

SUPPLY	242
origin of food	242
farmstead	243

PLANT-DERIVED FOOD	244
mushrooms	244
seaweed	244
bulb vegetables	245
tuber vegetables	245
leaf vegetables	246
fruit vegetables	248
stalk vegetables	250
root vegetables	251
inflorescence vegetables	251
legumes	252
fruits	254
spices	260
herbs	262
cereals	263
coffee and infusions	264

ANIMAL-DERIVED FOOD	265
mollusks	265
crustaceans	266
marine fishes	266
freshwater fishes	269
fish presentation	270
eggs	270
meat	271

PROCESSED FOOD	277
delicatessen	277
cereal products	278
dairy products	280
pasta	282
Asian noodles	283
rice	283
soybean products	284
fats and oils	284
sugar	285
chocolate	285
condiments	286

FOOD BUSINESS	288
supermarket	288
restaurant	290
self-service restaurant	292
food presentation	294

KITCHEN	296
kitchen: general view	296

TABLEWARE	297
glassware	297
knife	298
spoon	299
fork	300
silverware accessories	301
dinnerware	301
place setting	304

KITCHEN EQUIPMENT	306
kitchen utensils	306
cooking utensils	312
small domestic appliances	314

origin of food

origen^M de alimento^M

animal husbandry
ganadería^F

harvesting
recogida^F

hunting
caza^F

cultivation
cultivo^M

fishing
pesca^F

food industry
industria^F alimentaria

supermarket
supermercado^M

farmstead

granja^F

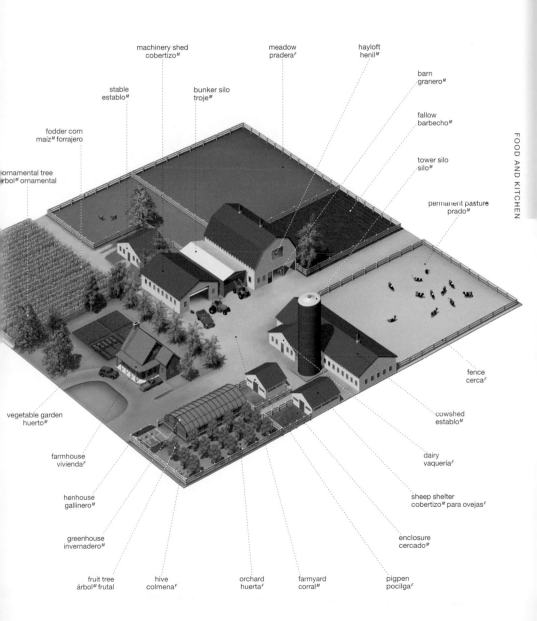

machinery shed
cobertizo^M

meadow
pradera^F

hayloft
henil^M

stable
establo^M

bunker silo
troje^M

barn
granero^M

fallow
barbecho^M

fodder corn
maíz^M forrajero

tower silo
silo^M

ornamental tree
árbol^M ornamental

permanent pasture
prado^M

fence
cerca^F

vegetable garden
huerto^M

cowshed
establo^M

farmhouse
vivienda^F

dairy
vaquería^F

henhouse
gallinero^M

sheep shelter
cobertizo^M para ovejas^F

greenhouse
invernadero^M

enclosure
cercado^M

fruit tree
árbol^M frutal

hive
colmena^F

orchard
huerta^F

farmyard
corral^M

pigpen
pocilga^F

mushrooms
hongos^M

truffle
trufa^F

wood ear
hongo^M oreja^F de
madera^F

royal agaric
oronja^F

saffron milk cap
níscalo^M

enoki mushroom
seta^F enoki

oyster mushroom
orellana^F

cultivated mushroom
champiñón^M

green russula
rusula^F verde

morel
morilla^F

porcini
porcini^M

shiitake
shitake^M

chanterelle
rebozuelo^M

portobello
portobello^M

cremini
champiñón^M café

seaweed
algas^F

arame
arame^M

wakame
wakame^M

kombu
kombu^M

spirulina
espirulina^F

Irish moss
Irish moss^M

hijiki
hijiki^M

sea lettuce
lechuga^F marina

agar
agar^M

nori
nori^M

dulse
dulse^M

bulb vegetables

bulbos^M

water chestnut
castaña^F de agua^F

shallot
chalote^M

chive
cebollino^M

garlic
ajo^M

scallion
cebolla^F tierna

green onion
cebolla^F tierna

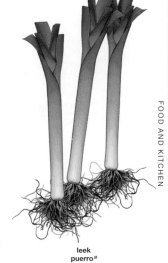

leek
puerro^M

pearl onion
cebolleta^F

white onion
cebolla^F blanca

red onion
cebolla^F roja

yellow onion
cebolla^F amarilla

FOOD AND KITCHEN

tuber vegetables

tubérculos^M

jicama
jícama^F

taro
taro^M

crosne
crosne^M

cassava
mandioca^F

yautia
malanga^F

potato
papa^F

sweet potato
batata^F

Jerusalem artichoke
aguaturma^F

yam
ñame^M

leaf vegetables

verduras^F de hojas^F

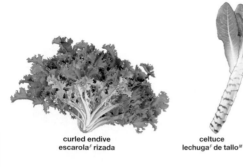

curled endive
escarola^F rizada

celtuce
lechuga^F de tallo^M

radicchio
achicoria^F de Treviso

iceberg lettuce
lechuga^F iceberg

romaine lettuce
lechuga^F romana

escarole
escarola^F

butter lettuce
lechuga^F de cogollo^M

leaf lettuce
lechuga^F rizada

collards
berzas^F

curled kale
col^F rizada

bok choy
pak-choi^M

Chinese cabbage
col^F china

Brussels sprout
col^M de Bruselas^F

sea kale
col^F marina

ornamental kale
col^F ornamental

leaf vegetables

savoy cabbage
col^F rizada de otoño^M

green cabbage
col^F verde/repollo^M
verde

red cabbage
col^F lombarda

white cabbage
col^F/repollo^M

spinach
espinaca^F

arugula
ruqueta^F

corn salad
colloja^F

dandelion
diente^M de león^M

garden cress
berros^M de jardín^M

nettle
ortiga^F

watercress
berro^M

purslane
verdolaga^F

garden sorrel
acedera^F

grape leaf
hoja^F de parra^F

Belgian endive
endivia^F

fruit vegetables

hortalizas*ᶠ* de fruto*ᴹ*

cherry tomato
tomate*ᴹ* cherry

olive
aceituna*ᶠ*

hot pepper
chile*ᴹ*

okra
gombo*ᴹ*, quingombó*ᴹ*

tomatillo
tomatillo*ᴹ*

plum tomato
tomate*ᴹ* italiano

tomato
tomate*ᴹ*

grape tomato
tomate*ᴹ* en rama*ᶠ*

avocado
aguacate*ᴹ*

yellow pepper
pimiento*ᴹ* dulce
amarillo

red pepper
pimiento*ᴹ* dulce rojo

green pepper
pimiento*ᴹ* dulce verde

cucumber
pepino*ᴹ*

seedless cucumber
pepino*ᴹ* sin pepitas*ᶠ*

gherkin
pepinillo*ᴹ*

bitter melon
pepino*ᴹ* amargo

wax gourd
calabaza*ᶠ* de China*ᶠ*

eggplant
berenjena*ᶠ*

fruit vegetables

summer squashes
calabazas^F de verano^M

straightneck squash
calabaza^F de cuello^M largo

crookneck squash
calabaza^F de cuello^M retorcido

pattypan squash
calabaza^F bonetera amarilla

zucchini
calabacín^M

vegetable marrow
calabacín^M

chayote
chayote^M

winter squashes
calabazas^F de invierno^M

pumpkin
calabaza^F común

spaghetti squash
calabaza^F romana

acorn squash
calabaza^F bonetera

buttercup squash
calabaza^F botón^M de oro^M

stalk vegetables

hortalizas^F de tallos^M

asparagus
espárrago^M

tip
punta^F

leaf
hoja^F

spear
turión^M

bundle
manojo^M

Swiss chard
acelga^F

rib
tallo^M

kohlrabi
colinabo^M

bamboo shoot
brote^M de bambú^M

fennel
hinojo^M

stalk
tallo^M

bulb
bulbo^M

cardoon
cardo^M

celery
apio^M

branch
tallo^M

fiddlehead fern
helecho^M canela

head
base^F

rhubarb
ruibarbo^M

root vegetables
raíces[F]

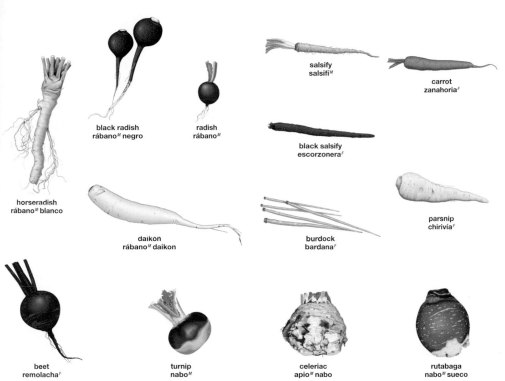

salsify
salsifí[M]

carrot
zanahoria[F]

black radish
rábano[M] negro

radish
rábano[M]

black salsify
escorzonera[F]

horseradish
rábano[M] blanco

daikon
rábano[M] daikon

burdock
bardana[F]

parsnip
chirivía[F]

beet
remolacha[F]

turnip
nabo[M]

celeriac
apio[M] nabo

rutabaga
nabo[M] sueco

inflorescence vegetables
hortalizas[F]

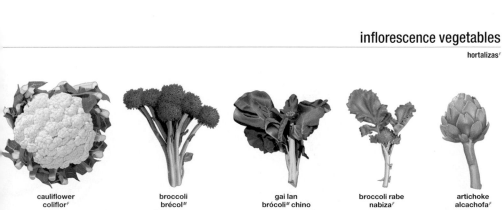

cauliflower
coliflor[F]

broccoli
brécol[M]

gai lan
brócoli[M] chino

broccoli rabe
nabiza[F]

artichoke
alcachofa[F]

legumes

legumbres^F

miscellaneous legumes
legumbres^F variadas

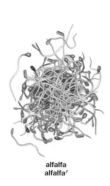

lupine
altramuz^M

lentil
lenteja^F

peanut
cacahuete^M

broad bean
haba^F

alfalfa
alfalfa^F

peas
guisantes^M

dolichos beans
dolichos^M

chickpea
garbanzo^M

split pea
guisante^M partido

black-eyed pea
judía^F de ojo^M

hyacinth bean
judía^F de Egipto^M

green pea
guisante^M verde

snow pea
guisante^M arveja^F

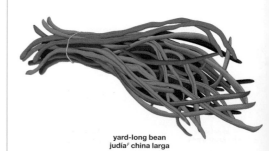

yard-long bean
judía^F china larga

FOOD AND KITCHEN

beans
judías^F

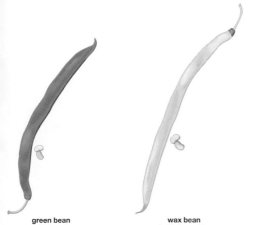

green bean
judía^F verde

wax bean
judía^F amarilla

roman bean
judía^F romana

pinto bean
judía^F roja

scarlet runner bean
ayocote^M

adzuki bean
judía^F adzuki

flageolet
frijol^M

mung bean
judía^F mungo

lima bean
judía^F de Lima

black bean
judía^F negra

urd
judía^F mungo negra

red kidney bean
judía^F roja

fruits

frutas^F

berries
bayas^F

currant
grosella^F

black currant
grosella^F negra

gooseberry
grosella^F espinosa

grape
uva^F

blueberry
arándano^M

bilberry
arándano^M negro

lingonberry
arándano^M rojo

goji
gogi^M

Cape gooseberry
grosella^M amarilla

cranberry
arándano^M agrio

raspberry
frambuesa^F

blackberry
moras^F

strawberry
fresa^F

stone fruits
drupas^F

plum
ciruela^F

peach
durazno^M

nectarine
nectarina^F

apricot
albaricoque^M

cherry
cereza^F

date
dátil^M

dry fruits
frutas*ᶠ* secas

macadamia nut
nuez*ᶠ* de macadamia*ᶠ*

ginkgo nut
nuez*ᶠ* de ginkgo*ᴹ*

pistachio
pistacho*ᴹ*

pine nut
piñón*ᴹ*

kola nut
nuez*ᶠ* de cola*ᶠ*

pecan
pacana*ᶠ*

cashew
anacardo*ᴹ*

almond
almendra*ᶠ*

hazelnut
avellana*ᶠ*

walnut
nuez*ᶠ*

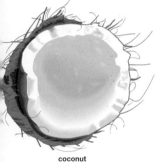

coconut
coco*ᴹ*

chestnut
castaña*ᶠ*

beechnut
hayuco*ᴹ*

Brazil nut
nuez*ᶠ* del Brasil*ᴹ*

FOOD AND KITCHEN

pome fruits
frutas*ᶠ* pomo

pear
pera*ᶠ*

quince
membrillo*ᴹ*

apple
manzana*ᶠ*

loquat
níspero*ᴹ*

FOOD AND KITCHEN

fruits

citrus fruits
cítricos^M

clementine
clementina^M

kumquat
naranja^F china

lime
lima^F

tangerine
mandarina^F

lemon
limón^M

orange
naranja^F

blood orange
naranja^F sanguina

mandarin
mandarina^F

bergamot
bergamota^F

grapefruit
toronja^F

pomelo
pomelo^M

citron
limón^M

fruits

melons
melones^M

charentais
melón^M cantalupo

casaba melon
melón^M invernal

honeydew melon
melón^M de miel^F

FOOD AND KITCHEN

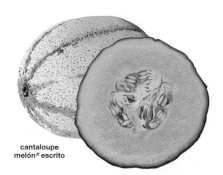

cantaloupe
melón^M escrito

Canary melon
melón^M

watermelon
sandía^F

Ogen melon
melón^M de Ogen

fruits

tropical fruits
frutas^f tropicales

plantain
plátano^M

banana
banana^f

longan
longan^M

tamarillo
tamarillo^M

passion fruit
fruta^f de la pasión^f

mangosteen
mangostán^M

kiwi
kiwi^M

horned melon
kiwano^M

pomegranate
granada^f

cherimoya
chirimoya^f

jackfruit
fruta^f de jack

pineapple
piña^f

fruits

jaboticaba
jaboticaba^F

lychee
lichi^M

fig
higo^M

jujube
jojoba^F

sapodilla
zapote^M

guava
guayaba^F

rambutan
rambután^M

Japanese persimmon
caqui^M

prickly pear
higo^M chumbo

carambola
carambola^F

Asian pear
pera^F asiática

mango
mango^M

durian
durión^M

papaya
papaya^F

pepino
pepino^M dulce

feijoa
feijoa^F

FOOD AND KITCHEN

spices

especias[F]

juniper berry
bayas[F] de enebro[M]

clove
clavo[M]

allspice
pimienta[F] de Jamaica[F]

white mustard
mostaza[F] blanca

black mustard
mostaza[F] negra

black pepper
pimienta[F] negra

white pepper
pimienta[F] blanca

pink pepper
pimienta[F] rosa

green pepper
pimienta[F] verde

nutmeg
nuez[F] moscada

caraway
alcaravea[F]

cardamom
cardamomo[M]

cinnamon
canela[F]

saffron
azafrán[M]

cumin
comino[M]

curry powder
curry[M]

turmeric
cúrcuma[F]

fenugreek
fenogreco[M]

jalapeño
chile^M jalapeño

bird's eye chile
guindilla^F

crushed chile
pimienta^F roja machacada

dried chile
pimienta^F roja seca

cayenne pepper
pimienta^F cayena^F

ground pepper
pimienta^F molida

ajowan
ajowán^M

asafetida
asafétida^F

garam masala
garam masala^M

cajun spice seasoning
condimento^M de especias^F
cajún

marinade spice seasoning
especias^F para salmuera^F

five spice powder
cinco especias^F chinas

chili powder
guindilla^F molida

paprika
pimentón^M

ras el hanout
ras el hanout^M

sumac
zumaque^M

poppy seed
semillas^F de adormidera^F

ginger
jengibre^M

herbs
hierbas^F aromáticas

dill
eneldo^M

anise
anís^M

sweet bay
laurel^M

oregano
orégano^M

tarragon
estragón^M

basil
albahaca^F

sage
salvia^F

thyme
tomillo^M

mint
hierbabuena^F

parsley
perejil^M

chervil
perifollo^M

coriander
cilantro^M

rosemary
romero^M

hyssop
hisopo^M

borage
borraja^F

lovage
alheña^F

savory
ajedrea^F

lemon balm
melisa^F

cereals

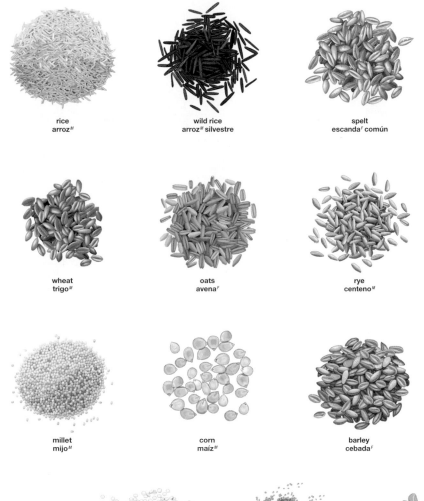

rice
arroz^M

wild rice
arroz^M silvestre

spelt
escanda^F común

wheat
trigo^M

oats
avena^F

rye
centeno^M

millet
mijo^M

corn
maíz^M

barley
cebada^F

buckwheat
trigo^M sarraceno

quinoa
quinua^F

amaranth
amaranto^M

triticale
triticale^M

coffee and infusions

café^M e infusiones^F

herbal teas
tisanas^F

FOOD AND KITCHEN

linden
tila^F

chamomile
manzanilla^F

verbena
verbena^F

mint
menta^F

coffee
café^M

green coffee beans
granos^M verdes de café^M

roasted coffee beans
granos^M torrefactos de
café^M

ground coffee
café^M molido

tea
té^M

green tea
té^M verde

black tea
té^M negro

oolong tea
té^M oolong

mollusks
moluscos^M

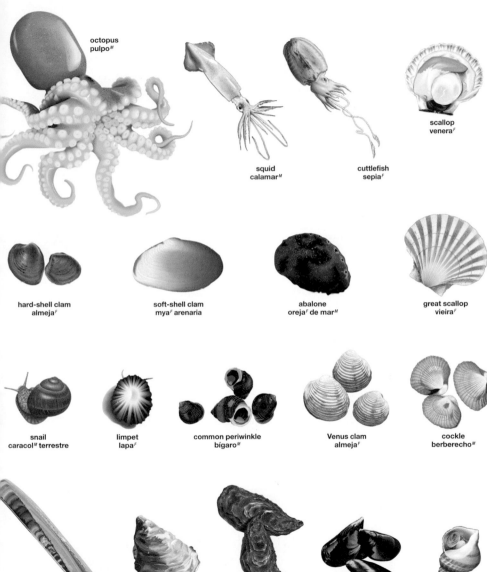

octopus
pulpo^M

squid
calamar^M

cuttlefish
sepia^F

scallop
venera^F

hard-shell clam
almeja^F

soft-shell clam
mya^F arenaria

abalone
oreja^F de mar^M

great scallop
vieira^F

snail
caracol^M terrestre

limpet
lapa^F

common periwinkle
bígaro^M

Venus clam
almeja^F

cockle
berberecho^M

razor clam
navaja^F

flat oyster
ostra^F

cupped Pacific oyster
ostra^F

blue mussel
mejillón^M

whelk
buccino^M

crustaceans

crustáceos^M

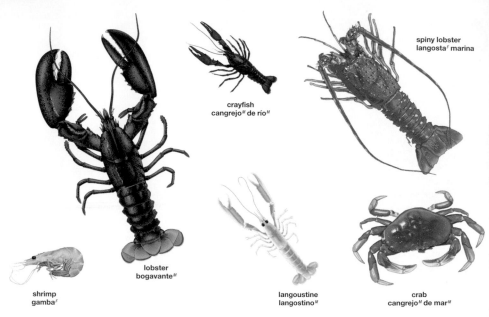

spiny lobster
langosta^F marina

crayfish
cangrejo^M de río^M

lobster
bogavante^M

shrimp
gamba^F

langoustine
langostino^M

crab
cangrejo^M de mar^M

marine fishes

peces^M de mar^M

larger spotted dogfish
alitán^M

skate
raya^F

smooth hound
musola^F

sturgeon
esturión^M

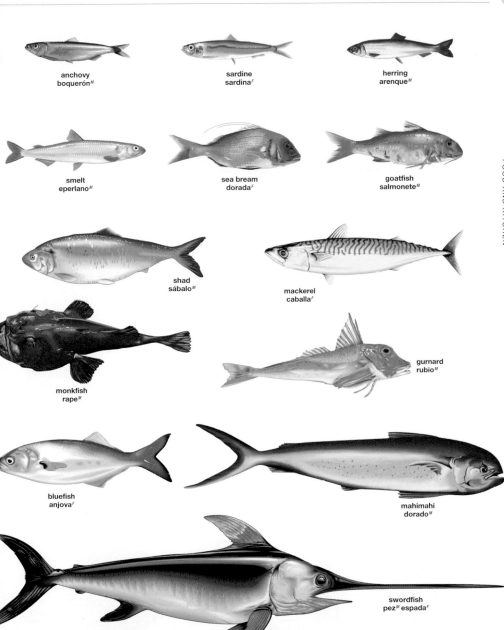

anchovy
boquerón^M

sardine
sardina^F

herring
arenque^M

smelt
eperlano^M

sea bream
dorada^F

goatfish
salmonete^M

shad
sábalo^M

mackerel
caballa^F

monkfish
rape^M

gurnard
rubio^M

bluefish
anjova^F

mahimahi
dorado^M

swordfish
pez^M espada^F

FOOD AND KITCHEN

marine fishes

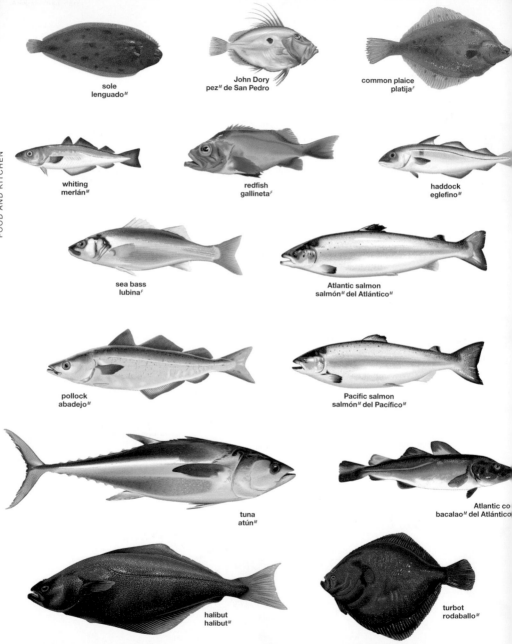

sole
lenguado[M]

John Dory
pez[M] de San Pedro

common plaice
platija[F]

whiting
merlán[M]

redfish
gallineta[F]

haddock
eglefino[M]

sea bass
lubina[F]

Atlantic salmon
salmón[M] del Atlántico[M]

pollock
abadejo[M]

Pacific salmon
salmón[M] del Pacífico[M]

tuna
atún[M]

Atlantic co
bacalao[M] del Atlántico

halibut
halibut[M]

turbot
rodaballo[M]

meat

cuts of veal
cortes^M de ternera^F

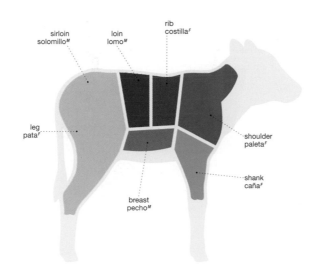

sirloin
solomillo^M

loin
lomo^M

rib
costilla^F

leg
pata^F

shoulder
paleta^F

shank
caña^F

breast
pecho^M

FOOD AND KITCHEN

examples of pieces
ejemplos^M de piezas^F

cutlet
chuleta^F

round steak
carne^M para asar

loin chop
chuleta^F de lomo^M

rib chop
chuleta^F de aguja^F

blade roast
paletilla^F

boneless shoulder
roast
paletilla^F deshuesada

breast
pecho^M

shank
paleta^F

meat

cuts of lamb
cortes^M de cordero^M

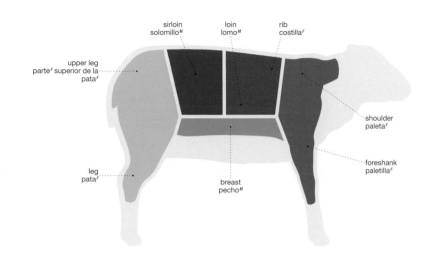

sirloin
solomillo^M

loin
lomo^M

rib
costilla^F

upper leg
parte^F superior de la
pata^F

shoulder
paleta^F

foreshank
paletilla^F

leg
pata^F

breast
pecho^M

examples of pieces
ejemplos^M de piezas^F

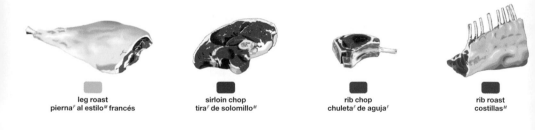

leg roast
pierna^F al estilo^M francés

sirloin chop
tira^F de solomillo^M

rib chop
chuleta^F de aguja^F

rib roast
costillas^M

shank
paletilla^F

boneless shoulder
roast
paletilla^F deshuesada

rolled breast
rotí^F de panceta^F

meat

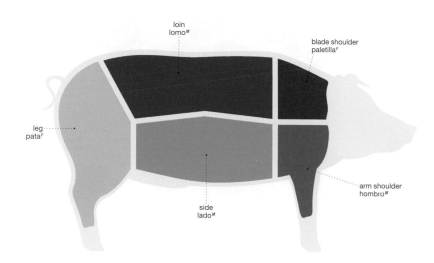

loin
lomo^M

blade shoulder
paletilla^F

leg
pata^F

arm shoulder
hombro^M

side
lado^M

FOOD AND KITCHEN

examples of pieces
ejemplos^M **de piezas**^F

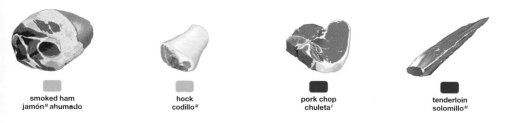

smoked ham
jamón^M ahumado

hock
codillo^M

pork chop
chuleta^F

tenderloin
solomillo^M

blade roast
paletilla^F

spareribs
costillar^M

smoked picnic roast
asado^M picnic^M
ahumado

meat

meat presentation
presentación^F de carne^F

ground meat
carne^M picada

meatballs
albóndigas^F

medaillons
medallones^M

tournedos
medallones^M

scallop
granadina^F

aiguillette
cuadril^M

round steak
carne^M para asar

paupiette
popieta^F

steak
filete^M

cubes
tacos^M

variety meat
despojos^M

marrow
médula^F

sweetbread
mollejas^F

heart
corazón^M

liver
hígado^M

tongue
lengua^F

kidney
riñones^M

brain
sesos^M

tripe
tripa^F

delicatessen
charcutería^F

mortadella
mortadela^F

kielbasa
salchicha^F kielbasa^F

Genoa salami
salami^M de Génova^F

foie gras
foie gras^M

rillettes
rillettes^F

German salami
salami^M alemán

blood sausage
morcilla^F

white pudding
morcilla^F blanca

pepperoni
pepperoni^M

chorizo
chorizo^M

Toulouse sausage
salchicha^F de Toulouse^M

merguez
merguez^M

andouillette
andouillete^F

chipolata
chipolata^F

frankfurter
salchicha^F de Frankfurt^M

pancetta
panceta^F

cooked ham
jamón^M de York

prosciutto
jamón^M serrano

Canadian bacon
bacón^M canadiense

bacon
bacón^M americano

FOOD AND KITCHEN

cereal products

cereales^M

flour and semolina
harina^F y sémola^F

semolina
sémola^F

all-purpose flour
harina^F común

whole-wheat flour
harina^F integral

unbleached flour
harina^F sin blanquear

corn flour
harina^F de maíz^M

wheat germ
germen^M de trigo^M

couscous
cuscús^M

bulgur
bulgur^M

buckwheat flour
harina^F de trigo^M
sarraceno

oat flour
harina^F de avena^F

bread
pan^M

naan
naan^M

chapati
chapati^M

tortilla
tortilla^F

pita bread
pan^M de pita^F

unleavened bread
pan^M ácimo

Danish rye bread
pan^M danés de centeno^M

sourdough bread
pan^M campesino

Russian black bread
pan^M negro ruso

bagel
rosquilla^F

pumpernickel
pan^M de centeno^M negro

challah
pan^M jalá

croissant
cruasán^M

French bread
baguette^F

baguette
baguette^F

epi bread
pan^M espiga^F

corn bread
pan^M de maíz^M

whole wheat bread
pan^M integral

multigrain bread
pan^M multicereales

German rye bread
pan^M alemán de centeno^M

brioche
pan^M de huevo^M

bread loaf
pan^M inglés

soda bread
pan^M irlandés

Greek bread
pan^M griego

bread crumbs
migas^F de pan^M

white bread
pan^M blanco

rye cracker
pan^M de centeno^M

cracker
pan^M crujiente

phyllo
pasta^F filo^M

dairy products

productos^M lácteos

yogurt
yogur^M

ghee
mantequilla^F clarificada

butter
mantequilla^F

cream
nata^F

whipping cream
nata^F de montar

sour cream
nata^F agria

milk
leche^F

cow's milk
leche^F de vaca^F

goat's milk
leche^F de cabra^F

milk forms
estados^M de leche^F

homogenized milk
leche^F homogeneizada

buttermilk
suero^M de la leche^F

evaporated milk
leche^F evaporada

powdered milk
leche^F en polvo^M

goat's-milk cheeses
quesos^M de cabra^F

goat cheese
queso^M de cabra^F

Crottin de Chavignol
Crottin^M de Chavignol

feta
feta^M

fresh cheeses
quesos^M frescos

cottage cheese
queso^M cottage

mozzarella
mozzarella^F

ricotta
ricotta^F

cream cheese
queso^M cremoso

dairy products

pressed cheeses
quesos^M **prensados**

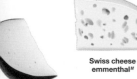

Swiss cheese
emmenthal^M

Romano
pecorino romano^M

raclette
raclette^F

Gouda
Gouda^M

Edam
Edam^M

Gruyère
gruyère^M

Oka
queso^M Oka^F

cheddar
Cheddar^M

Jarlsberg
jarlsberg^M

Parmesan
parmesano^M

blue cheeses
quesos^M **azules**

Roquefort
roquefort^M

Stilton
stilton^M

Danish blue
azul danés^M

Gorgonzola
gorgonzola^M

soft cheeses
quesos^M **blandos**

Pont-l'Évêque
Pont-l'Éveque^M

Coulommiers
coulommiers^M

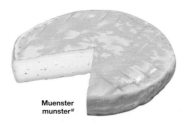

Camembert
camembert^M

Brie
brie^M

Muenster
munster^M

pasta

pasta*F*

rigatoni
rigatoni*M*

ravioli
raviolis*M*

conchiglie
conchitas*F*

fusilli
fusilli*M*

spaghetti
espagueti*M*

ditali
dedalitos*M*

rotini
sacacorchos*M*

tortellini
tortellini*M*

spaghettini
fideos*M*

elbow macaroni
tiburones*M*

penne
penne*M*

cannelloni
canelones*M*

lasagna
lasañas*F*

gnocchi
ñoquis*M*

spinach tagliatelle
tagliatelle*M* de
espinacas*F*

fettucine
fetuchinas*F*

Asian noodles
fideos^M asiáticos

soba
fideos^M soba

somen
fideos^M de somen^M

udon
fideos^M udón

rice papers
galletas^F de arroz^M

rice noodles
fideos^M de arroz^M

bean threads
fideos^M de frijol^M

chow mein noodles
fideos^M chow mein

rice vermicelli
vermicelli^M de arroz^M

wonton skins
wonton^M

ramen
ramen^M

rice
arroz^M

white rice
arroz^M blanco

brown rice
arroz^M integral

parboiled rice
arroz^M vaporizado

basmati rice
arroz^M basmati

FOOD AND KITCHEN

soybean products

productos^M de soja^F

soybean oil
aceite^M de soja^F

soybeans
soja^F

soybean milk
leche^M de soja^F

soybean sprouts
brotes^M de soja^F

tofu
tofu^M

fats and oils

grasas^F y aceites^M

corn oil
aceite^M de maíz^M

olive oil
aceite^M de oliva^F

sunflower oil
aceite^M de girasol^M

peanut oil
aceite^M de cacahuete^M

sesame oil
aceite^M de sésamo^M

shortening
grasa^F para cocinar

lard
manteca^F de cerdo^M

margarine
margarina^F

sugar
azúcar^M

granulated sugar
azúcar^M granulado

powdered sugar
azúcar^M glas

caster sugar
azúcar^M en polvo^M

molasses
melazas^F

corn syrup
jarabe^M de maíz^M

vanilla sugar
azúcar^M de vainilla^F

brown sugar
azúcar^M moreno

honey
miel^F

maple syrup
jarabe^M de arce^M

rock candy
azúcar^M candi

chocolate
chocolate^M

dark chocolate
chocolate^M amargo

milk chocolate
chocolate^M con leche^F

white chocolate
chocolate^M blanco

cocoa
cacao^M

condiments

condimentos^M

miso
miso^M

caper
alcaparra^F

tamarind paste
salsa^F de tamarindo^M

Tabasco® sauce
salsa^F Tabasco®

Worcestershire sauce
salsa^F Worcertershire

vanilla extract
extracto^M de vainilla^F

tomato paste
concentrado^M de
tomate^M

tomato coulis
salsa^F de tomate^M

hummus
hummus^M

tahini
tajín^M

hoisin sauce
salsa^F hoisin

soy sauce
salsa^F de soja^F

relish
condimento^M

mustard powder
mostaza^F en polvo^M

Dijon mustard
mostaza^F de Dijon

German mustard
mostaza^F alemana

English mustard
mostaza^F inglesa

American mustard
mostaza^F americana

wholegrain mustard
mostaza^F en grano^M

ketchup
ketchup^M

plum sauce
salsa^F de ciruelas^F

mango chutney
chutney^M de mango^M

harissa
harissa^F

sambal oelek
sambal oelek^M

chili sauce
salsa^F picante

wasabi
wasabi^M

table salt
sal^F de mesa^F

coarse salt
sal^F gorda

sea salt
sal^F marina

white balsamic vinegar
vinagre^M balsámico
blanco

malt vinegar
vinagre^M de malta^F

rice vinegar
vinagre^M de arroz^M

balsamic vinegar
vinagre^M balsámico

apple cider vinegar
vinagre^M de manzana^F

wine vinegar
vinagre^M de vino^M

white vinegar
vinagre^M blanco

supermarket

supermercado^M

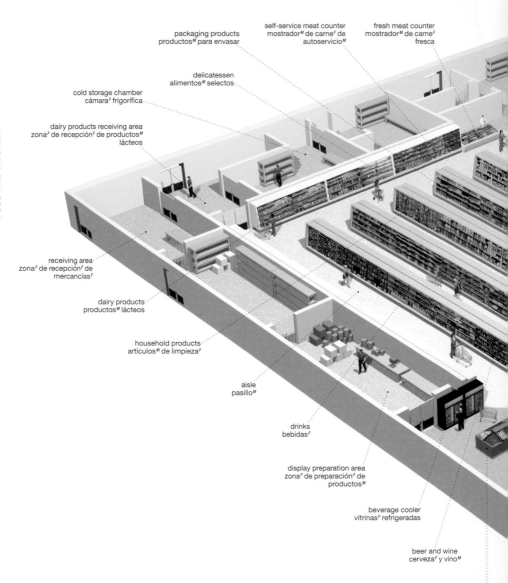

packaging products
productos^M para envasar

self-service meat counter
mostrador^M de carne^F de
autoservicio^M

fresh meat counter
mostrador^M de carne^F
fresca

delicatessen
alimentos^M selectos

cold storage chamber
cámara^F frigorífica

dairy products receiving area
zona^F de recepción^F de productos^M
lácteos

receiving area
zona^F de recepción^F de
mercancías^F

dairy products
productos^M lácteos

household products
artículos^M de limpieza^F

aisle
pasillo^M

drinks
bebidas^F

display preparation area
zona^F de preparación^F de
productos^M

beverage cooler
vitrinas^F refrigeradas

beer and wine
cerveza^F y vino^M

fruits and vegeta
frutas^F y verdur

supermarket

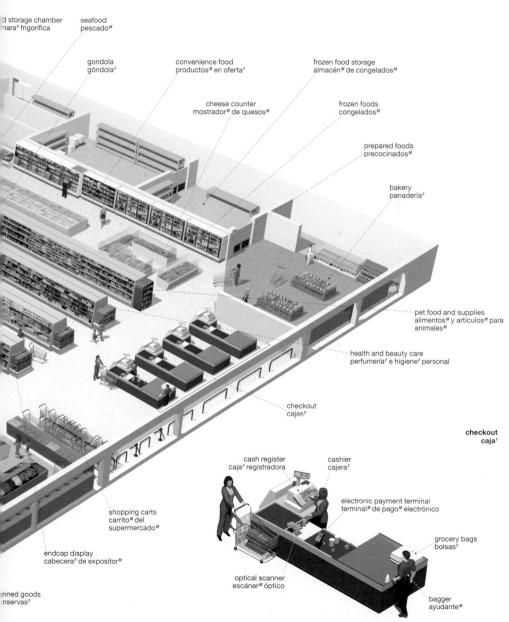

d storage chamber
nara^F frigorífica

seafood
pescado^M

gondola
góndola^F

convenience food
productos^M en oferta^F

frozen food storage
almacén^M de congelados^M

cheese counter
mostrador^M de quesos^M

frozen foods
congelados^M

prepared foods
precocinados^M

bakery
panadería^F

pet food and supplies
alimentos^M y artículos^M para
animales^M

health and beauty care
perfumería^F e higiene^F personal

checkout
cajas^F

checkout
caja^F

cash register
caja^F registradora

cashier
cajera^F

electronic payment terminal
terminal^M de pago^M electrónico

grocery bags
bolsas^F

shopping carts
carrito^M del
supermercado^M

endcap display
cabecera^F de expositor^M

optical scanner
escáner^M óptico

bagger
ayudante^M

nned goods
nservas^F

restaurant

restaurante^M

general view
vista^F general

FOOD AND KITCHEN

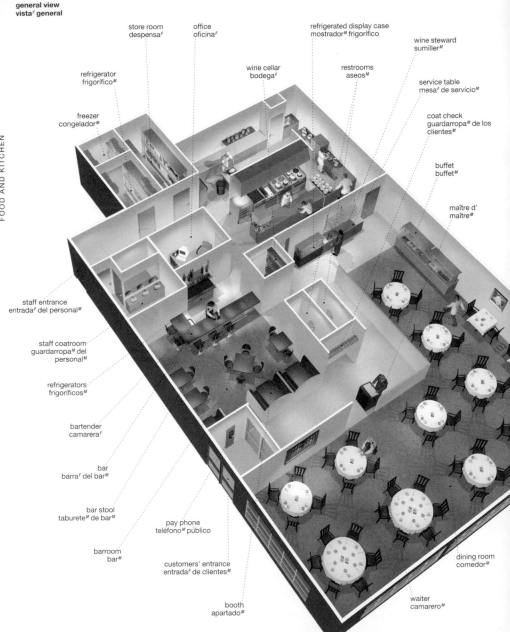

store room
despensa^F

office
oficina^F

refrigerated display case
mostrador^M frigorífico

wine steward
sumiller^M

refrigerator
frigorífico^M

wine cellar
bodega^F

restrooms
aseos^M

service table
mesa^F de servicio^M

freezer
congelador^M

coat check
guardarropa^M de los
clientes^M

buffet
buffet^M

maître d'
maître^M

staff entrance
entrada^F del personal^M

staff coatroom
guardarropa^M del
personal^M

refrigerators
frigoríficos^M

bartender
camarera^F

bar
barra^F del bar^M

bar stool
taburete^M de bar^M

pay phone
teléfono^M público

barroom
bar^M

customers' entrance
entrada^F de clientes^M

booth
apartado^M

dining room
comedor^M

waiter
camarero^M

restaurant

kitchen
cocina^F

hood
campana^F

pot-and-pan sink
fregadero^M para las cazuelas^F

dishwasher
lavavajillas^M

cleaning supplies
productos^M de limpieza^F

line cook
chef^M

dishwasher
lavavajillas^M

preparation counter
encimera^F

prerinse sink
fregadero^M de prelavado^M

ice machine
máquina^F de hielo^M

dirty dish table
mesa^F para la vajilla^F
sucia

FOOD AND KITCHEN

hot plate
placa^F calientaplatos^M

busboy
pinche^M de cocina^F

oven
horno^M

clean dish table
mesa^F para la vajilla^F
limpia

deep fryer
freidora^F

waiter
camarero^M

gas range
cocina^F

electric range
cocina^F eléctrica

chef
chef^M

hot food table
mesa^F caliente

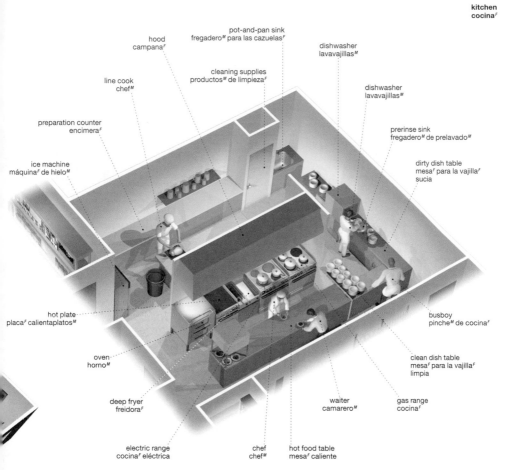

menu
menú^M

wine list
carta^F **de vinos**^M

check
cuenta^F

self-service restaurant

restaurante^M de autoservicio^M

general view
vista^F general

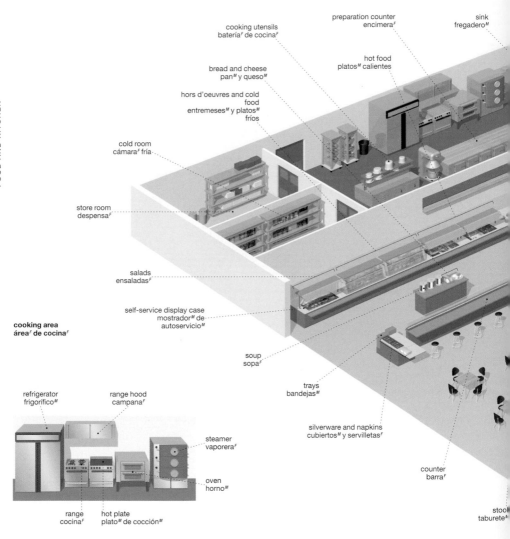

cooking utensils
batería^F de cocina^F

preparation counter
encimera^F

sink
fregadero^M

bread and cheese
pan^M y queso^M

hot food
platos^M calientes

hors d'oeuvres and cold
food
entremeses^M y platos^M
fríos

cold room
cámara^F fría

store room
despensa^F

salads
ensaladas^F

self-service display case
mostrador^M de
autoservicio^M

cooking area
área^F de cocina^F

soup
sopa^F

trays
bandejas^M

refrigerator
frigorífico^M

range hood
campana^F

silverware and napkins
cubiertos^M y servilletas^F

steamer
vaporera^F

oven
horno^M

counter
barra^F

range
cocina^F

hot plate
plato^M de cocción^M

stool
taburete^M

self-service restaurant

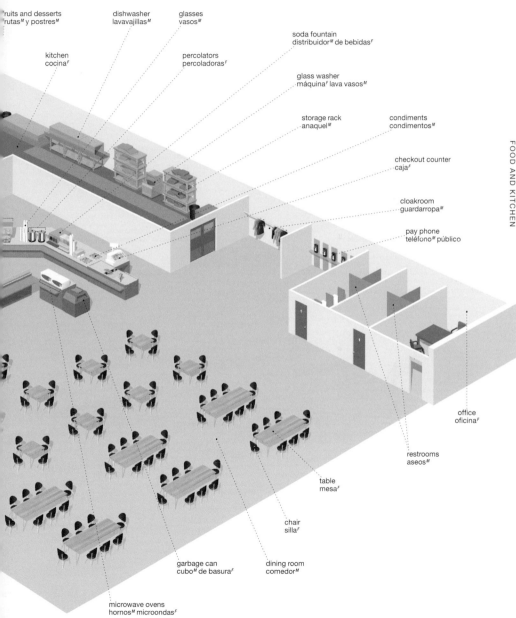

fruits and desserts
rutas* y postres*

dishwasher
lavavajillas*

glasses
vasos*

soda fountain
distribuidor* de bebidas*

kitchen
cocina*

percolators
percoladoras*

glass washer
máquina* lava vasos*

storage rack
anaquel*

condiments
condimentos*

checkout counter
caja*

cloakroom
guardarropa*

pay phone
teléfono* público

office
oficina*

restrooms
aseos*

table
mesa*

chair
silla*

garbage can
cubo* de basura*

dining room
comedor*

microwave ovens
hornos* microondas*

food presentation

presentación^F de alimentos^M

wraps and linings
envoltorios^M

parchment paper
papel^M para el horno^M

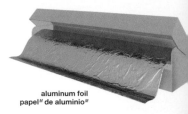

aluminum foil
papel^M de aluminio^M

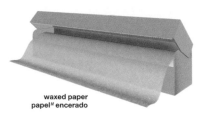

waxed paper
papel^M encerado

plastic wrap
envoltorio^M de plástico^M

containers
recipiente^M

heat-sealed film
película^F termosoldada

plastic food storage container
fiambrera^F de plástico^M

cup
copa^F

pouch
bolsa^F

small crate
caja^F

canisters
botes^M herméticos

mesh bag
bolsa^F de malla^F

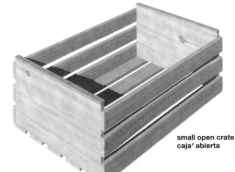

small open crate
caja^F abierta

egg carton
caja^F de cartón^M para
huevos^M

food presentation

snack bag
bolsa^F para aperitivo^M

sandwich bag
bolsa^F para sandwich^M

vegetable bag
bolsa^F para verduras^F

freezer bag
bolsa^F para
congelados^M

can
lata^F

glass bottle
botella^F de vidrio^M

screw cap
tapón^M de rosca^F

package
paquete^M

mason jar
bote^M de conservas^F

FOOD AND KITCHEN

tube
tubo^M

multipack
multipack^M

pull tab
tirador^M

beverage can
lata^F

drink box
brick^M pequeño

gable top
cierre^M en relieve^M

straw
pajita^F

butter cup
terrina^F para
mantequilla^F

tea bag
bolsa^F de té^M

cheese box
caja^F para queso^M

carton
cartón^M

small carton
cartón^M pequeño

milk/cream cup
miniporción^F de leche^F/
nata^F

food tray
barqueta^F

brick carton
brick^M

FOOD AND KITCHEN

kitchen: general view

cocina^F : vista^F general

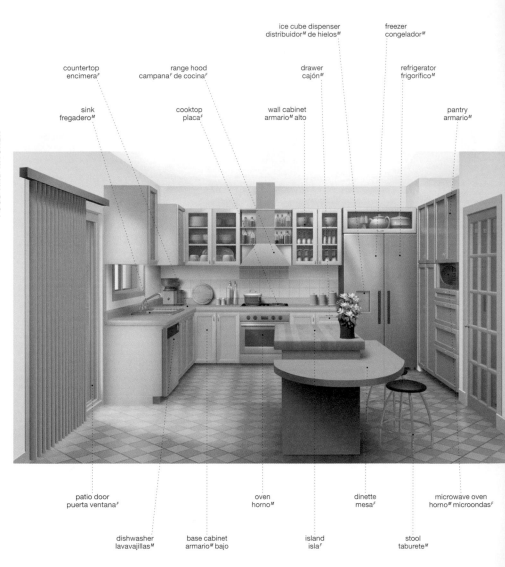

ice cube dispenser
distribuidor^M de hielos^M

freezer
congelador^M

countertop
encimera^F

range hood
campana^F de cocina^F

drawer
cajón^M

refrigerator
frigorífico^M

sink
fregadero^M

cooktop
placa^F

wall cabinet
armario^M alto

pantry
armario^M

patio door
puerta ventana^F

oven
horno^M

dinette
mesa^F

microwave oven
horno^M microondas^F

dishwasher
lavavajillas^M

base cabinet
armario^M bajo

island
isla^F

stool
taburete^M

glassware
cristalería^f

liqueur glass
copa^f para licores^M

port glass
copa^f para oporto^M

champagne glass
copa^f de champaña^f

brandy snifter
copa^f para brandy^M

FOOD AND KITCHEN

Hock glass
copa^f para vino^M de Alsacia

burgundy glass
copa^f para vino^M de Borgoña

bordeaux glass
copa^f para vino^M de Burdeos

white wine glass
copa^f para vino^M blanco

water goblet
copa^f de agua^f

cocktail glass
copa^f de cóctel^M

highball glass
vaso^M largo

old-fashioned glass
vaso^M corto

champagne flute
copa^f de flauta^f

beer mug
jarra^M de cerveza^f

small decanter
decantador^M

decanter
garrafa^f

knife

cuchillo*M*

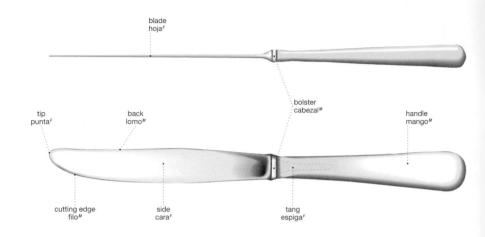

blade
hoja*F*

tip
punta*F*

back
lomo*M*

bolster
cabezal*M*

handle
mango*M*

cutting edge
filo*M*

side
cara*F*

tang
espiga*F*

examples of knives
ejemplos*M* de cuchillos*M*

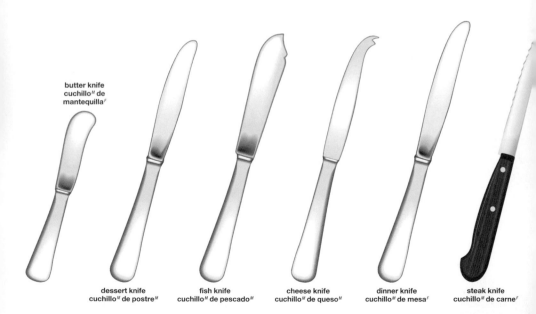

butter knife
cuchillo*M* de
mantequilla*F*

dessert knife
cuchillo*M* de postre*M*

fish knife
cuchillo*M* de pescado*M*

cheese knife
cuchillo*M* de queso*M*

dinner knife
cuchillo*M* de mesa*F*

steak knife
cuchillo*M* de carne*F*

spoon

cuchara^F

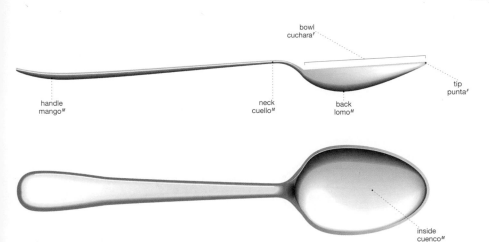

bowl
cuchara^F

tip
punta^F

handle
mango^M

neck
cuello^M

back
lomo^M

inside
cuenco^M

examples of spoons
ejemplos^M de cucharas^F

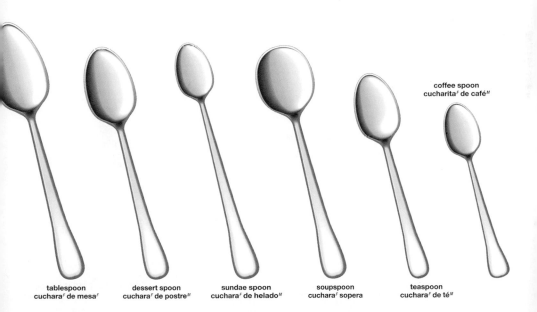

coffee spoon
cucharita^F de café^M

tablespoon
cuchara^F de mesa^F

dessert spoon
cuchara^F de postre^M

sundae spoon
cuchara^F de helado^M

soupspoon
cuchara^F sopera

teaspoon
cuchara^F de té^M

FOOD AND KITCHEN

fork
tenedor^M

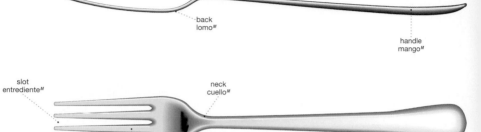

back
lomo^M

handle
mango^M

slot
entrediente^M

neck
cuello^M

root
raíz^F

point
punta^F

tine
diente^M

examples of forks
ejemplos^M de tenedores^M

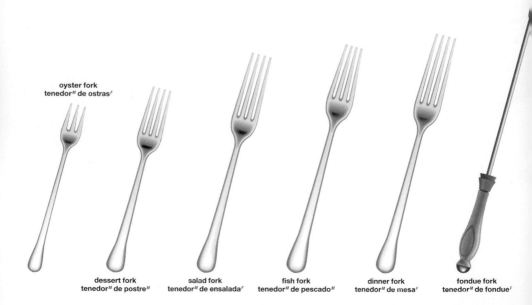

oyster fork
tenedor^M de ostras^F

dessert fork
tenedor^M de postre^M

salad fork
tenedor^M de ensalada^F

fish fork
tenedor^M de pescado^M

dinner fork
tenedor^M de mesa^F

fondue fork
tenedor^M de fondue^F

FOOD AND KITCHEN

silverware accessories
accesorios^M de cubertería^F

table napkin
servilleta^F

napkin ring
servilletero^M

knife-rest
reposa-cuchillos^M

dinnerware
vajilla^F y servicio^M de mesa^F

coffee mug
jarra^F para café^M

teacup
taza^F

demitasse
tacita^F de café^M

water pitcher
jarra^F de agua^F

teapot
tetera^F

creamer
jarrita^F de leche^F

sugar bowl
azucarero^M

dinnerware

salt shaker
salero*M*

pepper shaker
pimentero*M*

gravy boat
salsera*F*

butter dish
mantequera*F*

ramekin
cuenco*M* de queso*M*
blando

soup bowl
escudilla*F*

dessert plate
plato*M* de postre*M*

saucer
platillo*M*

salad plate
plato*M* de postre*M*

dinner plate
plato*M* llano

rim soup bowl
plato*M* sopero

dinnerware

chopsticks
palillos*M*

rice bowl
cuenco*M* para arroz*M*

vegetable bowl
fuente*F* de verdura*F*

sushi set
combinado*M* de sushi*M*

snail dish
plato*M* para caracoles*M*

hors d'oeuvre dish
bandeja*F* para los
entremeses*M*

FOOD AND KITCHEN

soup tureen
sopera*F*

salad dish
bol*M* para ensalada*F*

salad bowl
ensaladera*F*

platter
fuente*F* de servir

fish platter
fuente*F* para pescado*M*

cheese platter
plato*M* de queso*M*

place setting

mesa^F **puesta**

in the French style
estilo^M **francés**

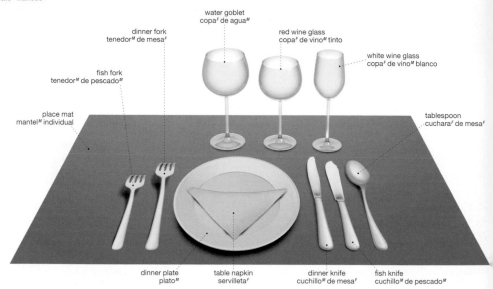

water goblet
copa^F de agua^M

dinner fork
tenedor^M de mesa^F

red wine glass
copa^F de vino^M tinto

fish fork
tenedor^M de pescado^M

white wine glass
copa^F de vino^M blanco

place mat
mantel^M individual

tablespoon
cuchara^F de mesa^F

dinner plate
plato^M

table napkin
servilleta^F

dinner knife
cuchillo^M de mesa^F

fish knife
cuchillo^M de pescado^M

in the English style
estilo^M **inglés**

dessert fork
tenedor^M de postre^M

water goblet
copa^F de agua^M

red wine glass
copa^F de vino^M tinto

dinner fork
tenedor^M de mesa^F

white wine glass
copa^F de vino^M blanco

place mat
mantel^M individual

tablespoon
cuchara^F de mesa^F

table napkin
servilleta^F

bread and butter plate
plato^M para pan^M y
mantequilla^F

dinner plate
plato^M

dessert knife
cuchillo^M de postre^M

dinner knife
cuchillo^M de mesa^F

FOOD AND KITCHEN

place setting

in the American style
estilo^M americano

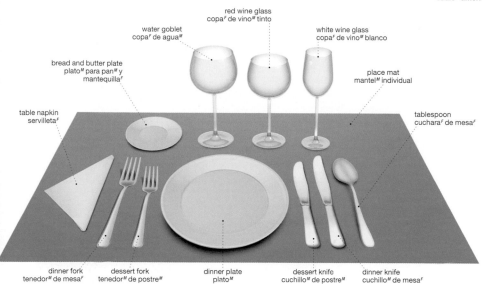

red wine glass
copa^F de vino^M tinto

water goblet
copa^F de agua^M

white wine glass
copa^F de vino^M blanco

bread and butter plate
plato^M para pan^M y
mantequilla^F

place mat
mantel^M individual

table napkin
servilleta^F

tablespoon
cuchara^F de mesa^F

dinner fork
tenedor^M de mesa^F

dessert fork
tenedor^M de postre^M

dinner plate
plato^M

dessert knife
cuchillo^M de postre^M

dinner knife
cuchillo^M de mesa^F

in the Chinese style
estilo^M chino

saucer
platillo^M

rice bowl
cuenco^M para arroz^M

teapot
tetera^F

bamboo place mat
mantel^M de bambú^M

ceramic spoon
cuchara^F de cerámica^F

chopstick rest
reposa-palillos^M

teacup
taza^F

dinner plate
plato^M

chopsticks
palillos^M

FOOD AND KITCHEN

kitchen utensils

utensilios*ᴹ* de cocina*ᶠ*

kitchen knife
cuchillo*ᴹ* de cocina*ᶠ*

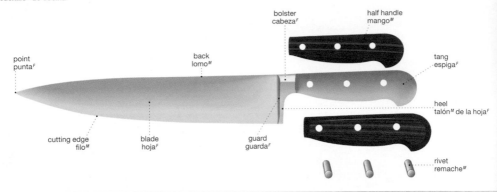

bolster
cabeza*ᶠ*

half handle
mango*ᴹ*

point
punta*ᶠ*

back
lomo*ᴹ*

tang
espiga*ᶠ*

heel
talón*ᴹ* de la hoja*ᶠ*

cutting edge
filo*ᴹ*

blade
hoja*ᶠ*

guard
guarda*ᶠ*

rivet
remache*ᴹ*

cutting and peeling utensils
ejemplos*ᴹ* de cuchillos*ᴹ* de cocina*ᶠ*

chef's knife
cuchillo*ᴹ* de carnicero*ᴹ*

cleaver
hacha*ᶠ* de cocinero*ᴹ*

bread knife
cuchillo*ᴹ* de pan*ᴹ*

carving knife
cuchillo*ᴹ* de trinchar

ham knife
cuchillo*ᴹ* para jamón*ᴹ*

paring knife
cuchillo*ᴹ* de pelar

filleting knife
cuchillo*ᴹ* filetero

boning knife
cuchillo*ᴹ* para
deshuesar

grapefruit knife
cuchillo*ᴹ* para pomelos*ᴹ*

oyster knife
cuchillo*ᴹ* para ostras*ᶠ*

zester
rallador*ᴹ*

kitchen utensils

for opening
utensilios^M para abrir y
descorchar

lever corkscrew
sacacorchos^M con
brazos^M

wine waiter corkscrew
sacacorchos^M

bottle opener
abrebotellas^M

can opener
abrelatas^M

for grinding and grating
para moler y rallar

nutcracker
cascanueces^M

mortar
almirez^M

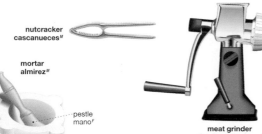

pestle
mano^F

meat grinder
picadora^F de carne^F

garlic press
triturador^M de ajos^M

manual coffee grinder
molinillo^M manual de
café^M

nutmeg grater
rallador^M de nuez^F
moscada

citrus juicer
exprimidor^M

rotary cheese grater
rallador^M cilíndrico de
queso^M

pusher
empujador^M

crank
manivela^F

grater
rallador^M

pepper mill
molinillo^F de pimienta^F

drum
tambor^M

handle
mango^M

pasta maker
máquina^F para hacer pasta^F italiana

food mill
pasapurés^M

mandoline
mandolina^F

kitchen utensils

for measuring
utensilios^M para medir

meat thermometer
termómetro^M para carne^F

measuring cup
jarra^F medidora

instant-read thermometer
termómetro^M de medida^F instantán

candy thermometer
termómetro^M de azúcar^M

measuring beaker
vaso^M medidor

measuring spoons
cucharas^F dosificadoras

egg timer
reloj^M de arena^F

measuring cups
tazas^F medidoras

kitchen timer
minutero^M

oven thermometer
termómetro^M de horno^M

kitchen scale
báscula^F de cocina^F

---

for straining and draining
coladores^M y escurridores^M

mesh strainer
colador^M fino

chinois
chino^M

muslin
muselina^F

funnel
embudo^M

colander
escurridor^M

frying basket
cesta^F de freír

sieve
tamiz^M

salad spinner
secadora^F de ensalada^F

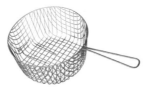

kitchen utensils

miscellaneous utensils
utensilios diversos

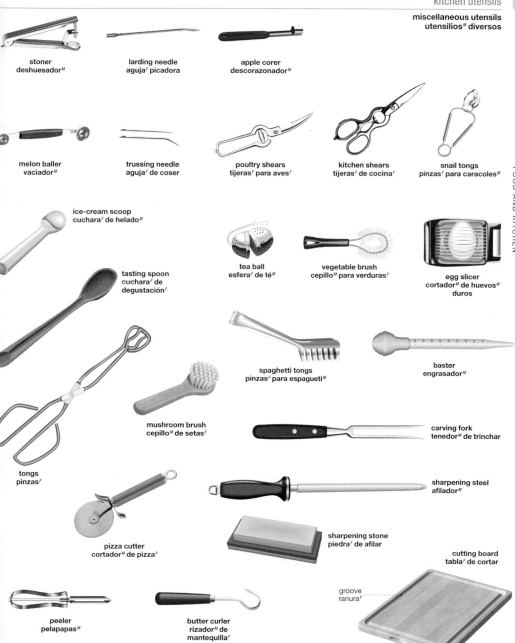

stoner
deshuesador^M

larding needle
aguja^F picadora

apple corer
descorazonador^M

melon baller
vaciador^M

trussing needle
aguja^F de coser

poultry shears
tijeras^F para aves^F

kitchen shears
tijeras^F de cocina^F

snail tongs
pinzas^F para caracoles^M

ice-cream scoop
cuchara^F de helado^M

tasting spoon
cuchara^F de
degustación^F

tea ball
esfera^F de té^M

vegetable brush
cepillo^M para verduras^F

egg slicer
cortador^M de huevos^M
duros

spaghetti tongs
pinzas^F para espagueti^M

baster
engrasador^M

mushroom brush
cepillo^M de setas^F

carving fork
tenedor^M de trinchar

tongs
pinzas^F

sharpening steel
afilador^M

pizza cutter
cortador^M de pizza^F

sharpening stone
piedra^F de afilar

cutting board
tabla^F de cortar

groove
ranura^F

peeler
pelapapas^M

butter curler
rizador^M de
mantequilla^F

FOOD AND KITCHEN

FOOD AND KITCHEN

kitchen utensils

baking utensils
utensilios^M para repostería^F

icing syringe
jeringa^F de decoración^F

pastry cutting wheel
cortapastas^M

pastry brush
pincel^M de repostería^F

egg beater
batidor^M mecánico

whisk
batidor^M

pastry bag and nozzles
manga^F y boquillas^F

shaker
mezclador^M

sifter
tamiz^M

baking sheet
bandeja^F de pastelería^F

mixing bowls
boles^M para batir

pastry blender
mezclador^M de
pastelería^F

cookie cutters
moldes^M de pastas^F

rolling pin
rodillo^M

soufflé dish
molde^M de soufflé^M

kitchen utensils

cake pan
molde*M* para bizcocho*M*

pie plate
molde*F* para tartas*F*

springform pan
molde*M* redondo con muelles*M*

tart pan
molde*F* para quiche*F*

bread pan
bandeja*F* de pan*F*

charlotte mold
molde*M* de carlota*F*

muffin pan
molde*M* para
magdalenas*F*

FOOD AND KITCHEN

set of kitchen utensils
conjunto*M* de utensilios*M* de cocina*F*

spatula
paleta*F*

ladle
cazo*M*

potato masher
pasapuré*M*

icing spatula
espátula*F*

draining spoon
escurridera*F*

skimmer
•spumadera*F*

FOOD AND KITCHEN

cooking utensils

utensilios^M de cocina^F

wok set
wok^M

lid
tapa^F

rack
rejilla^F

wok
wok^M

burner ring
quemador^M

tajine
tajina^F

fondue set
servicio^M **para fondue**^F

fondue pot
cacerola^F para fondue^F

stand
soporte^M

burner
quemador^M

fish poacher
besuguera^F

rack
rejilla^F desmontable

lid
tapa^F

terrine
terrina^F

drip pan
bandeja^F **de horno**^M

pressure cooker
olla^F **a presión**^F

pressure regulator
regulador^M de presión^F

safety valve
válvula^F de seguridad^F

roasting pans
asadores^M

cooking utensils

Dutch oven
cacerola[F] refractaria

stock pot
olla[F]

couscous steamer
olla[F] para cuscús[M]

frying pan
sartén[F]

cast-iron casserole
cazuela[F] de hierro[M]
fundido

steamer
cazuela[F] vaporera

sauté pan
sartén[F] honda

egg poacher
escalfador[M] de huevos[M]

pancake pan
sartén[F] para crepes[M]

skillet
sartén[F] pequeña

clay cooker
sartén[F] doble

steamer basket
cesto[M] de cocción[F] al vapor[M]

double boiler
cacerola[F] para baño[M] María

saucepan
cacerola[F]

pizza pan
bandeja[F] de pizza[F]

FOOD AND KITCHEN

small domestic appliances

pequeños*ᴹ* electrodomésticos*ᴹ*

for mixing and blending
para mezclar y batir

hand mixer
batidora*ᶠ* de mano*ᶠ*

beater ejector
eyector*ᴹ* de las varillas*ᶠ*

speed selector
selector*ᴹ* de velocidad*ᶠ*

handle
asa*ᶠ*

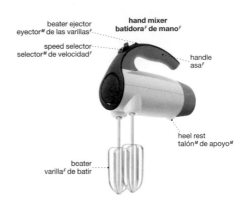

heel rest
talón*ᴹ* de apoyo*ᴹ*

beater
varilla*ᶠ* de batir

immersion blender
batidora*ᶠ*

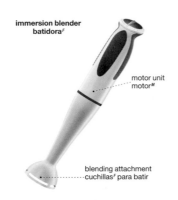

motor unit
motor*ᴹ*

blending attachment
cuchillas*ᶠ* para batir

stand mixer
batidora*ᶠ* de pie*ᴹ*

tilt-back head
cabeza*ᶠ* móvil

beater ejector
eyector*ᴹ* de las varillas*ᶠ*

blender
batidora*ᶠ* de vaso*ᴹ*

cap
tapa*ᶠ*

beater
varilla*ᶠ* de batir

container
vaso*ᴹ* mezclador

speed control
selector*ᴹ* de veloci

cutting blade
cuchilla*ᶠ*

control buttons
botones*ᴹ* de control*ᴹ*

mixing bowl
bol*ᴹ* mezclador

motor unit
motor*ᴹ*

turntable
disco*ᴹ* giratorio

stand
pie*ᴹ*

beaters
tipos*ᴹ* de varillas*ᶠ*

four blade beater
de aspas*ᶠ*

spiral beater
en espiral*ᶠ*

whisk attachment
circular

dough hook
de gancho*ᴹ*

small domestic appliances

for cutting
para cortar

food processor
robot^M de cocina^F

feed tube
tubo^M de entrada^F

disks
disco^M

lid
tapa^F

bowl
bol^M

spindle
eje^M

handle
asa^F

blade
cuchilla^F

motor unit
motor^M

FOOD AND KITCHEN

for juicing
para exprimir

electric knife
cuchillo^M eléctrico

power cord
cordón^M de alimentación^F

on-off switch
interruptor^M

blade
cuchilla^F

citrus juicer
exprimidor^M de cítricos^M

reamer
exprimidor^M

strainer
colador^M

bowl with serving spout
recipiente^M con vertedor^M

motor unit
motor^M

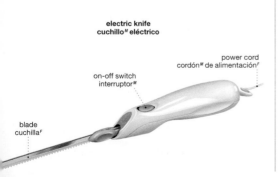

FOOD AND KITCHEN

small domestic appliances

for cooking
para cocinar

microwave oven
horno*M* microondas

door
puerta*F*

window
ventana*F*

clock timer
reloj*M* programador

control panel
panel*M* de mandos*M*

latch
seguro*M*

waffle iron
gofrera*F*

handle
asa*F*

plate
parrilla*F*

lid
plancha*F* superior

hinge
bisagra*F*

plate
parrilla*F*

temperature selector
selector*M* de
temperatura*F*

bread guide
rejilla*F*

toaster
tostador

slot
ranura*F* para el pan

lever
palanca*F*

thermostat
termostato*M*

deep fryer
freidora*F*

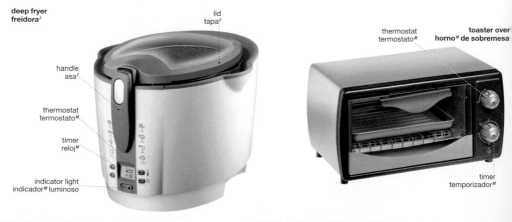

lid
tapa*F*

handle
asa*F*

thermostat
termostato*M*

timer
reloj*M*

indicator light
indicador*M* luminoso

thermostat
termostato*M*

toaster oven
horno*M* de sobremesa

timer
temporizador*M*

small domestic appliances

FOOD AND KITCHEN

slow cooker
olla^F de cocción^F lenta

lid
tapa^F

removable ceramic pot
gres^M extraíble

handle
asa^M

control panel
panel^M de control^M

heating base
base^F de calefacción^F

electric steamer
vaporera^F eléctrica

lid
tapa^F

fish tray
bandeja^F de pescado^M

cooking dishes
platos^M de cocción^F

drip tray
bandeja^F de zumo^M

base
base^F

indicator light
indicador^M luminoso

water level indicator
indicador^M del nivel^M del
agua^F

timer
minutero^M

bread machine
amasadora^F

window
ventana^F

lid
tapa^F

loaf pan
molde^M de pan^M

control panel
panel^M de mandos^M

raclette grill
parrilla^F raclette

cooking plate
placa^F de cocción^F

dish
bandeja^F

base
base^F

griddle
plancha^F eléctrica

handle
asa^F

detachable control
enchufe^M y selector^M
desmontables

cooking surface
plancha^F

grease well
colector^M de grasa^F

indoor electric grill
parrilla^F eléctrica

insulated handle
asa^F aislante

cooking surface
superficie^F de cocción^F

drip pan
grasera^F

thermostat
termostato^M

FOOD AND KITCHEN

small domestic appliances

miscellaneous appliances
aparatos*ᴹ* diversos

kettle
hervidor*ᴹ*

spout
vertedor*ᴹ*

handle
asa*ᶠ*

body
cuerpo*ᴹ*

on-off switch
interruptor*ᴹ*

base
base*ᶠ*

indicator light
indicador*ᴹ* luminoso

juicer
licuadora*ᶠ*

pusher
empujador*ᴹ*

feed tube
tubo*ᴹ* alimentador

lid
tapa*ᶠ*

strainer
colador*ᴹ*

bowl
recipiente*ᴹ*

motor unit
motor*ᴹ*

can opener
abrelatas*ᴹ*

pierce lever
palanca*ᶠ* de perforación*ᶠ*

cutting blade
cuchilla*ᶠ*

drive wheel
engranaje*ᴹ* de avance*ᴹ*

magnetic lid holder
retén*ᴹ* imantado

electric coffee grinder
molinillo*ᴹ* eléctrico de café*ᴹ*

lid
tapa*ᶠ*

bean container
recipiente*ᴹ* de granos*ᴹ* de café*ᴹ*

blade
cuchilla*ᶠ*

grinding control
control*ᴹ* del molinillo*ᴹ*

timer
temporizador*ᴹ*

motor unit
motor*ᴹ*

ground coffee container
recipiente*ᴹ* de café*ᴹ*
molido

ice-cream maker
heladera*ᶠ*

motor unit
motor*ᴹ*

cover
cubierta*ᶠ*

handle
asa*ᶠ*

freezer bucket
cubeta*ᶠ* congeladora

small domestic appliances

coffee makers
cafeteras^F

automatic drip coffee maker
cafetera^F de filtro^M automática

lid
tapa^F

reservoir
depósito^M de agua^F

basket
filtro^M

water level
nivel^M de agua^F

carafe
cafetera^F

indicator light
indicador^M luminoso

on-off switch
interruptor^M

warming plate
placa^F térmica

Neapolitan coffee maker
cafetera^F napolitana

vacuum coffee maker
cafetera^F de infusión^F

upper bowl
recipiente^M superior

stem
tubo^M de subida^F del
agua^F

lower bowl
recipiente^M inferior

espresso machine
máquina^F de café^M exprés

on-off switch
interruptor^M

steam control knob
manecilla^F de vapor^M

tamper
prensa-café^M

filter holder
porta-filtro^M

drip tray
beta^F colectora de
gotas^F

water tank
depósito^M de agua^F

steam nozzle
tubo^M de vapor^M

percolator
percoladora^F

spout
pitorro^M

indicator light
indicador^M luminoso

coffee press
cafetera^F de émbolo^M

stovetop espresso
maker
cafetera^F expreso

HOUSE
casa

LOCATION 322

exterior of a house 322
pool 324

ELEMENTS OF A HOUSE 325

exterior door 325
lock 326
window 327

STRUCTURE OF A HOUSE 328

site plan 328
main rooms 328
frame 332
roof truss 333
foundation 333
wood flooring 334
textile floor coverings 334
stairs 335

HEATING 336

wood firing 336
forced warm-air system 338
forced hot-water system 339
auxiliary heating 340
heat pump 341

AIR CONDITIONING 342

control devices 342
air-conditioning appliances 342

PLUMBING 344

plumbing system 344
pedestal-type sump pump 345
septic tank 345
bathroom 346
toilet 347
water-heater tank 348
faucets 350
fittings 351
examples of branching 352

ELECTRICITY 354

distribution panel 354
electricity meter 355
network connection 356
contact devices 358
lighting 359

HOUSE FURNISHINGS 360

armchair 360
side chair 361
seats 361
table 362
bed 363
storage furniture 364
children's furniture 366
window accessories 367
lights 372
home appliances 374
household equipment 381

exterior of a house

exterior^M de una casa^F

HOUSE

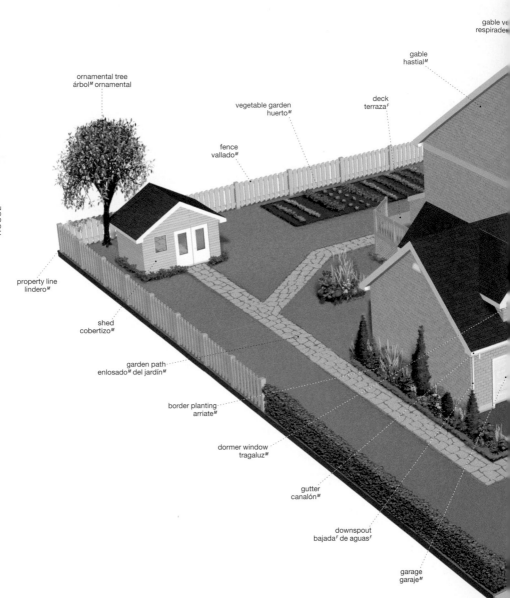

gable ve
respirade

gable
hastial^M

ornamental tree
árbol^M ornamental

vegetable garden
huerto^M

deck
terraza^F

fence
vallado^M

property line
lindero^M

shed
cobertizo^M

garden path
enlosado^M del jardín^M

border planting
arriate^M

dormer window
tragaluz^M

gutter
canalón^M

downspout
bajada^F de aguas^F

garage
garaje^M

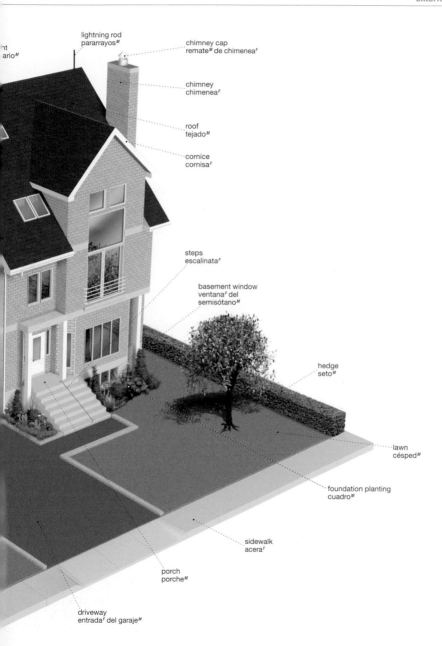

lightning rod
pararrayos^M

chimney cap
remate^M de chimenea^F

chimney
chimenea^F

roof
tejado^M

cornice
cornisa^F

steps
escalinata^F

basement window
ventana^F del
semisótano^M

hedge
seto^M

lawn
césped^M

foundation planting
cuadro^M

sidewalk
acera^F

porch
porche^M

driveway
entrada^F del garaje^M

pool

piscina^F

HOUSE

hot tub
jacuzzi^M

aboveground swimming pool
piscina^F **para el exterior**^M

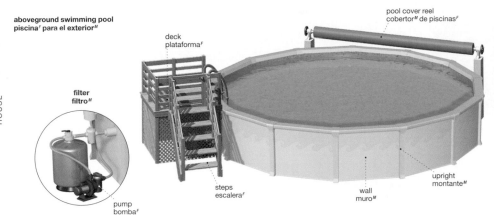

pool cover reel
cobertor^M de piscinas^F

deck
plataforma^F

filter
filtro^M

steps
escalera^F

pump
bomba^F

wall
muro^M

upright
montante^M

inground swimming pool
piscina^F

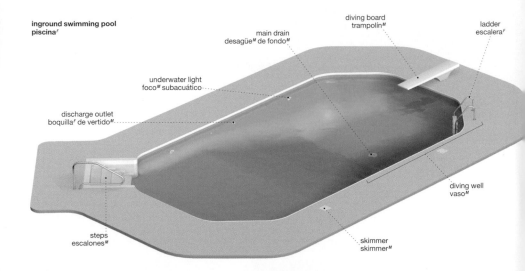

diving board
trampolín^M

main drain
desagüe^M de fondo^M

ladder
escalera^F

underwater light
foco^M subacuático

discharge outlet
boquilla^F de vertido^M

diving well
vaso^M

steps
escalones^M

skimmer
skimmer^M

exterior door

puerta^F de entrada^F

cornice
cornisa^F

entablature
entablamento^M

head casing
dintel^M

top rail
cabio^M alto

side casing
jamba^F

panel
entrepaño^M vertical

mullion
mainel^M

shutting stile
montante^M de la cerradura^F

lock rail
peinazo^M de la cerradura^F

lock
cerradura^F

middle panel
entrepaño^M horizontal

door handle
manilla^F

hanging stile
montante^M de la bisagra^F

hinge
bisagra^F

weather strip
vierteguas^M

bottom rail
cabio^M bajo

threshold
umbral^M

HOUSE

lock

cerrajería^F

general view
vista^F general

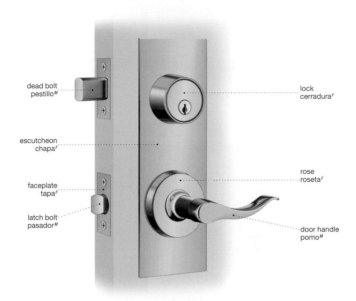

dead bolt
pestillo^M

escutcheon
chapa^F

faceplate
tapa^F

latch bolt
pasador^M

lock
cerradura^F

rose
roseta^F

door handle
pomo^M

tubular lock
cerradura^F tubular con
seguro^M

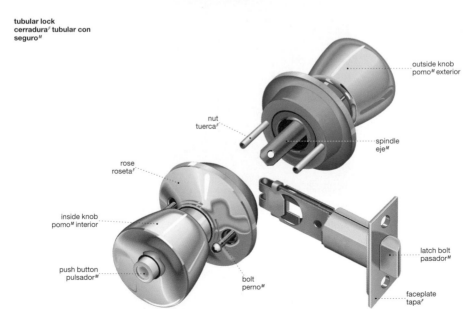

nut
tuerca^F

rose
roseta^F

inside knob
pomo^M interior

push button
pulsador^M

bolt
perno^M

outside knob
pomo^M exterior

spindle
eje^M

latch bolt
pasador^M

faceplate
tapa^F

HOUSE

lock

mortise lock
cerradura^F **embutida**

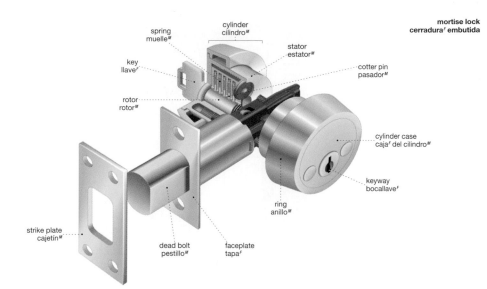

spring
muelle^M

cylinder
cilindro^M

stator
estator^M

key
llave^F

cotter pin
pasador^M

rotor
rotor^M

cylinder case
caja^F del cilindro^M

keyway
bocallave^F

strike plate
cajetín^M

ring
anillo^M

dead bolt
pestillo^M

faceplate
tapa^F

HOUSE

window

ventana^F

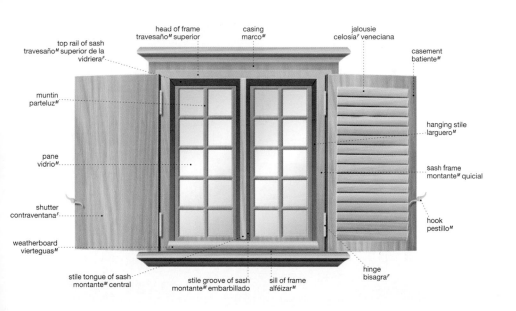

head of frame
travesaño^M superior

casing
marco^M

jalousie
celosía^F veneciana

top rail of sash
travesaño^M superior de la
vidriera^F

casement
batiente^M

muntin
parteluz^M

hanging stile
larguero^M

pane
vidrio^M

sash frame
montante^M quicial

shutter
contraventana^F

hook
pestillo^M

weatherboard
vierteaguas^M

stile tongue of sash
montante^M central

stile groove of sash
montante^M embarbillado

sill of frame
alféizar^M

hinge
bisagra^F

site plan

plano^M **del terreno**^M

HOUSE

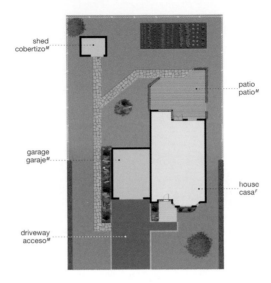

shed
cobertizo^M

patio
patio^M

garage
garaje^M

house
casa^F

driveway
acceso^M

main rooms

habitaciones^F **principales**

elevation
alzado^M

lawn
jardín^M

shed
cobertizo^M

garage
garaje^M

finished attic
entresuelo^M

second floor
planta^F alta

first floor
planta^F baja

basement
semisótano^M

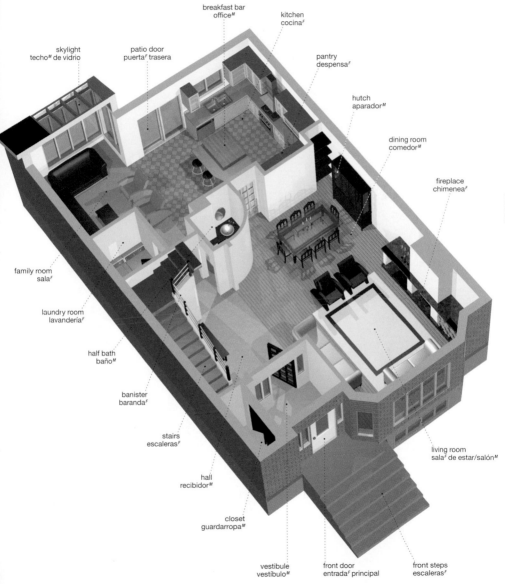

breakfast bar
officeᴹ

kitchen
cocinaᶠ

skylight
techoᴹ de vidrio

patio door
puertaᶠ trasera

pantry
despensaᶠ

hutch
aparadorᴹ

dining room
comedorᴹ

fireplace
chimeneaᶠ

family room
salaᶠ

laundry room
lavanderíaᶠ

half bath
bañoᴹ

banister
barandaᶠ

stairs
escalerasᶠ

living room
salaᶠ de estar/salónᴹ

hall
recibidorᴹ

closet
guardarropaᴹ

vestibule
vestíbuloᴹ

front door
entradaᶠ principal

front steps
escalerasᶠ

main rooms

second floor
planta^F alta

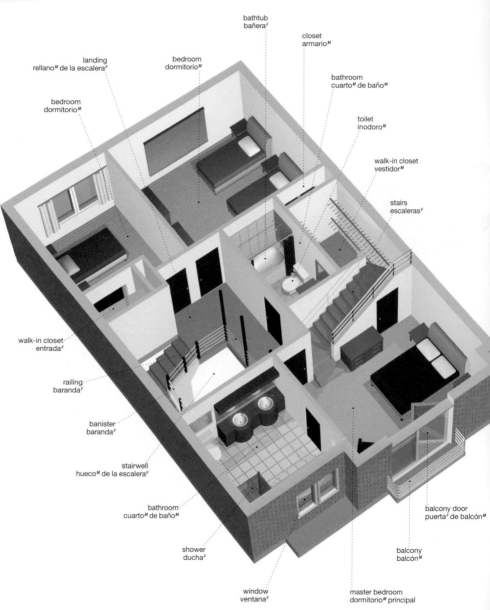

bathtub
bañera^F

closet
armario^M

bathroom
cuarto^M de baño^M

toilet
inodoro^M

walk-in closet
vestidor^M

stairs
escaleras^F

landing
rellano^M de la escalera^F

bedroom
dormitorio^M

bedroom
dormitorio^M

HOUSE

walk-in closet
entrada^F

railing
baranda^F

banister
baranda^F

stairwell
hueco^M de la escalera^F

bathroom
cuarto^M de baño^M

shower
ducha^F

window
ventana^F

master bedroom
dormitorio^M principal

balcony
balcón^M

balcony door
puerta^F de balcón^M

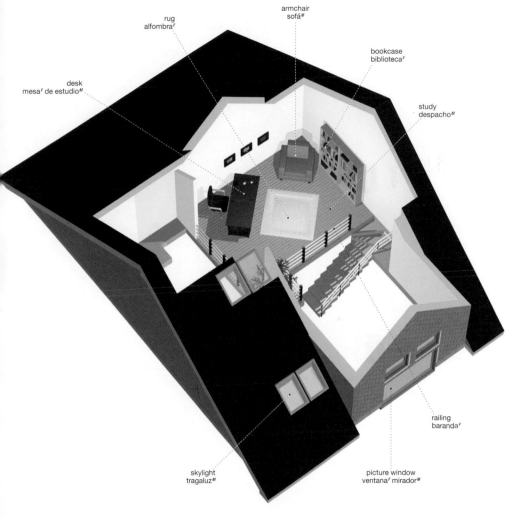

rug
alfombra^F

armchair
sofá^M

bookcase
biblioteca^F

desk
mesa^F de estudio^M

study
despacho^M

railing
baranda^F

skylight
tragaluz^M

picture window
ventana^F mirador^M

frame

armazón^M

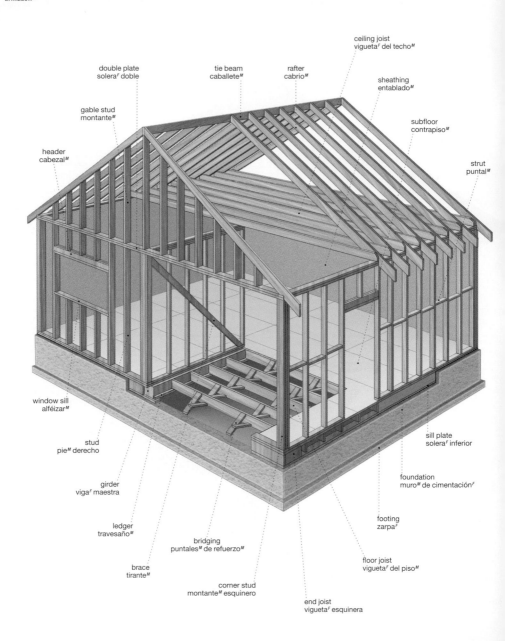

ceiling joist
vigueta^F del techo^M

double plate
solera^F doble

tie beam
caballete^M

rafter
cabrio^M

sheathing
entablado^M

gable stud
montante^M

subfloor
contrapiso^M

header
cabezal^M

strut
puntal^M

window sill
alféizar^M

sill plate
solera^F inferior

stud
pie^M derecho

foundation
muro^M de cimentación^F

girder
viga^F maestra

footing
zarpa^F

ledger
travesaño^M

bridging
puntales^M de refuerzo^M

floor joist
vigueta^F del piso^M

brace
tirante^M

corner stud
montante^M esquinero

end joist
vigueta^F esquinera

roof truss

armadura^F **del techo**^M

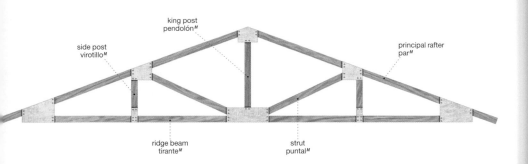

king post
pendolón^M

side post
virotillo^M

principal rafter
par^M

ridge beam
tirante^M

strut
puntal^M

foundation

cimientos^M

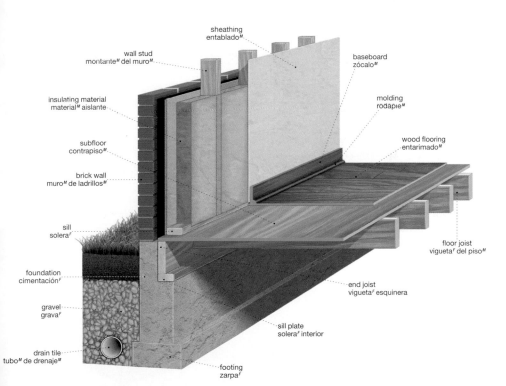

sheathing
entablado^M

wall stud
montante^M del muro^M

baseboard
zócalo^M

insulating material
material^M aislante

molding
rodapié^M

subfloor
contrapiso^M

wood flooring
entarimado^M

brick wall
muro^M de ladrillos^M

sill
solera^F

floor joist
vigueta^F del piso^M

foundation
cimentación^F

end joist
vigueta^F esquinera

gravel
grava^F

sill plate
solera^F interior

drain tile
tubo^M de drenaje^M

footing
zarpa^F

wood flooring

pisos^M de madera^F

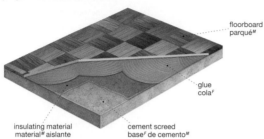

wood flooring on cement screed
parqué^M sobre base^F de cemento^M

floorboard
parqué^M

glue
cola^F

insulating material
material^M aislante

cement screed
base^F de cemento^M

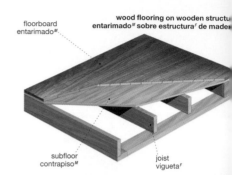

floorboard
entarimado^M

wood flooring on wooden structu
entarimado^M sobre estructura^F de made

subfloor
contrapiso^M

joist
vigueta^F

wood flooring arrangements
tipos^M de parqué^M

overlay flooring
parqué^M sobrepuesto

strip flooring with alternate joints
parqué^M alternado a la inglesa

herringbone parquet
parqué^M espinapez^M

herringbone patter
parqué^M en punta^F (
Hungría

inlaid parquet
parqué^M de mosaico^M

basket weave pattern
parqué^M de cestería^F

Arenberg parquet
parqué^M Arenberg

Chantilly parquet
parqué^M Chantilly

Versailles parquet
parqué^M Versalles

textile floor coverings

revestimientos^M textiles del suelo^M

rug
alfombra^F

pile carp
moquet

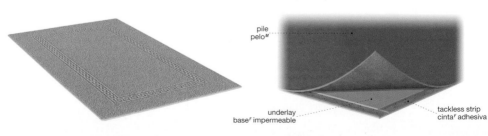

pile
pelo^M

underlay
base^F impermeable

tackless strip
cinta^F adhesiva

stairs

escalera^F

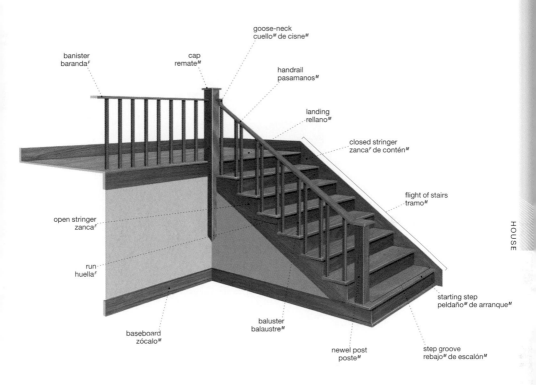

goose-neck
cuello^M de cisne^M

banister
baranda^F

cap
remate^M

handrail
pasamanos^M

landing
rellano^M

closed stringer
zanca^F de contén^M

flight of stairs
tramo^M

open stringer
zanca^F

run
huella^F

starting step
peldaño^M de arranque^M

baseboard
zócalo^M

baluster
balaustre^M

newel post
poste^M

step groove
rebajo^M de escalón^M

HOUSE

step
peldaño^M

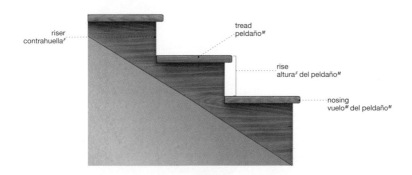

riser
contrahuella^F

tread
peldaño^M

rise
altura^F del peldaño^M

nosing
vuelo^M del peldaño^M

wood firing

calefacción^F de leña^F

fireplace
chimenea^F

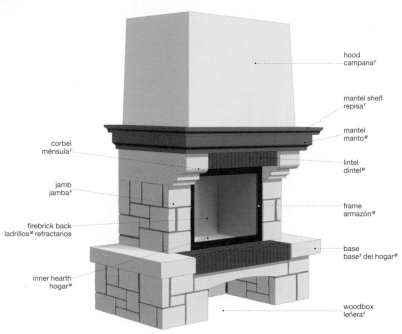

hood
campana^F

mantel shelf
repisa^F

mantel
manto^M

corbel
ménsula^F

lintel
dintel^M

jamb
jamba^F

frame
armazón^M

firebrick back
ladrillos^M refractarios

base
base^F del hogar^M

inner hearth
hogar^M

woodbox
leñera^F

slow-burning stove
estufa^F de leña^F a
fuego^M lento

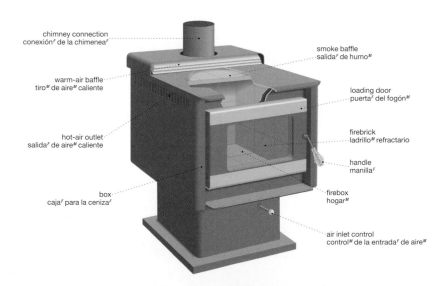

chimney connection
conexión^F de la chimenea^F

smoke baffle
salida^F de humo^M

warm-air baffle
tiro^M de aire^M caliente

loading door
puerta^F del fogón^M

firebrick
ladrillo^M refractario

hot-air outlet
salida^F de aire^M caliente

handle
manilla^F

box
caja^F para la ceniza^F

firebox
hogar^M

air inlet control
control^M de la entrada^F de aire^M

HOUSE

chimney
chimenea^F

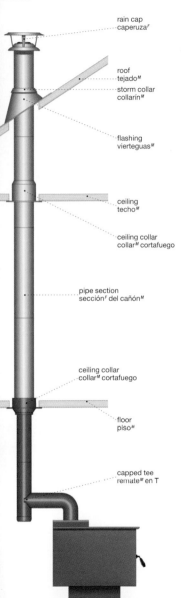

rain cap
caperuza^F

roof
tejado^M

storm collar
collarín^M

flashing
vierteguas^M

ceiling
techo^M

ceiling collar
collar^M cortafuego

pipe section
sección^F del cañón^M

ceiling collar
collar^M cortafuego

floor
piso^M

capped tee
remate^M en T

fire irons
utensilios^M **para la chimenea**^{F}

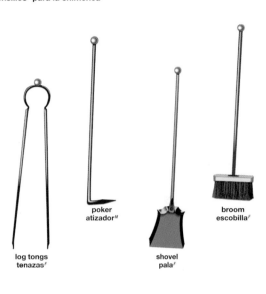

poker
atizador^M

broom
escobilla^F

log tongs
tenazas^F

shovel
pala^F

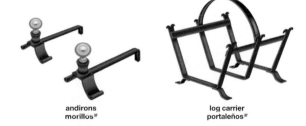

andirons
morillos^M

log carrier
portaleños^M

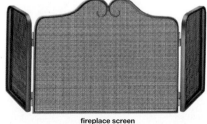

fireplace screen
pantalla^F

forced warm-air system

sistemaᴹ **de aire**ᴹ **caliente a presión**ᶠ

plan of a system
planoᴹ **de una**
instalaciónᴹ

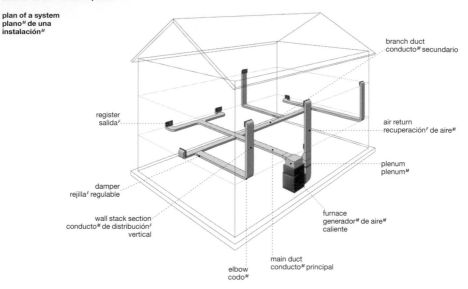

branch duct
conducto ᴹ secundario

register
salida ᶠ

air return
recuperación ᶠ de aire ᴹ

damper
rejilla ᶠ regulable

plenum
plenum ᴹ

wall stack section
conducto ᴹ de distribución ᶠ
vertical

furnace
generador ᴹ de aire ᴹ
caliente

elbow
codo ᴹ

main duct
conducto ᴹ principal

electric furnace
generadorᴹ **eléctrico de aire**ᴹ
caliente

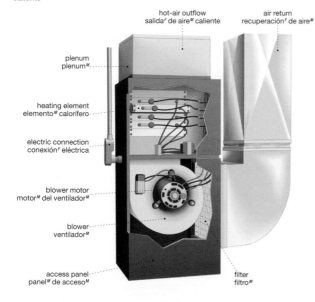

hot-air outflow
salida ᶠ de aire ᴹ caliente

air return
recuperación ᶠ de aire ᴹ

plenum
plenum ᴹ

heating element
elemento ᴹ calorífero

electric connection
conexión ᶠ eléctrica

blower motor
motor ᴹ del ventilador ᴹ

blower
ventilador ᴹ

access panel
panel ᴹ de acceso ᴹ

filter
filtro ᴹ

types of registers
tiposᴹ **de rejillas**ᶠ

baseboard register
rejillaᶠ **de piso**ᴹ

wall register
rejillaᶠ **de pared**ᶠ

ceiling register
rejillaᶠ **de techo**ᴹ

forced hot-water system

sistema^M **de agua**^F **caliente a presión**^F

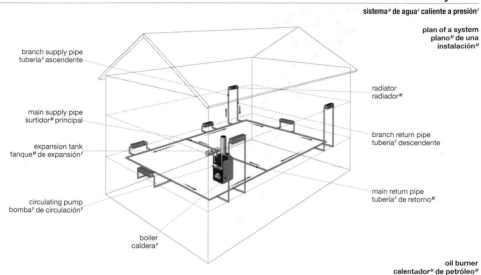

plan of a system
plano^M de una
instalación^M

branch supply pipe
tubería^F ascendente

radiator
radiador^M

main supply pipe
surtidor^M principal

branch return pipe
tubería^F descendente

expansion tank
tanque^M de expansión^F

main return pipe
tubería^F de retorno^M

circulating pump
bomba^F de circulación^F

boiler
caldera^F

oil burner
calentador^M **de petróleo**^M

HOUSE

oil boiler
caldera^F **de aceite**^M

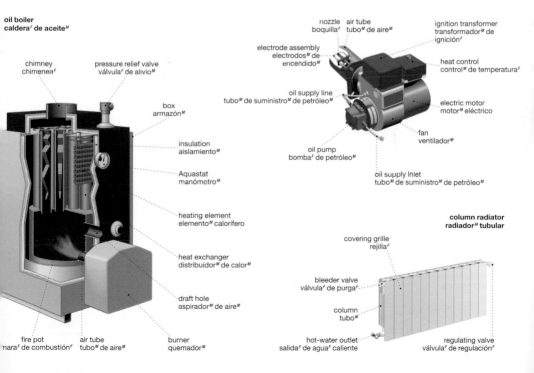

nozzle
boquilla^F

air tube
tubo^M de aire^M

ignition transformer
transformador^M de
ignición^F

electrode assembly
electrodos^M de
encendido^M

chimney
chimenea^F

pressure relief valve
válvula^F de alivio^M

heat control
control^M de temperatura^F

oil supply line
tubo^M de suministro^M de petróleo^M

box
armazón^M

electric motor
motor^M eléctrico

insulation
aislamiento^M

fan
ventilador^M

oil pump
bomba^F de petróleo^M

Aquastat
manómetro^M

oil supply Inlet
tubo^M de suministro^M de petróleo^M

heating element
elemento^M calorífero

column radiator
radiador^M **tubular**

covering grille
rejilla^F

heat exchanger
distribuidor^M de calor^M

bleeder valve
válvula^F de purga^F

draft hole
aspirador^M de aire^M

column
tubo^M

fire pot
...mara^F de combustión^F

air tube
tubo^M de aire^M

burner
quemador^M

hot-water outlet
salida^F de agua^F caliente

regulating valve
válvula^F de regulación^F

HOUSE

forced hot-water system

gas-fired boiler
calentador^M de gas^M

exhaust duct
conducto^M de
evacuación^F

expansion tank
tanque^M de expansión^M

plate-type heat exchanger
intercambiador^M de calor^M de
placas^F

gas and water connections
conexiones^M de gas^M y agua^M

burner
quemador^M

heat exchanger
intercambiador^M de
calor^M

combustion fan
turbina^F de aire^M de
combustión^F

circulating pump
bomba^F de circulación^F

digital boiler control unit
regulador^M digital^F del calentador^M

gas burner
quemador^M de gas^M

auxiliary heating

calefacción^F auxiliar

convector
radiador^M de convexión^F

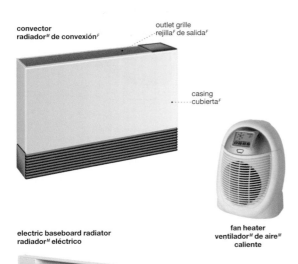

outlet grille
rejilla^F de salida^F

casing
cubierta^F

radiant heater
calefactor^M eléctrico a
infrarrojos^M

fan heater
ventilador^M de aire^M
caliente

electric baseboard radiator
radiador^M eléctrico

deflector
deflector^M

fin
aleta^F

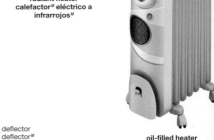

oil-filled heater
calefactor^M de aceite^M

heat pump

sistema de bomba de calor

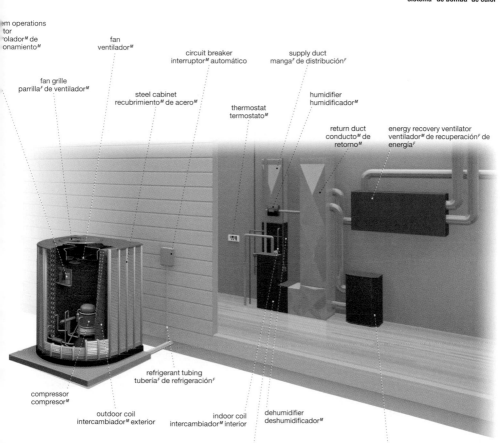

em operations
tor
olador de
onamiento

fan
ventilador

circuit breaker
interruptor automático

supply duct
manga de distribución

fan grille
parrilla de ventilador

steel cabinet
recubrimiento de acero

thermostat
termostato

humidifier
humidificador

return duct
conducto de
retorno

energy recovery ventilator
ventilador de recuperación de
energía

HOUSE

compressor
compresor

outdoor coil
intercambiador exterior

refrigerant tubing
tubería de refrigeración

indoor coil
intercambiador interior

dehumidifier
deshumidificador

furnace
generador de aire
caliente

filtration system
sistema de filtrado

utdoor unit
nidad exterior

indoor unit
unidad interior

control devices

dispositivos^M de control^M

**programmable
thermostat
termostato^M
programable**

housing
carcasa^F

display
display^M

arrow key
tecla^F de dirección^F

programming control
programador^M

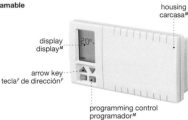

**room thermosta[
termostato**

cover
tapa^F

temperature control
control^M de temperatura^F

desired temperature
temperatura^F deseada

actual temperature
temperatura^F real

pointer
aguja^F indicadora

air-conditioning appliances

aparatos^M acondicionadores^M

**dehumidifier
deshumidificador^M**

humidistat
higróstato^M

front grille
rejilla^F frontal

bucket
recipiente^M

water level
nivel^M del agua^F

**ceiling fa
ventilador^M de techo**

rod
flecha^F

motor
motor^M

blade
aspa^F

**air purifier
purificador^M de aire^M**

**hygrometer
higrómetro^M**

temperature
temperatura^F

humidity
humedad^F del aire^M

**portable humidifie
humidificador^M portát[**

control panel
tablero^M de control^M

vaporizer
vaporizador^M

water tank
recipiente^M de agua^F

air filter
filtro^M de aire^M

water level
nivel^M de agua^F

vaporizing grille
rejilla^F de vaporizac[

tray
bandeja^F

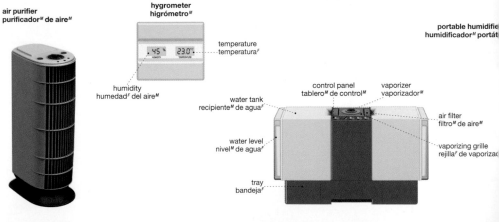

air-conditioning appliances

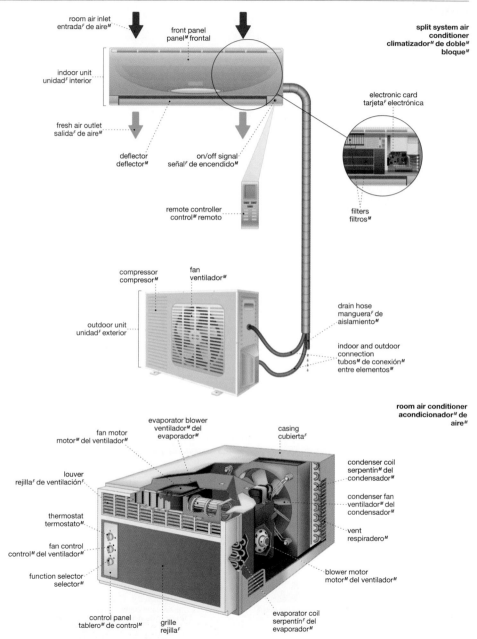

room air inlet
entrada^F de aire^M

front panel
panel^M frontal

split system air conditioner
climatizador^M de doble^M bloque^M

indoor unit
unidad^F interior

electronic card
tarjeta^F electrónica

fresh air outlet
salida^F de aire^M

deflector
deflector^M

on/off signal
señal^F de encendido^M

remote controller
control^M remoto

filters
filtros^M

compressor
compresor^M

fan
ventilador^M

outdoor unit
unidad^F exterior

drain hose
manguera^F de aislamiento^M

indoor and outdoor connection
tubos^M de conexión^M entre elementos^M

room air conditioner
acondicionador^M de aire^M

fan motor
motor^M del ventilador^M

evaporator blower
ventilador^M del evaporador^M

casing
cubierta^F

louver
rejilla^F de ventilación^F

condenser coil
serpentín^M del condensador^M

condenser fan
ventilador^M del condensador^M

thermostat
termostato^M

vent
respiradero^M

fan control
control^M del ventilador^M

function selector
selector^M

blower motor
motor^M del ventilador^M

control panel
tablero^M de control^M

grille
rejilla^F

evaporator coil
serpentín^F del evaporador^M

HOUSE

plumbing system

cañerías^f

HOUSE

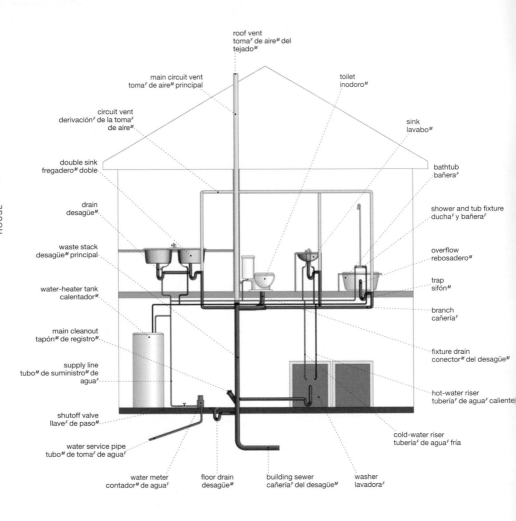

roof vent
toma^F de aire^M del tejado^M

main circuit vent
toma^F de aire^M principal

toilet
inodoro^M

circuit vent
derivación^F de la toma^F de aire^M

sink
lavabo^M

double sink
fregadero^M doble

bathtub
bañera^F

drain
desagüe^M

shower and tub fixture
ducha^F y bañera^F

waste stack
desagüe^M principal

overflow
rebosadero^M

water-heater tank
calentador^M

trap
sifón^M

branch
cañería^F

main cleanout
tapón^M de registro^M

fixture drain
conector^M del desagüe^M

supply line
tubo^M de suministro^M de agua^F

hot-water riser
tubería^F de agua^F caliente

shutoff valve
llave^F de paso^M

cold-water riser
tubería^F de agua^F fría

water service pipe
tubo^M de toma^F de agua^F

water meter
contador^M de agua^F

floor drain
desagüe^M

building sewer
cañería^F del desagüe^M

washer
lavadora^F

ventilating circuit
circuito^M de ventilación^F

draining circuit
circuito^M de desagüe^M

cold-water circuit
circuito^M de agua^F fría

hot-water circuit
circuito^M de agua^F caliente

pedestal-type sump pump

bombaᶠ tipoᴹ pedestalᴹ para sumideroᴹ

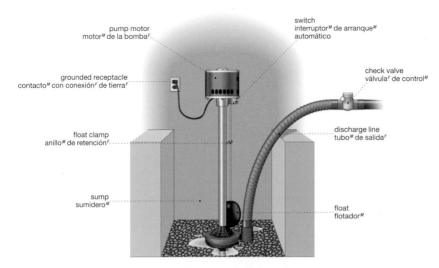

pump motor
motorᴹ de la bombaᶠ

switch
interruptorᴹ de arranqueᴹ
automático

grounded receptacle
contactoᴹ con conexiónᶠ de tierraᶠ

check valve
válvulaᶠ de controlᴹ

float clamp
anilloᴹ de retenciónᶠ

discharge line
tuboᴹ de salidaᶠ

sump
sumideroᴹ

float
flotadorᴹ

HOUSE

septic tank

fosaᶠ séptica

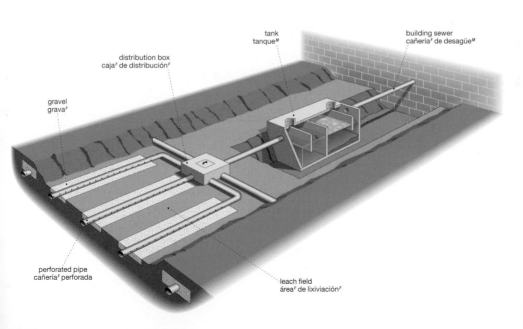

tank
tanqueᴹ

building sewer
cañeríaᶠ de desagüeᴹ

distribution box
cajaᶠ de distribuciónᶠ

gravel
gravaᶠ

perforated pipe
cañeríaᶠ perforada

leach field
áreaᶠ de lixiviaciónᶠ

bathroom

cuarto^M de baño^M

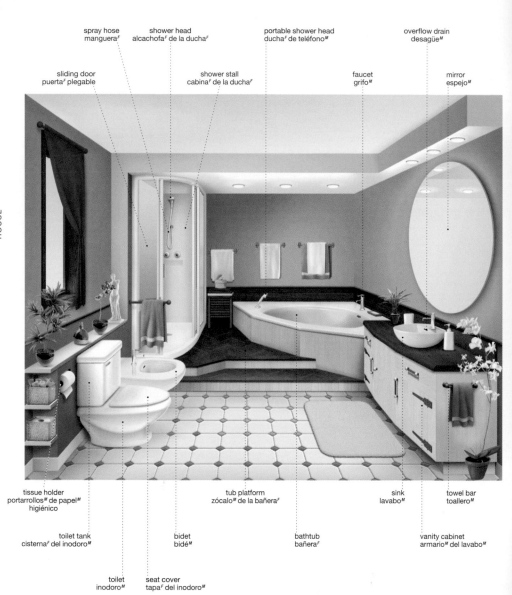

spray hose
manguera^F

shower head
alcachofa^F de la ducha^F

portable shower head
ducha^F de teléfono^M

overflow drain
desagüe^M

sliding door
puerta^F plegable

shower stall
cabina^F de la ducha^F

faucet
grifo^M

mirror
espejo^M

tissue holder
portarrollos^M de papel^M
higiénico

tub platform
zócalo^M de la bañera^F

sink
lavabo^M

towel bar
toallero^M

toilet tank
cisterna^F del inodoro^M

bidet
bidé^M

bathtub
bañera^F

vanity cabinet
armario^M del lavabo^M

toilet
inodoro^M

seat cover
tapa^F del inodoro^M

toilet
inodoro^M

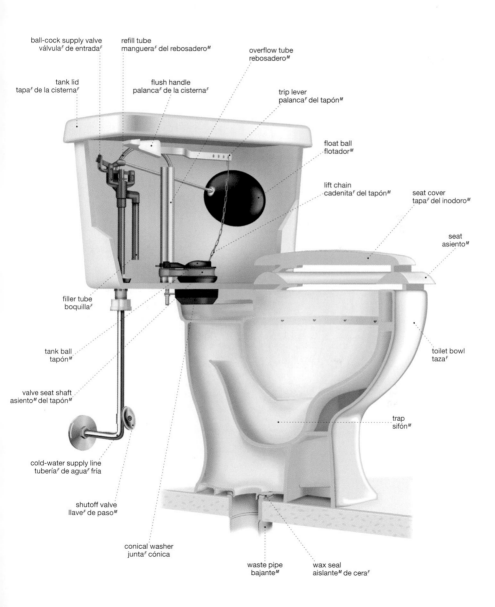

ball-cock supply valve
válvula^F de entrada^F

refill tube
manguera^F del rebosadero^M

overflow tube
rebosadero^M

tank lid
tapa^F de la cisterna^F

flush handle
palanca^F de la cisterna^F

trip lever
palanca^F del tapón^M

float ball
flotador^M

lift chain
cadenita^F del tapón^M

seat cover
tapa^F del inodoro^M

seat
asiento^M

filler tube
boquilla^F

tank ball
tapón^M

toilet bowl
taza^F

valve seat shaft
asiento^M del tapón^M

trap
sifón^M

cold-water supply line
tubería^F de agua^F fría

shutoff valve
llave^F de paso^M

conical washer
junta^F cónica

waste pipe
bajante^M

wax seal
aislante^M de cera^F

HOUSE

water-heater tank

calentador^M de agua^F eléctrico

electric water-heater tank
calentador^M eléctrico

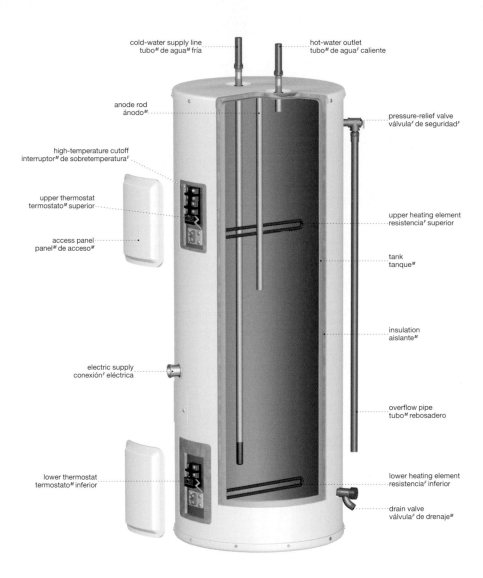

cold-water supply line
tubo^M de agua^M fría

hot-water outlet
tubo^M de agua^F caliente

anode rod
ánodo^M

pressure-relief valve
válvula^F de seguridad^F

high-temperature cutoff
interruptor^M de sobretemperatura^F

upper thermostat
termostato^M superior

upper heating element
resistencia^F superior

access panel
panel^M de acceso^M

tank
tanque^M

insulation
aislante^M

electric supply
conexión^F eléctrica

overflow pipe
tubo^M rebosadero

lower thermostat
termostato^M inferior

lower heating element
resistencia^F inferior

drain valve
válvula^F de drenaje^M

gas water-heater tank
caldera^F **de gas**^{M}

hot-water outlet
salida^F de agua^F caliente

flue hat
caperuza^F

outer jacket
envoltura^F metálica

pressure-relief valve
válvula^F de seguridad^F

overflow pipe
tubo^M de desagüe^M

insulation
aislante^M

cold-water supply line
entrada^F de agua^F fría

flue
tubo^M

glass-lined tank
revestimiento^M de fibra^F de vidrio^M

reset button
botón^M de seguridad^F

gas cock
llave^F de gas^M

control box
cajita^F reguladora

temperature control
control^M de temperatura^F

drain valve
válvula^F de drenaje^M

thermostat
termostato^M

gas burner
quemador^M de gas^M

HOUSE

faucets

grifos^M **y mezcladores**^M

stem faucet
grifo^M **de plato**^M

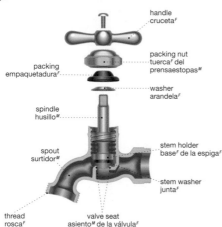

handle
cruceta^F

packing nut
tuerca^F del
prensaestopas^M

packing
empaquetadura^F

washer
arandela^F

spindle
husillo^M

spout
surtidor^M

stem holder
base^F de la espiga^F

stem washer
junta^F

thread
rosca^F

valve seat
asiento^M de la válvula^F

disc faucet
mezclador^M **de disco**^M

handle
palanca^F

bonnet
casquete^M

cylinder
cilindro^M

spout
surtidor^M

seal
junta^F de estanquidad

water inlet
entrada^F de agua^F

aerator
filtro^M

escutcheon
placa^F

ball-type faucet
grifo^M **de bola**^F

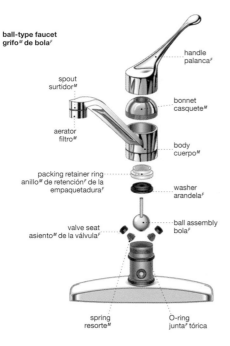

handle
palanca^F

spout
surtidor^M

bonnet
casquete^M

aerator
filtro^M

body
cuerpo^M

packing retainer ring
anillo^M de retención^F de la
empaquetadura^F

washer
arandela^F

valve seat
asiento^M de la válvula^F

ball assembly
bola^F

spring
resorte^M

O-ring
junta^F tórica

cartridge faucet
grifo^M **de cartucho**^M

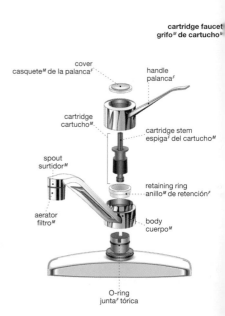

cover
casquete^M de la palanca^F

handle
palanca^F

cartridge
cartucho^M

cartridge stem
espiga^F del cartucho^M

spout
surtidor^M

retaining ring
anillo^M de retención^F

aerator
filtro^M

body
cuerpo^M

O-ring
junta^F tórica

HOUSE

fittings

conexiones[F]

plastic to steel
de plástico[M] a acero[M]

copper to plastic
de cobre[M] a plástico[M]

copper to steel
de cobre[M] a acero[M]

examples of transition
fittings
ejemplos[M] de adaptadores[M]

examples of fittings
ejemplos[M] de racores[M]

offset
codo[M] de cambio[M] de
eje[M]

tee
derivación[F] en T

Y-branch
derivación[F] en Y

trap
sifón[M]

cap
tapón[M]

U-bend
derivación[F] en U

threaded cap
tapón[M] hembra[F]

90° elbow
codo[M] de 90°

45° elbow
codo[M] de 45°

pipe coupling
unión[F]

hexagon bushing
tor[M] con cabeza[F] hexagonal

flush bushing
reductor[M]

nipple
entrerrosca[F]

reducing coupling
reductor[M] de calibre[M]

square head plug
tapón[M] macho[M]

HOUSE

mechanical connectors
racores[M] mecánicas

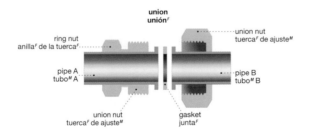

union
unión[F]

ring nut
anilla[F] de la tuerca[F]

union nut
tuerca[F] de ajuste[M]

pipe A
tubo[M] A

pipe B
tubo[M] B

union nut
tuerca[F] de ajuste[M]

gasket
junta[F]

compression fitting
racor[M] por compresión[F]

flare joint
racor[M] abocinado

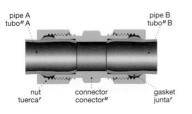

pipe A
tubo[M] A

pipe B
tubo[M] B

nut
tuerca[F]

connector
conector[M]

gasket
junta[F]

pipe A
tubo[M] A

pipe B
tubo[M] B

nut
tuerca[F]

connector
conector[M]

tube end
extremo[M] abocinado

examples of branching

ejemplos^M de conexiones^F

garbage disposal sink
fregadero^M con triturador^M de basura^F

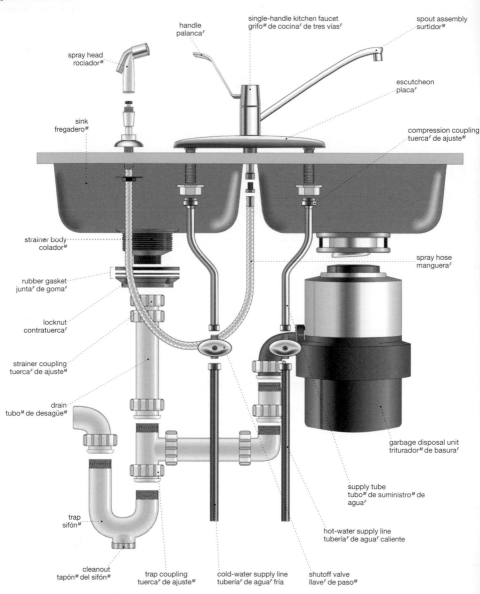

spray head
rociador^M

handle
palanca^F

single-handle kitchen faucet
grifo^M de cocina^F de tres vías^F

spout assembly
surtidor^M

escutcheon
placa^F

sink
fregadero^M

compression coupling
tuerca^F de ajuste^M

strainer body
colador^M

spray hose
manguera^F

rubber gasket
junta^F de goma^F

locknut
contratuerca^F

strainer coupling
tuerca^F de ajuste^M

drain
tubo^M de desagüe^M

garbage disposal unit
triturador^M de basura^F

trap
sifón^M

supply tube
tubo^M de suministro^M de
agua^F

cleanout
tapón^M del sifón^M

trap coupling
tuerca^F de ajuste^M

cold-water supply line
tubería^F de agua^F fría

shutoff valve
llave^F de paso^M

hot-water supply line
tubería^F de agua^F caliente

washer
lavadora^F

air chamber
cámara^F de aire^M

shutoff valve
llave^F de paso^M

tee
derivación^M en T

flexible rubber hose
manguera^F

cold-water supply line
tubería^F de agua^F fría

hot-water supply line
tubería^F de agua^F caliente

washer
lavadora^F

standpipe
toma^F de aire^M

house drain
sifón^M de desagüe^M

drain hose
manguera^F de desagüe^M

dishwasher
lavavajillas^F

drain hose
manguera^F de desagüe^M

dishwasher
lavavajillas^F

air chamber
cámara^F de aire^M

cold-water supply line
cañería^F de agua^F fría

hot-water supply line
ería^F de agua^F caliente

waste tee
derivación^F en T del desagüe^M

shutoff valve
llave^F de paso^M

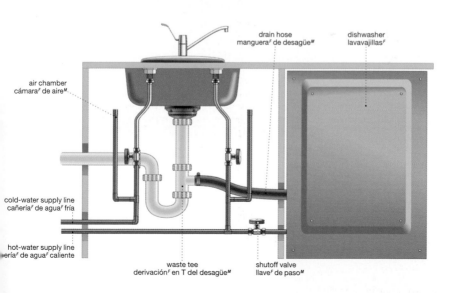

distribution panel

cuadro^M de distribución^F

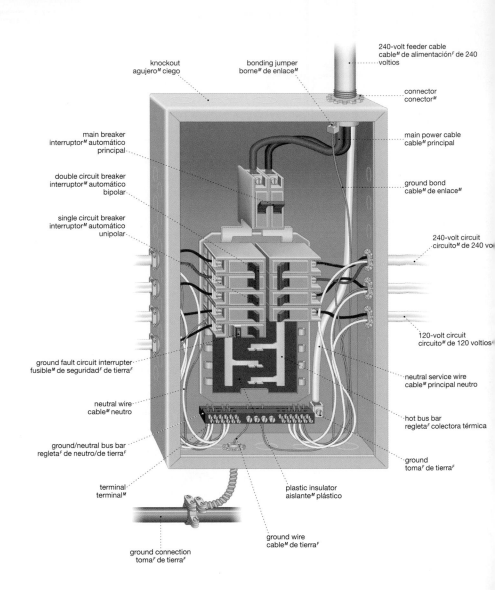

knockout
agujero^M ciego

bonding jumper
borne^M de enlace^M

240-volt feeder cable
cable^M de alimentación^F de 240
voltios

connector
conector^M

main breaker
interruptor^M automático
principal

double circuit breaker
interruptor^M automático
bipolar

single circuit breaker
interruptor^M automático
unipolar

main power cable
cable^M principal

ground bond
cable^M de enlace^M

240-volt circuit
circuito^M de 240 vo

120-volt circuit
circuito^M de 120 voltios

ground fault circuit interrupter
fusible^M de seguridad^F de tierra^F

neutral wire
cable^M neutro

ground/neutral bus bar
regleta^F de neutro/de tierra^F

terminal
terminal^M

neutral service wire
cable^M principal neutro

hot bus bar
regleta^F colectora térmica

ground
toma^F de tierra^F

plastic insulator
aislante^M plástico

ground wire
cable^M de tierra^F

ground connection
toma^F de tierra^F

distribution panel

examples of fuses
ejemplos de fusibles**

cartridge fuse
fusible de cartucho**

plug fuse
fusible de rosca**

knife-blade cartridge fuse
fusible de bayoneta**

electricity meter

contador de kilovatio-hora

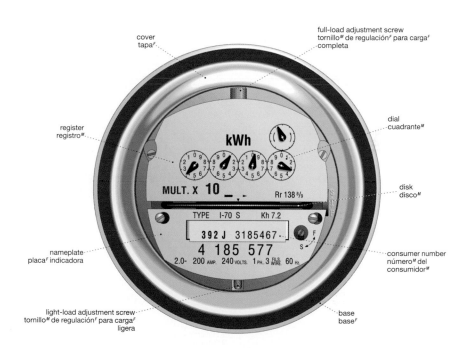

cover
tapa**

full-load adjustment screw
tornillo** de regulación** para carga**
completa

register
registro**

dial
cuadrante**

kWh

MULT. X **10**

Rr 138 ⁸/₉

disk
disco**

TYPE I-70 S   Kh 7.2

392 J 3185467

4 185 577

2.0- 200 AMP. 240 VOLTS. 1 PH. 3 FILS WIRE 60 Hz.

F
S

nameplate
placa** indicadora

consumer number
número** del
consumidor**

light-load adjustment screw
tornillo** de regulación** para carga**
ligera

base
base**

network connection

conexión^F a la red^F

**overhead distribution
system
distribución^F eléctrica
aérea**

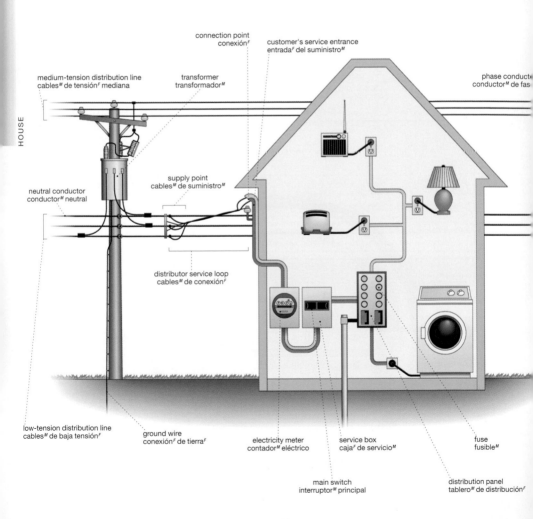

connection point
conexión^F

customer's service entrance
entrada^F del suministro^M

medium-tension distribution line
cables^M de tensión^F mediana

transformer
transformador^M

phase conductor
conductor^M de fase

HOUSE

supply point
cables^M de suministro^M

neutral conductor
conductor^M neutral

distributor service loop
cables^M de conexión^F

low-tension distribution line
cables^M de baja tensión^F

ground wire
conexión^F de tierra^F

electricity meter
contador^M eléctrico

service box
caja^F de servicio^M

fuse
fusible^M

main switch
interruptor^M principal

distribution panel
tablero^M de distribución^F

underground distribution system
distribución^F eléctrica subterránea

disconnect cabinet
armario^M de interruptor^M

enclosure
cajetín^M de conexión^F

pad-mounted
transformer
transformador^M sobre
base^F

HOUSE

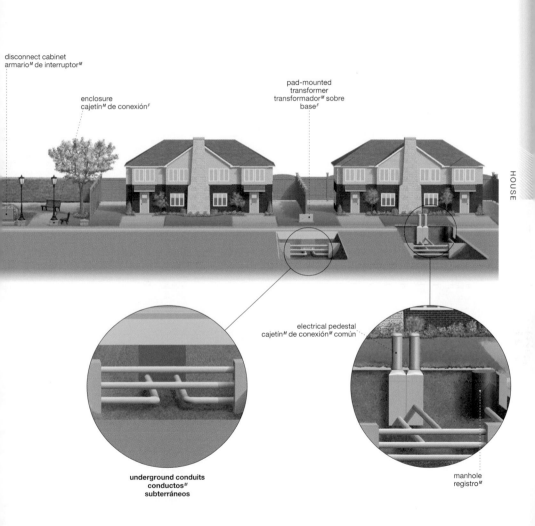

electrical pedestal
cajetín^M de conexión^M común

underground conduits
conductos^M
subterráneos

manhole
registro^M

contact devices

dispositivosᴹ **de contacto**ᴹ

European plug
clavijaᶠ **de tipo**ᴹ
europeo

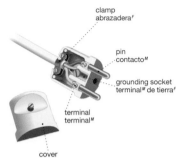

clamp
abrazadera ᶠ

pin
contacto ᴹ

grounding socket
terminal ᴹ de tierra ᶠ

terminal
terminal ᴹ

cover
tapa ᶠ

European outlet
enchufeᴹ **europeo**

socket-contact
alveolo ᴹ

grounding prong
conector ᴹ de tierra ᶠ macho

American outlet
enchufeᴹ **americano**

American plug
clavijaᶠ **de tipo**ᴹ
americano

blade
contacto ᴹ

grounding prong
contacto ᴹ de conexión ᶠ a
tierra ᶠ

parts of a lamp socket
componentesᶠ **del portalámpara**ᴹ

cap
tapa ᶠ

socket
casquillo ᴹ

insulating sleeve
manga ᶠ de aislamiento ᴹ

outer shell
cubierta ᶠ

plug adapter
adaptadorᴹ **de enchufes**ᴹ

screw base
bombillaᶠ **de rosca**ᶠ

bayonet base
bombillaᶠ **de bayoneta**ᶠ

switch
interruptorᴹ

lamp socket
portalámparasᴹ

switch plate
placaᶠ **del interruptor**

dimmer switch
conmutadorᴹ **de**
intensidadᶠ

electrical box
cajaᶠ **de conexiones**ᶠ

lighting

iluminación^F

tungsten-halogen lamp
lámpara^F halógena

bulb
ampolla^F

filament support
filamento^M

tungsten filament
filamento^M de tungsteno^M

inert gas
gas^M inerte

electric circuit
circuito^M eléctrico

base
casquillo^M

contact
contacto^M

incandescent lamp
bombilla^F incandescente

filament
filamento^M

inert gas
gas^M inerte

support
soporte^M

button
botón^M

lead-in wire
entrada^F de corriente^F

stem
varilla^F

pinch
pie^M

heat deflecting disc
disco^M desviador de
calor^M

exhaust tube
tubo^M de escape^M

base
casquillo^M

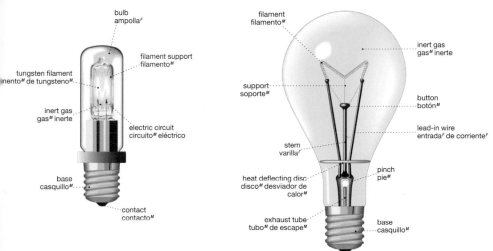

fluorescent tube
tubo^M fluorescente

electrode
electrodo^M

phosphorescent coating
revestimiento^M de
fósforo^M

pin base
base^F del tubo^M

lead-in wire
entrada^F de corriente^F

pin
pata^F

exhaust tube
tubo^M de escape^M

pinch
pie^M del electrodo^M

mercury
mercurio^M

gas
gas^M inerte

bulb
tubo^M

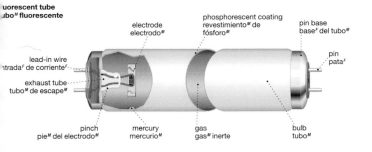

mini halogen lamp
mini lámpara^F halógena

pin
contacto^M

compact fluorescent
lamp
lámpara^F fluorescente

light-emitting diode (LED)
lamp
lámpara^F de LED^M

light-emitting diode (LED)
LED^M

base
base^F

bulb
bombilla^F

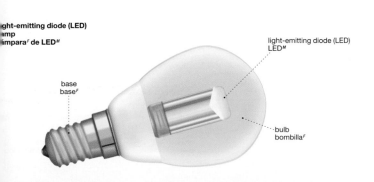

HOUSE

HOUSE

armchair
silla^F de brazos^M

parts of an armchair
partes^F de un sofá^M

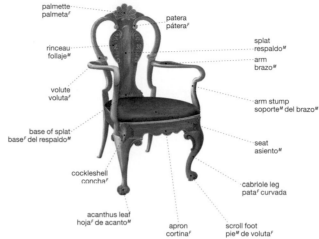

palmette
palmeta^F

patera
pátera^F

splat
respaldo^M

rinceau
follaje^M

arm
brazo^M

volute
voluta^F

arm stump
soporte^M del brazo^M

base of splat
base^F del respaldo^M

seat
asiento^M

cockleshell
concha^F

cabriole leg
pata^F curvada

acanthus leaf
hoja^F de acanto^M

apron
cortina^F

scroll foot
pie^M de voluta^F

examples of armchairs
ejemplos^M de divanes^M y butacas^F

Wassily chair
silla^F Wassily

director's chair
silla^F plegable de lona^F

cabriolet
silla^F cabriolé

rocking chair
mecedora^F

chair bed
sofá^M cama^F

club chair
butaca^F

bergère
silla^F poltrona

Voltaire chair
sillón^M Voltaire

tub chair
sillón^M clásico

méridienne
meridiano^M

love seat
sofá^M de dos plazas^F

sofa
sofá^M

chesterfield
chesterfield^M

récamier
sofá^M tipo^M imperio

side chair

silla^F sin brazos^M

parts of a side chair
partes^F de una silla^F

top rail
peinazo^M superior

cross rail
peinazo^M inferior

stile
larguero^M

apron
guarnición^F

rear leg
pata^F trasera

spindle
travesaño^M

ear
pomo^M

back
respaldo^M

seat
asiento^M

support
pata^F

front leg
pata^F delantera

examples of chairs
ejemplos^M de sillas^F

HOUSE

Windsor chair
silla^F Windsor

rocking chair
mecedora^F

chaise longue
tumbona^F

stacking chairs
sillas^F apilables

folding chair
silla^F plegable

seats

asientos^M

stool
escabel^M

barstool
taburete^M

beanbag chair
puf^M

ottoman
puf^M

storage bench
sillón^M baúl^M

bench
banco^M

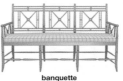

banquette
banqueta^F

step chair
silla^F escalera^F

table

mesa*F*

HOUSE

gateleg table
mesa*F* extensible

top
tablero*M*

apron
guarnición*F*

drawer
cajón*M*

knob
pomo*M*

drop leaf
panel*F* abatible

stretcher
travesaño*M*

leg
pata*F*

gateleg
soporte*M* de panel*M*

crosspiece
travesaño*M*

examples of tables
ejemplos*M* de mesas*F*

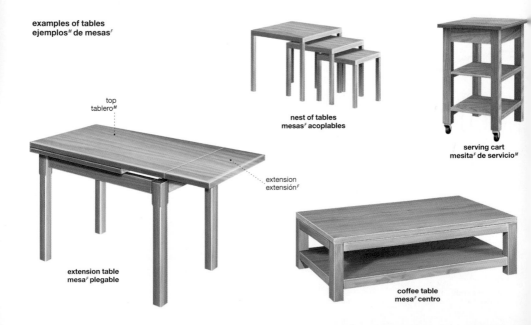

top
tablero*M*

nest of tables
mesas*F* acoplables

serving cart
mesita*F* de servicio*M*

top
tablero*M*

extension
extensión*F*

extension table
mesa*F* plegable

coffee table
mesa*F* centro

bed

cama^F

parts of a bed
partes^F de una cama^F

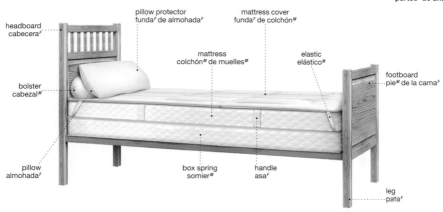

headboard
cabecera^F

pillow protector
funda^F de almohada^F

mattress cover
funda^F de colchón^M

mattress
colchón^M de muelles^M

elastic
elástico^M

footboard
pie^M de la cama^F

bolster
cabezal^M

pillow
almohada^F

box spring
somier^M

handle
asa^F

leg
pata^F

HOUSE

linen
ropa^F de cama^F

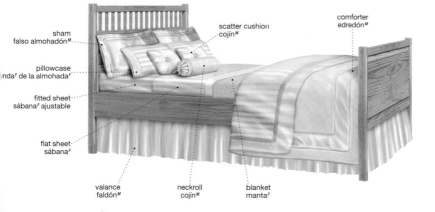

sham
falso almohadón^M

scatter cushion
cojín^M

comforter
edredón^M

pillowcase
funda^F de la almohada^F

fitted sheet
sábana^F ajustable

flat sheet
sábana^F

valance
faldón^M

neckroll
cojín^M

blanket
manta^F

futon
futón^M

futon
futón^M

frame
armazón^M

storage furniture

muebles^M contenedores

armoire
armario^M

frame
armazón^M

door
puerta^F

cornice
cornisa^F

door panel
entrepaño^M

hanging stile
larguero^M de la bisagra^F

frame stile
larguero^M del marco^M

hinge
bisagra^F

frieze
friso^M

top rail
peinazo^M superior

rail
peinazo^M

handle
asa^M

bracket base
rodapié^M

bottom rail
peinazo^M inferior

compartment
casillero^M

fall front
escritorio^M

secretary
bufete^M

linen chest
baúl^M

dresser
cómoda^F

storage furniture

dressing table
tocador^M

bedside table
mesita^F de noche^F

cellar
alacena^F

closet
guardarropa^M

shelf
anaquel^M

wardrobe
ropero^M

HOUSE

corner cupboard
rinconera^F

drawer
cajón^M

chiffonier
chifonier^M

display cabinet
vitrina^F

liquor cabinet
mueble^M bar^M

buffet
aparador^M

glass-fronted display
cabinet
aparador^M con vitrina^F

children's furniture

muebles^M infantiles

playpen
cuna^F plegable

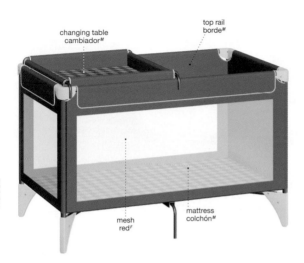

changing table
cambiador^M

top rail
borde^M

mesh
red^F

mattress
colchón^M

booster seat
silla^F alzador

back
respaldo^M

armrest
brazos^M

seat
asiento^M

changing table
cambiador

contour changing pad
cambiador^M

high chair
trona^F

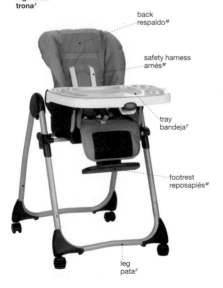

back
respaldo^M

safety harness
arnés^M

tray
bandeja^F

footrest
reposapiés^M

leg
pata^F

crib
cuna

barrier
barrera^F

slat
barrote^M

headboard
cabecera^F

caster
rueda^F giratoria

drawer
cajón^M

mattress
colchón^M

HOUSE

window accessories

accesorios^M para las ventanas^F

poles
varillas^F

plain pole
barra^F **lisa**

curtain pole
barra^F **de cortina**^F

pole
barra^F

block bracket
abrazadera^F

ring
anillo^M

fluted pole
barra^F **acanalada**

eyelet
ojete^M

end cap
tope^M

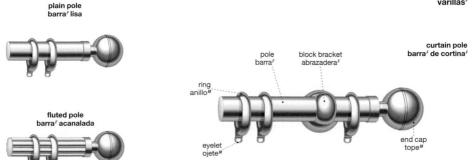

single curtain rod
barra^F **de varilla**^F **simple**

double curtain rod
barra^F **de varilla**^F **doble**

HOUSE

curtain track
riel^M

wall bracket
soporte^M de pared^F

roller
corredera^F

ceiling bracket
soporte^M de techo^M

track
riel^M

end stop
tope^M

bridge
puente^M

hook
gancho^M

clip
clip^M

ring
anilla^F

carrier
carro^M

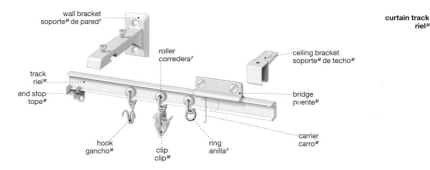

traverse rod
cortina^F **de riel**^M

end bracket
tope^M

master carrier
corredera^F

operating cord
cordón^M

yoke
balancín^M

support
soporte^M

tension pulley wheel
polea^F tensora

pulley
polea^F

overlap carrier
corredera^F con
enganches^M

spring housing
resorte^M

fastening device
sujeción^F

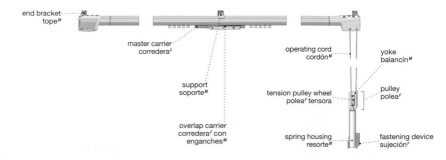

window accessories

glass curtain
cortina[F] **de ventana**[F]

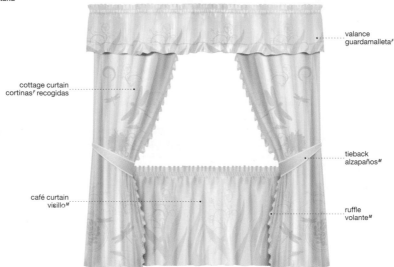

valance
guardamalleta[F]

cottage curtain
cortinas[F] recogidas

tieback
alzapaños[M]

café curtain
visillo[M]

ruffle
volante[M]

curtain
cortina[F]

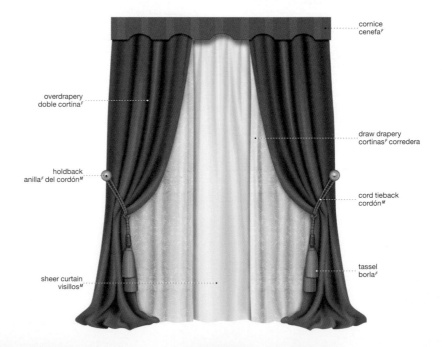

cornice
cenefa[F]

overdrapery
doble cortina[F]

draw drapery
cortinas[F] corredera

holdback
anilla[F] del cordón[M]

cord tieback
cordón[M]

sheer curtain
visillos[M]

tassel
borla[F]

window accessories

examples of curtains
ejemplos^M de cortinas^F

crisscross curtains
cortinas^F cruzadas

attached curtain
cortina^F sujeta de doble
barra^F

loose curtain
cortina^F suelta
corrediza

balloon curtain
cortina^F abombada

examples of headings
ejemplos^M de cenefas^F

HOUSE

grommet curtain
cortina^F con ojales^M

tab top heading
cortina^F con
pasadores^M

draped swag
cenefa^F drapeada

pleated heading
cenefa^F plisada

pencil pleat heading
cenefa^F plisada de
canotillo^M

shirred heading
cenefa^F fruncida

window accessories

examples of pleats
ejemplos*M* de fruncidos*M*

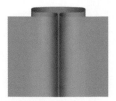

box pleat
pliegue*M* de cajón*M*

inverted pleat
pliegue*M* de cajón*M*
invertido

pinch pleat
pliegue*M* de pinza*F*

indoor shutters
postigos*M* interiores

panel
panel*M*

lath
listón*M*

blinds
persianas*F* enrollables

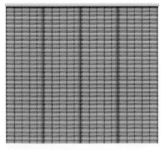

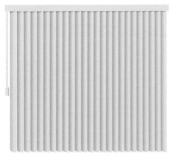

Japanese blind
estor*M* japonés

vertical blind
estor*M* vertical

HOUSE

roller shade
persiana^F enrollable
automática

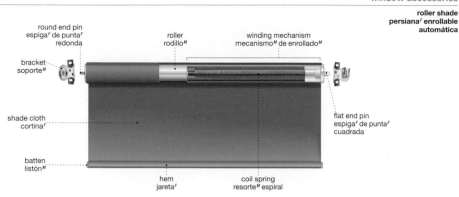

round end pin
espiga^F de punta^F
redonda

bracket
soporte^M

roller
rodillo^M

winding mechanism
mecanismo^M de enrollado^M

shade cloth
cortina^F

flat end pin
espiga^F de punta^F
cuadrada

batten
listón^M

hem
jareta^F

coil spring
resorte^M espiral

venetian blind
estor^M veneciano

HOUSE

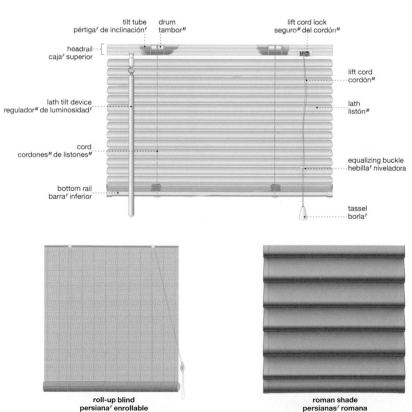

tilt tube
pértiga^F de inclinación^F

drum
tambor^M

lift cord lock
seguro^M del cordón^M

headrail
caja^F superior

lift cord
cordón^M

lath tilt device
regulador^M de luminosidad^F

lath
listón^M

cord
cordones^M de listones^M

equalizing buckle
hebilla^F niveladora

bottom rail
barra^F inferior

tassel
borla^F

roll-up blind
persiana^F enrollable

roman shade
persianas^F romana

lights
lámparas^f

clamp spotlight
lámpara^f de pinza^f

bed lamp
lámpara^f de cabecera^f

ceiling fitting
plafón^M

hanging pendant
lámpara^f de techo^M

HOUSE

adjustable lamp
flexo^M

on-off switch
interruptor^M

arm
brazo^M

spring
resorte^M

adjustable clamp
tornillo^M de ajuste^M

table lamp
lámpara^f de mesa^f

shade
pantalla^f

stand
pedestal^M

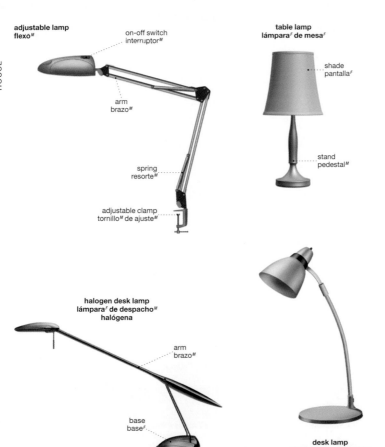

halogen desk lamp
lámpara^f de despacho^M
halógena

arm
brazo^M

base
base^f

desk lamp
lámpara^f de escritorio^M

base
base^f

floor lamp
lámpara^f de pie^M

post lantern
farola^F

chandelier
araña^F

bobeche
arandela^F

crystal drop
colgante^M

column
columna^F

crystal button
gota^F

HOUSE

track lighting
riel^M de iluminación^F

bar frame
armazón^M

transformer
transformador^M

spot
foco^M

wall lantern
farol^M

sconce
aplique^M

strip light
lámparas^F en serie^F

swivel wall lamp
lámpara^F orientable de pared^F

home appliances

aparatos^M electrodomésticos

steam iron
plancha^F de vapor^M

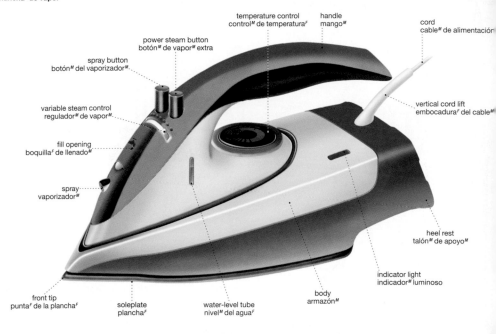

temperature control
control^M de temperatura^F

handle
mango^M

cord
cable^M de alimentación^F

power steam button
botón^M de vapor^M extra

spray button
botón^M del vaporizador^M

variable steam control
regulador^M de vapor^M

vertical cord lift
embocadura^F del cable^M

fill opening
boquilla^F de llenado^M

spray
vaporizador^M

heel rest
talón^M de apoyo^M

indicator light
indicador^M luminoso

front tip
punta^F de la plancha^F

soleplate
plancha^F

water-level tube
nivel^M del agua^F

body
armazón^M

HOUSE

hand vacuum cleaner
aspirador^M manual

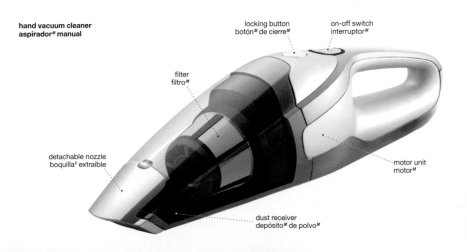

locking button
botón^M de cierre^M

on-off switch
interruptor^M

filter
filtro^M

detachable nozzle
boquilla^F extraíble

motor unit
motor^M

dust receiver
depósito^M de polvo^M

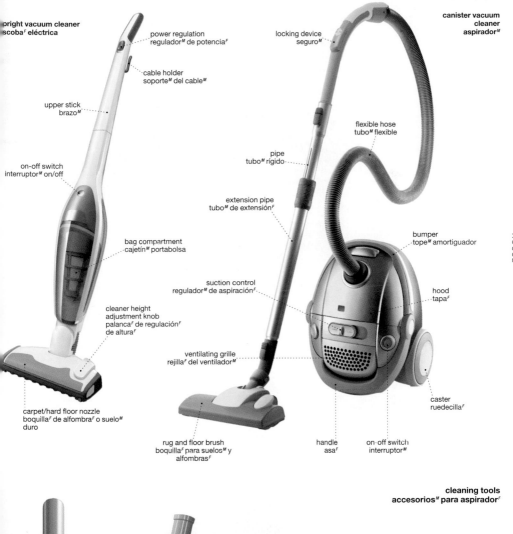

upright vacuum cleaner
escoba^F eléctrica

power regulation
regulador^M de potencia^F

cable holder
soporte^M del cable^M

upper stick
brazo^M

on-off switch
interruptor^M on/off

bag compartment
cajetín^M portabolsa

cleaner height
adjustment knob
palanca^F de regulación^F
de altura^F

carpet/hard floor nozzle
boquilla^F de alfombra^F o suelo^M
duro

**canister vacuum
cleaner
aspirador^M**

locking device
seguro^M

flexible hose
tubo^M flexible

pipe
tubo^M rígido

extension pipe
tubo^M de extensión^F

suction control
regulador^M de aspiración^F

ventilating grille
rejilla^F del ventilador^M

bumper
tope^M amortiguador

hood
tapa^F

caster
ruedecilla^F

rug and floor brush
boquilla^F para suelos^M y
alfombras^F

handle
asa^F

on-off switch
interruptor^M

HOUSE

**cleaning tools
accesorios^M para aspirador^F**

**upholstery nozzle
boquilla^F para tapicería^F**

**dusting brush
cepillo^M-plumero^M**

**crevice tool
boquilla^F rinconera**

**floor brush
cepillo^M para suelos^M**

HOUSE

home appliances

range hood
campana^F

filter
filtro^M

cooking unit   clock timer
zona^F de cocción^F   reloj^M

electric range
cocina^F **eléctrica**

cooktop
encimera^F

control panel
panel^M de mandos^M

cooktop edge
borde^M

control knob
botón^M de mando^M

oven
horno^M

handle
asa^F

window
visor^M

rack
parrilla^F

drawer
cajón^M calientaplatos

gas range
cocina^F **de gas**^M

burner
quemador^M

grate
rejilla^F

burner control knobs
mandos^M de los quemadores^M

cooktop
encimera^F

control panel
panel^M de mandos^M

oven
horno^M

handle
tirador^M

rack
parrilla^F

window
visor^M

door
puerta^F

home appliances

chest freezer
arcón^M congelador

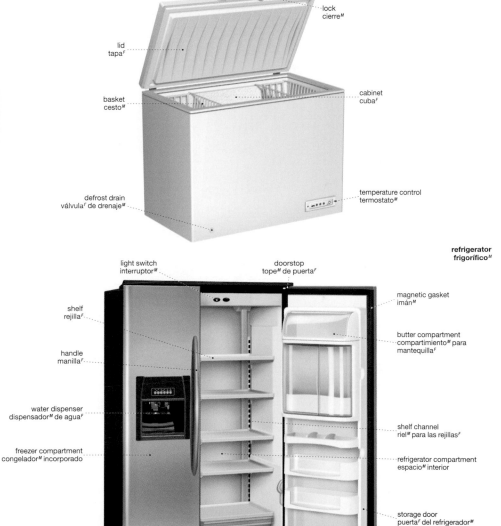

lock
cierre^M

lid
tapa^F

basket
cesto^M

cabinet
cuba^F

defrost drain
válvula^F de drenaje^M

temperature control
termostato^M

HOUSE

refrigerator
frigorífico^M

light switch
interruptor^M

doorstop
tope^M de puerta^F

magnetic gasket
imán^M

shelf
rejilla^F

butter compartment
compartimiento^M para
mantequilla^F

handle
manilla^F

water dispenser
dispensador^M de agua^F

shelf channel
riel^M para las rejillas^F

freezer compartment
congelador^M incorporado

refrigerator compartment
espacio^M interior

storage door
puerta^F del refrigerador^M

meat keeper
cajón^M para carnes^F

guardrail
bandeja^F de sujeción^F

crisper
cesto^M para verdura^F

dairy compartment
compartimiento^M para lácteos^M

home appliances

front-loading washer
lavadora^F de carga^F frontal

control knob
programador^M

door
puerta^F

control panel
panel^M de control^M

water-level selector
selector^M de nivel^M de agua^F

temperature selector
selector^M de
temperatura^F

HOUSE

top-loading washer mechanism
mecanismo^M de una lavadora^F de carga^F superior

backguard
alzado^M

basket
tambor^M

lint filter
filtro^M de pelusa^F

transmission
transmisión^F

spring
resorte^M

motor
motor^M

torque converter
convertidor^M de tensión^F

drive belt
correa^F del tambor^M

lid
tapa^F

agitator
agitador^M de aspas^F

cabinet
armazón^M

tub
cuba^F

suspension arm
brazo^M de suspensión^F

drain hose
manguera^F de desagüe^M

emptying hose
manguera^F de vaciado^M

pump
bomba^F

leveling foot
pie^M ajustable

home appliances

dryer
secadora^F

control knob
programador^M

start switch
interruptor^M

door
puerta^F

control panel
panel^M de control^M

temperature selector
selector^M de
temperatura^F

dryer mechanism
mecanismo^M de una secadora^F

HOUSE

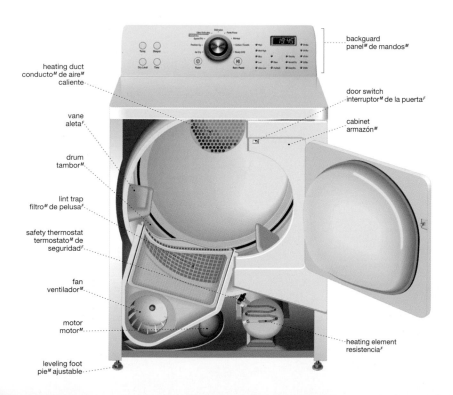

heating duct
conducto^M de aire^M
caliente

vane
aleta^F

drum
tambor^M

lint trap
filtro^M de pelusa^F

safety thermostat
termostato^M de
seguridad^F

fan
ventilador^M

motor
motor^M

leveling foot
pie^M ajustable

backguard
panel^M de mandos^M

door switch
interruptor^M de la puerta^F

cabinet
armazón^M

heating element
resistencia^F

home appliances

dishwasher: control panel
lavavajillas^F **: panel**^{M} **de control**^{M}

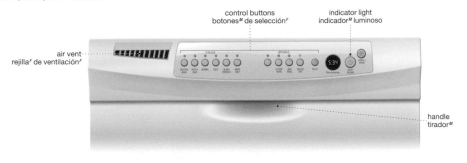

control buttons
botones^M de selección^F

indicator light
indicador^M luminoso

air vent
rejilla^F de ventilación^F

handle
tirador^M

dishwasher mechanism
mecanismo^M **de un**
lavavajillas^F

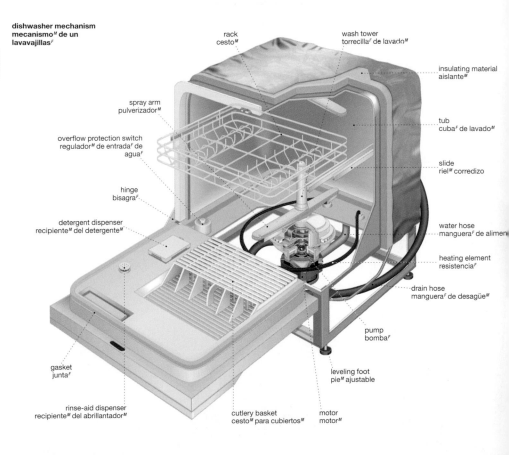

rack
cesto^M

wash tower
torrecilla^F de lavado^M

insulating material
aislante^M

spray arm
pulverizador^M

overflow protection switch
regulador^M de entrada^F de
agua^F

tub
cuba^F de lavado^M

slide
riel^M corredizo

hinge
bisagra^F

detergent dispenser
recipiente^M del detergente^M

water hose
manguera^F de alimen

heating element
resistencia^F

drain hose
manguera^F de desagüe^M

pump
bomba^F

gasket
junta^F

leveling foot
pie^M ajustable

rinse-aid dispenser
recipiente^M del abrillantador^M

cutlery basket
cesto^M para cubiertos^M

motor
motor^M

HOUSE

household equipment

artículos*M* **de limpieza***F*

kitchen towel
bayeta*F* **de cocina***F*

duster
plumero*M*

broom
escoba*F*

mop
fregona*F*

scrub brush
cepillo*M*

scouring sponge
estropajo*M* **con esponja***F*

block
lomo*M*

bristles
cerdas*F*

handle
palo*M*

trash can
cubo*M* **de basura***F*

dustpan
recogedor*M*

bristles
cerdas*F*

lid
tapa*F*

handle
asa*F*

pail
cubo*M*

pouring spout
pitorro*M*

handle
asa*F*

rubber gloves
guantes*M* **de goma***F*

HOUSE

DO-IT-YOURSELF AND GARDENING

bricolaje y jardinería

ATERIALS 384

basic building materials 384
covering materials 385
insulating materials 385
wood 386

ARPENTRY 387

accessories 387
measuring and marking tools 387
nailing tools 388
screwdriving tools 390
sawing tools 391
drilling tools 394
shaping tools 396
gripping and tightening tools 399

UMBING AND MASONRY 402

plumbing tools 402
masonry tools 403

ELECTRICITY 404

electrical tools 404

SOLDERING 406

soldering tools 406

PAINTING UPKEEP 408

painting material 408

LADDERS AND STEPLADDERS 409

ladders 409
stepladders 409

PLEASURE GARDEN 410

garden 410

YARD AND GARDEN EQUIPMENT 411

miscellaneous equipment 411
tools for loosening the earth 412
watering tools 414
pruning and cutting tools 416
hand tools 418
seeding and planting tools 418
lawn care 419

SNOW REMOVAL 421

snow removal tools 421

basic building materials

materiales^M básicos

brick
ladrillo^M

solid brick
ladrillo^M macizo

perforated brick
ladrillo^M perforado

hollow brick
ladrillo^M hueco

partition tile
ladrillo^M tabiquero

mortar
mortero^M

brick wall
muro^M de ladrillos^M

mortar
mortero^M

firebrick
ladrillo^M refractario

stone
piedra^F

flagstone
losa^F de piedra^F

rubble
morrillo^M

cut stone
piedra^M tallada

stone wall
muro^M de piedras^F

concrete and steel
hormigón^M y acero^M

concrete block
bloque^M de hormigón^M

prestressed concrete
hormigón^M pretensado

reinforced concrete
hormigón^M armado

steel
acero^M

covering materials

materiales^M de revestimiento^M

asphalt shingle
teja^F de asfalto^M

wooden shingle
ripia^F

diamond mesh metal lath
mallas^F de metal^M expandido

tar paper
fieltro^M asfáltico

roof tile
teja^F

gypsum tile
panel^M de yeso^M

tile
teja^F

drywall
paneles^M de yeso^M

insulating materials

materiales^M aislantes

loose-fill insulation
aislante^M granulado

spring-metal insulation
cinta^F metálica

vinyl insulation
aislante^M vinílico

pipe-wrapping insulation
cinta^F aislante para tubería^F

molded insulation
aislante^M premoldeado

foam weather stripping
aislante^M de gomaespuma^F

blanket insulation
lana^F de vidrio^M aislante

board insulation
tablero^M rígido aislante

foam insulation
espuma^F aislante^M

DO-IT-YOURSELF AND GARDENING

wood

madera^F

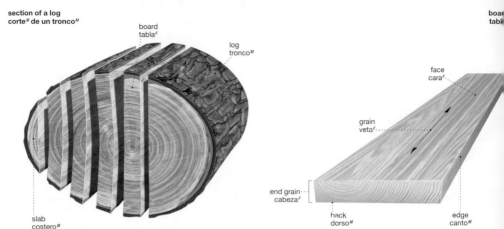

section of a log
corte^M de un tronco^M

board
tabla^F

log
tronco^M

slab
costero^M

boar
tabl

face
cara^F

grain
veta^F

end grain
cabeza^F

back
dorso^M

edge
canto^M

wood-based materials
láminas^F y tableros^M

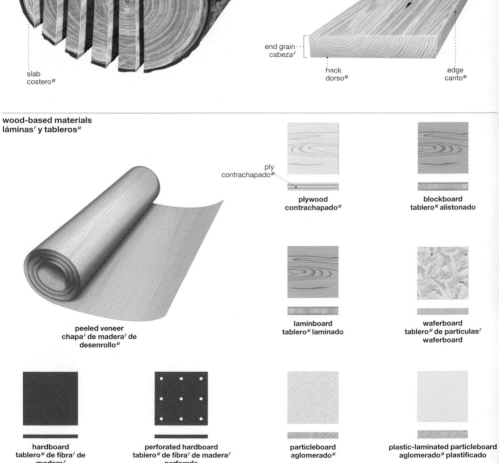

ply
contrachapado^M

plywood
contrachapado^M

blockboard
tablero^M alistonado

peeled veneer
chapa^F de madera^F de
desenrollo^M

laminboard
tablero^M laminado

waferboard
tablero^M de partículas^F
waferboard

hardboard
tablero^M de fibra^F de
madera^F

perforated hardboard
tablero^M de fibra^F de madera^F
perforada

particleboard
aglomerado^M

plastic-laminated particleboard
aglomerado^M plastificado

accessories

accesorios^M

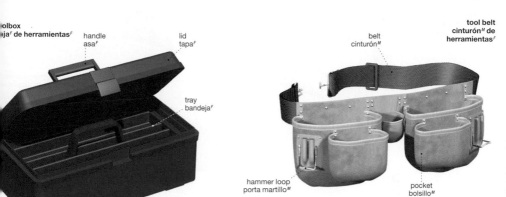

oolbox
aja^F **de herramientas^F**

handle
asa^F

lid
tapa^F

tray
bandeja^F

**tool belt
cinturón^M de
herramientas^F**

belt
cinturón^M

hammer loop
porta martillo^M

pocket
bolsillo^M

DO-IT-YOURSELF AND GARDENING

measuring and marking tools

herramientas^F de medida^F y marcado^M

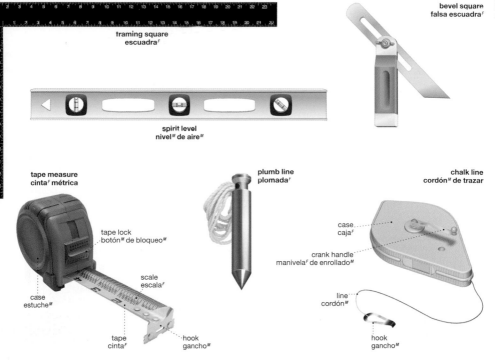

**bevel square
falsa escuadra^F**

**framing square
escuadra^F**

**spirit level
nivel^M de aire^M**

**tape measure
cinta^F métrica**

**plumb line
plomada^F**

**chalk line
cordón^M de trazar**

tape lock
botón^M de bloqueo^M

scale
escala^F

case
estuche^M

tape
cinta^F

hook
gancho^M

case
caja^F

crank handle
manivela^F de enrollado^M

line
cordón^M

hook
gancho^M

nailing tools

herramientas^F de clavado^M

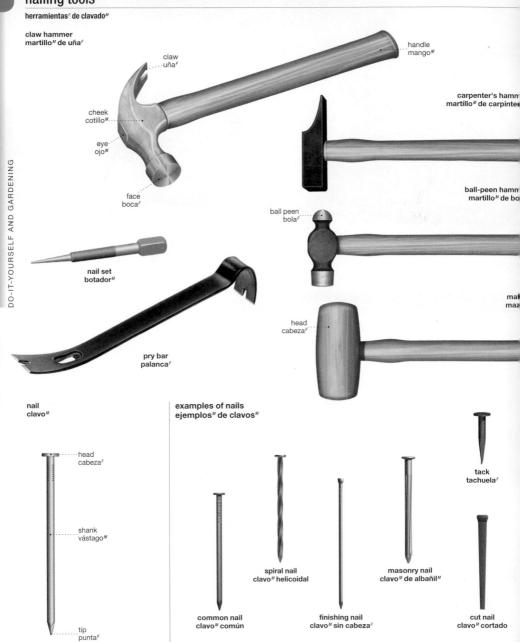

claw hammer
martillo^M de uña^F

claw
uña^F

handle
mango^M

cheek
cotillo^M

eye
ojo^M

face
boca^F

carpenter's hamm
martillo^M de carpinter

ball-peen hamm
martillo^M de bo

ball peen
bola^F

nail set
botador^M

ma
maz

head
cabeza^F

pry bar
palanca^F

nail
clavo^M

head
cabeza^F

shank
vástago^M

tip
punta^F

examples of nails
ejemplos^M de clavos^M

spiral nail
clavo^M helicoidal

masonry nail
clavo^M de albañil^M

tack
tachuela^F

common nail
clavo^M común

finishing nail
clavo^M sin cabeza^F

cut nail
clavo^M cortado

nailgun
clavadora^M **de batería**^F

motor
motor^M

jam-clearing latch
desatascador^M

contact trip
seguro^M por contacto^M

trigger switch
interruptor^M de gatillo^M

magazine
cargador^M

strip of nails
banda^F de puntas^F

battery pack
batería^F

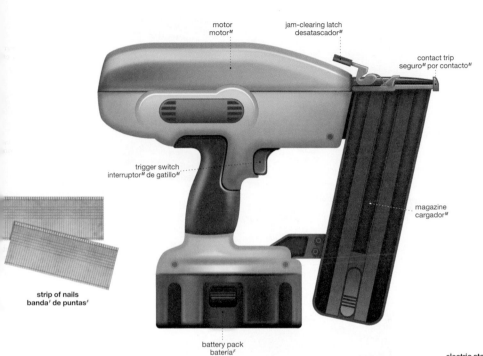

DO-IT-YOURSELF AND GARDENING

electric stapler
grapadora^F **eléctrica**

power cord
cable^M de alimentación^F

trigger switch
interruptor^M de gatillo^M

strip of staples
banda^F de grapas^F

magazine
cargador^M

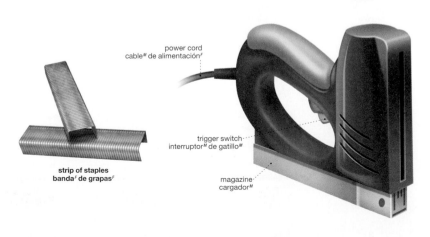

screwdriving tools

herramientasᶠ **de atornillado**ᴹ

screwdriver
destornilladorᴹ

shank
vástagoᴹ

blade
hojaᶠ

tip
puntaᶠ

handle
mangoᴹ

spiral screwdriver
destornilladorᴹ **de trinquete**ᴹ

ratchet
trinqueteᴹ

spiral
espiralᶠ

blade
hojaᶠ

handle
mangoᴹ

locking ring
anilloᴹ de ajusteᴹ

jaw
mordazaᶠ

chuck
mandrilᴹ

examples of tips
tiposᴹ **de puntas**ᶠ

square-headed tip
puntaᶠ **de caja**ᶠ **cuadrada**

Phillips-headed tip
puntaᶠ **cruciforme**

flat tip
puntaᶠ **de hoja**ᶠ **plana**

cordless screwdriver
destornilladorᴹ **inalámbrico**

reversing switch
inversorᴹ

handle
mangoᴹ

spring wing
mariposaᶠ de resorteᴹ

battery
bateríaᶠ

tip
puntaᶠ

bit
brocaᶠ

toggle bolt
pernoᴹ **para falso**
plafónᴹ

expansion bolt
pernoᴹ **de expansión**ᶠ

screw
tornilloᴹ

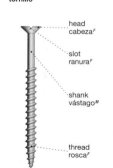

head
cabezaᶠ

slot
ranuraᶠ

shank
vástagoᴹ

thread
roscaᶠ

examples of heads
tiposᴹ **de cabeza**ᶠ

flat head
tornilloᴹ **de cabeza**ᶠ
avellanada

round head
tornilloᴹ **de cabeza**ᶠ
redonda

one-way head
tornilloᴹ **de un solo**
sentidoᴹ

Phillips head
tornilloᴹ **cruciforme**
(Phillips)

socket head
tornilloᴹ **de caja**ᶠ **cuadrada**

oval head
tornilloᴹ **de cabeza**ᶠ
achaflanada

sawing tools
herramientas^f de serrado^M

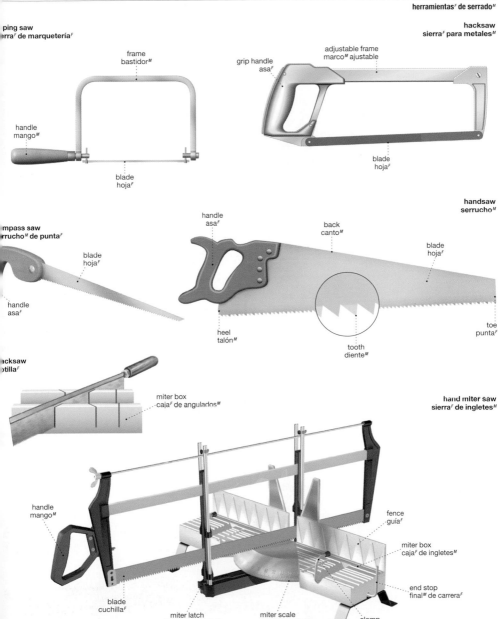

ping saw
erra^f de marquetería^f

hacksaw
sierra^f para metales^M

frame
bastidor^M

adjustable frame
marco^M ajustable

grip handle
asa^f

handle
mango^M

blade
hoja^f

blade
hoja^f

mpass saw
rrucho^M de punta^f

handle
asa^f

back
canto^M

handsaw
serrucho^M

blade
hoja^f

blade
hoja^f

handle
asa^f

toe
punta^f

heel
talón^M

tooth
diente^M

acksaw
tilla^f

miter box
caja^f de angulados^M

hand miter saw
sierra^f de ingletes^M

handle
mango^M

fence
guía^f

miter box
caja^f de ingletes^M

end stop
final^M de carrera^f

blade
cuchilla^f

miter latch
pestillo^M de ingletes^M

miter scale
escala^f de ingletes^M

clamp
mordaza^f

DO-IT-YOURSELF AND GARDENING

sawing tools

DO-IT-YOURSELF AND GARDENING

circular saw
sierra^F circular de mano^F

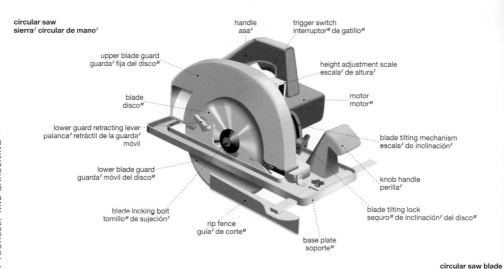

handle
asa^F

trigger switch
interruptor^M de gatillo^M

upper blade guard
guarda^F fija del disco^M

height adjustment scale
escala^F de altura^F

blade
disco^M

motor
motor^M

lower guard retracting lever
palanca^F retráctil de la guarda^F
móvil

blade tilting mechanism
escala^F de inclinación^F

lower blade guard
guarda^F móvil del disco^M

knob handle
perilla^F

blade locking bolt
tornillo^M de sujeción^F

rip fence
guía^F de corte^M

base plate
soporte^M

blade tilting lock
seguro^M de inclinación^F del disco^M

circular saw blade
disco^M

electric miter saw
sierra^F ingletadora eléctrica

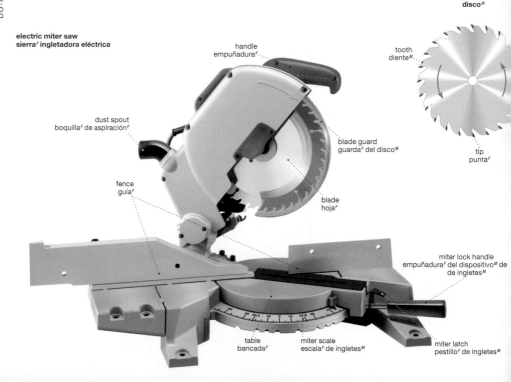

handle
empuñadura^F

tooth
diente^M

dust spout
boquilla^F de aspiración^F

blade guard
guarda^F del disco^M

tip
punta^F

fence
guía^F

blade
hoja^F

miter lock handle
empuñadura^F del dispositivo^M de
de ingletes^M

table
bancada^F

miter scale
escala^F de ingletes^M

miter latch
pestillo^F de ingletes^M

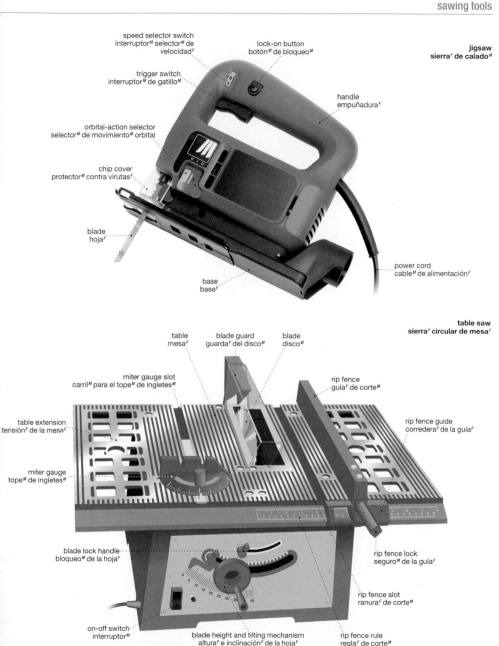

jigsaw
sierra^F de calado^M

speed selector switch
interruptor^M selector^M de
velocidad^F

lock-on button
botón^M de bloqueo^M

trigger switch
interruptor^M de gatillo^M

handle
empuñadura^F

orbital-action selector
selector^M de movimiento^M orbital

chip cover
protector^M contra virutas^F

blade
hoja^F

power cord
cable^M de alimentación^F

base
base^F

table saw
sierra^F circular de mesa^F

table
mesa^F

blade guard
guarda^F del disco^M

blade
disco^M

miter gauge slot
carril^M para el tope^M de ingletes^M

rip fence
guía^F de corte^M

table extension
tensión^F de la mesa^F

rip fence guide
corredera^F de la guía^F

miter gauge
tope^M de ingletes^M

blade lock handle
bloqueo^M de la hoja^F

rip fence lock
seguro^M de la guía^F

rip fence slot
ranura^F de corte^M

on-off switch
interruptor^M

blade height and tilting mechanism
altura^F e inclinación^F de la hoja^F

rip fence rule
regla^F de corte^M

DO-IT-YOURSELF AND GARDENING

drilling tools

herramientas^F de taladrado^M

cordless drill/driver
taladro^M de batería^F

speed selector switch
selector^M de velocidad^F

torque adjustment collar
anillo^M de reglaje^M del par^M de apriete^M

screwdriver bit
broca^F de atornillado^M

keyless chuck
mandril^M de sujeción^F

trigger switch
interruptor^M de gatillo^M

reversing switch
inversor^M

battery pack
batería^F

battery pack
batería^F

charger
cargador^M

12V

electric drill
taladro^M eléctrico

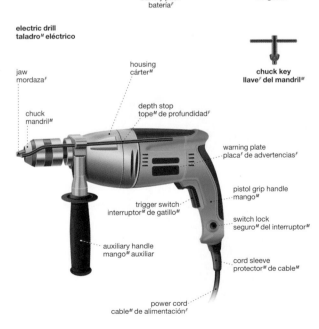

jaw
mordaza^F

chuck
mandril^M

housing
cárter^M

depth stop
tope^M de profundidad^F

warning plate
placa^F de advertencias^F

pistol grip handle
mango^M

trigger switch
interruptor^M de gatillo^M

switch lock
seguro^M del interruptor^M

auxiliary handle
mango^M auxiliar

cord sleeve
protector^M de cable^M

power cord
cable^M de alimentación^F

chuck key
llave^F del mandril^M

examples of bits and drills
ejemplos^M de brocas^F y
barrenas^F

twist bit
broca^F helicoidal

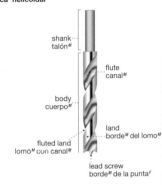

shank
talón^M

flute
canal^M

body
cuerpo^M

land
borde^M del lomo^M

fluted land
lomo^M con canal^M

lead screw
borde^M de la punta^F

solid center auger bit
broca^F helicoidal central

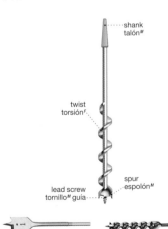

shank
talón^M

twist
torsión^F

lead screw
tornillo^M guía

spur
espolón^M

spade bit
broca^F de pala^F

double-twist auger bit
broca^F salomónica de canal^M
angosto

masonry drill
barrena^F de muro^M

twist drill
broca^F helicoidal

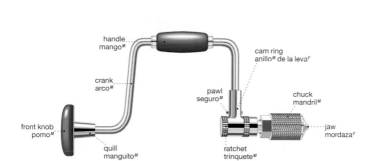

hand drill
taladro*M* **de mano***F*

turning handle
manivela*F*

side handle
perilla*F*

main handle
mango*M*

jaw
mordaza*F*

drill
broca*F*

chuck
mandril*M*

pinion
piñón*M*

drive wheel
cremallera*F*

brace
berbiquí*M*

handle
mango*M*

cam ring
anillo*M* de la leva*F*

crank
arco*M*

pawl
seguro*M*

chuck
mandril*M*

front knob
pomo*M*

jaw
mordaza*F*

quill
manguito*M*

ratchet
trinquete*M*

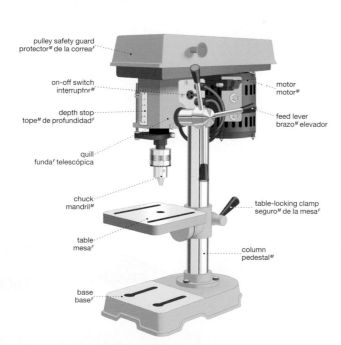

drill press
taladro*M* **vertical**

pulley safety guard
protector*M* de la correa*F*

on-off switch
interruptor*M*

depth stop
tope*M* de profundidad*F*

quill
funda*F* telescópica

chuck
mandril*M*

table
mesa*F*

base
base*F*

motor
motor*M*

feed lever
brazo*M* elevador

table-locking clamp
seguro*M* de la mesa*F*

column
pedestal*M*

DO-IT-YOURSELF AND GARDENING

shaping tools
herramientas^F de lijado^M

random orbit sander
lijadora^F excéntrica

angle grind
amoladora^F de ángul

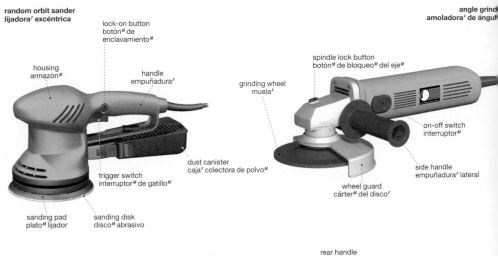

lock-on button
botón^M de
enclavamiento^M

housing
armazón^M

handle
empuñadura^F

spindle lock button
botón^M de bloqueo^M del eje^M

grinding wheel
muela^F

on-off switch
interruptor^M

dust canister
caja^F colectora de polvo^M

trigger switch
interruptor^M de gatillo^M

side handle
empuñadura^F lateral

wheel guard
cárter^M del disco^F

sanding pad
plato^M lijador

sanding disk
disco^M abrasivo

belt sander
lijadora^F de banda^F

trigger switch
interruptor^M de gatillo^M

rear handle
mango^M trasero

dust collection bag
bolsa^F del polvo^M

front handle
mango^M delantero

cord sleeve
protector^M de cable^M

power cord
cordón^M de alimentació

small pulley
rodillo^M pequeño

large pulley
rodillo^M principal

abrasive belt
banda^F de lija^F

timing belt
correa^F

tension release lever
palanca^F de liberación^F de
tensión^F

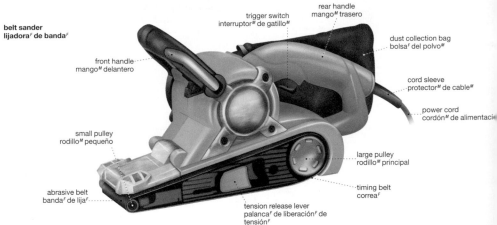

abrasive material
material^M de lijado^M

grinding wheel
muela^F

sanding disk
disco^M abrasivo

sandpaper
papel^M de lija^F

abrasive belt
banda^F de lija^F

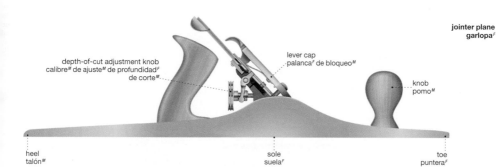

jointer plane
garlopa^F

depth-of-cut adjustment knob
calibre^M de ajuste^M de profundidad^F
de corte^M

lever cap
palanca^F de bloqueo^M

knob
pomo^M

heel
talón^M

sole
suela^F

toe
puntera^F

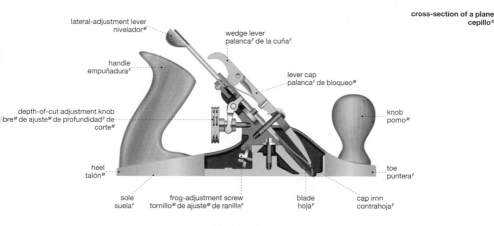

cross-section of a plane
cepillo^M

lateral-adjustment lever
nivelador^M

wedge lever
palanca^F de la cuña^F

handle
empuñadura^F

lever cap
palanca^F de bloqueo^M

depth-of-cut adjustment knob
bre^M de ajuste^M de profundidad^F de
corte^M

knob
pomo^M

heel
talón^M

toe
puntera^F

sole
suela^F

frog-adjustment screw
tornillo^M de ajuste^M de ranilla^F

blade
hoja^F

cap iron
contrahoja^F

electric plane
cepilladora^F **eléctrica**

trigger switch
interruptor^M de gatillo^M

dust outlet
salida^F de virutas^M

guide handle
mango^M guía^F

toothed belt cover
cubierta^F de la correa^F

sole
base^F

shaping tools

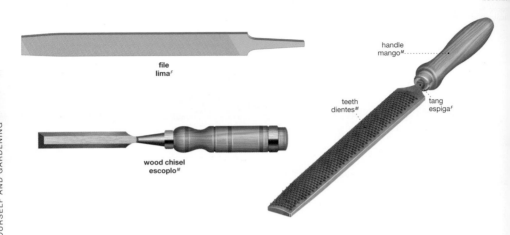

file
lima^F

handle
mango^M

teeth
dientes^M

tang
espiga^F

wood chisel
escoplo^M

DO-IT-YOURSELF AND GARDENING

router
fresadora^F

depth adjustment
ajuste^M de profundidad^F

motor
motor^M

power cord
cable^M de alimentación^F

on-off switch
interruptor^M

guide handle
asa^F

collet
collarín^M

chuck
mordaza^F

base
base^F

examples of bits
ejemplos^F **de fresas**^F

rounding-over bit
fresa^F **de redondeo**^M

rabbet bit
fresa^F **de acanalar**

core box bit
fresa^F **de enrasar**

dovetail bit
fresa^F **de cola**^F **de**
milano^M

cove bit
fresa^F **de caveto**^M

chamfer bit
fresa^F **de biselar**

gripping and tightening tools
herramientas^F de agarre^M

pliers
alicates^M

roove joint pliers
icates^M regulables

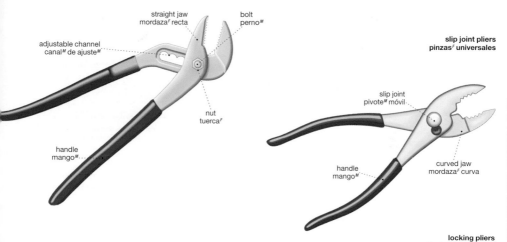

straight jaw
mordaza^F recta

bolt
perno^M

adjustable channel
canal^M de ajuste^M

nut
tuerca^F

handle
mango^M

slip joint pliers
pinzas^F universales

slip joint
pivote^M móvil

handle
mango^M

curved jaw
mordaza^F curva

locking pliers
alicates^M de presión^F

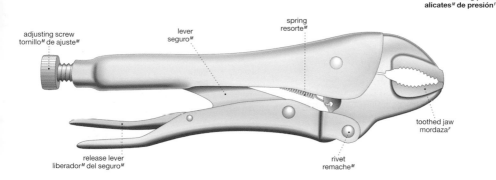

adjusting screw
tornillo^M de ajuste^M

lever
seguro^M

spring
resorte^M

release lever
liberador^M del seguro^M

rivet
remache^M

toothed jaw
mordaza^F

washers
arandelas^F

nternal tooth lock washer
dela^F de presión^F de dientes^M
internos

external tooth lock washer
arandela^F de presión^F de dientes^M
externos

lock washer
arandela^F de presión^F

flat washer
arandela^F plana

gripping and tightening tools

wrenches
llaves^F

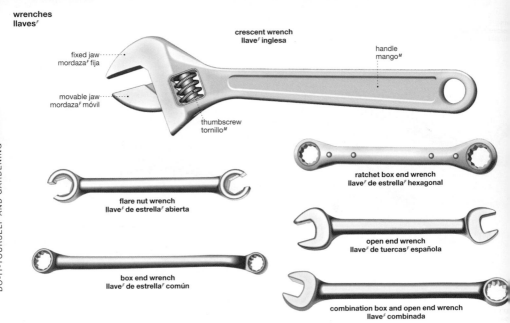

crescent wrench
llave^F inglesa

fixed jaw
mordaza^F fija

handle
mango^M

movable jaw
mordaza^F móvil

thumbscrew
tornillo^M

ratchet box end wrench
llave^F de estrella^F hexagonal

flare nut wrench
llave^F de estrella^F abierta

open end wrench
llave^F de tuercas^F española

box end wrench
llave^F de estrella^F común

combination box and open end wrench
llave^F combinada

ratchet socket wrench
llave^F **de carraca**^F

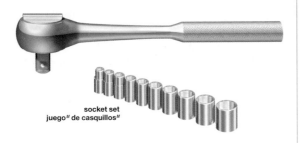

socket set
juego^M de casquillos^M

bolts
pernos^M

bolt
perno^M

nut
tuerca^F

head
cabeza^F

shoulder bolt
perno^M con collarín^M

threaded rod
rosca^F

shoulder
collarín^M

nuts
tuercas^F

hex nut
tuerca^F hexagonal

acorn nut
tuerca^F cerrada

wing nut
tuerca^F de mariposa^F

gripping and tightening tools

vise
orno^M de banco^M

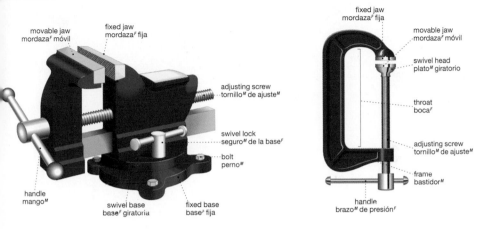

movable jaw
mordaza^F móvil

fixed jaw
mordaza^F fija

adjusting screw
tornillo^M de ajuste^M

swivel lock
seguro^M de la base^F

bolt
perno^M

handle
mango^M

swivel base
base^F giratoria

fixed base
base^F fija

**C-clamp
prensa^F en C**

fixed jaw
mordaza^F fija

movable jaw
mordaza^F móvil

swivel head
plato^M giratorio

throat
boca^F

adjusting screw
tornillo^M de ajuste^M

frame
bastidor^M

handle
brazo^M de presión^F

pipe clamp
sargento^M

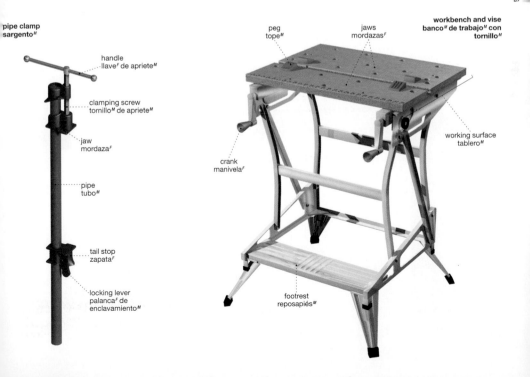

handle
llave^F de apriete^M

clamping screw
tornillo^M de apriete^M

jaw
mordaza^F

pipe
tubo^M

tail stop
zapata^F

locking lever
palanca^F de
enclavamiento^M

peg
tope^M

jaws
mordazas^F

**workbench and vise
banco^M de trabajo^M con
tornillo^M**

crank
manivela^F

working surface
tablero^M

footrest
reposapiés^M

plumbing tools

herramientas^f de fontanería^f

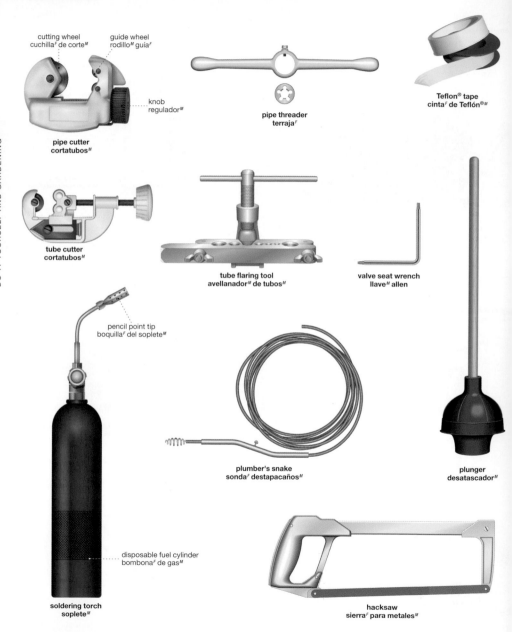

cutting wheel
cuchilla^f de corte^M

guide wheel
rodillo^M guía^f

knob
regulador^M

pipe cutter
cortatubos^M

pipe threader
terraja^f

Teflon® tape
cinta^f de Teflón®^M

tube cutter
cortatubos^M

tube flaring tool
avellanador^M de tubos^M

valve seat wrench
llave^M allen

pencil point tip
boquilla^f del soplete^M

plumber's snake
sonda^f destapacaños^M

plunger
desatascador^M

disposable fuel cylinder
bombona^f de gas^M

soldering torch
soplete^M

hacksaw
sierra^f para metales^M

DO-IT-YOURSELF AND GARDENING

plumbing tools

wrenches
llaves^F

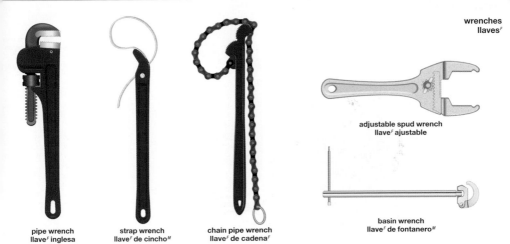

pipe wrench
llave^F inglesa

strap wrench
llave^F de cincho^M

chain pipe wrench
llave^F de cadena^F

adjustable spud wrench
llave^F ajustable

basin wrench
llave^F de fontanero^M

masonry tools

herramientas^F de albañilería^F

caulking gun
pistola^F para calafateo^M

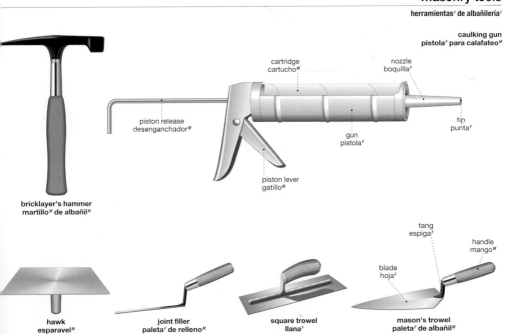

cartridge
cartucho^M

nozzle
boquilla^F

piston release
desenganchador^M

tip
punta^F

gun
pistola^F

piston lever
gatillo^M

bricklayer's hammer
martillo^M de albañil^M

tang
espiga^F

handle
mango^M

blade
hoja^F

hawk
esparavel^M

joint filler
paleta^F de relleno^M

square trowel
llana^F

mason's trowel
paleta^F de albañil^M

electrical tools

herramientas^F de electricista^F

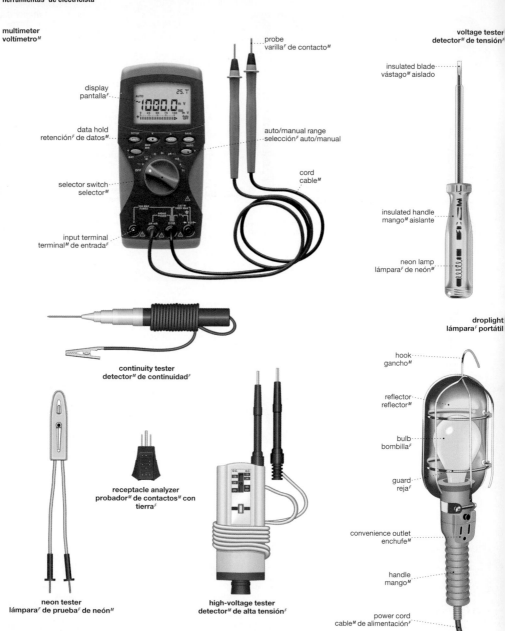

multimeter
voltímetro^M

probe
varilla^F de contacto^M

display
pantalla^F

data hold
retención^F de datos^M

auto/manual range
selección^F auto/manual

selector switch
selector^M

cord
cable^M

input terminal
terminal^M de entrada^F

voltage tester
detector^M de tensión^F

insulated blade
vástago^M aislado

insulated handle
mango^M aislante

neon lamp
lámpara^F de neón^M

continuity tester
detector^M de continuidad^F

droplight
lámpara^F portátil

hook
gancho^M

reflector
reflector^M

bulb
bombilla^F

guard
reja^F

receptacle analyzer
probador^M de contactos^M con tierra^F

convenience outlet
enchufe^M

handle
mango^M

neon tester
lámpara^F de prueba^F de neón^M

high-voltage tester
detector^M de alta tensión^F

power cord
cable^M de alimentación^F

DO-IT-YOURSELF AND GARDENING

electrical tools

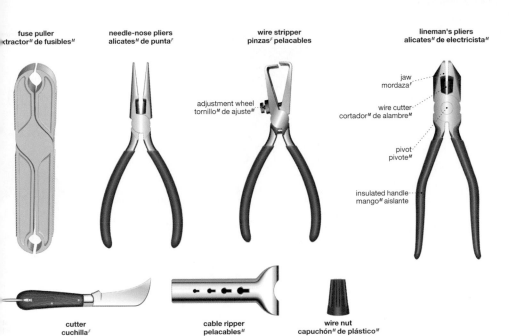

fuse puller
xtractor^M de fusibles^M

needle-nose pliers
alicates^M de punta^F

wire stripper
pinzas^F pelacables

adjustment wheel
tornillo^M de ajuste^M

lineman's pliers
alicates^M de electricista^M

jaw
mordaza^F

wire cutter
cortador^M de alambre^M

pivot
pivote^M

insulated handle
mango^M aislante

cutter
cuchilla^F

cable ripper
pelacables^M

wire nut
capuchón^M de plástico^M

DO-IT-YOURSELF AND GARDENING

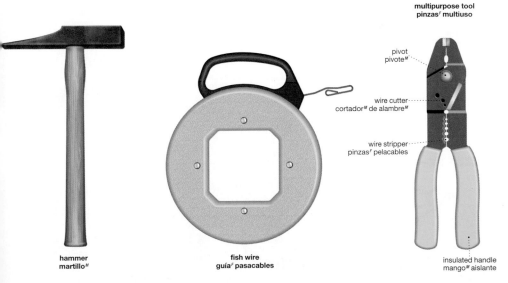

multipurpose tool
pinzas^F multiuso

pivot
pivote^M

wire cutter
cortador^M de alambre^M

wire stripper
pinzas^F pelacables

hammer
martillo^M

fish wire
guía^F pasacables

insulated handle
mango^M aislante

soldering tools

material^M de soldadura^M

soldering gun
pistola^F para soldar

tip
punta^F

housing
caja^F

heating element
resistencia^F

on-off switch
interruptor^M

pistol grip handle
mango^M

soldering iron
soldador^M

power cord
cable^M de alimentación^F

welding curtain
biombo^M para soldar

solder
estaño^M de soldar

tip cleaners
limpiador^M de boquillas^F

striker
encendedor^M

friction strip
frotador^M

flint
pedernal^M

arc welding
equipo^M de soldadura^F eléctrica

electrode holder
pinza^F del electrodo^M

electrode lead
cable^M de corriente^F

electrode
electrodo^M

work lead
cable^M de tierra^F

ground clamp
pinza^F de conexión^F a
tierra^F

arc welder
máquina^F de soldar eléctrica

protective clothing
ropa^F de protección^M

goggles
gafas^F protectoras

face shield
careta^F

hand shield
careta^F de mano^F

gauntlet
guantes^M

mitten
manoplas^F

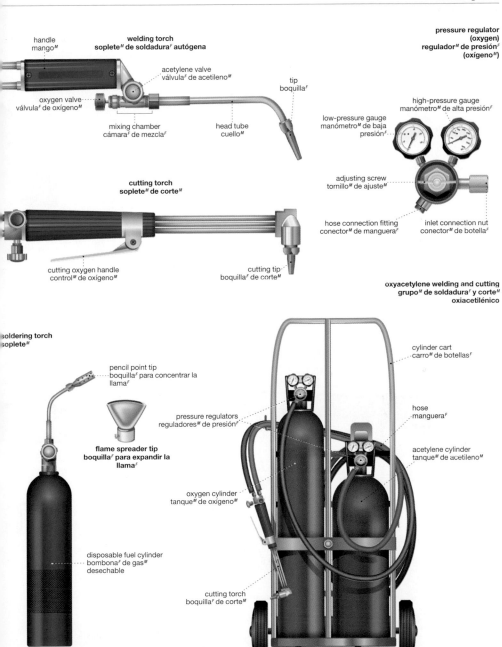

handle
mango^M

**welding torch
soplete^M de soldadura^F autógena**

acetylene valve
válvula^F de acetileno^M

tip
boquilla^F

oxygen valve
válvula^F de oxígeno^M

mixing chamber
cámara^F de mezcla^F

head tube
cuello^M

**pressure regulator
(oxygen)
regulador^M de presión^F
(oxígeno^M)**

high-pressure gauge
manómetro^M de alta presión^F

low-pressure gauge
manómetro^M de baja
presión^F

adjusting screw
tornillo^M de ajuste^M

hose connection fitting
conector^M de manguera^F

inlet connection nut
conector^M de botella^F

**cutting torch
soplete^M de corte^M**

cutting oxygen handle
control^M de oxígeno^M

cutting tip
boquilla^F de corte^M

**oxyacetylene welding and cutting
grupo^M de soldadura^F y corte^M
oxiacetilénico**

soldering torch
soplete^M

pencil point tip
boquilla^F para concentrar la
llama^F

cylinder cart
carro^M de botellas^F

pressure regulators
reguladores^M de presión^F

hose
manguera^F

**flame spreader tip
boquilla^F para expandir la
llama^F**

acetylene cylinder
tanque^M de acetileno^M

oxygen cylinder
tanque^M de oxígeno^M

disposable fuel cylinder
bombona^F de gas^M
desechable

cutting torch
boquilla^F de corte^M

DO-IT-YOURSELF AND GARDENING

painting material
material^M de pintura^F

spray paint gun
pistola^F de pintar

spreader adjustment screw
válvula^F de ajuste^M

fluid adjustment screw
regulador^M de fluidos^M

nozzle
boquilla^F

air cap
anillo^M de ajuste^M

air valve
válvula^F de aire^M

trigger
gatillo^M

gun body
empuñadura^F de pistola^F

vent hole
orificio^M de entrada^F de
aire^M

air hose connection
conexión^F para la manguera^F de
aire^M

container
depósito^M de pintura^F

brush
brocha^F

handle
mango^M

ferrule
collar^M

bristles
cerdas^F

air compressor
compresor^M de aire^M

pump
bomba^F

motor
motor^M

handle
empuñadura^F

air tank
tanque^M de aire^M

wheel
rueda^F

scraper
rasqueta^F

knurled bolt
tornillo^M

blade
hoja^F

handle
mango^M

heat gun
pistola^F de calor^M

nozzle
boquilla^F

on-off switch
interruptor^M

tray
bandeja^F de pintura^F

paint roller
rodillo^M de pintor^M

handle
mango^M

roller frame
armazón^M

roller cover
rodillo^M

ladders

escaleras^F

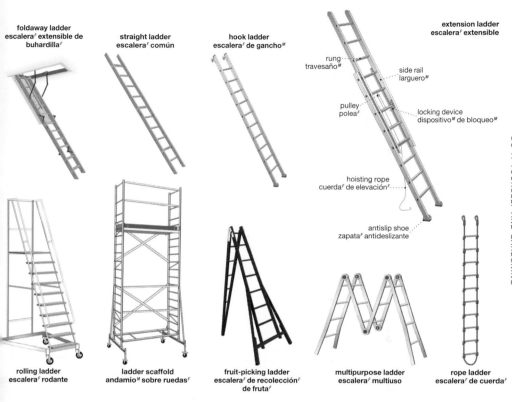

foldaway ladder
escalera^F extensible de buhardilla^F

straight ladder
escalera^F común

hook ladder
escalera^F de gancho^M

extension ladder
escalera^F extensible

rung
travesaño^M

side rail
larguero^M

pulley
polea^F

locking device
dispositivo^M de bloqueo^M

hoisting rope
cuerda^F de elevación^F

antislip shoe
zapata^F antideslizante

rolling ladder
escalera^F rodante

ladder scaffold
andamio^M sobre ruedas^F

fruit-picking ladder
escalera^F de recolección^F de fruta^F

multipurpose ladder
escalera^F multiuso

rope ladder
escalera^F de cuerda^F

DO-IT-YOURSELF AND GARDENING

stepladders

escalera^F de mano^F

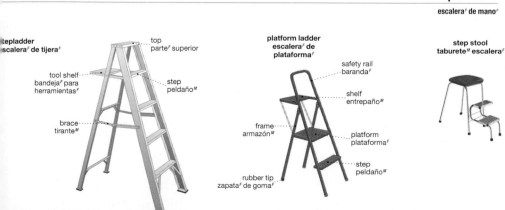

stepladder
escalera^F de tijera^F

top
parte^F superior

tool shelf
bandeja^F para herramientas^F

step
peldaño^M

brace
tirante^M

platform ladder
escalera^F de plataforma^F

safety rail
baranda^F

shelf
entrepaño^M

frame
armazón^M

platform
plataforma^F

step
peldaño^M

rubber tip
zapata^F de goma^F

step stool
taburete^M escalera^F

garden

jardín^M

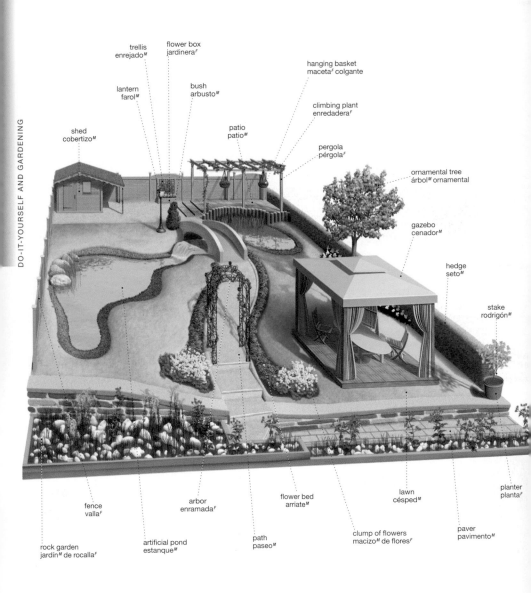

trellis
enrejado^M

flower box
jardinera^F

hanging basket
maceta^F colgante

lantern
farol^M

bush
arbusto^M

climbing plant
enredadera^F

shed
cobertizo^M

patio
patio^M

pergola
pérgola^F

ornamental tree
árbol^M ornamental

gazebo
cenador^M

hedge
seto^M

stake
rodrigón^M

fence
valla^F

arbor
enramada^F

flower bed
arriate^M

lawn
césped^M

planter
planta^F

rock garden
jardín^M de rocalla^F

artificial pond
estanque^M

path
paseo^M

clump of flowers
macizo^M de flores^F

paver
pavimento^M

miscellaneous equipment

equipamiento^M vario

leaf blower
soplador^M de hojas^F

motorized earth auger
taladro^M de motor^M

DO-IT-YOURSELF AND GARDENING

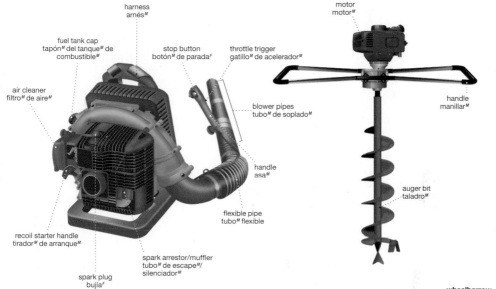

harness
arnés^M

motor
motor^M

fuel tank cap
tapón^M del tanque^M de
combustible^M

stop button
botón^M de parada^F

throttle trigger
gatillo^M de acelerador^M

air cleaner
filtro^M de aire^M

blower pipes
tubo^M de soplado^M

handle
manillar^M

handle
asa^M

recoil starter handle
tirador^M de arranque^M

flexible pipe
tubo^M flexible

auger bit
taladro^M

spark arrestor/muffler
tubo^M de escape^M/
silenciador^M

spark plug
bujía^F

wheelbarrow
carretilla^F

compost bin
cajón^M de abono^M compuesto

tray
caja^F

handle
brazo^M

leg
pata^F

wheel
rueda^F

tools for loosening the earth

herramientasⁱ para remover la tierraⁱ

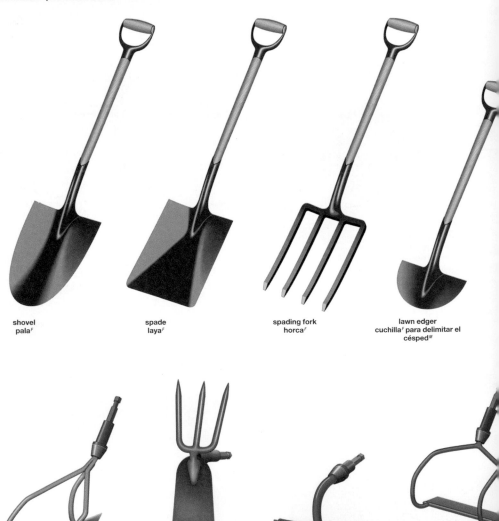

shovel
palaᶠ

spade
layaᶠ

spading fork
horcaᶠ

lawn edger
cuchillaᶠ para delimitar el
céspedᴹ

weeding hoe
cultivadorᴹ

hoe-fork
azuelaᶠ

draw hoe
azadaᶠ

collinear hoe
azadaᶠ de doble filoᴹ

tools for loosening the earth

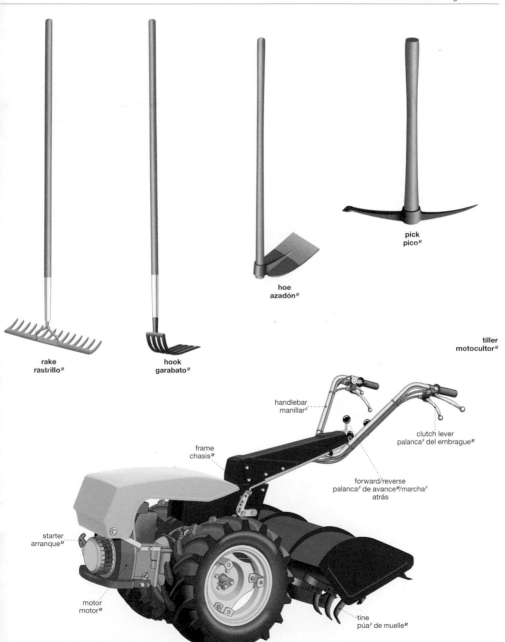

pick
pico^M

hoe
azadón^M

tiller
motocultor^M

rake
rastrillo^M

hook
garabato^M

handlebar
manillar^F

clutch lever
palanca^F del embrague^M

frame
chasis^M

forward/reverse
palanca^F de avance^M/marcha^F
atrás

starter
arranque^M

motor
motor^M

tine
púa^F de muelle^M

DO-IT-YOURSELF AND GARDENING

watering tools

herramientas^F para regar

hose reel cart
carro^M de enrollado^M de
manguera^F

sprinkler hos
manguera^F de riego

garden hose
manguera^F

hand crank
manivela^F

reel
carrete^M

tap connector
toma^F

hose nozzle
boquilla^F de riego^M

bottle sprayer
pulverizador^M

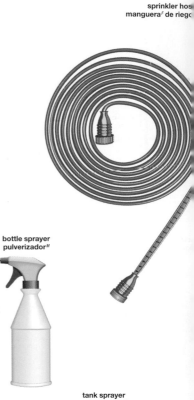

watering can
regadera^F

rose
roseta^F

handle
asa^F

tank sprayer
pulverizador^M

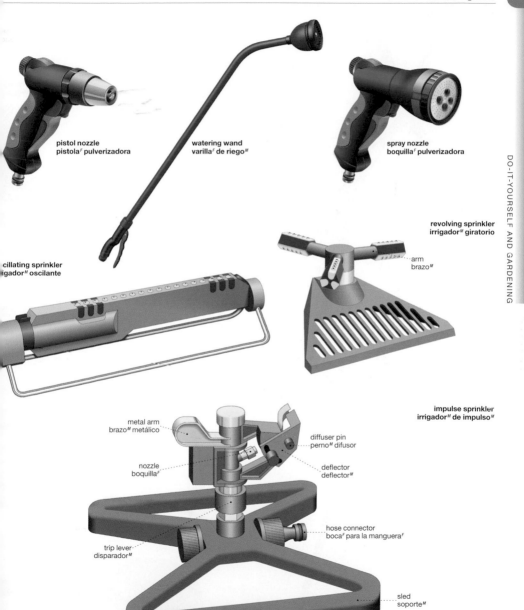

DO-IT-YOURSELF AND GARDENING

pistol nozzle
pistola^F pulverizadora

watering wand
varilla^F de riego^M

spray nozzle
boquilla^F pulverizadora

revolving sprinkler
irrigador^M giratorio

arm
brazo^M

cillating sprinkler
igador^M oscilante

impulse sprinkler
irrigador^M de impulso^M

metal arm
brazo^M metálico

diffuser pin
perno^M difusor

nozzle
boquilla^F

deflector
deflector^M

hose connector
boca^F para la manguera^F

trip lever
disparador^M

sled
soporte^M

pruning and cutting tools

herramientas^F para cortar

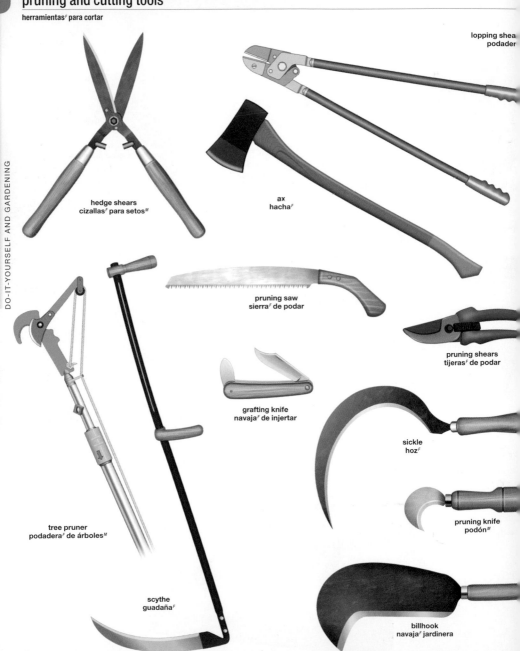

lopping shea
podader

hedge shears
cizallas^F para setos^M

ax
hacha^F

pruning saw
sierra^F de podar

pruning shears
tijeras^F de podar

grafting knife
navaja^F de injertar

sickle
hoz^F

pruning knife
podón^M

tree pruner
podadera^F de árboles^M

scythe
guadaña^F

billhook
navaja^F jardinera

pruning and cutting tools

hedge trimmer
cortasetosᴹ **eléctrico**

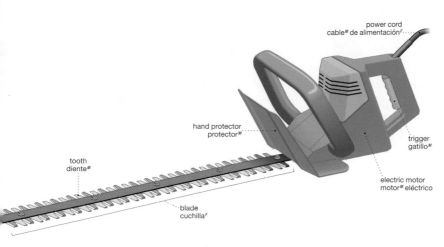

power cord
cable ᴹ de alimentación ᶠ

hand protector
protector ᴹ

trigger
gatillo ᴹ

electric motor
motor ᴹ eléctrico

tooth
diente ᴹ

blade
cuchilla ᶠ

chainsaw
sierraᶠ **de cadena**ᶠ

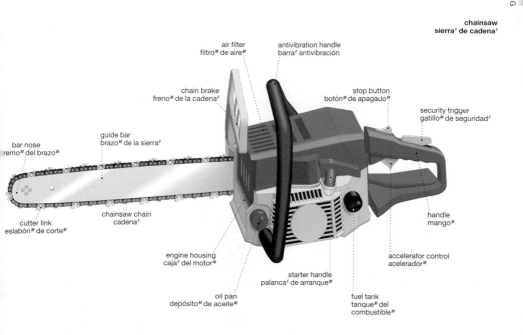

air filter
filtro ᴹ de aire ᴹ

antivibration handle
barra ᶠ antivibración

chain brake
freno ᴹ de la cadena ᶠ

stop button
botón ᴹ de apagado ᴹ

security trigger
gatillo ᴹ de seguridad ᶠ

bar nose
remo ᴹ del brazo ᴹ

guide bar
brazo ᴹ de la sierra ᶠ

cutter link
eslabón ᴹ de corte ᴹ

chainsaw chain
cadena ᶠ

handle
mango ᴹ

engine housing
caja ᶠ del motor ᴹ

accelerator control
acelerador ᴹ

starter handle
palanca ᶠ de arranque ᴹ

oil pan
depósito ᴹ de aceite ᴹ

fuel tank
tanque ᴹ del
combustible ᴹ

hand tools

juego^M de pequeñas herramientas^F

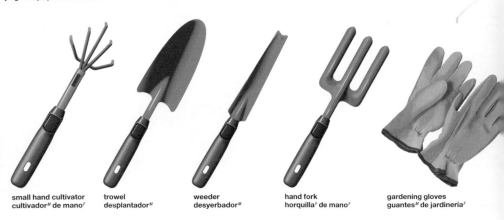

small hand cultivator
cultivador^M de mano^F

trowel
desplantador^M

weeder
desyerbador^M

hand fork
horquilla^F de mano^F

gardening gloves
guantes^M de jardinería^F

seeding and planting tools

herramientas^F para sembrar y plantar

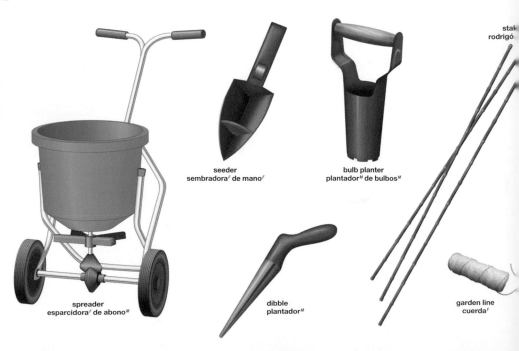

spreader
esparcidora^F de abono^M

seeder
sembradora^F de mano^F

bulb planter
plantador^M de bulbos^M

stak
rodrigó

dibble
plantador^M

garden line
cuerda^F

lawn care
cuidado^M **del césped**^M

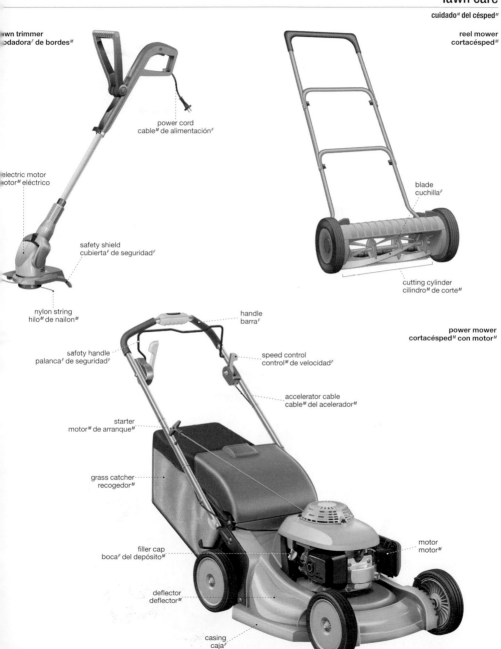

wn trimmer
odadora^F **de bordes**^M

power cord
cable^M de alimentación^F

electric motor
motor^M eléctrico

safety shield
cubierta^F de seguridad^F

nylon string
hilo^M de nailon^M

reel mower
cortacésped^M

blade
cuchilla^F

cutting cylinder
cilindro^M de corte^M

handle
barra^F

safoty handle
palanca^F de seguridad^F

speed control
control^M de velocidad^F

power mower
cortacésped^M **con motor**^M

accelerator cable
cable^M del acelerador^M

starter
motor^M de arranque^M

grass catcher
recogedor^M

filler cap
boca^F del depósito^M

motor
motor^M

deflector
deflector^M

casing
caja^F

DO-IT-YOURSELF AND GARDENING

lawn care

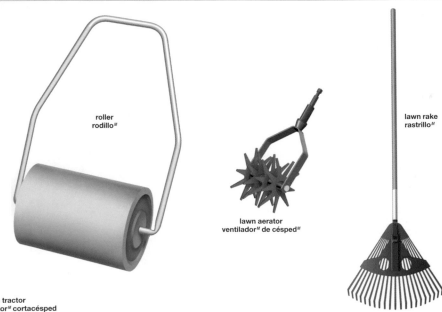

roller
rodillo^M

lawn aerator
ventilador^M de césped^M

lawn rake
rastrillo^M

lawn tractor
tractor^M cortacésped

seat
asiento^M

ignition key
llave^M de inyección^F

steering wheel
volante^F

brake pedal
pedal^M del freno^M

mower deck lift lever
palanca^F de levantamiento^M del tablero^M
de corte^M

cruise control lever
regulador^M de velocidad^F

hood
capó^M

rear wheel
rueda^F trasera

headlight
faro^M

forward travel pedal
pedal^M de marcha^M atrás

reverse travel pedal
pedal^M de marcha^F
adelante

deflector
deflector^M

front wheel
rueda^F frontal

mower deck
plataforma^F de corte^M

gauge wheel
rueda^F de calibrado^M

snow removal tools
herramientas^F de retirada^F de nieve^F

DO-IT-YOURSELF AND GARDENING

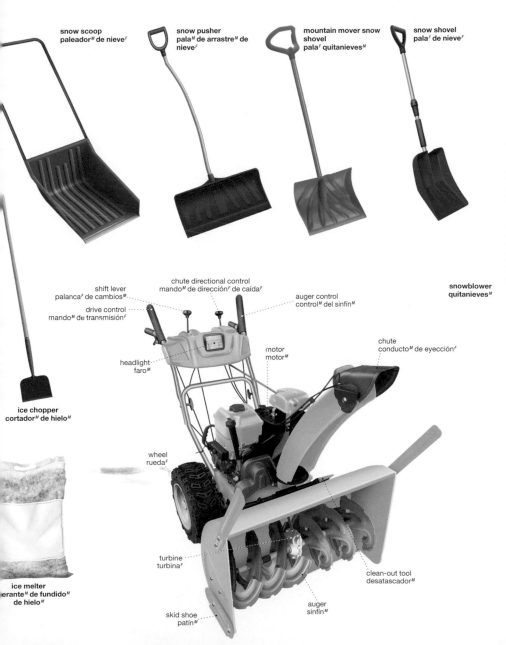

snow scoop
paleador^M de nieve^F

snow pusher
pala^M de arrastre^M de
nieve^F

mountain mover snow
shovel
pala^F quitanieves^M

snow shovel
pala^F de nieve^F

shift lever
palanca^F de cambios^M

chute directional control
mando^M de dirección^F de caída^F

auger control
control^M del sinfín^M

drive control
mando^M de transmisión^F

snowblower
quitanieves^M

headlight
faro^M

motor
motor^M

chute
conducto^M de eyección^F

ice chopper
cortador^M de hielo^M

wheel
rueda^F

ice melter
erante^M de fundido^M
de hielo^M

turbine
turbina^F

clean-out tool
desatascador^M

auger
sinfín^M

skid shoe
patín^M

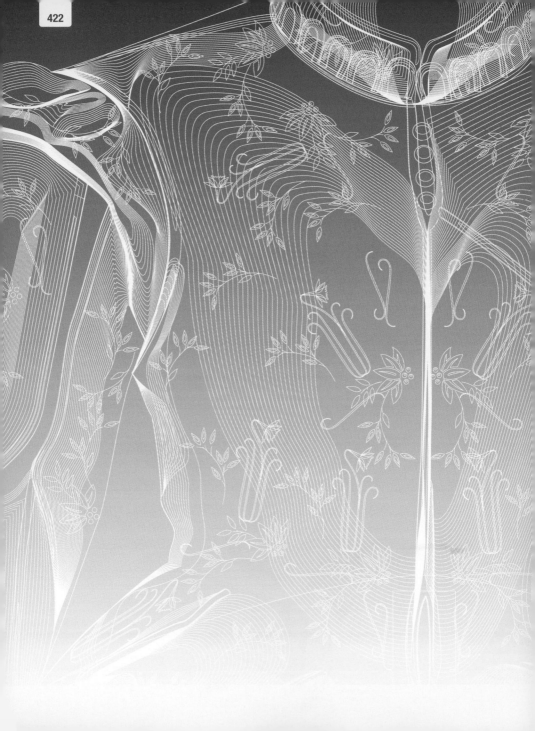

CLOTHING
vestido

XTILES 424

fibers 424
woven goods 424
fabric care symbols 425

STORICAL CLOTHES 426

examples of ancient costumes 426
examples of traditional clothing 429

EN'S CLOTHING 430

jackets 430
shirt 431
pants 432
sock 433
underwear 434
coats 435

NISEX CLOTHING 437

sweaters 437

WOMEN'S CLOTHING 438

dresses 438
skirts 439
tops 440
pants 441
jackets, vest and sweaters 442
coats 442
underwear 444
hose 446
nightclothes 447

SPECIALTY CLOTHING 448

children's clothing 448
sportswear 450

DESIGN AND FINISHING 452

pockets 452
sleeves 452
pleats 454
collars 454
necks 456
necklines 456

HEADGEAR 457

men's headgear 457
women's headgear 458
unisex headgear 458

SHOES 459

men's shoes 459
women's shoes 460
unisex shoes 462
accessories 463

DRESS ACCESSORIES 464

gloves 464
miscellaneous accessories 465

CLOTHING

fibers

fibras^F

natural fibers
fibras^F naturales

cotton
algodón^M

flax
lino^M

hemp
cáñamo^M

jute
yute^M

silk
seda^F

wool
lana^F

synthetic fibers
fibras^F sintéticas

polyester
poliéster^M

viscose
viscosa^F

nylon
nailon^M

acrylic fiber
fibra^F acrílica

spandex
spandex^M

woven goods

tejidos^M

flannel
franela^F

denim
tela^F vaquera

satin
satén^M

serge
sarga^F

tulle
tul^M

velvet
terciopelo^M

tweed
tweed^M

fabric care symbols

símbolos^M del cuidado^M de los tejidos^M

do not wash
no lavar

hand wash in lukewarm water
lavar a mano^F con agua^F tibia

machine wash in lukewarm water at a gentle setting/reduced
agitation
lavar a máquina^F con agua^F tibia en el ciclo^M para ropa^F delicada

machine wash in warm water at a gentle setting/
reduced agitation
lavar a máquina^F con agua^F caliente en el ciclo^M para
ropa^F delicada

machine wash in warm water at a normal setting
lavar a máquina^F con agua^F caliente, en el ciclo^M
normal

machine wash in hot water at a normal setting
lavar en lavadora^F con agua^F muy caliente, en el ciclo^M normal

do not use chlorine bleach
no blanquear con cloro

use chlorine bleach as directed
blanquear con cloro^M, siguiendo las indicaciones^F

CLOTHING

hang to dry
colgar al aire^M libre después de escurrir

dry flat
secar extendido sobre una toalla^F
después de escurrir

do not tumble dry
no secar en secadora^F
mecánica

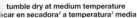

tumble dry at medium temperature
secar en secadora^F a temperatura^F media

tumble dry at low temperature
secar en secadora^F a baja temperatura^F

drip dry
secar sin escurrir

do not iron
no planchar

iron at low setting
usar plancha^F tibia

iron at medium setting
usar plancha^F caliente

iron at high setting
usar plancha^F muy caliente

American symbols
símbolos^M americanos

European symbols
símbolos^M europeos

examples of ancient costumes

ejemplos^M de trajes^M antiguos

peplos
peplo^M

fibula
fíbula^F

fold
pliegue^M

loincloth
taparrabos^M

toga
toga^F

sinus
seno^M

purple border
orla^F de púrpura^F

stola
stola^F

palla
palla^F

chlamys
clámide^F

chiton
quitón^M

examples of ancient costumes

vertical pocket
bolsillo^M vertical

floating sleeve
manga^F flotante

cotehardie
túnica^F de manga^F larga

farthingale
verdugado^M

short sleeve
manga^F corta

sleeve
manga^F

fringe
orla^F

dress with crinoline
vestido^M con crinolina^F

corset
corsé^M

underskirt
enaguas^F

shawl
chal^M

caraco jacket
blusa^F caracó

ruffle
manga^F de volante^M

stomacher
peto^M

bustle
polisón^M

surcoat
sobreveste^M

dress with panniers
vestido^M con miriñaque^M

dress with bustle
vestido^M con polisón^M

CLOTHING

examples of ancient costumes

frock coat costume
traje^M **con frack**^{M}

frock coat
levita^F

waistcoat
chaleco^M

breeches
calzones^M

justaucorps costume
traje^M **justaucorps**

justaucorps
casaca^F

vest
chaleco^M

cuff
puño^M

breeches
calzones^M

cape
capa^F

jacket
aljuba^F

houppelande
toga^F

doublet suit
traje^M **jublot**

doublet
jubón^M

wing
hombrera^F

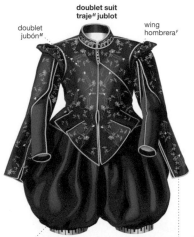

trunk hose
gregüescos^M

hanging sleeve
manga^F colgante

braies
calzas^F

examples of ancient costumes

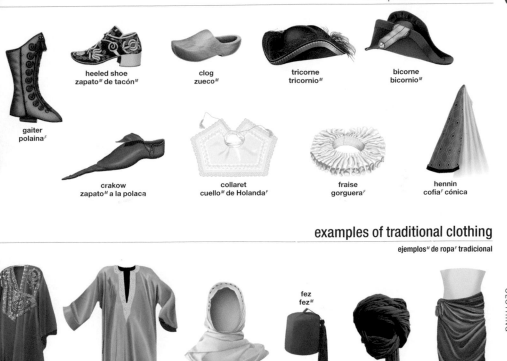

gaiter
polaina^F

heeled shoe
zapato^M de tacón^M

clog
zueco^M

tricorne
tricornio^M

bicorne
bicornio^M

crakow
zapato^M a la polaca

collaret
cuello^M de Holanda^F

fraise
gorguera^F

hennin
cofia^F cónica

examples of traditional clothing
ejemplos^M de ropa^F tradicional

CLOTHING

boubou
boubou^M

caftan
caftán^M

hijab
hiyab^M

fez
fez^M

turban
turbante^M

sarong
pareo^M

yarmulke
yarmulke^M

moccasin
mocasín^M

kimono
quimono^M

qipao
qipao^M

sari
sari^M

sombrero
sombrero^M

jackets

chaquetas^F y chalecos^M

double-breasted jacket
chaqueta^F cruzada

collar
cuello^M

peaked lapel
solapa^F puntiaguda

lining
forro^M

breast welt pocket
bolsillo^M de ojal^M

sleeve
manga^F

flap
solapa^F

outside ticket pocket
bolsillo^M del cambio^M

patch pocket
bolsillo^M de parche^M

double-breasted
jacket: back
chaqueta^F cruzada :
espalda^F

side back vent
abertura^F trasera lateral

vest
chaleco^M

V-neck
cuello^M en V

lining
forro^M

welt
ribete^M

seam
costura^F

front
delantero^M

welt pocket
bolsillo^M de ribete^M

adjustable waist tab
trincha^F

single-breasted jacket
chaqueta^F recta

lining
forro^M

notch
muesca^F

lapel
solapa^F

pocket handkerchief
pañuelo^M de bolsillo^M

front
delantero^M

sleeve
manga^F

flap pocket
lsillo^M con cartera^F

single-breasted jacket:
back
chaqueta^F sin cruzar :
espalda^F

back
espalda^F

center back vent
abertura^F trasera central

CLOTHING

shirt

camisa^F

examples of collars
ejemplos^M de
cuellos^M

button-down collar
cuello^M con puntas^F
abotonadas

spread collar
cuello^M italiano

parts of a shirt
partes^F de una camisa^F

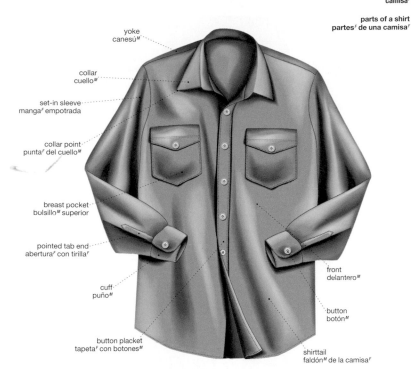

yoke
canesú^M

collar
cuello^M

set-in sleeve
manga^F empotrada

collar point
punta^F del cuello^M

breast pocket
bolsillo^M superior

pointed tab end
abertura^F con tirilla^F

cuff
puño^M

button placket
tapeta^F con botones^M

front
delantero^M

button
botón^M

shirttail
faldón^M de la camisa^F

accessories
accesorios^M

ascot tie
corbata^F inglesa

bow tie
pajarita^F

necktie
corbata^F

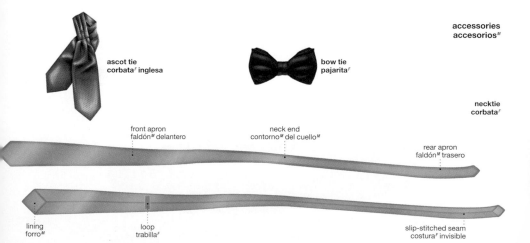

front apron
faldón^M delantero

neck end
contorno^M del cuello^M

rear apron
faldón^M trasero

lining
forro^M

loop
trabilla^F

slip-stitched seam
costura^F invisible

pants

pantalones^M

parts of pants
partes^F de pantalones^M

belt loop
trabilla^F

waistband extension
trabilla^F de la pretina^F

front top pocket
bolsillo^M delantero

knife pleat
pinza^F

waistband
pretina^F

fly
bragueta^F

crease
raya^F

cuff
vuelta^F

back pocket
bolsillo^M trasero

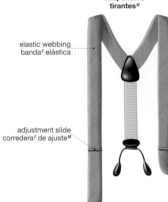

suspenders
tirantes^M

elastic webbing
banda^F elástica

adjustment slide
corredera^F de ajuste^M

leather end
lengüeta^F de cuero^M

button loop
presilla^F

suspender clip
pinza^F

belt
cinturón^M

panel
cuero^M

tip
punta^F

punch hole
ojete^M

belt loop
trabilla^F

tongue
pasador^M

buckle
hebilla^F

CLOTHING

pants

examples of pants
ejemplos^M de
pantalones^M

Bermuda shorts
bermudas^F

knickers
bragas^F

jeans
vaqueros^M

convertible pants
pantalones^M
convertibles

shorts
pantalones^M **cortos**

sock

calcetín^M

examples of socks
ejemplos^M de calcetines^M

arts of a sock
artes^F de un calcetín^M

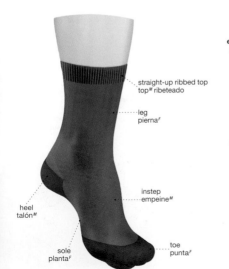

straight-up ribbed top
top^M ribeteado

leg
pierna^F

instep
empeine^M

heel
talón^M

sole
planta^F

toe
punta^F

executive length
calcetín^M largo
ejecutivo

ankle length
calcetín^M corto

anklet
tobillera^M

mid-calf length
calcetín^M **a media**
pantorrilla^F

underwear

ropa^F interior

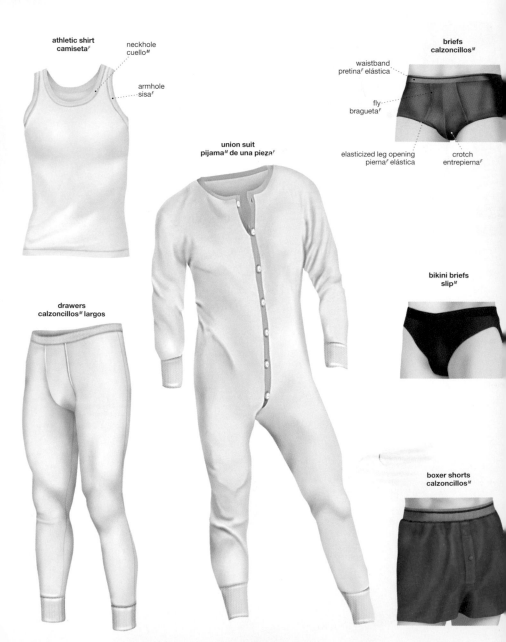

athletic shirt
camiseta^F

neckhole
cuello^M

armhole
sisa^F

briefs
calzoncillos^M

waistband
pretina^F elástica

fly
bragueta^F

elasticized leg opening
pierna^F elástica

crotch
entrepierna^F

union suit
pijama^M **de una pieza**^F

drawers
calzoncillos^M **largos**

bikini briefs
slip^M

boxer shorts
calzoncillos^M

CLOTHING

coats

raincoat
impermeable^M

collar
cuello^M

raglan sleeve
manga^F raglán

notched lapel
solapa^F con ojal^M

tab
lengüeta^F

d welt side pocket
^M de ribete^M ancho

buttonhole
ojal^M

side panel
paño^M lateral

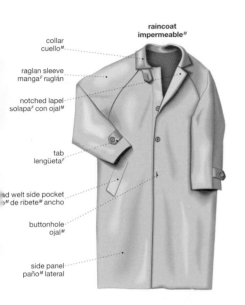

overcoat
abrigo^M

notched lapel
solapa^F con ojal^M

breast pocket
bolsillo^M superior

breast dart
pinza^F

flap pocket
bolsillo^M con cartera^F

trench coat
trinchera^F

epaulet
hombrera^F

two-way collar
cuello^M de doble vista^F

raglan sleeve
manga^F raglán

gun flap
protector^M

sleeve strap loop
presilla^F de la manga^F

double-breasted
buttoning
botonadura^F cruzada

belt
cinturón^M

sleeve strap
correa^F de la manga^F

belt loop
presilla^F del cinturón^M

broad welt side pocket
bolsillo^M de ribete^M ancho

frame
hebilla^F

three-quarter coat
abrigo^M de tres
cuartos^M

coats

parka
parka^F

snap-fastening tab
botón^M de presión^F

zipper
cremallera^F

sheepskin jacket
zamarra^F

duffle coat
trenca^F

hood
capucha^F

yoke
hombrillo^M

frog
alamar^M

patch pocket
bolsillo^M de solapa^F

toggle fastening
botón^M de madera^F

jacket
cazadora^F

snap fastener
botón^M de presión^F

windbreaker
cazadora^F

hand-warmer pocket
bolsillo^M de ojal^M

elastic waistband
pretina^F elástica

waistband
pretina^F

drawstring
cordón^M

CLOTHING

sweaters
suéteres^M

hanger loop
trabilla^F de suspensión^F

**V-neck cardigan
cárdigan**^M

V-neck
cuello^M de pico^M

button
botón^M

ribbing
tirilla^F elástica

welt pocket
bolsillo^M

buttoned placket
tirilla^F

**sweater vest
chaleco**^M **de punto**^M

**knit shirt
polo**^M

**turtleneck
suéter**^M **de cuello**^M **de
tortuga**^F

**crew neck sweater
suéter**^M **de cuello**^M **redondo**

**cardigan
chaqueta**^F **de punto**^M

CLOTHING

dresses

vestidos^M

sheath dress
recto^M entallado

princess dress
corte^M princesa^F

coat dress
traje^M cruzado

shift dress
vestido^M tubo^M

cocktail dress
vestido^M de fiesta^F

shirtwaist dress
vestido^M camisero

drop waist dress
vestido^M de talle^M bajo

trapeze dress
vestido^M acampanado

sundress
vestido^M de tirantes^M

wraparound dress
vestido^M cruzado

tunic dress
túnica^F

jumper
pichi^M

CLOTHING

skirts

ruffled skirt
falda^F de volantes^M

culottes
falda^F pantalón^M

yoke skirt
falda^F acampanada

gather skirt
falda^F fruncida

pencil skirt
falda^F recta

skort
falda^F short^M

straight skirt
falda^F recta

gored skirt
falda^F de piezas^F

kilt
falda^F escocesa

sarong
falda^F sarong^M

wraparound skirt
falda^F cruzada

tops

tops^M

body shirt
body^M

crotch piece
entrepierna^F

middy
camisa^F marinera

camisole
camisola^F

gather
fruncido^M

yoke
canesú^M

classic blouse
camisera^F clásica

smock
blusón^M

mini shirtdress
camisa^F

tunic
blusón^M con tirilla^F

wrapover top
chaqueta^F cruzada

polo shirt
polo^M

overblouse
casaca^F

pants
pantalones^M

knickers
bombachos^M

pedal pushers
pirata^M

Bermuda shorts
bermudas^M

shorts
pantalón^M **corto**

ski pants
pantalones^M **de tubo**^M

footstrap
trabilla^F

jeans
vaqueros^M

overalls
pantalón^M **peto**^M

jumpsuit
mono^M

bell bottoms
pantalones^M **acampanados**

cargo pants
pantalones^M **cargo**

capri pants
pantalones^M **capri**

slim slacks
pantalones^M **pitillo**^M

CLOTHING

jackets, vest and sweaters

chalecos*ᴹ*, suéteres*ᴹ* y chaquetas*ᶠ*

bolero
bolero*ᴹ*

safari jacket
saharianaᶠ

gusset pocket
bolsilloᴹ de fuelleᴹ

spencer
boleroᴹ con botonesᴹ

cardigan
chaquetaᶠ de puntoᴹ

crew neck sweater
suéterᴹ de cuelloᴹ redondo

twinset
conjuntoᴹ

pullover
suéterᴹ

vest
chalecoᴹ

blazer
americanaᶠ

coats

chaquetonesᴹ y abrigosᴹ

topcoat
abrigoᴹ redingote

parka
parkaᶠ

hood
capuchaᶠ

zipper
cremalleraᶠ

duffle coat
trencaᶠ

suit
traje^M de chaqueta^F

jacket
chaqueta^F

skirt
falda^F

raglan
abrigo^M raglán

raglan sleeve
manga^F raglán

fly front closing
pestaña^F

broad welt side pocket
bolsillo^M de ribete^M ancho

jacket
chaquetón^M

poncho
poncho^M

car coat
chaquetón^M de tres cuartos^M

pea jacket
chaquetón^M marinero

tailored collar
cuello^M hechura^F sastre^M

hand-warmer pocket
bolsillo^M de ojal^M

mock pocket
bolsillo^M simulado

CLOTHING

pelerine
abrigo^M con esclavina^F

pelerine
esclavina^F

seam pocket
bolsillo^M disimulado

cape
capa^F

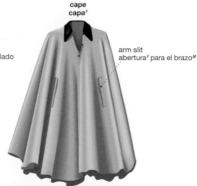

arm slit
abertura^F para el brazo^M

overcoat
abrigo^M

underwear
ropa^F interior

corselette
faja^F con sostén^M

camisole
camisola^F

teddy
canesú^M

bodysuit
body^M

panty corselette
faja^F corsé^M

princess seaming
costura^F de corte^M
princesa^F

half-slip
falda^F combinación^F

foundation slip
combinación^F

slip
combinación^F con
sujetador^M

underwire
varilla^F

strapless bra
sujetador^M sin tirantes^M

push-up bra
sujetador^M de aros^M

steel
varilla^F

bikini
braga^F

garter
liga^F

hose
medias^F

shoulder strap
tirante^M

cup
copa^F

midriff band
talle^M corto

wasp-waisted corset
corsé^M de cintura^F de
avispa^F

bra
sujetador^M

panel
refuerzo^M

décolleté bra
sujetador^M de escote^M bajo

girdle
faja^F

briefs
braga^F

panty girdle
faja^F braga

corset
faja^F con liguero^M

garter belt
liguero^M

G-string
tanga^F

tanga
tanga^F brasileño

hose

medias^F

short sock
calcetín^M

anklet
tobillera^F

sock
calcetín^M

knee-high sock
calcetín^M largo

net stocking
media^F de malla^F

thigh-high stocking
media^F antideslizante

stocking
media^F

panty hose
pantis^M/medias^F

nightclothes

ropa^f de dormir

bathrobe
albornoz^M

nightgown
camisón^M

baby doll
picardía^M

pajamas
pijama^M

negligee
bata^f

CLOTHING

children's clothing
ropa^F de niños^M

jumpsuit
pantalón^M de peto^M

hood
capuchón^M

false tuck
falsa doblez^F

bathing wrap
toalla^F con capuchón^M

bodysuit
body^M

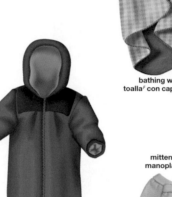

newborn hat
gorro^M de bebé^M

bunting bag
saco^M portabebé^M

mittens
manoplas^F

bootees
patucos^M

high-back overalls
pantalón^M de peto^M

adjustable strap
tirante^M ajustable

sleepers
pelele^M

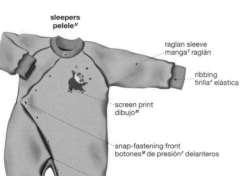

raglan sleeve
manga^F raglán

ribbing
tirilla^F elástica

screen print
dibujo^M

snap-fastening front
botones^M de presión^F delanteros

inside-leg snap-fastening
botones^M de presión^F de la pierna^F

bib
peto^M.

patch pocket
bolsillo^M de parche^M

top stitching
pespunte^M

inside-leg snap-fastening
botón^M de presión^F

bib
babero^M

disposable diaper
pañal^M desechable

Velcro closure
adhesivo^M

anti-leak guard
protector^M impermeable

waterproof pants
cubierta^F antihumedad^F

diaper
pañal^M

shirt
camiseta^F

sleep sack
saco^M de dormir

rompers
ranita^F

snowsuit
traje^M para nieve^F

crossover back straps overalls
pantalones^M de peto^M

button strap
tirante^M con botones^M

bib
peto^M

pajamas
pijama^M

drawstring hood
capucha^F

snow pants
pantalón^M de peto^M

sportswear

ropa^M de deporte^M

running shoe
zapatilla^F deportiva

loop
trabilla^F

lining
forro^M

nose of the quarter
ala^F del cuarto^M

eyelet
ojete^M

counter
contrafuerte^M

tongue
lengüeta^F

collar
ribete^M

vamp
empella^F

quarter
cuarto^M

punch hole
perforación^F

stitch
pespunteado^M

heel
talón^M

middle sole
cambrillón^M

shoelace
cordón^M

tag
herrete^M

stud
montante^M

outsole
suela^F

T-shirt
camiseta^F

tank top
camiseta^F con tirantes^M

swimsuit
traje^M de baño^M

swimming cap
gorro^M de natación^F

sandal
chándal^M

boxer shorts
pantalón^M de boxeo^M

bicycle pants
pantalón^M de ciclista^M

brief
traje^M de baño^M

hiking boot
bota^F de montaña^F

training suit
traje^M de entrenamiento^M

anorak
anorak^M

sweatshirt
sudadera^F

fleece jacket
forro^M polar

sweatpants
pantalón^M de chándal^M

pants
pantalones^M

hooded sweatshirt
sudadera^F con capucha^F

CLOTHING

CLOTHING

pockets

bolsillos^M

gusset pocket
bolsillo^M de fuelle^M

inset pocket
bolsillo^M simulado

welt pocket
bolsillo^M de ojal^M de
sastre^M

seam pocket
bolsillo^M disimulado

flap pocket
bolsillo^M de parche^M con
cartera^F

broad welt side pocket
bolsillo^M de ojal^M con
ribete^M

patch pocket
bolsillo^M de parche^M

hand-warmer pouch
bolsillo^M de manguito^M

sleeves

mangas^F

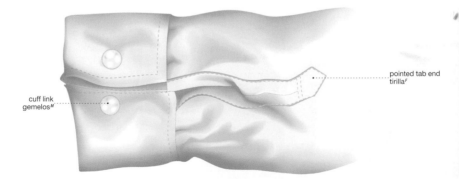

pointed tab end
tirilla^F

cuff link
gemelos^M

French cuff
puño^M para gemelos^M

puff sleeve
manga^F farol

leg-of-mutton sleeve
manga^F de jamón^M

bishop sleeve
manga^F común fruncida

three-quarter sleeve
manga^F recta de tres
cuartos^M

batwing sleeve
manga^F de murciélago^M

cap sleeve
manga^F corta sencilla

kimono sleeve
manga^F kimono^M

saddle sleeve
manga^M japonesa

raglan sleeve
manga^F raglán

shirtsleeve
manga^F de camisa^F

pagoda sleeve
manga^F de pagoda^F

tailored sleeve
manga^F de hechura^F
sastre^M

CLOTHING

pleats

pliegues^M

knife pleat tablas^F	topstitched pleat pliegue^M pespunteado	accordion pleat plisada	inverted pleat tabla^F delantera	kick pleat tabla^F abierta

collars

cuellos^M

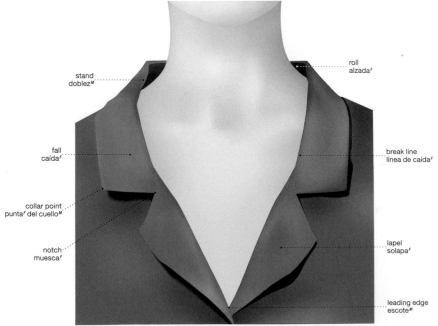

roll
alzada^F

stand
doblez^M

fall
caída^F

break line
línea de caída^F

collar point
punta^F del cuello^M

notch
muesca^F

lapel
solapa^F

leading edge
escote^M

parts of a collar
partes^F de un cuello^M

**examples of collars
ejemplos^M de
cuellos^M**

**collaret
cuello^M de volantes^M**

**bertha collar
cuello^M Berta**

**mandarin collar
cuello^M chino**

**dog-ear collar
cuello^M mariposa^F**

**shawl collar
cuello^M de chal^M**

**Peter Pan collar
cuello^M plano tipo^M
Peter Pan**

**shirt collar
cuello^M camisero**

**tailored collar
cuello^M de hechura^F de
sastre^M**

**bow collar
cuello^M de lazo^M**

**jabot
chorrera^F**

**sailor collar
cuello^M marinero**

**turtleneck
cuello^M de tortuga^F**

**cowl neck
cuello^M tipo^M de grulla^F**

**polo collar
cuello^M de polo^M**

**stand-up collar
cuello^M Mao**

CLOTHING

necks

cuellos^M

boatneck
escote^M de barco^M

round neck
cuello^M redondo

draped neck
cuello^M drapeado

necklines

escotes^M

V-shaped neck
escote^M de pico^M

square neck
escote^M cuadrado

draped neckline
descote^M rapeado

plunging neckline
escote^M bajo

sweetheart neckline
escote^M de corazón^M

men's headgear

sombreros^M de hombre^M

fedora
sombrero^M de fieltro^M

bow
lazo^M

hatband
cinta^F

binding
ribete^M

crown
copa^F

brim
ala^F

CLOTHING

boater
canotier^M

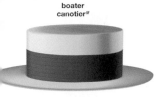

skullcap
solideo^M

cap
gorra^F

garrison cap
gorra^F de cuartel^M

top hat
chistera^F

shapka
chapka^F

hunting cap
gorra^F noruega

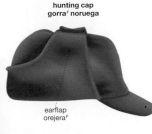

earflap
orejera^F

peak
visera^F

derby
sombrero^M de hongo^M

panama
panamá^M

women's headgear

sombreros^M de mujer^F

cloche
sombrero^M de campana^F

cartwheel hat
pamela^F

pillbox hat
sombrero^M sin alas^F

toque
toca^F

sailor's hat
gorro^M de marinero^M

crown
copa^F

turban
turbante^M

brim
ala^F

southwester
sueste^M

CLOTHING

unisex headgear

sombreros^M unisex

cap
gorra^F

stocking cap
gorro^M

balaclava
pasamontañas^F

face mask
máscara^F

beret
boina^F

men's shoes

zapatos^M de hombre^M

parts of a shoe
partes^F de un zapato^M

heel grip
refuerzo^M del talón^M

cuff
ribete^M

quarter
cuarto^M

outside counter
afuerte^M del talón^M

heel
talón^M

top lift
tapa^F

nose of the quarter
ala^F del cuarto^M

waist
enfranque^M

tag
herrete^M

eyelet tab
oreja^F

lining
forro^M

tongue
lengüeta^F

shoelace
cordón^M

vamp
empella^F

stitch
costura^F

punch hole
perforaciones^F

eyelet
ojete^M

outsole
suela^F

welt
vira^F

perforated toe cap
puntera^F perforada

CLOTHING

examples of shoes
ejemplos^M de
zapatos^M

bootee
botín^M

oxford shoe
Balmoral^M

chukka
media bota^F

work boot
bota^F de trabajo^M

blucher oxford
zapato^M de cordones^M

cowboy boot
bota^F de cowboy^M

rubber
chanclo^M de goma^F

women's shoes

zapatos^M de mujer^F

examples of shoes
ejemplos^M de
zapatos^M

T-strap shoe
zapato^M de correa^F

pump
zapato^M de salón^M

thigh boot
bota^F de caña^F alta

strap
correa^F

one-bar shoe   heel
zapato^F Mary Jane   tacón^M

sling back shoe
zapato^M de talón^M abierto

casual shoe
zapato^M con cordones^M

ankle boot
botín^M

CLOTHING

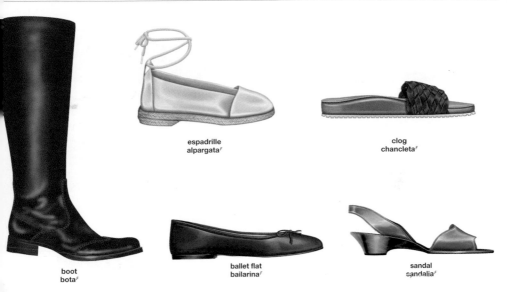

espadrille
alpargata^F

clog
chancleta^F

boot
bota^F

ballet flat
bailarina^F

sandal
sandalia^F

CLOTHING

examples of heels
ejemplos^M de
tacones^M

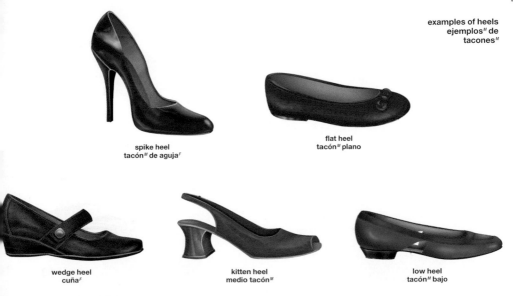

spike heel
tacón^M de aguja^F

flat heel
tacón^M plano

wedge heel
cuña^F

kitten heel
medio tacón^M

low heel
tacón^M bajo

unisex shoes

calzado^M unisex

CLOTHING

mule
pantufla^F

loafer
mocasín^M

tennis shoe
zapatilla^F de tenis^M

moccasin
mocasín^M

sandal
sandalia^F

rain boot
bota^F de agua^F

thong
chancleta^F playera

sandal
sandalia^F

hiking boot
bota^F de montaña^F

accessories

accesorios^M

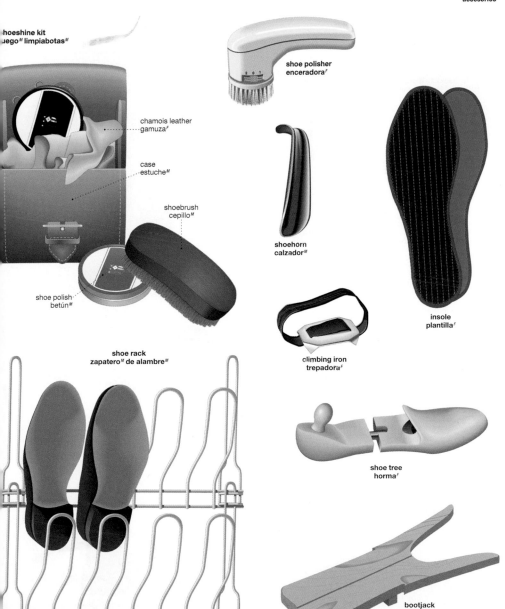

shoeshine kit
juego^M limpiabotas^M

shoe polisher
enceradora^F

chamois leather
gamuza^F

case
estuche^M

shoebrush
cepillo^M

shoehorn
calzador^M

shoe polish
betún^M

insole
plantilla^F

shoe rack
zapatero^M de alambre^M

climbing iron
trepadora^F

shoe tree
horma^F

bootjack
sacabotas^F

CLOTHING

CLOTHING

gloves

guantes^M

men's gloves
guantes^M de
hombre^M

back of a glove
dorso^M de un guante^M

palm of a glove
palma^F de un guante^M

fourchette
horquilla^F

glove finger
dedo^M

thumb
pulgar^M

palm
palma^F

seam
costura^F

snap fastener
botón^M de presión^F

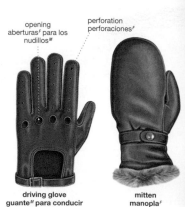

opening
aberturas^F para los
nudillos^M

perforation
perforaciones^F

driving glove
guante^M para conducir

mitten
manopla^F

women's gloves
guantes^M de mujer^F

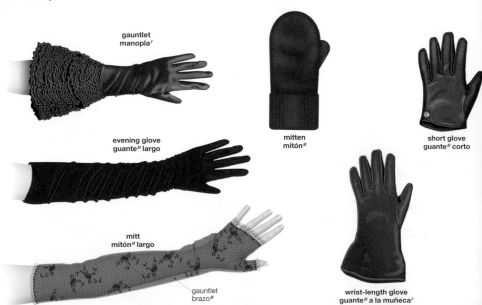

gauntlet
manopla^F

evening glove
guante^M largo

mitt
mitón^M largo

gauntlet
brazo^M

mitten
mitón^M

short glove
guante^M corto

wrist-length glove
guante^M a la muñeca^F

miscellaneous accessories

accesorios^M diversos

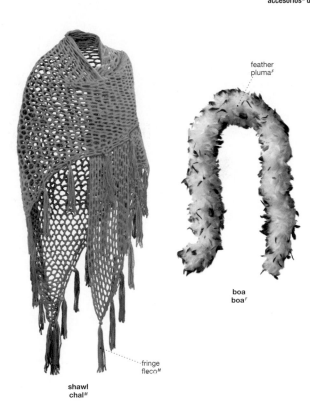

feather
pluma^F

scarf
bufanda^F

boa
boa^F

fringe
fleco^M

shawl
chal^M

headband
cinta^F de pelo^M

ear covering
orejera^F

neck warmer
braga^F de cuello^M

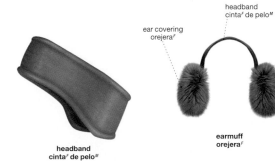

headband
cinta^F de pelo^M

earmuff
orejera^F

PERSONAL ACCESSORIES AND ARTICLES

accesorios y artículos personales

PERSONAL ACCESSORIES   **468**

jewelry	468
nail care	472
makeup	473
body care	474
hairdressing	476

PERSONAL ARTICLES   **479**

shaving	479
eyeglasses	480
contact lenses	481
dental care	482
smoking accessories	483
leather goods	484
handbags	486
luggage	488
umbrella and stick	490
child care	491
pet care	493

jewelry
joyería^F

earrings
aretes^M

clip earrings
aretes^M de clip^M

screw earrings
aretes^M de tuerca^F

pierced earrings
aretes^M de espiga^F

drop earrings
aretes^M

hoop earrings
aretes^M de aro^M

necklaces
collares^M

matinee-length necklace
collar^M de una vuelta^F, matinée^F

velvet-band choker
gargantilla^F de
terciopelo^M

pendant
arete^M

rope
lazo^M

opera-length necklace
collar^M de una vuelta^F, ópera^F

bib necklace
collar^M de 5 vueltas^F, peto^M

choker
gargantilla^F

locket
medallón^M

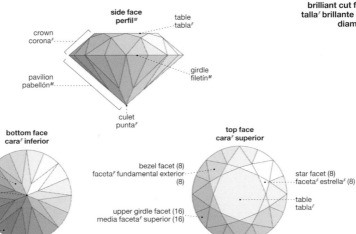

**brilliant cut facets
talla^f brillante de un
diamante^M**

side face
perfil^M

table
tabla^f

crown
corona^f

girdle
filetín^M

pavilion
pabellón^M

culet
punta^f

bottom face
cara^f inferior

top face
cara^f superior

pavilion facet (8)
faceta^f de pabellón^M (8)

culet
culata^f

lower girdle facet (16)
faceta^f inferior del contorno^M (16)

bezel facet (8)
faceta^f fundamental exterior (8)

upper girdle facet (16)
media faceta^f superior (16)

star facet (8)
faceta^f estrella^f (8)

table
tabla^f

**cut for gemstones
tallas^f de piedras^f preciosas**

step cut
talla^f escalonada

rose cut
talla^f en rosa^f
holandesa

table cut
talla^f en tabla^f

cabochon cut
talla^f en cabujón^M

pear-shaped cut
talla^f en pera^f

emerald cut
esmeralda^f

brilliant full cut
brillante^M

eight cut
talla^f octógono^M

scissors cut
en tijera^f

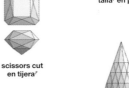

briolette cut
talla^f en briolette^f

baguette cut
talla^f en baguette^f

French cut
talla^f francesa

oval cut
talla^f oval

navette cut
marquesa^f

jewelry

semiprecious stones
piedras^F semipreciosas

amethyst
amatista^F

lapis lazuli
lapislázuli^M

aquamarine
aguamarina^F

topaz
topacio^M

tourmaline
turmalina^F

opal
ópalo^M

turquoise
turquesa^F

garnet
granate^M

precious stones
piedras^F preciosas

emerald
esmeralda^F

sapphire
zafiro^M

diamond
diamante^M

ruby
rubí^M

rings
anillos^M

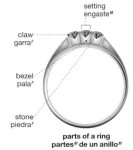

setting
engaste^M

claw
garra^F

bezel
pala^F

stone
piedra^F

parts of a ring
partes^F de un anillo^M

band ring
alianza^F

class ring
anillo^M de graduación^F

signet ring
sortija^F de sello^M

engagement ring
anillo^M de compromiso^M

wedding ring
alianza^F

solitaire ring
solitario^M

jewelry

bracelets
brazaletes^M

charm bracelet
pulsera^F de dijes^M

bangle
brazalete^M tubular

identification bracelet
brazalete^M de identificación^F

pins
alfileres^M

tie bar
pisacorbatas^M

tiepin
alfiler^M de corbata^F

collar bar
yugo^M

stickpin
alfiler^M de corbata^F

brooch
broche^M

charms
dijes^M

nameplate
placa^F de identificación^F

horn
cuerno^M

horseshoe
herradura^F

nail care

manicura^F

manicure set
estuche^M de manicura^F

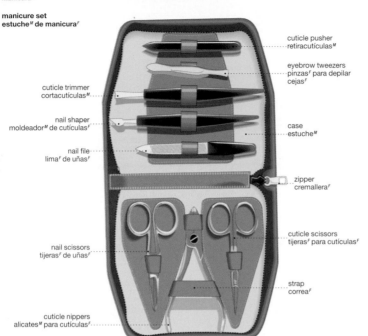

cuticle trimmer
cortacutículas^M

nail shaper
moldeador^M de cutículas^F

nail file
lima^F de uñas^F

cuticle pusher
retiracutículas^M

eyebrow tweezers
pinzas^F para depilar
cejas^F

case
estuche^M

zipper
cremallera^F

cuticle scissors
tijeras^F para cutículas^F

strap
correa^F

nail scissors
tijeras^F de uñas^F

cuticle nippers
alicates^M para cutículas^F

toenail scissors
tijeras^F de pedicura^F

safety scissors
tijeras^F de punta^F roma

nail buffer
lima^F de uñas^F

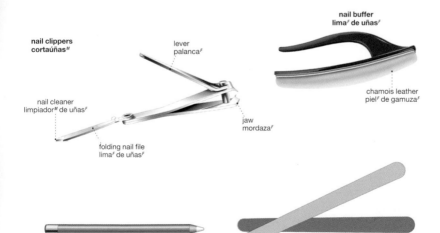

nail clippers
cortaúñas^M

lever
palanca^F

nail cleaner
limpiador^M de uñas^F

jaw
mordaza^F

folding nail file
lima^F de uñas^F

chamois leather
piel^F de gamuza^F

nail polish
esmalte^M de uñas^F

nail whitener pencil
lápiz^M blanco para uñas^F

emery boards
lima^F de uñas^F

nail polish remover
quitaesmaltes^M

makeup
maquillaje^M

facial makeup
maquillaje^M

compact
polvera^F

pressed powder
polvo^M compacto

blusher brush
brocha^F aplicadora de
colorete^M

powder blusher
colorete^M en polvo^M

powder puff
borla^F

liquid foundation
base^F líquida

loose powder brush
brocha^F

loose powder
polvos^M sueltos

synthetic sponge
esponja^F sintética

fan brush
brocha^F en forma^F de
abanico^M

eye makeup
maquillaje^M para ojos^M

brow brush and lash comb
cepillo^M para cejas^F y pestañas^F

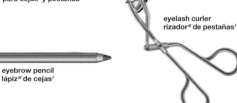

eyelash curler
rizador^M de pestañas^F

concealer
corrector^M

eyebrow pencil
lápiz^M de cejas^F

liquid eyeliner
delineador^M

mascara brush
cepillo^M aplicador de
rímel^M

sponge-tipped applicator
aplicador^M de esponja^F

liquid mascara
rímel^M líquido

cake mascara
rímel^M en pasta^F

eyeshadow
sombra^F de ojos^M

makeup

lip makeup
maquillaje *M* **labial**

lip gloss
barra *F* de labios *M*

lip liner
delineador *M* de labios *M*

lipstick
pintalabios *M*

lip brush
pincel *M* para labios *F*

body care

cuidado *M* personal

cotton swab
bastoncillo *M* de
algodón *M*

stopper
tapón *M*

absorbent cotton
algodón *M*

bottle
botella *F*

eau de toilette
agua *F* de colonia *F*

makeup remover pad
discos *M*
desmaquillantes

deodorant
desodorante *M*

eau de parfum
agua *F* de perfume *M*

toilet soap
jabón *M* de tocador *M*

scrub
exfoliante *M*

bath salts
sales *F* de baño *M*

moisturizer
crema *F* hidratante

hair coloring
tinte *M* capilar

PERSONAL ACCESSORIES AND ARTICLES

shampoo
champú^M

hair conditioner
acondicionador^M

shower gel
gel^M de ducha^F

bubble bath
gel^M de baño^M

lip balm
bálsamo^M labial

bath brush
cepillo^M de baño^M

bath sheet
toalla^F de baño^M

bath towel
toalla^F de lavabo^M

natural sponge
esponja^F natural

back brush
cepillo^M de espalda^F

washcloth
manopla^F de baño^M

washcloth
toalla^F para la cara^F

massage glove
guante^M de crin^M

loofah
esponja^F

hairdressing
peinado*M*

hairbrushes
cepillos*M*

flat-back brush
cepillo*M* con base*F* de goma*F*

round brush
cepillo*M* redondo

quill brush
cepillo*M* de púas*F*

vent brush
cepillo*M* de esqueleto*M*

combs
peines*M*

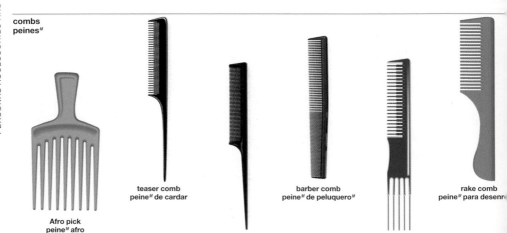

teaser comb
peine*M* de cardar

barber comb
peine*M* de peluquero*M*

rake comb
peine*M* para desenr

Afro pick
peine*M* afro

tail comb
peine*M* de mango*M*

pitchfork comb
peine*M* combinado

hair roller
rulo*M* para el cabello*M*

roller
rulo*M*

hair roller pin
alfiler*M*

hairpin
horquilla*F* de moño*M*

bobby pin
horquilla*F*

wave clip
pinza*F* para rizar

hair clip
pinza*F* para el cabello*M*

barrette
pasador*M*

scissors
tijeras^F

haircutting scissors
tijeras^F **de peluquero**^M

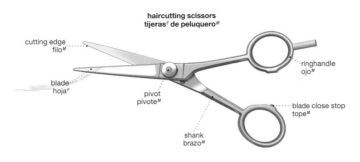

cutting edge
filo^M

ringhandle
ojo^M

blade
hoja^F

blade close stop
tope^M

pivot
pivote^M

shank
brazo^M

notched single-edged thinning scissors
tijeras^F con filo^M simple para entresacar

notched double-edged thinning
scissors
tijeras^F **con doble filo**^M **para entresacar**

blade
cuchilla^F

notched edge
hoja^F dentada

tooth
diente^M

miscellaneous accessories
accesorios^M **diversos**

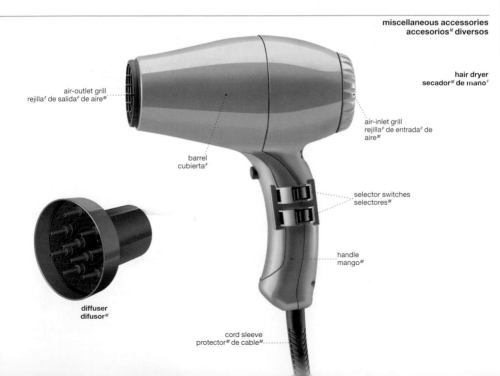

hair dryer
secador^M **de mano**^F

air-outlet grill
rejilla^F de salida^F de aire^M

air-inlet grill
rejilla^F de entrada^F de
aire^M

barrel
cubierta^F

selector switches
selectores^M

handle
mango^M

diffuser
difusor^M

cord sleeve
protector^M de cable^M

hairdressing

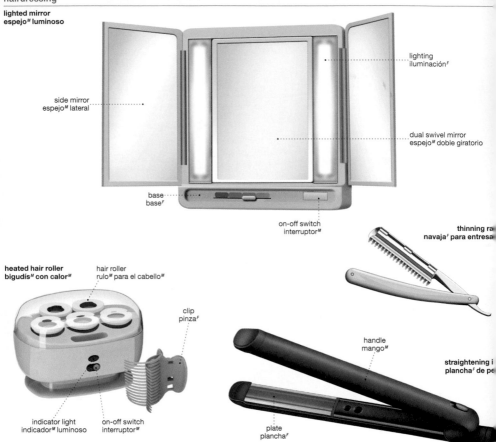

lighted mirror
espejo^M **luminoso**

lighting
iluminación^F

side mirror
espejo^M lateral

dual swivel mirror
espejo^M doble giratorio

base
base^F

on-off switch
interruptor^M

thinning ra
navaja^F para entresa

heated hair roller
bigudís^M **con calor**^M

hair roller
rulo^M para el cabello^M

clip
pinza^F

handle
mango^M

straightening i
plancha^F **de pe**

indicator light
indicador^M luminoso

on-off switch
interruptor^M

plate
plancha^F

cord sle
protector^M de ca

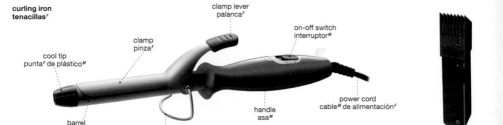

curling iron
tenacillas^F

clamp lever
palanca^F

on-off switch
interruptor^M

clamp
pinza^F

cool tip
punta^F de plástico^M

barrel
varilla^F rizadora

stand
soporte^M

handle
asa^M

power cord
cable^M de alimentación^F

clippers
maquinilla^F **para cortar el**
cabello^M

shaving
afeitado^M

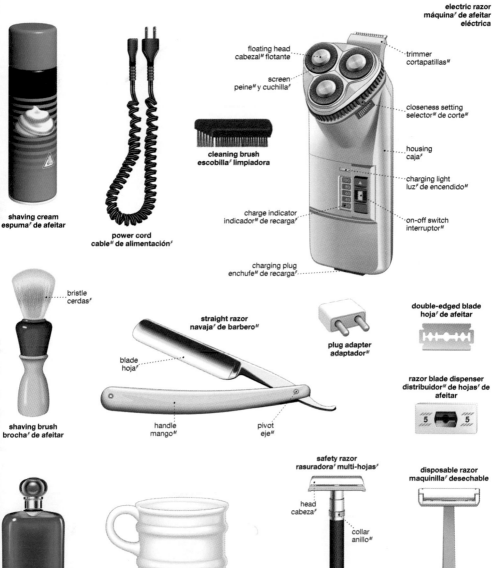

electric razor
máquina^F de afeitar
eléctrica

floating head
cabezal^M flotante

screen
peine^M y cuchilla^F

trimmer
cortapatillas^M

closeness setting
selector^M de corte^M

housing
caja^F

charging light
luz^F de encendido^M

on-off switch
interruptor^M

charge indicator
indicador^M de recarga^F

charging plug
enchufe^M de recarga^F

cleaning brush
escobilla^F limpiadora

shaving cream
espuma^F de afeitar

power cord
cable^M de alimentación^F

bristle
cerdas^F

shaving brush
brocha^F de afeitar

straight razor
navaja^F de barbero^M

blade
hoja^F

handle
mango^M

pivot
eje^M

plug adapter
adaptador^M

double-edged blade
hoja^F de afeitar

razor blade dispenser
distribuidor^M de hojas^F de
afeitar

aftershave
ción^M para después del
afeitado^M

shaving mug
jabonera^F

safety razor
rasuradora^F multi-hojas^F

head
cabeza^F

collar
anillo^M

handle
mango^M

disposable razor
maquinilla^F desechable

PERSONAL ACCESSORIES AND ARTICLES

eyeglasses

gafas[F]

eyeglasses parts
gafas[F]: partes[F]

frames
montura[F]

lens
lente[F]

bend
codo[M]

bridge
puente[M]

bar
barra[F]

temple
patilla[F]

endpiece
espiga[F]

butt-strap
extremo[M]

earpiece
gafa[F]

nose pad
plaqueta[F]

pad plate
soporte[M] de la plaqueta[F]

pad arm
brazo[M] de la plaqueta[F]

rim
aro[M]

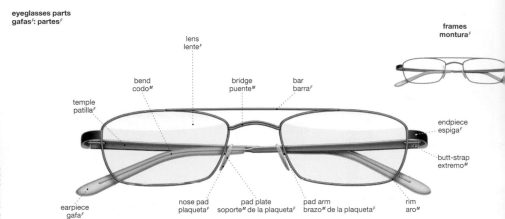

eyeglasses accessories
accesorios[M] de gafas[F]

clip-on sunglasses
gafas[F] de sol[M] de clip[M]

lens cleaning cloth
gamuza[F] para limpiar
lentes[F]

eyeglasses retainer
cordón[M] de gafas[F]

eyeglasses case
funda[F] de gafas[F]

eyeglasses

examples of eyeglasses
ejemplos^M de gafas^F

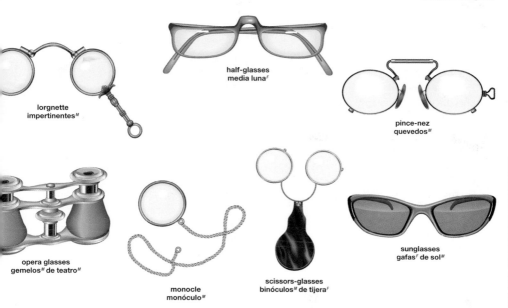

half-glasses
media luna^F

lorgnette
impertinentes^M

pince-nez
quevedos^M

opera glasses
gemelos^M de teatro^M

monocle
monóculo^M

scissors-glasses
binóculos^M de tijera^F

sunglasses
gafas^F de sol^M

contact lenses

lentes^F de contacto^M

disposable contact lens
lentes^F de contacto^M
desechables

soft contact lens
lentes^F de contacto^M
blandas

hard contact lens
lentes^F de contacto^M
duras

left side
lado^M izquierdo

right side
lado^M derecho

lubricant eye drops
gotas^F oftalmológicas lubricantes

multipurpose solution
solución^F
multipropósito

lens case
estuche^M portalentes

dental care

higiene^F **dental**

PERSONAL ACCESSORIES AND ARTICLES

manual toothbrush
cepillo^M **de dientes**^M
manual

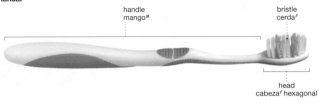

handle
mango^M

bristle
cerda^F

head
cabeza^F hexagonal

dental floss
hilo^M **dental**

replacement brushhead
cabezal^M de repuesto^M

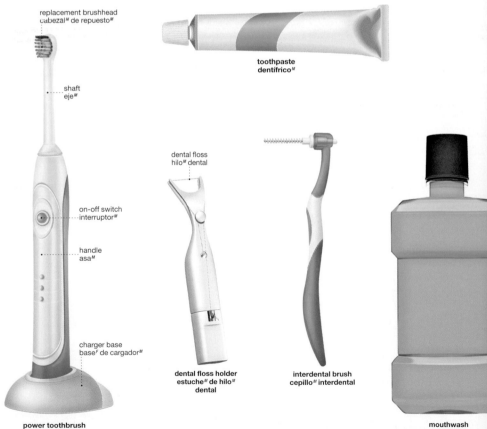

shaft
eje^M

on-off switch
interruptor^M

handle
asa^M

charger base
base^F de cargador^M

power toothbrush
cepillo^M **de dientes**^M
eléctrico

toothpaste
dentífrico^M

dental floss
hilo^M dental

dental floss holder
estuche^M **de hilo**^M
dental

interdental brush
cepillo^M **interdental**

mouthwash
colutorio^M

smoking accessories
artículos^M de fumador^M

pe
pa^F

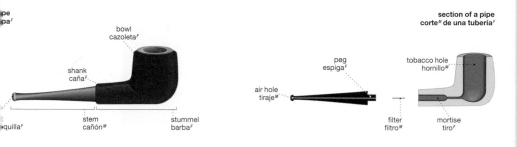

bowl
cazoleta^F

shank
caña^F

quilla^F

stem
cañón^M

stummel
barba^F

section of a pipe
corte^M de una tubería^F

peg
espiga^F

tobacco hole
hornillo^M

air hole
tiraje^M

filter
filtro^M

mortise
tiro^F

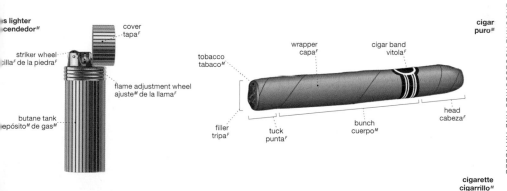

s lighter
cendedor^M

striker wheel
cilla^F de la piedra^F

cover
tapa^F

flame adjustment wheel
ajuste^M de la llama^F

butane tank
epósito^M de gas^M

**cigar
puro^M**

tobacco
tabaco^M

wrapper
capa^F

cigar band
vitola^F

head
cabeza^F

filler
tripa^F

tuck
punta^F

bunch
cuerpo^M

**cigarette
cigarrillo^M**

atchbook
rterita^F de cerillas^F

cover
tapa^F

matchstick
cerilla^F

head
cabeza^F

front flap
solapa^F

paper
papel^M

filter tip
filtro^M

tobacco
tabaco^M

seam
costura^F

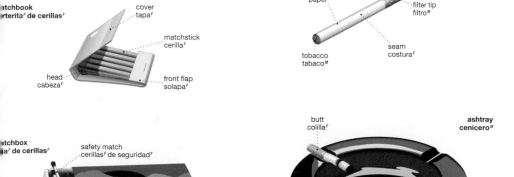

atchbox
ja^F de cerillas^F

safety match
cerillas^F de seguridad^F

butt
colilla^F

**ashtray
cenicero^M**

ash
ceniza^F

leather goods
artículos^M de marroquinería^F

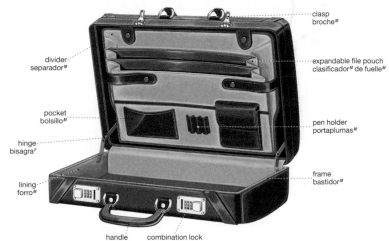

attaché case
maletín^M

clasp
broche^M

divider
separador^M

expandable file pouch
clasificador^M de fuelle^M

pocket
bolsillo^M

pen holder
portaplumas^M

hinge
bisagra^F

frame
bastidor^M

lining
forro^M

handle
asa^F

combination lock
cerradura^F de
combinación^F

bottom-fold portfolio
cartera^F de fondo^M plegable

retractable handle
asa^F extensible

exterior pocket
bolsillo^M delantero

briefca
carte

tab
lengüeta^F

key lock
cerradura^F

gusset
fuelle^M

checkbook/secretary clutch
chequera^F con calculadora^F

trimming
broche^M automático

card case
tarjetero^M

calculator
calculadora^F

pen holder
portaplumas^M

hidden pocket
bolsillo^M secreto

checkbook
talonario^M de cheques^M

card ca
tarjete

bill compartment
billetera^F

windows
plásticos^M transp

tab
lengüeta^F

slot
ranura^F

ID window
plástico^M transparente

wallet
billetero_M_

billfold
billetera_F_

coin purse
portamonedas_M_

key case
llavero_M_

purse
monedero_M_

passport case
porta pasaportes_M_

eyeglasses case
funda_F_ **de gafas**_F_

checkbook case
talonario_M_ **de cheques**_M_

underarm portfolio
cartera_F_
portadocumentos_M_

writing case
agenda_F_

PERSONAL ACCESSORIES AND ARTICLES

handbags

bolsos^M

drawstring bag
bolso^M tipo cubo^M

eyelet
ojal^M

drawstring
cordón^M

front pocket
bolsillo^M exterior

handle
asa^F

satchel b
bolso^M clási

flap
ala^F

clasp
broche^M

lock
cierre^M

tote bag
bolsa^F de lona^F

carrier bag
bolso^M de la compra^F

box bag
bolso^M de vestir

drawstring bag
bolso^M saco

messenger bag
bolsa^F de mensajero^M

sea bag
saco^M de marinero^M

money belt
cinturón*M* porta dinero*M*

fanny pack
riñonera*F*

muff
bolso*M* manguito*M*

gusset
fuelle*M*

accordion bag
bolso*M* de fuelle*M*

shopping bag
capazo*M*

men's bag
bolso*M* de hombre*M*

duffel bag
bolso*M* de viaje*M*

shoulder strap
bandolera*F*

buckle
hebilla*F*

shoulder bag
bolso*M* de bandolera*F*

hobo bag
morral*M*

luggage
equipaje^M

carry-on bag
bolso^M de viaje^M

handle
asa^F

shoulder strap
bandolera^F

exterior pocket
bolsillo^M exterior

utility case
neceser^M

tote b
malet

garment bag
portatrajes^M

zipper
cremallera^F

identification tag
etiqueta^F de
identificación^F

handle
asa^F

frame
bastidor^M

pull strap
correa^F

trim
guarnición^F

wheel
ruedecilla^F

suitca
maleta^F clás

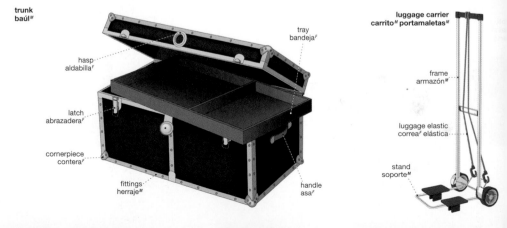

trunk
baúl^M

tray
bandeja^F

hasp
aldabilla^F

latch
abrazadera^F

cornerpiece
contera^F

fittings
herraje^M

handle
asa^F

luggage carrier
carrito^M portamaletas^M

frame
armazón^M

luggage elastic
correa^F elástica

stand
soporte^M

luggage

retractable handle
asa^M retráctil

garment bag on wheels
bolsa^F de ropa^F

top carrying handle
asa^F superior

front pocket
bolsillo^M delantero

backpack
mochila^F

shoulder strap
correa^F de transporte

hip belt
cinturón^M

retractable handle
asa^F retráctil

upright suitcase
maleta^F vertical

weekender
maleta^F de fin^M de semana^F

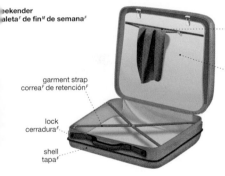

interior pocket
bolso^M interior

garment strap
correa^F de retención^F

curtain
panel^M de separación^F

lock
cerradura^F

shell
tapa^F

laptop computer briefcase
maletín^M para computadora^F
portátil

computer compartment
compartimiento^M para
computadora^F

document compartment
compartimiento^M de
documentos^M

duffel bag on wheels
bolsa^F de lona^F

shoulder strap
bandolera^F

umbrella and stick

paraguas^M y bastones^M

umbrella
paraguas^M

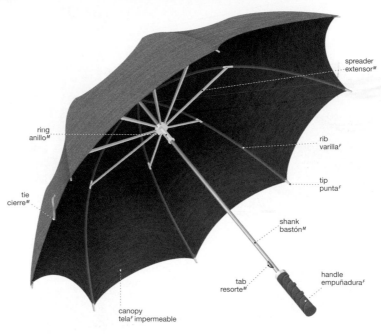

spreader
extensor^M

ring
anillo^M

rib
varilla^F

tip
punta^F

tie
cierre^M

shank
bastón^M

tab
resorte^M

handle
empuñadura^F

canopy
tela^F impermeable

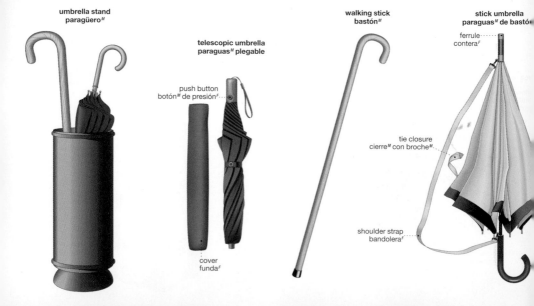

umbrella stand
paragüero^M

telescopic umbrella
paraguas^M plegable

push button
botón^M de presión^F

cover
funda^F

walking stick
bastón^M

stick umbrella
paraguas^M de bastó

ferrule
contera^F

tie closure
cierre^M con broche^M

shoulder strap
bandolera^F

child care

cuidado^M de niños^M

fant car seat
la^F portabebés^M de
che^M

carrying handle
asa^F de transporte^M

hood
capota^F

cloth baby carrier
portabebés^M de tela^F

wrap baby carrier
fular^M portabebés^M

stay-in-car base
base^M de silla^F
portabebés^M de coche^M

harness
arnés^M

stroller
cochecito^M

ckpack baby carrier
ochila^F portabebés^M

hood
capota^F

hood
capota^F

handle
asa^M

headrest
reposacabezas^F

harness
arnés^M

shoulder strap
rea^F de transporte

child's harness
arnés^M de niño^M

padded hip belt
inturón^M acolchado

kickstand
pata^F de cabra^F

basket
cesta^F

child care

pacifier
chupete^M

nipple
pezón^M

ring
anillo^M

bottle
botella^F

baby bottle
biberón^M

cap
tapa^F

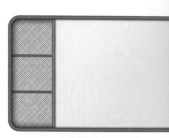

portable changing pad
cambiador^M **de viaje**^M

pacifier clip
clip^M **de chupete**^M

splash guard
antisalpicaduras^M

toilet seat reducer
reductor^M **de asiento**^M **de**
inodoro^M

diaper bag
bolsa^F **para pañales**^M

potty-chair
bacinilla^F

nursing pillow
almohada^F **de maternidad**^F

bassinet
moisés^M

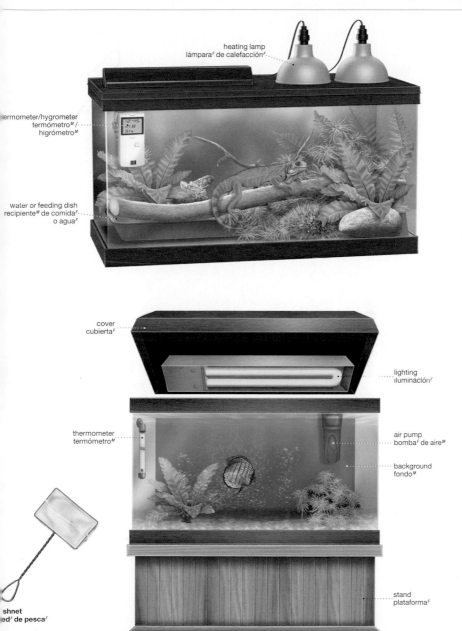

heating lamp
lámpara^F de calefacción^F

**terrarium
terrario**^M

ermometer/hygrometer
termómetro^M /
higrómetro^M

water or feeding dish
recipiente^M de comida^F
o agua^F

cover
cubierta^F

**aquarium
acuario**^M

lighting
iluminación^F

thermometer
termómetro^M

air pump
bomba^F de aire^M

background
fondo^M

stand
plataforma^F

shnet
ed^F de pesca^F

ANCIENT ARCHITECTURE 498

pyramid 498
Greek theater 498
Greek temple 499
architectural styles 500
Roman house 502
Roman amphitheater 503

MILITARY ARCHITECTURE 504

castle 504
Vauban fortification 505

WESTERN ARCHITECTURE 506

Gothic cathedral 506
Romanesque church 508
Renaissance villa 509
Baroque church 510
art deco building 511
international style skyscraper 512

ASIAN AND PRE-COLUMBIAN ARCHITECTURE 513

pagoda 513
Aztec temple 513

ELEMENTS OF ARCHITECTURE 51

examples of arches 51
examples of doors 51
examples of roofs 51
examples of windows 51
escalator 51
elevator 51

HOUSING 52

traditional houses 52
city houses 52

ARTS AND ARCHITECTURE
arte y arquitectura

INE ARTS — 522

museum — 522
painting and drawing — 524
wood carving — 531

RAPHIC ARTS — 532

printing — 532
relief printing process — 533
intaglio printing process — 534
lithography — 535
screen printing — 536
fine bookbinding — 537

PERFORMING ARTS — 540

theater — 540
movie set — 542
movie theater — 544

MUSIC — 545

symphony orchestra — 545
examples of instrumental groups — 546
stringed instruments — 547
wind instruments — 550
keyboard instruments — 552
percussion instruments — 556
electronic music — 558
traditional musical instruments — 560
musical notation — 562
musical accessories — 564

CRAFTS — 565

embroidery — 565
sewing — 566
knitting — 570
weaving — 572
pottery — 576
bobbin lace — 578
stained glass — 579

pyramid

pirámide[F]

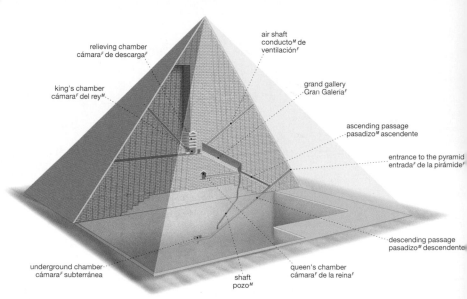

relieving chamber
cámara[F] de descarga[F]

king's chamber
cámara[F] del rey[M]

air shaft
conducto[M] de
ventilación[F]

grand gallery
Gran Galería[F]

ascending passage
pasadizo[M] ascendente

entrance to the pyramid
entrada[F] de la pirámide[F]

descending passage
pasadizo[M] descendente

underground chamber
cámara[F] subterránea

shaft
pozo[M]

queen's chamber
cámara[F] de la reina[F]

Greek theater

teatro[M] griego

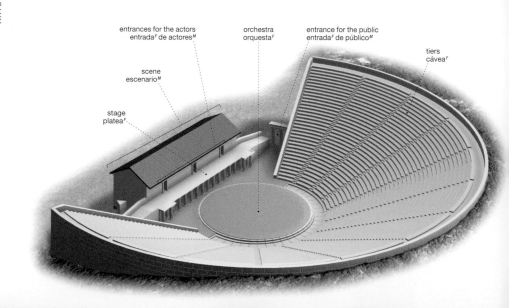

entrances for the actors
entrada[F] de actores[M]

scene
escenario[M]

stage
platea[F]

orchestra
orquesta[F]

entrance for the public
entrada[F] de público[M]

tiers
cávea[F]

Greek temple

templo^M griego

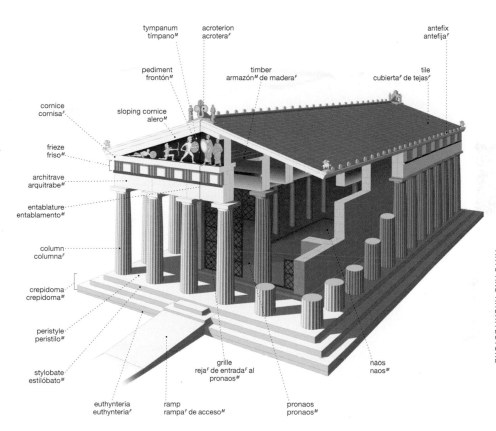

tympanum
tímpano^M

acroterion
acrotera^F

antefix
antefija^F

pediment
frontón^M

timber
armazón^M de madera^F

tile
cubierta^F de tejas^F

cornice
cornisa^F

sloping cornice
alero^M

frieze
friso^M

architrave
arquitrabe^M

entablature
entablamento^M

column
columna^F

crepidoma
crepidoma^M

peristyle
peristilo^M

stylobate
estilóbato^M

euthynteria
euthynteria^F

ramp
rampa^F de acceso^M

grille
reja^F de entrada^F al
pronaos^M

naos
naos^M

pronaos
pronaos^M

ARTS AND ARCHITECTURE

plan of a Greek temple
plano^M de un templo^M
griego

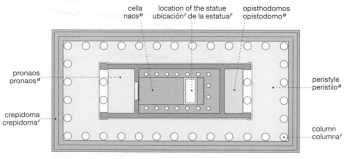

cella
naos^M

location of the statue
ubicación^F de la estatua^F

opisthodomos
opistodomo^M

pronaos
pronaos^M

peristyle
peristilo^M

crepidoma
crepidoma^F

column
columna^F

architectural styles

estilos^M arquitectónicos

Doric order
orden^M dórico

Ionic order
orden^M jónico

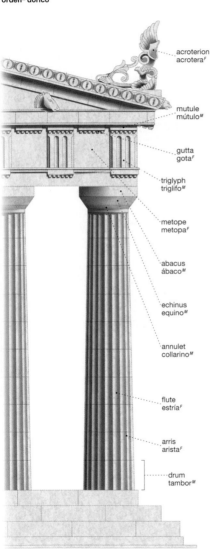

acroterion
acrotera^F

mutule
mútulo^M

gutta
gota^F

triglyph
triglifo^M

metope
metopa^F

abacus
ábaco^M

echinus
equino^M

annulet
collarino^M

flute
estría^F

arris
arista^F

drum
tambor^M

ARTS AND ARCHITECTURE

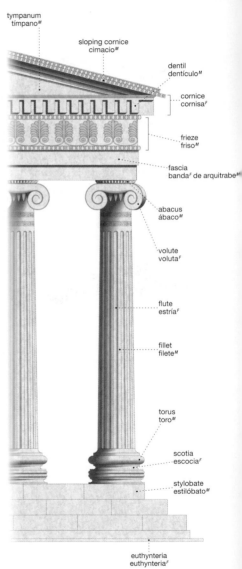

tympanum
tímpano^M

sloping cornice
cimacio^M

dentil
dentículo^M

cornice
cornisa^F

frieze
friso^M

fascia
banda^F de arquitrabe^M

abacus
ábaco^M

volute
voluta^F

flute
estría^F

fillet
filete^M

torus
toro^M

scotia
escocia^F

stylobate
estilóbato^M

euthynteria
euthynteria^F

Corinthian order
orden ^M **corintio**

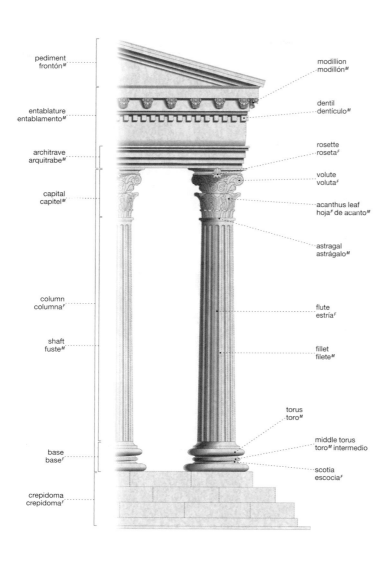

pediment
frontón^M

entablature
entablamento^M

architrave
arquitrabe^M

capital
capitel^M

column
columna^F

shaft
fuste^M

base
base^F

crepidoma
crepidoma^F

modillion
modillón^M

dentil
dentículo^M

rosette
roseta^F

volute
voluta^F

acanthus leaf
hoja^F de acanto^M

astragal
astrágalo^M

flute
estría^F

fillet
filete^M

torus
toro^M

middle torus
toro^M intermedio

scotia
escocia^F

ARTS AND ARCHITECTURE

castle

castillo^M

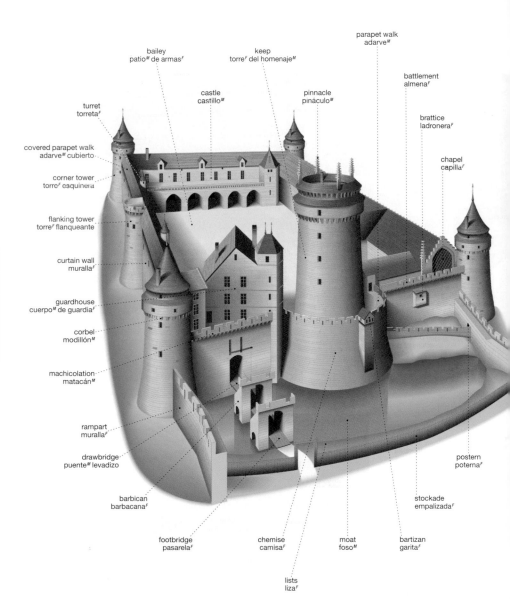

parapet walk
adarve^M

bailey
patio^M de armas^F

keep
torre^F del homenaje^M

battlement
almena^F

castle
castillo^M

pinnacle
pináculo^M

turret
torreta^F

brattice
ladronera^F

covered parapet walk
adarve^M cubierto

chapel
capilla^F

corner tower
torre^F esquinera

flanking tower
torre^F flanqueante

curtain wall
muralla^F

guardhouse
cuerpo^M de guardia^F

corbel
modillón^M

machicolation
matacán^M

rampart
muralla^F

drawbridge
puente^M levadizo

postern
poterna^F

barbican
barbacana^F

stockade
empalizada^F

footbridge
pasarela^F

chemise
camisa^F

moat
foso^M

bartizan
garita^F

lists
liza^F

Vauban fortification

fortificación^F de Vauban

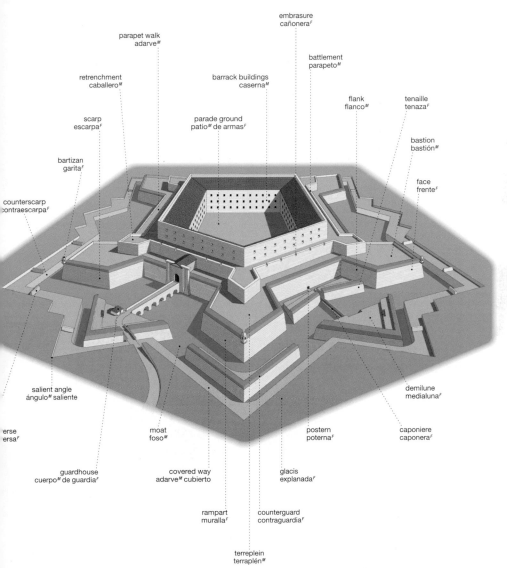

embrasure
cañonera^F

parapet walk
adarve^M

battlement
parapeto^M

retrenchment
caballero^M

barrack buildings
caserna^M

flank
flanco^M

tenaille
tenaza^F

scarp
escarpa^F

parade ground
patio^M de armas^F

bastion
bastión^M

bartizan
garita^F

face
frente^F

counterscarp
contraescarpa^F

salient angle
ángulo^M saliente

demilune
medialuna^F

erse
ersa^F

moat
foso^M

postern
poterna^F

caponiere
caponera^F

guardhouse
cuerpo^M de guardia^F

covered way
adarve^M cubierto

glacis
explanada^F

rampart
muralla^F

counterguard
contraguardia^F

terreplein
terraplén^M

Gothic cathedral

catedralᶠ gótica

general view
vista ᶠ general

vau
bóveda

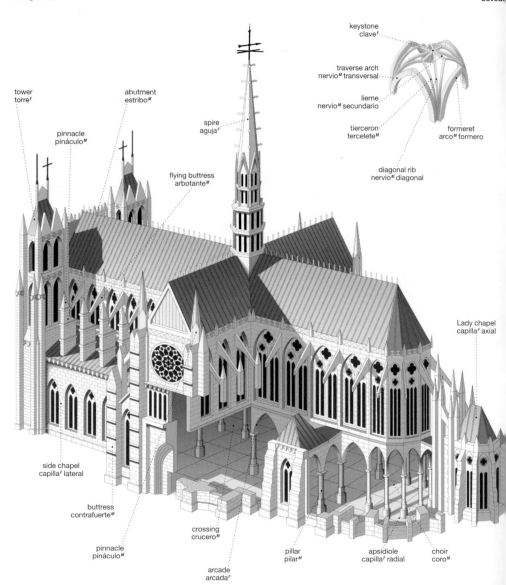

tower
torre ᶠ

abutment
estribo ᴹ

pinnacle
pináculo ᴹ

spire
aguja ᶠ

flying buttress
arbotante ᴹ

keystone
clave ᶠ

traverse arch
nervio ᴹ transversal

lierne
nervio ᴹ secundario

tierceron
tercelete ᴹ

diagonal rib
nervio ᴹ diagonal

formeret
arco ᴹ formero

Lady chapel
capilla ᶠ axial

side chapel
capilla ᶠ lateral

buttress
contrafuerte ᴹ

pinnacle
pináculo ᴹ

crossing
crucero ᴹ

arcade
arcada ᶠ

pillar
pilar ᴹ

apsidiole
capilla ᶠ radial

choir
coro ᴹ

Gothic cathedral

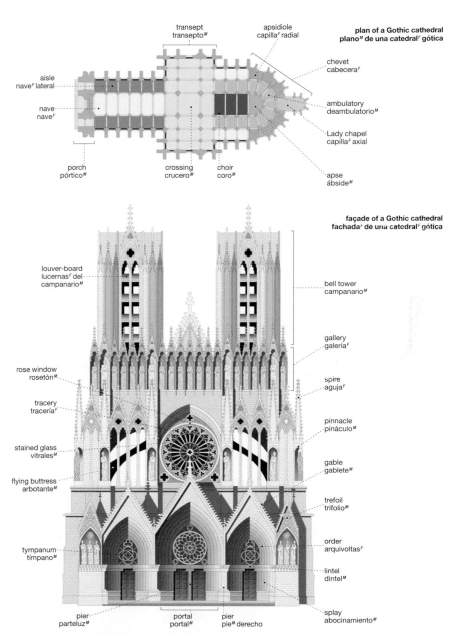

plan of a Gothic cathedral
plano ᴹ **de una catedral** ᶠ **gótica**

transept
transepto ᴹ

apsidiole
capilla ᶠ radial

chevet
cabecera ᶠ

aisle
nave ᶠ lateral

nave
nave ᶠ

ambulatory
deambulatorio ᴹ

Lady chapel
capilla ᶠ axial

porch
pórtico ᴹ

crossing
crucero ᴹ

choir
coro ᴹ

apse
ábside ᴹ

façade of a Gothic cathedral
fachada ᶠ **de una catedral** ᶠ **gótica**

louver-board
lucernas ᶠ del
campanario ᴹ

bell tower
campanario ᴹ

gallery
galería ᶠ

rose window
rosetón ᴹ

spire
aguja ᶠ

tracery
tracería ᶠ

pinnacle
pináculo ᴹ

stained glass
vitrales ᴹ

gable
gablete ᴹ

flying buttress
arbotante ᴹ

trefoil
trifolio ᴹ

order
arquivoltas ᶠ

tympanum
tímpano ᴹ

lintel
dintel ᴹ

pier
parteluz ᴹ

portal
portal ᴹ

pier
pie ᴹ derecho

splay
abocinamiento ᴹ

ARTS AND ARCHITECTURE

Romanesque church

iglesia^f románica

façade of a Romanesque church
fachada^f de una iglesia^f románica

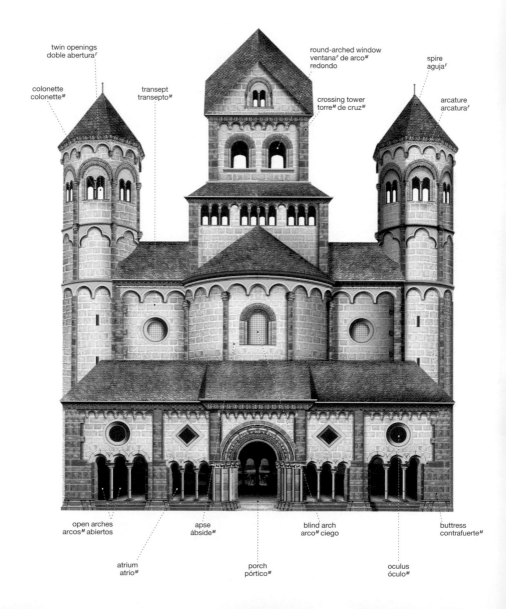

twin openings
doble abertura^f

colonette
colonette^M

transept
transepto^M

round-arched window
ventana^f de arco^M
redondo

spire
aguja^f

crossing tower
torre^M de cruz^M

arcature
arcatura^f

open arches
arcos^M abiertos

apse
ábside^M

blind arch
arco^M ciego

buttress
contrafuerte^M

atrium
atrio^M

porch
pórtico^M

oculus
óculo^M

Renaissance villa

casa^F renacentista

façade of a Renaissance villa
fachada^F de casa^F renacentista

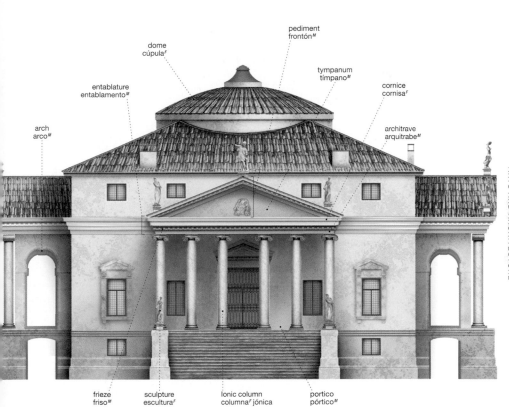

pediment
frontón^M

dome
cúpula^F

tympanum
tímpano^M

entablature
entablamento^M

cornice
cornisa^F

arch
arco^M

architrave
arquitrabe^M

frieze
friso^M

sculpture
escultura^F

Ionic column
columna^F jónica

portico
pórtico^M

ARTS AND ARCHITECTURE

Baroque church

iglesia^F barroca

façade of a Baroque church
fachada^F de una iglesia^F barroca

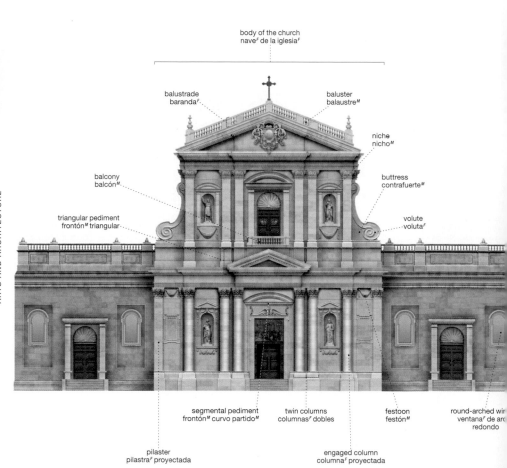

body of the church
nave^F de la iglesia^F

balustrade
baranda^F

baluster
balaustre^M

niche
nicho^M

balcony
balcón^M

buttress
contrafuerte^M

triangular pediment
frontón^M triangular

volute
voluta^F

segmental pediment
frontón^M curvo partido^M

twin columns
columnas^F dobles

festoon
festón^M

round-arched win
ventana^F de arc
redondo

pilaster
pilastra^F proyectada

engaged column
columna^F proyectada

art deco building

edificio^M art deco^M

façade of an art deco building
fachada^F de un edificio^M art deco^M

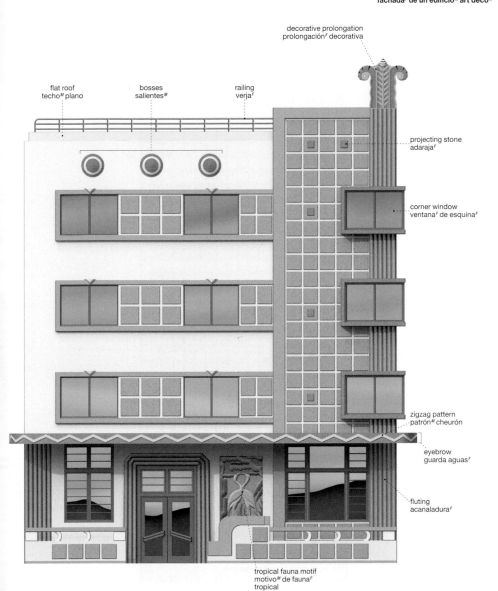

decorative prolongation
prolongación^F decorativa

flat roof
techo^M plano

bosses
salientes^M

railing
verja^F

projecting stone
adaraja^F

corner window
ventana^F de esquina^F

zigzag pattern
patrón^M cheurón

eyebrow
guarda aguas^F

fluting
acanaladura^F

tropical fauna motif
motivo^M de fauna^F
tropical

international style skyscraper

rascacielos^M de estilo^M internacional

façade of an international style skyscraper
fachada^F de rascacielos^M de estilo^M
internacional

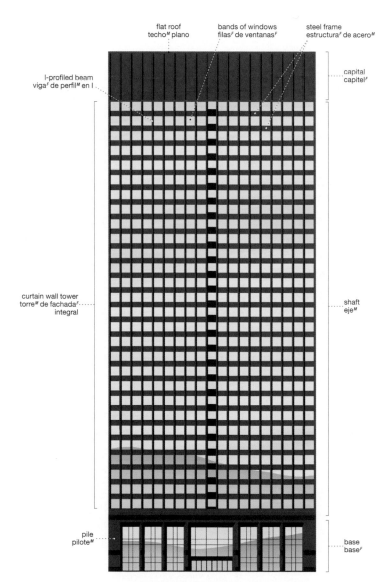

flat roof
techo^M plano

bands of windows
filas^F de ventanas^F

steel frame
estructura^F de acero^M

capital
capitel^F

I-profiled beam
viga^F de perfil^M en I

curtain wall tower
torre^M de fachada^F
integral

shaft
eje^M

pile
pilote^M

base
base^F

pagoda
pagoda^F

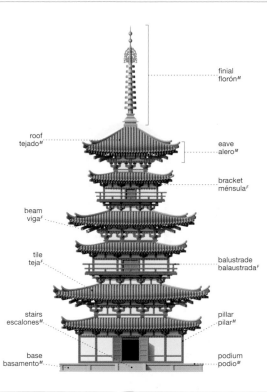

finial
florón^M

roof
tejado^M

eave
alero^M

bracket
ménsula^F

beam
viga^F

tile
teja^F

balustrade
balaustrada^F

stairs
escalones^M

pillar
pilar^M

base
basamento^M

podium
podio^M

Aztec temple
templo^M **azteca**

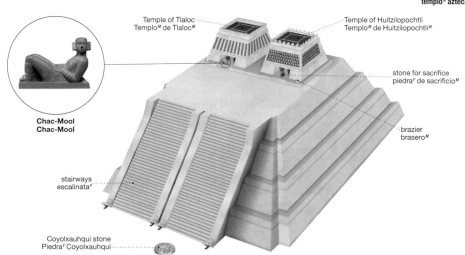

Temple of Tlaloc
Templo^M de Tlaloc^M

Temple of Huitzilopochtli
Templo^M de Huitzilopochtli^M

stone for sacrifice
piedra^F de sacrificio^M

brazier
brasero^M

Chac-Mool
Chac-Mool

stairways
escalinata^F

Coyolxauhqui stone
Piedra^F Coyolxauhqui

examples of roofs

cubiertas^f

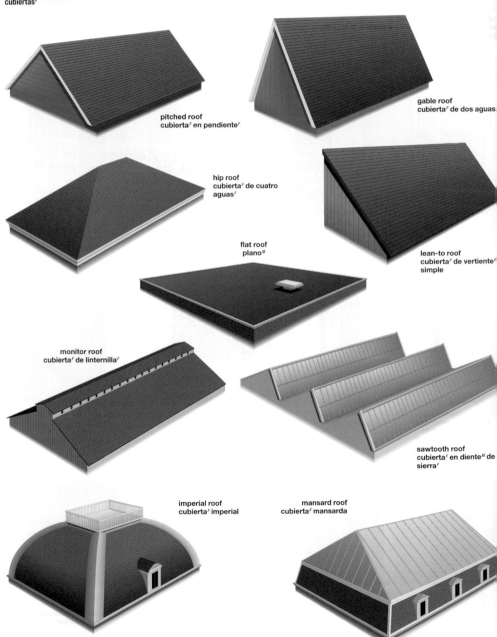

pitched roof
cubierta^f en pendiente^f

gable roof
cubierta^f de dos aguas

hip roof
cubierta^f de cuatro
aguas^f

lean-to roof
cubierta^f de vertiente^f
simple

flat roof
plano^M

monitor roof
cubierta^f de linternilla^f

sawtooth roof
cubierta^f en diente^M de
sierra^f

imperial roof
cubierta^f imperial

mansard roof
cubierta^f mansarda

conical broach roof
cubierta^f cónica

sloped turret
cubierta^f de torrecilla^f

helm roof
cubierta^f piramidal

bell roof
cubierta^f de cúpula^f
peraltada

ARTS AND ARCHITECTURE

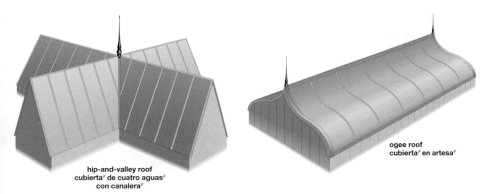

hip-and-valley roof
cubierta^f de cuatro aguas^f
con canalera^f

ogee roof
cubierta^f en artesa^f

dome roof
cúpula^f

rotunda roof
cubierta^f de rotonda^f

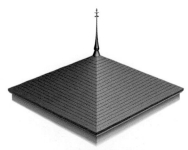

pavilion roof
cubierta^f de pabellón^m

examples of windows

ejemplos^M de ventanas^F

sliding folding window
ventana^F de librillo^M

French casement window
ventana^F a la francesa^F

casement window
ventana^F a la inglesa^F

louvered window
ventana^F de celosía^F

sliding window
ventana^F corredera

double-hung window
ventana^F de guillotina^F

horizontal pivoting window
ventana^F basculante

vertical pivoting window
ventana^F pivotante

escalator

escalera^F mecánica

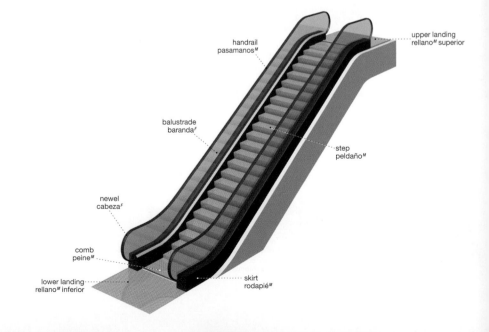

handrail
pasamanos^M

upper landing
rellano^M superior

balustrade
baranda^F

step
peldaño^M

newel
cabeza^F

comb
peine^M

lower landing
rellano^M inferior

skirt
rodapié^M

elevator

ascensor[M]

elevator mechanism
mecanismo[M] del
ascensor[M]

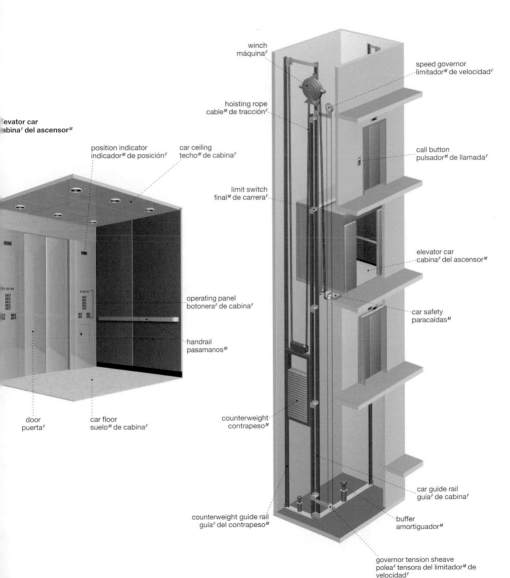

winch
máquina[F]

speed governor
limitador[M] de velocidad[F]

hoisting rope
cable[M] de tracción[F]

elevator car
cabina[F] del ascensor[M]

position indicator
indicador[M] de posición[F]

car ceiling
techo[M] de cabina[F]

call button
pulsador[M] de llamada[F]

limit switch
final[M] de carrera[F]

elevator car
cabina[F] del ascensor[M]

operating panel
botonera[F] de cabina[F]

car safety
paracaídas[M]

handrail
pasamanos[M]

door
puerta[F]

car floor
suelo[M] de cabina[F]

counterweight
contrapeso[M]

car guide rail
guía[F] de cabina[F]

counterweight guide rail
guía[F] del contrapeso[M]

buffer
amortiguador[M]

governor tension sheave
polea[F] tensora del limitador[M] de
velocidad[F]

traditional houses

viviendas^F tradicionales

igloo
iglú^M

yurt
yurta^F

hut
choza^F indígena

wigwam
wigwam^M

hut
choza^F

isba
isba^F

tepee
tipi^M

pile dwelling
palafito^M

adobe house
casa^F de adobes

viga
viga^F

ladder
escalera^F

ARTS AND ARCHITECTURE

city houses
viviendas^f urbanas

two-story house
casa*f* de dos plantas*f*

one-story house
casa*f* de una planta*F*

duplex
casas*f* pareadas

town houses
casas*f* adosadas

condominiums
viviendas*f* plurifamiliares

high-rise apartment
bloque*M* de apartamentos*M*

ARTS AND ARCHITECTURE

museum

museo^M

general view
vista^F **general**

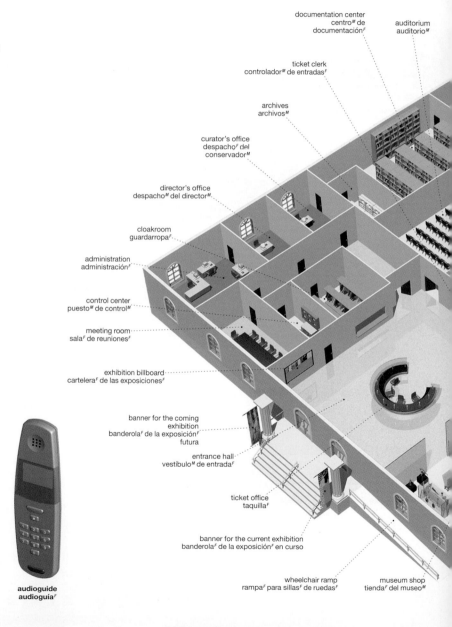

documentation center
centro^M de
documentación^F

auditorium
auditorio^M

ticket clerk
controlador^M de entradas^F

archives
archivos^M

curator's office
despacho^F del
conservador^M

director's office
despacho^M del director^M

cloakroom
guardarropa^F

administration
administración^F

control center
puesto^M de control^M

meeting room
sala^F de reuniones^F

exhibition billboard
cartelera^F de las exposiciones^F

banner for the coming
exhibition
banderola^F de la exposición^F
futura

entrance hall
vestíbulo^M de entrada^F

ticket office
taquilla^F

banner for the current exhibition
banderola^F de la exposición^F en curso

wheelchair ramp
rampa^F para sillas^F de ruedas^F

museum shop
tienda^F del museo^M

audioguide
audioguía^F

unloading dock
muelle^M de carga^F

receiving area
área^F de recepción^F

conservation laboratory
laboratorio^M de
conservación^F

surveillance camera
cámara^F de vigilancia^F

sculpture
escultura^F

interactive terminals
terminales^M interactivos

installation work
instalación^F

temporary exhibition rooms
salas^F de exposición^F
temporal

painting
pintura^F

projection room
sala^F de proyección^F

permanent exhibition rooms
salas^F de exposición^F
permanente

restrooms
aseos^M

library
biblioteca^F

frame
marco^M

painting
pintura^F

label
etiqueta^F

ARTS AND ARCHITECTURE

painting and drawing
pintura^F y dibujo^M

drawing material
material^M de dibujo^M

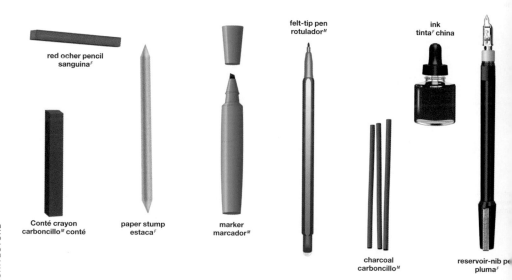

red ocher pencil
sanguina^F

felt-tip pen
rotulador^M

ink
tinta^F china

Conté crayon
carboncillo^M conté

paper stump
estaca^F

marker
marcador^M

charcoal
carboncillo^M

reservoir-nib pe
pluma^F

oil pastel
pastel^M al óleo^M

wax crayons
ceras^F

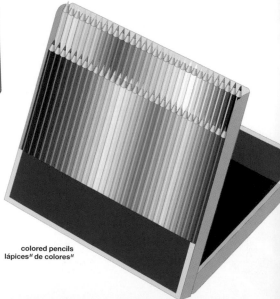

dry pastel
pastel^M

colored pencils
lápices^M de colores^M

ARTS AND ARCHITECTURE

palette with dipper
aleta^F con tarrito^M

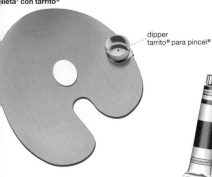

dipper
tarrito^M para pincel^M

painting material
material^M de pintura^F

palette with hollows
aleta^F con huecos^M para
pintura^F

oil/acrylic paint
óleo^M

watercolor/gouache tube
tubo^M de acuarela^F/de guache^M

watercolor/gouache cakes
pastillas^F de acuarela^F/de guaches^M

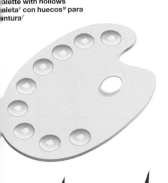

palette knife
espátula^F

fan brush
brocha^F

brush
pincel^M

sumi-e brush
sumie^M

flat brush
pincel^M plano

painting knife
cuchillo^M paleta^F

ARTS AND ARCHITECTURE

painting and drawing

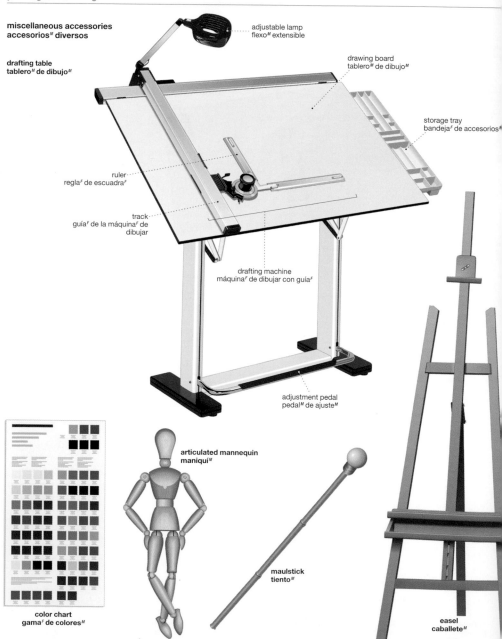

miscellaneous accessories
accesorios^M diversos

drafting table
tablero^M de dibujo^M

adjustable lamp
flexo^M extensible

drawing board
tablero^M de dibujo^M

storage tray
bandeja^F de accesorios^M

ruler
regla^F de escuadra^F

track
guía^F de la máquina^F de
dibujar

drafting machine
máquina^F de dibujar con guía^F

adjustment pedal
pedal^M de ajuste^M

articulated mannequin
maniquí^M

maulstick
tiento^M

color chart
gama^F de colores^M

easel
caballete^M

painting and drawing

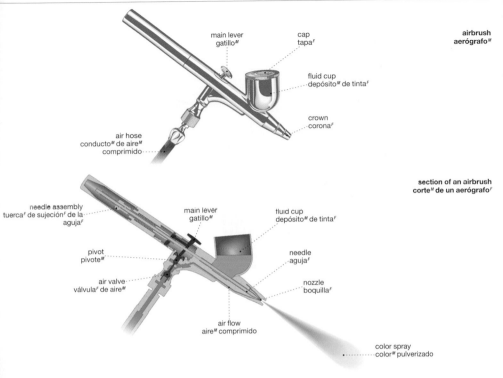

main lever
gatillo^M

cap
tapa^F

fluid cup
depósito^M de tinta^F

crown
corona^F

air hose
conducto^M de aire^M
comprimido

**airbrush
aerógrafo^M**

**section of an airbrush
corte^M de un aerógrafo^F**

needle assembly
tuerca^F de sujeción^F de la
aguja^F

main lever
gatillo^M

fluid cup
depósito^M de tinta^F

pivot
pivote^M

needle
aguja^F

air valve
válvula^F de aire^M

nozzle
boquilla^F

air flow
aire^M comprimido

color spray
color^M pulverizado

**utility liquids
líquidos^M accesorios**

**turpentine
aguarrás^M**

**fixative
fijador^M**

**varnish
barniz^M**

**linseed oil
aceite^M de linaza^F**

ARTS AND ARCHITECTURE

painting and drawing

color wheel
círculo^M **de los colores**^{M}

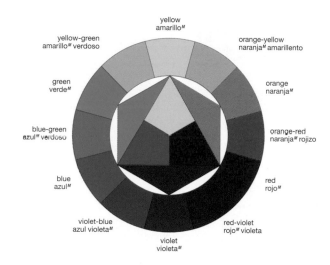

yellow
amarillo^M

yellow-green
amarillo^M verdoso

orange-yellow
naranja^M amarillento

green
verde^M

orange
naranja^M

blue-green
azul^M verdoso

orange-red
naranja^M rojizo

blue
azul^M

red
rojo^M

violet-blue
azul violeta^M

red-violet
rojo^M violeta

violet
violeta^M

primary colors
colores^M **primarios**

secondary co
colores^M secune

tertiary colors
colores^M **terciarios**

major techniques
técnicas^F **principales**

gouache
guache

watercolor
acuarela^F

oil painting
pintura^F **al óleo**^{M}

charcoal drawing
dibujo^M **al carboncillo**^{M}

ink drawing
dibujo^M **de tinta**^{F} **ch**

wax crayon drawing
dibujo^M **a la cera**^{F}

colored pencil drawing
dibujo^M **de lápices**^{M} **de**
colores^M

oil pastel drawing
pintura^F **al pastel**^{M} **al**
óleo^M

dry pastel drawing
pintura^F **al pastel**^{M}
blando

felt-tip pen drawin
pintura^F **con**
rotuladores^M

ARTS AND ARCHITECTURE

painting and drawing

**main supports
soportes***M*
principales

**panel
tabla***F*

**canvas
lienzo***M*

**cardboard
cartón***M*

**paper
papel***M*

**painting: examples of
styles
pintura***F*: **ejemplos***M* **de
estilos***M*

**Baroque
barroco***M*

**classicism
clasicismo***M*

painting and drawing

painting: examples of styles

Impressionism
impresionismo*ᴹ*

Expressionism
expresionismo*ᴹ*

Cubism
cubismo*ᴹ*

abstract art
arte*ᴹ* abstracto

naive art
naïf*ᴹ*

realism
realismo*ᴹ*

ARTS AND ARCHITECTURE

wood carving

talla[F] en madera[F]

steps
etapas[F]

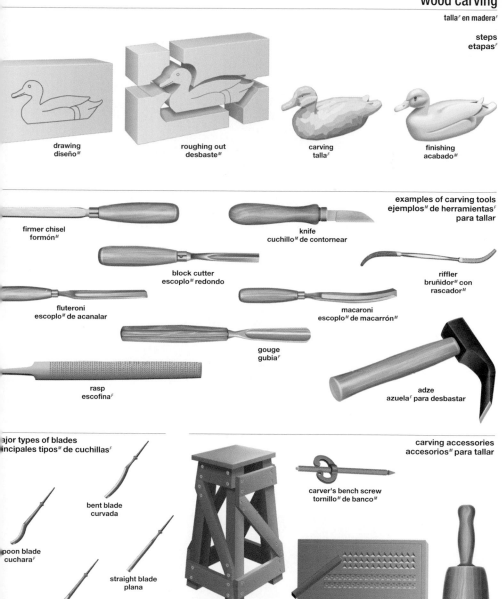

drawing
diseño[M]

roughing out
desbaste[M]

carving
talla[F]

finishing
acabado[M]

examples of carving tools
ejemplos[M] de herramientas[F]
para tallar

firmer chisel
formón[M]

knife
cuchillo[M] de contornear

block cutter
escoplo[M] redondo

riffler
bruñidor[M] con
rascador[M]

fluteroni
escoplo[M] de acanalar

macaroni
escoplo[M] de macarrón[M]

gouge
gubia[F]

rasp
escofina[F]

adze
azuela[F] para desbastar

ARTS AND ARCHITECTURE

ajor types of blades
incipales tipos[M] de cuchillas[F]

carving accessories
accesorios[M] para tallar

bent blade
curvada

carver's bench screw
tornillo[M] de banco[M]

poon blade
cuchara[F]

straight blade
plana

blade with two beveled edges
escoplo[M]

stand
taburete[M]

punch and pattern
punteo[M]

mallet
mazo[M]

printing

impresión^F

relief printing
impresión^F en relieve^M

paper
papel^M

printed image
imagen^F impresa

inked surface
entintado^M

raised figure
matriz^F en relieve^M

intaglio printing
huecograbado^M

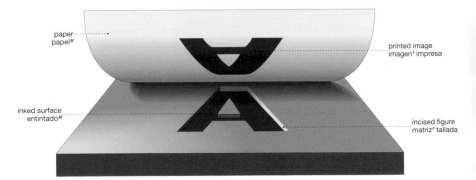

paper
papel^M

printed image
imagen^F impresa

inked surface
entintado^M

incised figure
matriz^F tallada

lithographic printing
impresión^F litográfica

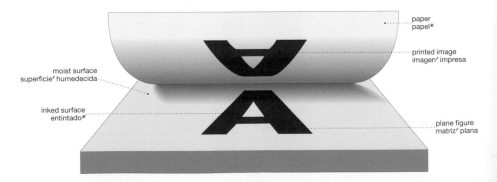

paper
papel^M

printed image
imagen^F impresa

moist surface
superficie^F humedecida

inked surface
entintado^M

plane figure
matriz^F plana

relief printing process

impresión^F en relieve^M

equipment
equipo^M

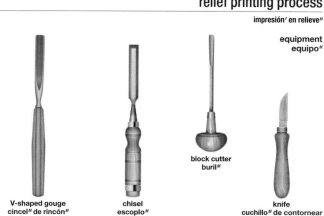

mallet
maza^F

U-shaped gouge
gubia^F

V-shaped gouge
cincel^M de rincón^M

chisel
escoplo^M

block cutter
buril^M

knife
cuchillo^M de contornear

ink
tinta^F

spatula
espátula^F

inking slab
plancha^F de entintado^M

ink
tinta^F

brayer
rodillo^M entintador

baren
frotador^M

woodcut
bloque^M de madera^F
grabado

wood engraving
que^M de madera^F para grabar

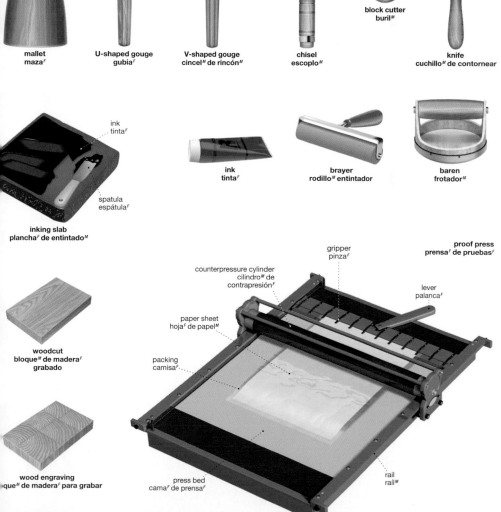

gripper
pinza^F

proof press
prensa^F de pruebas^F

counterpressure cylinder
cilindro^M de
contrapresión^F

lever
palanca^F

paper sheet
hoja^F de papel^M

packing
camisa^F

rail
raíl^M

press bed
cama^F de prensa^F

ARTS AND ARCHITECTURE

intaglio printing process
impresión^F en huecograbado^M

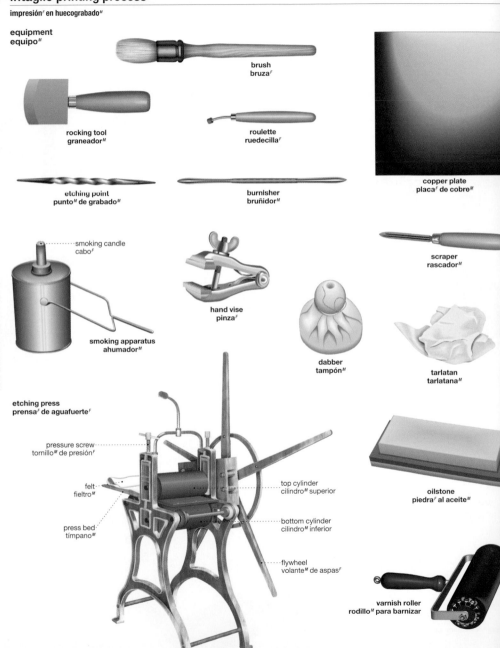

equipment
equipo^M

brush
bruza^F

rocking tool
graneador^M

roulette
ruedecilla^F

etching point
punto^M de grabado^M

burnisher
bruñidor^M

copper plate
placa^F de cobre^M

smoking candle
cabo^F

scraper
rascador^M

smoking apparatus
ahumador^M

hand vise
pinza^F

dabber
tampón^M

tarlatan
tarlatana^M

etching press
prensa^F de aguafuerte^F

pressure screw
tornillo^M de presión^F

felt
fieltro^M

top cylinder
cilindro^M superior

oilstone
piedra^F al aceite^M

press bed
tímpano^M

bottom cylinder
cilindro^M inferior

flywheel
volante^M de aspas^F

varnish roller
rodillo^M para barnizar

lithography
litografía^F

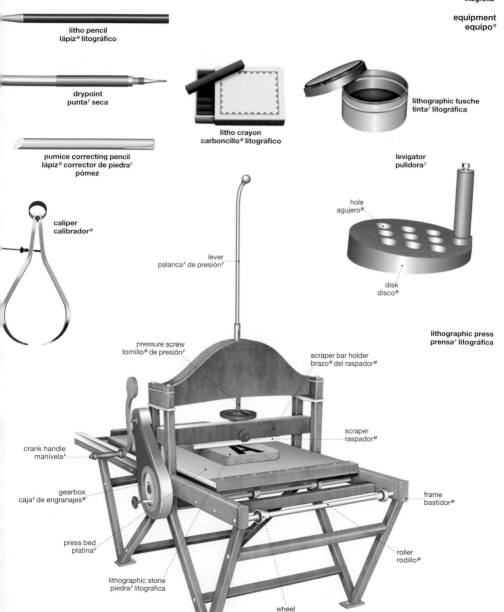

equipment
equipo^M

litho pencil
lápiz^M litográfico

drypoint
punta^F seca

pumice correcting pencil
lápiz^M corrector de piedra^F
pómez

litho crayon
carboncillo^M litográfico

lithographic tusche
tinta^F litográfica

levigator
pulidora^F

hole
agujero^M

disk
disco^M

caliper
calibrador^M

lever
palanca^F de presión^F

lithographic press
prensa^F litográfica

pressure screw
tornillo^M de presión^F

scraper bar holder
brazo^M del raspador^M

scraper
raspador^M

crank handle
manivela^F

gearbox
caja^F de engranajes^M

frame
bastidor^M

press bed
platina^F

roller
rodillo^M

lithographic stone
piedra^F litográfica

wheel
rueda^F

ARTS AND ARCHITECTURE

screen printing
impresión^f de pantalla^f

equipment
equipo^M

screen printing ink
tinta^f de impresión^f en pantalla^f

photo emulsion
emulsión^f fotográfica

sensitizer
sensibilizante^M

stencil
matriz^f

squeegee
escobilla^f para secar

silk screen frame
marco^M de pantalla^f de seda^f

fabric screen mesh
malla^f de pantalla^f de tela^f

aluminum frame
marco^M de aluminio^M

textile printing
prensa^f de impresión

design
diseño^M

silk screen frame
marco^M de pantalla^f de seda^f

screen holder
soporte^M para pantalla^f

removable pallet
palé^M extraíble

pivoting tray
bandeja^f pivotante

scoop coater
aplicador^M de emulsiones^f

vacuum printing table
tabla^f de impresión^f en vacío^M

silk screen frame
marco^M de pantalla^f de seda^f

vacuum table
tabla^f de vacío^M

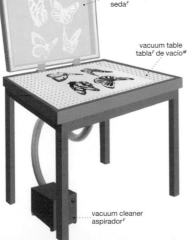

vacuum cleaner
aspirador^f

exposure ta
tabla^f de exposici

rubber lid
tapa^f de caucho^M

transparent working surface
superficie^f de trabajo^M transparente

fluorescent lamp
luz^f fluorescente

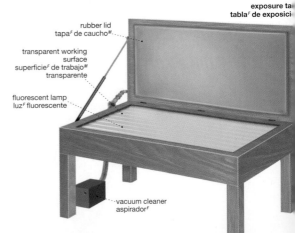

vacuum cleaner
aspirador^f

fine bookbinding
encuadernación^f a mano^f

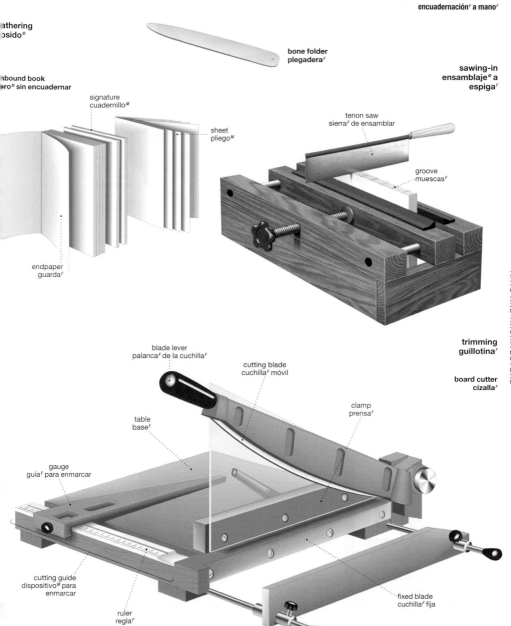

athering
osido^M

bone folder
plegadera^F

nbound book
ro^M sin encuadernar

signature
cuadernillo^M

sheet
pliego^M

endpaper
guarda^F

sawing-in
ensamblaje^M a
espiga^F

tenon saw
sierra^F de ensamblar

groove
muescas^F

trimming
guillotina^F

board cutter
cizalla^F

blade lever
palanca^F de la cuchilla^F

cutting blade
cuchilla^F móvil

clamp
prensa^F

table
base^F

gauge
guía^F para enmarcar

cutting guide
dispositivo^M para
enmarcar

ruler
regla^F

fixed blade
cuchilla^F fija

ARTS AND ARCHITECTURE

theater

teatro[M]

general view
vista[F] **general**

ARTS AND ARCHITECTURE

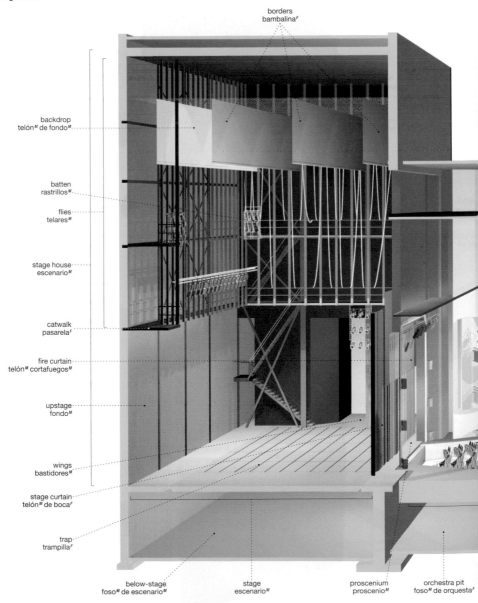

borders
bambalina[F]

backdrop
telón[M] de fondo[M]

batten
rastrillos[M]

flies
telares[M]

stage house
escenario[M]

catwalk
pasarela[F]

fire curtain
telón[M] cortafuegos[M]

upstage
fondo[M]

wings
bastidores[M]

stage curtain
telón[M] de boca[F]

trap
trampilla[F]

below-stage
foso[M] de escenario[M]

stage
escenario[M]

proscenium
proscenio[M]

orchestra pit
foso[M] de orquesta[F]

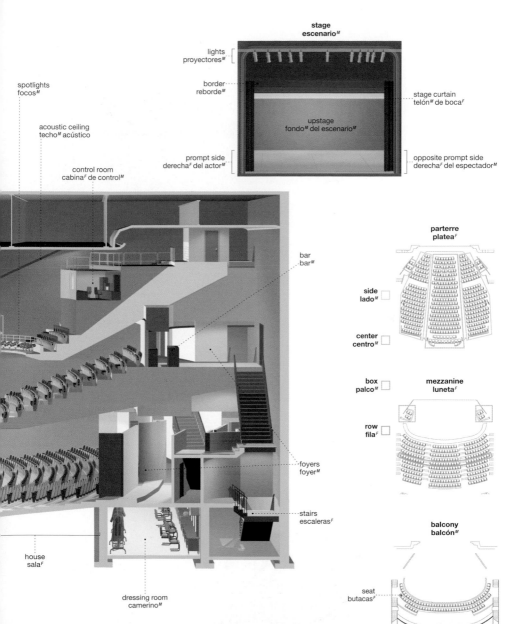

stage
escenario^M

lights
proyectores^M

border
reborde^M

stage curtain
telón^M de boca^F

upstage
fondo^M del escenario^M

prompt side
derecha^F del actor^M

opposite prompt side
derecha^F del espectador^M

spotlights
focos^M

acoustic ceiling
techo^M acústico

control room
cabina^F de control^M

bar
bar^M

parterre
platea^F

side
lado^M

center
centro^M

box
palco^M

mezzanine
luneta^F

row
fila^F

foyers
foyer^M

stairs
escaleras^F

house
sala^F

dressing room
camerino^M

balcony
balcón^M

seat
butacas^F

ARTS AND ARCHITECTURE

movie set

platóᴹ de rodajeᴹ

general view
vistaꟳ general

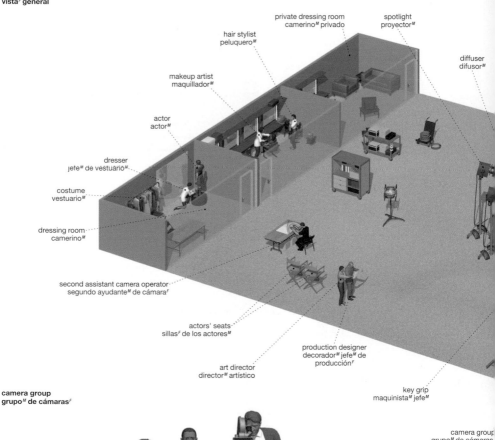

private dressing room
camerinoᴹ privado

spotlight
proyectorᴹ

hair stylist
peluqueroᴹ

diffuser
difusorᴹ

makeup artist
maquilladorᴹ

actor
actorᴹ

dresser
jefeᴹ de vestuarioᴹ

costume
vestuarioᴹ

dressing room
camerinoᴹ

second assistant camera operator
segundo ayudanteᴹ de cámaraꟳ

actors' seats
sillasꟳ de los actoresᴹ

production designer
decoradorᴹ jefeᴹ de
producciónꟳ

art director
directorᴹ artístico

key grip
maquinistaᴹ jefeᴹ

camera group
grupoᴹ de cámarasꟳ

grip
maquinistaᴹ

first assistant camera
operator
primer ayudanteᴹ de
cámaraꟳ

camera
cámaraꟳ

camera group
grupoᴹ de cámaras

camera operator
operadorᴹ de cámaraꟳ

dolly
travelínᴹ

dolly tracks
raílesᴹ del travelínᴹ

movie set

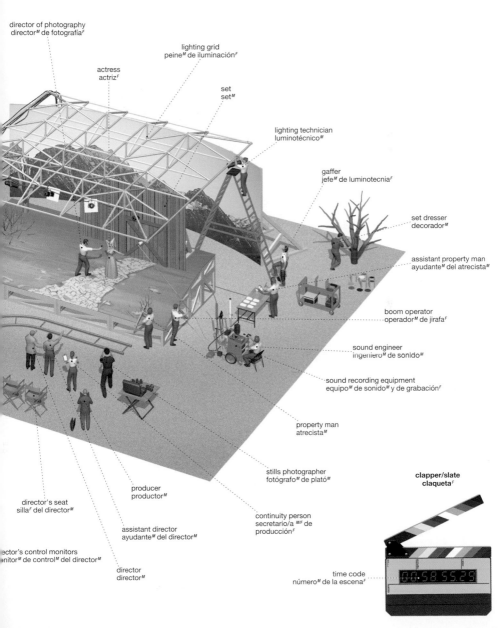

director of photography
director^M de fotografía^F

lighting grid
peine^M de iluminación^F

actress
actriz^F

set
set^M

lighting technician
luminotécnico^M

gaffer
jefe^M de luminotecnia^F

set dresser
decorador^M

assistant property man
ayudante^M del atrecista^F

boom operator
operador^M de jirafa^F

sound engineer
ingeniero^M de sonido^M

sound recording equipment
equipo^M de sonido^M y de grabación^F

property man
atrecista^M

stills photographer
fotógrafo^M de plató^M

clapper/slate
claqueta^F

producer
productor^M

continuity person
secretario/a ^{M/F} de
producción^F

director's seat
silla^F del director^M

assistant director
ayudante^M del director^M

ector's control monitors
onitor^M de control^M del director^M

director
director^M

time code
número^M de la escena^F

00:58:55:29

movie theater

cine^M

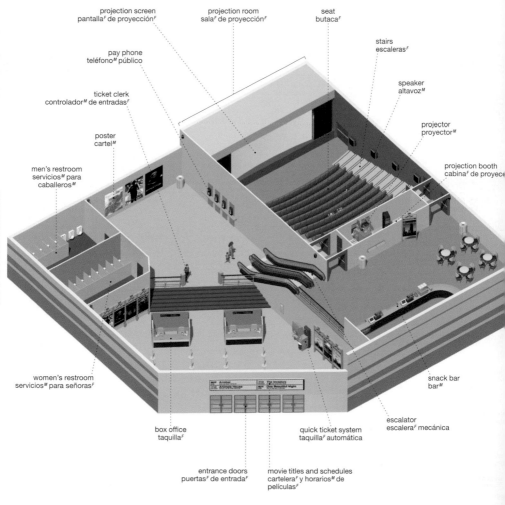

projection screen
pantalla^F de proyección^F

projection room
sala^F de proyección^F

seat
butaca^F

stairs
escaleras^F

pay phone
teléfono^M público

speaker
altavoz^M

ticket clerk
controlador^M de entradas^F

projector
proyector^M

poster
cartel^M

projection booth
cabina^F de proyec

men's restroom
servicios^M para
caballeros^M

women's restroom
servicios^M para señoras^F

snack bar
bar^M

box office
taquilla^F

quick ticket system
taquilla^F automática

escalator
escalera^F mecánica

entrance doors
puertas^F de entrada^F

movie titles and schedules
cartelera^F y horarios^M de
películas^F

symphony orchestra

orquesta^F sinfónica

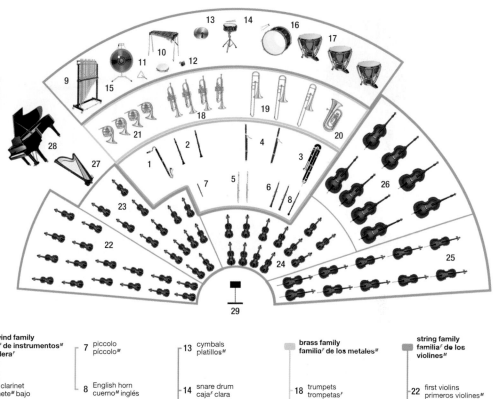

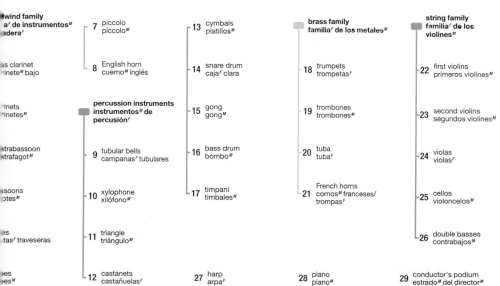

wind family
a^F de instrumentos^M
adera^F

ss clarinet
rinete^M bajo

rinets
rinetes^M

trabassoon
trafagot^M

ssoons
otes^M

es
tas^F traveseras

es
es^M

7 piccolo
  píccolo^M

8 English horn
  cuerno^M inglés

percussion instruments
instrumentos^M de
percusión^F

9 tubular bells
  campanas^F tubulares

10 xylophone
   xilófono^M

11 triangle
   triángulo^M

12 castanets
   castañuelas^F

13 cymbals
   platillos^M

14 snare drum
   caja^F clara

15 gong
   gong^M

16 bass drum
   bombo^M

17 timpani
   timbales^M

27 harp
   arpa^F

brass family
familia^F de los metales^M

18 trumpets
   trompetas^F

19 trombones
   trombones^M

20 tuba
   tuba^F

21 French horns
   cornos^M franceses/
   trompas^F

28 piano
   piano^M

string family
familia^F de los
violines^M

22 first violins
   primeros violines^M

23 second violins
   segundos violines^M

24 violas
   violas^F

25 cellos
   violoncelos^M

26 double basses
   contrabajos^M

29 conductor's podium
   estrado^M del director^M

examples of instrumental groups

ejemplos^M de conjuntos^M instrumentales

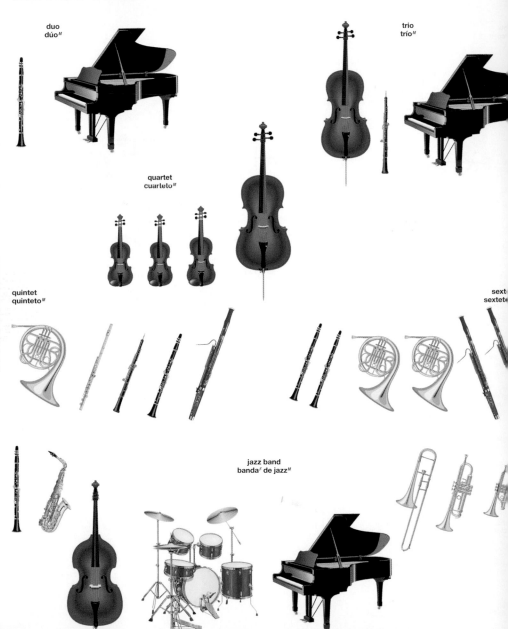

duo
dúo^M

trio
trío^M

quartet
cuarleto^M

quintet
quinteto^M

sext
sextet

jazz band
banda^F de jazz^M

stringed instruments
instrumentos^M **de cuerda**^F

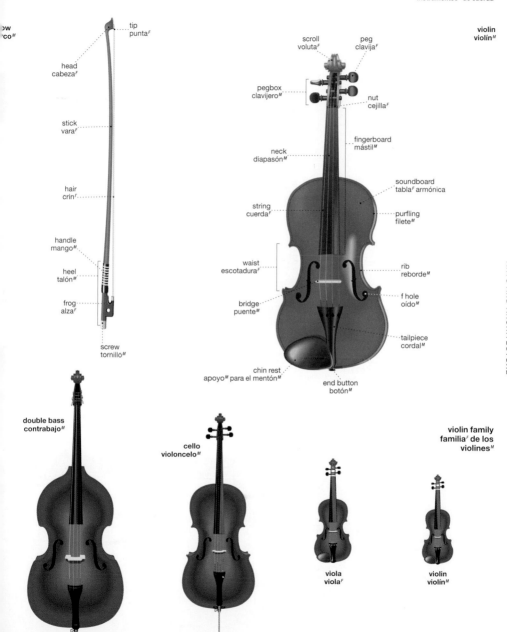

ɔw
co^M

tip
punta^F

head
cabeza^F

stick
vara^F

hair
crin^F

handle
mango^M

heel
talón^M

frog
alza^F

screw
tornillo^M

violin
violín^M

scroll
voluta^F

peg
clavija^F

pegbox
clavijero^M

nut
cejilla^F

fingerboard
mástil^M

neck
diapasón^M

soundboard
tabla^F armónica

string
cuerda^F

purfling
filete^M

waist
escotadura^F

rib
reborde^M

bridge
puente^M

f hole
oído^M

tailpiece
cordal^M

chin rest
apoyo^M para el mentón^M

end button
botón^M

double bass
contrabajo^M

cello
violoncelo^M

violin family
familia^F de los
violines^M

viola
viola^F

violin
violín^M

stringed instruments

harp
arpa^F

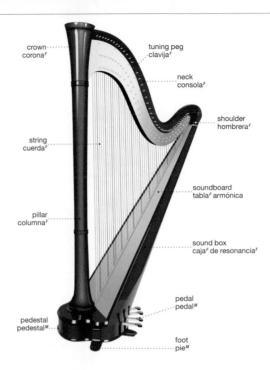

crown ········ corona^F

tuning peg ·clavija^F

neck consola^F

shoulder hombrera^F

string cuerda^F

soundboard tabla^F armónica

pillar columna^F

sound box caja^F de resonancia^F

pedal ·pedal^M

pedestal pedestal^M·

foot ·pie^M

acoustic guitar
guitarra^F **clásica**

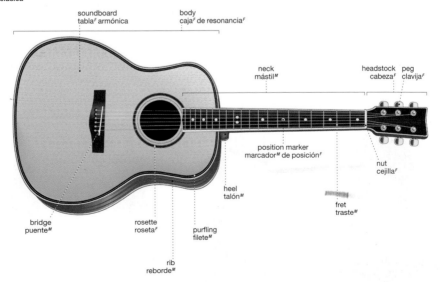

soundboard tabla^F armónica

body caja^F de resonancia^F

neck mástil^M

headstock cabeza^F

peg clavija^F

position marker marcador^M de posición^F

nut cejilla^F

heel talón^M

fret traste^M

bridge puente^M

rosette roseta^F

purfling filete^M

rib reborde^M

ARTS AND ARCHITECTURE

stringed instruments

electric guitar
guitarra^F eléctrica

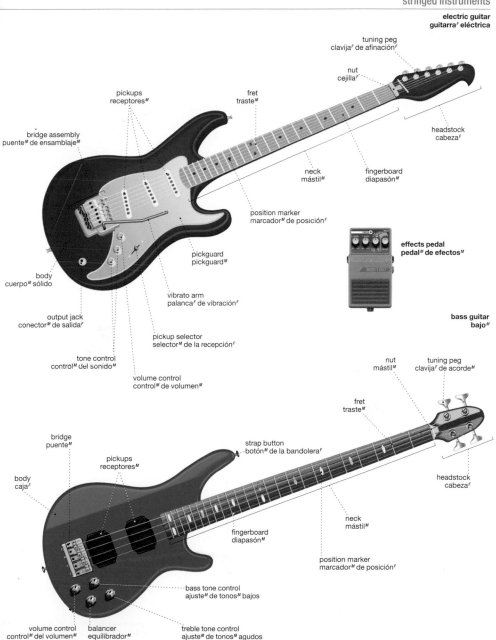

tuning peg
clavija^F de afinación^F

nut
cejilla^F

pickups
receptores^M

fret
traste^M

bridge assembly
puente^M de ensamblaje^M

headstock
cabeza^F

neck
mástil^M

fingerboard
diapasón^M

position marker
marcador^M de posición^F

effects pedal
pedal^M de efectos^M

pickguard
pickguard^M

body
cuerpo^M sólido

vibrato arm
palanca^F de vibración^F

bass guitar
bajo^M

output jack
conector^M de salida^F

pickup selector
selector^M de la recepción^F

nut
mástil^M

tuning peg
clavija^F de acorde^M

tone control
control^M del sonido^M

fret
traste^M

volume control
control^M de volumen^M

bridge
puente^M

strap button
botón^M de la bandolera^F

pickups
receptores^M

body
caja^F

headstock
cabeza^F

neck
mástil^M

fingerboard
diapasón^M

position marker
marcador^M de posición^F

bass tone control
ajuste^M de tonos^M bajos

volume control
control^M del volumen^M

balancer
equilibrador^M

treble tone control
ajuste^M de tonos^M agudos

ARTS AND ARCHITECTURE

wind instruments

instrumentos^M de viento^M

saxophone
saxofón^M

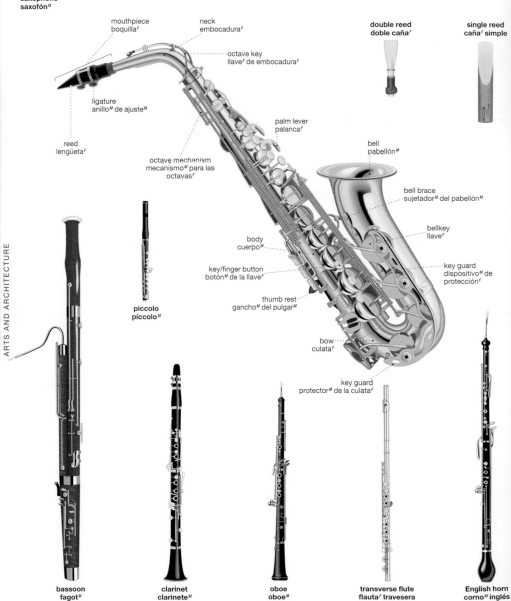

mouthpiece
boquilla^F

neck
embocadura^F

octave key
llave^F de embocadura^F

ligature
anillo^M de ajuste^M

reed
lengüeta^F

octave mechanism
mecanismo^M para las
octavas^F

palm lever
palanca^F

body
cuerpo^M

key/finger button
botón^M de la llave^F

thumb rest
gancho^M del pulgar^M

bow
culata^F

key guard
protector^M de la culata^F

bell
pabellón^M

bell brace
sujetador^M del pabellón^M

bellkey
llave^F

key guard
dispositivo^M de
protección^F

double reed
doble caña^F

single reed
caña^F simple

piccolo
píccolo^M

bassoon
fagot^M

clarinet
clarinete^M

oboe
oboe^M

transverse flute
flauta^F travesera

English horn
corno^M inglés

ARTS AND ARCHITECTURE

wind instruments

finger button
llave^F

little finger hook
gancho^M del meñique^M

bell
pabellón^M

trumpet
trompeta^F

mouthpiece receiver
empate^M de la boquilla^F

leadpipe
tubo^M

ring
anillo^M

mouthpiece
boquilla^F

tuning slide
corredera^F de
afinamiento^M

first valve slide
primer pistón^M móvil

third valve slide
tercer pistón^M móvil

euphonium
llave^F para agua^F

thumb hook
gancho^M del pulgar^M

valve
pistón^M

mute
sordina^F

valve casing
tubo^M del pistón^M

second valve slide
segundo pistón^M móvil

French horn
corno^M **francés/trompa**^F

cornet
cornetín^M

bugle
clarín^M

euphonium
tuba^F

saxhorn
bombardino^M

trombone
trombón^M

ARTS AND ARCHITECTURE

keyboard instruments

instrumentos^M **de teclado**^M

upright piano
piano^M **vertical**

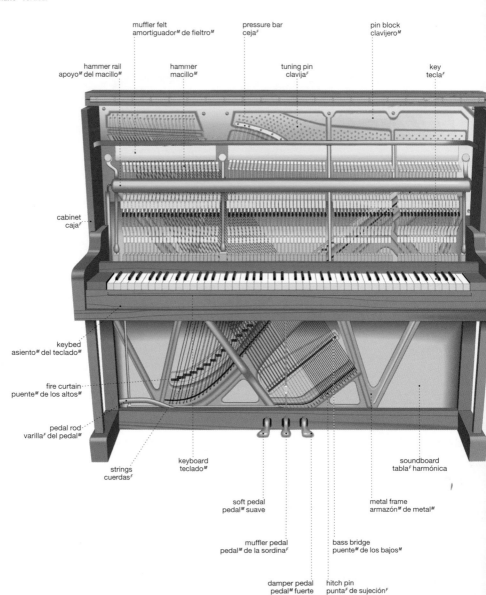

muffler felt
amortiguador^M de fieltro^M

pressure bar
ceja^F

pin block
clavijero^M

hammer rail
apoyo^M del macillo^M

hammer
macillo^M

tuning pin
clavija^F

key
tecla^F

cabinet
caja^F

keybed
asiento^M del teclado^M

fire curtain
puente^M de los altos^M

pedal rod
varilla^F del pedal^M

strings
cuerdas^F

keyboard
teclado^M

soundboard
tabla^F harmónica

soft pedal
pedal^M suave

metal frame
armazón^M de metal^M

muffler pedal
pedal^M de la sordina^F

bass bridge
puente^M de los bajos^M

damper pedal
pedal^M fuerte

hitch pin
punta^F de sujeción^F

keyboard instruments

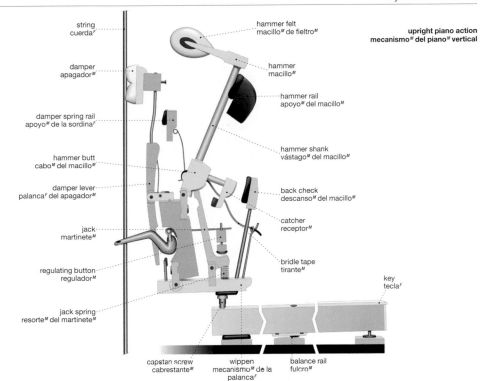

string
cuerda^F

hammer felt
macillo^M de fieltro^M

upright piano action
mecanismo^M del piano^M vertical

damper
apagador^M

hammer
macillo^M

hammer rail
apoyo^M del macillo^M

damper spring rail
apoyo^M de la sordina^F

hammer shank
vástago^M del macillo^M

hammer butt
cabo^M del macillo^M

damper lever
palanca^F del apagador^M

back check
descanso^M del macillo^M

catcher
receptor^M

jack
martinete^M

bridle tape
tirante^M

regulating button
regulador^M

key
tecla^F

jack spring
resorte^M del martinete^M

capstan screw
cabrestante^M

wippen
mecanismo^M de la
palanca^F

balance rail
fulcro^M

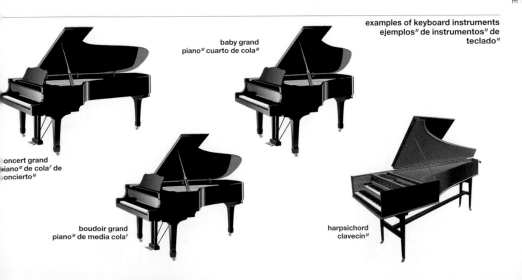

examples of keyboard instruments
ejemplos^M de instrumentos^M de
teclado^M

baby grand
piano^M cuarto de cola^M

concert grand
piano^M de cola^F de
concierto^M

boudoir grand
piano^M de media cola^F

harpsichord
clavecín^M

keyboard instruments

organ console
consola^F

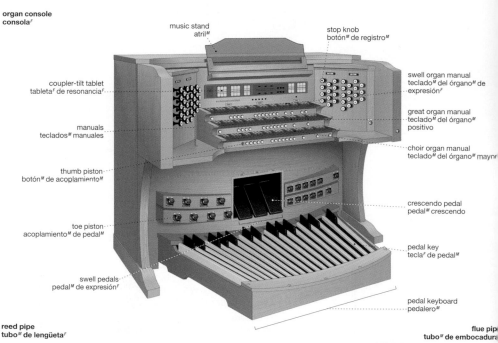

music stand
atril^M

stop knob
botón^M de registro^M

coupler-tilt tablet
tableta^F de resonancia^F

manuals
teclados^M manuales

thumb piston
botón^M de acoplamiento^M

toe piston
acoplamiento^M de pedal^M

swell pedals
pedal^M de expresión^F

swell organ manual
teclado^M del órgano^M de expresión^F

great organ manual
teclado^M del órgano^M positivo

choir organ manual
teclado^M del órgano^M mayor

crescendo pedal
pedal^M crescendo

pedal key
tecla^F de pedal^M

pedal keyboard
pedalero^M

reed pipe
tubo^M **de lengüeta**^{F}

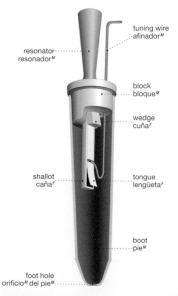

tuning wire
afinador^M

resonator
resonador^M

block
bloque^M

wedge
cuña^F

shallot
caña^F

tongue
lengüeta^F

boot
pie^M

foot hole
orificio^M del pie^M

flue pipe
tubo^M **de embocadura**^{F}

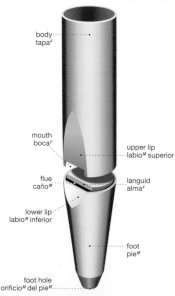

body
tapa^F

mouth
boca^F

flue
caño^M

lower lip
labio^M inferior

upper lip
labio^M superior

languid
alma^F

foot
pie^M

foot hole
orificio^M del pie^M

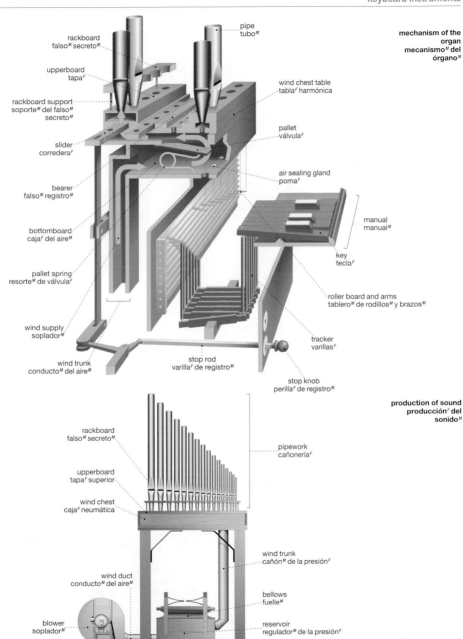

mechanism of the
organ
mecanismo^M del
órgano^M

rackboard
falso^M secreto^M

upperboard
tapa^F

rackboard support
soporte^M del falso^M
secreto^M

slider
corredera^F

bearer
falso^M registro^M

bottomboard
caja^F del aire^M

pallet spring
resorte^M de válvula^F

wind supply
soplador^M

wind trunk
conducto^M del aire^M

pipe
tubo^M

wind chest table
tabla^F harmónica

pallet
válvula^F

air sealing gland
poma^F

manual
manual^M

key
tecla^F

roller board and arms
tablero^M de rodillos^M y brazos^M

tracker
varillas^F

stop rod
varilla^F de registro^M

stop knob
perilla^F de registro^M

ARTS AND ARCHITECTURE

production of sound
producción^F del
sonido^M

rackboard
falso^M secreto^M

upperboard
tapa^F superior

wind chest
caja^F neumática

pipework
cañonería^F

wind trunk
cañón^M de la presión^F

bellows
fuelle^M

wind duct
conducto^M del aire^M

blower
soplador^M

reservoir
regulador^M de la presión^F

percussion instruments

instrumentos^M **de percusión**^F

drum kit
batería^M

tom-tom
tam-tam^M

cymbal
platillo^M suspendido

high-hat cymbal
platillo^M high hat

batter head
parche^M superior

snare drum
caja^F clara

tripod stand
trípode^M

bass drum
bombo^M

tension screw
clavija^F de tensión^F

stand
soporte^M

mallet
palillo^M

floor tom
tamboril^M

spur
espolón^M

footplate
pedal^M

leg
pata^F

kettledrum
timbal

snare drum
caja^F **clara**

tension casing
sujetador^M

tension rod
varilla^F de tensión^F

snare strainer
tensor^M de las cuerdas^F

snare
cuerdas^F

snare head
parche^M inferior

tuning bolt
barra^F sujetadora

head
parche^M superior

metal counterhoop
arco^M tensor

tuning gauge
afinación^F

kettle
concha^F

strut
puntal^M

tension rod
varilla^F de tensión^F

crown
corona^F

pedal
pedal^M

caster
ruedecilla^F

foot
pata^F

sleigh bells
cascabeles^M

set of bells
campanillas^F

sistrum
sistro^M

castanets
castañuelas^F

cymbals
platillos^M

tambourine
pandereta^F

triangle
triángulo^M

bongos
bongos^M

head
parche^M

jingle
cascabel^M

beater
maza^F

wire brush
escobilla^F metálica

tubular bells
campanas^F tubulares

gong
gong^M

xylophone
xilófono^M

resonator
resonador^M

drumsticks
baquetas^F

frame
armazón^M

bar
barra^F

mallets
maza^F

ARTS AND ARCHITECTURE

electronic music

música^f electrónica

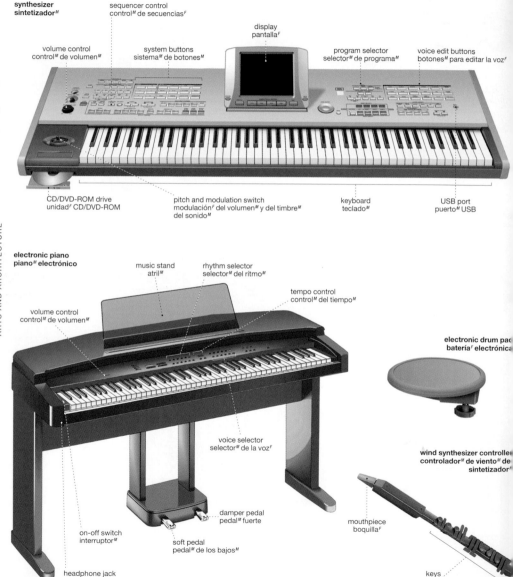

synthesizer
sintetizador^M

sequencer control
control^M de secuencias^F

display
pantalla^F

volume control
control^M de volumen^M

system buttons
sistema^M de botones^M

program selector
selector^M de programa^M

voice edit buttons
botones^M para editar la voz^F

CD/DVD-ROM drive
unidad^F CD/DVD-ROM

pitch and modulation switch
modulación^F del volumen^M y del timbre^M
del sonido^M

keyboard
teclado^M

USB port
puerto^M USB

electronic piano
piano^M electrónico

music stand
atril^M

rhythm selector
selector^M del ritmo^M

tempo control
control^M del tiempo^M

volume control
control^M de volumen^M

electronic drum pad
batería^F electrónica

voice selector
selector^M de la voz^F

wind synthesizer controller
controlador^M de viento^M de
sintetizador^M

on-off switch
interruptor^M

damper pedal
pedal^M fuerte

soft pedal
pedal^M de los bajos^M

mouthpiece
boquilla^F

headphone jack
toma^F para auriculares^M

keys
teclas^F

ARTS AND ARCHITECTURE

electronic music

accessories and mixing
devices
accesorios^M y dispositivos^M de
mezcla^F

drum machine
máquina^F de percusión^F

amplifier
amplificador^M

input jack
conector^M de entrada^F

headphone jack
toma^F para auriculares^M

sequencer
secuenciador^M

speaker
altavoz^M

expander
amplificador^M

musical instrument digital interface (MIDI) cable
cable^M de interfaz^F digital para instrumentos^M musicales
(MIDI)

SB turntable
cadiscos^M USB

tone arm
brazo^M fonocaptor

sampler
muestreador^M

pitch fader
atenuador^M de tonos^M

platter
plato^M

pitch slider
potenciómetro^M de velocidad^F de
lectura^F

DJ console
consola^F de DJ

miniature joystick
minijoystick^M

scratch/jog wheel
rueda^F para scratch^M

cue point button
botón^M de punto^M de
referencia^F

headphone jack
toma^F para auriculares^M

play/pause button
botón^M de reproducción^F/
pausa^F

volume control
control^M de volumen^M

microphone jack
toma^F del micrófono^M

pre-listening button
botón^M de escucha^F
previa

volume control
control^M de volumen^M

crossfader
mezclador^M

traditional musical instruments

instrumentos*ᴹ* musicales tradicionales

accordion
acordeón*ᴹ*

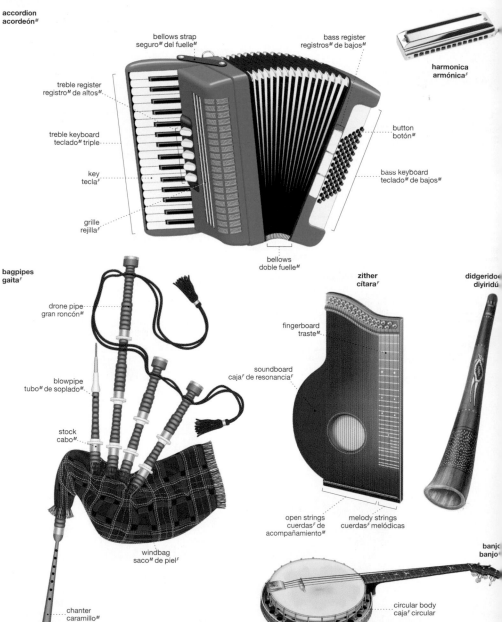

bellows strap
seguro*ᴹ* del fuelle*ᴹ*

bass register
registros*ᴹ* de bajos*ᴹ*

harmonica
armónica*ᶠ*

treble register
registro*ᴹ* de altos*ᴹ*

button
botón*ᴹ*

treble keyboard
teclado*ᴹ* triple

bass keyboard
teclado*ᴹ* de bajos*ᴹ*

key
tecla*ᶠ*

grille
rejilla*ᶠ*

bellows
doble fuelle*ᴹ*

bagpipes
gaita*ᶠ*

zither
cítara*ᶠ*

didgeridoo
diyiridú

drone pipe
gran roncón*ᴹ*

fingerboard
traste*ᴹ*

soundboard
caja*ᶠ* de resonancia*ᶠ*

blowpipe
tubo*ᴹ* de soplado*ᴹ*

stock
cabo*ᴹ*

open strings
cuerdas*ᶠ* de
acompañamiento*ᴹ*

melody strings
cuerdas*ᶠ* melódicas

banjo
banjo

windbag
saco*ᴹ* de piel*ᶠ*

chanter
caramillo*ᴹ*

circular body
caja*ᶠ* circular

kora
kora^F

neck
mástil^M

strings
cuerdas^F

tuning chords
anillos^M de sonido^M

hand post
porte^M de la mano^F

head
piel^F armónica

sound box
caja^F de resonancia^F

bridge
puente^M

tailpiece
cordal^M

mallet
mazo^M

panpipe
zampoña^F

lyre
lira^F

crossbar
travesaño^M

arm
brazo^M

sound box
caja^F de resonancia^F

balalaika
balalaika^F

triangular body
caja^F triangular

erhu
erhu^M

bow
arco^M

ratchet
leva^F

djembe
yembé^M

head
piel^F

shell
caja^F de resonancia^F

tension rope
cuerda^F de tensión^F

plectrum
púa^F

mandolin
mandolina^F

pear-shaped body
caja^F media pera^F

Jew's harp
birimbao^M

tongue
lengüeta^F de la caña^F

frame
estructura^F

talking drum
tambor^M hablante

musical notation

notación^F musical

staff
pentagrama^M

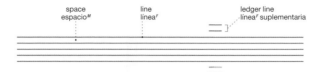

space
espacio^M

line
línea^F

ledger line
línea^F suplementaria

clefs
claves^F

G clef
clave^F de sol^M

F clef
clave^F de fa^M

C clef
clave^F de do^M

time signatures
compás^M

two-two time
de dos mitades^F

four-four time
de cuatro cuartos^M

repeat sign
barra^F de repetición^F

three-four time
de tres cuartos^M

bar line
barra^F de compás^M

intervals
intervalos^M

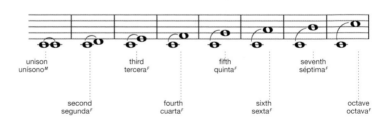

unison
unísono^M

third
tercera^F

fifth
quinta^F

seventh
séptima^F

second
segunda^F

fourth
cuarta^F

sixth
sexta^F

octave
octava^F

scale
escala^F

C	D	E	F	G	A	B	C
do(C)	re(D)	mi(E)	fa(F)	sol(G)	la(A)	si(B)	do(C)

musical notation

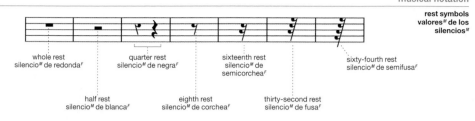

whole rest
silencio^M de redonda^F

quarter rest
silencio^M de negra^F

sixteenth rest
silencio^M de
semicorchea^F

sixty-fourth rest
silencio^M de semifusa^F

half rest
silencio^M de blanca^F

eighth rest
silencio^M de corchea^F

thirty-second rest
silencio^M de fusa^F

ornaments
adornos^M

appoggiatura
apoyatura^F

trill
trino^M

turn
grupeto^M

mordent
mordente^M

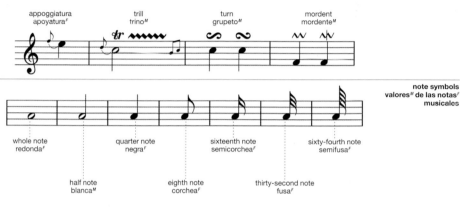

note symbols
valores^M **de las notas**^F
musicales

whole note
redonda^F

quarter note
negra^F

sixteenth note
semicorchea^F

sixty-fourth note
semifusa^F

half note
blanca^M

eighth note
corchea^F

thirty-second note
fusa^F

accidentals
accidentales^M

flat
bemol^M

double sharp
doble sostenido^M

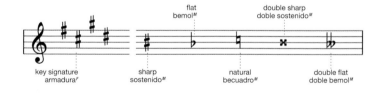

key signature
armadura^F

sharp
sostenido^M

natural
becuadro^M

double flat
doble bemol^M

other signs
otros signos^M

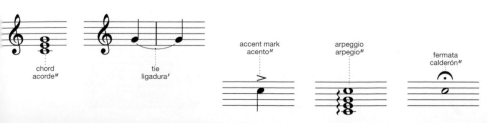

chord
acorde^M

tie
ligadura^F

accent mark
acento^M

arpeggio
arpegio^M

fermata
calderón^M

ARTS AND ARCHITECTURE

musical accessories

accesorios^M musicales

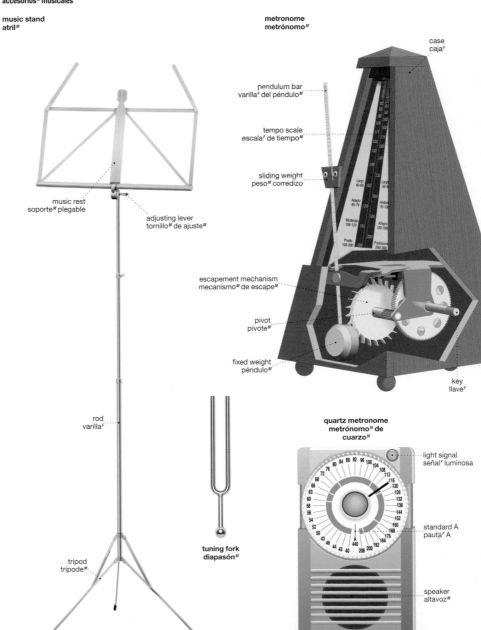

music stand
atril^M

music rest
soporte^M plegable

adjusting lever
tornillo^M de ajuste^M

rod
varilla^F

tripod
trípode^M

metronome
metrónomo^M

case
caja^F

pendulum bar
varilla^F del péndulo^M

tempo scale
escala^F de tiempo^M

sliding weight
peso^M corredizo

escapement mechanism
mecanismo^M de escape^M

pivot
pivote^M

fixed weight
péndulo^M

key
llave^F

tuning fork
diapasón^M

quartz metronome
metrónomo^M de
cuarzo^M

light signal
señal^F luminosa

standard A
pauta^F A

speaker
altavoz^M

embroidery
bordado^M

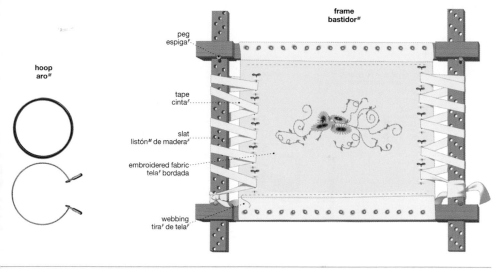

frame
bastidor^M

peg
espiga^F

tape
cinta^F

slat
listón^M de madera^F

embroidered fabric
tela^F bordada

webbing
tira^F de tela^F

hoop
aro^M

stitch patterns
puntos^M **de bordado**^M

cross stitches
puntos^M **de cruz**^F

couched stitches
bordados^M **planos**

loop stitches
puntos^M **de malla**^F

flat stitches
puntos^M **de relleno**^M

knot stitches
puntos^M **de relleno**^M **sueltos**

chevron stitch
punto^M de cruz^F

Oriental couching stitch
relleno^M alternado

chain stitch
cadeneta^F

long and short stitch
lanzado^M desigual

bullion stitch
pespunte^M

herringbone stitch
punto^M de escapulario^M

feather stitch
pata^F de gallo^M

French knot stitch
punto^M de nudos^M

Romanian couching stitch
bordado^M plano

fishbone stitch
punto^M de espiga^F

sewing
costura^F

sewing machine
máquina^F de coser

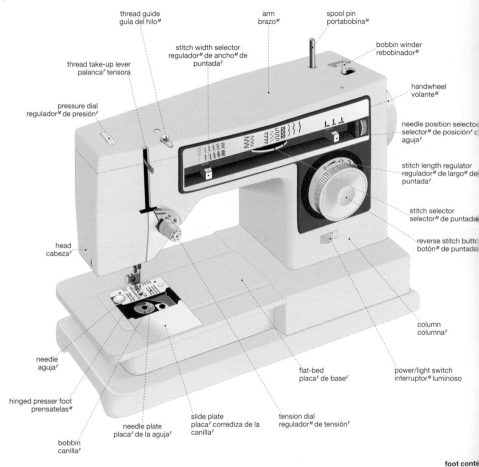

thread guide
guía del hilo^M

arm
brazo^M

spool pin
portabobina^M

stitch width selector
regulador^M de ancho^M de
puntada^F

bobbin winder
rebobinador^M

thread take-up lever
palanca^F tensora

handwheel
volante^M

pressure dial
regulador^M de presión^F

needle position selector
selector^M de posición^F de
aguja^F

stitch length regulator
regulador^M de largo^M de
puntada^F

stitch selector
selector^M de puntada

head
cabeza^F

reverse stitch button
botón^M de puntada

column
columna^F

needle
aguja^F

power/light switch
interruptor^M luminoso

flat-bed
placa^F de base^F

hinged presser foot
prensatelas^M

slide plate
placa^F corrediza de la
canilla^F

tension dial
regulador^M de tensión^F

needle plate
placa^F de la aguja^F

bobbin
canilla^F

foot control
pedal^M eléctrico

bobbin case
bobinas^F

bobbin
canilla^F

latch lever
lengüeta^F

hook
portacanilla^M

speed controller
pedal^M de velocidad^F

connecting terminal
enchufe^M

sewing

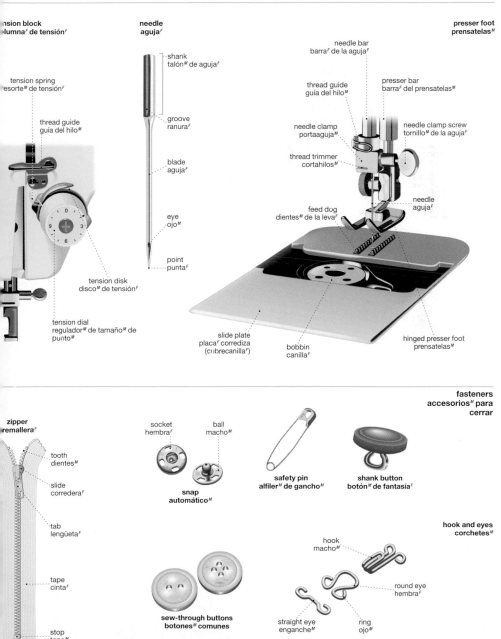

tension block
columna^F de tensión^F

tension spring
resorte^M de tensión^F

thread guide
guía del hilo^M

tension disk
disco^M de tensión^F

tension dial
regulador^M de tamaño^M de punto^M

needle
aguja^F

shank
talón^M de aguja^F

groove
ranura^F

blade
aguja^F

eye
ojo^M

point
punta^F

presser foot
prensatelas^M

needle bar
barra^F de la aguja^F

thread guide
guía del hilo^M

presser bar
barra^F del prensatelas^M

needle clamp
portaaguja^M

needle clamp screw
tornillo^M de la aguja^F

thread trimmer
cortahilos^M

needle
aguja^F

feed dog
dientes^M de la leva^F

slide plate
placa^F corrediza
(cubrecanilla^F)

bobbin
canilla^F

hinged presser foot
prensatelas^M

ARTS AND ARCHITECTURE

fasteners
accesorios^M para
cerrar

zipper
cremallera^F

tooth
dientes^M

slide
corredera^F

tab
lengüeta^F

tape
cinta^F

stop
tope^M

socket
hembra^F

ball
macho^M

snap
automático^M

safety pin
alfiler^M de gancho^M

shank button
botón^M de fantasía^F

hook and eyes
corchetes^M

hook
macho^M

round eye
hembra^F

sew-through buttons
botones^M comunes

straight eye
enganche^M

ring
ojo^M

sewing

ARTS AND ARCHITECTURE

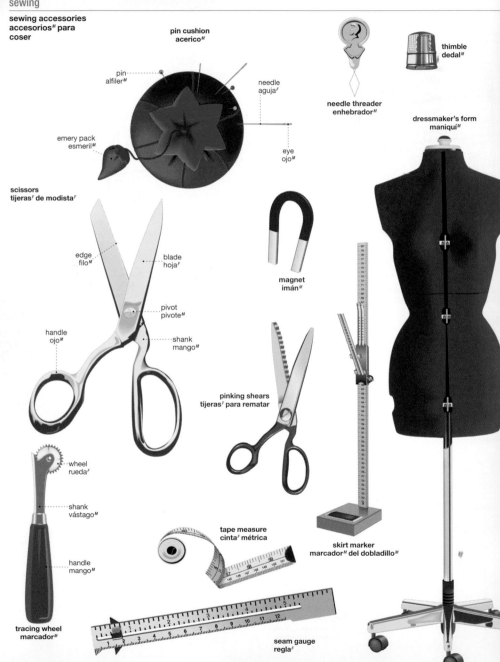

sewing accessories
accesoriosᴹ **para**
coser

pin cushion
acericoᴹ

pin
alfilerᴹ

needle
agujaᶠ

emery pack
esmerilᴹ

eye
ojoᴹ

needle threader
enhebradorᴹ

thimble
dedalᴹ

dressmaker's form
maniquíᴹ

scissors
tijerasᶠ **de modista**ᶠ

edge
filoᴹ

blade
hojaᶠ

magnet
imánᴹ

pivot
pivoteᴹ

handle
ojoᴹ

shank
mangoᴹ

pinking shears
tijerasᶠ **para rematar**

wheel
ruedaᶠ

shank
vástagoᴹ

tape measure
cintaᶠ **métrica**

skirt marker
marcadorᴹ **del dobladillo**ᴹ

handle
mangoᴹ

tracing wheel
marcadorᴹ

seam gauge
reglaᶠ

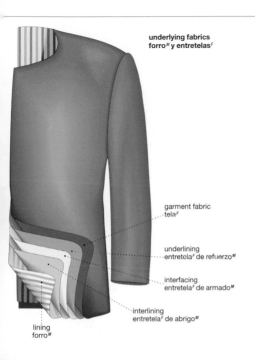

underlying fabrics
forro^M y entretelas^F

garment fabric
tela^F

underlining
entretela^F de refuerzo^M

interfacing
entretela^F de armado^M

interlining
entretela^F de abrigo^M

lining
forro^M

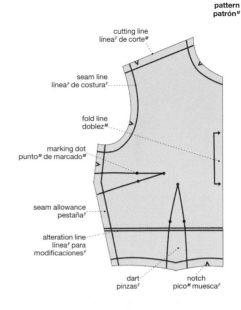

pattern
patrón^M

cutting line
línea^F de corte^M

seam line
línea^F de costura^F

fold line
doblez^M

marking dot
punto^M de marcado^M

seam allowance
pestaña^F

alteration line
línea^F para
modificaciones^F

dart
pinzas^F

notch
pico^M muesca^F

fabric structure
tejidos^M

bias
bies^M

selvage
orillo^M

crosswise grain
contrahílo^M de la tela^F

lengthwise grain
hilo^M de la tela^F

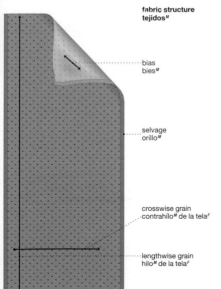

zipper line
posición^F de la cremallera^F

lengthwise grain
pinzas^F verticales

hemline
línea^F del dobladillo^M

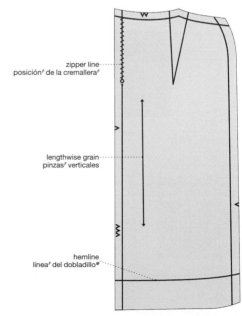

ARTS AND ARCHITECTURE

knitting

tejido M **de punto** M

knitting needle
aguja F **de punto** M

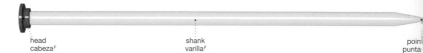

head
cabeza F

shank
varilla F

poin
punta

hook
gancho M

flat part
parte F plana

crochet ho
ganchill

circular needle
aguja F **circular**

cast-on stitches
puntos M **de montado** M

knitting gauge
regla F **para medir puntos** M

CM
1 1 2 3 4 5 6 7 8 9 10 11 12 13 14 15

7.5 7 6.5 6 5.5 5 4.5 4 3.75 3.25 3 2.75 2.25 2 8 9 10

stitch patterns
tipos M **de punto** M

swatch
muestra F

stockinette stitch
punto M **del derecho** M

garter stitch
punto M **del revés** M

moss stitch
punto M **de arroz** M

rib stitch
punto M **de respiguilla** F

basket stitch
punto M **de malla** F

cable stitch
punto M **de ochos** M

ARTS AND ARCHITECTURE

knitting machine
máquina^f tricotar

needle bed and carriages
máquinas^f de tejer

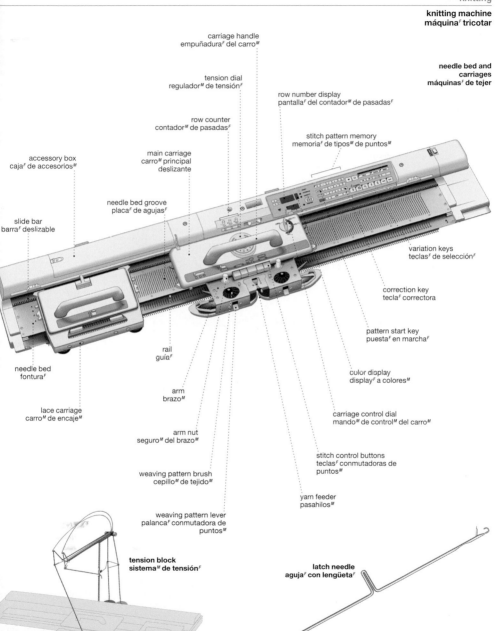

carriage handle
empuñadura^f del carro^M

tension dial
regulador^M de tensión^F

row number display
pantalla^F del contador^M de pasadas^F

row counter
contador^M de pasadas^F

stitch pattern memory
memoria^F de tipos^M de puntos^M

accessory box
caja^F de accesorios^M

main carriage
carro^M principal
deslizante

needle bed groove
placa^F de agujas^F

slide bar
barra^F deslizable

variation keys
teclas^F de selección^F

correction key
tecla^F correctora

pattern start key
puesta^F en marcha^F

needle bed
fontura^F

rail
guía^F

color display
display^F a colores^M

lace carriage
carro^M de encaje^M

arm
brazo^M

carriage control dial
mando^M de control^M del carro^M

arm nut
seguro^M del brazo^M

stitch control buttons
teclas^F conmutadoras de
puntos^M

weaving pattern brush
cepillo^M de tejido^M

yarn feeder
pasahilos^M

weaving pattern lever
palanca^F conmutadora de
puntos^M

tension block
sistema^M de tensión^F

latch needle
aguja^F con lengüeta^F

weaving
tejido^M

low-warp loom
telar^M de cuatro
marcos^M

general view
vista^F general

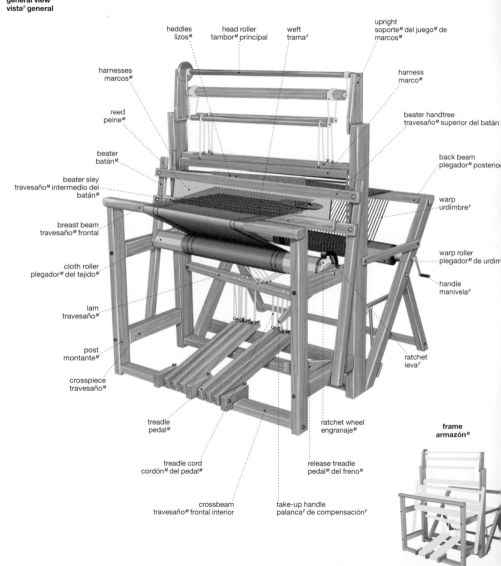

heddles
lizos^M

head roller
tambor^M principal

weft
trama^F

upright
soporte^M del juego^M de
marcos^M

harnesses
marcos^M

harness
marco^M

reed
peine^M

beater handtree
travesaño^M superior del batán

beater
batán^M

back beam
plegador^M posterio

beater sley
travesaño^M intermedio del
batán^M

warp
urdimbre^F

breast beam
travesaño^M frontal

warp roller
plegador^M de urdim

cloth roller
plegador^M del tejido^M

handle
manivela^F

lam
travesaño^M

post
montante^M

ratchet
leva^F

crosspiece
travesaño^M

treadle
pedal^M

ratchet wheel
engranaje^M

frame
armazón^M

treadle cord
cordón^M del pedal^M

release treadle
pedal^M del freno^M

crossbeam
travesaño^M frontal interior

take-up handle
palanca^F de compensación^F

weaving

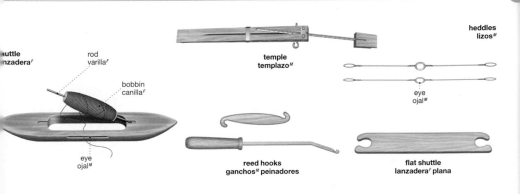

shuttle
lanzadera^F

rod
varilla^F

bobbin
canilla^F

eye
ojal^M

temple
templazo^M

heddles
lizos^M

eye
ojal^M

reed hooks
ganchos^M peinadores

flat shuttle
lanzadera^F plana

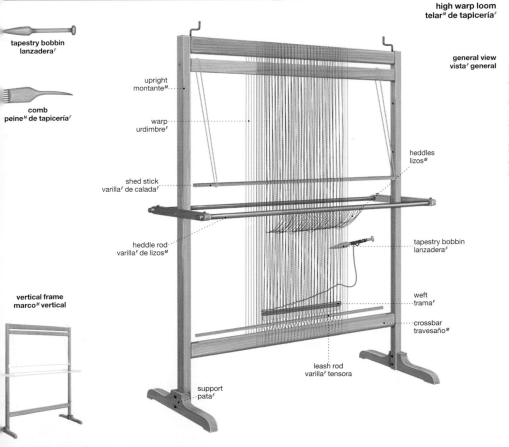

high warp loom
telar^M **de tapicería**^F

tapestry bobbin
lanzadera^F

comb
peine^M de tapicería^F

general view
vista^F **general**

upright
montante^M

warp
urdimbre^F

heddles
lizos^M

shed stick
varilla^F de calada^F

heddle rod
varilla^F de lizos^M

tapestry bobbin
lanzadera^F

vertical frame
marco^M **vertical**

weft
trama^F

crossbar
travesaño^M

leash rod
varilla^F tensora

support
pata^F

ARTS AND ARCHITECTURE

weaving

**weaving accessories
accesorios^M de
tejidos^F**

**bobbin winder
devanador^M de
bobinas^F**

shaft
eje^M

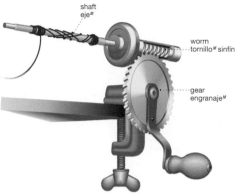

worm
tornillo^M sinfín

gear
engranaje^M

**swift
devanadera^F**

**motorized bobbin
winder
devanador^M**

driving wheel
polea^F de transmisión^F

clamp
tornillo^M

ball
huso^M

**warping frame
urdidor^M**

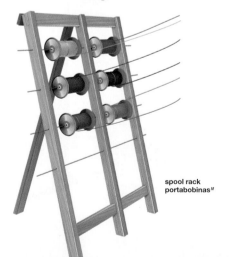

**spool rack
portabobinas^M**

peg
espiga^F

weaving

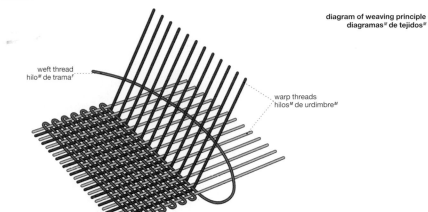

diagram of weaving principle
diagramas^M de tejidos^M

weft thread
hilo^M de trama^F

warp threads
hilos^M de urdimbre^M

basic weaves
ligamentos^M textiles básicos

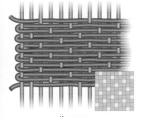

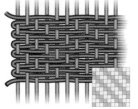

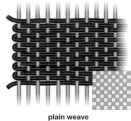

satin weave
satén^M

twill weave
sarga^F

plain weave
tafetán^M

other techniques
otros ligamentos^M
textiles

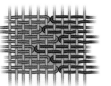

knot
anudado

hatching
punteado

slit
vertical

interlock
entrecruzado

pottery
cerámica^F

throwing
alfarería^F

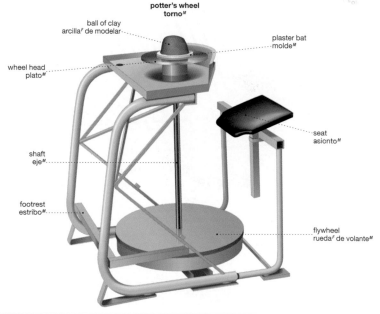

potter's wheel
torno^M

ball of clay
arcilla^F de modelar

plaster bat
molde^M

wheel head
plato^M

seat
asiento^M

shaft
eje^M

footrest
estribo^M

flywheel
rueda^F de volante^M

pottery tools
herramientas^F **para**
cerámica^F

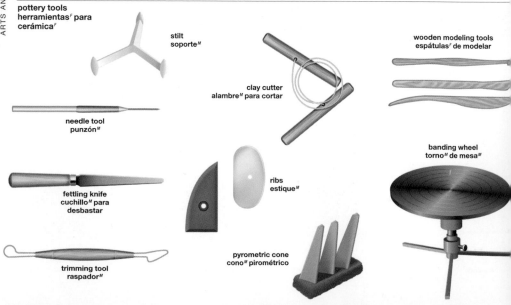

stilt
soporte^M

wooden modeling tools
espátulas^F de modelar

clay cutter
alambre^M para cortar

needle tool
punzón^M

banding wheel
torno^M de mesa^M

fettling knife
cuchillo^M para
desbastar

ribs
estique^M

trimming tool
raspador^M

pyrometric cone
cono^M pirométrico

slab building
rodillo^M

coiling
cordón^M **para espirales**^F

firing
cocción^F

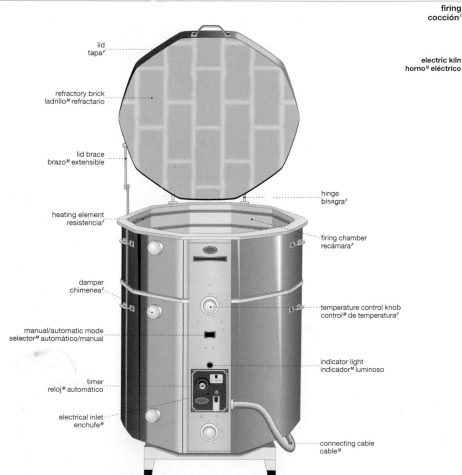

electric kiln
horno^M **eléctrico**

lid
tapa^F

refractory brick
ladrillo^M refractario

lid brace
brazo^M extensible

heating element
resistencia^F

damper
chimenea^F

manual/automatic mode
selector^M automático/manual

timer
reloj^M automático

electrical inlet
enchufe^M

hinge
bisagra^F

firing chamber
recámara^F

temperature control knob
control^M de temperatura^F

indicator light
indicador^M luminoso

connecting cable
cable^M

ARTS AND ARCHITECTURE

bobbin lace

encaje^M de bolillos^M

pillow
bolillos^M

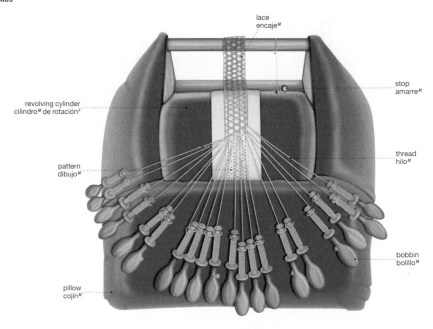

lace
encaje^M

stop
amarre^M

revolving cylinder
cilindro^M de rotación^F

thread
hilo^M

pattern
dibujo^M

bobbin
bolillo^M

pillow
cojín^M

needle
aguja^F

handle
bolillo^M

pricker
punzón^M

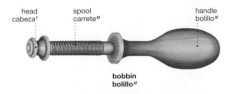

head
cabeza^F

spool
carrete^M

handle
bolillo^M

bobbin
bolillo^M

stained glass
vitral^M

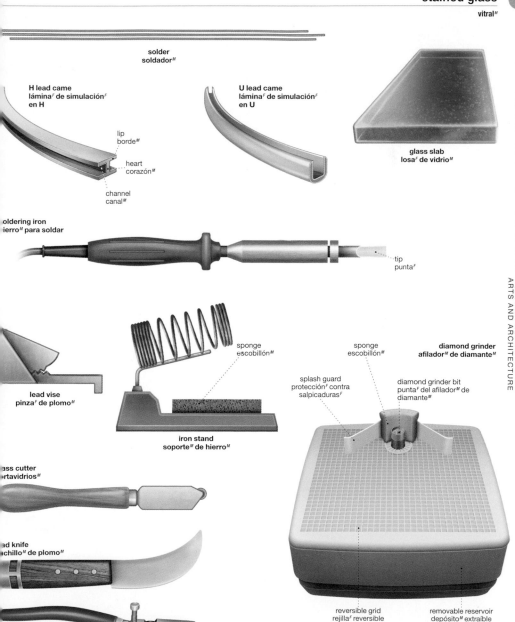

solder
soldador^M

H lead came
lámina^F de simulación^F
en H

U lead came
lámina^F de simulación^F
en U

glass slab
losa^F de vidrio^M

lip
borde^M

heart
corazón^M

channel
canal^M

soldering iron
hierro^M para soldar

tip
punta^F

lead vise
pinza^F de plomo^M

sponge
escobillón^M

sponge
escobillón^M

diamond grinder
afilador^M de diamante^M

splash guard
protección^F contra
salpicaduras^F

diamond grinder bit
punta^F del afilador^M de
diamante^M

iron stand
soporte^M de hierro^M

glass cutter
cortavidrios^M

lead knife
cuchillo^M de plomo^M

runner
tenazas^F de sujeción^F

reversible grid
rejilla^F reversible

removable reservoir
depósito^M extraíble

ARTS AND ARCHITECTURE

COMMUNICATIONS

comunicaciones

LANGUAGES OF THE WORLD 582

major language families 582

WRITTEN COMMUNICATION 584

writing 584
typography 586
symbols 587
postal service network 588
newspaper 590

PHOTOGRAPHY 591

film cameras 591
films 591
film reflex camera 592
digital non-reflex cameras 592
digital reflex camera 593
memory cards 594
batteries 595
photographic accessories 596
lenses 598
digital photo management 599
film processing 600
transparency viewing 601

TELECOMMUNICATIONS 602

broadcast satellite communication 602
telecommunication satellites 602
telecommunications by satellite 603

RADIO 604

studio and control room 604
microphones and accessories 604

TELEVISION 605

program production 605
television reception 609
camcorders 612

SOUND REPRODUCING SYSTEM 614

elements of a sound reproducing system 614
mini stereo sound system 619
portable sound systems 619

WIRELESS COMMUNICATION 621

walkie-talkie 621
numeric pager 621
CB radio 621

TELEPHONY 622

cellular telephone 622
examples of telephones 623

major language families

grandes familias[f] linguisticas

geographic distribution
distribución[f] geográfica

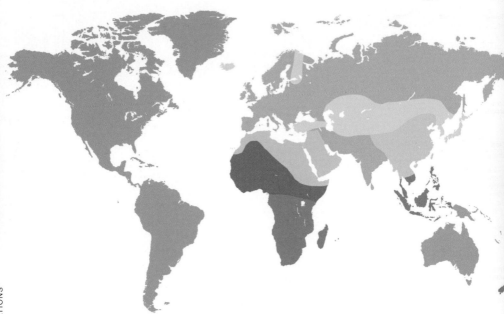

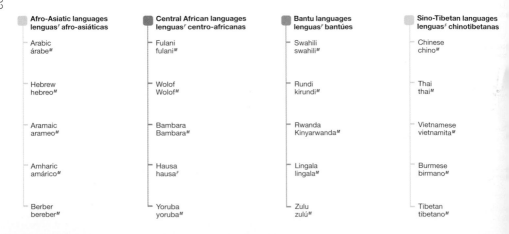

Afro-Asiatic languages lenguas[f] afro-asiáticas	**Central African languages** lenguas[f] centro-africanas	**Bantu languages** lenguas[f] bantúes	**Sino-Tibetan languages** lenguas[f] chinotibetanas
Arabic árabe[M]	Fulani fulani[M]	Swahili swahili[M]	Chinese chino[M]
Hebrew hebreo[M]	Wolof Wolof[M]	Rundi kirundi[M]	Thai thai[M]
Aramaic arameo[M]	Bambara Bambara[M]	Rwanda Kinyarwanda[M]	Vietnamese vietnamita[M]
Amharic amárico[M]	Hausa hausa[F]	Lingala lingala[M]	Burmese birmano[M]
Berber bereber[M]	Yoruba yoruba[M]	Zulu zulú[M]	Tibetan tibetano[M]

major language families

Indo-European languages
lenguas*f* indoeuropeas

Romance languages lenguas*f* romances	Germanic languages lenguas*f* germánicas	Celtic languages lenguas*f* célticas	Slavic languages lenguas*f* eslavas	Indo-Iranian languages lenguas*f* indoiranias
French francés*M*	English inglés*M*	Breton bretón*M*	Czech checo*M*	Persian persa*M*
Spanish español*M*	German alemán*M*	Welsh galés*M*	Slovak eslovaco*M*	Urdu urdu*M*
Catalan catalán*M*	Dutch holandés*M*	Scottish escocés*M*	Polish polaco*M*	Hindi Hindi*M*
Portuguese portugués*M*	Danish danés*M*	Irish irlandés*M*	Russian ruso*M*	

				Amerindian languages lenguas*f* amerindias
Italian italiano*M*	Swedish sueco*M*	**isolated languages** lenguas*f* aisladas	Ukrainian ucranio*M*	Inuktitut inuktitut*M*
Romanian rumano*M*	Norwegian noruego*M*	Greek griego*M*	Bulgarian búlgaro*M*	Cree cree*M*
	Icelandic islandés*M*	Albanian albanés*M*	Slovene esloveno*M*	Montagnais montagnais*M*

Ural-Altaic languages
lenguas*f* uraloaltaicas

	Yiddish yidish*M*	Armenian armeno*M*	Serbo-Croatian serbio*M* y croata*M*	Navajo navajo*M*
Japanese japonés*M*				
Korean coreano*M*	**Malayo-Polynesian languages** lenguas*f* malayo-polinesias			Nahuatl nahualt*M*
Mongolian mogol*M*	Indonesian indonesio*M*	Tahitian tahitiano*M*	**Oceanian languages** lenguas*f* oceánicas	Maya maya*M*
Turkish turco*M*	Tagalog tagalo*M*	Hawaiian hawaiano*M*	Melanesian melanesia	Quechua quechua*M*
Hungarian húngaro*M*	Malagasy malgache*M*	Maori maori*M*	Papuan languages lenguas*f* papúas	Aymara aymara*M*
Finnish finlandés*M*	Samoan samoano*M*		Australian aboriginal languages lenguas*f* australianas aborígenas	Guarani guaraní*M*

COMMUNICATIONS

writing
escritura^F

traditional writing instruments
instrumentos^M de escritura^F
tradicionales

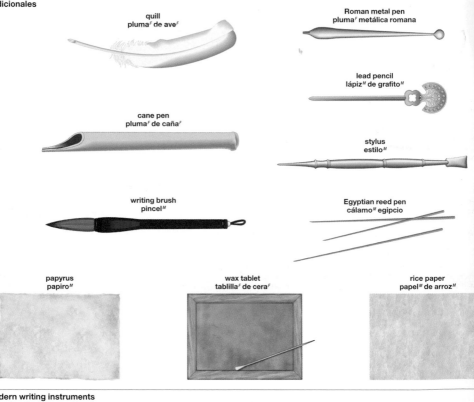

quill
pluma^F de ave^F

Roman metal pen
pluma^F metálica romana

lead pencil
lápiz^M de grafito^M

cane pen
pluma^F de caña^F

stylus
estilo^M

writing brush
pincel^M

Egyptian reed pen
cálamo^M egipcio

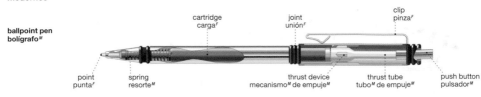

papyrus
papiro^M

wax tablet
tablilla^F de cera^F

rice paper
papel^M de arroz^M

modern writing instruments
instrumentos^M de escritura^F
modernos

ballpoint pen
bolígrafo^M

cartridge
carga^F

joint
unión^F

clip
pinza^F

point
punta^F

spring
resorte^M

thrust device
mecanismo^M de empuje^M

thrust tube
tubo^M de empuje^M

push button
pulsador^M

section of the point
corte^M de la punta^F

ball bearing
bola^F de rodamiento^M

ink
tinta^F

refill
repuesto^M

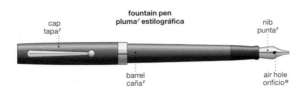

fountain pen
pluma^F estilográfica

cap
tapa^F

nib
punta^F

barrel
caña^F

air hole
orificio^M

marker
marcador^M

pencil
lápiz^M

mechanical pencil
portaminas^M

steel pen
pluma^F metálica

highlighter
rotulador^M

paper
papel^M

COMMUNICATIONS

examples of writing systems
ejemplos^M de sistemas^M de
escritura^F

abcd

Latin characters
caracteres^M latinos

ابثت

Arabic script
escritura^F árabe

אבגד

Hebrew characters
caracteres^M hebreos

абвг

Cyrillic characters
caracteres^M cirílicos

汉字

Chinese characters
caracteres^M chinos

αβγδ

Greek characters
caracteres^M griegos

braille
braille^M

typography

tipografía[F]

characters of a font
caracteres[M] de una fundición[F]

sans serif type
tipo[M] sans serif

abcdefghijklmnopqrstuvwxyz 0123456789

letters
letras[F]

figures
cifras[F]

serif type
tipo[M] serif

abcdefghijklmnopqrstuvwxyz 01234567

shape of characters
forma[F] de los
caracteres[M]

ABCDEF
uppercase
mayúscula

ABCDEF
small capital
versalita

abcdef
lowercase
minúscula

abcdef
italic
cursiva

weight
tamaño[M]

a
light
fina

a
semi-bold
semi-negrita

a
extra-bold
extra-negrita

a
extra-light
extra-fina

a
medium
media

a
bold
negrita

a
black
negro

set width
espacio[M]

a
condensed
condensada

a
narrow
estrecha

a
normal
normal

a
wide
ancha

a
extended
alargada

leading
interlineado[M]

position of a charact
posición[F] de un carácte

Lorem ipsum dolor sit
amet, consectetuer
adipiscing elit, sed
simple spacing
interlineado[M] sencillo

Lorem ipsum dolor sit
amet, consectetuer
adipiscing elit, sed
1.5 spacing
interlineado[M] 1.5

Lorem ipsum dolor sit
amet, consectetuer
adipiscing elit, sed
double spacing
interlineado[M] doble

H_2SO_4
inferior
subíndice

XXe
superior
superíndice

symbols
signos*M* y símbolos*M*

diacritic symbols
signos*M* diacríticos

grave accent
acento*M* grave

acute accent
acento*M* agudo

cedilla
cedilla*F*

umlaut
diéresis*F*

circumflex accent
acento*M* circunflejo

tilde
tilde*F*

miscellaneous symbols
varios

registered trademark
marca*F* registrada

copyright
copyright (derechos*M* de autor*M*)

ampersand
y

apostrophe
apóstrofe*M*

at sign
símbolo*M* de arroba*F*

punctuation marks
signos*M* de puntuación*F*

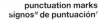

dash
guión*M* largo

hyphen
guión*M*

period
punto*M*

semicolon
punto*M* y coma*F*

comma
coma*F*

ellipses
puntos*M* suspensivos

colon
dos puntos*M*

asterisk
asterisco*M*

braces
llaves*M*

parentheses
paréntesis*M*

square brackets
corchetes*M*

virgule
diagonal*F*

exclamation point
exclamación*F*

question mark
interrogación*F*

single quotation marks
comillas*F* sencillas

quotation marks
comillas*F* inglesas

quotation marks (French)
comillas*F* españolas

CCMMUNICATIONS

COMMUNICATIONS

postal service network

red^M de servicio^M postal

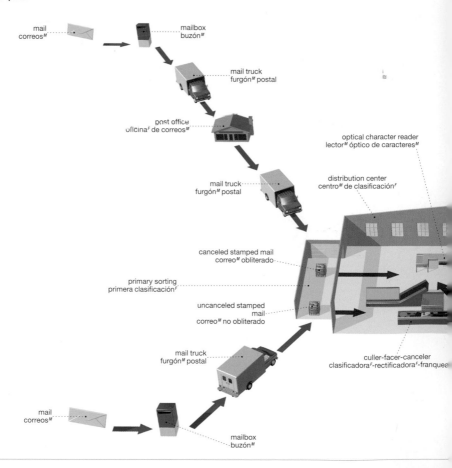

mail
correos^M

mailbox
buzón^M

mail truck
furgón^M postal

post office
oficina^F de correos^M

mail truck
furgón^M postal

optical character reader
lector^M óptico de caracteres^M

distribution center
centro^M de clasificación^F

canceled stamped mail
correo^M obliterado

primary sorting
primera clasificación^F

uncanceled stamped mail
correo^M no obliterado

culler-facer-canceler
clasificadora^F-rectificadora^F-franquea

mail truck
furgón^M postal

mail
correos^M

mailbox
buzón^M

---

mail
correo^M

postage stamp
sello^M de correos^M

letter
carta^F

postcard
postal^F

postal service network

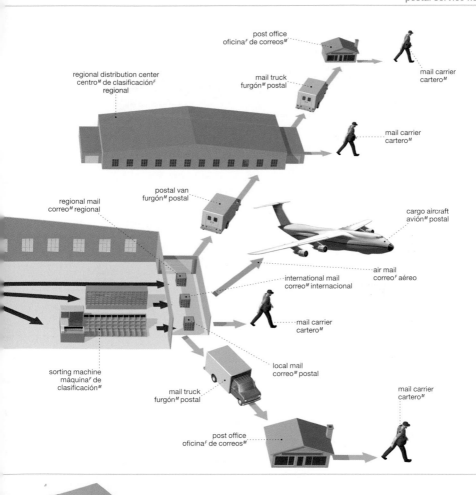

post office
oficina^F de correos^M

mail carrier
cartero^M

regional distribution center
centro^M de clasificación^F
regional

mail truck
furgón^M postal

mail carrier
cartero^M

postal van
furgón^M postal

regional mail
correo^M regional

cargo aircraft
avión^M postal

air mail
correo^F aéreo

international mail
correo^M internacional

mail carrier
cartero^M

local mail
correo^M postal

mail carrier
cartero^M

sorting machine
máquina^F de
clasificación^M

mail truck
furgón^M postal

post office
oficina^F de correos^M

mail

postal parcel
paquete^M postal

bulk mail
correo^M de masa^F

postal money order
giro^M postal

newspaper

periódico[M]

layout
diseño[M]

heading
cabecera[F]

section
sección[F]

article
artículo[M]

literary supplement
suplemento[M] literario

tabloid
tabloide[M]

color supplement
suplemento[M] a color[M]

magazine
revista[F]

index
sumario[M]

front page
primera plana[F]

nameplate
nombre[M] del periódico[M]

banner
grandes titulares[M]

front picture
foto[F] de primera plana[F]

caption
pie[M] de foto[F]

kicker
ladillo[M]

headline
titular[M]

deck
subtítulo[M]

subhead
intertítulo[M]

columns
columnas[F]

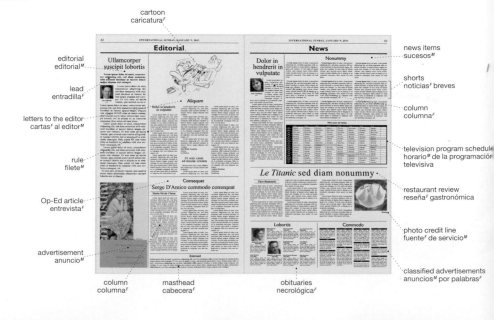

cartoon
caricatura[F]

editorial
editorial[M]

lead
entradilla[F]

letters to the editor
cartas[F] al editor[M]

rule
filete[M]

Op-Ed article
entrevista[F]

advertisement
anuncio[M]

column
columna[F]

masthead
cabecera[F]

obituaries
necrológica[F]

news items
sucesos[M]

shorts
noticias[F] breves

column
columna[F]

television program schedule
horario[M] de la programación televisiva

restaurant review
reseña[F] gastronómica

photo credit line
fuente[F] de servicio[M]

classified advertisements
anuncios[M] por palabras[F]

film cameras

cámaras^f analógicas

disposable camera
cámara^f desechable

medium-format SLR (6 X 6)
cámara^f reflex de formato^M medio SLR
(6X6)

rangefinder
telémetro^M

single-lens reflex (SLR) camera
cámara^f reflex de un solo objetivo^M

Polaroid® camera
cámara^f Polaroid® Land

view camera
cámara^f de fuelle^M

COMMUNICATIONS

films

películas^f

film pack
paquete^M de placas^f
fotográficas

roll film
rollo^M de película^f

cartridge film
cartucho^M de la película^f

transparency slide
diapositiva^f

film reflex camera

cámara^F réflex analógica

front view
vista^F frontal

exposure adjustment knob
botón^M de compensación^M de la
exposición^F

accessory shoe
zapata^F de accesorios^M

hot-shoe contact
contacto^M central

control panel
panel^M de controles^M

film advance mode
modo^M dispositivo^M

command control dial
selector^M de programa^M

exposure mode
modalidad^F de exposición

on-off switch
interruptor^M de encendido/
apagado

multiple exposure mode
modalidad^F de exposición
múltiple

shutter release button
disparador^M

film speed
sensibilidad^F

self-timer indicator
indicador^M de tiempo^M

remote control terminal
terminal^M del control^M remo

camera body
caja^F

depth-of-field preview button
botón^M de previsionado de profundid
campo^M

lens release button
botón^M de desbloqueo^M del
objetivo^M

focus mode selector
selector^M de focalización^F

lens
objetivo^M

digital non-reflex cameras

cámaras^F digitales que no son réflex

ultracompact camera
cámara^F ultracompacta

compact camera
cámara^F compacta

digital reflex camera
cámara^f réflex digital

back view
vista^f trasera

viewfinder
visor^M

menu button
botón^M de selección^F del menú^M

shutter release button
disparador^M

settings display button
botón^M de visualización^F de
ajustes^M

mode dial
disco^M de modo^M

on-off switch
interruptor^M

enlarge button
botón^M para aumentar

strap eyelet
ojete^M para la correa^F

cover
tapa^F

video and digital
terminals
tomas^F vídeo y digital

four-way selector
selector^M cuadro-
direccional

display
pantalla^F

memory card
tarjeta^F de memoria^F

remote control terminal
botón^M de control^M
remoto

eject button
botón^M de expulsión^F

multi-image jump button
botón^M de salto^M de
imágenes^F

display button
botón^M de visualización^F

erase button
botón^M de cancelación^F

image review button
botón^M de visualización^F de imágenes^F

COMMUNICATIONS

main functions
funciones^F principales

image-recording quality
calidad^F de grabación^F de imágenes^F

sensitivity
velocidad^F de la película^F

shutter speed
velocidad^F de
obturación^F

metering mode
modo^M de medición^F

aperture
apertura^F

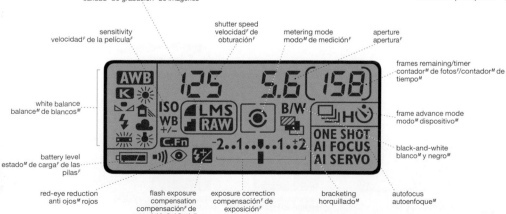

frames remaining/timer
contador^M de fotos^F/contador^M de
tiempo^M

white balance
balance^M de blancos^M

frame advance mode
modo^M dispositivo^M

battery level
estado^M de carga^F de las
pilas^F

black-and-white
blanco^M y negro^M

red-eye reduction
anti ojos^M rojos

flash exposure
compensation
compensación^F de
exposición^F al flash^M

exposure correction
compensación^F de
exposición^F

bracketing
horquillado^M

autofocus
autoenfoque^M

digital reflex camera

framing
enmarcadoᴹ

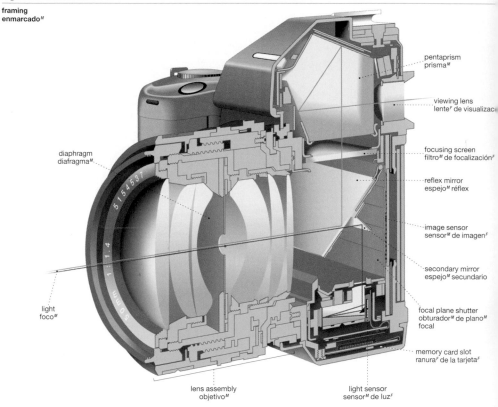

pentaprism
prisma ᴹ

viewing lens
lente ᶠ de visualizac

focusing screen
filtro ᴹ de focalización ᶠ

diaphragm
diafragma ᴹ

reflex mirror
espejo ᴹ réflex

image sensor
sensor ᴹ de imagen ᶠ

secondary mirror
espejo ᴹ secundario

light
foco ᴹ

focal plane shutter
obturador ᴹ de plano ᴹ
focal

memory card slot
ranura ᶠ de la tarjeta ᶠ

lens assembly
objetivo ᴹ

light sensor
sensor ᴹ de luz ᶠ

COMMUNICATIONS

memory cards

tarjetas ᶠ de memoria

Memory Stick
tarjeta ᶠ Memory Stick

xD-Picture card
tarjeta ᶠ xD Picture

Secure Digital card
tarjeta ᶠ Digital Segura

compact flash card
tarjeta ᶠ flash compacta

digital reflex camera

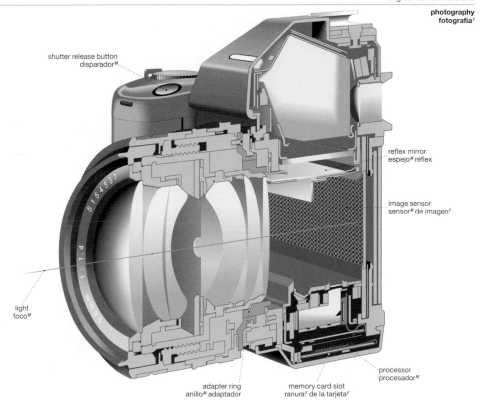

shutter release button
disparador[M]

reflex mirror
espejo[M] réflex

image sensor
sensor[M] de imagen[F]

light
foco[M]

processor
procesador[M]

adapter ring
anillo[M] adaptador

memory card slot
ranura[F] de la tarjeta[F]

COMMUNICATIONS

batteries

baterías[F]

battery
pila[F]

battery pack
batería[F]

battery
pila[F] de botón[M]

photographic accessories

accesorios^M fotográficos

waterproof case
estuche^M sumergible

cable shutter release
disparador^M de cable^M

electronic flash
flash^M electrónico

flashtube
tubo^M de flash^M

photoelectric cell
celda^F fotoeléctrica

mounting foot
pie^M de montura^F

tripod
trípode^M

camera platform
plataforma^F

camera screw
tornillo^M de fijación^F

plate
placa^F

quick release system
sistema^M de disparo^M rápido

panoramic head
cabeza^F panorámica

side-tilt lock
bloqueo^M de inclinación^F
lateral

camera platform lock
bloqueo^M de la plataforma^F

horizontal motion lock
bloqueo^M de movimiento^M
horizontal

column lock
bloqueo^M de la columna^F

column crank
manivela^F de la columna^F

camera bag
bolsa^F de viaje^M

column
columna^F

collet
anillo^M

telescoping leg
pata^F telescópica

digital photo frame
marco^M para fotos^M
digitales

COMMUNICATIONS

photographic accessories

exposure meter
fotómetro^M

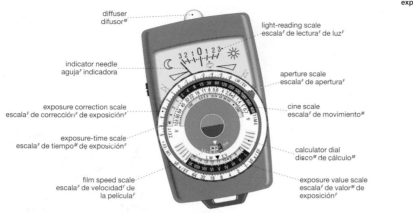

diffuser
difusor^M

light-reading scale
escala^F de lectura^F de luz^F

indicator needle
aguja^F indicadora

aperture scale
escala^F de apertura^F

exposure correction scale
escala^F de corrección^F de exposición^F

cine scale
escala^F de movimiento^M

exposure-time scale
escala^F de tiempo^M de exposición^F

calculator dial
disco^M de cálculo^M

film speed scale
escala^F de velocidad^F de
la película^F

exposure value scale
escala^F de valor^M de
exposición^F

digital exposure meter
fotómetro^M

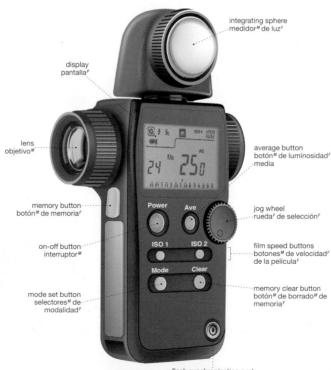

integrating sphere
medidor^M de luz^F

display
pantalla^F

average button
botón^M de luminosidad^F
media

lens
objetivo^M

memory button
botón^M de memoria^F

jog wheel
rueda^F de selección^F

on-off button
interruptor^M

film speed buttons
botones^M de velocidad^F
de la película^F

mode set button
selectores^M de
modalidad^F

memory clear button
botón^M de borrado^M de
memoria^F

flash synchronization port
terminal^M de sincronización^F
de flash^M

COMMUNICATIONS

lenses

objetivos^M

standard lens
objetivo^M normal

lens
objetivo^M

focus setting ring
anillo^M de ajuste^M del
enfoque^M

depth-of-field scale
escala^F de profundidad^F de campo^M
de visión^F

lens aperture scale
escala^F de abertura^F del
diafragma^M

distance scale
escala^F de distancia^F

bayonet mount
montura^F de bayoneta^F

zoom lens
objetivo^M zoom^M

lens accessories
accesorios^M para el objetivo^M

lens cap
tapa^F del objetivo^M

lens hood
capuchón^M

macro lens
objetivo^M macro

wide-angle lens
objetivo^M gran angula

color filter
filtro^M de color^M

telephoto lens
teleobjetivo^M

close-up lens
lente^M de acercamiento^M

polarizing filter
filtro^M de polarización^F

objective lens
objetivo^M

tele-converter
teleconvertidor^M

semi-fisheye lens
objetivo^M ojo^M de pez^M

fisheye lens
lente^M de 180 grados^M

digital photo management

gestión^F de fotos^F digitales

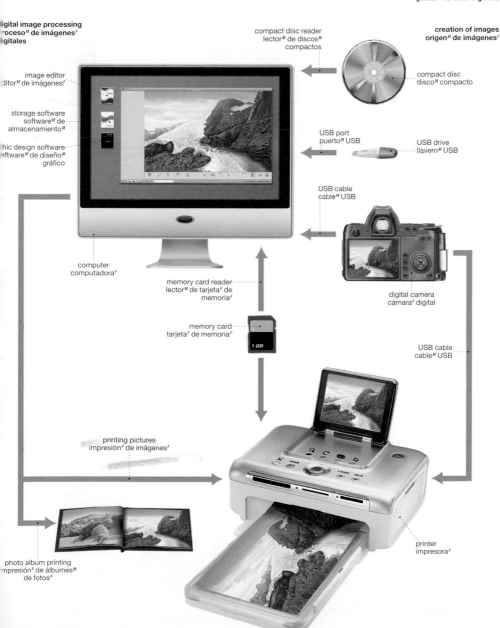

digital image processing
proceso^M de imágenes^F
digitales

compact disc reader
lector^M de discos^M
compactos

creation of images
origen^M de imágenes^F

image editor
editor^M de imágenes^F

compact disc
disco^M compacto

storage software
software^M de
almacenamiento^M

USB port
puerto^M USB

USB drive
llavero^M USB

graphic design software
software^M de diseño^M
gráfico

USB cable
cable^M USB

computer
computadora^F

memory card reader
lector^M de tarjeta^F de
memoria^F

digital camera
cámara^F digital

memory card
tarjeta^F de memoria^F

1 GB

USB cable
cable^M USB

printing pictures
impresión^F de imágenes^F

photo album printing
impresión^F de álbumes^M
de fotos^F

printer
impresora^F

COMMUNICATIONS

film processing

proceso^M de películas^F

darkroom equipment
material^M de cuarto^M oscuro

timer
reloj^M

enlarger
ampliadora^F

column
columna^F

lamphouse head
cabeza^F de la caja^F de
iluminación^F

negative carrier
portanegativos^M

window
ventana^F

lamphouse elevation control
control^M de elevación^F de la caja^F de
iluminación^F

developing tank
tanque^M de revelado

height control
control^M de altura^F

negative
negativo^M

cap
capuchón^M

bellows
fuelle^M

negative carrier
portanegativos^M

lid
tapa^F

enlarging lens
lente^F de ampliación^F

reel
espiral^F

red safelight filter
filtro^M rojo^M de seguridad^F

height scale
escala^F de ampliación^F

safelight
luz^F de seguridad^F

tank
cubeta^F

baseboard
tablero^M de base^F

COMMUNICATIONS

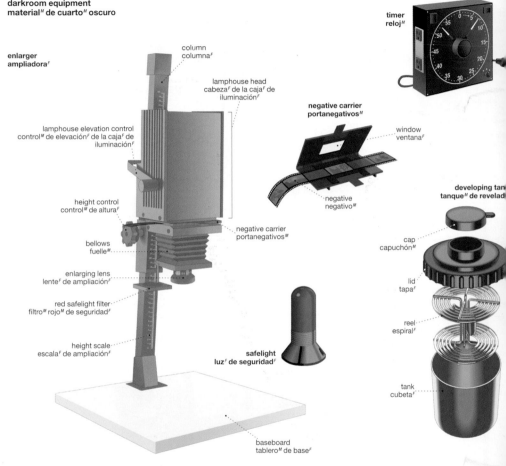

developing baths
baños^M de revelado^M

developer bath
baño^M de revelado^M

stop bath
baño^M de stop^M

fixing bath
baño^M de fijación^F

print drying rack
secadora^F de pruebas^F

transparency viewing

visualización^F de diapositivas^F

**slide projector
proyector^M de
diapositivas^F**

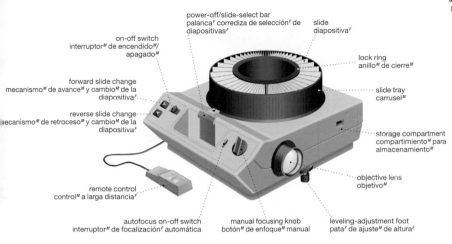

power-off/slide-select bar
palanca^F corrediza de selección^F de
diapositivas^F

slide
diapositiva^F

on-off switch
interruptor^M de encendido^M/
apagado^M

lock ring
anillo^M de cierre^M

forward slide change
mecanismo^M de avance^M y cambio^M de la
diapositiva^F

slide tray
carrusel^M

reverse slide change
mecanismo^M de retroceso^M y cambio^M de la
diapositiva^F

storage compartment
compartimiento^M para
almacenamiento^M

objective lens
objetivo^M

remote control
control^M a larga distancia^F

autofocus on-off switch
interruptor^M de focalización^F automática

manual focusing knob
botón^M de enfoque^M manual

leveling-adjustment foot
pata^F de ajuste^M de altura^F

**projection screen
pantalla^F de
proyección^F**

hanger
gancho^M

saddle
soporte^M

screen
pantalla^F

screen case
caja^F de la pantalla^F

tripod
trípode^M

shoe
contera^F

COMMUNICATIONS

broadcast satellite communication

comunicación^F vía satélite^M

broadcasting system
sistema^M de difusión^F

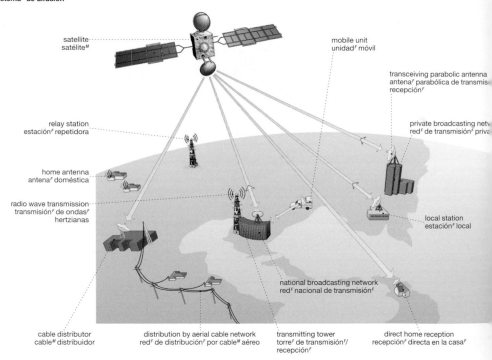

satellite
satélite^M

mobile unit
unidad^F móvil

transceiving parabolic antenna
antena^F parabólica de transmisión
recepción^F

relay station
estación^F repetidora

private broadcasting network
red^F de transmisión^F privada

home antenna
antena^F doméstica

radio wave transmission
transmisión^F de ondas^F
hertzianas

local station
estación^F local

national broadcasting network
red^F nacional de transmisión^F

cable distributor
cable^M distribuidor

distribution by aerial cable network
red^F de distribución^F por cable^M aéreo

transmitting tower
torre^F de transmisión^F/
recepción^F

direct home reception
recepción^F directa en la casa^F

COMMUNICATIONS

telecommunication satellites

satélites^M de telecomunicaciones^F

Eutelsat
Eutelsat^M

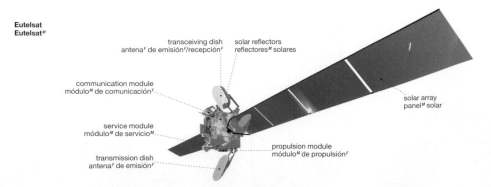

transceiving dish
antena^F de emisión^F/recepción^F

solar reflectors
reflectores^M solares

communication module
módulo^M de comunicación^F

solar array
panel^M solar

service module
módulo^M de servicio^M

propulsion module
módulo^M de propulsión^F

transmission dish
antena^F de emisión^F

telecommunications by satellite

telecomunicaciones^F vía satélite^M

telecommunications system
sistema^M de telecomunicaciones^F

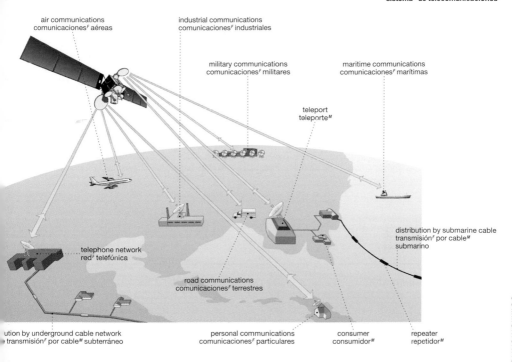

air communications
comunicaciones^F aéreas

industrial communications
comunicaciones^F industriales

military communications
comunicaciones^F militares

maritime communications
comunicaciones^F marítimas

teleport
teleporte^M

distribution by submarine cable
transmisión^F por cable^M
submarino

telephone network
red^F telefónica

road communications
comunicaciones^F terrestres

...ution by underground cable network
...transmisión^F por cable^M subterráneo

personal communications
comunicaciones^F particulares

consumer
consumidor^M

repeater
repetidor^M

telecommunication satellites

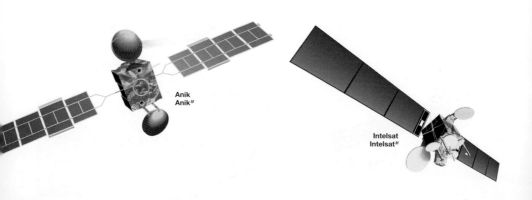

Anik
Anik^M

Intelsat
Intelsat^M

studio and control room

estudio^M y cabina^F de control^M

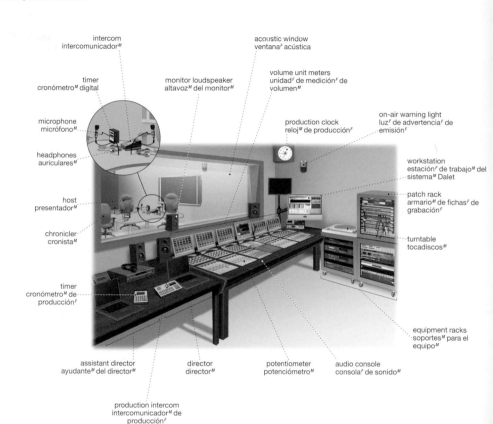

intercom
intercomunicador^M

acoustic window
ventana^F acústica

timer
cronómetro^M digital

monitor loudspeaker
altavoz^M del monitor^M

volume unit meters
unidad^F de medición^F de
volumen^M

microphone
micrófono^M

production clock
reloj^F de producción^F

on-air warning light
luz^F de advertencia^F de
emisión^F

headphones
auriculares^M

workstation
estación^F de trabajo^M del
sistema^M Dalet

host
presentador^M

patch rack
armario^M de fichas^F de
grabación^F

chronicler
cronista^M

turntable
tocadiscos^M

timer
cronómetro^M de
producción^F

equipment racks
soportes^M para el
equipo^M

assistant director
ayudante^M del director^M

director
director^M

potentiometer
potenciómetro^M

audio console
consola^F de sonido^M

production intercom
intercomunicador^M de
producción^F

microphones and accessories

micrófonos^M y accesorios^M

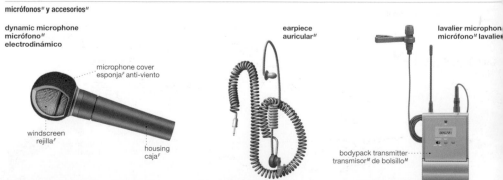

**dynamic microphone
micrófono^M
electrodinámico**

**earpiece
auricular^M**

**lavalier microphone
micrófono^M lavalier**

microphone cover
esponja^F anti-viento

windscreen
rejilla^F

housing
caja^F

bodypack transmitter
transmisor^M de bolsillo^M

program production

producción^F del programa^M

studio set and control rooms
estudio^M

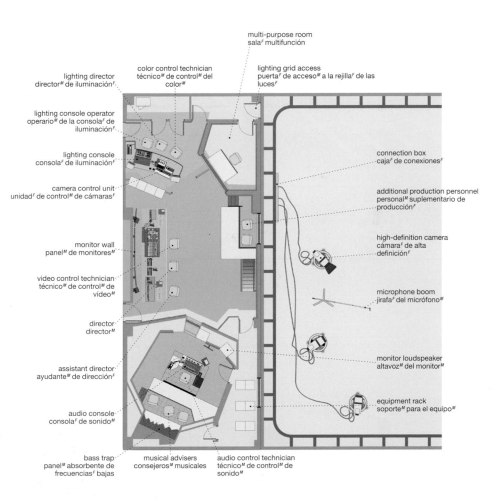

multi-purpose room
sala^F multifunción

lighting director
director^M de iluminación^F

color control technician
técnico^M de control^M del
color^M

lighting grid access
puerta^F de acceso^M a la rejilla^F de las
luces^F

lighting console operator
operario^M de la consola^F de
iluminación^F

connection box
caja^F de conexiones^F

lighting console
consola^F de iluminación^F

additional production personnel
personal^M suplementario de
producción^F

camera control unit
unidad^F de control^M de cámaras^F

high-definition camera
cámara^F de alta
definición^F

monitor wall
panel^M de monitores^M

video control technician
técnico^M de control^M de
vídeo^M

microphone boom
jirafa^F del micrófono^M

director
director^M

assistant director
ayudante^M de dirección^F

monitor loudspeaker
altavoz^M del monitor^M

audio console
consola^F de sonido^M

equipment rack
soporte^M para el equipo^M

bass trap
panel^M absorbente de
frecuencias^F bajas

musical advisers
consejeros^M musicales

audio control technician
técnico^M de control^M de
sonido^M

COMMUNICATIONS

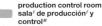 audio control room
control^M de sonido^M

production control room
sala^F de producción^F y
control^M

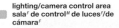 lighting/camera control area
sala^F de control^M de luces^F/de
cámara^F

studio set
estudio^M

program production

studio set
estudio^M

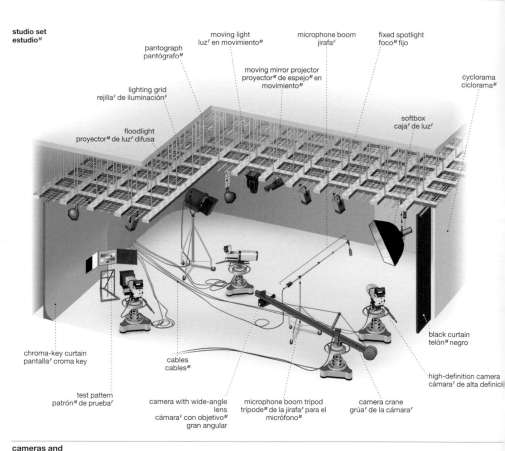

pantograph
pantógrafo^M

moving light
luz^F en movimiento^M

microphone boom
jirafa^F

fixed spotlight
foco^M fijo

moving mirror projector
proyector^M de espejo^M en
movimiento^M

cyclorama
ciclorama^F

lighting grid
rejilla^F de iluminación^F

softbox
caja^F de luz^F

floodlight
proyector^M de luz^F difusa

chroma-key curtain
pantalla^F croma key

cables
cables^M

black curtain
telón^M negro

high-definition camera
cámara^F de alta definició

test pattern
patrón^M de prueba^F

camera with wide-angle
lens
cámara^F con objetivo^M
gran angular

microphone boom tripod
trípode^M de la jirafa^F para el
micrófono^M

camera crane
grúa^F de la cámara^F

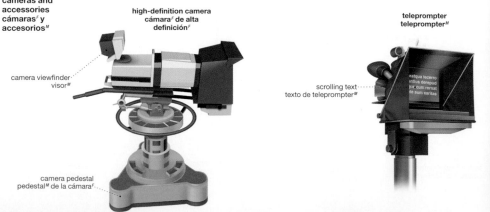

cameras and
accessories
cámaras^F y
accesorios^M

high-definition camera
cámara^F de alta
definición^F

teleprompter
teleprompter^M

camera viewfinder
visor^M

scrolling text
texto de teleprompter^M

camera pedestal
pedestal^M de la cámara^F

program production

COMMUNICATIONS

production control room
sala^F de control^M de producción^F

monitor loudspeaker
altavoz^M del monitor^M

program monitor
monitor^M de programas^M

production clock
reloj^M de producción^F

preview monitor
monitor^M de
visualización^F previa

monitor wall
el^M de monitores^M

rcom microphone
micrófono^M del
ntercomunicador^M

intercom
ntercomunicador^M

special effects monitor
monitor^M de efectos^M
especiales

production desk
mesa^F de producción^F

digital console
consola^F digital

camera monitors
monitores^M de cámaras^F

switcher console
consola^F de producción^F
de vídeo^M

cameras and
accessories

Steadicam
estabilizador^M de
cámara^F

shoulder mount
camcorder
videocámara^F de
hombro^M

program production

mobile production truck
unidad^F móvil

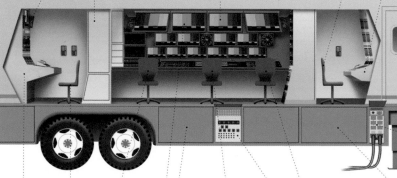

microwave antenna
antena^F microondas^F

audio control room
sala^F de control^M de sonido^M

production control room
sala^F de control^M de la
producción^F

video control room
sala^F de control^M de vídeo^M

monitor loudspeaker
altavoz^M del monitor^M

monitor wall
panel^M de control^M

color control technician
técnico^M de control^M del color^M

equipment rack
soporte^M para el equipo^M

preview monitor
monitor^M de visualización^F
previa

camera control unit
unidad^F de control^M de
cámaras^F

electrical connection pane
panel^M de conexiones^F elé

COMMUNICATIONS

audio console
consola^F de sonido^M

director
director^M

video control technician
técnico^M de control^M de vídeo^M

technical director
director^M técnico

equipment compartment
compartimento^M para los equipo

audio control technician
técnico^M de control^M de
sonido^M

program monitor
monitor^M de programas^M

cable reels compartment
compartimento^M de
bobina^F de cables^M

video connection panel
panel^M de conexión^F del
vídeo^M

television reception
recepción^F de programas^M

analog television
televisión^F **analógica**

on-off button
interruptor^M

cathode-ray tube television
televisor^M **con pantalla**^F **catódica**

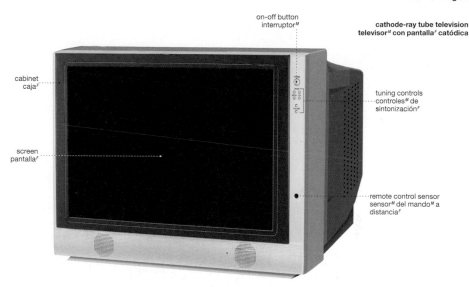

cabinet
caja^F

tuning controls
controles^M de
sintonización^F

screen
pantalla^F

remote control sensor
sensor^M del mando^M a
distancia^F

electron gun
cañón^M **de electrones**^M

grid
rejilla^F

red beam
haz^M rojo

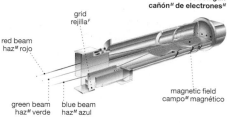

magnetic field
campo^M magnético

green beam
haz^M verde

blue beam
haz^M azul

cture tube
oo^M **de pantalla**^F

funnel
cono^M

color selection filter
filtro^M selector del color^M

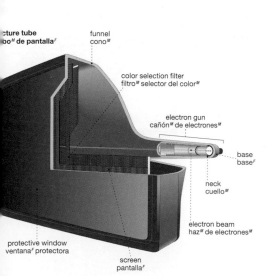

electron gun
cañón^M de electrones^M

base
base^F

neck
cuello^M

electron beam
haz^M de electrones^M

protective window
ventana^F protectora

screen
pantalla^F

digital-to-analog converter box
caja^F **de conversión**^F **de señal**^F
digital-analógica

television reception

digital television
televisión^F digital

liquid crystal display (LCD) television
televisor^M de cristal^M líquido

plasma televisi
televisor^M plasm

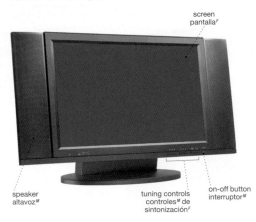

screen
pantalla^F

speaker
altavoz^M

tuning controls
controles^M de
sintonización^F

on-off button
interruptor^M

digital video recorder/receiver
receptor^M/grabadora^F de
vídeo^M digital

instant replay button
botón^M de reproducción^F
instantánea

fast rewind button
botón^M de rebobinado^M

stop button
tecla^F de parada^F

fast-forward button
botón^M de avance^M rápido

return to live programming button
botón^M de programación^F de vuelta^F
al directo^M

function buttons
botones^M de funciones^F

on-off button
interruptor^M

display
pantalla^F

record button
botón^M de inicio^M de
grabación^F

input device switching button
botón^M de visualización^F de TV^F/DVD^M

remote contro
mando^M a distanc

dish antenna
antena^F de recepción^F
parabólica

dish
parábola^M

feedhorn
alimentador^M

pole
mástil^M

portable DVD play
reproductor^M portátil de DV

television reception

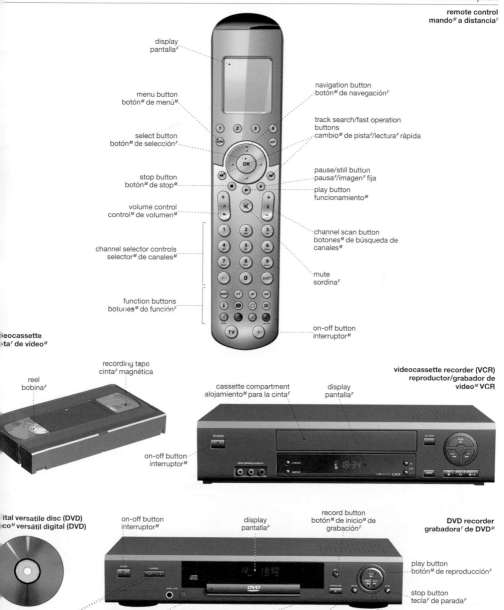

remote control
mando^M a distancia^F

display
pantalla^F

navigation button
botón^M de navegación^F

menu button
botón^M de menú^M

track search/fast operation
buttons
cambio^M de pista^F/lectura^F rápida

select button
botón^M de selección^F

pause/still button
pausa^F/imagen^F fija

stop button
botón^M de stop^M

play button
funcionamiento^M

volume control
control^M de volumen^M

channel scan button
botones^M de búsqueda de
canales^M

channel selector controls
selector^M de canales^M

mute
sordina^F

function buttons
botones^M do función^F

on-off button
interruptor^M

eocassette
ta^F de vídeo^M

recording tape
cinta^F magnética

reel
bobina^F

videocassette recorder (VCR)
reproductor/grabador de
video^M VCR

cassette compartment
alojamiento^M para la cinta^F

display
pantalla^F

on-off button
interruptor^M

ital versatile disc (DVD)
co^M versátil digital (DVD)

on-off button
interruptor^M

display
pantalla^F

record button
botón^M de inicio^M de
grabación^F

DVD recorder
grabadora^F de DVD^M

play button
botón^M de reproducción^F

stop button
tecla^F de parada^F

annel select buttons
tones^M de selección^F
de canal^M

disc tray
bandeja^F de carga^F

disc tray control
control^M de bandeja^F de
carga^F

pause/still button
pausa^F/imagen^F fija

track search/fast operation buttons
cambio^M de pista^F/lectura^F rápida

television reception

home theater
home^M **theater**

surround loudspeaker
altavoz^M surround

main loudspeaker
altavoz^M principal

wide-screen television
televisor^M de pantalla^F
panorámica

center loudspeaker
altavoz^M central

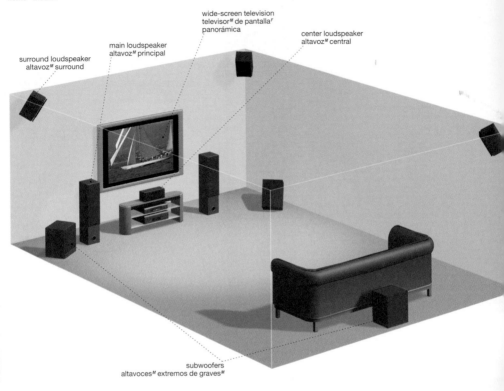

subwoofers
altavoces^M extremos de graves^M

camcorders

videocámaras^F

DVD camcorder
videocámara^F **DVD**^{M}

hard disk drive camcorder
videocámara^F **con disco**^{M}
duro

miniDV cassette
cassette^F **mini DV**

miniDV camcorder: front view
videocámara^F miniDV : vista^F frontal

electronic viewfinder
visor^M electrónico

zoom button
botón^M de zoom^M
eléctrico

recording mode
botón^M de modo^M
grabación^F

photoshot button
disparador^M de fotos^F

zoom lens
objetivo^M zoom

power/function switch
interruptor^M alimentación^F/
funciones^F

lamp
lámpara^F

hand strap
correa^F para la mano^F

microphone
micrófono^M

terminal cover
tapa^F de conexión^F

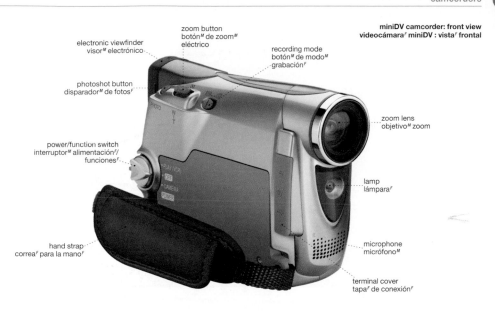

miniDV camcorder: rear view
videocámara^F miniDV : vista^F
posterior

videotape operation controls
mandos^M de la cinta^F de
vídeo^M

focus button
botón^M de enfoque^M

nightshot button
botón^M de grabación^F nocturna

eyepiece
ocular^M

display
pantalla^F

recording start/stop button
tecla^F de inicio/stop de
grabación^F

rechargeable battery
pack
pila^F recargable

card slot
ranura^F de la tarjeta^F de memoria^F

speaker
altavoz^M

backlighting button
botón^M de contraluz^F

widescreen/data code button
botón^M de pantalla^F ancha/código^M
de datos^M

menu button
botón^M de menú^M

COMMUNICATIONS

elements of a sound reproducing system

elementos^M de un sistema^M de audio-estéreo

amplifier with tuner
amplificador^M/sintonizador^M: vista^F
frontal

standby/on button
botón^M de encendido^M/espera^F

input select buttons
teclas^F de selección^F de
entrada^F

display
display^M

control select butto
botones^M de selecc
de control^M

input selector
selector^M de entrada^F

headphone jack
toma^F para auriculares^M

listening mode buttons
botones^M de modo^M de
escucha^F

visual mode buttons
botones^M de modo^M
visual

master volume dial
control^M del volumen^M

ampli-tuner: back view
amplificador^M/sintonizador^M: vista^F
posterior

RS connector
conector^M RS

AM and FM antenna terminals
terminales^M de antena^F de OM^F y FM^F

AC power inl
toma^F de corrient

HDMI connector
conector^M HDMI

coaxial digital audio input
entrada^F de sonido^M digital
coaxial

audio/video source inputs/
outputs
entradas^F/salidas^F de fuente^F de
audio^M/vídeo^M

optical digital audio output/input
entrada^F/salida^F de sonido^M digital óptico

multichannel audio
inputs
entradas^F de sonido^M
multicanal

speaker terminals
terminales^M del altavoz^M

multichannel outputs
salidas^F multicanal

elements of a sound reproducing system

compact disc
disco^M compacto

technical identification band
banda^F de identificación^F
técnica

compact disc reading
lectura^M de disco^M
compacto

objective lens
objetivo^M

asperity
pit^M

laser beam
rayo^M láser^M

pressed area
área^F grabada

reading start
comienzo^M de lectura^F

aluminum layer
capa^F de aluminio^M

resin surface
superficie^F de resina^F

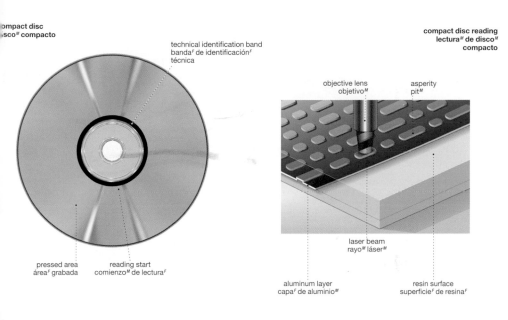

COMMUNICATIONS

shuffle play button
botón^M de reproducción^F
aleatoria

compact disc player
lector^M de discos^M compactos

track search/fast operation
buttons
botón^M de cambio^M de pista^F y
botón^M de lectura^F rápida

on-off button
interruptor^M

direct disc access
buttons
teclas^F numéricas

repeat button
botón^M de repetición^F

stop button
botón^M de stop^M

pause button
botón^M de pausa^F

play button
botón^M de lectura^F

disc skip
botón^M de cambio^M de
disco^M

headphone jack
toma^F para los
auriculares^M

disc compartment
alojamiento^M para el disco^M

display
pantalla^F

disc compartment control
botón^M de control^M del alojamiento^M del
disco^M

elements of a sound reproducing system

cassette
casete^F

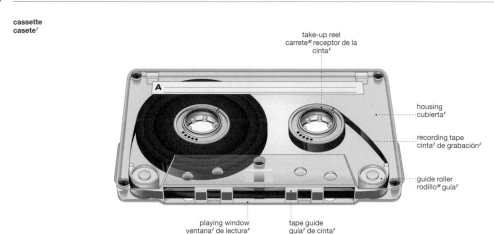

take-up reel
carrete^M receptor de la
cinta^F

housing
cubierta^F

recording tape
cinta^F de grabación^F

guide roller
rodillo^M guía^F

playing window
ventana^F de lectura^F

tape guide
guía^F de cinta^F

cassette tape deck
pletina^F de casete^F

play button
botón^M de reproducción^F

tape counter
contador^M

fast-forward button
botón^M de avance^M rápido

eject button
botón^M de expulsión^F

counter reset button
botón^M de ajuste^M a cero^M del contador^M

tape selector
selector^M de tipo^M de cinta^F

peak level meter
medidor^M de altos niveles^M de
frecuencia^F

cassette holder
alojamiento^M de la
casete^F

rewind button
botón^M de rebobinado^M

stop button
botón^M de stop^M

record muting button
botón^M de grabación^F silenciosa

record button
botón^M de inicio^M de
grabación^F

pause button
botón^M de pausa^F

recording level control
botón^M de nivel^M de grabación^F

COMMUNICATIONS

OFFICE AUTOMATION

ofimática

COMPUTING EQUIPMENT	628	NETWORKING	640	OFFICE	644
all-in-one computer	628	examples of networks	640	office organization	644
tower case computer	629	Internet	642	office furniture	645
laptop computer	630	Internet uses	643	photocopier	647
connection devices	631			stationery	648
connecting cables	631				
input devices	632				
output devices	636				
data storage devices	638				
protection devices	638				
miscellaneous computer tools	639				

all-in-one computer

computadora^F todo en uno

front view
vista^F frontal

display
pantalla^F

enclosure
armazón^M

tapered pedestal
pie^M

OFFICE AUTOMATION

side view
vista^F lateral

back view
vista^F trasera

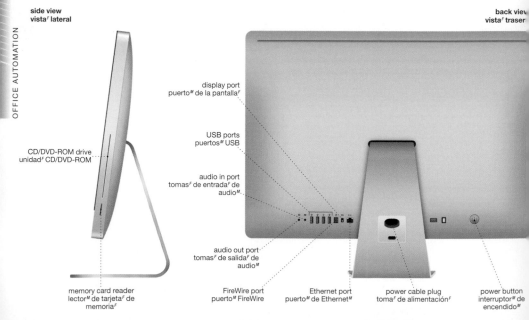

display port
puerto^M de la pantalla^F

USB ports
puertos^M USB

CD/DVD-ROM drive
unidad^F CD/DVD-ROM

audio in port
tomas^F de entrada^F de
audio^M

audio out port
tomas^F de salida^F de
audio^M

memory card reader
lector^M de tarjeta^F de
memoria^F

FireWire port
puerto^M FireWire

Ethernet port
puerto^M de Ethernet^M

power cable plug
toma^F de alimentación^F

power button
interruptor^M de
encendido^M

tower case computer
computadora^F de torre^F

monitor
pantalla^M

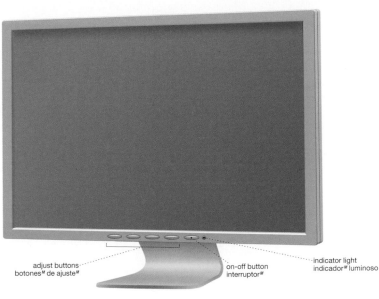

adjust buttons
botones^M de ajuste^M

on-off button
interruptor^M

indicator light
indicador^M luminoso

tower case: back view
computadora^F : vista^F
posterior

tower case: front view
computadora^F : vista^F frontal

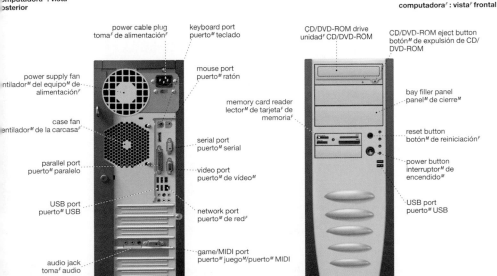

power cable plug
toma^F de alimentación^F

keyboard port
puerto^M teclado

CD/DVD-ROM drive
unidad^F CD/DVD-ROM

CD/DVD-ROM eject button
botón^M de expulsión de CD/
DVD-ROM

mouse port
puerto^M ratón

power supply fan
ventilador^M del equipo^M de
alimentación^F

memory card reader
lector^M de tarjeta^F de
memoria^F

bay filler panel
panel^M de cierre^M

case fan
ventilador^M de la carcasa^F

serial port
puerto^M serial

reset button
botón^M de reiniciación^F

parallel port
puerto^M paralelo

video port
puerto^M de vídeo^M

power button
interruptor^M de
encendido^M

USB port
puerto^M USB

network port
puerto^M de red^F

USB port
puerto^M USB

audio jack
toma^F audio

game/MIDI port
puerto^M juego^M/puerto^M MIDI

laptop computer
computadora*f* portátil

front view
vista*f* frontal

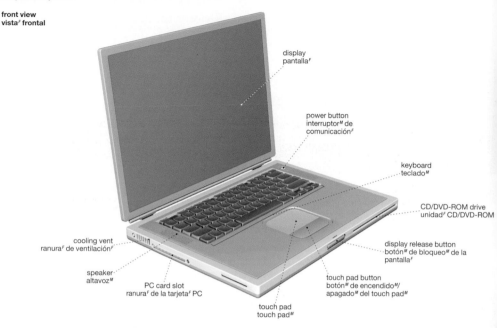

display
pantalla*f*

power button
interruptor*M* de
comunicación*f*

keyboard
teclado*M*

CD/DVD-ROM drive
unidad*f* CD/DVD-ROM

cooling vent
ranura*f* de ventilación*f*

display release button
botón*M* de bloqueo*M* de la
pantalla*f*

speaker
altavoz*M*

PC card slot
ranura*f* de la tarjeta*f* PC

touch pad button
botón*M* de encendido*M*/
apagado*M* del touch pad*M*

touch pad
touch pad*M*

OFFICE AUTOMATION

back view
vista*f* trasera

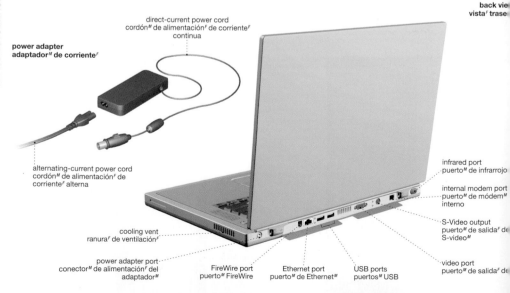

direct-current power cord
cordón*M* de alimentación*f* de corriente*f*
continua

power adapter
adaptador*M* de corriente*f*

alternating-current power cord
cordón*M* de alimentación*f* de
corriente*f* alterna

infrared port
puerto*M* de infrarrojo

internal modem port
puerto*M* de módem*M*
interno

S-Video output
puerto*M* de salida*f* de
S-video*M*

cooling vent
ranura*f* de ventilación*f*

power adapter port
conector*M* de alimentación*f* del
adaptador*M*

FireWire port
puerto*M* FireWire

Ethernet port
puerto*M* de Ethernet*M*

USB ports
puertos*M* USB

video port
puerto*M* de salida*f* de

connection devices
dispositivos^M de conexión^M

wireless network interface card
tarjeta^F de interfaz^F de red^F sin hilos^M

network interface card
tarjeta^F de interfaz^F de
red^F

Internet stick
Internet^M USB

network access point transceiver
emisor^M-receptor^M de acceso^M a
la red^F

modem
módem^M

OFFICE AUTOMATION

connecting cables
cables^M de conexión^F

coaxial cable
cable^M coaxial

twisted-pair cable
cable^M de par^M

fiber-optic cable
cable^M de fibra^F óptica

USB cable
cable^M USB

input devices

unidades[F] de entrada[F] de información[F]

keyboard and pictograms
teclado[M] y pictogramas[M]

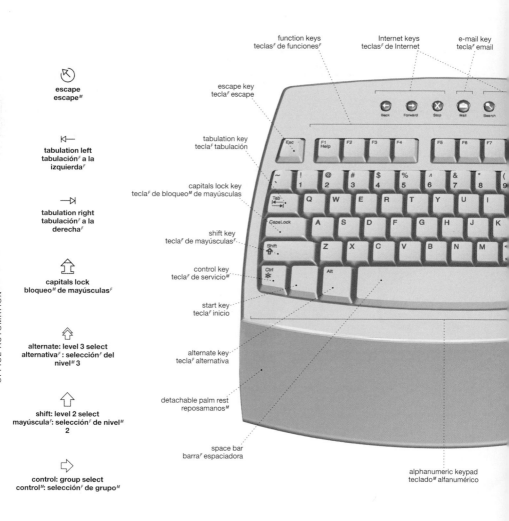

escape
escape[M]

tabulation left
tabulación[F] a la
izquierda[F]

tabulation right
tabulación[F] a la
derecha[F]

capitals lock
bloqueo[M] de mayúsculas[F]

alternate: level 3 select
alternativa[F]: selección[F] del
nivel[M] 3

shift: level 2 select
mayúscula[F]: selección[F] de nivel[M]
2

control: group select
control[M]: selección[F] de grupo[M]

function keys
teclas[F] de funciones[F]

Internet keys
teclas[F] de Internet

e-mail key
tecla[F] email

escape key
tecla[F] escape

tabulation key
tecla[F] tabulación

capitals lock key
tecla[F] de bloqueo[M] de mayúsculas

shift key
tecla[F] de mayúsculas[F]

control key
tecla[F] de servicio[M]

start key
tecla[F] inicio

alternate key
tecla[F] alternativa

detachable palm rest
reposamanos[M]

space bar
barra[F] espaciadora

alphanumeric keypad
teclado[M] alfanumérico

control
control[M]

alternate
alternativa[F]

space
espacio[M]

nonbreaking space
espacio[M] sin pausa[F]

cursor left
cursor[M] hacia la
izquierda[F]

OFFICE AUTOMATION

input devices

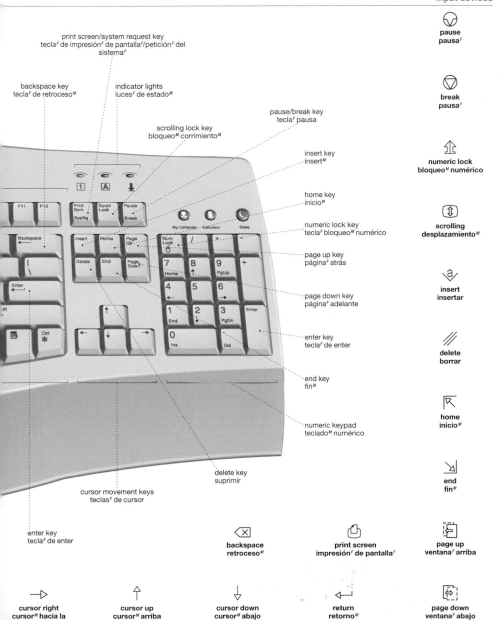

pause
pausa^f

break
pausa^f

numeric lock
bloqueo^M numérico

scrolling
desplazamiento^M

insert
insertar

delete
borrar

home
inicio^M

end
fin^M

page up
ventana^f arriba

page down
ventana^f abajo

print screen/system request key
tecla^f de impresión^f de pantalla^f/petición^f del
sistema^M

backspace key
tecla^f de retroceso^M

indicator lights
luces^f de estado^M

pause/break key
tecla^f pausa

scrolling lock key
bloqueo^M corrimiento^M

insert key
insert^M

home key
inicio^M

numeric lock key
tecla^f bloqueo^M numérico

page up key
página^f atrás

page down key
página^f adelante

enter key
tecla^f de enter

end key
fin^M

numeric keypad
teclado^M numérico

delete key
suprimir

cursor movement keys
teclas^f de cursor

enter key
tecla^f de enter

backspace
retroceso^M

print screen
impresión^f de pantalla^f

cursor right
cursor^M hacia la
derecha^f

cursor up
cursor^M arriba

cursor down
cursor^M abajo

return
retorno^M

page down
ventana^f abajo

OFFICE AUTOMATION

input devices

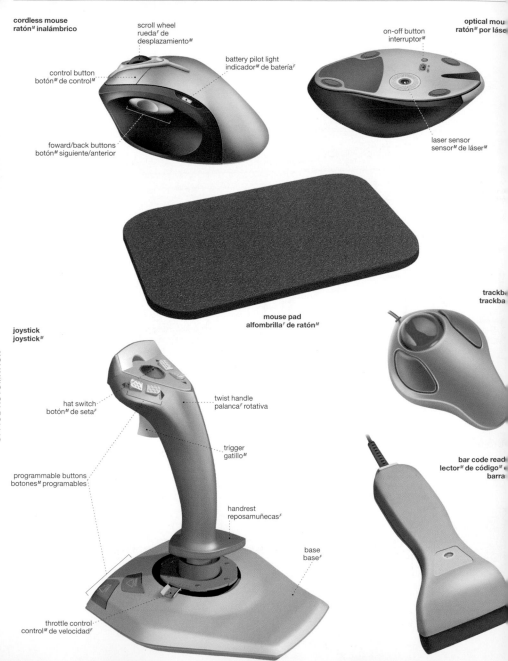

cordless mouse
ratón^M **inalámbrico**

scroll wheel
rueda^F de
desplazamiento^M

control button
botón^M de control^M

battery pilot light
indicador^M de batería^F

foward/back buttons
botón^M siguiente/anterior

optical mou
ratón^M **por láser**

on-off button
interruptor^M

laser sensor
sensor^M de láser^M

mouse pad
alfombrilla^F **de ratón**^{M}

trackba
trackba

joystick
joystick^M

hat switch
botón^M de seta^F

twist handle
palanca^F rotativa

trigger
gatillo^M

programmable buttons
botones^M programables

handrest
reposamuñecas^F

base
base^F

bar code read
lector^M **de código**^{M}
barra

throttle control
control^M de velocidad^F

OFFICE AUTOMATION

input devices

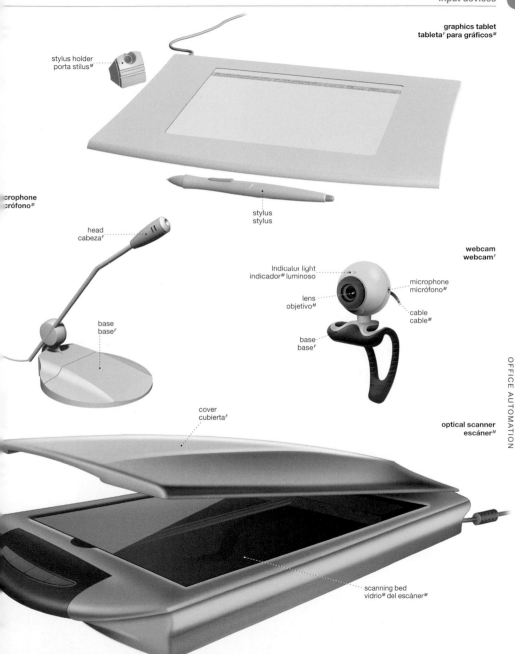

graphics tablet
tabletaᶠ para gráficosᴹ

stylus holder
porta stilusᴹ

microphone
micrófonoᴹ

stylus
stylus

head
cabezaᶠ

base
baseᶠ

webcam
webcamᶠ

Indicator light
indicadorᴹ luminoso

microphone
micrófonoᴹ

lens
objetivoᴹ

cable
cableᴹ

base
baseᶠ

cover
cubiertaᶠ

optical scanner
escánerᴹ

scanning bed
vidrioᴹ del escánerᴹ

OFFICE AUTOMATION

output devices

unidades^F de salida^F de información^F

projector
proyector^M

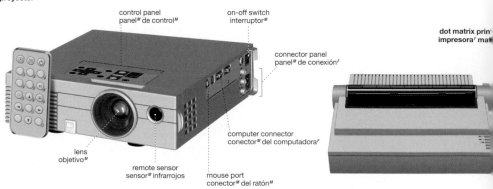

control panel
panel^M de control^M

on-off switch
interruptor^M

dot matrix prin
impresora^F mat

connector panel
panel^M de conexión^F

computer connector
conector^M del computadora^F

lens
objetivo^M

remote sensor
sensor^M infrarrojos

mouse port
conector^M del ratón^M

plotter
plotter^M

output devices

ink cartridge
cartucho^M de tinta^F

toner cartridge
cartucho^M de tóner^M

laser printer
impresora^F láser

output tray
bandeja^F de
alimentación^F

front panel
panel^M frontal

control panel
panel^M de control^M

cooling vent
ranura^F de ventilación^F

paper guide
guía^F papel^M

input tray
bandeja^F de
alimentación^F

cover
cubierta^F

input paper tray
bandeja^F de entrada^F de papel^M

combination printer and scanner
impresora^F de líneas^F

display
pantalla^F

operation panel
panel^M de control^M

platen glass
vidrio^M del escáner^M

memory card slot
puerto^M de tarjeta^F de
memoria^F

USB port
puertos^M USB

output tray
bandeja^F de salida^F

OFFICE AUTOMATION

data storage devices

unidades*f* de almacenamiento*M* de información*f*

external hard drive
disco*M* duro externo

USB port
puerto*M* USB

DVD burner
grabadora*f* de DVD*M*

rewritable DVD
DVD*M* regrabable

disc tray
alojamiento*f* de disco*M*

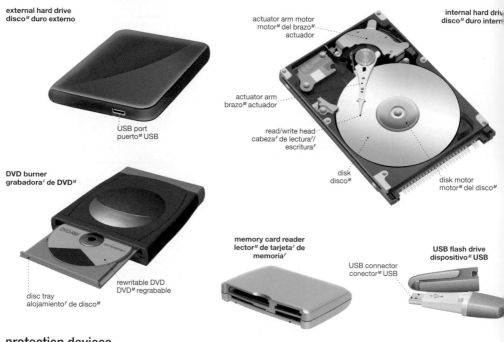

actuator arm motor
motor*M* del brazo*M* actuador

internal hard drive
disco*M* duro interno

actuator arm
brazo*M* actuador

read/write head
cabeza*f* de lectura*f*/
escritura*f*

disk
disco*M*

disk motor
motor*M* del disco*M*

memory card reader
lector*M* de tarjeta*f* de memoria*f*

USB connector
conector*M* USB

USB flash drive
dispositivo*M* USB

protection devices

dispositivos*M* de protección*f*

uninterruptible power supply (UPS):
back view
sistema*f* de alimentación*f*
ininterrumpida : parte*f* posterior

telephone surge protection jacks
tomas*f* telefónicas contra
sobretensiones*f*

computer interface port
puerto*M* de interfaz*f* de
computadora*f*

surge protection receptacle
toma*f* contra sobretensión*f*

input receptacle
toma*f* de entrada*f*

battery backup/surge protection receptacles
toma*f* contra sobretensión*f* alimentadas por
baterías*f*

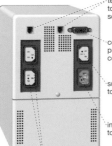

uninterruptible power supply (UPS): front
view
sistema*f* de alimentación*f* ininterrumpida :
parte*f* frontal

control lights
indicadores*M* de control*M*

on/off/test button
botón*M* de encendido/
apagado/test*M*

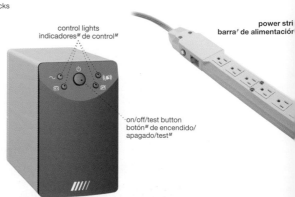

power strip
barra*f* de alimentación*f*

miscellaneous computer tools
herramientas^F informáticas diversas

interactive whiteboard
pizarra^F interactiva

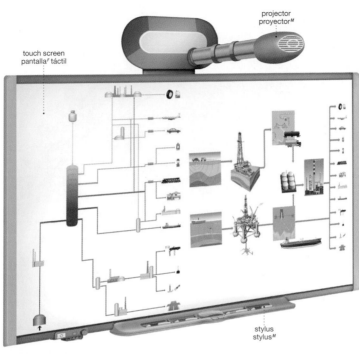

projector
proyector^M

touch screen
pantalla^F táctil

stylus
stylus^M

OFFICE AUTOMATION

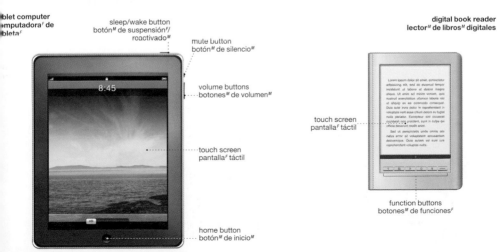

tablet computer
computadora^F de
tableta^F

sleep/wake button
botón^M de suspensión^F/
reactivado^M

mute button
botón^M de silencio^M

volume buttons
botones^M de volumen^M

8:45

touch screen
pantalla^F táctil

home button
botón^M de inicio^M

digital book reader
lector^M de libros^M digitales

touch screen
pantalla^F táctil

function buttons
botones^M de funciones^F

examples of networks

ejemplos^M de redes^F

ring network
red^F en anillo^M

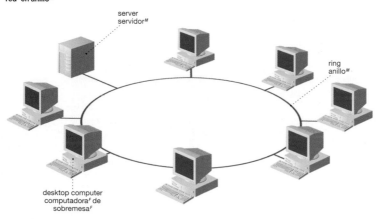

server
servidor^M

ring
anillo^M

desktop computer
computadora^F de
sobremesa^F

OFFICE AUTOMATION

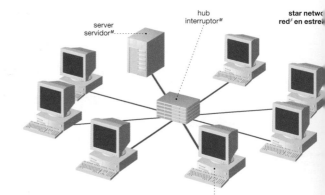

hub
interruptor^M

server
servidor^M

star netwo
red^F en estre

desktop computer
computadora^F de
sobremesa^F

bus network
red^F en bus^M

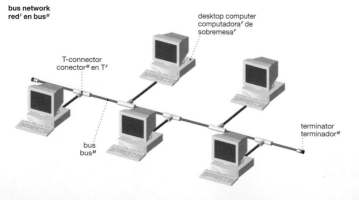

desktop computer
computadora^F de
sobremesa^F

T-connector
conector^M en T^F

terminator
terminador^M

bus
bus^M

examples of networks

wide area network
red^f de área^f amplia

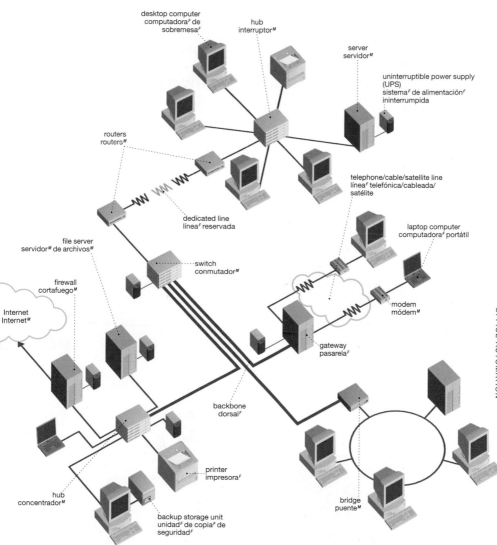

desktop computer
computadora^F de
sobremesa^F

hub
interruptor^M

server
servidor^M

uninterruptible power supply
(UPS)
sistema^F de alimentación^F
ininterrumpida

routers
routers^M

telephone/cable/satellite line
línea^F telefónica/cableada/
satélite

dedicated line
línea^F reservada

laptop computer
computadora^F portátil

file server
servidor^M de archivos^M

firewall
cortafuego^M

switch
conmutador^M

modem
módem^M

Internet
Internet^M

gateway
pasarela^F

backbone
dorsal^F

printer
impresora^F

hub
concentrador^M

backup storage unit
unidad^F de copia^F de
seguridad^F

bridge
puente^M

OFFICE AUTOMATION

Internet

Internet^M

uniform resource locator (URL)
URL localizador^M universal de recursos^M

communication protocol
protocolo^M de comunicación^F

domain name
nombre^M del dominio^M

file format
formato^M del archivo^M

http://www.un.org/aboutun/index.html

double slash
doble barra^F oblicua

second-level domain
dominio^M de segundo
nivel^M

file
archivo^M

server
servidor^M

top-level domain
dominio^M de primer nivel^M

directory
directorio^M

OFFICE AUTOMATION

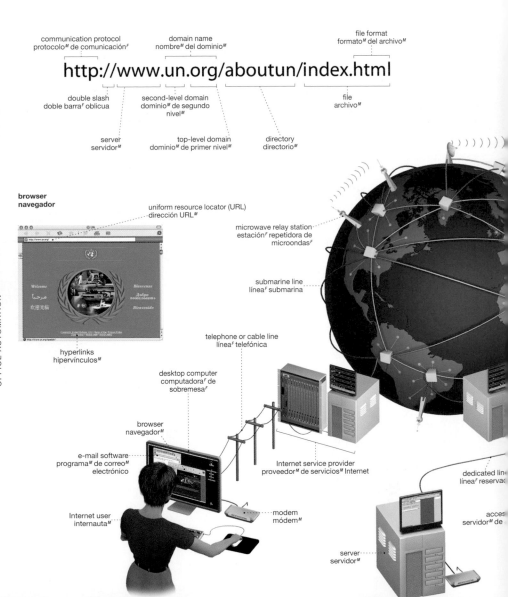

browser
navegador

uniform resource locator (URL)
dirección URL^M

microwave relay station
estación^F repetidora de
microondas^F

submarine line
línea^F submarina

telephone or cable line
línea^F telefónica

hyperlinks
hipervínculos^M

desktop computer
computadora^F de
sobremesa^F

browser
navegador^M

Internet service provider
proveedor^M de servicios^M Internet

dedicated line
línea^F reservada

e-mail software
programa^M de correo^M
electrónico

Internet user
internauta^M

modem
módem^M

access
servidor^M de

server
servidor^M

Internet uses

usos^M de Internet^M

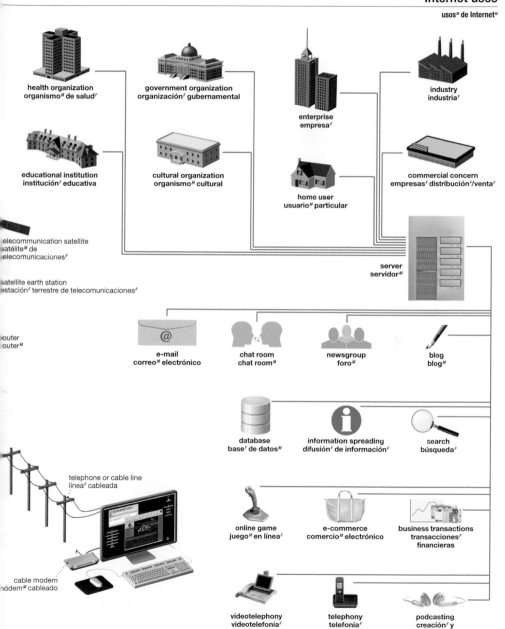

health organization
organismo^M de salud^F

government organization
organización^F gubernamental

industry
industria^F

enterprise
empresa^F

educational institution
institución^F educativa

cultural organization
organismo^M cultural

commercial concern
empresas^F distribución^F/venta^F

home user
usuario^M particular

telecommunication satellite
satélite^M de
telecomunicaciones^F

satellite earth station
estación^F terrestre de telecomunicaciones^F

server
servidor^M

router
router^M

e-mail
correo^M electrónico

chat room
chat room^M

newsgroup
foro^M

blog
blog^M

database
base^F de datos^M

information spreading
difusión^F de información^F

search
búsqueda^F

telephone or cable line
línea^F cableada

online game
juego^M en línea^F

e-commerce
comercio^M electrónico

business transactions
transacciones^F
financieras

cable modem
módem^M cableado

videotelephony
videotelefonía^F

telephony
telefonía^F

podcasting
creación^F y
distribución^F de
archivos^M de sonido^M
digital

OFFICE AUTOMATION

office organization

organización[F] de oficina[F]

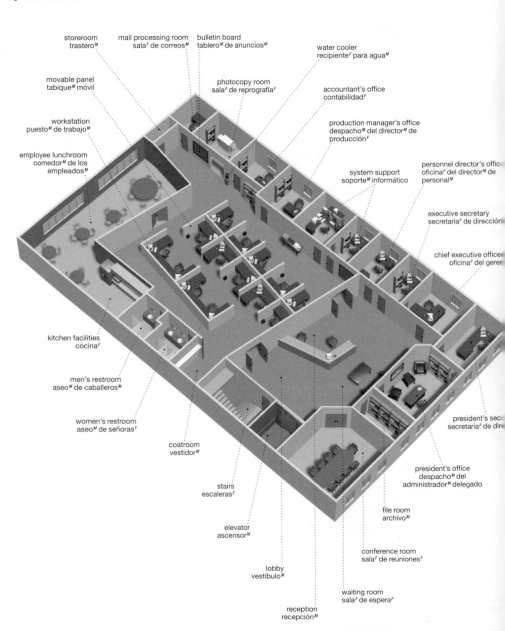

storeroom
trastero[M]

mail processing room
sala[F] de correos[M]

bulletin board
tablero[M] de anuncios[M]

water cooler
recipiente[F] para agua[M]

movable panel
tabique[M] móvil

photocopy room
sala[F] de reprografía[F]

accountant's office
contabilidad[F]

workstation
puesto[M] de trabajo[M]

production manager's office
despacho[M] del director[M] de
producción[F]

employee lunchroom
comedor[M] de los
empleados[M]

personnel director's office
oficina[F] del director[M] de
personal[M]

system support
soporte[M] informático

executive secretary
secretaria[F] de dirección

chief executive office
oficina[F] del gere

kitchen facilities
cocina[F]

men's restroom
aseo[M] de caballeros[M]

women's restroom
aseo[M] de señoras[F]

president's sec
secretaría[F] de dir

coatroom
vestidor[M]

stairs
escaleras[F]

president's office
despacho[M] del
administrador[M] delegado

elevator
ascensor[M]

file room
archivo[M]

conference room
sala[F] de reuniones[F]

lobby
vestíbulo[M]

waiting room
sala[F] de espera[F]

reception
recepción[M]

office furniture

muebles^M de oficina^F

filing furniture
archivadores^M

lateral filing cabinet
archivador^M lateral

mobile drawer unit
cajonera^F móvil

mobile filing unit
archivador^M móvil

storage furniture
muebles^M contenedores

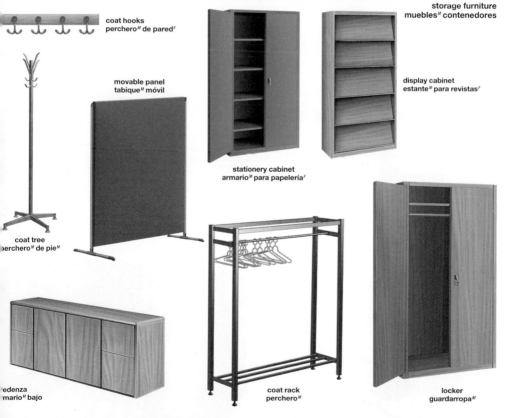

coat hooks
perchero^M de pared^F

movable panel
tabique^M móvil

display cabinet
estante^M para revistas^F

stationery cabinet
armario^M para papelería^F

coat tree
perchero^M de pie^M

credenza
armario^M bajo

coat rack
perchero^M

locker
guardarropa^M

OFFICE AUTOMATION

office furniture

work furniture
muebles^M de trabajo^M

return
mesa^M auxiliar de
escritorio^M

des
mesa^F de estudie

desk mat
vade^M

typist's chair
silla^F de secretaria^F

swivel-tilter armchair
sillón^M giratorio

computer de
escritorio^M para
computador

printer table
mesa^F de la impresora^F

pull-out keyboard shelf
bandeja^F extraible para
teclado^M

central unit platform
plataforma^F de unidad^F
central

shelf
tablilla^F

footrest
reposapiés^M

executive de
escritorio^M e
ejecutiv

kneeling chair
silla^F ergonómica

OFFICE AUTOMATION

photocopier

fotocopiadora[F]

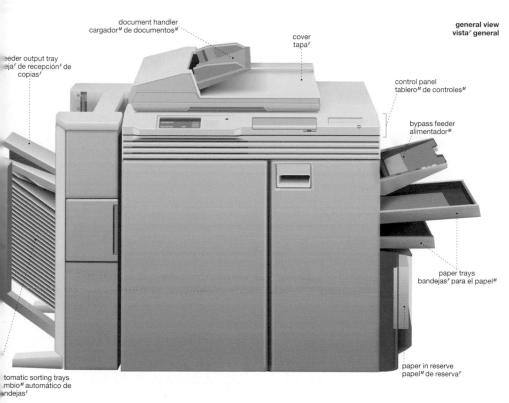

general view
vista[F] **general**

document handler
cargador[M] de documentos[M]

cover
tapa[F]

control panel
tablero[M] de controles[M]

feeder output tray
eja[F] de recepción[F] de copias[F]

bypass feeder
alimentador[M]

paper trays
bandejas[F] para el papel[M]

paper in reserve
papel[M] de reserva[F]

tomatic sorting trays
mbio[M] automático de
andejas[F]

OFFICE AUTOMATION

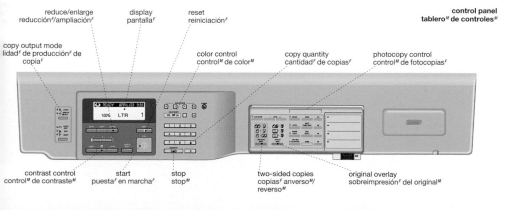

control panel
tablero[M] **de controles**[M]

reduce/enlarge
reducción[F]/ampliación[F]

display
pantalla[F]

reset
reiniciación[F]

copy output mode
lidad[F] de producción[F] de
copia[F]

color control
control[M] de color[M]

copy quantity
cantidad[F] de copias[F]

photocopy control
control[M] de fotocopias[F]

contrast control
control[M] de contraste[M]

start
puesta[F] en marcha[F]

stop
stop[M]

two-sided copies
copias[F] anverso[M]/
reverso[M]

original overlay
sobreimpresión[F] del original[M]

stationery

artículos^M de escritorio^M

electronic typewriter
máquina^F de escribir
electrónica

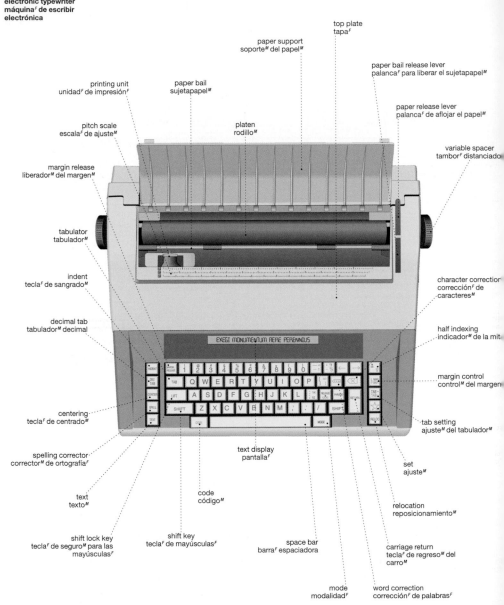

top plate
tapa^F

paper support
soporte^M del papel^M

paper bail release lever
palanca^F para liberar el sujetapapel^M

printing unit
unidad^F de impresión^F

paper bail
sujetapapel^M

paper release lever
palanca^F de aflojar el papel^M

pitch scale
escala^F de ajuste^M

platen
rodillo^M

variable spacer
tambor^F distanciado

margin release
liberador^M del margen^M

tabulator
tabulador^M

indent
tecla^F de sangrado^M

character correction
corrección^F de
caracteres^M

decimal tab
tabulador^M decimal

half indexing
indicador^M de la mit

margin control
control^M del margen

EXEGI MONUMENTUM RERE PERENNIUS

centering
tecla^F de centrado^M

tab setting
ajuste^M del tabulador^M

spelling corrector
corrector^M de ortografía^F

set
ajuste^M

text
texto^M

text display
pantalla^F

code
código^M

relocation
reposicionamiento^M

shift lock key
tecla^F de seguro^M para las
mayúsculas^F

shift key
tecla^F de mayúsculas^F

space bar
barra^F espaciadora

carriage return
tecla^F de regreso^M del
carro^M

mode
modalidad^F

word correction
corrección^F de palabras^F

stationery

**for calculating
para calcular**

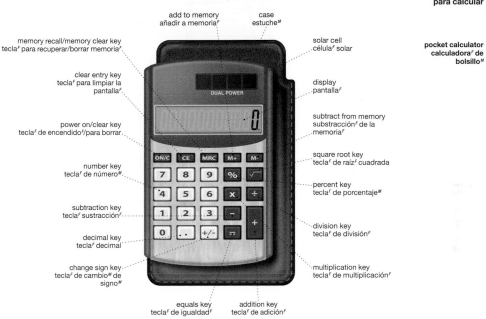

add to memory
añadir a memoria^F

case
estuche^M

memory recall/memory clear key
tecla^F para recuperar/borrar memoria^F.

solar cell
célula^F solar

**pocket calculator
calculadora^F de
bolsillo^M**

clear entry key
tecla^F para limpiar la
pantalla^F.

display
pantalla^F

power on/clear key
tecla^F de encendido^F/para borrar.

subtract from memory
substracción^F de la
memoria^F

number key
tecla^F de número^M.

square root key
tecla^F de raíz^F cuadrada

subtraction key
tecla^F sustracción^F.

percent key
tecla^F de porcentaje^M

decimal key
tecla^F decimal.

division key
tecla^F de división^F

change sign key
tecla^F de cambio^M de
signo^M

multiplication key
tecla^F de multiplicación^F

equals key
tecla^F de igualdad^F

addition key
tecla^F de adición^F

**printing calculator
calculadora^F con
impresora^F**

**graphing calculator
calculadora^F de gráficos^M**

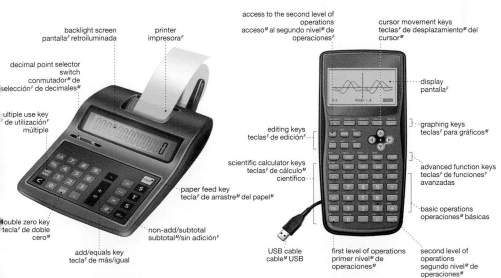

access to the second level of
operations
acceso^M al segundo nivel^M de
operaciones^F

cursor movement keys
teclas^F de desplazamiento^M del
cursor^M

backlight screen
pantalla^F retroiluminada

printer
impresora^F

display
pantalla^F

decimal point selector
switch
conmutador^M de
selección^F de decimales^M

graphing keys
teclas^F para gráficos^M

multiple use key
de utilización^F
múltiple

editing keys
teclas^F de edición^F

advanced function keys
teclas^F de funciones^F
avanzadas

scientific calculator keys
teclas^F de cálculo^M
científico

basic operations
operaciones^M básicas

paper feed key
tecla^F de arrastre^M del papel^M

double zero key
tecla^F de doble
cero^M

non-add/subtotal
subtotal^M/sin adición^F

add/equals key
tecla^F de más/igual

USB cable
cable^M USB

first level of operations
primer nivel^M de
operaciones^M

second level of
operations
segundo nivel^M de
operaciones^M

OFFICE AUTOMATION

stationery

for time management and notetaking
para el empleo^M **del tiempo**^M **y la**
toma^F **de anotaciones**^F

OFFICE AUTOMATION

calendar pad
calendario^M de sobremesa^F

tear-off calendar
calendario^M de sobremesa^F

dater
fechador^M

appointment book
agenda^F

memo pad
libreta^F

sticky note
nota^F adhesiva

display
pantalla^F

time cloc
timbradora

spiral binder
carpeta^F de espiral^F

clipboard
tabla^F con pinza^F

time card
calendario^M

stationery

for correspondence
para la
correspondencia^F

added envelope
sobre^M almohadillado

self-sealing flap
solapa^F autoadhesiva

letter opener
abrecartas^M

numbering machine
foliador^M

letter scale
balanza^F para cartas^F

air bubbles
burbujas^F de aire^M

steno book
cuaderno^M de
taquigrafía^F

fingertip
dedal^M

moistener
rueda^F humedecedora

rubber stamp
sello^M de goma^F

signature book
libro^M de firmas^M

stamp pad
cojín^M para sellos^M

stamp rack
portasellos^M

rotary file
fichero^M giratorio

blotting paper
papel^M secante

telephone index
agenda^F telefónica

OFFICE AUTOMATION

postage meter
máquina^F franqueadora

postmarking module
módulo^M de franqueado^M

desk tray
bandeja^F de
correspondencia^F

feed deck
plataforma^F de
alimentación^F

base
base^F

stationery

for filing
para archivar

window tab
indicador^M transparente

self-adhesive labels
etiquetas^F adhesivas

tab
indicador^M

index cards
fichas^F

sheet protector
protector^M de folios^M

fastener binder
carpeta^F de broches^M

dividers
divisores^M

folder
carpeta^F de archivo^M

spring binder
carpeta^F de costilla^F de
resorte^M

clamp binder
carpeta^F con mecanismo^M de
presión^F

hanging file
archivador^M colgante

file guides
guías^F de archivo^M

ring binder
carpeta^F de argollas^F

document folder
carpeta^F con guardas^F

post binder
carpeta^F de tornillos^M

index card drawer
gaveta^F de archivador^M

archboard
tabla^F con argollas^F

art and photo envelope
sobre^M con cierre^M de cremallera^F

index card cabinet
archivador^M de fichas^F

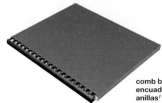

carry folder
portafolios^M

compressor
compresor^M

label holder
soporte^M del rótulo^M

metal rail
riel^M metálico

filing box
caja^F archivo^M

label maker
rotulador^M

comb binding
encuadernación^F de
anillas^F

expanding file
archivador^M de fuelle^M

stationery

**miscellaneous
articles
artículos**ᴹ **varios**

tape guide
guía ᶠ de cinta ᶠ

paper clips
clip ᴹ

thumbtacks and pushpins
chinchetas ᶠ

electric penc
sharpene
sacapuntas ᴹ eléctric

**box sealing tape
dispenser
porta-cinta**ᴹ **adhesiva**

tension adjusting screw
tornillo ᴹ de ajuste ᴹ de
tensión ᶠ

cutting blade
cuchilla ᶠ

hub
cubo ᴹ

tape
cinta ᶠ

handle
empuñadura ᶠ

pencil sharpener
sacapuntas ᴹ

receptacle for shavings
receptáculo ᴹ

**leads tube
estuche**ᴹ **de minas**ᶠ

**paper fasteners
tachuelas**ᶠ **para papel**ᴹ

paper clip holder
distribuidor ᴹ de clips ᴹ

eraser
goma ᶠ

magnet
imán ᴹ

clip
pinza ᶠ

**correction pen
bolígrafo**ᴹ **corrector**

glue stick
lápiz ᴹ adhesivo

tape dispenser
porta-celo ᴹ

staple remover
quitagrapas ᴹ

digital voice recorder
grabadora ᶠ digital

pencil sharpener
sacapuntas ᴹ

**correction tape
cinta**ᶠ **correctora**

bill-file
pinchador ᴹ

staples
grapas ᶠ

stapler
grapadora ᶠ

OFFICE AUTOMATION

overhead projector
royector

projection head
cabeza^F de proyección^M

optical lens
lente^F

mirror
espejo^M

optical stage
pletina^F de proyección^F

account book
agenda^F de caja^F

cutting head
cabeza^F cortadora

wastebasket
papelera^F

wastebasket
papelera^F

ulletin board
ablero^M de anuncios^M

paper shredder
trituradora^F de documentos^M

bookends
sujetalibros^M

lightbox
caja^F de luz^F

posting surface
superficie^F de fijación^F

paper punch
perforadora^F

flap
solapa^F

slotted box
caja^F de cartón^M

aper cutter
uillotina^F

hand hole
empuñadura^F recortada

OFFICE AUTOMATION

ROAD TRANSPORT 658

road system 65
fixed bridges 66
movable bridges 66
road tunnel 66
road signs 66

AUTOMOTIVE ROAD TRANSPORT 668

service station 66
automobile 66
electric automobile 67
hybrid automobile 67
brakes 67
types of engines 68
radiator 68
spark plug 68
tire 68
battery 68
accessories 68
campers 68
bus 68
trucking 69
motorcycle 69
4x4 all-terrain vehicle 69

TRANSPORT AND MACHINERY

transporte y vehículos

CYCLING ROAD TRANSPORT 698

bicycle 698

RAIL TRANSPORT 703

railroad station 703
passenger station 704
types of passenger cars 705
diesel-electric locomotive 706
high-speed train 707
yard 708
freight car 709
railroad track 712
crossing gate 713

URBAN RAIL TRANSPORT 714

subway 714
streetcar 717

MARITIME TRANSPORT 718

harbor 718
canal lock 719
ancient ships 720
traditional ships 721
examples of sails 723
examples of rigs 723
four-masted bark 724
examples of boats and ships 726
anchor 732
life-saving equipment 733
navigation devices 734
maritime signals 736
maritime buoyage system 738

AIR TRANSPORT 740

airport 740
long-range jet 746
examples of airplanes 750
examples of tail shapes 751
examples of wing shapes 752
movements of an airplane 752
forces acting on an airplane 752
helicopter 753
examples of helicopters 753

MATERIAL HANDLING 754

typical devices 754
cranes 756
container 757

HEAVY MACHINERY 758

bulldozer 758
backhoe loader 759
scraper 760
power shovel 760
grader 761
dump truck 761
asphalt paver 762
road roller 762
snowblower 763
street sweeper 763
tractor 764
agricultural machinery 765

road system

sistema^M de carreteras^F

cross section of a road
corte^M de una carretera^F

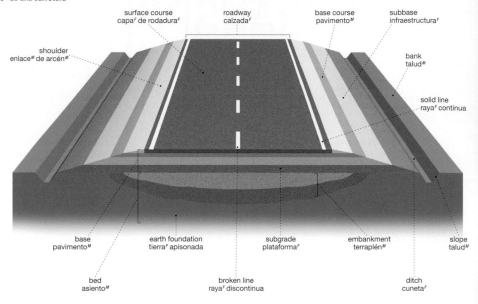

shoulder
enlace^M de arcén^M

surface course
capa^F de rodadura^F

roadway
calzada^F

base course
pavimento^M

subbase
infraestructura^F

bank
talud^M

solid line
raya^F continua

base
pavimento^M

earth foundation
tierra^F apisonada

subgrade
plataforma^F

embankment
terraplén^M

slope
talud^M

bed
asiento^M

broken line
raya^F discontinua

ditch
cuneta^F

examples of interchanges
ejemplos^M de enlaces^M de carreteras^F

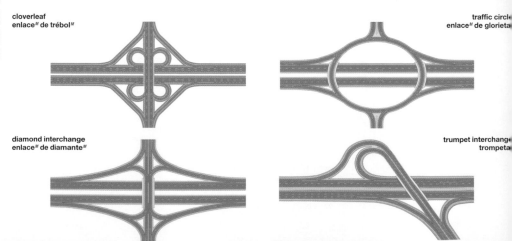

cloverleaf
enlace^M de trébol^M

traffic circle
enlace^M de glorieta

diamond interchange
enlace^M de diamante^M

trumpet interchange
trompeta

road system

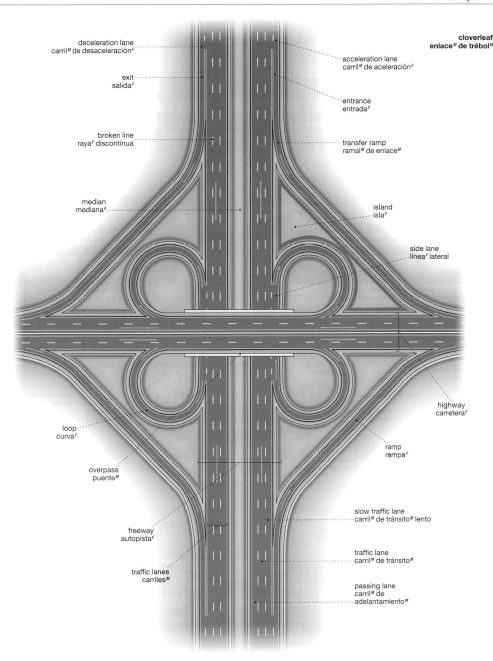

deceleration lane
carril^M de desaceleración^F

exit
salida^F

broken line
raya^F discontinua

median
mediana^F

loop
curva^F

overpass
puente^M

freeway
autopista^F

traffic lanes
carriles^M

cloverleaf
enlace^M de trébol^M

acceleration lane
carril^M de aceleración^F

entrance
entrada^F

transfer ramp
ramal^M de enlace^M

island
isla^F

side lane
línea^F lateral

highway
carretera^F

ramp
rampa^F

slow traffic lane
carril^M de tránsito^M lento

traffic lane
carril^M de tránsito^M

passing lane
carril^M de
adelantamiento^M

automobile

body
carrocería^F

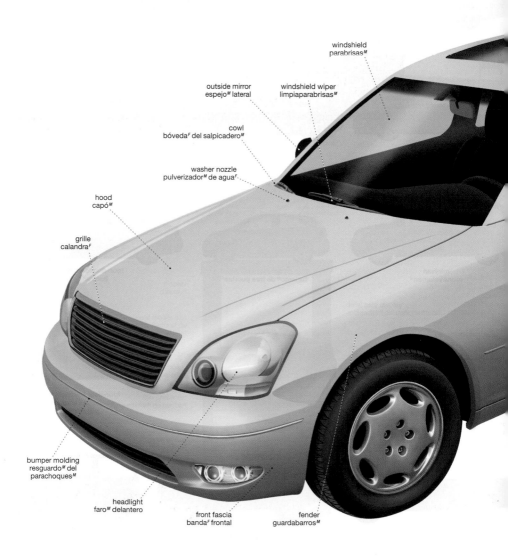

windshield
parabrisas^M

outside mirror
espejo^M lateral

windshield wiper
limpiaparabrisas^M

cowl
bóveda^F del salpicadero^M

washer nozzle
pulverizador^M de agua^F

hood
capó^M

grille
calandra^F

bumper molding
resguardo^M del
parachoques^M

headlight
faro^M delantero

front fascia
banda^F frontal

fender
guardabarros^M

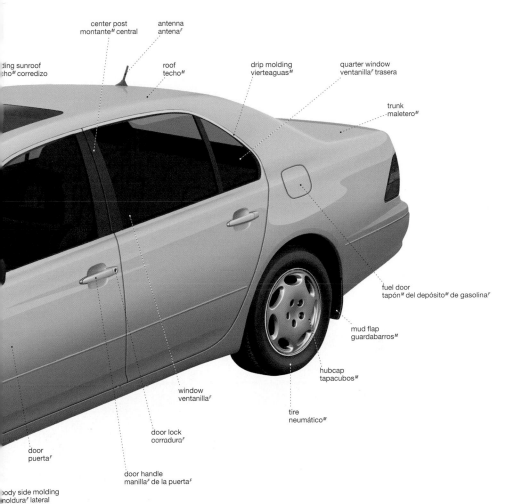

center post
montante^M central

antenna
antena^F

ding sunroof
cho^M corredizo

roof
techo^M

drip molding
vierteaguas^M

quarter window
ventanilla^F trasera

trunk
maletero^M

fuel door
tapón^M del depósito^M de gasolina^F

mud flap
guardabarros^M

hubcap
tapacubos^M

window
ventanilla^F

tire
neumático^M

door lock
cerradura^F

door
puerta^F

door handle
manilla^F de la puerta^F

body side molding
moldura^F lateral

automobile

automobile systems: main parts
automóviles^M: componentes^M principales

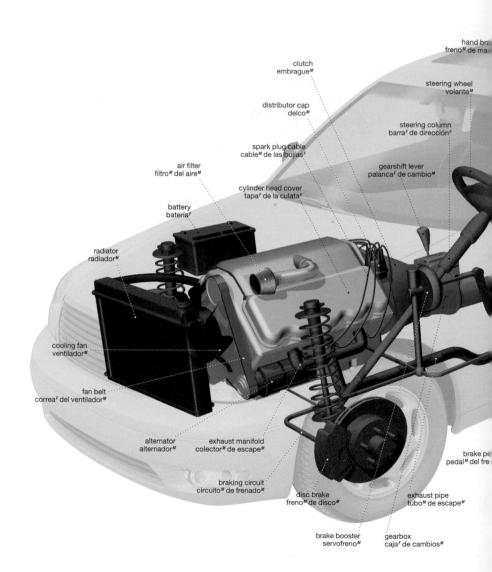

hand bra
freno^M de ma

clutch
embrague^M

steering wheel
volante^M

distributor cap
delco^M

steering column
barra^F de dirección^F

spark plug cable
cable^M de las bujías^F

gearshift lever
palanca^F de cambio^M

air filter
filtro^M del aire^M

cylinder head cover
tapa^F de la culata^F

battery
batería^F

radiator
radiador^M

cooling fan
ventilador^M

fan belt
correa^F del ventilador^M

alternator
alternador^M

exhaust manifold
colector^M de escape^M

brake pe
pedal^M del fre

braking circuit
circuito^M de frenado^M

disc brake
freno^M de disco^M

exhaust pipe
tubo^M de escape^M

brake booster
servofreno^M

gearbox
caja^F de cambios^M

TRANSPORT AND MACHINERY

automobile

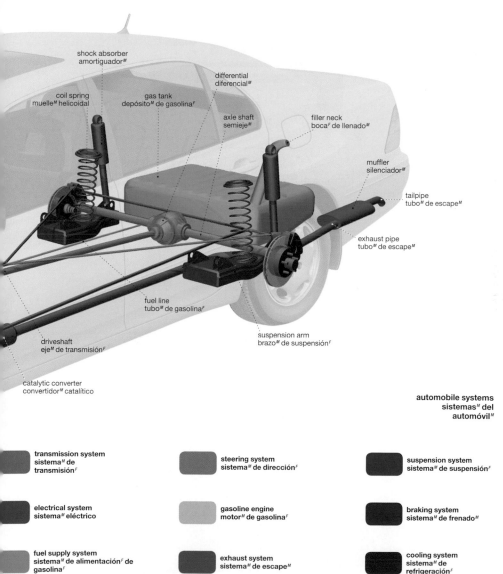

shock absorber
amortiguador^M

coil spring
muelle^M helicoidal

gas tank
depósito^M de gasolina^F

differential
diferencial^M

axle shaft
semieje^M

filler neck
boca^F de llenado^M

muffler
silenciador^M

tailpipe
tubo^M de escape^M

exhaust pipe
tubo^M de escape^M

fuel line
tubo^M de gasolina^F

driveshaft
eje^M de transmisión^F

suspension arm
brazo^M de suspensión^F

catalytic converter
convertidor^M catalítico

automobile systems
sistemas^M del
automóvil^M

transmission system
sistema^M de
transmisión^F

steering system
sistema^M de dirección^F

suspension system
sistema^M de suspensión^F

electrical system
sistema^M eléctrico

gasoline engine
motor^M de gasolina^F

braking system
sistema^M de frenado^M

fuel supply system
sistema^M de alimentación^F de
gasolina^F

exhaust system
sistema^M de escape^M

cooling system
sistema^M de
refrigeración^F

TRANSPORT AND MACHINERY

automobile

headlights
faros *M* **delanteros**

high beam
luz *F* larga

low beam
luz *F* de cruce *M*

fog light
luz *F* antiniebla

turn signal
intermitente *M*

side marker light
luz *F* de posición *F*

taillights
luces *F* **traseras**

center high-mounted
stop light
luz *F* de freno *M*

turn signal
intermitente *M*

back-up light
luz *F* de marcha *F* atrás

brake light
luz *F* de freno *M*

taillight
luz *F* trasera

license plate light
iluminación *F* de la placa *F* de
matrícula *F*

side marker light
luz *F* de posición *F*

door
puerta *F*

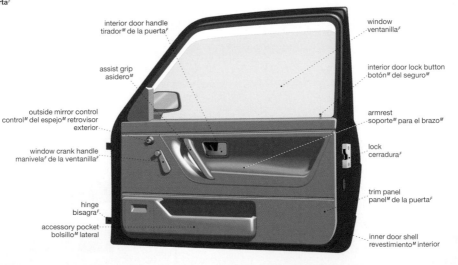

interior door handle
tirador *M* de la puerta *F*

window
ventanilla *F*

assist grip
asidero *M*

interior door lock button
botón *M* del seguro *M*

outside mirror control
control *M* del espejo *M* retrovisor
exterior

armrest
soporte *M* para el brazo *M*

window crank handle
manivela *F* de la ventanilla *F*

lock
cerradura *F*

hinge
bisagra *F*

trim panel
panel *M* de la puerta *F*

accessory pocket
bolsillo *M* lateral

inner door shell
revestimiento *M* interior

bucket seat: front view
asiento^M: **vista**^F **frontal**

bucket seat: side view
asiento^M: **vista**^F **lateral**

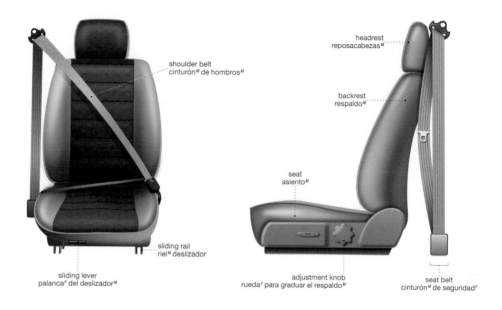

shoulder belt
cinturón^M de hombros^M

headrest
reposacabezas^M

backrest
respaldo^M

seat
asiento^M

sliding rail
riel^M deslizador

sliding lever
palanca^F del deslizador^M

adjustment knob
rueda^F para graduar el respaldo^M

seat belt
cinturón^M de seguridad^F

rear seat
asiento^M **trasero**

armrest
reposabrazos^M

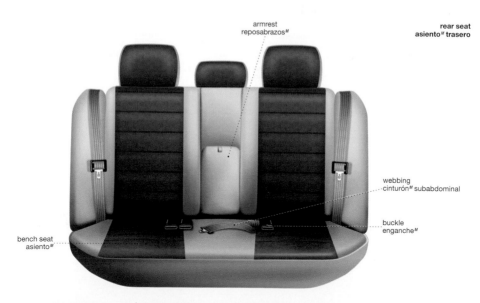

webbing
cinturón^M subabdominal

buckle
enganche^M

bench seat
asiento^M

TRANSPORT AND MACHINERY

automobile

dashboard
salpicadero^M

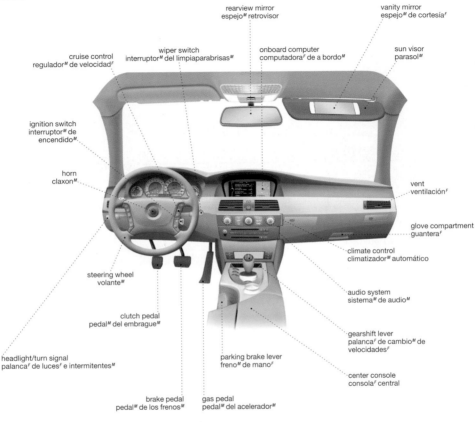

rearview mirror
espejo^M retrovisor

vanity mirror
espejo^M de cortesía^F

cruise control
regulador^M de velocidad^F

wiper switch
interruptor^M del limpiaparabrisas^M

onboard computer
computadora^F de a bordo^M

sun visor
parasol^M

ignition switch
interruptor^M de
encendido^M

horn
claxon^M

vent
ventilación^F

glove compartment
guantera^F

climate control
climatizador^M automático

steering wheel
volante^M

audio system
sistema^M de audio^M

clutch pedal
pedal^M del embrague^M

gearshift lever
palanca^F de cambio^M de
velocidades^F

headlight/turn signal
palanca^F de luces^F e intermitentes^M

parking brake lever
freno^M de mano^F

center console
consola^F central

brake pedal
pedal^M de los frenos^M

gas pedal
pedal^M del acelerador^M

air bag restraint system
sistema^M **de restricción**^F **del**
airbag^M

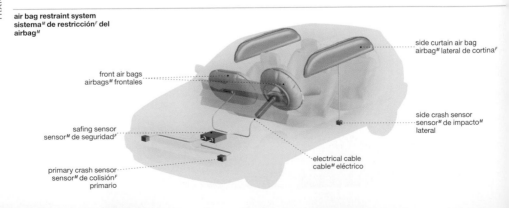

side curtain air bag
airbag^M lateral de cortina^F

front air bags
airbags^M frontales

side crash sensor
sensor^M de impacto^M
lateral

safing sensor
sensor^M de seguridad^F

primary crash sensor
sensor^M de colisión^F
primario

electrical cable
cable^M eléctrico

instrument panel
instrumentos del salpicadero**

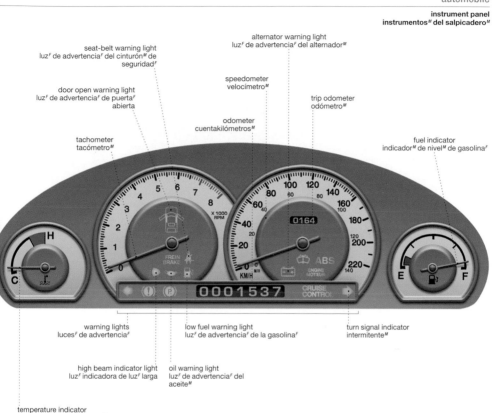

alternator warning light
luz de advertencia del alternador**

seat-belt warning light
luz de advertencia del cinturón de
seguridad

speedometer
velocímetro**

door open warning light
luz de advertencia de puerta
abierta

trip odometer
odómetro**

odometer
cuentakilómetros**

tachometer
tacómetro**

fuel indicator
indicador de nivel** de gasolina

warning lights
luces de advertencia

low fuel warning light
luz de advertencia de la gasolina

turn signal indicator
intermitente**

high beam indicator light
luz indicadora de luz larga

oil warning light
luz de advertencia del
aceite**

temperature indicator
indicador de temperatura

windshield wiper
limpiaparabrisas

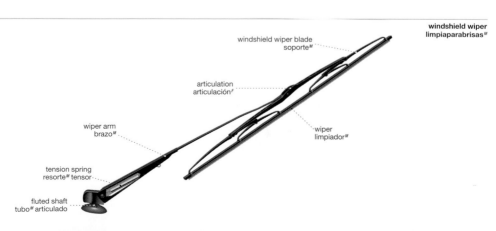

windshield wiper blade
soporte**

articulation
articulación

wiper arm
brazo**

wiper
limpiador**

tension spring
resorte** tensor

fluted shaft
tubo** articulado

TRANSPORT AND MACHINERY

electric automobile
automóvil*ᴹ* eléctrico

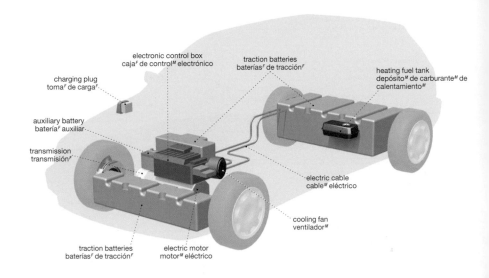

electronic control box
caja*ᶠ* de control*ᴹ* electrónico

traction batteries
baterías*ᶠ* de tracción*ᶠ*

heating fuel tank
depósito*ᴹ* de carburante*ᴹ* de
calentamiento*ᴹ*

charging plug
toma*ᶠ* de carga*ᶠ*

auxiliary battery
batería*ᶠ* auxiliar

transmission
transmisión*ᶠ*

electric cable
cable*ᴹ* eléctrico

cooling fan
ventilador*ᴹ*

traction batteries
baterías*ᶠ* de tracción*ᶠ*

electric motor
motor*ᴹ* eléctrico

hybrid automobile
automóvil*ᴹ* híbrido

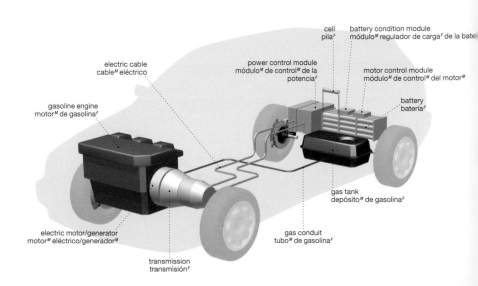

cell
pila*ᶠ*

battery condition module
módulo*ᴹ* regulador de carga*ᶠ* de la bate

electric cable
cable*ᴹ* eléctrico

power control module
módulo*ᴹ* de control*ᴹ* de la
potencia*ᶠ*

motor control module
módulo*ᴹ* de control*ᴹ* del motor*ᴹ*

battery
batería*ᶠ*

gasoline engine
motor*ᴹ* de gasolina*ᶠ*

gas tank
depósito*ᴹ* de gasolina*ᶠ*

electric motor/generator
motor*ᴹ* eléctrico/generador*ᴹ*

gas conduit
tubo*ᴹ* de gasolina*ᶠ*

transmission
transmisión*ᶠ*

brakes
frenos[M]

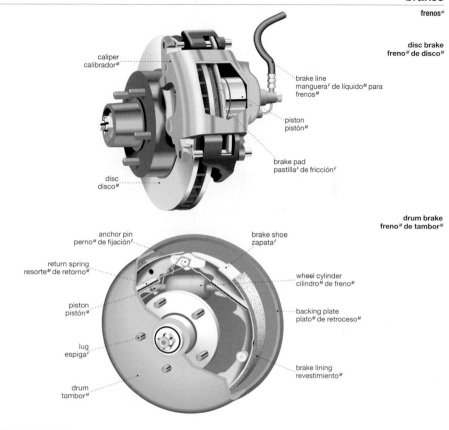

disc brake
freno[M] de disco[M]

caliper
calibrador[M]

brake line
manguera[F] de líquido[M] para
frenos[M]

piston
pistón[M]

brake pad
pastilla[F] de fricción[F]

disc
disco[M]

drum brake
freno[M] de tambor[M]

anchor pin
perno[M] de fijación[F]

brake shoe
zapata[F]

return spring
resorte[M] de retorno[M]

wheel cylinder
cilindro[M] de freno[M]

piston
pistón[M]

backing plate
plato[M] de retroceso[M]

lug
espiga[F]

brake lining
revestimiento[M]

drum
tambor[M]

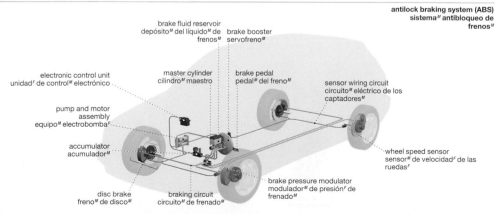

antilock braking system (ABS)
sistema[M] antibloqueo de
frenos[M]

brake fluid reservoir
depósito[M] del líquido[M] de
frenos[M]

brake booster
servofreno[M]

electronic control unit
unidad[F] de control[M] electrónico

master cylinder
cilindro[M] maestro

brake pedal
pedal[M] del freno[M]

sensor wiring circuit
circuito[M] eléctrico de los
captadores[M]

pump and motor
assembly
equipo[M] electrobomba[F]

accumulator
acumulador[M]

wheel speed sensor
sensor[M] de velocidad[F] de las
ruedas[F]

disc brake
freno[M] de disco[M]

braking circuit
circuito[M] de frenado[M]

brake pressure modulator
modulador[M] de presión[F] de
frenado[M]

types of engines

tipos^M de motores^M

turbo-compressor engine
motor^M turbocompresor

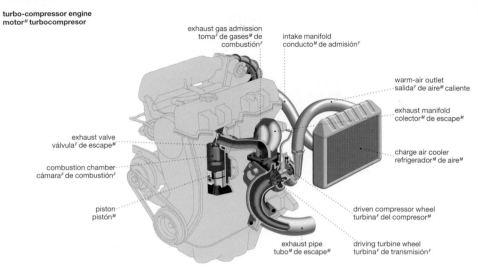

exhaust gas admission
toma^F de gases^M de
combustión^F

intake manifold
conducto^M de admisión^F

warm-air outlet
salida^F de aire^M caliente

exhaust manifold
colector^M de escape^M

exhaust valve
válvula^F de escape^M

combustion chamber
cámara^F de combustión^F

charge air cooler
refrigerador^M de aire^M

piston
pistón^M

driven compressor wheel
turbina^F del compresor^M

exhaust pipe
tubo^M de escape^M

driving turbine wheel
turbina^F de transmisión^F

---

four-stroke-cycle engine
ciclo^M de un motor^M de cuatro tiempos^M

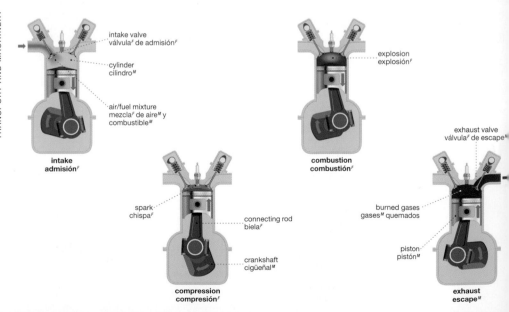

intake valve
válvula^F de admisión^F

cylinder
cilindro^M

air/fuel mixture
mezcla^F de aire^M y
combustible^M

explosion
explosión^F

exhaust valve
válvula^F de escape^M

intake
admisión^F

spark
chispa^F

connecting rod
biela^F

crankshaft
cigüeñal^M

combustion
combustión^F

burned gases
gases^M quemados

piston
pistón^M

compression
compresión^F

exhaust
escape^M

two-stroke-cycle engine cycle
ciclo^M de un motor^M de dos tiempos^M

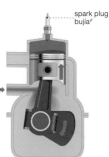

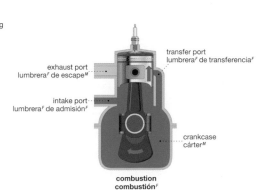

spark plug
bujía^F

exhaust port
lumbrera^F de escape^M

intake port
lumbrera^F de admisión^F

transfer port
lumbrera^F de transferencia^F

crankcase
cárter^M

compression/intake
compresión^F/admisión^F

combustion
combustión^F

exhaust/scavenging
escape^M

rotary engine cycle
ciclo^M de un motor^M rotatorio

intake manifold
colector^M de admisión^F

exhaust manifold
colector^M de escape^M

rotor
rotor^M

intake
admisión^F

compression
compresión^F

power
combustión^F

exhaust
escape^M

diesel engine cycle
ciclo^M de un motor^M diésel

air
aire^M

injection/combustion
inyección^F/combustión^F

fuel injector
inyector^M de
combustible^M

intake
admisión^F

compression
compresión^F

power
combustión^M

exhaust
escape^M

TRANSPORT AND MACHINERY

types of engines

interior of a gasoline engine
corte^M **de un motor**^{M} **de**
gasolina^F

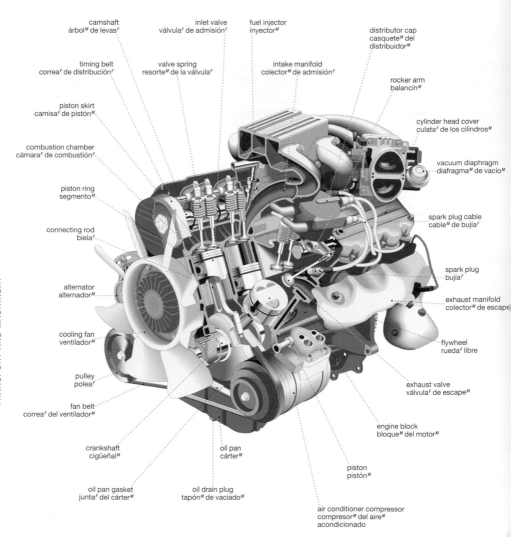

camshaft
árbol^M de levas^F

inlet valve
válvula^F de admisión^F

fuel injector
inyector^M

distributor cap
casquete^M del
distribuidor^M

timing belt
correa^F de distribución^F

valve spring
resorte^M de la válvula^F

intake manifold
colector^M de admisión^F

rocker arm
balancín^M

piston skirt
camisa^F de pistón^M

cylinder head cover
culata^F de los cilindros^M

combustion chamber
cámara^F de combustión^F

vacuum diaphragm
diafragma^M de vacío^M

piston ring
segmento^M

spark plug cable
cable^M de bujía^F

connecting rod
biela^F

spark plug
bujía^F

alternator
alternador^M

exhaust manifold
colector^M de escape

cooling fan
ventilador^M

flywheel
rueda^F libre

pulley
polea^F

exhaust valve
válvula^F de escape^M

fan belt
correa^F del ventilador^M

engine block
bloque^M del motor^M

crankshaft
cigüeñal^M

oil pan
cárter^M

piston
pistón^M

oil pan gasket
junta^F del cárter^M

oil drain plug
tapón^M de vaciado^M

air conditioner compressor
compresor^M del aire^M
acondicionado

radiator
radiador[M]

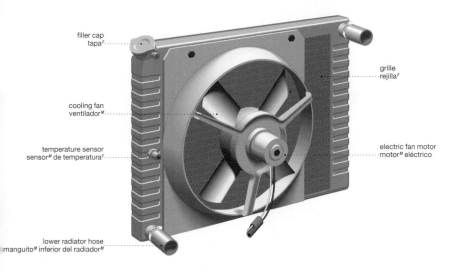

filler cap
tapa[F]

grille
rejilla[F]

cooling fan
ventilador[M]

temperature sensor
sensor[M] de temperatura[F]

electric fan motor
motor[M] eléctrico

lower radiator hose
manguito[M] inferior del radiador[M]

spark plug
bujía[F]

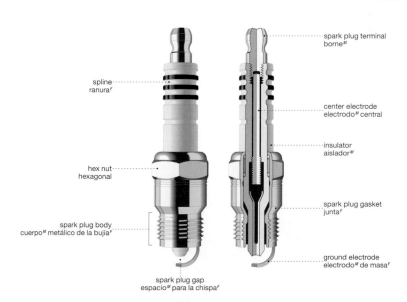

spline
ranura[F]

spark plug terminal
borne[M]

center electrode
electrodo[M] central

insulator
aislador[M]

hex nut
hexagonal

spark plug body
cuerpo[M] metálico de la bujía[F]

spark plug gasket
junta[F]

spark plug gap
espacio[M] para la chispa[F]

ground electrode
electrodo[M] de masa[F]

tire

neumático^M

parts of a tire
partes^F de un neumático^F

whe
rued

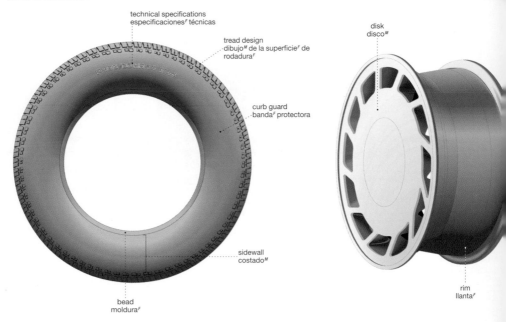

technical specifications
especificaciones^F técnicas

tread design
dibujo^M de la superficie^F de
rodadura^F

curb guard
banda^F protectora

disk
disco^M

sidewall
costado^M

bead
moldura^F

rim
llanta^F

examples of tires
ejemplos^M de neumáticos^M

performance tire
neumático^M de
rendimiento^M

all-season tire
neumático^M de todas las
estaciones^F

winter tire
neumático^M de
invierno^M

touring tire
neumático^M de turismo^M

studded tire
neumático^M de tac

TRANSPORT AND MACHINERY

tire

steel belted radial tire
neumático **radial con**
cinturones

bias-ply tire
neumático^M **de capas**^F **al sesgo**^M

radial tire
neumático^M **radial**

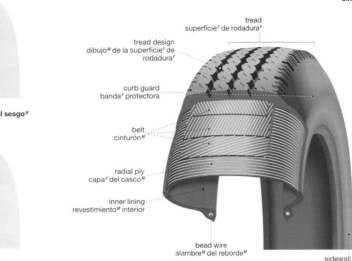

tread
superficie^F de rodadura^F

tread design
dibujo^M de la superficie^F de
rodadura^F

curb guard
banda^F protectora

belt
cinturón^M

radial ply
capa^F del casco^M

inner lining
revestimiento^M interior

bead wire
alambre^M del reborde^M

sidewall
costado^M

battery

batería^F

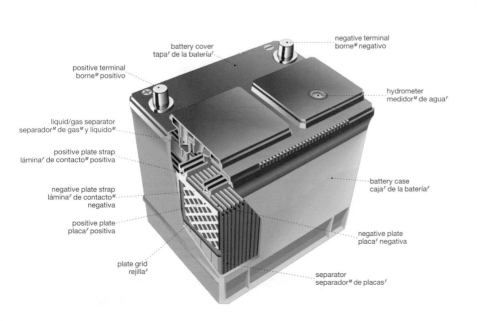

positive terminal
borne^M positivo

battery cover
tapa^F de la batería^F

negative terminal
borne^M negativo

hydrometer
medidor^M de agua^F

liquid/gas separator
separador^M de gas^M y líquido^M

positive plate strap
lámina^F de contacto^M positiva

negative plate strap
lámina^F de contacto^M
negativa

positive plate
placa^F positiva

battery case
caja^F de la batería^F

negative plate
placa^F negativa

plate grid
rejilla^F

separator
separador^M de placas^F

TRANSPORT AND MACHINERY

bus

autobús^M

school bus
autobús^M escolar

rearview mirror
espejo^M retrovisor exterior

blind spot mirror
retrovisor^M de gran
angular^M

flashing lights
faros^M intermitentes

crossover mirror
espejo^M de cercanías^F

crossing arm
barra^F distanciadora

coach
autocar^M

engine air intake
toma^F de aire^M del motor^M

door
puerta^F

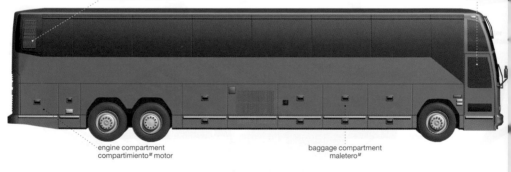

engine compartment
compartimiento^M motor

baggage compartment
maletero^M

city bus
autobús^M urbano

air intake
toma^F de aire^M

route sign
indicador^M de línea^F

two-leaf door
puerta^F de dos hojas^F

double-decker bus
autocar^M de dos pisos^M

upper deck
piso^M superior

route sign
indicador^M de línea^F

specialized transportation bus
autobús^M de transporte^M especial

lift door
puerta^F de la plataforma^F elevadora

West Coast mirror
espejo^M retrovisor

blind spot mirror
retrovisor^M de gran angular^M

handrail
pasamano^M

wheelchair lift
plataforma^F elevadora para silla^F de ruedas^F

entrance door
puerta^F de entrada^F

platform
plataforma^F

TRANSPORT AND MACHINERY

articulated bus
autobús^M articulado

rear rigid section
remolque^M rígido trasero

articulated joint
sección^F articulada

front rigid section
sección^F rígida de tracción^F delantera

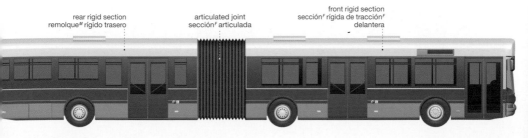
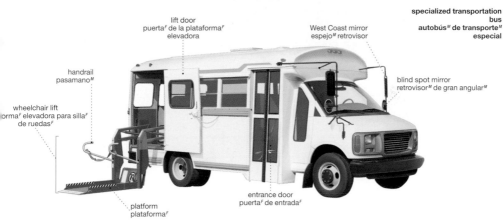

trucking

camionesᴹ

truck tractor
camiónᴹ tractorᴹ

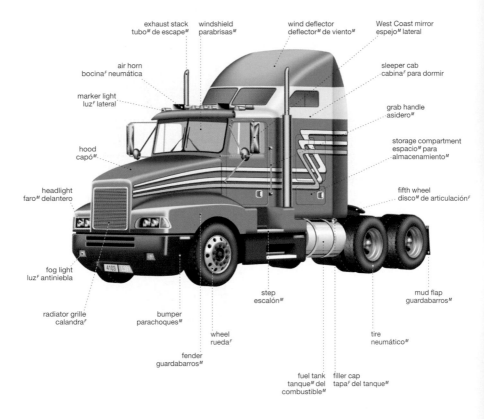

exhaust stack
tuboᴹ de escapeᴹ

windshield
parabrisasᴹ

wind deflector
deflectorᴹ de vientoᴹ

West Coast mirror
espejoᴹ lateral

air horn
bocinaᶠ neumática

sleeper cab
cabinaᶠ para dormir

marker light
luzᶠ lateral

grab handle
asideroᴹ

hood
capóᴹ

storage compartment
espacioᴹ para
almacenamientoᴹ

headlight
faroᴹ delantero

fifth wheel
discoᴹ de articulaciónᶠ

fog light
luzᶠ antiniebla

step
escalónᴹ

mud flap
guardabarrosᴹ

radiator grille
calandraᶠ

bumper
parachoquesᴹ

tire
neumáticoᴹ

wheel
ruedaᶠ

fender
guardabarrosᴹ

fuel tank
tanqueᴹ del
combustibleᴹ

filler cap
tapaᶠ del tanqueᴹ

tandem tractor trailer
camiónᴹ articulado

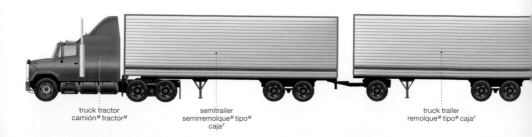

truck tractor
camiónᴹ tractorᴹ

semitrailer
semirremolqueᴹ tipoᴹ
cajaᶠ

truck trailer
remolqueᴹ tipoᴹ cajaᶠ

refrigerated semitrailer
semirremolque^M
frigorífico

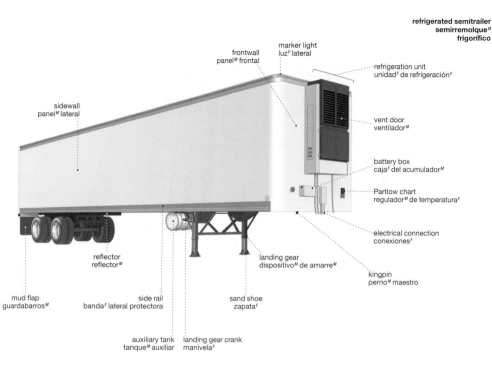

frontwall
panel^M frontal

marker light
luz^F lateral

refrigeration unit
unidad^F de refrigeración^F

sidewall
panel^M lateral

vent door
ventilador^M

battery box
caja^F del acumulador^M

Partlow chart
regulador^M de temperatura^F

electrical connection
conexiones^F

reflector
reflector^M

landing gear
dispositivo^M de amarre^M

kingpin
perno^M maestro

mud flap
guardabarros^M

side rail
banda^F lateral protectora

sand shoe
zapata^F

auxiliary tank
tanque^M auxiliar

landing gear crank
manivela^F

flatbed semitrailer
semirremolque^M tipo^M
plataforma^F

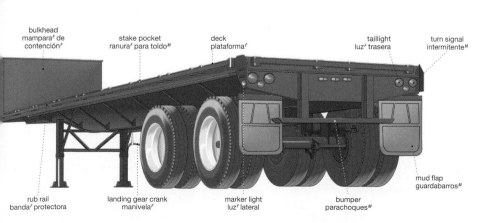

bulkhead
mampara^F de
contención^F

stake pocket
ranura^F para toldo^M

deck
plataforma^F

taillight
luz^F trasera

turn signal
intermitente^M

mud flap
guardabarros^M

rub rail
banda^F protectora

landing gear crank
manivela^F

marker light
luz^F lateral

bumper
parachoques^M

TRANSPORT AND MACHINERY

trucking

examples of semitrailers
ejemplos^M de camiones^M
articulados

automobile transport
semitrailer
trailer^M para transporte^M de
vehículos^M

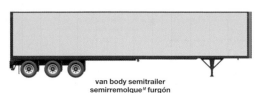

van body semitrailer
semirremolque^M furgón

tank body
cisterna^F

tank trailer
camión^M cisterna^F

chip van
semirremolque^M con lona^F

dump body
volquete^M basculante

dump semitrailer
camión^M volquete

twist lock
bloqueo^M giratorio

container semitrailer
semirremolque^M porta
container^M

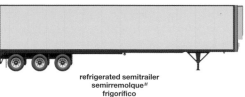

refrigerated semitrailer
semirremolque^M
frigorífico

log semitrailer
semirremolque^M para el
transporte^M de troncos^M

possum-belly body semitrailer
semirremolque^M jaula^F bajo para
transporte^M ganadero

double drop lowbed semitrailer
semirremolque^M bajo portamáquinas^M

TRANSPORT AND MACHINERY

examples of trucks
ejemplos de camiones**

loading hopper
tolva^F de carga^F

packer body
empaquetadora^F

garbage truck
compactadora^F

box van
camioneta^F

dump body
volquete^M

dump truck
camión^M **basculante**

septic truck
aspiradora^F **de fangos**^M

concrete mixer truck
hormigonera^F

tank body
cisterna^F

tank truck
camión^M **cisterna**^F

tow truck
grúa^F **remolque**

cable
cable^M

boom
brazo^M de elevación^F

hook
gancho^M

elevating cylinder
cilindro^M elevador

detachable body truck
carrocería^F **amovible**

towing device
dispositivo^M de
remolque^M

winch controls
mandos^M del
cabestrante^M

winch
cabestrante^M

TRANSPORT AND MACHINERY

motorcycle

motocicleta^F

side view
vista^F lateral

gas tar
depósito^M de gasolina

passenger's seat
asiento^M del
acompañante^M

driver's seat
asiento^M del piloto^M

fairing
carenado^M

taillight
luz^F trasera

rear turn signal
intermitente^M trasero

passenger's footrest
reposapiés^M del
acompañante^M

frame
bastidor^M

exhaust pipe
tubo^M de escape^M

rear brake pedal
pedal^M del freno^M trasero

carbure
carburad

kickstand
caballete^M lateral

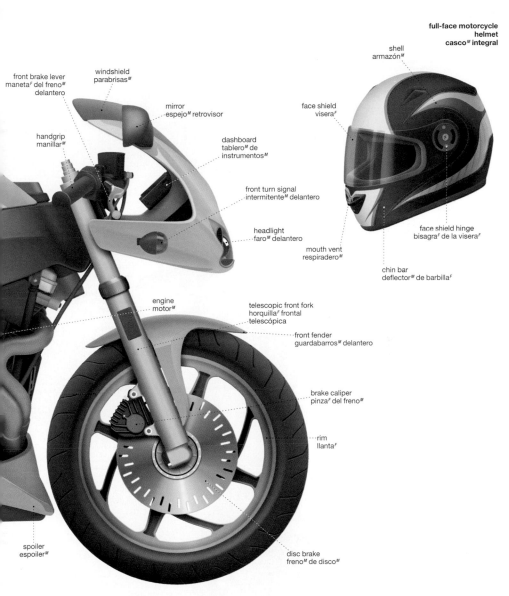

**full-face motorcycle
helmet
casco^M integral**

shell
armazón^M

windshield
parabrisas^M

front brake lever
maneta^F del freno^M
delantero

mirror
espejo^M retrovisor

face shield
visera^F

handgrip
manillar^M

dashboard
tablero^M de
instrumentos^M

front turn signal
intermitente^M delantero

face shield hinge
bisagra^F de la visera^F

headlight
faro^M delantero

mouth vent
respiradero^M

chin bar
deflector^M de barbilla^F

engine
motor^M

telescopic front fork
horquilla^F frontal
telescópica

front fender
guardabarros^M delantero

brake caliper
pinza^F del freno^M

rim
llanta^F

spoiler
espoiler^M

disc brake
freno^M de disco^M

TRANSPORT AND MACHINERY

motorcycle

dashboard
tablero de instrumentos**

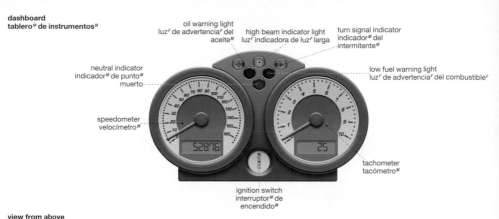

oil warning light
luz de advertencia del aceite**

high beam indicator light
luz indicadora de luz larga

turn signal indicator
indicador del intermitente**

neutral indicator
indicador de punto muerto

low fuel warning light
luz de advertencia del combustible

speedometer
velocímetro**

tachometer
tacómetro**

ignition switch
interruptor de encendido**

view from above
vista desde arriba

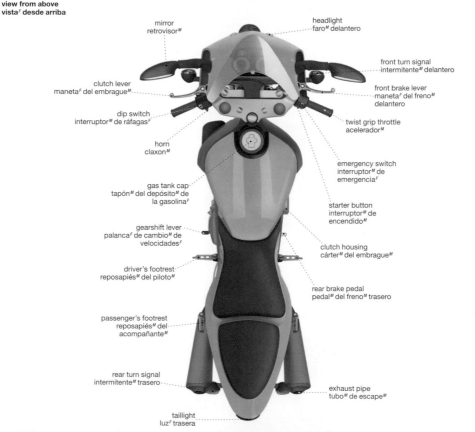

mirror
retrovisor**

headlight
faro** delantero

front turn signal
intermitente** delantero

clutch lever
maneta del embrague**

front brake lever
maneta del freno** delantero

dip switch
interruptor de ráfagas

twist grip throttle
acelerador**

horn
claxon**

emergency switch
interruptor de emergencia

gas tank cap
tapón del depósito de la gasolina

starter button
interruptor de encendido**

gearshift lever
palanca de cambio de velocidades

clutch housing
cárter del embrague**

driver's footrest
reposapiés del piloto**

rear brake pedal
pedal del freno** trasero

passenger's footrest
reposapiés del acompañante**

rear turn signal
intermitente** trasero

exhaust pipe
tubo de escape**

taillight
luz trasera

examples of motorcycles
ejemplos^M de motocicletas^F

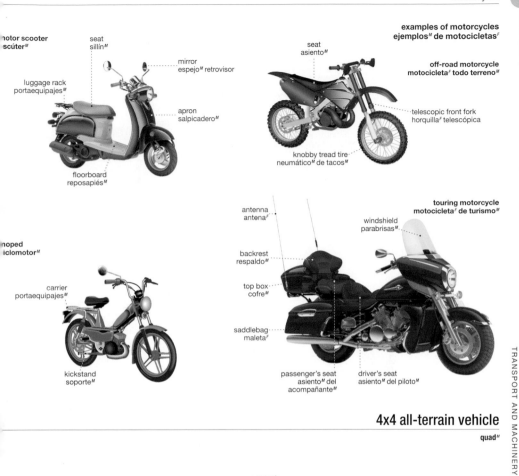

motor scooter
scúter^M

seat
sillín^M

mirror
espejo^M retrovisor

luggage rack
portaequipajes^M

apron
salpicadero^M

floorboard
reposapiés^M

off-road motorcycle
motocicleta^F todo terreno^M

seat
asiento^M

telescopic front fork
horquilla^F telescópica

knobby tread tire
neumático^M de tacos^M

touring motorcycle
motocicleta^F de turismo^M

antenna
antena^F

windshield
parabrisas^M

backrest
respaldo^M

top box
cofre^M

saddlebag
maleta^F

passenger's seat
asiento^M del
acompañante^M

driver's seat
asiento^M del piloto^M

moped
ciclomotor^M

carrier
portaequipajes^M

kickstand
soporte^M

4x4 all-terrain vehicle

quad^M

rear cargo rack
portaequipajes^M
posterior

seat
sillín^M

gas tank
depósito^M de gasolina^F

handgrip
manillar^M

rear fender
parachoques^M posterior

bumper
parachoques^M

muffler
tubo^M de escape^M

front shock absorber
amortiguador^M delantero

gearshift lever
palanca^F de cambio^M de
velocidades^F

TRANSPORT AND MACHINERY

bicycle

bicicleta^F

parts of a bicycle
partes^F de una
bicicleta^F

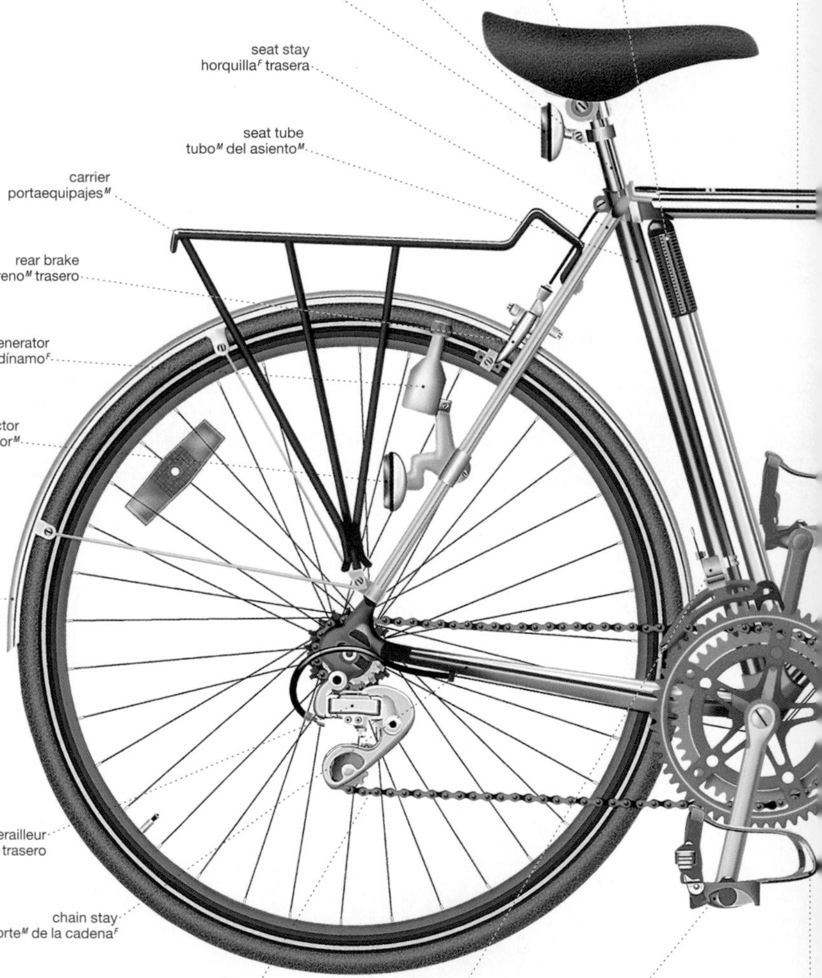

seat post
poste^M del asiento^M

seat
sillín^M

tire pump
bomba^F de aire^M

crossbar
barra^F

rear reflector
reflector^F trasero

seat stay
horquilla^F trasera

seat tube
tubo^M del asiento^M

carrier
portaequipajes^M

rear brake
freno^M trasero

generator
dínamo^F

reflector
reflector^M

fender
guardabarros^M

rear derailleur
cambio^M de marchas^F trasero

chain stay
soporte^M de la cadena^F

chain
cadena^F

front derailleur
cambio^M de marchas^F
delantero

pedal
pedal^M

toe clip
calzapié^M

bicycle

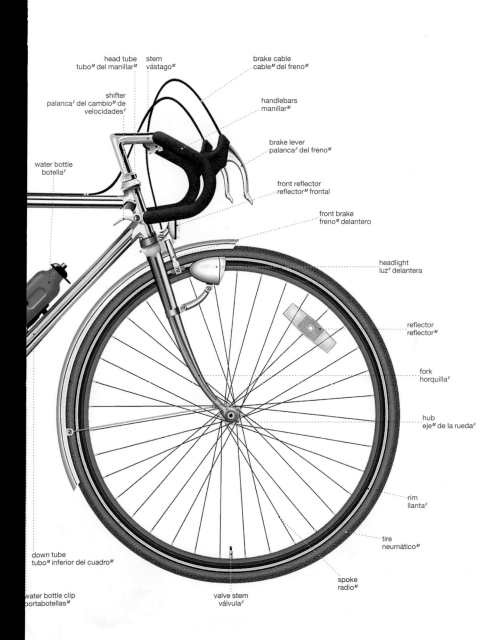

head tube
tubo^M del manillar^M

stem
vástago^M

brake cable
cable^M del freno^M

shifter
palanca^F del cambio^M de
velocidades^F

handlebars
manillar^M

water bottle
botella^F

brake lever
palanca^F del freno^M

front reflector
reflector^M frontal

front brake
freno^M delantero

headlight
luz^F delantera

reflector
reflector^M

fork
horquilla^F

hub
eje^M de la rueda^F

rim
llanta^F

tire
neumático^M

down tube
tubo^M inferior del cuadro^M

spoke
radio^M

water bottle clip
portabotellas^M

valve stem
válvula^F

TRANSPORT AND MACHINERY

bicycle

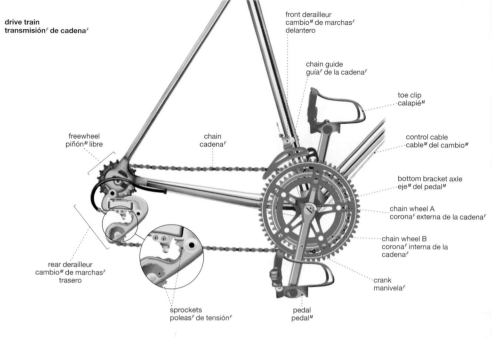

drive train
transmisión^F de cadena^F

front derailleur
cambio^M de marchas^F
delantero

chain guide
guía^F de la cadena^F

toe clip
calapié^M

freewheel
piñón^M libre

chain
cadena^F

control cable
cable^M del cambio^M

bottom bracket axle
eje^M del pedal^M

chain wheel A
corona^F externa de la cadena^F

chain wheel B
corona^F interna de la
cadena^F

rear derailleur
cambio^M de marchas^F
trasero

crank
manivela^F

sprockets
poleas^F de tensión^F

pedal
pedal^M

accessories
accesorios^M

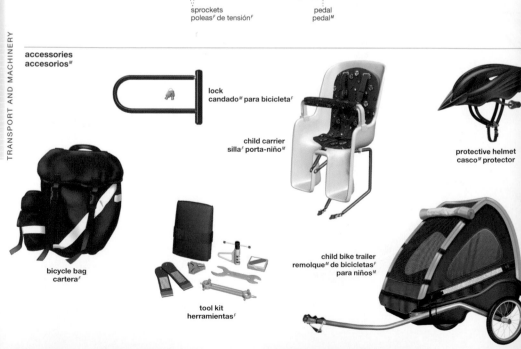

lock
candado^M para bicicleta^F

child carrier
silla^F porta-niño^M

protective helmet
casco^M protector

bicycle bag
cartera^F

child bike trailer
remolque^M de bicicletas^F
para niños^M

tool kit
herramientas^F

bicycle

examples of bicycles
ejemplos^M de
bicicletas^F

child's tricycle
triciclo^M

trailer bike
semi-tándem^M

training wheel
ruedas^F estabilizadoras

child's bicycle
bicicleta^F de niño^M

BMX bike
bicicleta^F BMX

road bicycle
bicicleta^F de carretera^F

mountain bike
bicicleta^F todo terreno^M

TRANSPORT AND MACHINERY

bicycle

examples of bicycles

rear basket
cesta^F trasera

adult tricycle
triciclo^M para adultos^M

recumbent bicycle
bicicleta^F reclinada

city bicycle
bicicleta^F de ciudad^F

battery
batería^F

electric bicycle
bicicleta^F eléctrica

touring bicycle
bicicleta^F de turismo^M

tandem bicycle
tándem^M

railroad station

estación^F de ferrocarril^M

passenger station
estación^F de ferrocarril^M

station platform
andén^M

commuter train
tren^M suburbano

main lines
vías^F principales

suburban commuter railroad
vía^F de tren^M suburbano

siding
vía^F subsidiaria

bumper
tope^M

grade crossing
paso^M a nivel^M

parking
estacionamiento^M

platform shelter
marquesina^F del andén^M

footbridge
pasarela^F

semaphore
semáforo^M

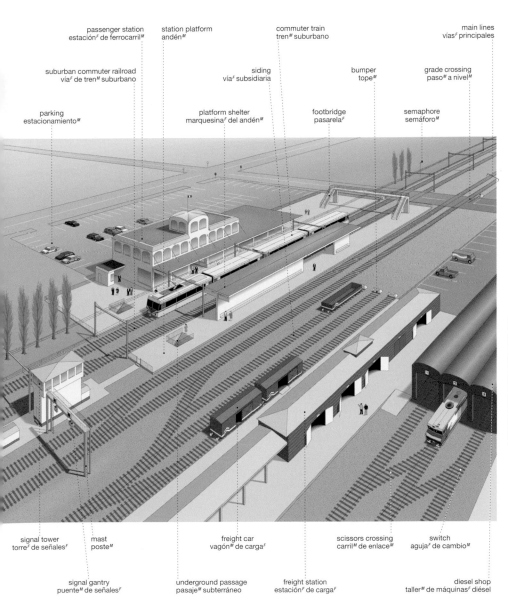

signal tower
torre^F de señales^F

mast
poste^M

freight car
vagón^M de carga^F

scissors crossing
carril^M de enlace^M

switch
aguja^F de cambio^M

signal gantry
puente^M de señales^F

underground passage
pasaje^M subterráneo

freight station
estación^F de carga^F

diesel shop
taller^M de máquinas^F diésel

TRANSPORT AND MACHINERY

passenger station

estación' de ferrocarril

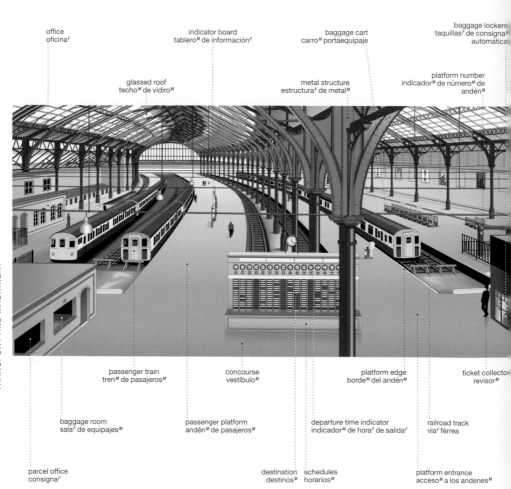

office
oficina

indicator board
tablero de información

baggage cart
carro portaequipaje

baggage lockers
taquillas de consigna
automática

glassed roof
techo de vidiro

metal structure
estructura de metal

platform number
indicador de número de
andén

baggage room
sala de equipajes

passenger train
tren de pasajeros

concourse
vestíbulo

platform edge
borde del andén

ticket collecto
revisor

passenger platform
andén de pasajeros

departure time indicator
indicador de hora de salida

railroad track
vía férrea

parcel office
consigna

destination
destinos

schedules
horarios

platform entrance
acceso a los andenes

types of passenger cars

vagones^M de pasajeros^M

coach car
vagón^M de pasajeros^M

luggage rack
compartimiento para el
equipaje^M

adjustable seat
asiento^M ajustable

center aisle
pasillo^M central

vestibule
plataforma^F

vestibule door
puerta^F de entrada^F

sleeping car
coche^M cama^F

berth
litera^F

restroom
aseos^M

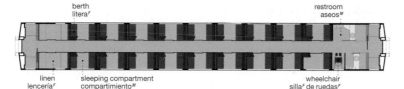

linen
lencería^F

sleeping compartment
compartimiento^M
dormitorio

wheelchair
silla^F de ruedas^F

corridor connection
pasillo^M de enlace^M

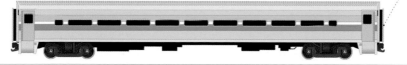

dining car
vagón^M comedor^M

dining section
comedor^M

steward's desk
barra^F de camareros^M

storage space
espacio^M de
almacenamiento^M

kitchen
cocina^F

crew's locker
armario^M para el personal^M

panoramic window
ventanilla^F panorámica

grab handle
asidero^M

TRANSPORT AND MACHINERY

diesel-electric locomotive

locomotora^F diésel eléctrica

**cross section of a
locomotive**
corte^M de una
locomotora^F

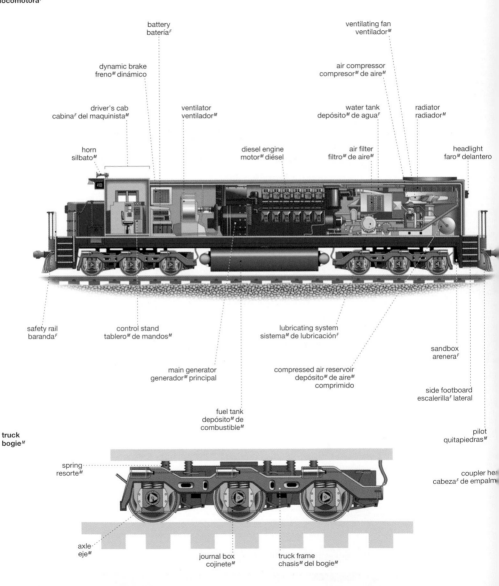

battery
batería^F

ventilating fan
ventilador^M

dynamic brake
freno^M dinámico

air compressor
compresor^M de aire^M

driver's cab
cabina^F del maquinista^M

ventilator
ventilador^M

water tank
depósito^M de agua^F

radiator
radiador^M

horn
silbato^M

diesel engine
motor^M diésel

air filter
filtro^M de aire^M

headlight
faro^M delantero

safety rail
baranda^F

control stand
tablero^M de mandos^M

lubricating system
sistema^M de lubricación^F

sandbox
arenera^F

main generator
generador^M principal

compressed air reservoir
depósito^M de aire^M
comprimido

side footboard
escalerilla^F lateral

fuel tank
depósito^M de
combustible^M

pilot
quitapiedras^M

**truck
bogie^M**

coupler he
cabeza^F de empalm

spring
resorte^M

axle
eje^M

journal box
cojinete^M

truck frame
chasis^M del bogie^M

TRANSPORT AND MACHINERY

high-speed train

tren^M de alta velocidad^F

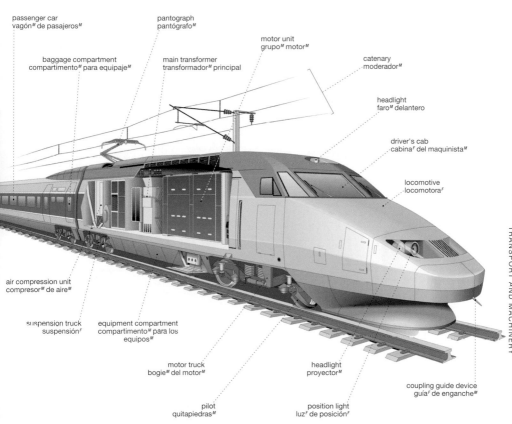

passenger car
vagón^M de pasajeros^M

pantograph
pantógrafo^M

motor unit
grupo^M motor^M

baggage compartment
compartimento^M para equipaje^M

main transformer
transformador^M principal

catenary
moderador^M

headlight
faro^M delantero

driver's cab
cabina^F del maquinista^M

locomotive
locomotora^F

air compression unit
compresor^M de aire^M

suspension truck
suspensión^F

equipment compartment
compartimento^M para los
equipos^M

motor truck
bogie^M del motor^M

headlight
proyector^M

coupling guide device
guía^F de enganche^M

pilot
quitapiedras^M

position light
luz^F de posición^F

TRANSPORT AND MACHINERY

yard

estación*de clasificación*

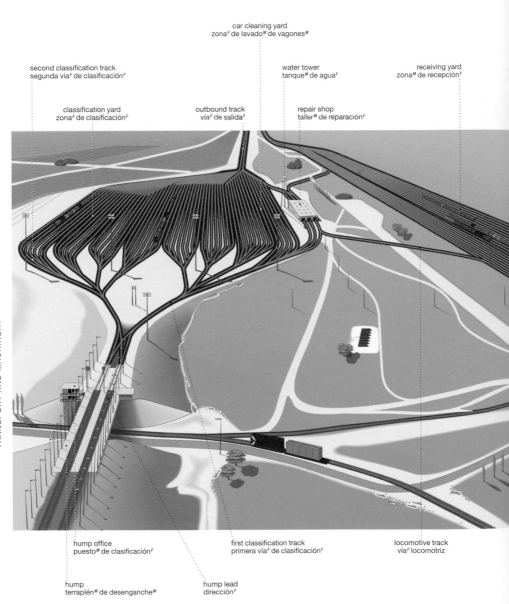

car cleaning yard
zona^F de lavado^M de vagones^M

second classification track
segunda vía^F de clasificación^F

water tower
tanque^M de agua^F

receiving yard
zona^M de recepción^F

classification yard
zona^F de clasificación^F

outbound track
vía^F de salida^F

repair shop
taller^M de reparación^F

hump office
puesto^M de clasificación^F

first classification track
primera vía^F de clasificación^F

locomotive track
vía^F locomotriz

hump
terraplén^M de desenganche^M

hump lead
dirección^F

freight car

vagón^M **de carga**^{F}

boxcar
vagón^M **de carga**^{F}

horizontal end handhold
asidero^M horizontal

and brake wheel
te^M del freno^M manual

corner cap
esquinera^F

routing cardboard
tarjeta^F de ruta^F

placard board
tablero^M de rótulo^M

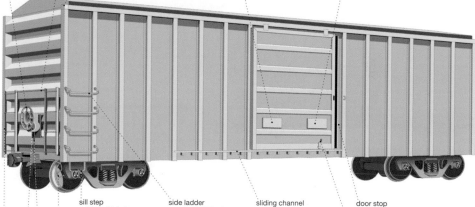

sill step
peldaño^M inferior

side ladder
escalerilla^F lateral

sliding channel
guía^F corrediza

door stop
tope^M de la puerta^F

telescoping uncoupling rod
varilla^F telescópica de
desenganche^M

locking lever
palanca^F de cierre^M

hand brake winding lever
palanca^F de accionamiento^M del freno^M
de mano^F

hand brake gear housing
cubierta^F del mecanismo^M del freno^M

end ladder
escalerilla^F de estribo^M

automatic coupler
enganche^M **automático**

coupler knuckle pin
pivote^M de la rótula^F

coupler knuckle
rótula^F de enganche^M

TRANSPORT AND MACHINERY

freight car

examples of freight cars
ejemplos^M **de vagones**^{M}

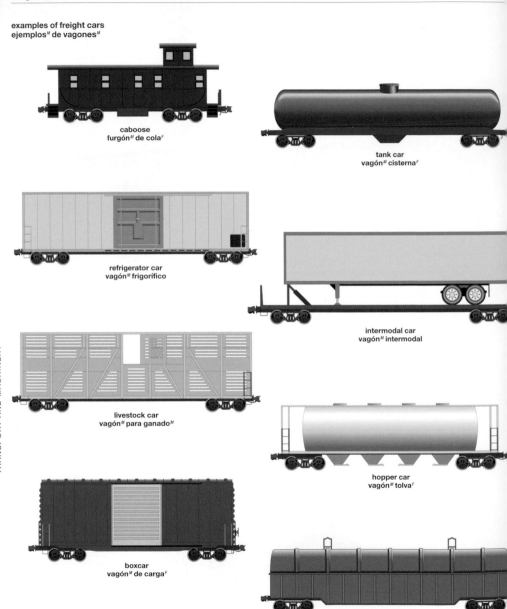

caboose
furgón^M de cola^F

tank car
vagón^M cisterna^F

refrigerator car
vagón^M frigorífico

intermodal car
vagón^M intermodal

livestock car
vagón^M para ganado^M

hopper car
vagón^M tolva^F

boxcar
vagón^M de carga^F

covered gondola car
vagón^M cerrado

freight car

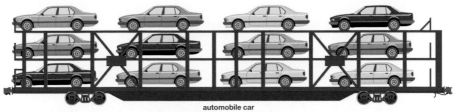

automobile car
vagón^M para automóviles^M

container car
vagón^M para contenedores^M

depressed-center flatcar
vagon^M plataforma^F de piso^M
bajo

gondola car
vagón^M de mercancías^F

bulkhead flatcar
vagón^M plataforma^F con retenedores^M

hopper ore car
vagón^M tolva^F para minerales^M

flatcar
vagón^M plataforma^F

wood chip car
vagón^M para madera^F

railroad track

vía^F férrea

rail joint
empalme^M de rieles^M

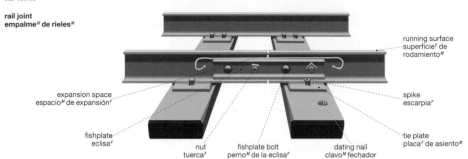

running surface
superficie^F de
rodamiento^M

expansion space
espacio^M de expansión^F

spike
escarpia^F

fishplate
eclisa^F

tie plate
placa^F de asiento^M

nut
tuerca^F

fishplate bolt
perno^M de la eclisa^F

dating nail
clavo^M fechador

remote-controlled switch
aguja^F de control^M a larga distancia^F

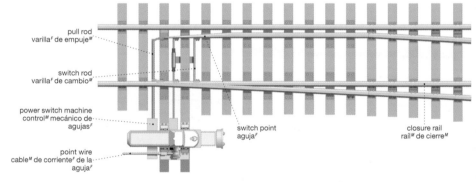

pull rod
varilla^F de empuje^M

switch rod
varilla^F de cambio^M

power switch machine
control^M mecánico de
agujas^F

switch point
aguja^F

closure rail
raíl^M de cierre^M

point wire
cable^M de corriente^F de la
aguja^F

manually operated switch
cambiador^M manual de vía^F

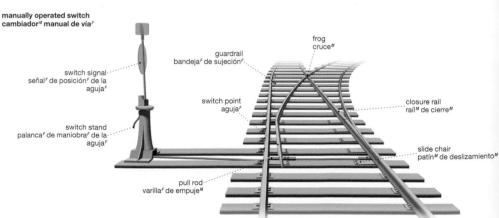

frog
cruce^M

guardrail
bandeja^F de sujeción^F.

switch signal
señal^F de posición^F de la
aguja^F

switch point
aguja^F

closure rail
raíl^M de cierre^M

switch stand
palanca^F de maniobra^F de la
aguja^F

slide chair
patín^M de deslizamiento^M

pull rod
varilla^F de empuje^M

railroad track

ailroad track
oundation
ase[F] de la vía[F] férrea

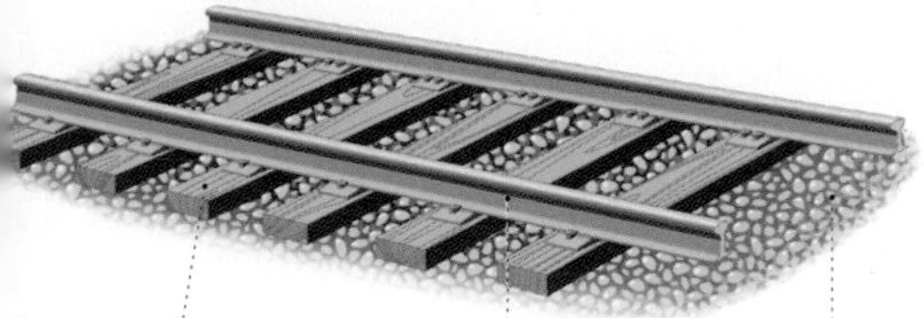
tie
traviesa[F]
rail
raíl[M]
ballast
balasto[M]

cross section of a rail
corte[M] de un raíl[M]

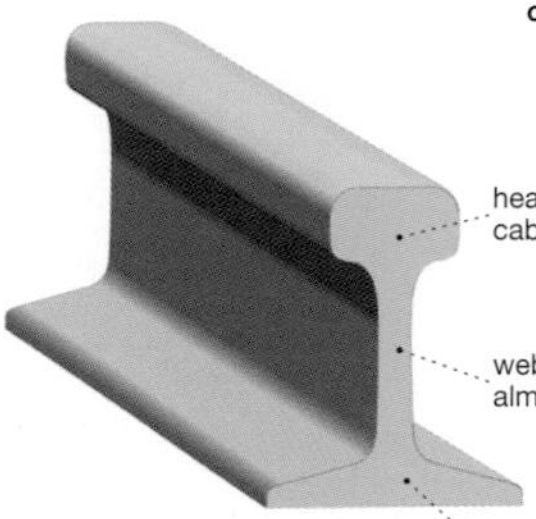
head
cabeza[F]
web
alma[F]
base
base[F]

crossing gate

paso[M] a nivel[M]

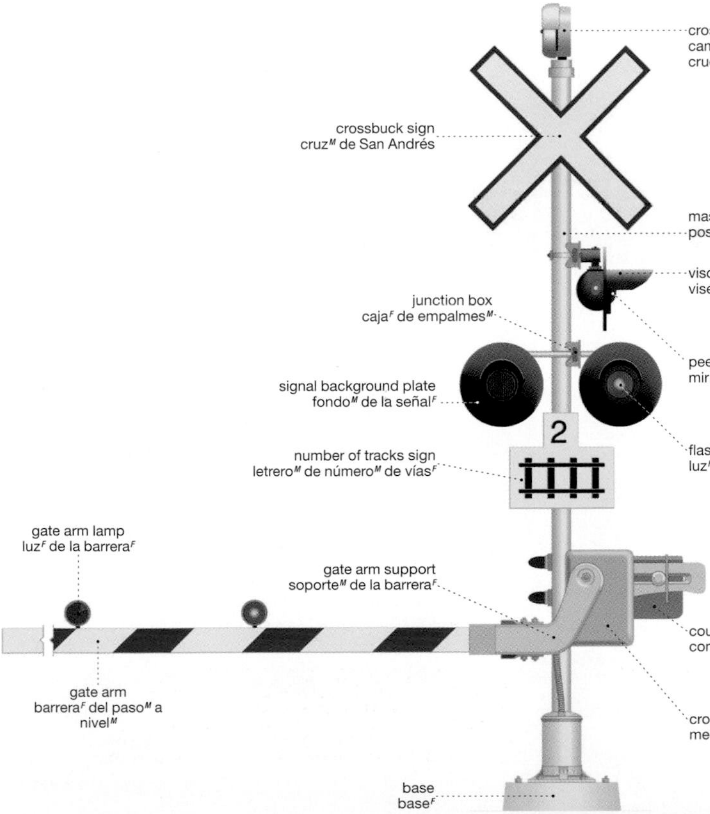
crossing bell
campana[F] de aviso[M] de cruce[M]
crossbuck sign
cruz[M] de San Andrés
mast
poste[M]
visor
visera[F]
junction box
caja[F] de empalmes[M]
peep hole
mirilla[F]
signal background plate
fondo[M] de la señal[F]
2
number of tracks sign
letrero[M] de número[M] de vías[F]
flashing light
luz[F] intermitente
gate arm lamp
luz[F] de la barrera[F]
gate arm support
soporte[M] de la barrera[F]
counterweight
contrapeso[M]
gate arm
barrera[F] del paso[M] a nivel[M]
crossing gate mechanism
mecanismo[M] de la barrera[F]
base
base[F]

subway

metro^M

subway station
estación^F de metro^M

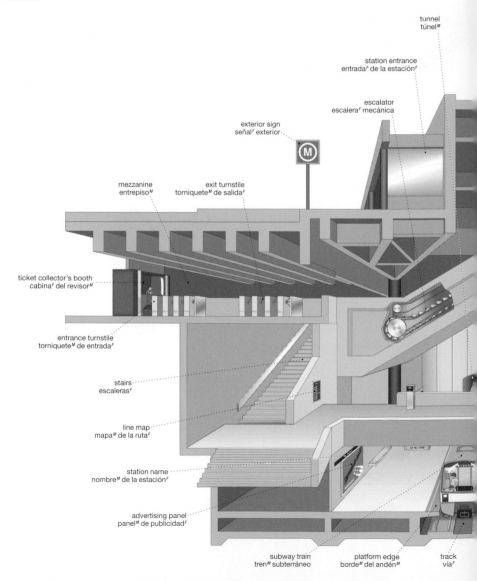

tunnel
túnel^M

station entrance
entrada^F de la estación^F

escalator
escalera^F mecánica

exterior sign
señal^F exterior

mezzanine
entrepiso^M

exit turnstile
torniquete^M de salida^F

ticket collector's booth
cabina^F del revisor^M

entrance turnstile
torniquete^M de entrada^F

stairs
escaleras^F

line map
mapa^M de la ruta^F

station name
nombre^M de la estación^F

advertising panel
panel^M de publicidad^F

subway train
tren^M subterráneo

platform edge
borde^M del andén^M

track
vía^F

TRANSPORT AND MACHINERY

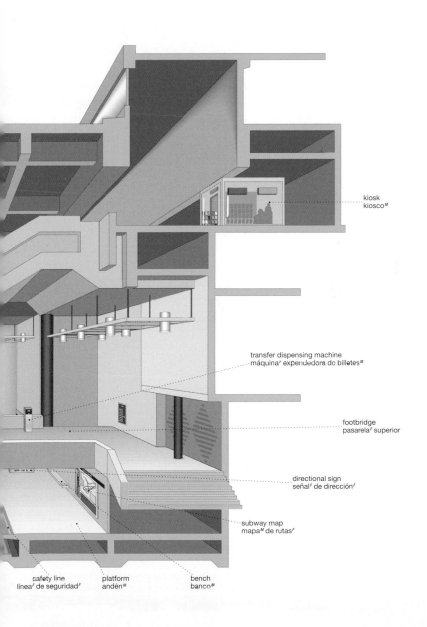

kiosk
kiosco^M

transfer dispensing machine
máquina^F expendedora de billetes^M

footbridge
pasarela^F superior

directional sign
señal^F de dirección^F

subway map
mapa^M de rutas^F

safety line
línea^F de seguridad^F

platform
andén^M

bench
banco^M

subway

passenger car
vagón^M de pasajeros^M

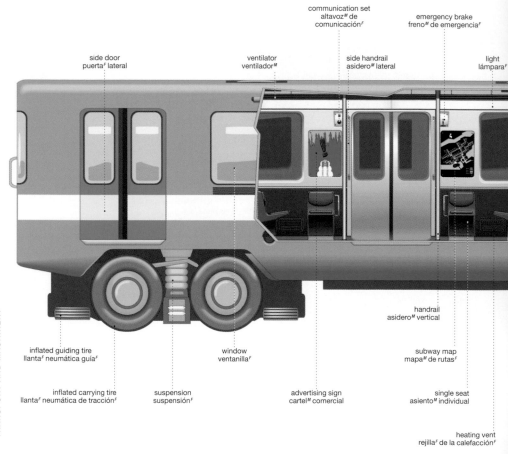

communication set
altavoz^M de
comunicación^F

emergency brake
freno^M de emergencia^F

side door
puerta^F lateral

ventilator
ventilador^M

side handrail
asidero^M lateral

light
lámpara^F

handrail
asidero^M vertical

inflated guiding tire
llanta^F neumática guía^F

window
ventanilla^F

subway map
mapa^M de rutas^F

inflated carrying tire
llanta^F neumática de tracción^F

suspension
suspensión^F

advertising sign
cartel^M comercial

single seat
asiento^M individual

heating vent
rejilla^F de la calefacción^F

subway train
tren^M subterráneo

double s
asiento^M do

motor car
vagón^M máquina^F

truck
bogie^M

trailer car
coche^M de tracción^F

motor car
vagón^M máquina^F

subway

truck and track
bogie^M y vía^F

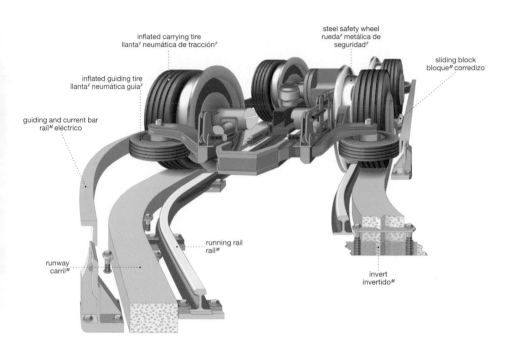

inflated carrying tire
llanta^F neumática de tracción^F

steel safety wheel
rueda^F metálica de
seguridad^F

sliding block
bloque^M corredizo

inflated guiding tire
llanta^F neumática guía^F

guiding and current bar
raíl^M eléctrico

running rail
raíl^M

runway
carril^M

invert
invertido^M

streetcar

tranvía^M

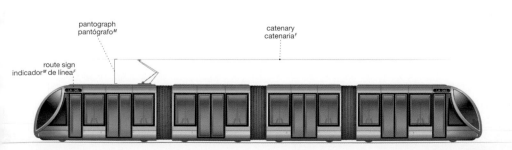

pantograph
pantógrafo^M

catenary
catenaria^F

route sign
indicador^M de línea^F

harbor

puerto^M

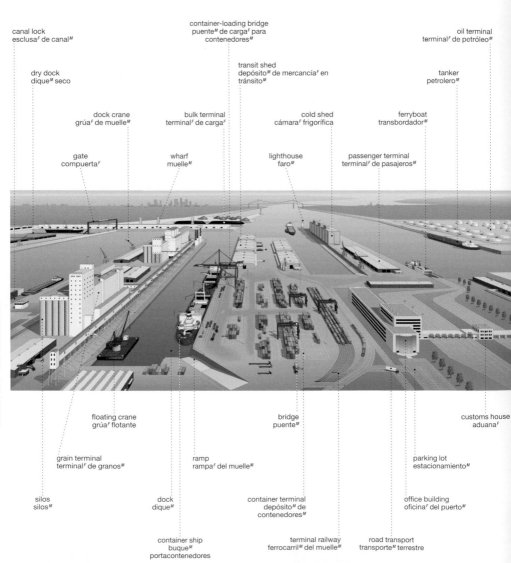

canal lock
esclusa^F de canal^M

container-loading bridge
puente^M de carga^F para
contenedores^M

oil terminal
terminal^F de petróleo^M

dry dock
dique^M seco

transit shed
depósito^M de mercancía^F en
tránsito^M

tanker
petrolero^M

dock crane
grúa^F de muelle^M

bulk terminal
terminal^F de carga^F

cold shed
cámara^F frigorífica

ferryboat
transbordador^M

gate
compuerta^F

wharf
muelle^M

lighthouse
faro^M

passenger terminal
terminal^F de pasajeros^M

TRANSPORT AND MACHINERY

floating crane
grúa^F flotante

bridge
puente^M

customs house
aduana^F

grain terminal
terminal^F de granos^M

ramp
rampa^F del muelle^M

parking lot
estacionamiento^M

silos
silos^M

dock
dique^M

container terminal
depósito^M de
contenedores^M

office building
oficina^F del puerto^M

container ship
buque^M
portacontenedores

terminal railway
ferrocarril^M del muelle^M

road transport
transporte^M terrestre

canal lock

esclusaᶠ de canalᴹ

parts of a canal lock
partesᶠ de una esclusaᶠ
de canalᴹ

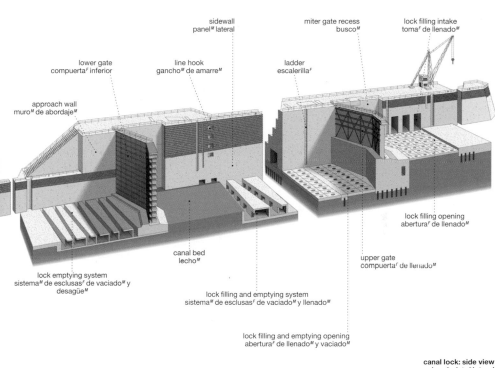

sidewall
panelᴹ lateral

miter gate recess
buscoᴹ

lock filling intake
tomaᶠ de llenadoᴹ

lower gate
compuertaᶠ inferior

line hook
ganchoᴹ de amarreᴹ

ladder
escalerillaᶠ

approach wall
muroᴹ de abordajeᴹ

lock filling opening
aberturaᶠ de llenadoᴹ

canal bed
lechoᴹ

upper gate
compuertaᶠ de llenadoᴹ

lock emptying system
sistemaᴹ de esclusasᶠ de vaciadoᴹ y
desagüeᴹ

lock filling and emptying system
sistemaᴹ de esclusasᶠ de vaciadoᴹ y llenadoᴹ

lock filling and emptying opening
aberturaᶠ de llenadoᴹ y vaciadoᴹ

canal lock: side view
esclusaᶠ: vistaᶠ lateral

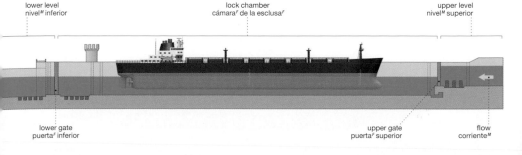

lower level
nivelᴹ inferior

lock chamber
cámaraᶠ de la esclusaᶠ

upper level
nivelᴹ superior

lower gate
puertaᶠ inferior

upper gate
puertaᶠ superior

flow
corrienteᴹ

TRANSPORT AND MACHINERY

ancient ships

embarcaciones^F antiguas

longship
dragón^M vikingo

stay
estay^M

stern
popa^F

stempost
estrave^F

steering oar
remo^M de dirección^F

oar
remo^M

galley
galera^F

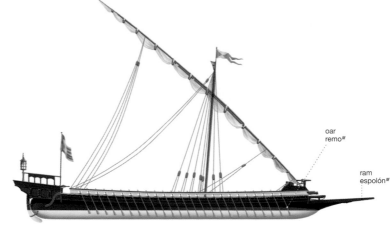

oar
remo^M

ram
espolón^M

trireme
trirreme^M

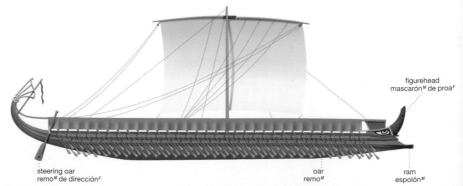

figurehead
mascarón^M de proa^F

steering oar
remo^M de dirección^F

oar
remo^M

ram
espolón^M

TRANSPORT AND MACHINERY

ancient ships

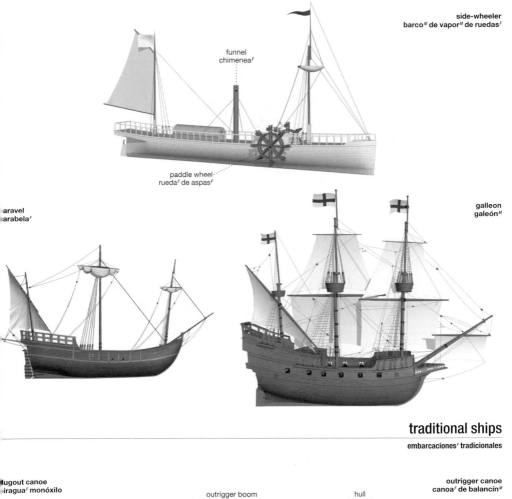

side-wheeler
barco^M **de vapor**^M **de ruedas**^F

funnel
chimenea^F

paddle wheel
rueda^F de aspas^F

caravel
carabela^F

galleon
galeón^M

traditional ships

embarcaciones^F tradicionales

dugout canoe
piragua^F **monóxilo**

outrigger boom
brazo^M de balancín^M

hull
casco^M

outrigger canoe
canoa^F **de balancín**^M

outrigger
balancín^M

TRANSPORT AND MACHINERY

traditional ships

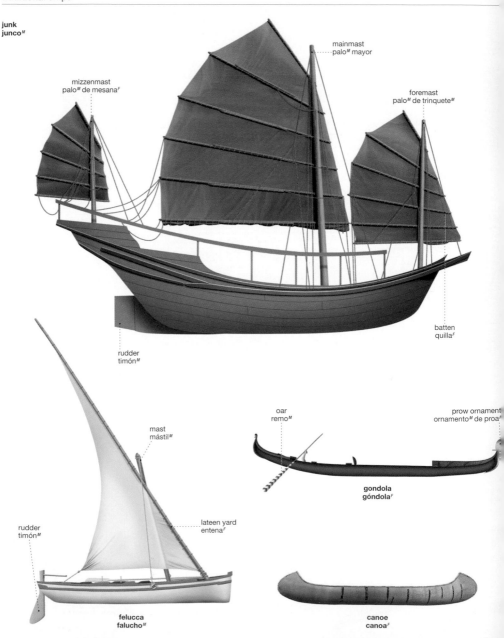

junk
junco^M

mizzenmast
palo^M de mesana^F

mainmast
palo^M mayor

foremast
palo^M de trinquete^M

rudder
timón^M

batten
quilla^F

mast
mástil^M

oar
remo^M

prow ornament
ornamento^M de proa^F

gondola
góndola^F

rudder
timón^M

lateen yard
entena^F

felucca
falucho^M

canoe
canoa^F

examples of sails

ejemplos^M de velas^F

gaff sail
vela^F áurica

Bermuda sail
vela^F Bermuda

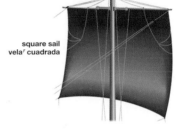

lug sail
vela^F al tercio^M

lateen sail
vela^F latina

square sail
vela^F cuadrada

spritsail
vela^F tarquina

examples of rigs

ejemplos^M de aparejos^M

yawl
cúter^M Marconi

ketch
queche^M

schooner
goleta^F

whale boat
ballenera^F

brigantine
bergantín^M goleta^F

brig
bergantín^M

TRANSPORT AND MACHINERY

four-masted bark

barco^M de vela^F de cuatro palos^M

upper section of mizzenmast
corte^M superior de un palo^M mayor

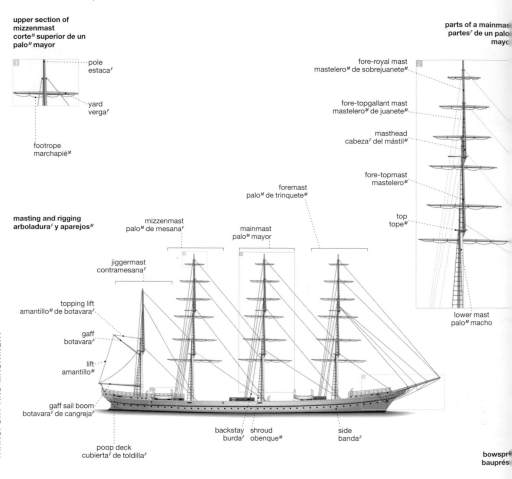

pole
estaca^F

yard
verga^F

footrope
marchapié^M

parts of a mainmast
partes^F de un palo
mayo

fore-royal mast
mastelero^M de sobrejuanete^M

fore-topgallant mast
mastelero^M de juanete^M

masthead
cabeza^F del mástil^M

fore-topmast
mastelero^M

top
tope^M

lower mast
palo^M macho

masting and rigging
arboladura^F y aparejos^M

mizzenmast
palo^M de mesana^F

mainmast
palo^M mayor

foremast
palo^M de trinquete^M

jiggermast
contramesana^F

topping lift
amantillo^M de botavara^F

gaff
botavara^F

lift
amantillo^M

gaff sail boom
botavara^F de cangreja^F

poop deck
cubierta^F de toldilla^F

backstay
burda^F

shroud
obenque^M

side
banda^F

bowspri
bauprés

lifeboat
bote^M salvavidas

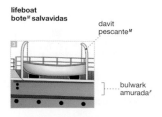

davit
pescante^M

bulwark
amurada^F

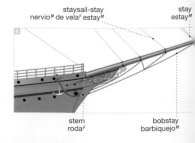

staysail-stay
nervio^M de vela^F estay^M

stay
estay^M

stem
roda^F

bobstay
barbiquejo^M

sails
velamen^M

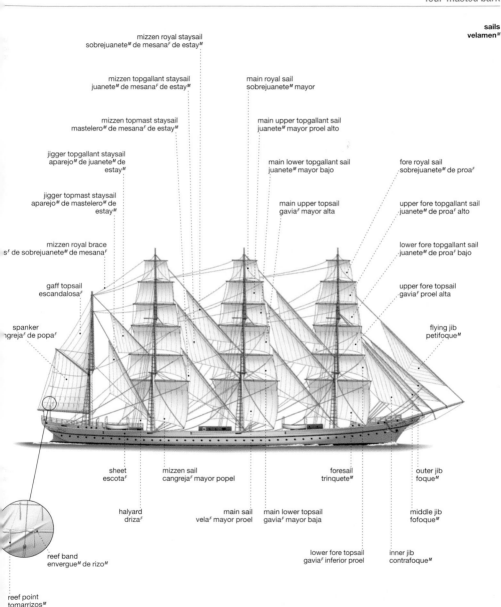

mizzen royal staysail
sobrejuanete^M de mesana^F de estay^M

mizzen topgallant staysail
juanete^M de mesana^F de estay^M

mizzen topmast staysail
mastelero^M de mesana^F de estay^M

jigger topgallant staysail
aparejo^M de juanete^M de
estay^M

jigger topmast staysail
aparejo^M de mastelero^M de
estay^M

mizzen royal brace
s^F de sobrejuanete^M de mesana^F

gaff topsail
escandalosa^F

spanker
ngreja^F de popa^F

main royal sail
sobrejuanete^M mayor

main upper topgallant sail
juanete^M mayor proel alto

main lower topgallant sail
juanete^M mayor bajo

main upper topsail
gavia^F mayor alta

fore royal sail
sobrejuanete^M de proa^F

upper fore topgallant sail
juanete^M de proa^F alto

lower fore topgallant sail
juanete^M de proa^F bajo

upper fore topsail
gavia^F proel alta

flying jib
petifoque^M

sheet
escota^F

halyard
driza^F

mizzen sail
cangreja^F mayor popel

main sail
vela^F mayor proel

main lower topsail
gavia^F mayor baja

foresail
trinquete^M

lower fore topsail
gavia^F inferior proel

outer jib
foque^M

middle jib
fofoque^M

inner jib
contrafoque^M

reef band
envergue^M de rizo^M

reef point
tomarrizos^M

TRANSPORT AND MACHINERY

examples of boats and ships

ejemplos^M de barcos^M y embarcaciones^F

drill ship
barco^M perforador

derrick
torre^F de perforación^F

bulk carrier
buque^M de carga^F

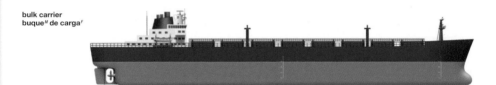

container ship
carguero^M
portacontenedores

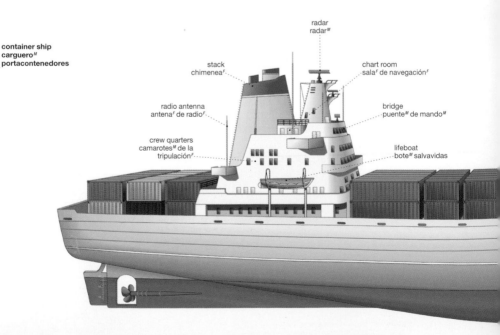

radar
radar^M

stack
chimenea^F

chart room
sala^F de navegación^F

radio antenna
antena^F de radio^F

bridge
puente^M de mando^M

crew quarters
camarotes^M de la
tripulación^F

lifeboat
bote^M salvavidas

examples of boats and ships

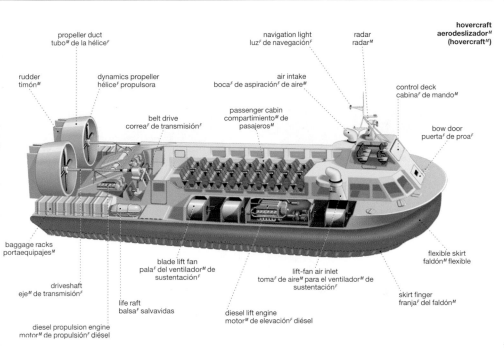

propeller duct
tubo^M de la hélice^F

navigation light
luz^F de navegación^F

radar
radar^M

hovercraft
aerodeslizador^M
(hovercraft^M)

rudder
timón^M

dynamics propeller
hélice^F propulsora

air intake
boca^F de aspiración^F de aire^M

control deck
cabina^F de mando^M

belt drive
correa^F de transmisión^F

passenger cabin
compartimiento^M de
pasajeros^M

bow door
puerta^F de proa^F

baggage racks
portaequipajes^M

flexible skirt
faldón^M flexible

blade lift fan
pala^F del ventilador^M de
sustentación^F

lift-fan air inlet
toma^F de aire^M para el ventilador^M de
sustentación^F

skirt finger
franja^F del faldón^M

driveshaft
eje^M de transmisión^F

life raft
balsa^F salvavidas

diesel lift engine
motor^M de elevación^F diésel

diesel propulsion engine
motor^M de propulsión^F diésel

masthead light
luz^F de tope^M

forecastle
castillo^M de proa^F

container
contenedor^M

container hold
bodega^F de contenedores^M

anchor-windlass room
escobén^M

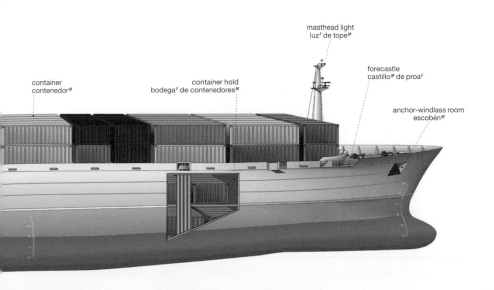

examples of boats and ships

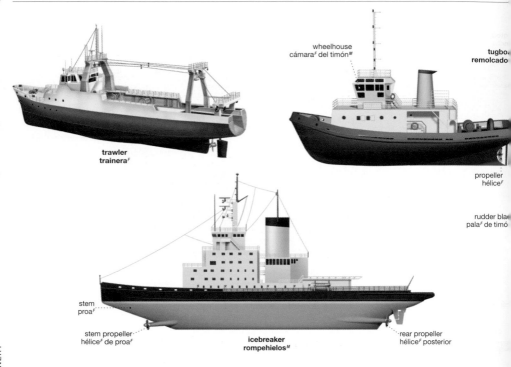

wheelhouse
cámara^F del timón^M

tugboat
remolcador

trawler
trainera^F

propeller
hélice^F

rudder blade
pala^F de timón

stem
proa^F

stem propeller
hélice^F de proa^F

icebreaker
rompehielos^M

rear propeller
hélice^F posterior

tanker
petrolero^M

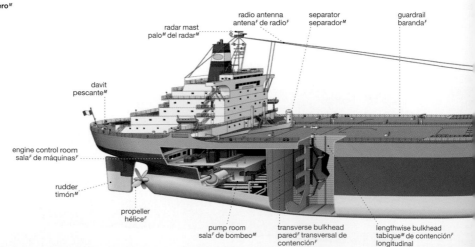

radio antenna
antena^F de radio^F

separator
separador^M

guardrail
baranda^F

radar mast
palo^M del radar^M

davit
pescante^M

engine control room
sala^F de máquinas^F

rudder
timón^M

propeller
hélice^F

pump room
sala^F de bombeo^M

transverse bulkhead
pared^F transversal de
contención^F

lengthwise bulkhead
tabique^M de contención^F
longitudinal

life-saving equipment
equipo^M salvavidas

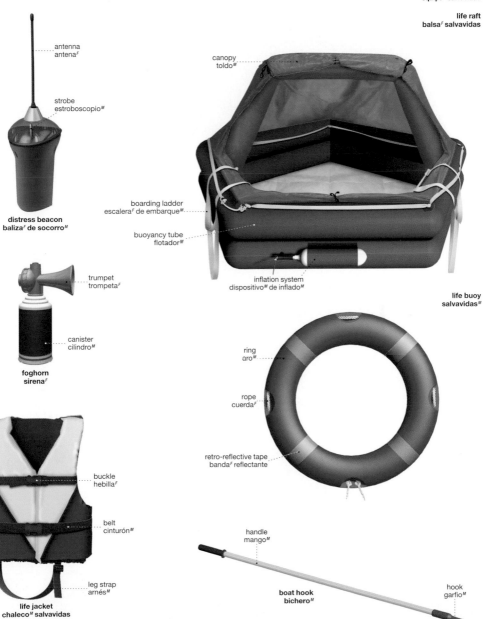

life raft
balsa^F salvavidas

antenna
antena^F

canopy
toldo^M

strobe
estroboscopio^M

boarding ladder
escalera^F de embarque^M

distress beacon
baliza^F de socorro^M

buoyancy tube
flotador^M

inflation system
dispositivo^M de inflado^M

trumpet
trompeta^F

life buoy
salvavidas^M

canister
cilindro^M

ring
aro^M

foghorn
sirena^F

rope
cuerda^F

retro-reflective tape
banda^F reflectante

buckle
hebilla^F

belt
cinturón^M

handle
mango^M

leg strap
arnés^M

hook
garfio^M

life jacket
chaleco^M salvavidas

boat hook
bichero^M

TRANSPORT AND MACHINERY

navigation devices

instrumentos^M de navegación^F

sextant
sextante^M

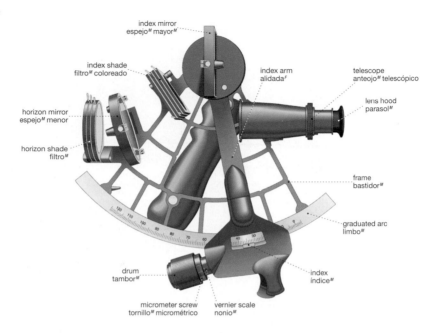

index mirror
espejo^M mayor^M

index shade
filtro^M coloreado

index arm
alidada^F

telescope
anteojo^M telescópico

horizon mirror
espejo^M menor

lens hood
parasol^M

horizon shade
filtro^M

frame
bastidor^M

graduated arc
limbo^M

drum
tambor^M

index
índice^M

micrometer screw
tornillo^M micrométrico

vernier scale
nonio^M

liquid compass
brújula^F **líquida**

sliding cover
cubierta^F deslizable

glass dome
domo^M de vidrio^M

compass card
rosa^F de los vientos^M

pivot
pivote^M

bowl
mortero^M

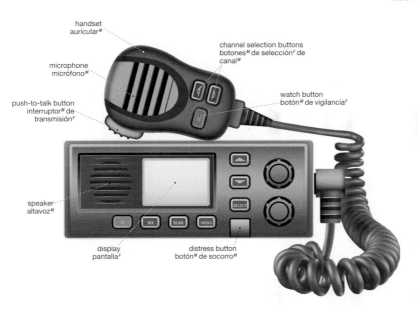

marine VHF radio
radio^F VHF marítima

handset
auricular^M

channel selection buttons
botones^M de selección^F de
canal^M

microphone
micrófono^M

watch button
botón^M de vigilancia^F

push-to-talk button
interruptor^M de
transmisión^F

speaker
altavoz^M

display
pantalla^F

distress button
botón^M de socorro^M

nar
nar^M

display
pantalla^F

satellite navigation system
sistema^M de navegación^F por
satélite^M

display
pantalla^F

GPS receiver-antenna
antena^F-receptor^M GPS

33⁹^m

3⁸^{mm}

power   mob   zoom-in   zoom-out
ctr

bracket
brida^F de sujeción^F

maritime signals

señales^F marítimas

lighthouse
faro^M marítimo

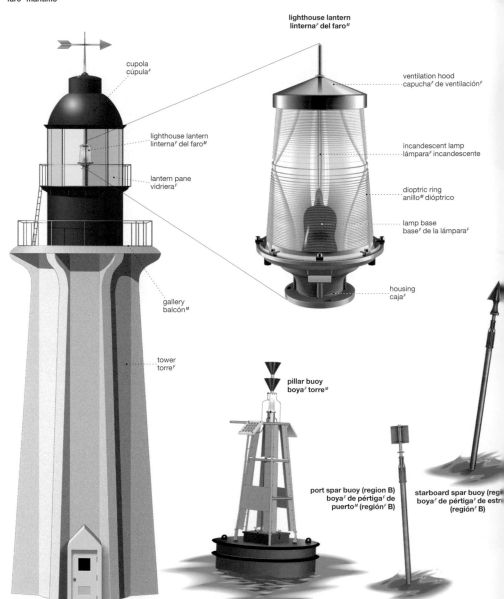

cupola
cúpula^F

lighthouse lantern
linterna^F del faro^M

lighthouse lantern
linterna^F del faro^M

ventilation hood
capucha^F de ventilación^F

lantern pane
vidriera^F

incandescent lamp
lámpara^F incandescente

dioptric ring
anillo^M dióptrico

lamp base
base^F de la lámpara^F

gallery
balcón^M

housing
caja^F

tower
torre^F

pillar buoy
boya^F torre^M

port spar buoy (region B)
boya^F de pértiga^F de
puerto^M (región^F B)

starboard spar buoy (regi
boya^F de pértiga^F de estr
(región^F B)

TRANSPORT AND MACHINERY

maritime signals

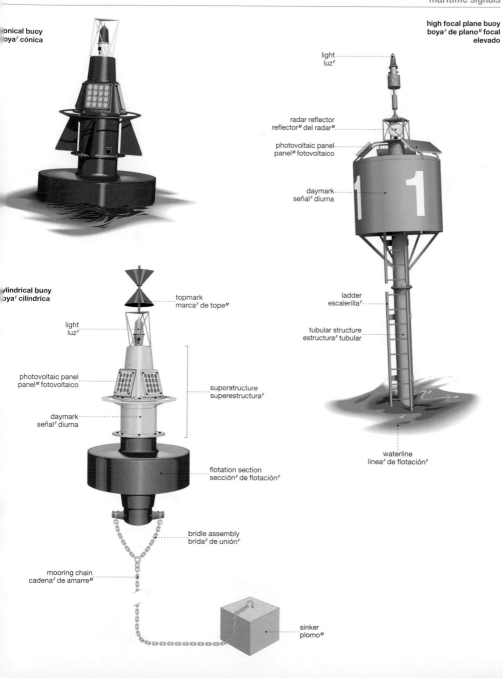

onical buoy
oya^F cónica

high focal plane buoy
boya^F de plano^M focal elevado

light
luz^F

radar reflector
reflector^M del radar^M

photovoltaic panel
panel^M fotovoltaico

daymark
señal^F diurna

ladder
escalerilla^F

tubular structure
estructura^F tubular

waterline
línea^F de flotación^F

ylindrical buoy
oya^F cilíndrica

topmark
marca^F de tope^M

light
luz^F

photovoltaic panel
panel^M fotovoltaico

superstructure
superestructura^F

daymark
señal^F diurna

flotation section
sección^F de flotación^F

bridle assembly
brida^F de unión^F

mooring chain
cadena^F de amarre^M

sinker
plomo^M

TRANSPORT AND MACHINERY

maritime buoyage system

sistema^M de boyas^F marítimas

cardinal marks
señales^F de los puntos^M
cardinales

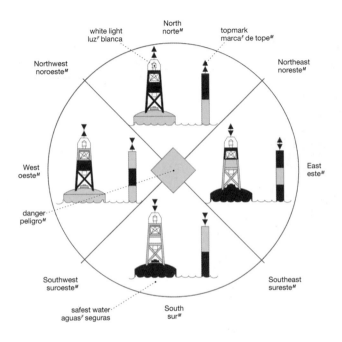

North
norte^M

white light
luz^F blanca

topmark
marca^F de tope^M

Northwest
noroeste^M

Northeast
noreste^M

West
oeste^M

East
este^M

danger
peligro^M

Southwest
suroeste^M

Southeast
sureste^M

safest water
aguas^F seguras

South
sur^M

buoyage regions
regiones^F de boyas^F

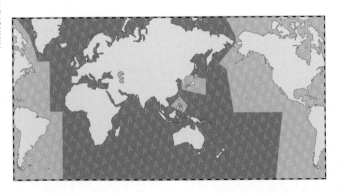

port side
babor^M

starboard side
estribor^M

region A
región^F A

region B
región^F B

maritime buoyage system

rhythm of marks by night
ritmo^M de las señales^F nocturnas

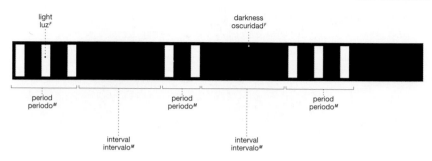

light
luz^F

darkness
oscuridad^F

period
periodo^M

period
periodo^M

period
periodo^M

interval
intervalo^M

interval
intervalo^M

seamarks (region B)
señales^F diurnas (región^F B)

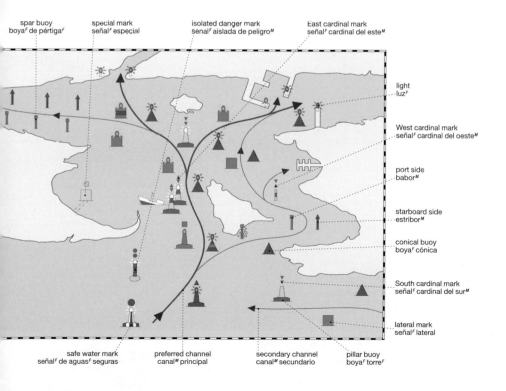

spar buoy
boya^F de pértiga^F

special mark
señal^F especial

isolated danger mark
señal^F aislada de peligro^M

East cardinal mark
señal^F cardinal del este^M

light
luz^F

West cardinal mark
señal^F cardinal del oeste^M

port side
babor^M

starboard side
estribor^M

conical buoy
boya^F cónica

South cardinal mark
señal^F cardinal del sur^M

lateral mark
señal^F lateral

safe water mark
señal^F de aguas^F seguras

preferred channel
canal^M principal

secondary channel
canal^M secundario

pillar buoy
boya^F torre^F

TRANSPORT AND MACHINERY

airport

aeropuerto^M

exterior view
vista^F **exterior**

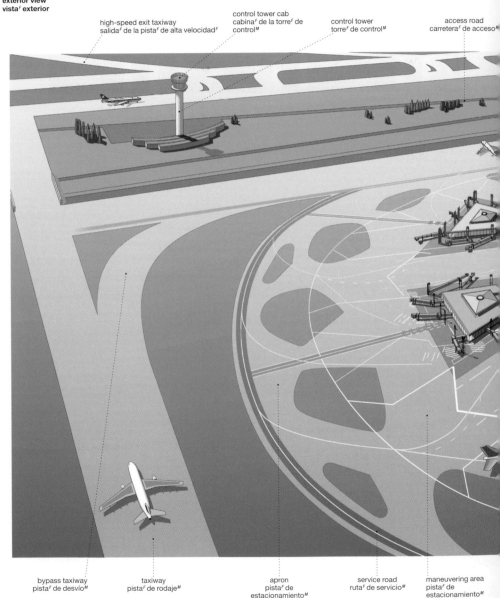

high-speed exit taxiway
salida^F de la pista^F de alta velocidad^F

control tower cab
cabina^F de la torre^F de
control^M

control tower
torre^F de control^M

access road
carretera^F de acceso^M

bypass taxiway
pista^F de desvío^M

taxiway
pista^F de rodaje^M

apron
pista^F de
estacionamiento^M

service road
ruta^F de servicio^M

maneuvering area
pista^F de
estacionamiento^M

TRANSPORT AND MACHINERY

airport

taxiway
pista^F de rodaje^M

passenger terminal
terminal^M de pasajeros^M

maintenance hangar
hangar^M de
mantenimiento^M

parking area
parque^M de
estacionamiento^M

TRANSPORT AND MACHINERY

jet bridge
pasarela^F telescópica

service area
zona^F de servicio^M

boarding walkway
túnel^M de embarque^M

taxiway line
línea^F de pista^F

satellite terminal
terminal^F satélite de pasajeros^M

airport

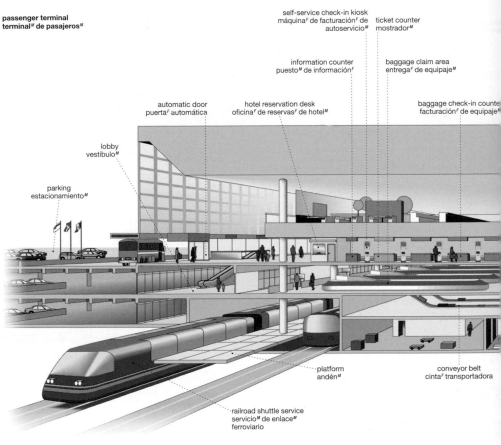

passenger terminal
terminal^M **de pasajeros**^{M}

self-service check-in kiosk
máquina^F de facturación^F de
autoservicio^M

ticket counter
mostrador^M

information counter
puesto^M de información^F

baggage claim area
entrega^F de equipaje^M

automatic door
puerta^F automática

hotel reservation desk
oficina^F de reservas^F de hotel^M

baggage check-in counter
facturación^F de equipaje^M

lobby
vestíbulo^M

parking
estacionamiento^M

platform
andén^M

conveyor belt
cinta^F transportadora

railroad shuttle service
servicio^M de enlace^M
ferroviario

runway
pista^F **de aterrizaje**^{M} **y**
despegue^M

TRANSPORT AND MACHINERY

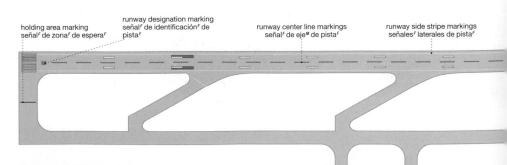

holding area marking
señal^F de zona^F de espera^F

runway designation marking
señal^F de identificación^F de
pista^F

runway center line markings
señal^F de eje^M de pista^F

runway side stripe markings
señales^F laterales de pista^F

airport

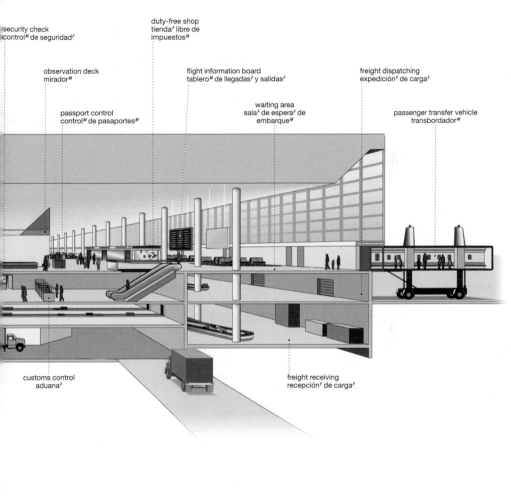

security check
control^M de seguridad^F

duty-free shop
tienda^F libre de
impuestos^M

observation deck
mirador^M

flight information board
tablero^M de llegadas^F y salidas^F

freight dispatching
expedición^F de carga^F

passport control
control^M de pasaportes^M

waiting area
sala^F de espera^F de
embarque^M

passenger transfer vehicle
transbordador^M

customs control
aduana^F

freight receiving
recepción^F de carga^F

TRANSPORT AND MACHINERY

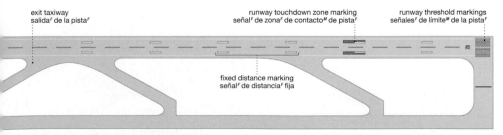

exit taxiway
salida^F de la pista^F

runway touchdown zone marking
señal^F de zona^F de contacto^M de pista^F

runway threshold markings
señales^F de límite^M de la pista^F

fixed distance marking
señal^F de distancia^F fija

airport

airport ground equipment
equipo^M de tierra^F del aeropuerto^M

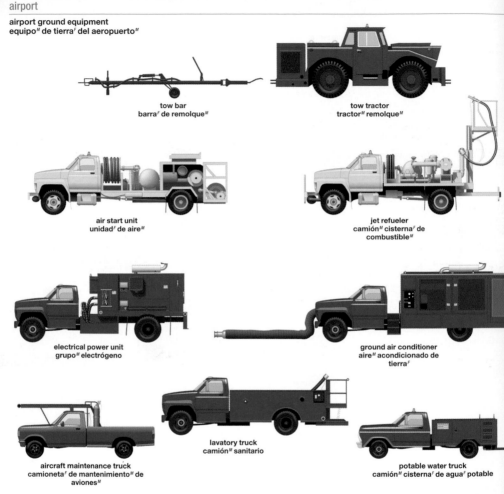

tow bar
barra^F de remolque^M

tow tractor
tractor^M remolque^M

air start unit
unidad^F de aire^M

jet refueler
camión^M cisterna^F de
combustible^M

electrical power unit
grupo^M electrógeno

ground air conditioner
aire^M acondicionado de
tierra^F

lavatory truck
camión^M sanitario

aircraft maintenance truck
camioneta^F de mantenimiento^M de
aviones^M

potable water truck
camión^M cisterna^F de agua^F potable

wheel chock
calzo^M de la rueda^F

boom truck
camioneta^F con canastilla^F
telescópica

TRANSPORT AND MACHINERY

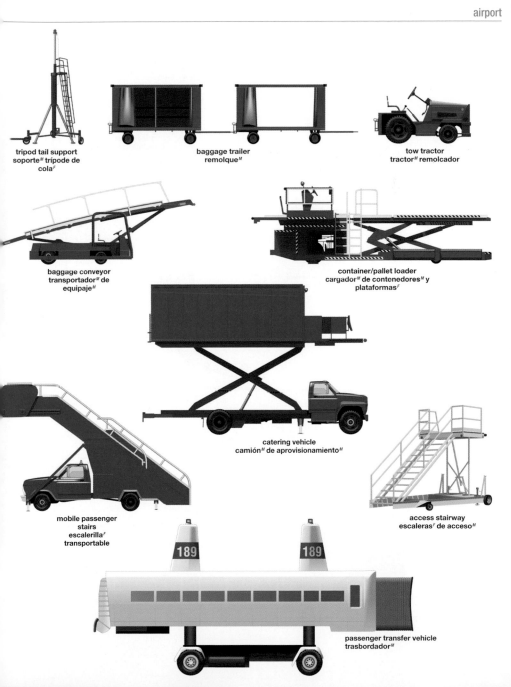

tripod tail support
soporte^M trípode de
cola^F

baggage trailer
remolque^M

tow tractor
tractor^M remolcador

baggage conveyor
transportador^M de
equipaje^M

container/pallet loader
cargador^M de contenedores^M y
plataformas^F

catering vehicle
camión^M de aprovisionamiento^M

mobile passenger
stairs
escalerilla^F
transportable

access stairway
escaleras^F de acceso^M

189

189

passenger transfer vehicle
trasbordador^M

TRANSPORT AND MACHINERY

long-range jet
avión^M turborreactor de pasajeros^M

general view
vista^F general

TRANSPORT AND MACHINERY

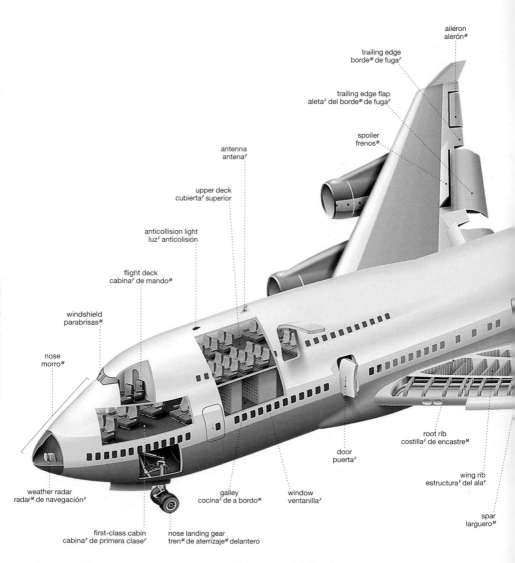

aileron
alerón^M

trailing edge
borde^M de fuga^F

trailing edge flap
aleta^F del borde^M de fuga^F

spoiler
frenos^M

antenna
antena^F

upper deck
cubierta^F superior

anticollision light
luz^F anticolisión

flight deck
cabina^F de mando^M

windshield
parabrisas^M

nose
morro^M

weather radar
radar^M de navegación^F

first-class cabin
cabina^F de primera clase^F

nose landing gear
tren^M de aterrizaje^M delantero

galley
cocina^F de a bordo^M

window
ventanilla^F

door
puerta^F

root rib
costilla^F de encastre^M

wing rib
estructura^F del ala^F

spar
larguero^M

long-range jet

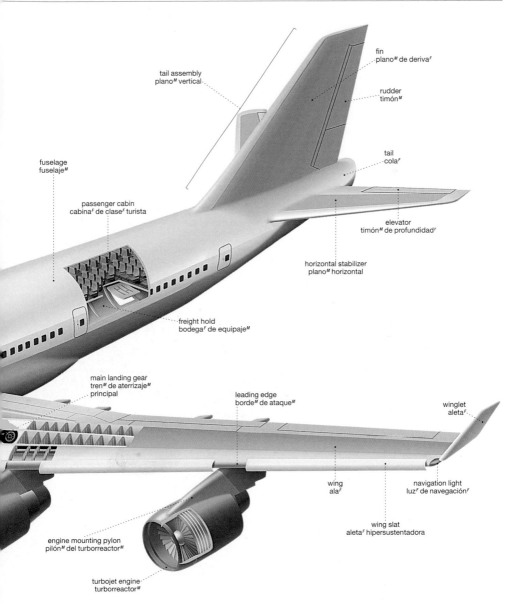

fin
plano^M de deriva^F

rudder
timón^M

tail assembly
plano^M vertical

tail
cola^F

fuselage
fuselaje^M

passenger cabin
cabina^F de clase^F turista

elevator
timón^M de profundidad^F

horizontal stabilizer
plano^M horizontal

freight hold
bodega^F de equipaje^M

main landing gear
tren^M de aterrizaje^M
principal

leading edge
borde^M de ataque^M

winglet
aleta^F

wing
ala^F

navigation light
luz^F de navegación^F

engine mounting pylon
pilón^M del turborreactor^M

wing slat
aleta^F hipersustentadora

turbojet engine
turborreactor^M

TRANSPORT AND MACHINERY

long-range jet

flight deck
puente^M de mando^M

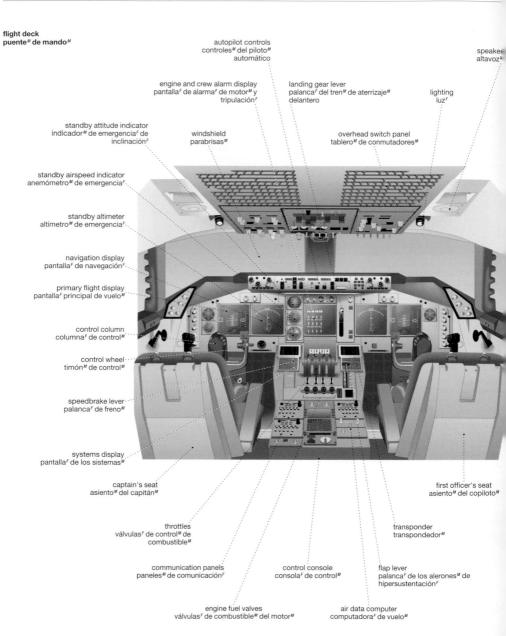

autopilot controls
controles^M del piloto^M
automático

speaker
altavoz^M

engine and crew alarm display
pantalla^F de alarma^F de motor^M y
tripulación^F

landing gear lever
palanca^F del tren^M de aterrizaje^M
delantero

lighting
luz^F

standby attitude indicator
indicador^M de emergencia^F de
inclinación^F

windshield
parabrisas^M

overhead switch panel
tablero^M de conmutadores^M

standby airspeed indicator
anemómetro^M de emergencia^F

standby altimeter
altímetro^M de emergencia^F

navigation display
pantalla^F de navegación^F

primary flight display
pantalla^F principal de vuelo^M

control column
columna^F de control^M

control wheel
timón^M de control^M

speedbrake lever
palanca^F de freno^M

systems display
pantalla^F de los sistemas^M

captain's seat
asiento^M del capitán^M

first officer's seat
asiento^M del copiloto^M

throttles
válvulas^F de control^M de
combustible^M

transponder
transpondedor^M

communication panels
paneles^M de comunicación^F

control console
consola^F de control^M

flap lever
palanca^F de los alerones^M de
hipersustentación^F

engine fuel valves
válvulas^F de combustible^M del motor^M

air data computer
computadora^F de vuelo^M

TRANSPORT AND MACHINERY

long-range jet

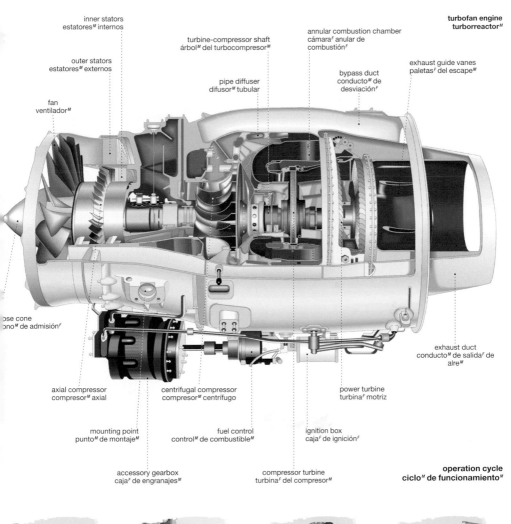

inner stators
estatores^M internos

turbine-compressor shaft
árbol^M del turbocompresor^M

annular combustion chamber
cámara^F anular de
combustión^F

**turbofan engine
turborreactor^M**

outer stators
estatores^M externos

pipe diffuser
difusor^M tubular

bypass duct
conducto^M de
desviación^F

exhaust guide vanes
paletas^F del escape^M

fan
ventilador^M

ose cone
ono^M de admisión^F

exhaust duct
conducto^M de salida^F de
alre^M

axial compressor
compresor^M axial

centrifugal compressor
compresor^M centrífugo

power turbine
turbina^F motriz

mounting point
punto^M de montaje^M

fuel control
control^M de combustible^M

ignition box
caja^F de ignición^F

accessory gearbox
caja^F de engranajes^M

compressor turbine
turbina^F del compresor^M

**operation cycle
ciclo^M de funcionamiento^M**

**air intake
boca^F de aspiración^F
de aire^M**

**compression
compresión^F**

**combustion
combustión^F**

**exhaust
escape^M**

examples of airplanes

ejemplos^M de aviones^M

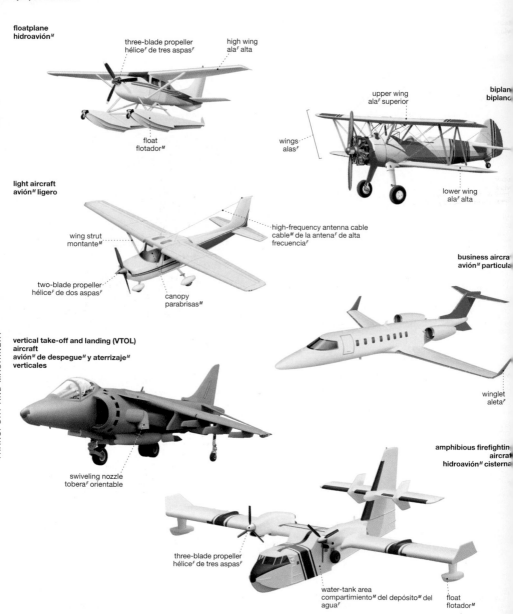

floatplane
hidroavión^M

three-blade propeller
hélice^F de tres aspas^F

high wing
ala^F alta

float
flotador^M

upper wing
ala^F superior

biplane
biplano

wings
alas^F

lower wing
ala^F alta

light aircraft
avión^M **ligero**

wing strut
montante^M

high-frequency antenna cable
cable^M de la antena^F de alta
frecuencia^F

two-blade propeller
hélice^F de dos aspas^F

canopy
parabrisas^M

business aircraft
avión^M particular

vertical take-off and landing (VTOL)
aircraft
avión^M **de despegue**^M **y aterrizaje**^M
verticales

winglet
aleta^F

swiveling nozzle
tobera^F orientable

amphibious firefighting
aircraft
hidroavión^M cisterna

three-blade propeller
hélice^F de tres aspas^F

water-tank area
compartimiento^M del depósito^M del
agua^F

float
flotador^M

examples of airplanes

stealth aircraft
avión^M stealth

facet
faceta^F

radar-absorbent material
material^M que absorbe las ondas^F
radar

rotodome
rotodomo

radar aircraft
avión^M radar

strut
montante^M

superjumbo
avión^M de gran fuselaje^M

variable ejector nozzle
tobera^F de sección^F
variable

supersonic liner
avión^M supersónico

droop nose
morro^M abatible

delta wing
ala^F delta^M

cargo aircraft
avión^M de carga^F

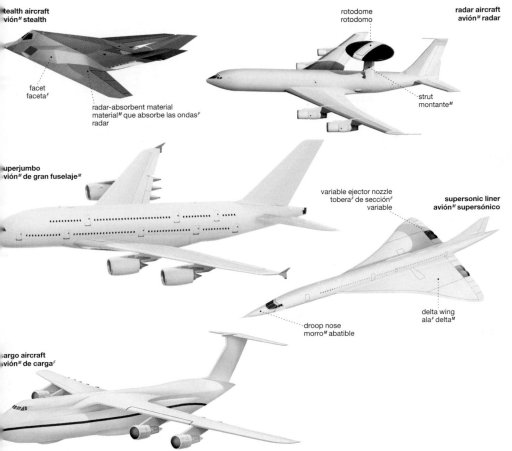

examples of tail shapes

ejemplos de empenajes^M de cola^F

T-tail unit
guías^F en T

triple tail unit
triple plano^M vertical

fuselage mounted tail unit
guías^F normales

cruciform tail unit
unidad^F cruciforme

TRANSPORT AND MACHINERY

examples of wing shapes
diferentes formas^F de alas^F

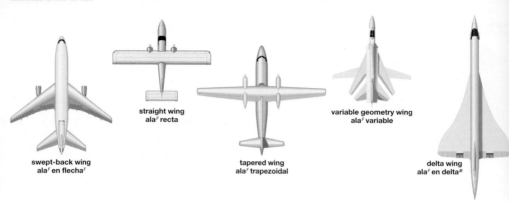

straight wing
ala^F recta

variable geometry wing
ala^F variable

swept-back wing
ala^F en flecha^F

tapered wing
ala^F trapezoidal

delta wing
ala^F en delta^M

movements of an airplane
movimientos^M de un avión^M

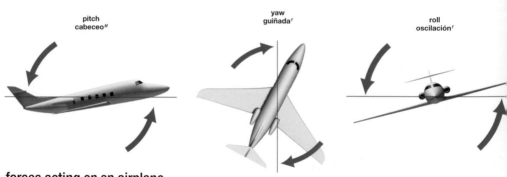

pitch
cabeceo^M

yaw
guiñada^F

roll
oscilación^F

forces acting on an airplane
fuerzas^F que actúan sobre un avión^M

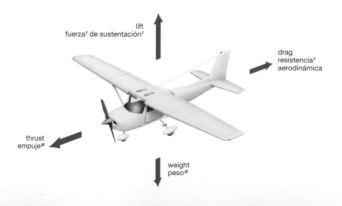

lift
fuerza^F de sustentación^F

drag
resistencia^F
aerodinámica

thrust
empuje^M

weight
peso^M

helicopter

helicóptero[M]

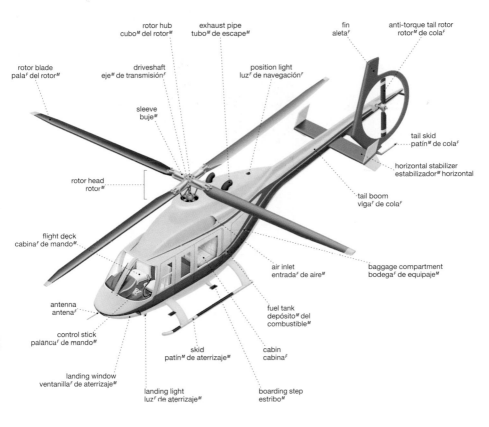

rotor hub
cubo[M] del rotor[M]

exhaust pipe
tubo[M] de escape[M]

fin
aleta[F]

anti-torque tail rotor
rotor[M] de cola[F]

rotor blade
pala[F] del rotor[M]

driveshaft
eje[M] de transmisión[F]

position light
luz[F] de navegación[F]

sleeve
buje[M]

tail skid
patín[M] de cola[F]

horizontal stabilizer
estabilizador[M] horizontal

rotor head
rotor[M]

tail boom
viga[F] de cola[F]

flight deck
cabina[F] de mando[M]

air inlet
entrada[F] de aire[M]

baggage compartment
bodega[F] de equipaje[M]

antenna
antena[F]

fuel tank
depósito[M] del
combustible[M]

control stick
palanca[F] de mando[M]

skid
patín[M] de aterrizaje[M]

cabin
cabina[F]

landing window
ventanilla[F] de aterrizaje[M]

landing light
luz[F] de aterrizaje[M]

boarding step
estribo[M]

examples of helicopters

ejemplos[M] de helicópteros[M]

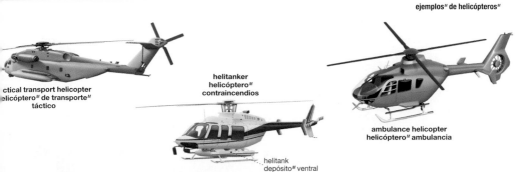

ctical transport helicopter
elicóptero[M] de transporte[M]
táctico

helitanker
helicóptero[M]
contraincendios

helitank
depósito[M] ventral

ambulance helicopter
helicóptero[M] ambulancia

TRANSPORT AND MACHINERY

typical devices

dispositivos^M habituales

**forklift
carretilla^F elevadora de
horquilla^F**

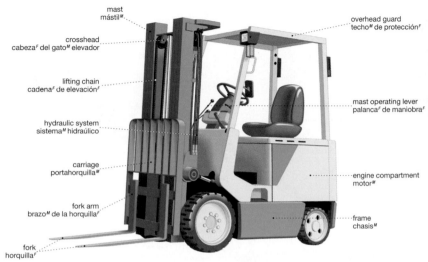

mast
mástil^M

crosshead
cabeza^F del gato^M elevador

lifting chain
cadena^F de elevación^F

hydraulic system
sistema^M hidraúlico

carriage
portahorquilla^M

fork arm
brazo^M de la horquilla^F

fork
horquilla^F

overhead guard
techo^M de protección^F

mast operating lever
palanca^F de maniobra^F

engine compartment
motor^M

frame
chasis^M

**pallets
palés^M**

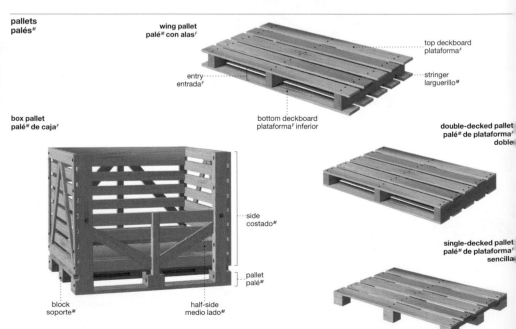

**wing pallet
palé^M con alas^F**

entry
entrada^F

top deckboard
plataforma^F

stringer
larguerillo^M

bottom deckboard
plataforma^F inferior

**box pallet
palé^M de caja^F**

**double-decked pallet
palé^M de plataforma^F
doble**

side
costado^M

pallet
palé^M

block
soporte^M

half-side
medio lado^M

**single-decked pallet
palé^M de plataforma^F
sencilla**

TRANSPORT AND MACHINERY

typical devices

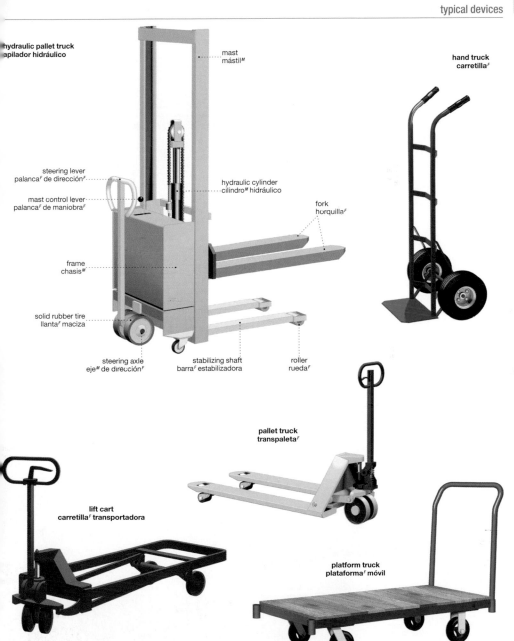

hydraulic pallet truck
apilador hidráulico

mast
mástil^M

hand truck
carretilla^F

steering lever
palanca^F de dirección^F

hydraulic cylinder
cilindro^M hidráulico

mast control lever
palanca^F de maniobra^F

fork
horquilla^F

frame
chasis^M

solid rubber tire
llanta^F maciza

steering axle
eje^M de dirección^F

stabilizing shaft
barra^F estabilizadora

roller
rueda^F

pallet truck
transpaleta^F

lift cart
carretilla^F transportadora

platform truck
plataforma^F móvil

TRANSPORT AND MACHINERY

cranes

grúas[f]

tower crane
grúa[f] torre[f]

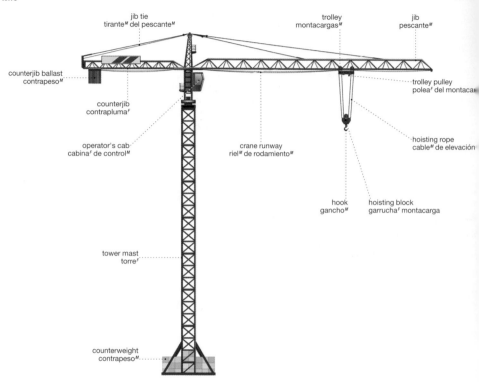

jib tie
tirante[M] del pescante[M]

trolley
montacargas[M]

jib
pescante[M]

counterjib ballast
contrapeso[M]

trolley pulley
polea[f] del montaca…

counterjib
contrapluma[f]

operator's cab
cabina[f] de control[M]

crane runway
riel[M] de rodamiento[M]

hoisting rope
cable[M] de elevación

hook
gancho[M]

hoisting block
garrucha[f] montacarga

tower mast
torre[f]

counterweight
contrapeso[M]

truck crane
grúa[f] móvil

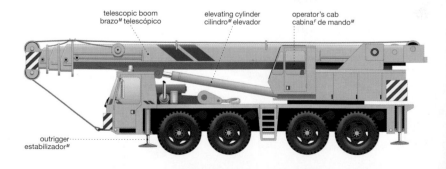

telescopic boom
brazo[M] telescópico

elevating cylinder
cilindro[M] elevador

operator's cab
cabina[f] de mando[M]

outrigger
estabilizador[M]

cranes

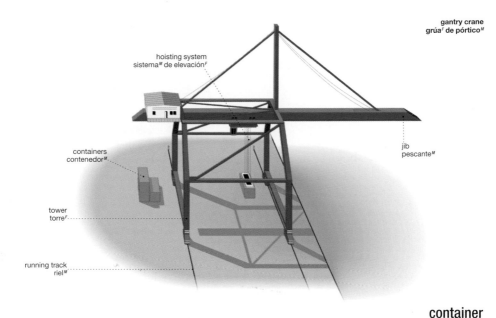

gantry crane
grúa^F de pórtico^M

hoisting system
sistema^M de elevación^F

containers
contenedor^M

jib
pescante^M

tower
torre^F

running track
riel^M

container

contenedor^M

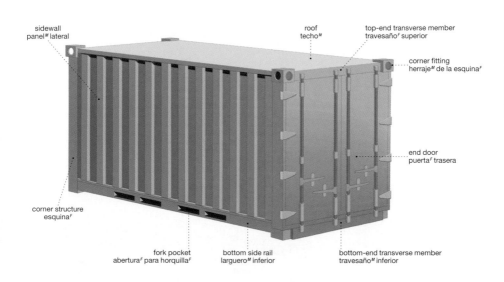

sidewall
panel^M lateral

roof
techo^M

top-end transverse member
travesaño^F superior

corner fitting
herraje^M de la esquina^F

end door
puerta^F trasera

corner structure
esquina^F

fork pocket
abertura^F para horquilla^F

bottom side rail
larguero^M inferior

bottom-end transverse member
travesaño^M inferior

TRANSPORT AND MACHINERY

bulldozer

bulldozer^M

general view
vista^F **general**

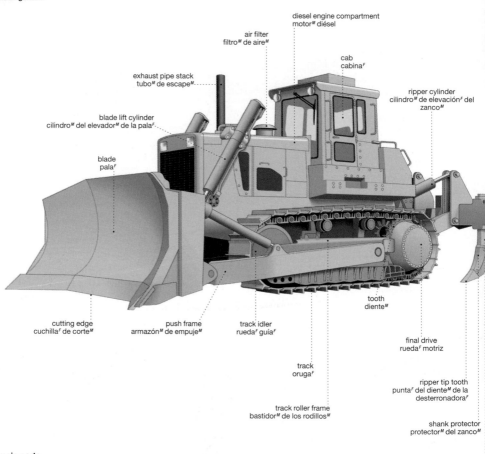

diesel engine compartment
motor^M diésel

air filter
filtro^M de aire^M

cab
cabina^F

exhaust pipe stack
tubo^M de escape^M

ripper cylinder
cilindro^M de elevación^F del
zanco^M

blade lift cylinder
cilindro^M del elevador^M de la pala^F

blade
pala^F

cutting edge
cuchilla^F de corte^M

push frame
armazón^M de empuje^M

track idler
rueda^F guía^F

tooth
diente^M

final drive
rueda^F motriz

track
oruga^F

ripper tip tooth
punta^F del diente^M de la
desterronadora^F

track roller frame
bastidor^M de los rodillos^M

shank protector
protector^M del zanco^M

ripper shank
diente^M de la
desterronadora^F

main parts
componentes^M
principales

crawler tractor
tractor^M **de orugas**^{F}

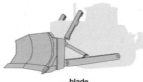

blade
pala^F

ripper
zanco^M

backhoe loader
cargadora^f-retroexcavadora^f

general view
vista^f general

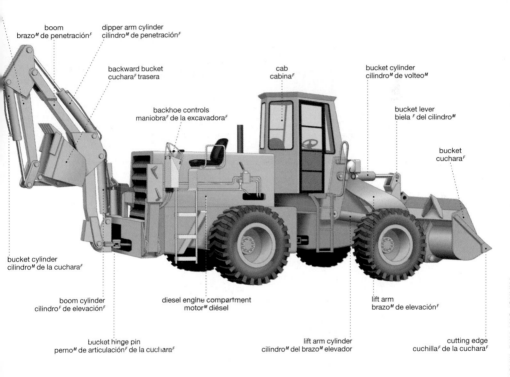

pper arm
azo^M de la cuchara^F

boom
brazo^M de penetración^F

dipper arm cylinder
cilindro^M de penetración^F

backward bucket
cuchara^F trasera

cab
cabina^F

bucket cylinder
cilindro^M de volteo^M

backhoe controls
maniobra^F de la excavadora^F

bucket lever
biela ^F del cilindro^M

bucket
cuchara^F

bucket cylinder
cilindro^M de la cuchara^F

boom cylinder
cilindro^F de elevación^F

diesel engine compartment
motor^M diésel

lift arm
brazo^M de elevación^F

bucket hinge pin
perno^M de articulación^F de la cuchara^F

lift arm cylinder
cilindro^M del brazo^M elevador

cutting edge
cuchilla^F de la cuchara^F

TRANSPORT AND MACHINERY

main parts
componentes^M
principales

front-end loader
cargador^M delantero

wheel tractor
tractor^M de ruedas^F

backhoe
excavadora^F

scraper

raspador^M

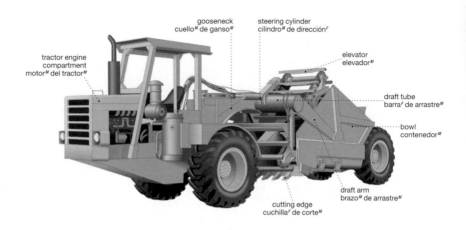

gooseneck
cuello^M de ganso^M

steering cylinder
cilindro^M de dirección^F

elevator
elevador^M

tractor engine
compartment
motor^M del tractor^M

draft tube
barra^F de arrastre^M

bowl
contenedor^M

draft arm
brazo^M de arrastre^M

cutting edge
cuchilla^F de corte^M

power shovel

pala^F hidráulica

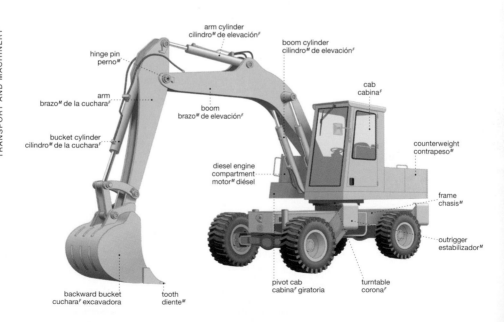

arm cylinder
cilindro^M de elevación^F

boom cylinder
cilindro^M de elevación^F

hinge pin
perno^M

cab
cabina^F

arm
brazo^M de la cuchara^F

boom
brazo^M de elevación^F

counterweight
contrapeso^M

bucket cylinder
cilindro^M de la cuchara^F

diesel engine
compartment
motor^M diésel

frame
chasis^M

outrigger
estabilizador^M

backward bucket
cuchara^F excavadora

tooth
diente^M

pivot cab
cabina^F giratoria

turntable
corona^F

grader

niveladora^f

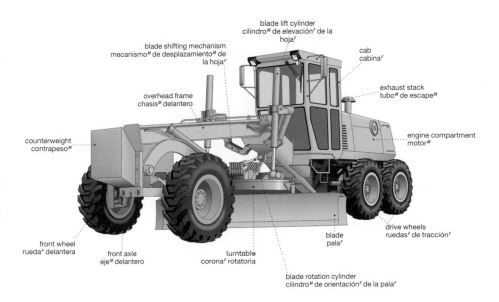

blade lift cylinder
cilindro^M de elevación^F de la hoja^F

blade shifting mechanism
mecanismo^M de desplazamiento^M de la hoja^F

cab
cabina^F

overhead frame
chasis^M delantero

exhaust stack
tubo^M de escape^M

counterweight
contrapeso^M

engine compartment
motor^M

front wheel
rueda^F delantera

front axle
eje^M delantero

turntable
corona^F rotatoria

blade
pala^F

drive wheels
ruedas^F de tracción^F

blade rotation cylinder
cilindro^M de orientación^F de la pala^F

dump truck

volcadora^f

canopy
cubierta^F protectora

cab
cabina^F

rib
nervio^M

diesel engine compartment
motor^M diésel

dump body
caja^F basculante

ladder
escalerilla^F

frame
chasis^M

asphalt paver

pavimentadora^F

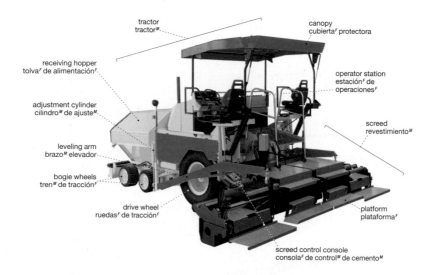

tractor
tractor^M

canopy
cubierta^F protectora

receiving hopper
tolva^F de alimentación^F

operator station
estación^F de
operaciones^F

adjustment cylinder
cilindro^M de ajuste^M

screed
revestimiento^M

leveling arm
brazo^M elevador

bogie wheels
tren^M de tracción^F

drive wheel
ruedas^F de tracción^F

platform
plataforma^F

screed control console
consola^F de control^M de cemento^M

road roller

apisonadora^F

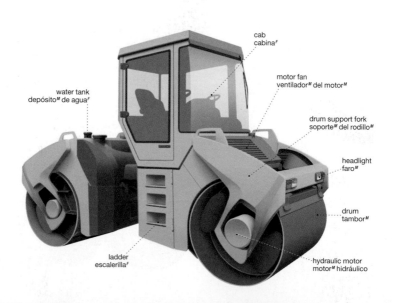

cab
cabina^F

water tank
depósito^M de agua^F

motor fan
ventilador^M del motor^M

drum support fork
soporte^M del rodillo^M

headlight
faro^M

drum
tambor^M

ladder
escalerilla^F

hydraulic motor
motor^M hidráulico

snowblower

quitanieves^M

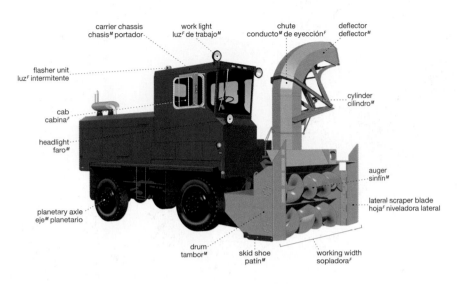

carrier chassis
chasis^M portador

work light
luz^F de trabajo^M

chute
conducto^M de eyección^F

deflector
deflector^M

flasher unit
luz^F intermitente

cylinder
cilindro^M

cab
cabina^F

headlight
faro^M

auger
sinfín^M

lateral scraper blade
hoja^F niveladora lateral

planetary axle
eje^M planetario

drum
tambor^M

skid shoe
patín^M

working width
sopladora^F

street sweeper

barredora^F

water tank
depósito^M de agua^F

rearview mirror
espejo^M retrovisor

rotating beacon
luz^F giratoria

debris hopper
tina^F de residuos^M

cab
cabina^F

parabolic rearview mirror
espejo^M retrovisor
parabólico

sweeping mirror
espejo^M de limpieza^F

headlight
faro^M

front spray bar
barra^F irrigadora frontal

pickup broom
cepillo^M central

watering tube
tubo^M de irrigación^F

gutter broom
cepillo^M de suelo^M

step
peldaño^M

tractor

tractor^M

front view
vista^F frontal

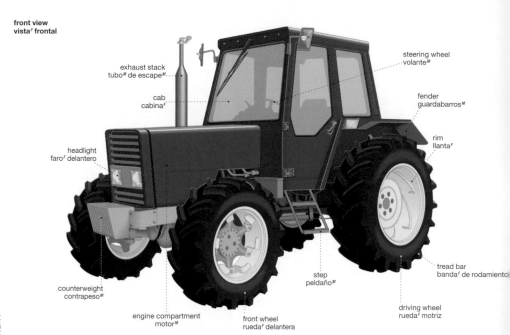

exhaust stack
tubo^M de escape^M

cab
cabina^F

headlight
faro^F delantero

counterweight
contrapeso^M

engine compartment
motor^M

front wheel
rueda^F delantera

step
peldaño^M

steering wheel
volante^M

fender
guardabarros^M

rim
llanta^F

tread bar
banda^F de rodamiento

driving wheel
rueda^F motriz

rear view
vista^F posterior

taillight
faros^M traseros

hydraulic coupler
empalme^M hidráulico

hydraulic cylinder
cilindro^M hidráulico

coupler head
cabeza^F de empalme^M

towing hitch
gancho^M del remolque^M

headlight
luces^F traseras

compression link
eslabón^M de compresión^F

rock shaft lift arm
brazo^M de elevación^M del árbol^M
oscilante

lifting link
vástago^M de elevación^F

power take-off
toma^F de fuerza^F

draft link
brazo^M de tracción^F

agricultural machinery
maquinaria^F agrícola

ribbing plow
arado^M de vertedera^F

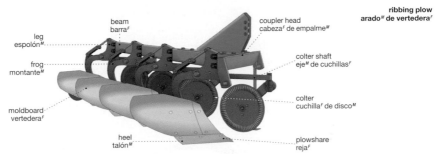

leg
espolón^M

beam
barra^F

coupler head
cabeza^F de empalme^M

frog
montante^M

colter shaft
eje^M de cuchillas^F

moldboard
vertedera^F

colter
cuchilla^F de disco^M

heel
talón^M

plowshare
reja^F

tandem disc harrow
pulverizador^M tándem

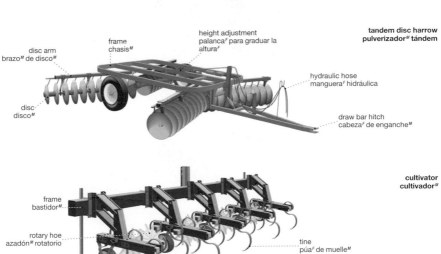

disc arm
brazo^M de disco^M

frame
chasis^M

height adjustment
palanca^F para graduar la
altura^F

hydraulic hose
manguera^F hidráulica

disc
disco^M

draw bar hitch
cabeza^F de enganche^M

cultivator
cultivador^M

frame
bastidor^M

rotary hoe
azadón^M rotatorio

tine
púa^F de muelle^M

manure spreader
esparcidora^M de
estiércol^M

box
cajón^M

beater
batidor^M

chain drive
cadena^F de transmisión^F

power take-off shaft
eje^M de toma^F de fuerza^F

frame
chasis^M

jack stand
pie^M de apoyo^M

hydraulic hose
manguera^F hidráulica

draw bar hitch
cabeza^F de enganche^M

agricultural machinery

rake
rastrillo^M

frame
chasis^M

height adjustment
palanca^F para graduar la
altura^F

rake bar
barra^F de rastrillos^M

tooth
diente^M

flail mower
segadora^F

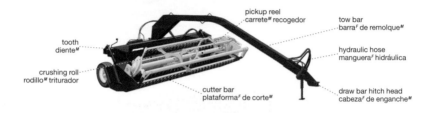

pickup reel
carrete^M recogedor

tow bar
barra^F de remolque^M

tooth
diente^M

hydraulic hose
manguera^F hidráulica

crushing roll
rodillo^M triturador

cutter bar
plataforma^F de corte^M

draw bar hitch head
cabeza^F de enganche^M

hay baler
empacadora^F **de heno**^M

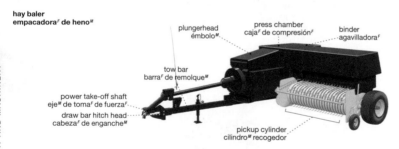

plungerhead
émbolo^M

press chamber
caja^F de compresión^F

binder
agavilladora^F

tow bar
barra^F de remolque^M

power take-off shaft
eje^M de toma^F de fuerza^F

draw bar hitch head
cabeza^F de enganche^M

pickup cylinder
cilindro^M recogedor

forage harvester
cosechera^F **de forraje**^M

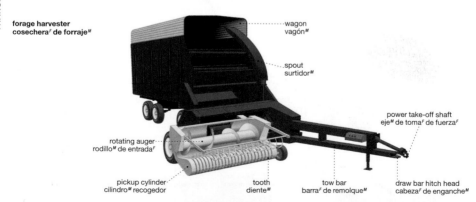

wagon
vagón^M

spout
surtidor^M

power take-off shaft
eje^M de toma^F de fuerza^F

rotating auger
rodillo^M de entrada^F

pickup cylinder
cilindro^M recogedor

tooth
diente^M

tow bar
barra^F de remolque^M

draw bar hitch head
cabeza^F de enganche^M

agricultural machinery

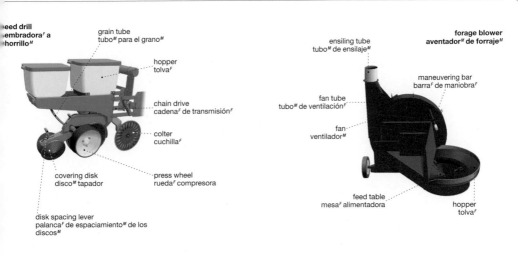

seed drill
sembradora^F a
chorrillo^M

grain tube
tubo^M para el grano^M

hopper
tolva^F

chain drive
cadena^F de transmisión^F

colter
cuchilla^F

covering disk
disco^M tapador

press wheel
rueda^F compresora

disk spacing lever
palanca^F de espaciamiento^M de los
discos^M

forage blower
aventador^M de forraje^M

ensiling tube
tubo^M de ensilaje^M

maneuvering bar
barra^F de maniobra^F

fan tube
tubo^M de ventilación^F

fan
ventilador^M

feed table
mesa^F alimentadora

hopper
tolva^F

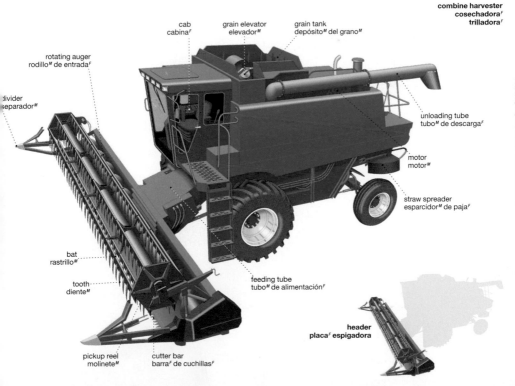

combine harvester
cosechadora^F
trilladora^F

cab
cabina^F

grain elevator
elevador^M

grain tank
depósito^M del grano^M

rotating auger
rodillo^M de entrada^F

divider
separador^M

unloading tube
tubo^M de descarga^F

motor
motor^M

straw spreader
esparcidor^M de paja^F

bat
rastrillo^M

tooth
diente^M

feeding tube
tubo^M de alimentación^F

pickup reel
molinete^M

cutter bar
barra^F de cuchillas^F

header
placa^F espigadora

TRANSPORT AND MACHINERY

ENERGY
energía

EOTHERMAL ENERGY 770

production of electricity from
  geothermal energy 770
geothermal house 770

OSSIL ENERGY 771

coal mine 771
thermal energy 775
oil 775
natural gas 783
alternative fuel 784

HYDROELECTRICITY 785

hydroelectric complex 785
steps in production of electricity 789
examples of dams 790
electricity transmission 792
tidal power plant 794

NUCLEAR ENERGY 795

production of electricity from nuclear energy 795
nuclear generating station 796
fuel handling sequence 798
fuel bundle 799
nuclear reactor 799
types of reactors 800

SOLAR ENERGY 802

solar cell 802
flat-plate solar collector 802
solar cell system 803
solar furnace 804
production of electricity from solar energy 804
solar house 805

WIND ENERGY 806

windmills 806
wind turbines and electricity production 807

production of electricity from geothermal energy

producción⁀ de electricidad⁀ por energía⁀ geotérmica

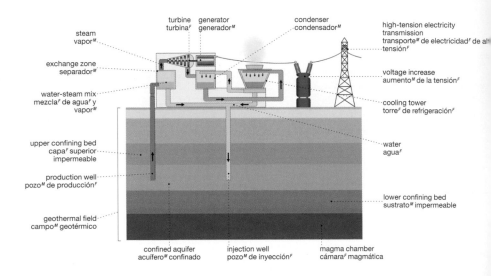

steam
vapor^M

exchange zone
separador^M

water-steam mix
mezcla⁀ de agua⁀ y
vapor^M

upper confining bed
capa⁀ superior
impermeable

production well
pozo^M de producción⁀

geothermal field
campo^M geotérmico

turbine
turbina⁀

generator
generador^M

condenser
condensador^M

high-tension electricity
transmission
transporte^M de electricidad⁀ de alt
tensión⁀

voltage increase
aumento^M de la tensión⁀

cooling tower
torre⁀ de refrigeración⁀

water
agua⁀

lower confining bed
sustrato^M impermeable

confined aquifer
acuífero^M confinado

injection well
pozo^M de inyección⁀

magma chamber
cámara⁀ magmática

geothermal house

casa⁀ geotérmica

independent geothermal heating
calor^M geotérmico autónomo

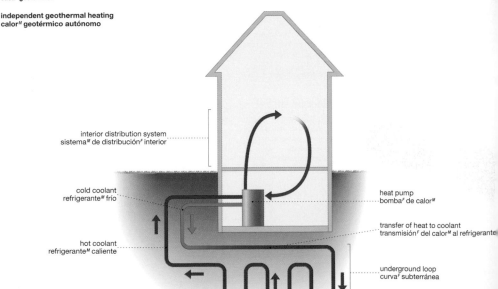

interior distribution system
sistema^M de distribución⁀ interior

cold coolant
refrigerante^M frío

hot coolant
refrigerante^M caliente

heat pump
bomba⁀ de calor^M

transfer of heat to coolant
transmisión⁀ del calor^M al refrigerante

underground loop
curva⁀ subterránea

ENERGY

coal mine

minas^F de carbón^M

strip mine
excavación^F a cielo^M
abierto

conveyor
cinta^F transportadora

dump
escombrera^M

trench
zanja^F

roof
terreno^M de
recubrimiento^M

mechanical shovel
pala^F mecánica

bucket wheel excavator
excavadora^F de rueda^F de
cangilones^M

overburden
relleno exterior^M

face
frente^M de corte^M

bulldozer
bulldozer^M

belt loader
cinta^F cargadora

open-pit mine
mina^F a cielo^M abierto

bench
banco^M

ground surface
superficie^F del terreno^M

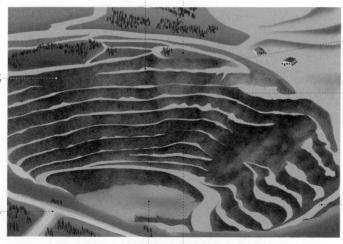

overburden
relleno^M exterior

face
frente^M de corte^M

bench height
altura^F del banco^M

haulage road
camino^M de arrastre^M

ramp
talud^M

crater
cráter^M

coal ore
mineral^M

ENERGY

coal mine

jackleg drill
perforadora^F **con empujador**^{M} **neumático**

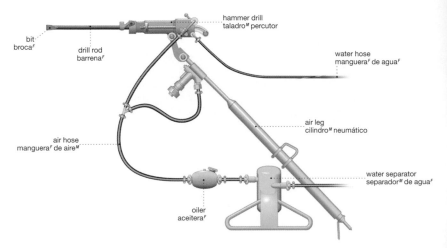

bit
broca^F

drill rod
barrena^F

hammer drill
taladro^M percutor

water hose
manguera^F de agua^F

air leg
cilindro^M neumático

air hose
manguera^F de aire^M

water separator
separador^M de agua^F

oiler
aceitera^F

pithead
planta^F **exterior de una**
mina^F

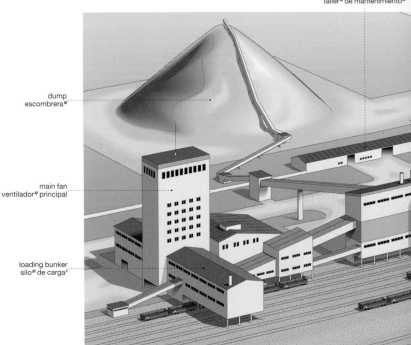

maintenance shop
taller^M de mantenimiento^M

dump
escombrera^M

main fan
ventilador^M principal

loading bunker
silo^M de carga^F

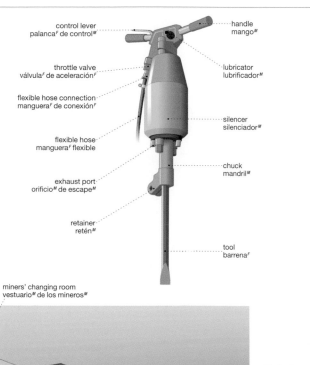

control lever
palanca^F de control^M

handle
mango^M

throttle valve
válvula^F de aceleración^F

lubricator
lubrificador^M

flexible hose connection
manguera^F de conexión^F

flexible hose
manguera^F flexible

silencer
silenciador^M

exhaust port
orificio^M de escape^M

chuck
mandril^M

retainer
retén^M

tool
barrena^F

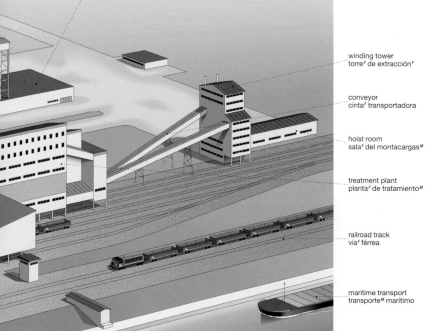

adframe
re^F de extracción^F

miners' changing room
vestuario^M de los mineros^M

winding tower
torre^F de extracción^F

conveyor
cinta^F transportadora

hoist room
sala^F del montacargas^M

treatment plant
planta^F de tratamiento^M

railroad track
vía^F férrea

maritime transport
transporte^M marítimo

ENERGY

coal mine

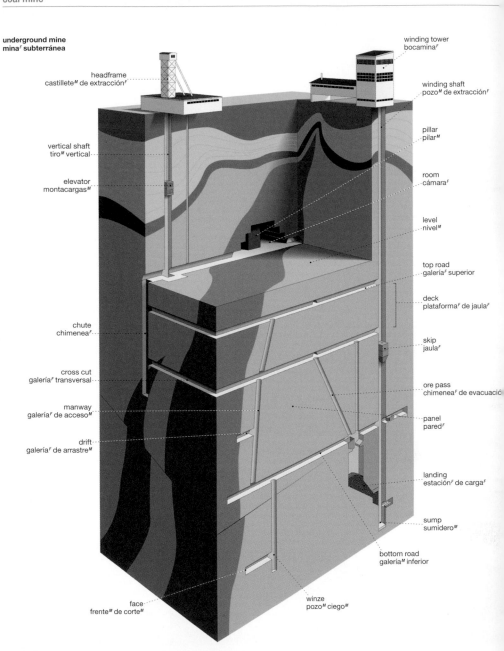

underground mine
mina^F subterránea

headframe
castillete^M de extracción^F

vertical shaft
tiro^M vertical

elevator
montacargas^M

chute
chimenea^F

cross cut
galería^F transversal

manway
galería^F de acceso^M

drift
galería^F de arrastre^M

face
frente^M de corte^M

winze
pozo^M ciego^M

bottom road
galería^M inferior

winding tower
bocamina^F

winding shaft
pozo^M de extracción^F

pillar
pilar^M

room
cámara^F

level
nivel^M

top road
galería^F superior

deck
plataforma^F de jaula^F

skip
jaula^F

ore pass
chimenea^F de evacuació

panel
pared^F

landing
estación^F de carga^F

sump
sumidero^M

ENERGY

thermal energy

energía^F **térmica**

**production of electricity from thermal energy
producción^F de electricidad^F por energía^F
térmica**

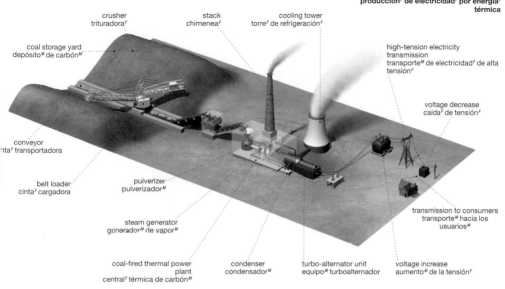

crusher
trituradora^F

stack
chimenea^F

cooling tower
torre^F de refrigeración^F

coal storage yard
depósito^M de carbón^M

high-tension electricity
transmission
transporte^M de electricidad^F de alta
tensión^F

voltage decrease
caída^F de tensión^F

conveyor
nta^F transportadora

belt loader
cinta^F cargadora

pulverizer
pulverizador^M

steam generator
generador^M de vapor^M

transmission to consumers
transporte^M hacia los
usuarios^M

coal-fired thermal power
plant
central^F térmica de carbón^M

condenser
condensador^M

turbo-alternator unit
equipo^M turboalternador

voltage increase
aumento^M de la tensión^F

oil

petróleo^M

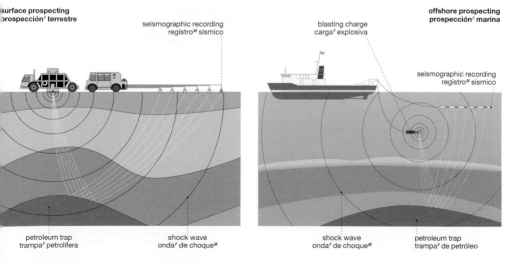

**surface prospecting
prospección^F terrestre**

seismographic recording
registro^M sísmico

blasting charge
carga^F explosiva

**offshore prospecting
prospección^F marina**

seismographic recording
registro^M sísmico

petroleum trap
trampa^F petrolífera

shock wave
onda^F de choque^M

shock wave
onda^F de choque^M

petroleum trap
trampa^F de petróleo

ENERGY

oil

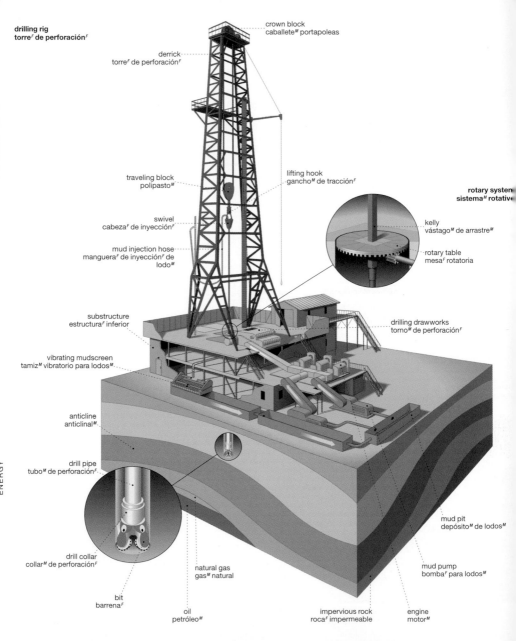

drilling rig
torre^F de perforación^F

crown block
caballete^M portapoleas

derrick
torre^F de perforación^F

lifting hook
gancho^M de tracción^F

traveling block
polipasto^M

rotary system
sistema^M rotativo

swivel
cabeza^F de inyección^F

kelly
vástago^M de arrastre^M

rotary table
mesa^F rotatoria

mud injection hose
manguera^F de inyección^F de
lodo^M

substructure
estructura^F inferior

drilling drawworks
torno^M de perforación^F

vibrating mudscreen
tamiz^M vibratorio para lodos^M

anticline
anticlinal^M

drill pipe
tubo^M de perforación^F

mud pit
depósito^M de lodos^M

drill collar
collar^M de perforación^F

mud pump
bomba^F para lodos^M

natural gas
gas^M natural

bit
barrena^F

oil
petróleo^M

impervious rock
roca^F impermeable

engine
motor^M

ENERGY

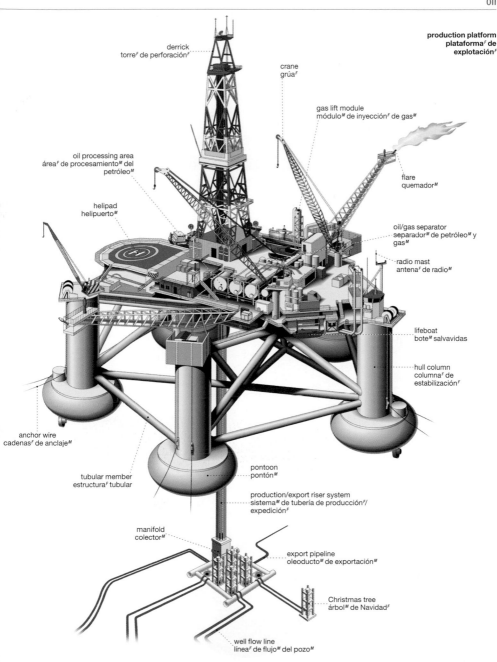

production platform
plataforma^F de
explotación^F

derrick
torre^F de perforación^F

crane
grúa^F

gas lift module
módulo^M de inyección^F de gas^M

oil processing area
área^F de procesamiento^M del
petróleo^M

flare
quemador^M

helipad
helipuerto^M

oil/gas separator
separador^M de petróleo^M y
gas^M

radio mast
antena^F de radio^M

lifeboat
bote^M salvavidas

hull column
columna^F de
estabilización^F

anchor wire
cadenas^F de anclaje^M

tubular member
estructura^F tubular

pontoon
pontón^M

production/export riser system
sistema^M de tubería de producción^F/
expedición^F

manifold
colector^M

export pipeline
oleoducto^M de exportación^M

Christmas tree
árbol^M de Navidad^F

well flow line
línea^F de flujo^M del pozo^M

ENERGY

oil

offshore drilling
perforaciónᶠ marina

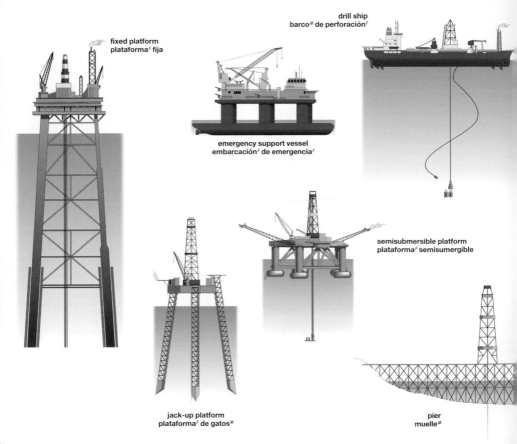

drill ship
barcoᴹ de perforaciónᶠ

fixed platform
plataformaᶠ fija

emergency support vessel
embarcaciónᶠ de emergenciaᶠ

semisubmersible platform
plataformaᶠ semisumergible

jack-up platform
plataformaᶠ de gatosᴹ

pier
muelleᴹ

oil extraction from oil sands
extracciónᶠ de petróleoᴹ de arenasᶠ
bituminosas

oil sand
arenaᶠ bituminosa

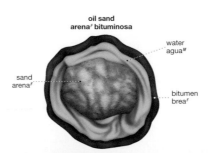

water
aguaᴹ

sand
arenaᶠ

bitumen
breaᶠ

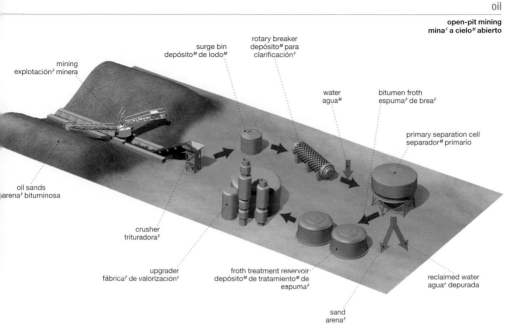

open-pit mining
mina ^{F} **a cielo** ^{M} **abierto**

mining
explotación ^{F} minera

surge bin
depósito ^{M} de lodo ^{M}

rotary breaker
depósito ^{M} para
clarificación ^{F}

water
agua ^{M}

bitumen froth
espuma ^{F} de brea ^{F}

primary separation cell
separador ^{M} primario

oil sands
arena ^{F} bituminosa

crusher
trituradora ^{F}

upgrader
fábrica ^{F} de valorización ^{F}

froth treatment reservoir
depósito ^{M} de tratamiento ^{M} de
espuma ^{F}

reclaimed water
agua ^{F} depurada

sand
arena ^{F}

cyclic steam injection
estimulación ^{F} **cíclica de vapor** ^{M}

steam-assisted gravity drainage
drenaje ^{M} **por infiltración** ^{F} **asistida por vapor** ^{M}

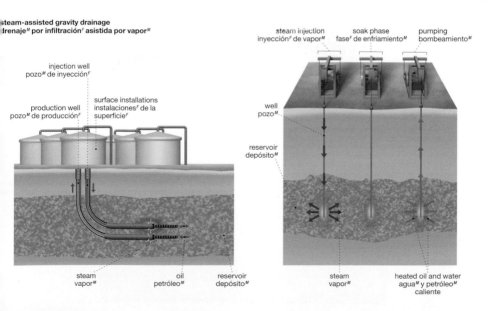

injection well
pozo ^{M} de inyección ^{F}

production well
pozo ^{M} de producción ^{F}

surface installations
instalaciones ^{F} de la
superficie ^{F}

steam
vapor ^{M}

oil
petróleo ^{M}

reservoir
depósito ^{M}

steam injection
inyección ^{F} de vapor ^{M}

soak phase
fase ^{F} de enfriamiento ^{F}

pumping
bombeamiento ^{M}

well
pozo ^{M}.

reservoir
depósito ^{M}

steam
vapor ^{M}

heated oil and water
agua ^{M} y petróleo ^{M}
caliente

ENERGY

oil

Christmas tree
árbol^M **de Navidad**^{F}

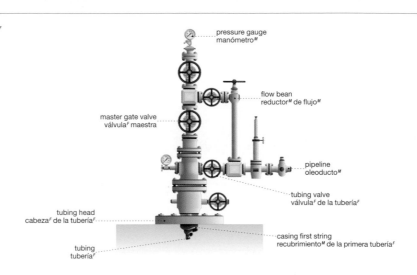

pressure gauge
manómetro^M

flow bean
reductor^M de flujo^M

master gate valve
válvula^F maestra

pipeline
oleoducto^M

tubing valve
válvula^F de la tubería^F

tubing head
cabeza^F de la tubería^F

casing first string
recubrimiento^M de la primera tubería^F

tubing
tubería^F

crude oil pipeline
oleoducto^M **de crudo**^{M}

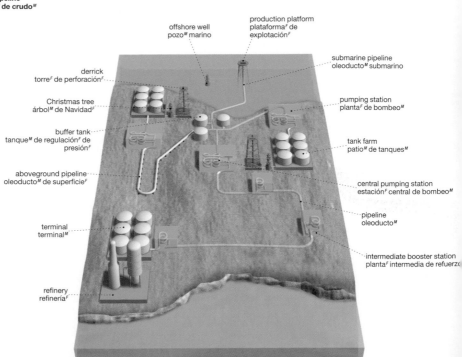

offshore well
pozo^M marino

production platform
plataforma^F de
explotación^F

submarine pipeline
oleoducto^M submarino

derrick
torre^F de perforación^F

Christmas tree
árbol^M de Navidad^F

pumping station
planta^F de bombeo^M

buffer tank
tanque^M de regulación^F de
presión^F

tank farm
patio^M de tanques^M

aboveground pipeline
oleoducto^M de superficie^F

central pumping station
estación^F central de bombeo^M

terminal
terminal^M

pipeline
oleoducto^M

intermediate booster station
planta^F intermedia de refuerzo

refinery
refinería^F

tanks
tanques^M

fixed-roof tank
tanque^M **de techo**^{M} **fijo**

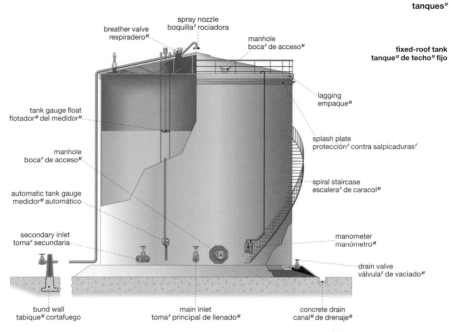

spray nozzle
boquilla^F rociadora

breather valve
respiradero^M

manhole
boca^F de acceso^M

tank gauge float
flotador^M del medidor^M

manhole
boca^F de acceso^M

automatic tank gauge
medidor^M automático

secondary inlet
toma^F secundaria

lagging
empaque^M

splash plate
protección^F contra salpicaduras^F

spiral staircase
escalera^F de caracol^M

manometer
manómetro^M

drain valve
válvula^F de vaciado^M

bund wall
tabique^M cortafuego

main inlet
toma^F principal de llenado^M

concrete drain
canal^M de drenaje^M

floating-roof tank
tanque^M **de techo**^{M} **pontón**

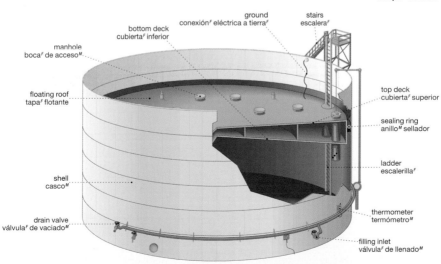

bottom deck
cubierta^F inferior

ground
conexión^F eléctrica a tierra^F

stairs
escalera^F

manhole
boca^F de acceso^M

floating roof
tapa^F flotante

shell
casco^M

drain valve
válvula^F de vaciado^M

top deck
cubierta^F superior

sealing ring
anillo^M sellador

ladder
escalerilla^F

thermometer
termómetro^M

filling inlet
válvula^F de llenado^M

ENERGY

oil

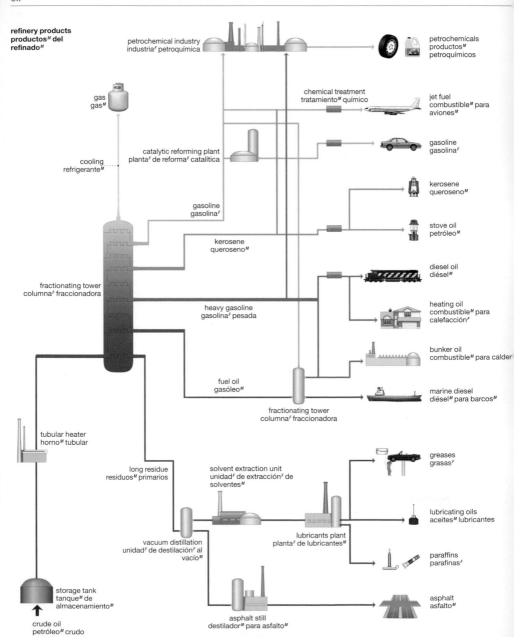

refinery products
productos^M **del**
refinado^M

petrochemical industry
industria^F petroquímica

petrochemicals
productos^M
petroquímicos

gas
gas^M

chemical treatment
tratamiento^M químico

jet fuel
combustible^M para
aviones^M

cooling
refrigerante^M

catalytic reforming plant
planta^F de reforma^F catalítica

gasoline
gasolina^F

gasoline
gasolina^F

kerosene
queroseno^M

stove oil
petróleo^M

kerosene
queroseno^M

diesel oil
diésel^M

fractionating tower
columna^F fraccionadora

heavy gasoline
gasolina^F pesada

heating oil
combustible^M para
calefacción^F

bunker oil
combustible^M para calder

fuel oil
gasóleo^M

marine diesel
diésel^M para barcos^M

fractionating tower
columna^F fraccionadora

tubular heater
horno^M tubular

greases
grasas^F

long residue
residuos^M primarios

solvent extraction unit
unidad^F de extracción^F de
solventes^M

lubricating oils
aceites^M lubricantes

ENERGY

vacuum distillation
unidad^F de destilación^F al
vacío^M

lubricants plant
planta^F de lubricantes^M

paraffins
parafinas^F

storage tank
tanque^M de
almacenamiento^M

asphalt
asfalto^M

crude oil
petróleo^M crudo

asphalt still
destilador^M para asfalto^M

natural gas

gas^M natural

natural gas pipeline
system
sistema^M de líneas^F
canalizadas de gas^M
natural

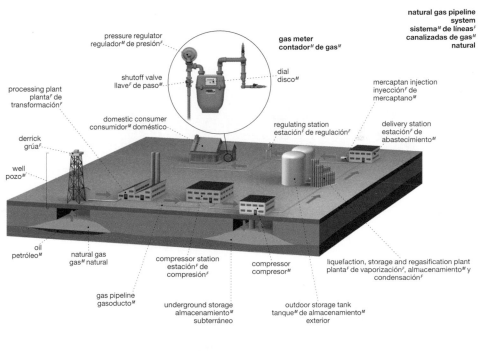

pressure regulator
regulador^M de presión^F

shutoff valve
llave^F de paso^M

processing plant
planta^F de
transformación^F

domestic consumer
consumidor^M doméstico

derrick
grúa^F

well
pozo^M

gas meter
contador^M de gas^M

dial
disco^M

mercaptan injection
inyección^F de
mercaptano^M

regulating station
estación^F de regulación^F

delivery station
estación^F de
abastecimiento^M

oil
petróleo^M

natural gas
gas^M natural

compressor station
estación^F de
compresión^F

compressor
compresor^M

liquefaction, storage and regasification plant
planta^F de vaporización^F, almacenamiento^M y
condensación^F

gas pipeline
gasoducto^M

underground storage
almacenamiento^M
subterráneo

outdoor storage tank
tanque^M de almacenamiento^M
exterior

shale gas extraction
extracción^F de gas^M de pizarra^F

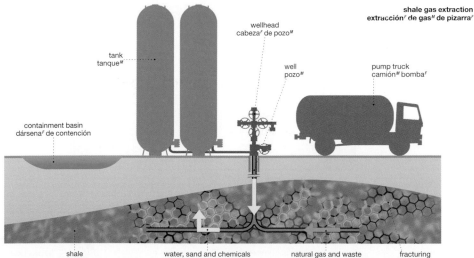

wellhead
cabeza^F de pozo^M

tank
tanque^M

well
pozo^M

pump truck
camión^M bomba^F

containment basin
dársena^F de contención^F

shale
pizarra^F

water, sand and chemicals
agua^F, arena^F y productos^M
químicos

natural gas and waste
gas^M natural y residuos^M

fracturing
fractura^F

ENERGY

alternative fuel

combustiblesᴹ **alternativos**

**biodiesel production
producción**ᶠ **de
biodiesel**ᴹ

**bioethanol production
producción**ᶠ **de
bioetanol**ᴹ

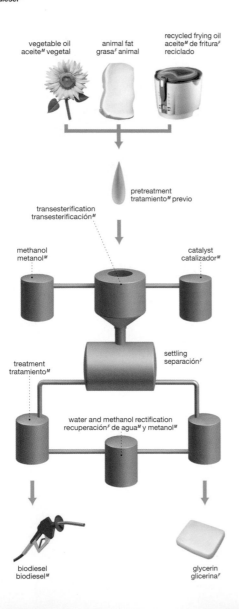

vegetable oil
aceiteᴹ vegetal

animal fat
grasaᶠ animal

recycled frying oil
aceiteᴹ de frituraᶠ
reciclado

pretreatment
tratamientoᴹ previo

transesterification
transesterificaciónᴹ

methanol
metanolᴹ

catalyst
catalizadorᴹ

settling
separaciónᶠ

treatment
tratamientoᴹ

water and methanol rectification
recuperaciónᶠ de aguaᴹ y metanolᴹ

biodiesel
biodieselᴹ

glycerin
glicerinaᶠ

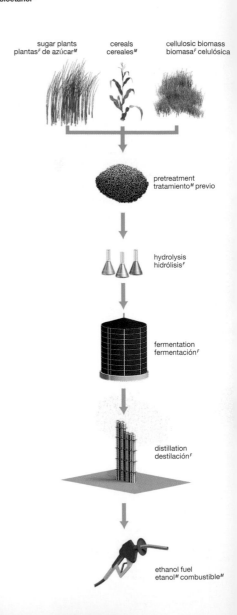

sugar plants
plantasᶠ de azúcarᴹ

cereals
cerealesᴹ

cellulosic biomass
biomasaᶠ celulósica

pretreatment
tratamientoᴹ previo

hydrolysis
hidrólisisᶠ

fermentation
fermentaciónᶠ

distillation
destilaciónᶠ

ethanol fuel
etanolᴹ combustibleᴹ

hydroelectric complex
complejoᴹ **hidroeléctrico**

exterior view
vistaᶠ **exterior**

crest of spillway
cresta ᶠ del aliviadero ᴹ

spillway gate
compuerta ᶠ del aliviadero ᴹ

top of dam
cresta ᶠ de la presa ᶠ

reservoir
embalse ᴹ

headbay
embalse ᴹ a monte ᴹ

spillway
aliviadero ᴹ

penstock
tubería ᶠ de carga ᶠ

gantry crane
grúa ᶠ de caballete ᴹ

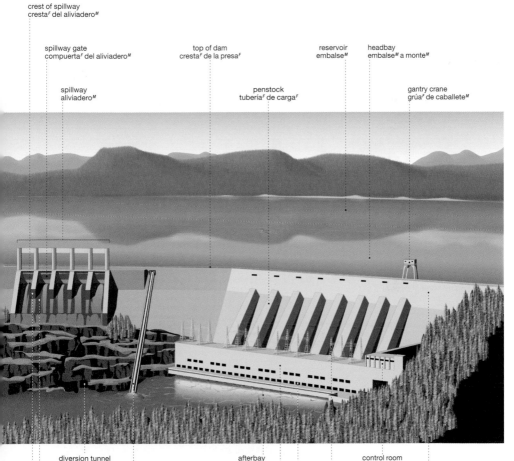

diversion tunnel
túnel ᴹ de desvío ᴹ

afterbay
embalse ᴹ de
compensación ᶠ

control room
sala ᶠ de control ᴹ

spillway chute
canal ᴹ del aliviadero ᴹ

power plant
central ᶠ eléctrica

bushing
boquilla ᶠ

training wall
muro ᴹ de
encauzamiento ᴹ

log chute
rebosadero ᴹ

machine hall
sala ᶠ de máquinas ᶠ

dam
presa ᶠ

ENERGY

hydroelectric complex

**cross section of a hydroelectric
power plant**
corte^M de una central^F hidroeléctrica

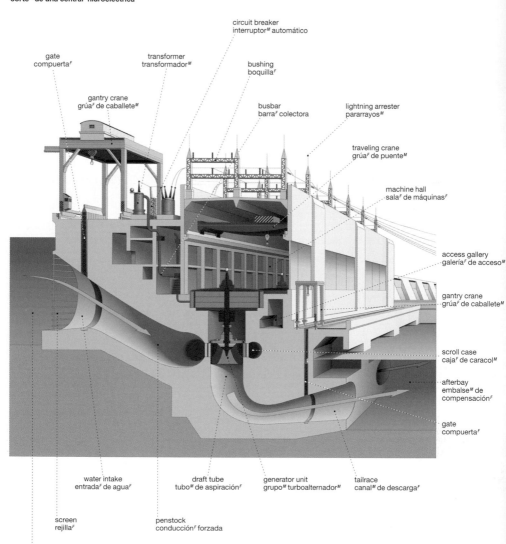

circuit breaker
interruptor^M automático

gate
compuerta^F

transformer
transformador^M

bushing
boquilla^F

gantry crane
grúa^F de caballete^M

busbar
barra^F colectora

lightning arrester
pararrayos^M

traveling crane
grúa^F de puente^M

machine hall
sala^F de máquinas^F

access gallery
galería^F de acceso^M

gantry crane
grúa^F de caballete^M

scroll case
caja^F de caracol^M

afterbay
embalse^M de
compensación^F

gate
compuerta^F

water intake
entrada^F de agua^F

draft tube
tubo^M de aspiración^F

generator unit
grupo^M turboalternador^M

tailrace
canal^M de descarga^F

screen
rejilla^F

penstock
conducción^F forzada

reservoir
embalse^M

ENERGY

hydroelectric complex

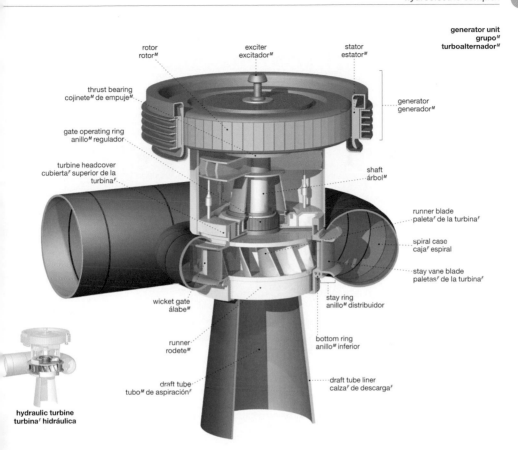

generator unit
grupo^M **turboalternador**^M

rotor
rotor^M

exciter
excitador^M

stator
estator^M

generator
generador^M

thrust bearing
cojinete^M de empuje^M

gate operating ring
anillo^M regulador

turbine headcover
cubierta^F superior de la
turbina^F

shaft
árbol^M

runner blade
paleta^F de la turbina^F

spiral case
caja^F espiral

stay vane blade
paletas^F de la turbina^F

wicket gate
álabe^M

stay ring
anillo^M distribuidor

runner
rodete^M

bottom ring
anillo^M inferior

draft tube
tubo^M de aspiración^F

draft tube liner
calza^F de descarga^F

hydraulic turbine
turbina^F **hidráulica**

runners
rodetes^M

Pelton runner
turbina^F **Pelton**

bucket
álabe^M

coupling bolt
perno^M de acoplamiento^M

Francis runner
turbina^F **Francis**

Kaplan runner
turbina^F **Kaplan**

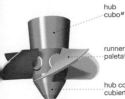

hub
cubo^M

runner blade
paleta^F del rodete^M

hub cover
cubierta^F del cubo^M

bucket ring
rueda^F **de alabes**^M

blade
paleta^F

ring
anillo^M

ENERGY

hydroelectric complex

types of power plants
tipos^M **de centrales**^{F}

run-of-the-river power plant
central^F **hidroeléctrica de agua**^{F} **fluyente**

floodgate
compuerta^F

dam
presa^M

spillway
aliviadero^M

power plant
central^F

transformer
transformador^M

powerline
cable^M de alta tensión^F

power station with reservoir
central^F **eléctrica con depósito**^{M}

reservoir
depósito^M

gravity dam
presa^M

steps in production of electricity

etapas*f* de la producción*f* de electricidad*f*

energy transmission at the generator voltage
transmisión*f* de energía*f* al generador*M* de
voltaje*M*

energy integration to the transmission
network
paso*M* de la energía*f* hacia la red*f* de
transmisión*f*

voltage increase
amplificador*M* de voltaje*M*

voltage decrease
reductor*M* de voltaje*M*

head of water
altura*f* del agua*f*

high-tension electricity transmission
transporte*M* de electricidad*f* de alta
tensión*f*

transmission to consumers
distribución*f* al consumidor*M*

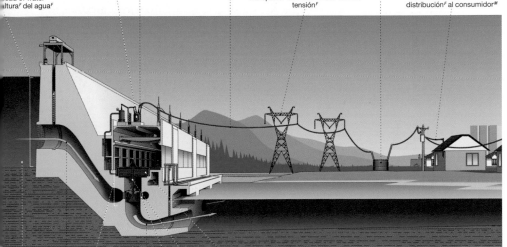

supply of water
suministro*M* de agua*f*

production of electricity by the
generator
producción*f* de electricidad*f* por
generador*M*

water under pressure
agua*f* a presión*f*

transmission of the rotative movement to
the rotor
transmisión*f* del movimiento*M* hacia el rotor*M*

transformation of mechanical work into
electricity
transformación*f* del trabajo*M* mecánico en
electricidad*f*

rotation of the turbine
rotación*f* de la turbina*f*

turbined water draining
desagüe*M* de la turbina*f*

ENERGY

examples of dams

ejemplos^M de presas^F

buttress dam
presa^F de contrafuertes^M

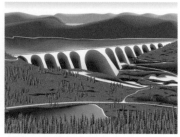

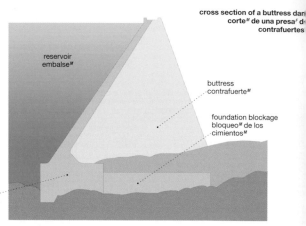

reservoir
embalse^M

buttress
contrafuerte^M

foundation blockage
bloqueo^M de los cimientos^M

foundation
cimientos^M

embankment dam
presa^F de tierra^F

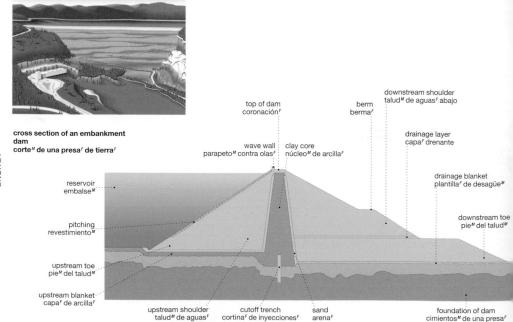

cross section of an embankment dam
corte^M de una presa^F de tierra^F

top of dam
coronación^F

berm
berma^F

downstream shoulder
talud^M de aguas^F abajo

wave wall
parapeto^M contra olas^F

clay core
núcleo^M de arcilla^F

drainage layer
capa^F drenante

drainage blanket
plantilla^F de desagüe^M

reservoir
embalse^M

downstream toe
pie^M del talud^M

pitching
revestimiento^M

upstream toe
pie^M del talud^M

upstream blanket
capa^F de arcilla^F

upstream shoulder
talud^M de aguas^F contenidas

cutoff trench
cortina^F de inyecciones^F

sand
arena^F

foundation of dam
cimientos^M de una presa^F

ENERGY

cross section of an arch dam
corte^M **de una presa**^{F} **de bóveda**^{F}

arch dam
presa^F **de bóveda**^{F}

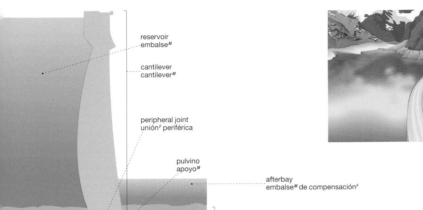

reservoir
embalse^M

cantilever
cantilever^M

peripheral joint
unión^F periférica

pulvino
apoyo^M

afterbay
embalse^M de compensación^F

soil
suelo^M

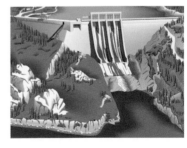

cross section of a gravity dam.
corte^M **de una presa**^{F} **de gravedad**^{F}

gravity dam
presa^F

reservoir
embalse^M

top of dam
coronamiento^M

upstream face
paramento^M de aguas^F
contenidas

downstream face
paramento^M de aguas^F
corrientes

afterbay
embalse^M de
compensación^F

cutoff trench
cortina^F de inyecciones^F

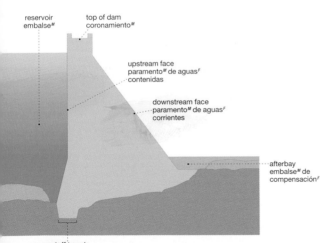

ENERGY

electricity transmission

transporte^M de electricidad^F

examples of towers
ejemplos^M de torres^F

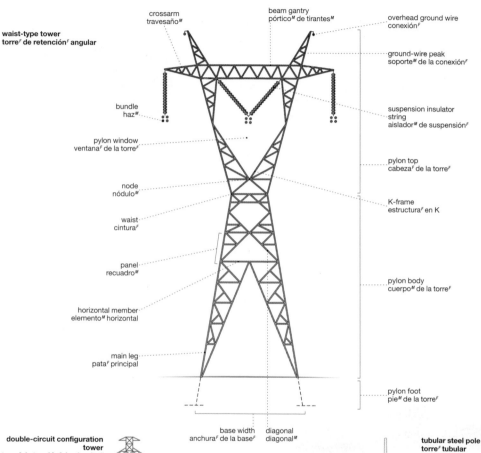

waist-type tower
torre^F de retención^F angular

crossarm
travesaño^M

beam gantry
pórtico^M de tirantes^M

overhead ground wire
conexión^F

ground-wire peak
soporte^M de la conexión^F

bundle
haz^M

suspension insulator
string
aislador^M de suspensión^F

pylon window
ventana^F de la torre^F

pylon top
cabeza^F de la torre^F

node
nódulo^M

K-frame
estructura^F en K

waist
cintura^F

panel
recuadro^M

pylon body
cuerpo^M de la torre^F

horizontal member
elemento^M horizontal

main leg
pata^F principal

pylon foot
pie^M de la torre^F

base width
anchura^F de la base^F

diagonal
diagonal^M

double-circuit configuration
tower
torre^F de tensión^F de circuito^M
doble

tubular steel pole
torre^F tubular

ENERGY

electricity transmission

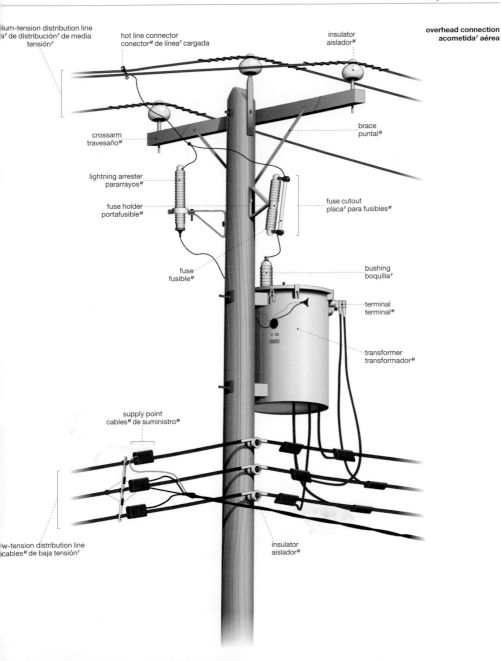

overhead connection
acometida aérea

ium-tension distribution line
a de distribución de media
tensión

hot line connector
conector de línea cargada

insulator
aislador

brace
puntal

crossarm
travesaño

lightning arrester
pararrayos

fuse cutout
placa para fusibles

fuse holder
portafusible

fuse
fusible

bushing
boquilla

terminal
terminal

transformer
transformador

supply point
cables de suministro

w-tension distribution line
cables de baja tensión

insulator
aislador

ENERGY

tidal power plant

planta^F **de energía**^F **maremotriz**

exterior view
vista^F **exterior**

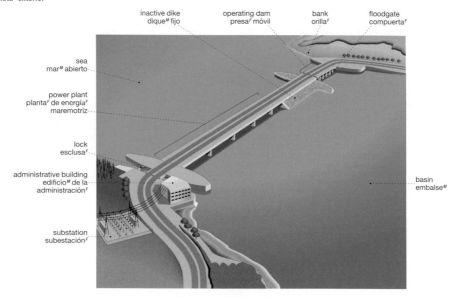

inactive dike
dique^M fijo

operating dam
presa^F móvil

bank
orilla^F

floodgate
compuerta^F

sea
mar^M abierto

power plant
planta^F de energía^F
maremotriz

lock
esclusa^F

administrative building
edificio^M de la
administración^F

substation
subestación^F

basin
embalse^M

cross section of a tidal power plant
corte^M **de una central**^F

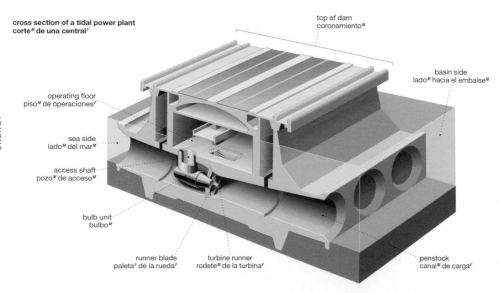

top of dam
coronamiento^M

basin side
lado^M hacia el embalse^M

operating floor
piso^M de operaciones^F

sea side
lado^M del mar^M

access shaft
pozo^M de acceso^M

bulb unit
bulbo^M

runner blade
paleta^F de la rueda^F

turbine runner
rodete^M de la turbina^F

penstock
canal^M de carga^F

production of electricity from nuclear energy
producción^F de electricidad^F por energía^F nuclear

coolant
refrigerante^M

moderator
moderador^M

fuel
combustible^M

heat production
producción^F de calor^M

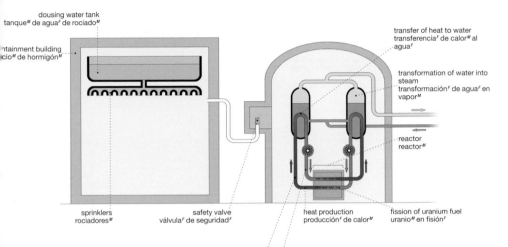

dousing water tank
tanque^M de agua^F de rociado^M

ntainment building
cio^M de hormigón^M

transfer of heat to water
transferencia^F de calor^M al
agua^F

transformation of water into
steam
transformación^F de agua^F en
vapor^M

reactor
reactor^M

sprinklers
rociadores^M

safety valve
válvula^F de seguridad^F

heat production
producción^F de calor^M

fission of uranium fuel
uranio^M en fisión^F

hot coolant
refrigerante^M caliente

cold coolant
refrigerante^M frío

electricity production
producción^F de
electricidad^F

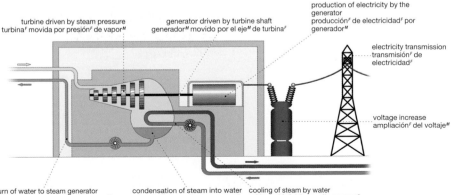

turbine driven by steam pressure
turbina^F movida por presión^F de vapor^M

generator driven by turbine shaft
generador^M movido por el eje^M de turbina^F

production of electricity by the
generator
producción^F de electricidad^F por
generador^M

electricity transmission
transmisión^F de
electricidad^F

voltage increase
ampliación^F del voltaje^M

return of water to steam generator
retorno^M del agua^F al generador^M de vapor^M

condensation of steam into water
el vapor^M se condensa en agua^F

cooling of steam by water
refrigeración^F del vapor^M con agua^F

ENERGY

nuclear generating station

central^F nuclear

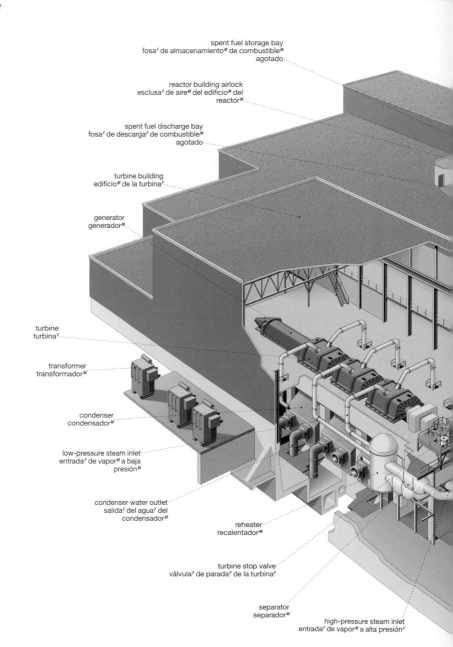

spent fuel storage bay
fosa^F de almacenamiento^M de combustible^M
agotado

reactor building airlock
esclusa^F de aire^M del edificio^M del
reactor^M

spent fuel discharge bay
fosa^F de descarga^F de combustible^M
agotado

turbine building
edificio^M de la turbina^F

generator
generador^M

turbine
turbina^F

transformer
transformador^M

condenser
condensador^M

low-pressure steam inlet
entrada^F de vapor^M a baja
presión^M

condenser water outlet
salida^F del agua^F del
condensador^M

reheater
recalentador^M

turbine stop valve
válvula^F de parada^F de la turbina^F

separator
separador^M

high-pressure steam inlet
entrada^F de vapor^M a alta presión^F

ENERGY

nuclear generating station

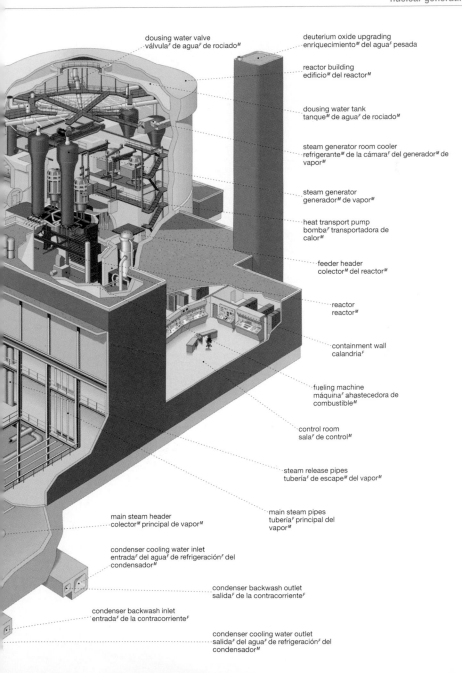

dousing water valve
válvula^F de agua^F de rociado^M

deuterium oxide upgrading
enriquecimiento^M del agua^F pesada

reactor building
edificio^M del reactor^M

dousing water tank
tanque^M de agua^F de rociado^M

steam generator room cooler
refrigerante^M de la cámara^F del generador^M de
vapor^M

steam generator
generador^M de vapor^M

heat transport pump
bomba^F transportadora de
calor^M

feeder header
colector^M del reactor^M

reactor
reactor^M

containment wall
calandria^F

fueling machine
máquina^F abastecedora de
combustible^M

control room
sala^F de control^M

steam release pipes
tubería^F de escape^M del vapor^M

main steam pipes
tubería^F principal del
vapor^M

main steam header
colector^M principal de vapor^M

condenser cooling water inlet
entrada^F del agua^F de refrigeración^F del
condensador^M

condenser backwash outlet
salida^F de la contracorriente^F

condenser backwash inlet
entrada^F de la contracorriente^F

condenser cooling water outlet
salida^F del agua^F de refrigeración^F del
condensador^M

fuel handling sequence

secuencia[F] en el manejo[M] de combustible[M]

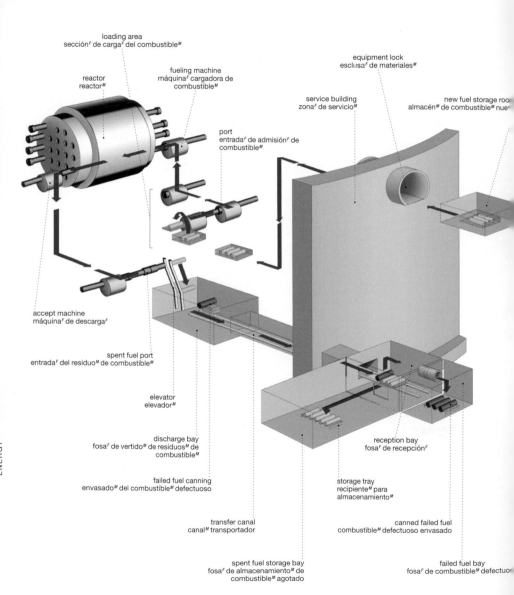

loading area
sección[F] de carga[F] del combustible[M]

equipment lock
esclusa[F] de materiales[M]

fueling machine
máquina[F] cargadora de
combustible[M]

service building
zona[F] de servicio[M]

new fuel storage roo
almacén[M] de combustible[M] nue

reactor
reactor[M]

port
entrada[F] de admisión[F] de
combustible[M]

accept machine
máquina[F] de descarga[F]

spent fuel port
entrada[F] del residuo[M] de combustible[M]

elevator
elevador[M]

discharge bay
fosa[F] de vertido[M] de residuos[M] de
combustible[M]

reception bay
fosa[F] de recepción[F]

failed fuel canning
envasado[M] del combustible[M] defectuoso

storage tray
recipiente[M] para
almacenamiento[M]

transfer canal
canal[M] transportador

canned failed fuel
combustible[M] defectuoso envasado

spent fuel storage bay
fosa[F] de almacenamiento[M] de
combustible[M] agotado

failed fuel bay
fosa[F] de combustible[M] defectuo

fuel bundle

elemento^M de combustible^M

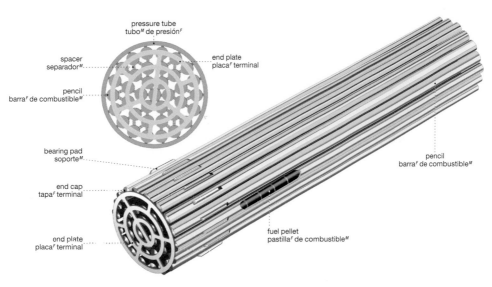

pressure tube
tubo^M de presión^F

spacer
separador^M

pencil
barra^F de combustible^M

end plate
placa^F terminal

bearing pad
soporte^M

end cap
tapa^F terminal

ond plate
placa^F terminal

fuel pellet
pastilla^F de combustible^M

pencil
barra^F de combustible^M

nuclear reactor

carga^F del reactor^M nuclear

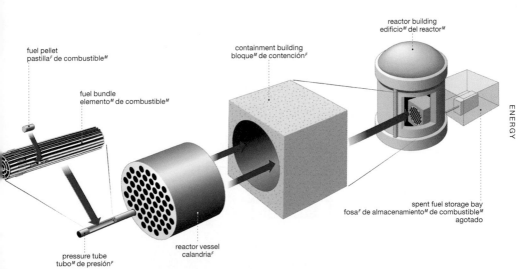

fuel pellet
pastilla^F de combustible^M

fuel bundle
elemento^M de combustible^M

containment building
bloque^M de contención^F

reactor building
edificio^M del reactor^M

pressure tube
tubo^M de presión^F

reactor vessel
calandria^F

spent fuel storage bay
fosa^F de almacenamiento^M de combustible^M
agotado

ENERGY

types of reactors

tipos^M de reactores^M

carbon dioxide reactor
reactor^M de bióxido^M de carbono^M

fuel: natural uranium
combustible^M: uranio^M nat…

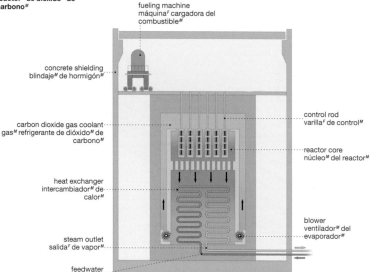

fueling machine
máquina^F cargadora del combustible^M

concrete shielding
blindaje^M de hormigón^M

carbon dioxide gas coolant
gas^M refrigerante de dióxido^M de carbono^M

heat exchanger
intercambiador^M de calor^M

steam outlet
salida^F de vapor^M

feedwater
alimentación^F de agua^F

control rod
varilla^F de control^M

reactor core
núcleo^M del reactor^M

blower
ventilador^M del evaporador^M

moderator: graphite
moderador^M: grafito^M

coolant: carbon dioxide
refrigerante^M: dióxido^M d…
carbono^M

heavy-water reactor
reactor^M de agua^F pesada

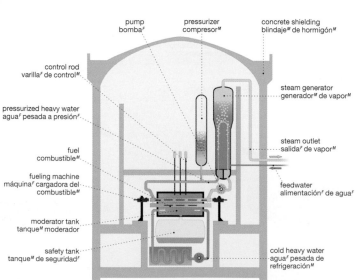

pump
bomba^F

pressurizer
compresor^M

concrete shielding
blindaje^M de hormigón^M

control rod
varilla^F de control^M

pressurized heavy water
agua^F pesada a presión^F

fuel
combustible^M

fueling machine
máquina^F cargadora del combustible^M

moderator tank
tanque^M moderador

safety tank
tanque^M de seguridad^F

steam generator
generador^M de vapor^M

steam outlet
salida^F de vapor^M

feedwater
alimentación^F de agua^F

cold heavy water
agua^F pesada de refrigeración^M

fuel: natural uranium
combustible^M: uranio^M natu…

moderator: heavy water
moderador^M: agua^F pesad…

coolant: pressurized heavy w…
refrigerante^M: agua^F pesad…
presurizada

fuel: enriched uranium
combustible^M: uranio^M
enriquecido

moderator: natural
water
moderador^M: agua^F
natural

coolant: pressurized water
refrigerante^M: agua^F
presurizada

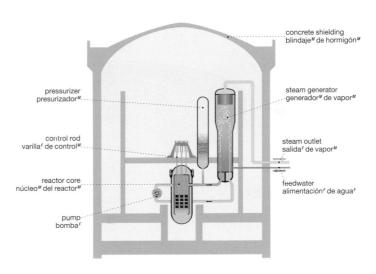

concrete shielding
blindaje^M de hormigón^M

pressurizer
presurizador^M

steam generator
generador^M de vapor^M

control rod
varilla^F de control^M

steam outlet
salida^F de vapor^M

reactor core
núcleo^M del reactor^M

feedwater
alimentación^F de agua^F

pump
bomba^F

---

fuel: enriched uranium
combustible^M: uranio^M
enriquecido

moderator: natural water
moderador^M: agua^F natural

coolant: boiling water
refrigerante^M: agua^F hirviente

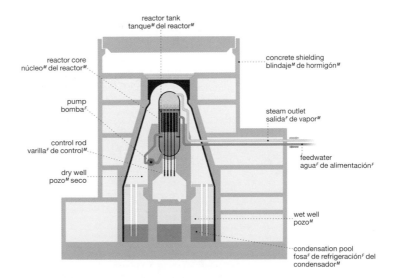

reactor tank
tanque^M del reactor^M

reactor core
núcleo^M del reactor^M

concrete shielding
blindaje^M de hormigón^M

pump
bomba^F

steam outlet
salida^F de vapor^M

control rod
varilla^F de control^M

feedwater
agua^F de alimentación^F

dry well
pozo^M seco

wet well
pozo^M

condensation pool
fosa^F de refrigeración^F del
condensador^M

ENERGY

solar cell
célula^F **solar**

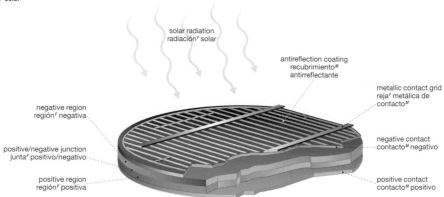

solar radiation
radiación^F solar

antireflection coating
recubrimiento^M
antirreflectante

metallic contact grid
reja^F metálica de
contacto^M

negative region
región^F negativa

negative contact
contacto^M negativo

positive/negative junction
junta^F positivo/negativo

positive region
región^F positiva

positive contact
contacto^M positivo

flat-plate solar collector
colector^M **solar plano**

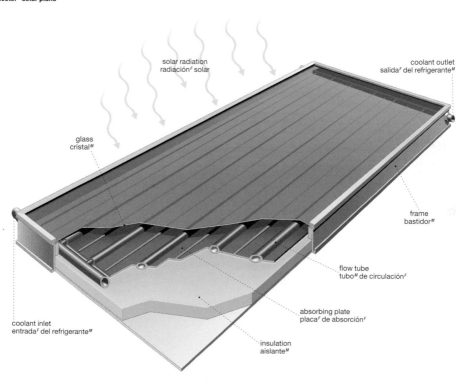

solar radiation
radiación^F solar

coolant outlet
salida^F del refrigerante^M

glass
cristal^M

frame
bastidor^M

flow tube
tubo^M de circulación^F

coolant inlet
entrada^F del refrigerante^M

absorbing plate
placa^F de absorción^F

insulation
aislante^M

ENERGY

solar cell system
sistema*ᴹ* fotovoltaico

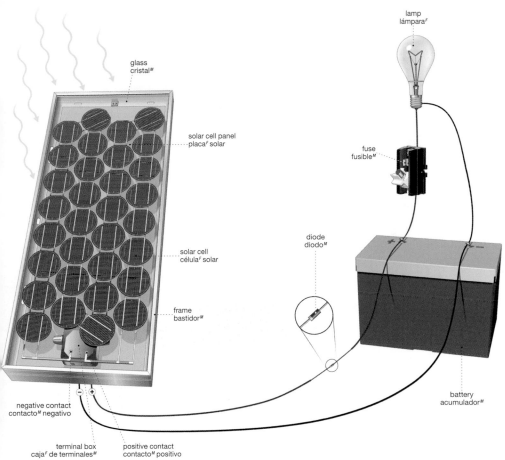

solar radiation
radiación*ᶠ* solar

glass
cristal*ᴹ*

lamp
lámpara*ᶠ*

solar cell panel
placa*ᶠ* solar

fuse
fusible*ᴹ*

solar cell
célula*ᶠ* solar

diode
diodo*ᴹ*

frame
bastidor*ᴹ*

negative contact
contacto*ᴹ* negativo

battery
acumulador*ᴹ*

terminal box
caja*ᶠ* de terminales*ᴹ*

positive contact
contacto*ᴹ* positivo

ENERGY

solar furnace
horno^M solar

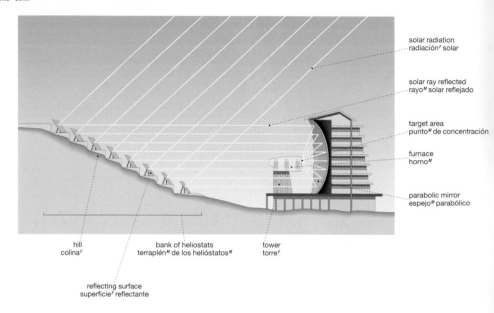

solar radiation
radiación^F solar

solar ray reflected
rayo^M solar reflejado

target area
punto^M de concentración

furnace
horno^M

parabolic mirror
espejo^F parabólico

hill
colina^F

bank of heliostats
terraplén^M de los helióstatos^M

tower
torre^F

reflecting surface
superficie^F reflectante

production of electricity from solar energy
producción^F de electricidad^F por energía^F solar

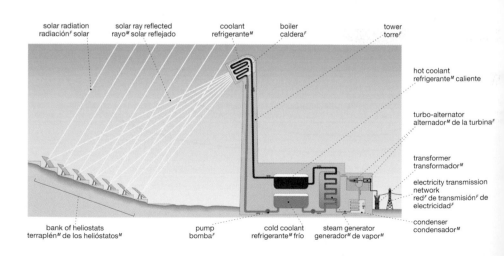

solar radiation
radiación^F solar

solar ray reflected
rayo^M solar reflejado

coolant
refrigerante^M

boiler
caldera^F

tower
torre^F

hot coolant
refrigerante^M caliente

turbo-alternator
alternador^M de la turbina^F

transformer
transformador^M

electricity transmission
network
red^F de transmisión^F de
electricidad^F

condenser
condensador^M

bank of heliostats
terraplén^M de los helióstatos^M

pump
bomba^F

cold coolant
refrigerante^M frío

steam generator
generador^M de vapor^M

ENERGY

solar house

casa^F solar

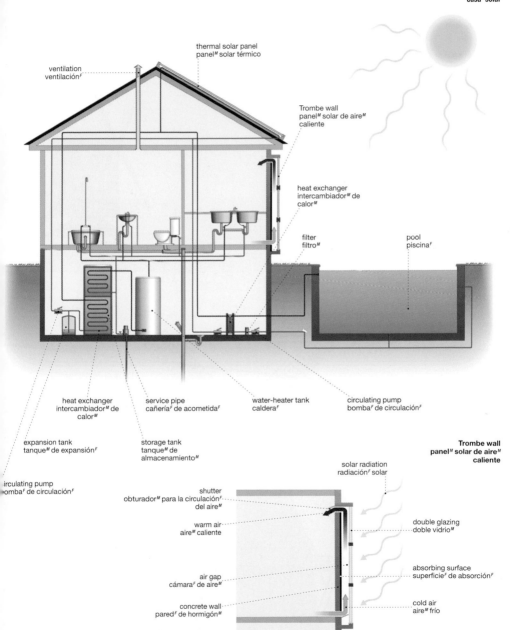

ventilation
ventilación^F

thermal solar panel
panel^M solar térmico

Trombe wall
panel^M solar de aire^M
caliente

heat exchanger
intercambiador^M de
calor^M

filter
filtro^M

pool
piscina^F

heat exchanger
intercambiador^M de
calor^M

service pipe
cañería^F de acometida^F

water-heater tank
caldera^F

circulating pump
bomba^F de circulación^F

expansion tank
tanque^M de expansión^F

storage tank
tanque^M de
almacenamiento^M

circulating pump
bomba^F de circulación^F

**Trombe wall
panel^M solar de aire^M
caliente**

solar radiation
radiación^F solar

shutter
obturador^M para la circulación^F
del aire^M

warm air
aire^M caliente

double glazing
doble vidrio^M

air gap
cámara^F de aire^M

absorbing surface
superficie^F de absorción^F

concrete wall
pared^F de hormigón^M

cold air
aire^M frío

ENERGY

windmills

molinos^M de viento^M

tower mill
molino^M de torre^F

post mi
molino^M de plataforma
giratori

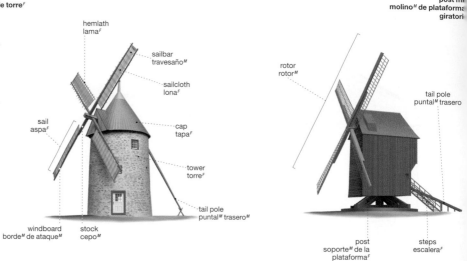

hemlath
lama^F

sailbar
travesaño^M

sailcloth
lona^F

sail
aspa^F

cap
tapa^F

tower
torre^F

tail pole
puntal^M trasero^M

windboard
borde^M de ataque^M

stock
cepo^M

rotor
rotor^M

tail pole
puntal^M trasero

post
soporte^M de la
plataforma^F

steps
escalera^F

smock mill
molino^M de plataforma^F

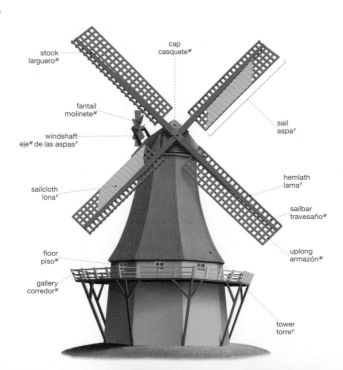

stock
larguero^M

cap
casquete^M

fantail
molinete^M

windshaft
eje^M de las aspas^F

sail
aspa^F

sailcloth
lona^F

hemlath
lama^F

sailbar
travesaño^M

floor
piso^M

uplong
armazón^M

gallery
corredor^M

tower
torre^F

wind turbines and electricity production
turbinas^f de viento^M y producción^f eléctrica

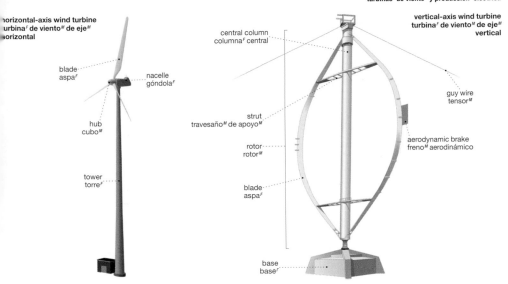

horizontal-axis wind turbine
turbina^f de viento^M de eje^M horizontal

blade
aspa^f

nacelle
góndola^f

hub
cubo^M

tower
torre^f

central column
columna^f central

strut
travesaño^M de apoyo^M

rotor
rotor^M

blade
aspa^f

base
base^f

vertical-axis wind turbine
turbina^f de viento^M de eje^M vertical

guy wire
tensor^M

aerodynamic brake
freno^M aerodinámico

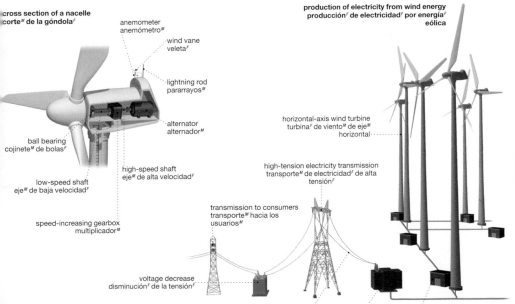

cross section of a nacelle
corte^M de la góndola^f

anemometer
anemómetro^M

wind vane
veleta^f

lightning rod
pararrayos^M

alternator
alternador^M

ball bearing
cojinete^M de bolas^f

low-speed shaft
eje^M de baja velocidad^f

high-speed shaft
eje^M de alta velocidad^f

speed-increasing gearbox
multiplicador^M

production of electricity from wind energy
producción^f de electricidad^f por energía^f eólica

horizontal-axis wind turbine
turbina^f de viento^M de eje^M horizontal

high-tension electricity transmission
transporte^M de electricidad^f de alta tensión^f

transmission to consumers
transporte^M hacia los usuarios^M

voltage decrease
disminución^f de la tensión^f

energy integration to the transmission network
integración^f de energía^f a la red^f de transporte^M

second voltage increase
segundo aumento^M de tensión^f

first voltage increase
primer aumento^M de la tensión^f

ENERGY

SCIENCE

ciencia

CHEMISTRY   810

matter   810
chemical elements   812
laboratory equipment   815

PHYSICS: MECHANICS   816

gearing systems   816
double pulley system   816
lever   816

PHYSICS: ELECTRICITY AND MAGNETISM   817

magnetism   817
electrical circuit   818
generators   819
dry cells   820
electronics   820

PHYSICS: OPTICS   821

electromagnetic spectrum   821
wave   821
color synthesis   821
light waves trajectory   822
lenses   822
mirror   823
optical devices   823

MEASURING DEVICES   827

measure of temperature   827
measure of time   828
measure of weight   830
measure of distance   832
measure of thickness   832
measure of length   833
measure of angles   833

SCIENTIFIC SYMBOLS   834

chemistry   834
biology   834
International System of Units (SI)   835
Roman numerals   836
geometry   836
mathematics   837
graphic representations   838

matter

materia^F

atom
átomo^M

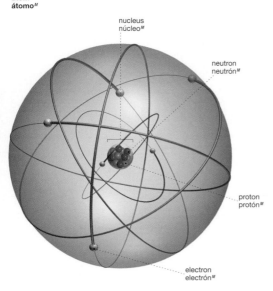

nucleus
núcleo^M

neutron
neutrón^M

proton
protón^M

electron
electrón^M

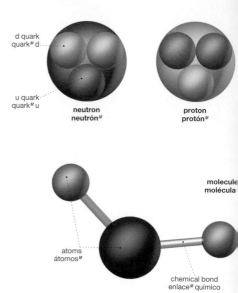

d quark
quark^M d

u quark
quark^M u

neutron
neutrón^M

proton
protón^M

molecule
molécula

atoms
átomos^M

chemical bond
enlace^M químico

states of matter
estados^M **de la materia**^F

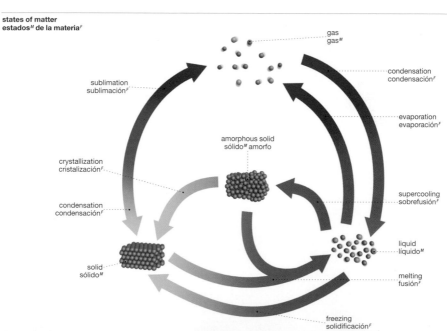

gas
gas^M

sublimation
sublimación^F

condensation
condensación^F

evaporation
evaporación^F

crystallization
cristalización^F

amorphous solid
sólido^M amorfo

supercooling
sobrefusión^F

condensation
condensación^F

liquid
líquido^M

solid
sólido^M

melting
fusión^F

freezing
solidificación^F

SCIENCE

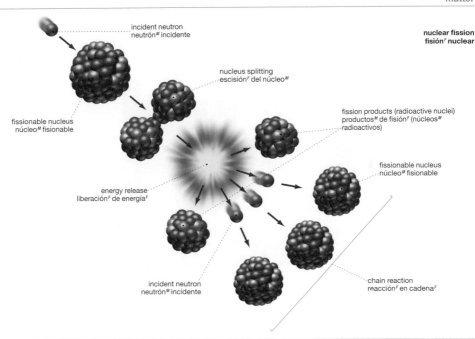

nuclear fission
fisión^F nuclear

incident neutron
neutrón^M incidente

nucleus splitting
escisión^F del núcleo^M

fission products (radioactive nuclei)
productos^M de fisión^F (núcleos^M
radioactivos)

fissionable nucleus
núcleo^M fisionable

fissionable nucleus
núcleo^M fisionable

energy release
liberación^F de energía^F

incident neutron
neutrón^M incidente

chain reaction
reacción^F en cadena^F

heat transfer
transmisión^F de calor^M

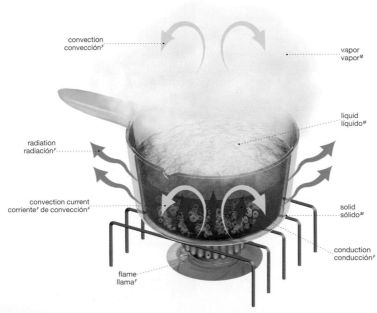

convection
convección^F

vapor
vapor^M

liquid
líquido^M

radiation
radiación^F

convection current
corriente^F de convección^F

solid
sólido^M

conduction
conducción^F

flame
llama^F

SCIENCE

chemical elements

elementos[M] químicos

periodic table of elements
tabla[F] periódica de los elementos[M]

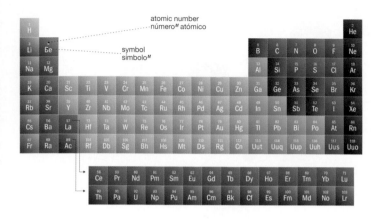

atomic number
número[M] atómico

symbol
símbolo[M]

other metals
otros metales[M]

13 Al	aluminum aluminio[M]
31 Ga	gallium galio[M]
49 In	indium indio[M]
50 Sn	tin estaño[M]
81 Tl	thallium talio[M]
82 Pb	lead plomo[M]
83 Bi	bismuth bismuto[M]
84 Po	polonium polonio[M]
113 Uut	ununtrium ununtrio[M]
114 Uuq	ununquadium ununquadio[M]
115 Uup	ununpentium ununpentio[M]
116 Uuh	ununhexium ununhexio[M]

1 H	hydrogen hidrógeno[M]

semimetals (metalloids)
semimetales[M] (metaloides[M])

5 B	boron boro[M]
14 Si	silicon silicio[M]
32 Ge	germanium germanio[M]
33 As	arsenic arsénico[M]
34 Se	selenium selenio[M]
51 Sb	antimony antimonio[M]
52 Te	tellurium telurio[M]

alkali metals
metales[M] alcalinos

3 Li	lithium litio[M]
11 Na	sodium sodio[M]
19 K	potassium potasio[M]
37 Rb	rubidium rubidio[M]
55 Cs	cesium cesio[M]
87 Fr	francium francio[M]

alkaline earth metals
metales[M] alcalinotérreos

4 Be	beryllium berilio[M]
12 Mg	magnesium magnesio[M]
20 Ca	calcium calcio[M]
38 Sr	strontium estroncio[M]
56 Ba	barium bario[M]
88 Ra	radium radio[M]

SCIENCE

transition metals
metales ^{M} de transición ^{F}

30 zinc
Zn cinc ^{M}

21 scandium
Sc escandio ^{M}

22 titanium
Ti titanio ^{M}

23 vanadium
V vanadio ^{M}

24 chromlum
Cr cromo ^{M}

25 manganese
Mn manganeso ^{M}

26 iron
Fe hierro ^{M}

27 cobalt
Co cobalto ^{M}

28 nickel
Ni níquel ^{M}

29 copper
Cu cobre ^{M}

39 yttrium
Y itrio ^{M}

40 zirconium
Zr zirconio ^{M}

41 niobium
Nb niobio ^{M}

42 molybdenum
Mo molibdeno ^{M}

43 technetium
Tc tecnecio ^{M}

44 ruthenium
Ru rutenio ^{M}

45 rhodium
Rh rodio ^{M}

46 palladium
Pd paladio ^{M}

47 silver
Ag plata ^{F}

48 cadmium
Cd cadmio ^{M}

72 hafnium
Hf hafnio ^{M}

73 tantalum
Ta tántalo ^{M}

74 tungsten
W tungsteno ^{M}

74 rhenium
Re renio ^{M}

76 osmium
Os osmio ^{M}

77 iridium
Ir iridio ^{M}

78 platinum
Pt platino ^{M}

79 gold
Au oro ^{M}

80 mercury
Hg mercurio ^{M}

104 rutherfordium
Rf rutherfodio ^{M}

105 dubnium
Db dubnio ^{M}

106 seaborgium
Sg seaborgio ^{M}

107 bohrium
Bh bohrio ^{M}

108 hassium
Hs hassio ^{M}

109 meitnerium
Mt meitnerio ^{M}

110 darmstadtium
Ds darmstadtio ^{M}

111 roentgenium
Rg roentgenio ^{M}

112 copernicium
Cn ununbio ^{M}

nonmetals
no metales ^{M}

6 carbon
C carbón ^{M}

7 nitrogen
N nitrógeno ^{M}

8 oxygen
O oxígeno ^{M}

9 fluorine
F flúor ^{M}

15 phosphorus
P fósforo ^{M}

16 sulfur
S azufre ^{M}

17 chlorine
Cl cloro ^{M}

35 bromine
Br bromo ^{M}

53 iodine
I yodo ^{M}

85 astatine
At ástato ^{M}

117 ununseptium
Uus ununseptio ^{M}

chemical elements

noble gases
gases^M **nobles**

| 2 He | helium helio^M | 18 Ar | argon argón^M | 54 Xe | xenon xenón^M | 118 Uuo | ununoctium ununoctio^M |
| 10 Ne | neon neón^M | 36 Kr | krypton criptón^M | 86 Rn | radon radón^M | | |

lanthanides (rare earth)
lantánidos^M **(tierras**^{F} **raras)**

57 La	lanthanum lantano^M	61 Pm	promethium promecio^M	65 Tb	terbium terbio^M	69 Tm	thulium tulio^M
58 Ce	cerium cerio^M	62 Sm	samarium samario^M	66 Dy	dysprosium disprosio^M	70 Yb	ytterbium iterbio^M
59 Pr	praseodymium praseodimio^M	63 Eu	europium europio^M	67 Ho	holmium holmio^M	71 Lu	lutetium lutecio^M
60 Nd	neodymium neodimio^M	64 Gd	gadolinium gadolinio^M	68 Er	erbium erbio^M		

actinides
actínidos^M **(tierras**^{F}
raras)

89 Ac	actinium actino^M	93 Np	neptunium neptunio^M	97 Bk	berkelium berquelio^M	101 Md	mendelevium mendelevio^M
90 Th	thorium torio^M	94 Pu	plutonium plutonio^M	98 Cf	californium californio^M	102 No	nobelium nobelio^M
91 Pa	protactinium protactinio^M	95 Am	americium americio^M	99 Es	einsteinium einstenio^M	103 Lr	lawrencium laurencio^M
92 U	uranium uranio^M	96 Cm	curium curio^M	100 Fm	fermium fermio^M		

laboratory equipment
material^M de laboratorio^M

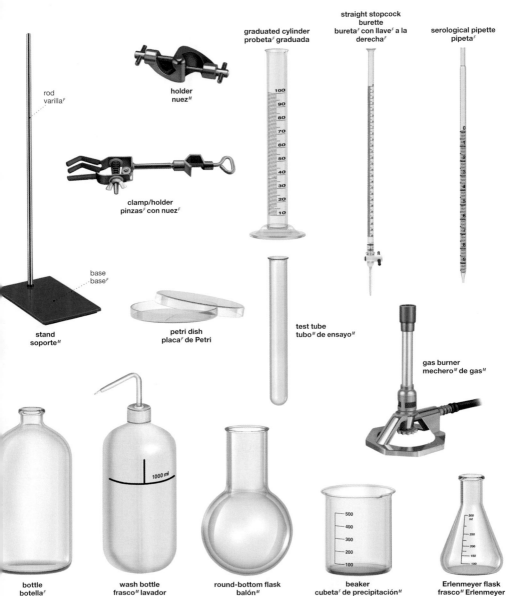

rod
varilla^F

holder
nuez^M

clamp/holder
pinzas^F con nuez^F

base
base^F

stand
soporte^M

petri dish
placa^F de Petri

graduated cylinder
probeta^F graduada

test tube
tubo^M de ensayo^M

straight stopcock
burette
bureta^F con llave^F a la
derecha^F

serological pipette
pipeta^F

gas burner
mechero^M de gas^M

bottle
botella^F

wash bottle
frasco^M lavador

round-bottom flask
balón^M

beaker
cubeta^F de precipitación^M

Erlenmeyer flask
frasco^M Erlenmeyer

SCIENCE

gearing systems

sistemas^M de engranajes^F

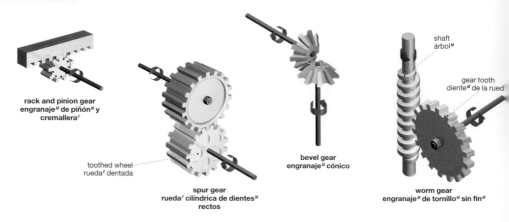

rack and pinion gear
engranaje^M de piñón^M y cremallera^F

toothed wheel
rueda^F dentada

spur gear
rueda^F cilíndrica de dientes^M rectos

bevel gear
engranaje^M cónico

shaft
árbol^M

gear tooth
diente^M de la rued

worm gear
engranaje^M de tornillo^M sin fin^M

double pulley system

sistema^F de doble polea^F

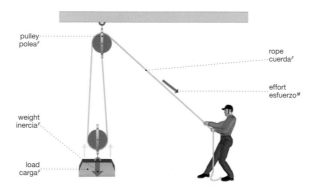

pulley
polea^F

rope
cuerda^F

effort
esfuerzo^M

weight
inercia^F

load
carga^F

lever

palanca^F

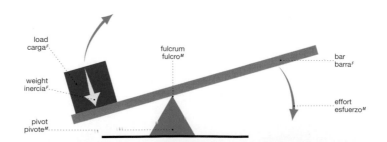

load
carga^F

fulcrum
fulcro^M

bar
barra^F

weight
inercia^F

effort
esfuerzo^M

pivot
pivote^M

magnetism

magnetismo^M

magnet
imán^M

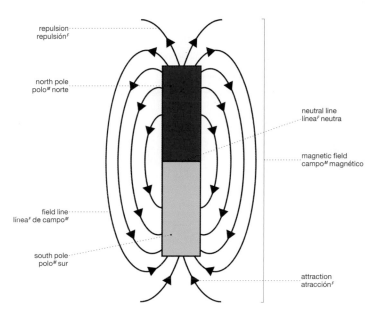

repulsion
repulsión^F

north pole
polo^M norte

neutral line
línea^F neutra

magnetic field
campo^M magnético

field line
línea^F de campo^M

south pole
polo^M sur

attraction
atracción^F

Earth's magnetic field
campo^M **magnético**
terrestre

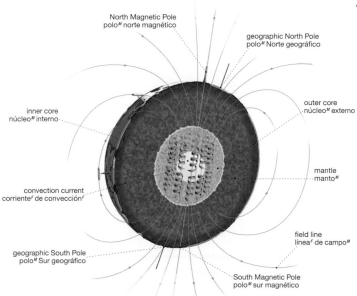

North Magnetic Pole
polo^M norte magnético

geographic North Pole
polo^M Norte geográfico

outer core
núcleo^M externo

inner core
núcleo^M interno

mantle
manto^M

convection current
corriente^F de convección^F

field line
línea^F de campo^M

geographic South Pole
polo^M Sur geográfico

South Magnetic Pole
polo^M sur magnético

SCIENCE

electrical circuit

circuito^M eléctrico

series circuit
circuito^M en serie^F

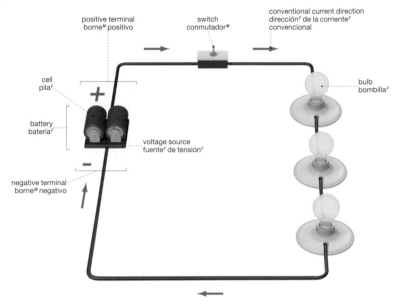

positive terminal
borne^M positivo

switch
conmutador^M

conventional current direction
dirección^F de la corriente^F
convencional

cell
pila^F

bulb
bombilla^F

battery
batería^F

voltage source
fuente^F de tensión^F

negative terminal
borne^M negativo

parallel circuit
circuito^M en paralelo^M

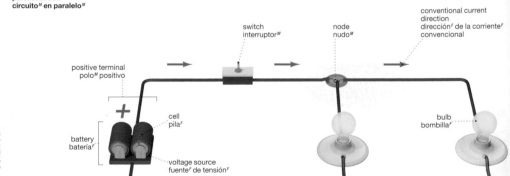

switch
interruptor^M

node
nudo^M

conventional current
direction
dirección^F de la corriente^F
convencional

positive terminal
polo^M positivo

cell
pila^F

bulb
bombilla^F

battery
batería^F

voltage source
fuente^F de tensión^F

negative terminal
borne^M negativo

branches
ramificaciones^F

SCIENCE

generators

generadores^M

dynamo
dínamo^M

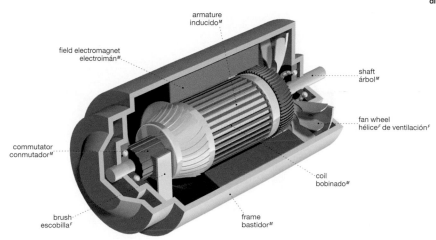

armature
inducido^M

field electromagnet
electroimán^M

shaft
árbol^M

fan wheel
hélice^F de ventilación^F

commutator
conmutador^M

coil
bobinado^M

brush
escobilla^F

frame
bastidor^M

alternator
alternador^M

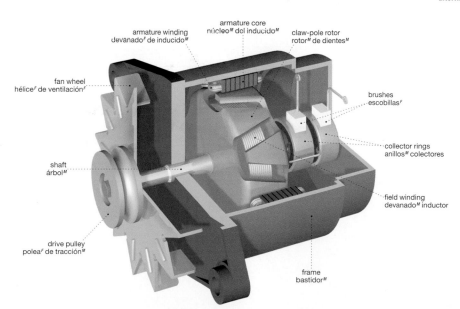

armature winding
devanado^F de inducido^M

armature core
núcleo^M del inducido^M

claw-pole rotor
rotor^M de dientes^M

fan wheel
hélice^F de ventilación^F

brushes
escobillas^F

collector rings
anillos^M colectores

shaft
árbol^M

field winding
devanado^M inductor

drive pulley
polea^F de tracción^M

frame
bastidor^M

SCIENCE

SCIENCE

dry cells
pilas^F secas

carbon-zinc cell
pila^F de carbón^M-cinc^M

alkaline manganese-zinc cell
pila^F alcalina de
manganeso^M-cinc

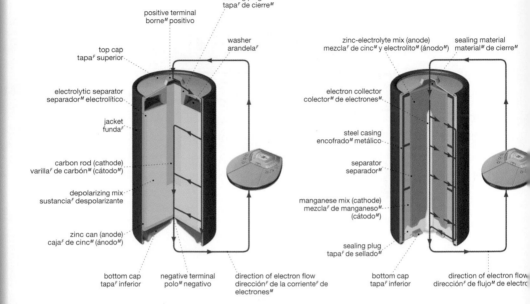

sealing plug
tapa^F de cierre^M

positive terminal
borne^M positivo

washer
arandela^F

top cap
tapa^F superior

electrolytic separator
separador^M electrolítico

jacket
funda^F

carbon rod (cathode)
varilla^F de carbón^M (cátodo^M)

depolarizing mix
sustancia^F despolarizante

zinc can (anode)
caja^F de cinc^M (ánodo^M)

bottom cap
tapa^F inferior

negative terminal
polo^M negativo

direction of electron flow
dirección^F de la corriente^F de
electrones^M

zinc-electrolyte mix (anode)
mezcla^F de cinc^M y electrolito^M (ánodo^M)

sealing material
material^M de cierre^M

electron collector
colector^M de electrones^M

steel casing
encofrado^M metálico

separator
separador^M

manganese mix (cathode)
mezcla^F de manganeso^M
(cátodo^M)

sealing plug
tapa^F de sellado^M

bottom cap
tapa^F inferior

direction of electron flow
dirección^F de flujo^M de electr

electronics
electrónica^F

printed circuit board
tarjeta^F de circuito^M
impreso

packaged integrated circuit
placa^F de circuito^M impreso

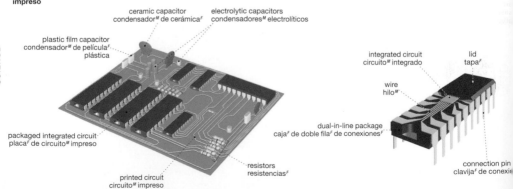

ceramic capacitor
condensador^M de cerámica^F

electrolytic capacitors
condensadores^M electrolíticos

plastic film capacitor
condensador^M de película^F
plástica

integrated circuit
circuito^M integrado

lid
tapa^F

wire
hilo^M

packaged integrated circuit
placa^F de circuito^M impreso

dual-in-line package
caja^F de doble fila^F de conexiones^F

resistors
resistencias^F

connection pin
clavija^F de conexi

printed circuit
circuito^M impreso

optical devices

microscopes
microscopios[M]

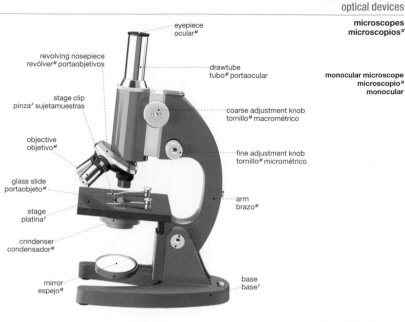

eyepiece
ocular[M]

revolving nosepiece
revólver[M] portaobjetivos

drawtube
tubo[M] portaocular

monocular microscope
microscopio[M]
monocular

stage clip
pinza[F] sujetamuestras

coarse adjustment knob
tornillo[M] macrométrico

objective
objetivo[M]

fine adjustment knob
tornillo[M] micrométrico

glass slide
portaobjeto[M]

stage
platina[F]

arm
brazo[M]

condenser
condensador[M]

mirror
espejo[M]

base
base[F]

binocular microscope
microscopio[M] **binocular**

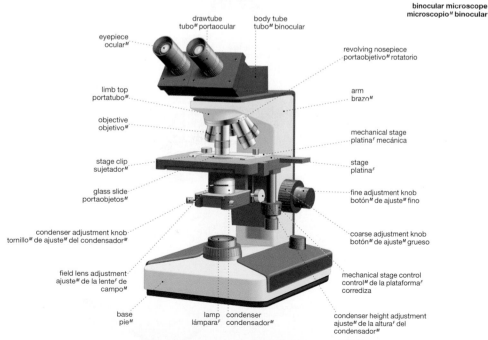

drawtube
tubo[M] portaocular

body tube
tubo[M] binocular

eyepiece
ocular[M]

revolving nosepiece
portaobjetivo[M] rotatorio

limb top
portatubo[M]

arm
brazo[M]

objective
objetivo[M]

mechanical stage
platina[F] mecánica

stage clip
sujetador[M]

stage
platina[F]

glass slide
portaobjetos[M]

fine adjustment knob
botón[M] de ajuste[M] fino

condenser adjustment knob
tornillo[M] de ajuste[M] del condensador[M]

coarse adjustment knob
botón[M] de ajuste[M] grueso

field lens adjustment
ajuste[M] de la lente[F] de
campo[M]

mechanical stage control
control[M] de la plataforma[F]
corrediza

base
pie[M]

lamp
lámpara[F]

condenser
condensador[M]

condenser height adjustment
ajuste[M] de la altura[F] del
condensador[M]

SCIENCE

optical devices

microscopes

cross section of an electron microscope
corte^M **transversal de un microscopio**^{M} **de**
electrones^M

electron gun
cañón^M de electrones^M

electron beam
haz^M de electrones^M

electron beam positioning
posición^F del haz^M de electrones^M

vacuum manifold
canalización^F de vacío^M

beam diameter reduction
reducción^F del diámetro^M del haz^M

condenser
condensador^M

aperture changer
abertura^F para el cambio^M de
gases^M

aperture diaphragm
abertura^F del diafragma^M

focusing lenses
lentes^F de enfoque^M

visual transmission
transmisión^F visual

stage
platina^F

vacuum chamber
cámara^F de vacío^M

electron microscope elements
elementos^M **del microscopio**^{M} **de**
electrones^M

liquid nitrogen tank
tanque^M del nitrógeno^M

electron gun
cañón^M de electrones^M

control visual display
pantalla^F de control^M

spectrometer
espectrómetro^M

data record system
sistema^M de registro^M de la
información^F

specimen chamber
cámara^F para la muestra^F

vacuum system console
consola^F para el sistema^M de
vacío^M

specimen positioning control
control^M de posición^F de la muestra^F

control panel
tablero^M de control^M

photographic chamber
cámara^F de fotografía^F

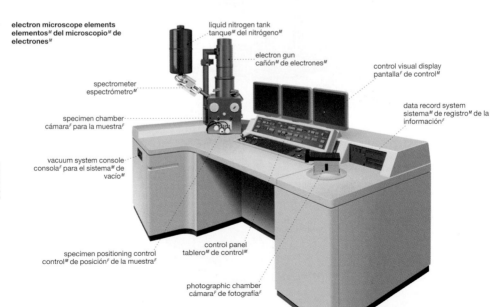

SCIENCE

measure of temperature

medición^r de la temperatura^r

alcohol thermometer
termómetro^M

clinical thermometer
termómetro^M clínico

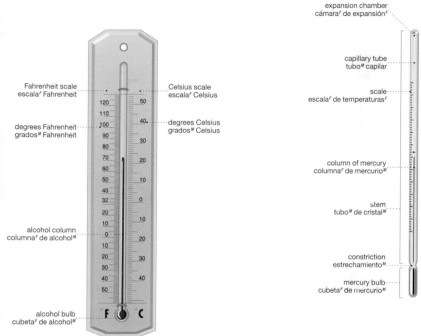

expansion chamber
cámara^r de expansión^r

Fahrenheit scale
escala^r Fahrenheit

Celsius scale
escala^r Celsius

capillary tube
tubo^M capilar

scale
escala^r de temperaturas^r

degrees Fahrenheit
grados^M Fahrenheit

degrees Celsius
grados^M Celsius

column of mercury
columna^r de mercurio^M

stem
tubo^M de cristal^M

alcohol column
columna^r de alcohol^M

constriction
estrechamiento^M

mercury bulb
cubeta^r de mercurio^M

alcohol bulb
cubeta^r de alcohol^M

cross section of a bimetallic
thermometer
sección^r de un termómetro^M
bimetálico

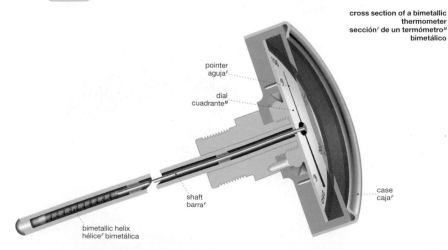

pointer
aguja^r

dial
cuadrante^M

case
caja^r

shaft
barra^r

bimetallic helix
hélice^r bimetálica

SCIENCE

measure of time

medición^F del tiempo^M

stopwatch
cronómetro^M

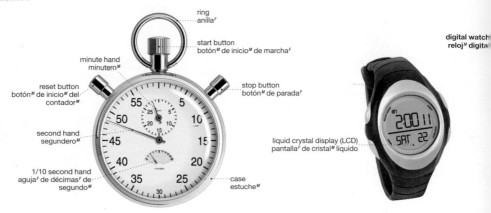

ring
anilla^F

start button
botón^M de inicio^M de marcha^F

minute hand
minutero^M

reset button
botón^M de inicio^M del
contador^M

stop button
botón^M de parada^F

second hand
segundero^M

liquid crystal display (LCD)
pantalla^F de cristal^M líquido

1/10 second hand
aguja^F de décimas^F de
segundo^M

case
estuche^M

digital watch
reloj^M digital

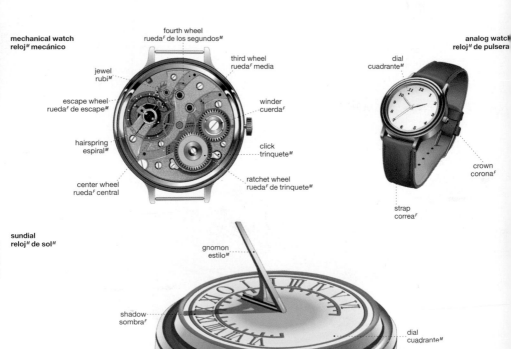

mechanical watch
reloj^M mecánico

fourth wheel
rueda^F de los segundos^M

third wheel
rueda^F media

jewel
rubí^M

escape wheel
rueda^F de escape^M

winder
cuerda^F

hairspring
espiral^M

click
trinquete^M

center wheel
rueda^F central

ratchet wheel
rueda^F de trinquete^M

analog watch
reloj^M de pulsera

dial
cuadrante^M

crown
corona^F

strap
correa^F

sundial
reloj^M de sol^M

gnomon
estilo^M

shadow
sombra^F

dial
cuadrante^M

SCIENCE

measure of time

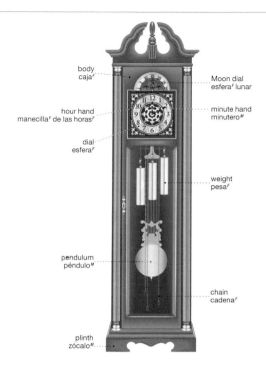

grandfather clock
reloj^M de péndulo^M

body
caja^F

Moon dial
esfera^F lunar

hour hand
manecilla^F de las horas^F

minute hand
minutero^M

dial
esfera^F

weight
pesa^F

pendulum
péndulo^M

chain
cadena^F

plinth
zócalo^M

weight-driven clock
mechanism
mecanismo^M del reloj^M de
pesas^F

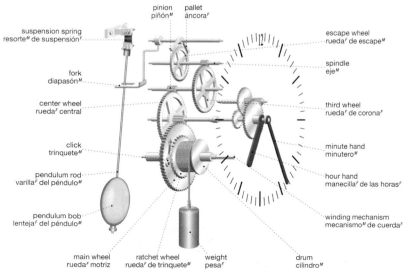

pinion
piñón^M

pallet
áncora^F

suspension spring
resorte^M de suspensión^F

escape wheel
rueda^F de escape^M

spindle
eje^M

fork
diapasón^M

center wheel
rueda^F central

third wheel
rueda^F de corona^F

click
trinquete^M

minute hand
minutero^M

pendulum rod
varilla^F del péndulo^M

hour hand
manecilla^F de las horas^F

pendulum bob
lenteja^F del péndulo^M

winding mechanism
mecanismo^M de cuerda^F

main wheel
rueda^F motriz

ratchet wheel
rueda^F de trinquete^M

weight
pesa^F

drum
cilindro^M

SCIENCE

graphic representations
representaciones gráficas
polygons
polígonos

angles
ángulos

trapezoid
trapecio*

rhombus
rombo*

right angle
ángulo* recto

square
cuadrado*

triangle
triángulo*

acute angle
ángulo* agudo

regular heptagon
heptágono* regular

regular hexagon
hexágono* regular

regular pentagon
pentágono* regular

quadrilateral
cuadrilátero*

parallelogram
paralelogramo*

circle
círculo*

arc
arco*

regular decagon
decágono* regular

obtuse angle
ángulo* obtuso

regular nonagon
nonágono* regular

regular octagon
octágono* regular

solids
cuerpos* sólidos

diameter
diámetro*

semicircle
semicírculo*

circumference
circunferencia*

cube
cubo*

sphere
esfera*

hemisphere
hemisferio*

torus
toro*

helix
hélice*

pie chart
gráfico* de sectores*

pyramid
pirámide*

cone
cono*

SOCIETY

sociedad

CITY 842

metropolitan area 842
downtown 844
street 846
office building 847
shopping mall 848
department store 850
convention center 852
hotel 854
common symbols 856

ECONOMY AND FINANCE 858

bank branch 858
examples of currency abbreviations 860
money and modes of payment 860

JUSTICE 862

court 862
prison 864

EDUCATION 866

library 866
school 868

common symbols

símbolos*ᴹ* de uso*ᴹ* común

men's restroom
servicios*ᴹ* para caballeros*ᴹ*

women's restroom
servicios*ᴹ* para señoras*ᶠ*

wheelchair access
acceso*ᴹ* para minusválidos*ᴹ*

no wheelchair access
prohibido usar silla*ᶠ* de ruedas

picnic area
zona*ᶠ* de comidas*ᶠ*
campestres

picnics prohibited
prohibido hacer comidas*ᶠ*
campestres

camping (tent)
zona*ᶠ* para acampar

camping prohibited
prohibido acampar

coffee shop
cafetería*ᶠ*

restaurant
restaurante*ᴹ*

service station
estación*ᶠ* de servicio*ᴹ*

camping (trailer)
zona*ᶠ* para caravanas*ᶠ*

camping (trailer and tent)
zona*ᶠ* para acampar y para
caravanas*ᶠ*

police
policía*ᶠ*

hospital
hospital*ᴹ*

first aid
puesto*ᴹ* de socorro*ᴹ*

pharmacy
farmacia*ᶠ*

fire extinguisher
extintor*ᴹ* de incendios*ᴹ*

escalator
escalera^F mecánica

stairs
escaleras^F

elevator
elevador^M

dogs prohibited
prohibido perros^M

car rental
alquiler^M de
automóviles^M

baggage lockers
taquillas^F de consigna^F

lodging
alojamiento^M

no smoking
prohibido fumar

bus stop
autobús^M

airport
aeropuerto^M

post office
correos^M

taxi transportation
servicio^M de taxis^M

telephone
teléfono^M

information
información^F

information
información^F

lost and found articles
oficina^F de objetos^M
perdidos

currency exchange
cambio^M

examples of currency abbreviations

ejemplos^M de abreviaciones^F de monedas^F

cent
centavo^M

euro
euro^M

peso
peso^M

pound
libra^F

dollar
dólar^M

rupee
rupia^F

new shekel
nuevo shekel^M

yen
yen^M

yuan
yuán^M

money and modes of payment

dinero^M y modos^M de pago^M

coin: obverse
moneda^F : anverso^M

edge
canto^M

date
fecha^F

coin: reverse
moneda^F : reverso^M

denomination
valor^M

rim
cordoncillo^M

check
cheque^M

traveler's check
cheque^M de viaje^M

money and modes of payment

Is of the issuing bank
iniciales^F del banco^M
emisor

security thread
hilo^M de seguridad^F

official signature
firma^F oficial

hologram foil strip
banda^F holográfica
metalizada

portrait
retrato^M

serial number
número^M de serie^F

watermark
filigrana^F

color shifting ink
tinta^F de color^M
cambiante

**banknote: front
billete^M: recto^M**

serial number
número^M de serie^F

motto
lema^M

name of the currency
nombre^M de la moneda^F

denomination
valor^M

**banknote: back
billete^M: verso^M**

**debit card
tarjeta^F de débito^M**

card number
número^M de tarjeta^F

magnetic stripe
banda^F magnética

cardholder's signature
firma^F del titular^M

chip
chip^M

card number
número^M de la tarjeta^F

**credit card
tarjeta^F de crédito^M**

cardholder's name
nombre^M del titular^M

expiration date
fecha^F de vencimiento^M

SOCIETY

court

tribunal^M

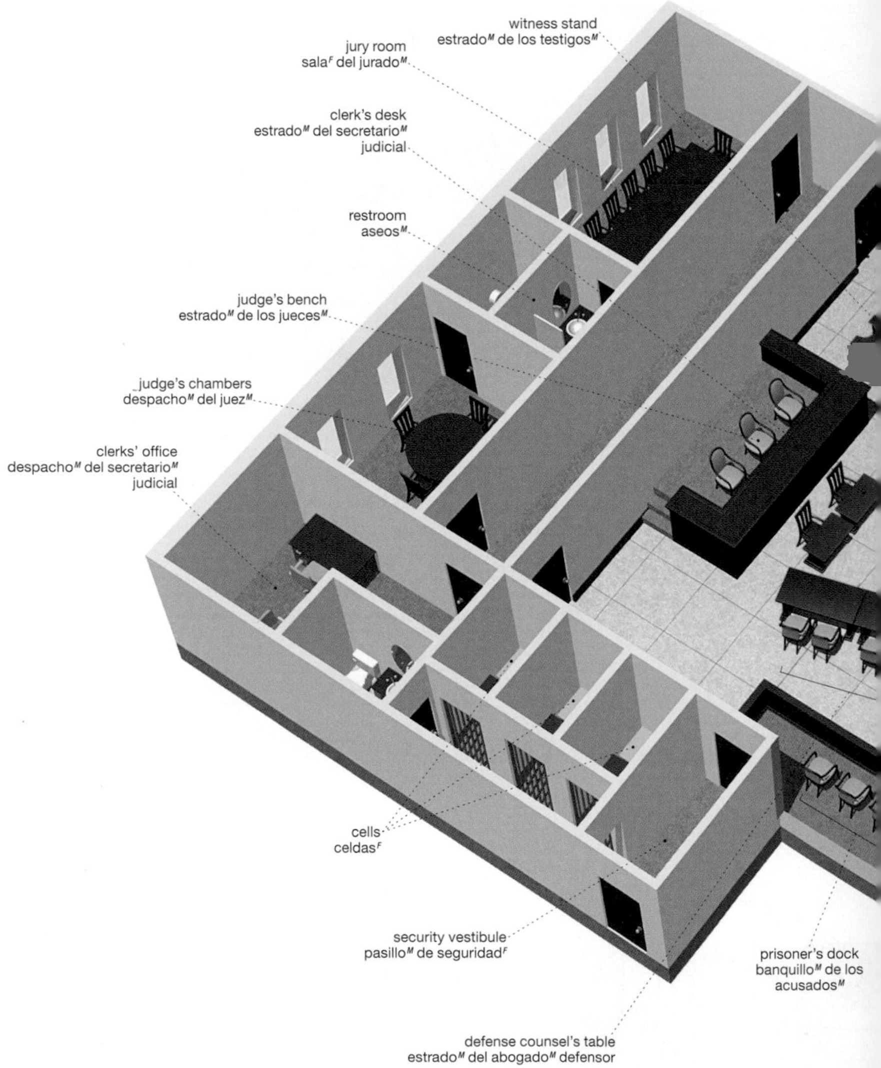

witness stand
estrado^M de los testigos^M

jury room
sala^F del jurado^M

clerk's desk
estrado^M del secretario^M
judicial

restroom
aseos^M

judge's bench
estrado^M de los jueces^M

judge's chambers
despacho^M del juez^M

clerks' office
despacho^M del secretario^M
judicial

cells
celdas^F

security vestibule
pasillo^M de seguridad^F

prisoner's dock
banquillo^M de los
acusados^M

defense counsel's table
estrado^M del abogado^M defensor

court

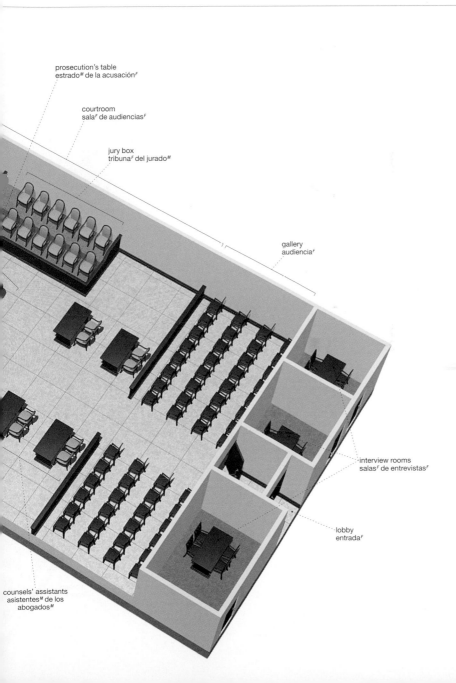

prosecution's table
estrado^M de la acusación^F

courtroom
sala^F de audiencias^F

jury box
tribuna^F del jurado^M

gallery
audiencia^F

interview rooms
salas^F de entrevistas^F

lobby
entrada^F

counsels' assistants
asistentes^M de los
abogados^M

prison
cárcel^F

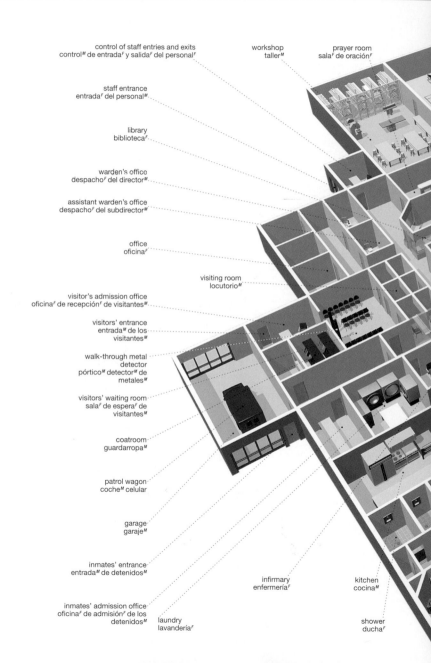

control of staff entries and exits
control^M de entrada^F y salida^F del personal^F

staff entrance
entrada^F del personal^M

library
biblioteca^F

warden's office
despacho^F del director^M

assistant warden's office
despacho^F del subdirector^M

office
oficina^F

visiting room
locutorio^M

visitor's admission office
oficina^F de recepción^F de visitantes^M

visitors' entrance
entrada^M de los visitantes^M

walk-through metal detector
pórtico^M detector^M de metales^M

visitors' waiting room
sala^F de espera^F de visitantes^M

coatroom
guardarropa^M

patrol wagon
coche^M celular

garage
garaje^M

inmates' entrance
entrada^M de detenidos^M

inmates' admission office
oficina^F de admisión^F de los detenidos^M

laundry
lavandería^F

workshop
taller^M

prayer room
sala^F de oración^F

infirmary
enfermería^F

kitchen
cocina^M

shower
ducha^F

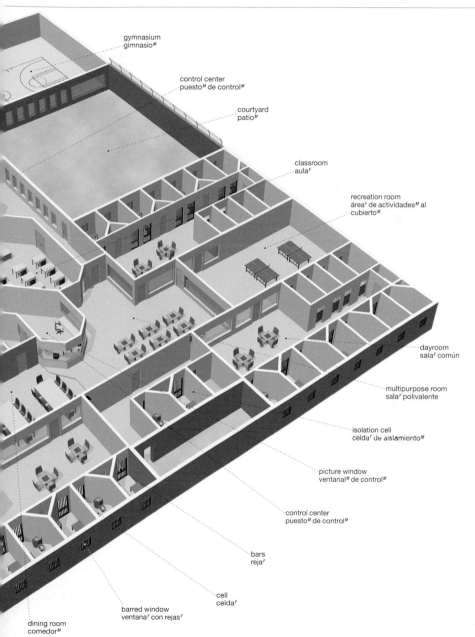

gymnasium
gimnasio^M

control center
puesto^M de control^M

courtyard
patio^M

classroom
aula^F

recreation room
área^F de actividades^M al
cubierto^M

dayroom
sala^F común

multipurpose room
sala^F polivalente

isolation cell
celda^F de aislamiento^M

picture window
ventanal^M de control^M

control center
puesto^M de control^M

bars
reja^F

cell
celda^F

barred window
ventana^F con rejas^F

dining room
comedor^M

library

biblioteca^F

monograph section
sección^M de monografías^F

technical services
servicios^M técnicos

reference books
libros^M de consulta^F

service entrance
entrada^F de servicio^M

director's office
despacho^M del director^M

librarian's office
despacho^M del
bibliotecario^M

microfilm reader
lector^M de microfilmes^M

microfilm room
sala^F de microfilmes^M

map library
sección^F cartográfica

computer workstations
puesto^M de
computadoras^F

children's books
libros^M para niños^M

reading room
sala^F de lectura^F

children's section
sección^F infantil

attendant's desk
escritorio^M del celador^M

auditorium
auditorio^M

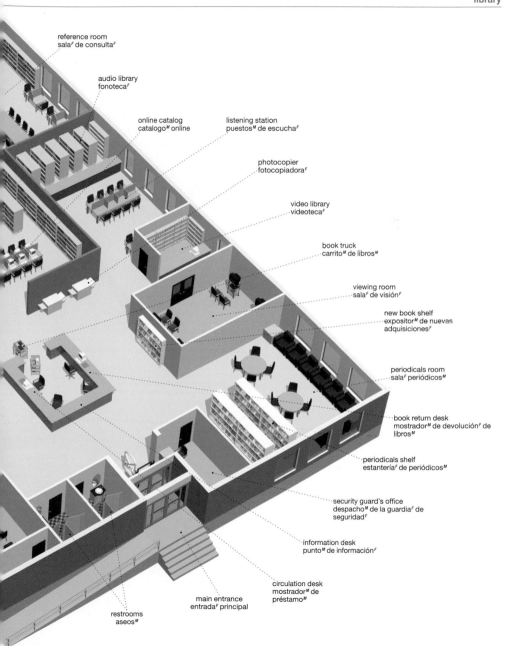

reference room
sala^F de consulta^F

audio library
fonoteca^F

online catalog
catalogo^M online

listening station
puestos^M de escucha^F

photocopier
fotocopiadora^F

video library
videoteca^F

book truck
carrito^M de libros^M

viewing room
sala^F de visión^F

new book shelf
expositor^M de nuevas
adquisiciones^F

periodicals room
sala^F periódicos^M

book return desk
mostrador^M de devolución^F de
libros^M

periodicals shelf
estantería^F de periódicos^M

security guard's office
despacho^M de la guardia^F de
seguridad^F

information desk
punto^M de información^F

circulation desk
mostrador^M de
préstamo^M

main entrance
entrada^F principal

restrooms
aseos^M

school

colegio^M

general view
vista^F **general**

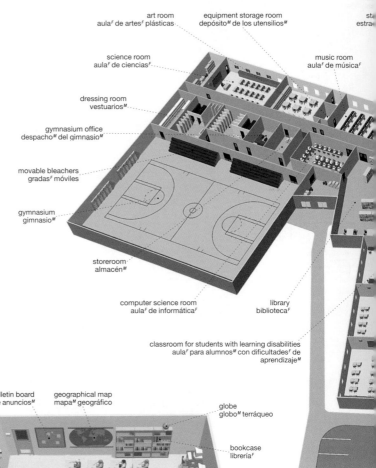

art room
aula^F de artes^F plásticas

equipment storage room
depósito^M de los utensilios^M

sta
estrac

science room
aula^F de ciencias^F

music room
aula^F de música^F

dressing room
vestuarios^M

gymnasium office
despacho^M del gimnasio^M

movable bleachers
gradas^F móviles

gymnasium
gimnasio^M

storeroom
almacén^M

computer science room
aula^F de informática^F

library
biblioteca^F

classroom
aula^F

classroom for students with learning disabilities
aula^F para alumnos^M con dificultades^F de
aprendizaje^M

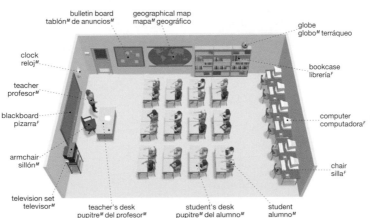

bulletin board
tablón^M de anuncios^M

geographical map
mapa^M geográfico

globe
globo^M terráqueo

clock
reloj^M

teacher
profesor^M

blackboard
pizarra^F

armchair
sillón^M

bookcase
librería^F

computer
computadora^F

chair
silla^F

television set
televisor^M

teacher's desk
pupitre^M del profesor^M

student's desk
pupitre^M del alumno^M

student
alumno^M

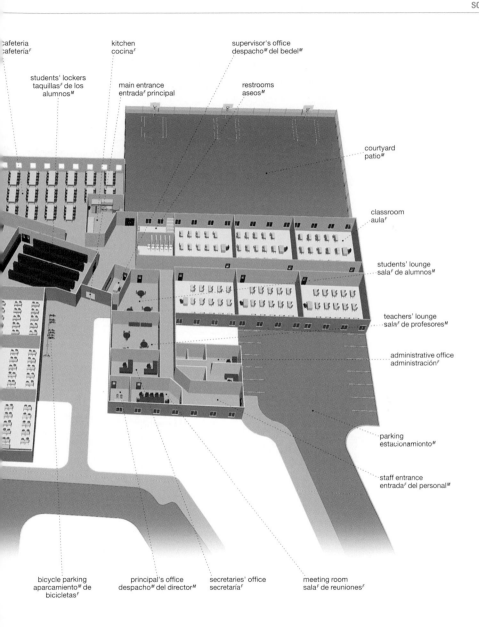

cafeteria
cafetería^F

students' lockers
taquillas^F de los
alumnos^M

kitchen
cocina^F

main entrance
entrada^F principal

supervisor's office
despacho^M del bedel^M

restrooms
aseos^M

courtyard
patio^M

classroom
aula^F

students' lounge
sala^F de alumnos^M

teachers' lounge
sala^F de profesores^M

administrative office
administración^F

parking
estacionamionto^M

staff entrance
entrada^F del personal^M

bicycle parking
aparcamiento^M de
bicicletas^F

principal's office
despacho^M del director^M

secretaries' office
secretaría^F

meeting room
sala^F de reuniones^F

chronology of religions

Cronología^r de las Religiones^r

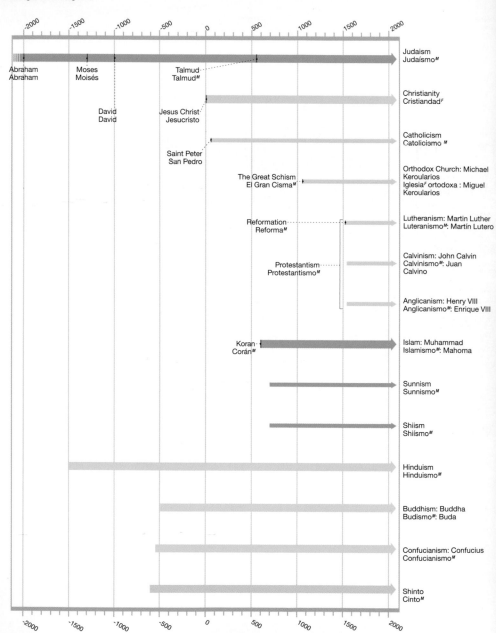

SOCIETY

church

iglesia^F

secondary altar
altar^M lateral

bell tower
campanario^M

Communion rail
comulgatorio^M

baptismal font
pila^F bautismal

Paschal candle
vela^F

votive offering
exvoto^M

stained glass window
vidriera^F

confessional
confesionario^M

sanctuary lamp
lámpara^F del santuario^M

crucifix
crucifijo^M

altarpiece
retablo^M

tabernacle
tabernáculo^M

statue
estatua^F

altar frontal
frontal^M

altar cross
cruz^F del altar^M

thurible
incensario^M

sacristy
sacristía^F

chalice
cáliz^M

lectern
atril^M

holy water font
pila^F de agua^F bendita

high altar
altar^M mayor

pulpit
púlpito^M

pew
banco^M

heraldry

shield divisions
divisiones^F **de los escudos**^M

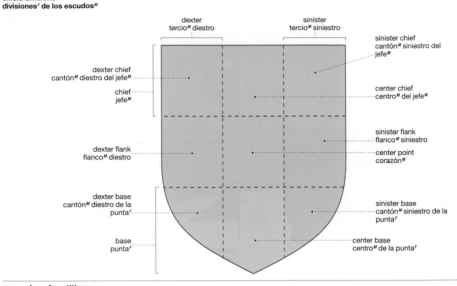

dexter
tercio^M diestro

sinister
tercio^M siniestro

sinister chief
cantón^M siniestro del
jefe^M

dexter chief
cantón^M diestro del jefe^M

chief
jefe^M

center chief
centro^M del jefe^M

sinister flank
flanco^M siniestro

dexter flank
flanco^M diestro

center point
corazón^M

dexter base
cantón^M diestro de la
punta^F

sinister base
cantón^M siniestro de la
punta^F

base
punta^F

center base
centro^M de la punta^F

examples of partitions
ejemplos^M **de**
particiones^F

per fess
escudo^M **cortado**

party
escudo^M **partido**

per bend
escudo^M **tronchado**

quarterly
escudo^M **acuartelado**

examples of ordinaries
ejemplos^M **de piezas**^F
honorables

chief
jefe^M

chevron
cheurón^M

pale
palo^M

cross
cruz^F

examples of metals
ejemplos^M de metales^M

examples of furs
ejemplos^M de forros^M

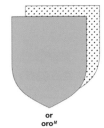

argent
plata^F

or
oro^M

ermine
armiño^M

vair
cerros^M

examples of charges
ejemplos^M de muebles^M

lion passant
león^M rampante

fleur-de-lis
flor^F de lis^F

eagle
águila^F

crescent
creciente^M

mullet
estrella^F

examples of colors
ejemplos^M de colores^M

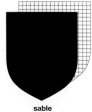

azure
azur^M

gules
gules^M

vert
sinople^M

purpure
púrpura^M

sable
sable^M

UN members flags

banderas^F de miembros^M de la ONU^F

Americas
Américas^F

1
Canada
Canadá^M

2
United States of
America
Estados^M Unidos de
América^F

3
Mexico
México^M

4
Honduras
Honduras^M

5
Guatemala
Guatemala^F

6
Belize
Belice^M

7
El Salvador
El Salvador^M

8
Nicaragua
Nicaragua^F

9
Costa Rica
Costa Rica^F

10
Panama
Panamá^M

11
Colombia
Colombia^F

12
Venezuela
Venezuela^F

13
Guyana
Guyana^F

14
Suriname
Surinam^M

15
Ecuador
Ecuador^M

16
Peru
Perú^M

17
Brazil
Brasil^M

18
Bolivia
Bolivia^F

19
Paraguay
Paraguay^M

20
Chile
Chile^M

21
Argentina
Argentina^F

22
Uruguay
Uruguay^M

Caribbean Islands
islas^F **del Caribe**^M

23
Bahamas
Bahamas^F

24
Cuba
Cuba^F

25
Jamaica
Jamaica^F

26
Haiti
Haití^M

27
Saint Kitts and Nevis
Saint Kitts and Nevis^M

28
Antigua and Barbuda
Antigua^F y Barbuda^F

29
Dominica
Dominica^F

30
Saint Lucia
Santa Lucía^F

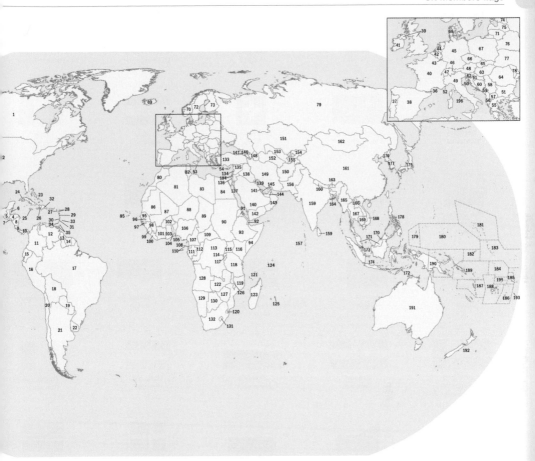

31 Saint Vincent and the Grenadines
an Vicente y las Grenadinas[f]

32 Dominican Republic
República[f] Dominicana

33 Barbados
Barbados[f]

34 Grenada
Granada[f]

35 Trinidad and Tobago
Trinidad[f] y Tobago[M]

SOCIETY

Europe
Europa[f]

36 Andorra
Principado[M] de Andorra[f]

37 Portugal
Portugal[M]

38 Spain
España[f]

39 United Kingdom of Great Britain and Northern Ireland
Reino[M] Unido de Gran Bretaña[f] e Irlanda[f] del Norte[M]

UN members flags

40 France
Francia[F]

41 Ireland
Irlanda[F]

42 Belgium
Bélgica[F]

43 Luxembourg
Luxemburgo[M]

44 Netherlands
Países[M] Bajos

45 Germany
Alemania[F]

46 Liechtenstein
Liechtenstein[M]

47 Switzerland
Suiza[F]

48 Austria
Austria[F]

49 Italy
Italia[F]

50 San Marino
República[F] de San
Marino[M]

51 Bulgaria
Bulgaria[F]

52 Monaco
Principado[M] de
Mónaco[M]

53 Malta
Malta[F]

54 Cyprus
Chipre[M]

55 Greece
Grecia[F]

56 Albania
Albania[F]

57 Macedonia
Antigua República[F] Yugoslava de
Macedonia[F]

58 Serbia
Serbia[F]

59 Montenegro
Montenegro[M]

60 Bosnia and
Herzegovina
Bosnia[F] y Herzegovina[F]

61 Croatia
Croacia[F]

62 Slovenia
Eslovenia[F]

63 Hungary
Hungría[F]

64 Romania
Rumanía[F]

65 Slovakia
Eslovaquia[F]

66 Czech Republic
República[F] Checa

67 Poland
Polonia[F]

68 Denmark
Dinamarca[F]

69 Iceland
Islandia[F]

70 Norway
Noruega[F]

71 Lithuania
Lituania[F]

72 Sweden
Suecia[F]

73 Finland
Finlandia[F]

74 Estonia
Estonia[F]

SOCIETY

75 Latvia
Letonia[F]

76 Belarus
Bielorrusia[F]

77 Ukraine
Ucrania[F]

78 Moldova
Moldavia[F]

79 Russia
Federación[F] Rusa

Africa
África^F

80
Morocco
Marruecos^M

81
Algeria
Argelia^F

82
Tunisia
Túnez^M

83
Libya
Libia^F

84
Egypt
Egipto^M

85
Cape Verde
Islas^F **de Cabo**^M **Verde**

86
Mauritania
Mauritania^F

87
Mali
República^F **de Malí**

88
Niger
Níger^M

89
Chad
Chad^M

90
Sudan
Sudán^M

91
Eritrea
Eritrea^F

92
Djibouti
Yibuti^M

93
Ethiopia
Etiopía^F

94
Somalia
Somalia^F

95
Senegal
Senegal^M

96
Gambia
Gambia^M

97
Guinea-Bissau
Guinea-Bissau^F

98
Guinea
Guinea^F

99
Sierra Leone
Sierra^F **Leona**

100
Liberia
Liberia^F

101
Côte d'Ivoire
Costa de Marfil^F

102
Burkina Faso
Burkina Faso^M

103
Ghana
Ghana^F

104
Togo
Togo^M

105
Benin
Benín^M

106
Nigeria
Nigeria^F

107
Cameroon
Camerún^M

108
Equatorial Guinea
Guinea^F **Ecuatorial**

109
Central African
Republic
República^F
Centroafricana

110
Sao Tome and Principe
Santo Tomé y Príncipe^M

111
Gabon
Gabón^M

112
Congo
Congo^M

113
Democratic Republic of the
Congo
República^F **Democrática del**
Congo^M

114
Rwanda
Ruanda^M

115
Uganda
Uganda^F

116
Kenya
Kenia^F

117
Burundi
Burundi^M

118
Tanzania
Tanzania^F

SOCIETY

UN members flags

119 Mozambique
Mozambique*M*

120 Swaziland
Suazilandia*M*

121 Comoros
Comoras*F*

122 Zambia
Zambia*F*

123 Madagascar
Madagascar*M*

124 Seychelles
Seychelles*F*

125 Mauritius
Mauricio*F*

126 Malawi
Malawi*M*

127 Zimbabwe
Zimbabwe*M*

128 Angola
Angola*F*

129 Namibia
Namibia*F*

130 Botswana
Bostuana*M*

131 Lesotho
Lesoto*M*

132 South Africa
Sudáfrica*F*

Asia
Asia*F*

133 Turkey
Turquía*F*

134 Lebanon
Líbano*M*

135 Syria
Siria*F*

136 Israel
Israel*M*

137 Jordan
Jordania*F*

138 Iraq
Iraq*M*

139 Kuwait
Kuwait*M*

140 Saudi Arabia
Arabia Saudí*F*

141 Bahrain
Bahrein*M*

142 Yemen
Yemen*M*

143 Oman
Omán*M*

144 United Arab Emirates
Emiratos*M* Árabes
Unidos

145 Qatar
Qatar*M*

146 Georgia
Georgia*F*

147 Armenia
Armenia*F*

148 Azerbaijan
Azerbaiyán*M*

149 Iran
Irán*M*

150 Afghanistan
Afganistán*M*

151 Kazakhstan
Kazajistán*M*

152 Turkmenistan
Turkmenistán*M*

153 Uzbekistan
Uzbekistán*M*

154 Kyrgyzstan
Kirguizistán*M*

155 Tajikistan
Tayikistán*M*

156 Pakistan
Pakistán*M*

157 Maldives
Maldivas*F*

UN members flags

158
India
India^F

159
Sri Lanka
Sri Lanka^M

160
Nepal
Nepal^M

161
China
China^F

162
Mongolia
Mongolia^F

163
Bhutan
Bután^M

164
Bangladesh
Bangladesh^M

165
Myanmar
Myanmar^M

166
Laos
Laos^M

167
Thailand
Tailandia^F

168
Vietnam
Vietnam^M

169
Cambodia
Camboya^F

170
Brunei
Brunei^M

171
Malaysia
Malasia^F

172
East Timor
Timor^M Oriental

173
Singapore
Singapur^M

174
Indonesia
Indonesia^F

175
Japan
Japón^M

176
Democratic People's Republic of Korea
República^F Democrática Popular de Corea^F

177
Republic of Korea
República^F de Corea^F

Oceania
Oceanía^F

178
Philippines
Filipinas^F

179
Palau
Palau^M

180
Micronesia
Micronesia^F

181
Marshall Islands
Islas^F Marshall

182
Nauru
Nauru^M

183
Kiribati
Kiribati^M

184
Tuvalu
Tuvalu^M

185
Samoa
Samoa^F

186
Tonga
Tonga^M

187
Vanuatu
Vanuatu^M

188
Fiji
Fiji^F

189
Solomon Islands
Islas Salomón^F

190
Papua New Guinea
Papúa Nueva Guinea^F

191
Australia
Australia^F

192
New Zealand
Nueva Zelanda^F

UN observers flags

banderas*f* de observadores*M* de la ONU*f*

193

Cook Islands
Islas*f* Cook

194

Palestine
Palestina*f*

195

Niue
Niue

196

Vatican City State
Ciudad*f* del Vaticano*M*

international organizations flags

banderas*f* de organizaciones*f* internacionales

United Nations (UN)
Organización*f* de las Naciones*f* Unidas
(ONU)

United Nations Educational, Scientific and Cultural Organization
(UNESCO)
Organización*f* de las Naciones*f* Unidas para la Educación*f*, la Ciencia*f* y
la Cultura*f* (UNESCO)

International Olympic Committee (IOC)
Comité*M* Olímpico Internacional (COI)

European Union (EU)
Unión*f* Europea (UE)

Commonwealth
Commonwealth*f*

Red Cross
Cruz*f* Roja

Red Crescent
Media Luna*f* Roja

North Atlantic Treaty Organization (NATO)
Organización*f* del Tratado*M* del Atlántico*M* Norte
(OTAN)

International Organisation of La Francophonie
Organización*f* internacional de la Francofonía*f*

Sovereign Military Order of Malta
Orden*f* de Malta*f*

African Union
Unión*f* africana

League of Arab States
Liga*f* de los Estados*M*
árabes

Organisation of the Islamic Conference
Organización*f* de la conferencia*f* Islámica

SOCIETY

weapons in the Stone Age

polished stone hand axe
hacha^F de piedra^F pulida

flint arrowhead
punta^F de flecha^F de sílex^M

flint knife
cuchillo^M de sílex^M

weapons in the age of the Romans

Roman legionnaire
legionario^M romano

crest
penacho^M

cuirass
loriga^F

shield
escudo^M

gladius
espada^F

javelin
jabalina^F

tunic
túnica^F

sandal
sandalia^F

Gallic warrior
guerrero^M galo

helmet
casco^M

shield
escudo^M

breeches
pantalones^M

spear
lanza^F

SOCIETY

armor

armadura^F

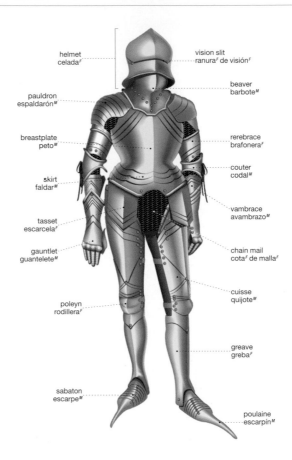

helmet
celada^F

vision slit
ranura^F de visión^F

beaver
barbote^M

pauldron
espaldarón^M

rerebrace
brafonera^F

breastplate
peto^M

couter
codal^M

skirt
faldar^M

vambrace
avambrazo^M

tasset
escarcela^F

chain mail
cota^F de malla^F

gauntlet
guantelete^M

cuisse
quijote^M

poleyn
rodillera^F

greave
greba^F

sabaton
escarpe^M

poulaine
escarpín^M

helmet
yelmo^M

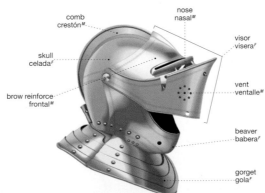

comb
crestón^M

nose
nasal^M

visor
visera^F

skull
celada^F

brow reinforce
frontal^M

vent
ventalle^M

beaver
babera^F

gorget
gola^F

SOCIETY

bows and crossbow

arcos^M y ballesta^F

crossbow
ballesta^F

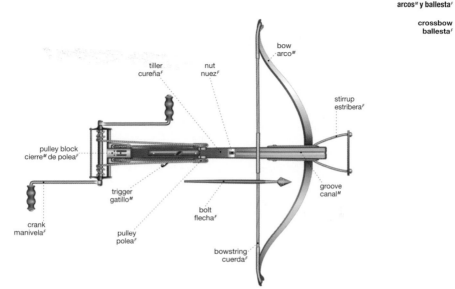

bow
arco^M

tiller
cureña^F

nut
nuez^F

stirrup
estribera^F

pulley block
cierre^M de polea^F

trigger
gatillo^M

groove
canal^M

crank
manivela^F

pulley
polea^F

bolt
flecha^F

bowstring
cuerda^F

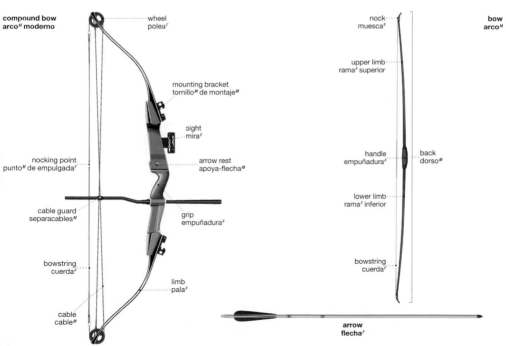

compound bow
arco^M moderno

wheel
polea^F

nock
muesca^F

bow
arco^M

upper limb
rama^F superior

mounting bracket
tornillo^M de montaje^M

sight
mira^F

nocking point
punto^M de empulgada^F

arrow rest
apoya-flecha^M

handle
empuñadura^F

back
dorso^M

cable guard
separacables^M

grip
empuñadura^F

lower limb
rama^F inferior

bowstring
cuerda^F

bowstring
cuerda^F

limb
pala^F

cable
cable^M

arrow
flecha^F

thrusting and cutting weapons

armas[F] **blancas**

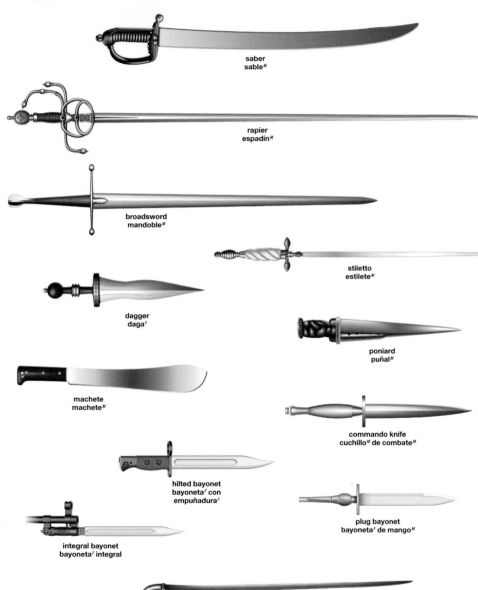

saber
sable[M]

rapier
espadín[M]

broadsword
mandoble[M]

stiletto
estilete[M]

dagger
daga[F]

poniard
puñal[M]

machete
machete[M]

commando knife
cuchillo[M] de combate[M]

hilted bayonet
bayoneta[F] con
empuñadura[F]

plug bayonet
bayoneta[F] de mango[M]

integral bayonet
bayoneta[F] integral

socket bayonet
bayoneta[F] de cubo[M]

hunting arms
armas^F de caza^F

rifle (rifled bore)
rifle^M

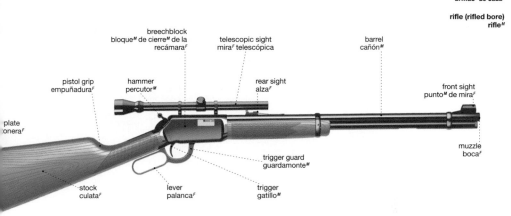

breechblock
bloque^M de cierre^M de la recámara^F

telescopic sight
mira^F telescópica

barrel
cañón^M

pistol grip
empuñadura^F

hammer
percutor^M

rear sight
alza^F

front sight
punto^M de mira^F

plate
onera^F

muzzle
boca^F

trigger guard
guardamonte^M

stock
culata^F

lever
palanca^F

trigger
gatillo^M

shotgun (smooth bore)
escopeta^F

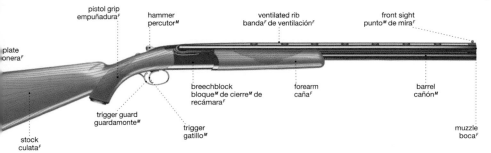

pistol grip
empuñadura^F

hammer
percutor^M

ventilated rib
banda^F de ventilación^F

front sight
punto^M de mira^F

plate
onera^F

breechblock
bloque^M de cierre^M de recámara^F

forearm
caña^F

barrel
cañón^M

trigger guard
guardamonte^M

trigger
gatillo^M

stock
culata^F

muzzle
boca^F

cartridge (rifle)
cartucho^M de rifle^M

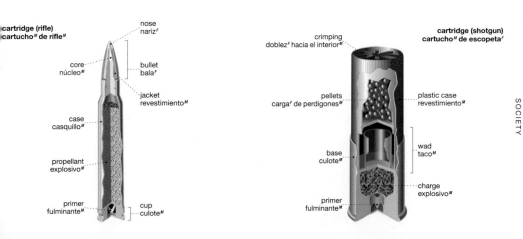

nose
nariz^F

core
núcleo^M

bullet
bala^F

jacket
revestimiento^M

case
casquillo^M

propellant
explosivo^M

primer
fulminante^M

cup
culote^M

cartridge (shotgun)
cartucho^M de escopeta^F

crimping
doblez^F hacia el interior^M

pellets
carga^F de perdigones^M

plastic case
revestimiento^M

base
culote^M

wad
taco^M

primer
fulminante^M

charge
explosivo^M

SOCIETY

handguns

pistolas^F

pistol
pistola^F

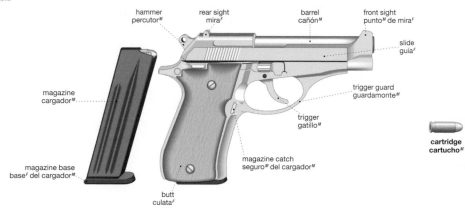

hammer
percutor^M

rear sight
mira^F

barrel
cañón^M

front sight
punto^M de mira^F

slide
guía^F

magazine
cargador^M

trigger guard
guardamonte^M

trigger
gatillo^M

**cartridge
cartucho^M**

magazine base
base^F del cargador^M

magazine catch
seguro^M del cargador^M

butt
culata^F

revolver
revólver^M

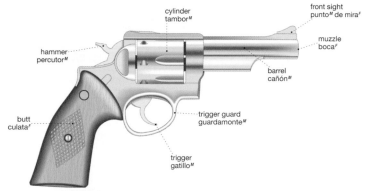

cylinder
tambor^M

front sight
punto^M de mira^F

hammer
percutor^M

muzzle
boca^F

barrel
cañón^M

butt
culata^F

trigger guard
guardamonte^M

trigger
gatillo^M

electroshock weapon
pistola^F eléctrica

replaceable cartridge
cartucho^M recargable

trigger
gatillo^M

seventeenth century firearms

armas^F de fuego^M del siglo^M XVII

harquebus
arcabuz^M

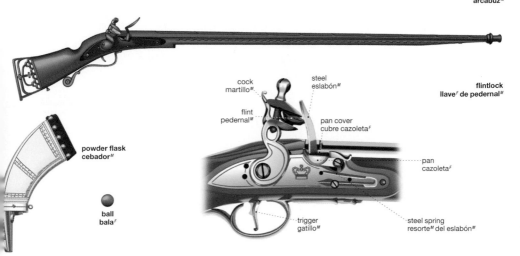

cock
martillo^M

steel
eslabón^M

flint
pedernal^M

pan cover
cubre cazoleta^F

flintlock
llave^F de pedernal^M

powder flask
cebador^M

pan
cazoleta^F

ball
bala^F

trigger
gatillo^M

steel spring
resorte^M del eslabón^M

seventeenth century cannon and mortar

cañón^M y mortero^M del siglo^M XVII

projectiles
proyectiles^M

firing accessories
accesorios^M de disparo^M

solid shot
bala^F sólida

hollow shot
bala^F con perdigones^M

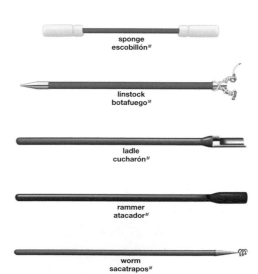

sponge
escobillón^M

linstock
botafuego^M

ladle
cucharón^M

rammer
atacador^M

grapeshot
metralla^F

bar shot
bala^F de barra^F

worm
sacatrapos^M

seventeenth century cannon and mortar

section of a muzzle loading
corte^F de un cañón^M de avancarga^F

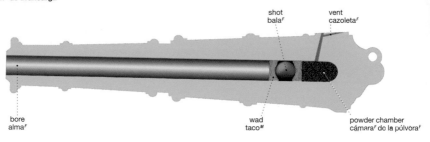

shot
bala^F

vent
cazoleta^F

bore
alma^F

wad
taco^M

powder chamber
cámara^F de la pólvora^F

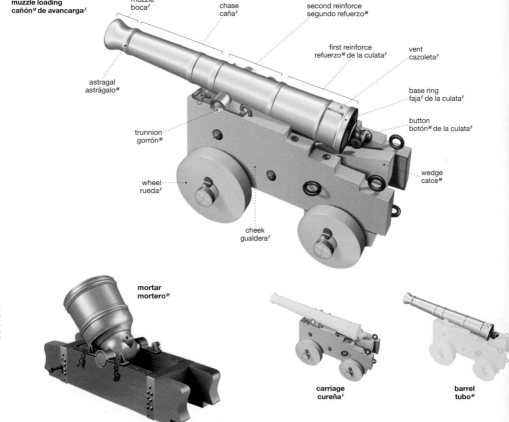

muzzle loading
cañón^M de avancarga^F

muzzle
boca^F

chase
caña^F

second reinforce
segundo refuerzo^M

first reinforce
refuerzo^M de la culata^F

vent
cazoleta^F

astragal
astrágalo^M

base ring
faja^F de la culata^F

button
botón^M de la culata^F

trunnion
gorrón^M

wedge
calce^M

wheel
rueda^F

cheek
gualdera^F

mortar
mortero^M

carriage
cureña^F

barrel
tubo^M

assault weapons
armasᶠ de asaltoᴹ

submachine gun
metralletaᶠ

rear sight
alzaᶠ

front sight
puntoᴹ de miraᶠ

barrel
cañónᴹ

pistol grip
pistoleteᴹ

trigger
gatilloᴹ

trigger guard
guardamonteᴹ

magazine
cargadorᴹ

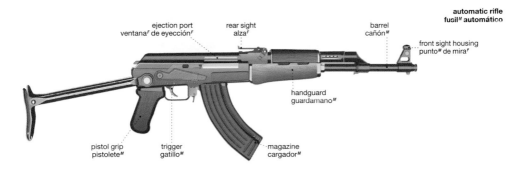

automatic rifle
fusilᴹ automático

ejection port
ventanaᶠ de eyecciónᶠ

rear sight
alzaᶠ

barrel
cañónᴹ

front sight housing
puntoᴹ de miraᶠ

handguard
guardamanoᴹ

pistol grip
pistoleteᴹ

trigger
gatilloᴹ

magazine
cargadorᴹ

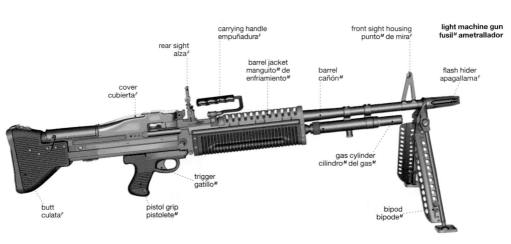

light machine gun
fusilᴹ ametrallador

carrying handle
empuñaduraᶠ

rear sight
alzaᶠ

front sight housing
puntoᴹ de miraᶠ

barrel jacket
manguitoᴹ de
enfriamientoᴹ

barrel
cañónᴹ

flash hider
apagallamaᶠ

cover
cubiertaᶠ

trigger
gatilloᴹ

gas cylinder
cilindroᴹ del gasᴹ

butt
culataᶠ

pistol grip
pistoleteᴹ

bipod
bípodeᴹ

SOCIETY

missiles

proyectiles^M

structure of a missile
estructura^F de un misil^M

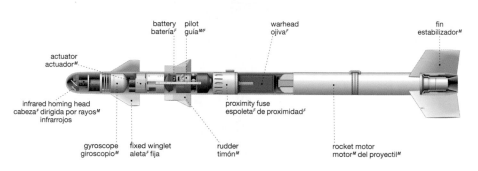

battery
batería^F

pilot
guía^{MF}

warhead
ojiva^F

fin
estabilizador^M

actuator
actuador^M

infrared homing head
cabeza^F dirigida por rayos^M
infrarrojos

proximity fuse
espoleta^F de proximidad^F

gyroscope
giroscopio^M

fixed winglet
aleta^F fija

rudder
timón^M

rocket motor
motor^M del proyectil^M

major types of missiles
principales tipos^M de misiles^M

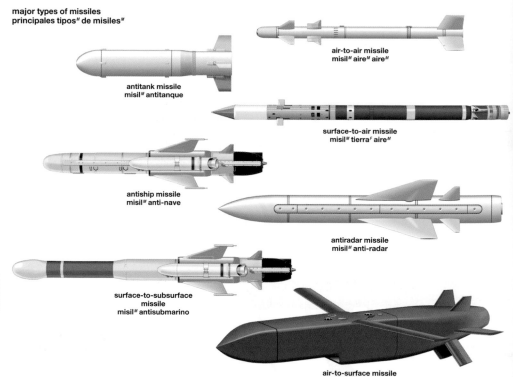

antitank missile
misil^M antitanque

air-to-air missile
misil^M aire^M aire^M

surface-to-air missile
misil^M tierra^F aire^M

antiship missile
misil^M anti-nave

antiradar missile
misil^M anti-radar

surface-to-subsurface
missile
misil^M antisubmarino

air-to-surface missile
misil^M aire^M tierra^F

tank

carro^M de combate^M

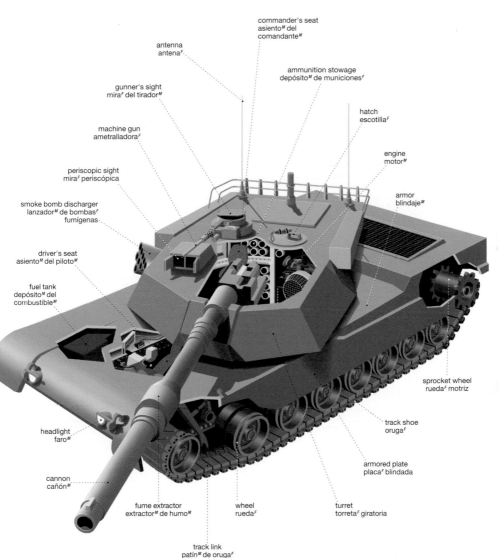

commander's seat
asiento^M del
comandante^M

antenna
antena^F

ammunition stowage
depósito^M de municiones^F

gunner's sight
mira^F del tirador^M

hatch
escotilla^F

machine gun
ametralladora^F

engine
motor^M

periscopic sight
mira^F periscópica

armor
blindaje^M

smoke bomb discharger
lanzador^M de bombas^F
fumígenas

driver's seat
asiento^M del piloto^M

fuel tank
depósito^M del
combustible^M

sprocket wheel
rueda^F motriz

track shoe
oruga^F

headlight
faro^M

armored plate
placa^F blindada

cannon
cañón^M

fume extractor
extractor^M de humo^M

wheel
rueda^F

turret
torreta^F giratoria

track link
patín^M de oruga^F

combat aircraft

avión^M de combate^M

in-flight refueling
repostaje^M de combustible^M en vuelo^M

tanker
avión^M nodriza^F

radar antenna
antena^F de radar^M

rudder
timón^M

parachute
paracaídas^F

fin
deriva^F

in-flight refueling probe
manguera^F de abastecimiento^M en
vuelo^M

exhaust nozzle
tobera^F de eyección^F

air brake
aerofreno^M

air-to-air missile
misil^M aire^M aire^M

stabilizer
estabilizador^M

missile launch rail
riel^M de lanzamiento^M de
proyectiles^M

turbojet engine
turborreactor^M

canopy
cúpula^F

ejection seat
asiento^M de eyección

wing
ala^F

flap hydraulic jack
gato^M hidráulico del alerón^M de
curvatura^F

trailing edge flap
alerón^M de
hipersustentación^F

main landing gear
tren^M de aterrizaje^M
principal

radar unit
unidad^F del radar^M

leading edge flap
alerón^M de
hipersustentación^F

fuel tank
depósito^M de
combustible^M

front landing gear
tren^M de aterrizaje^M delantero

motor air inlet
toma^F de aire^M del motor^M

wing box
cajón^M del plano^M de
sustentación^F

radome
radomo^M

warships
buques de guerra

aircraft carrier
portaaviones

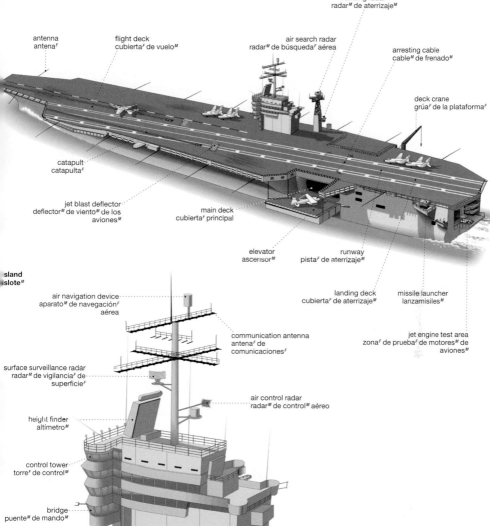

landing radar
radar de aterrizaje

antenna
antena

flight deck
cubierta de vuelo

air search radar
radar de búsqueda aérea

arresting cable
cable de frenado

deck crane
grúa de la plataforma

catapult
catapulta

jet blast deflector
deflector de viento de los
aviones

main deck
cubierta principal

elevator
ascensor

runway
pista de aterrizaje

island
islote

air navigation device
aparato de navegación
aérea

landing deck
cubierta de aterrizaje

missile launcher
lanzamisiles

communication antenna
antena de
comunicaciones

jet engine test area
zona de prueba de motores de
aviones

surface surveillance radar
radar de vigilancia de
superficie

air control radar
radar de control aéreo

height finder
altímetro

control tower
torre de control

bridge
puente de mando

SOCIETY

warships

frigate
fragata^F

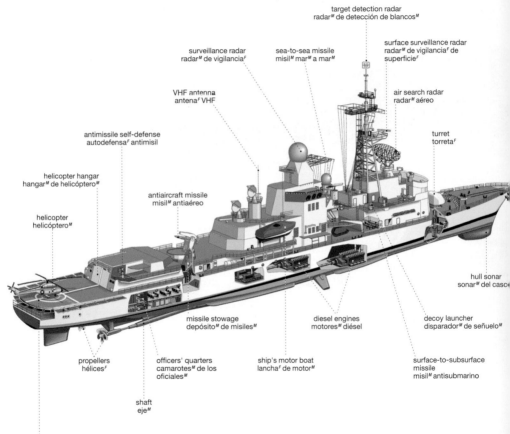

target detection radar
radar^M de detección de blancos^M

surveillance radar
radar^M de vigilancia^F

sea-to-sea missile
misil^M mar^M a mar^M

surface surveillance radar
radar^M de vigilancia^F de
superficie^F

VHF antenna
antena^F VHF

air search radar
radar^M aéreo

antimissile self-defense
autodefensa^F antimisil

turret
torreta^F

helicopter hangar
hangar^M de helicóptero^M

antiaircraft missile
misil^M antiaéreo

helicopter
helicóptero^M

hull sonar
sonar^M del casco

missile stowage
depósito^M de misiles^M

diesel engines
motores^M diésel

decoy launcher
disparador^M de señuelo^M

propellers
hélices^F

officers' quarters
camarotes^M de los
oficiales^M

ship's motor boat
lancha^F de motor^M

surface-to-subsurface
missile
misil^M antisubmarino

shaft
eje^M

helicopter flight deck
plataforma^F de vuelo^M del helicóptero^M

SOCIETY

nuclear submarine
submarino nuclear

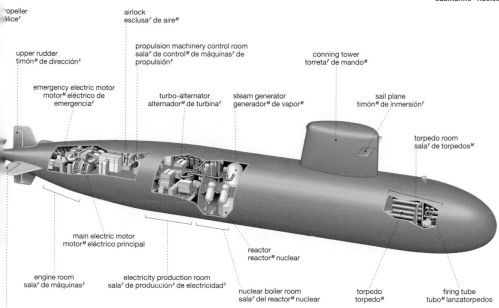

propeller
hélice

upper rudder
timón de dirección

emergency electric motor
motor eléctrico de
emergencia

airlock
esclusa de aire

propulsion machinery control room
sala de control de máquinas de
propulsión

turbo-alternator
alternador de turbina

steam generator
generador de vapor

conning tower
torreta de mando

sail plane
timón de inmersión

torpedo room
sala de torpedos

main electric motor
motor eléctrico principal

reactor
reactor nuclear

engine room
sala de máquinas

electricity production room
sala de producción de electricidad

nuclear boiler room
sala del reactor nuclear

torpedo
torpedo

firing tube
tubo lanzatorpedos

diving plane
timón de profundidad

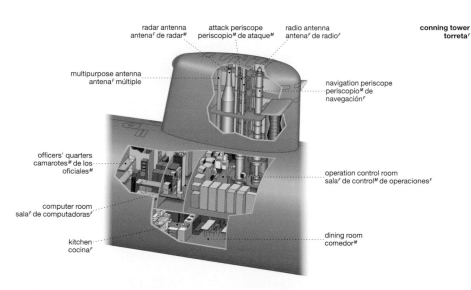

radar antenna
antena de radar

attack periscope
periscopio de ataque

radio antenna
antena de radio

conning tower
torreta

multipurpose antenna
antena múltiple

navigation periscope
periscopio de
navegación

officers' quarters
camarotes de los
oficiales

operation control room
sala de control de operaciones

computer room
sala de computadoras

kitchen
cocina

dining room
comedor

SOCIETY

fire prevention

prevención^F **de incendios**^M

fire station
parque^M **de bomberos**^M

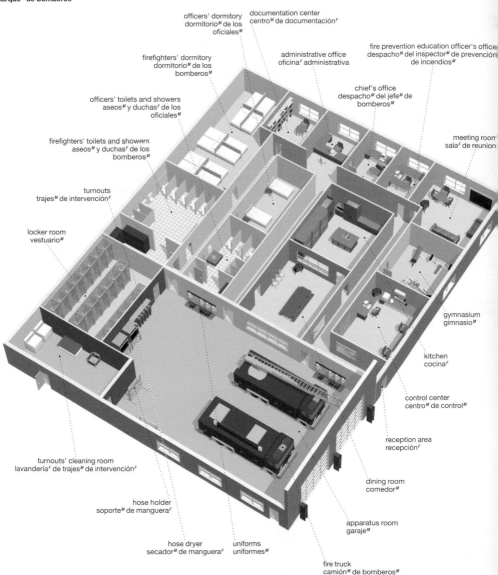

officers' dormitory
dormitorio^M de los
oficiales^M

documentation center
centro^M de documentación^F

firefighters' dormitory
dormitorio^M de los
bomberos^M

administrative office
oficina^F administrativa

fire prevention education officer's office
despacho^M del inspector^M de prevención^F
de incendios^M

officers' toilets and showers
aseos^M y duchas^F de los
oficiales^M

chief's office
despacho^M del jefe^M de
bomberos^M

firefighters' toilets and showers
aseos^M y duchas^F de los
bomberos^M

meeting room
sala^F de reunion

turnouts
trajes^M de intervención^F

locker room
vestuario^M

gymnasium
gimnasio^M

kitchen
cocina^F

control center
centro^M de control^M

reception area
recepción^F

turnouts' cleaning room
lavandería^F de trajes^M de intervención^F

dining room
comedor^M

hose holder
soporte^M de manguera^F

apparatus room
garaje^M

hose dryer
secador^M de manguera^F

uniforms
uniformes^M

fire truck
camión^M de bomberos^M

SOCIETY

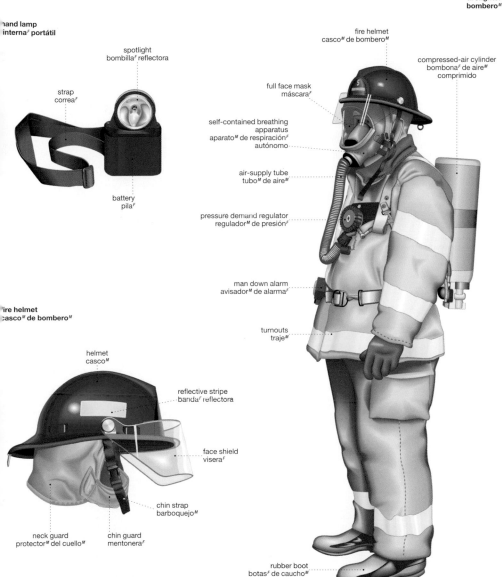

firefighter
bombero^M

hand lamp
linterna^F portátil

spotlight
bombilla^F reflectora

strap
correa^F

battery
pila^F

fire helmet
casco^M de bombero^M

fire helmet
casco^M de bombero^M

full face mask
máscara^F

self-contained breathing
apparatus
aparato^M de respiración^F
autónomo

air-supply tube
tubo^M de aire^M

pressure demand regulator
regulador^M de presión^F

man down alarm
avisador^M de alarma^F

compressed-air cylinder
bombona^F de aire^M
comprimido

turnouts
traje^M

helmet
casco^M

reflective stripe
banda^F reflectora

face shield
visera^F

chin strap
barboquejo^M

neck guard
protector^M del cuello^M

chin guard
mentonera^F

rubber boot
botas^F de caucho^M

SOCIETY

fire prevention

fire trucks
camiones^M **de**
bomberos^M

pumper
autobomba^M **tanque**

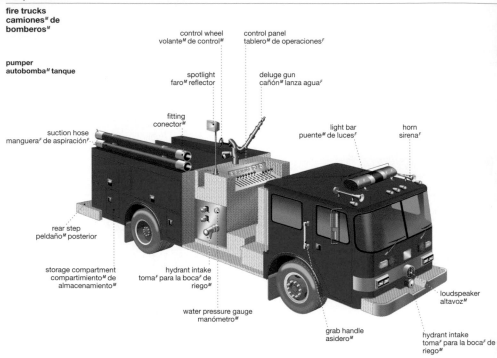

control wheel
volante^M de control^M

control panel
tablero^M de operaciones^F

spotlight
faro^M reflector

deluge gun
cañón^M lanza agua^F

fitting
conector^M

suction hose
manguera^F de aspiración^F

light bar
puente^M de luces^F

horn
sirena^F

rear step
peldaño^M posterior

storage compartment
compartimiento^M de
almacenamiento^M

hydrant intake
toma^F para la boca^F de
riego^M

water pressure gauge
manómetro^M

grab handle
asidero^M

loudspeaker
altavoz^M

hydrant intake
toma^F para la boca^F de
riego^M

ladder truck
autoescalera^M

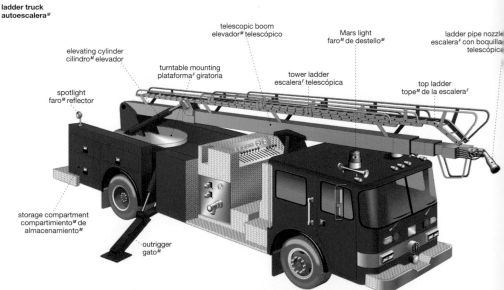

telescopic boom
elevador^M telescópico

Mars light
faro^M de destello^M

ladder pipe nozzle
escalera^F con boquilla
telescópica

elevating cylinder
cilindro^M elevador

turntable mounting
plataforma^F giratoria

tower ladder
escalera^F telescópica

top ladder
tope^M de la escalera^F

spotlight
faro^M reflector

storage compartment
compartimiento^M de
almacenamiento^M

outrigger
gato^M

fire prevention

cover
tapa^F

base
base^F

test button
botón^M de ensayo^M

indicator light
testigo^M luminoso

fire hydrant
boca^F de riego^M

smoke detector
detector^M de humo^M

fire-fighting material
material^M de lucha^F contra los
incendios^M

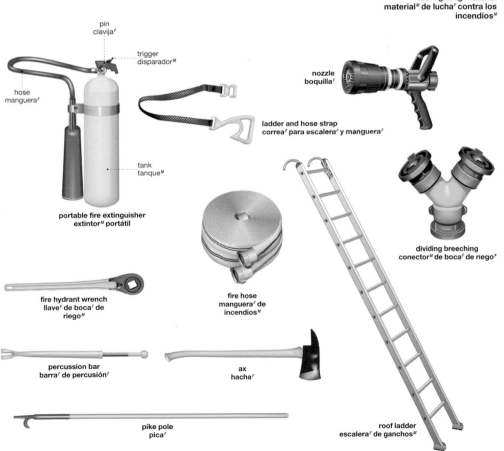

pin
clavija^F

trigger
disparador^M

nozzle
boquilla^F

hose
manguera^F

ladder and hose strap
correa^F para escalera^F y manguera^F

tank
tanque^M

portable fire extinguisher
extintor^M portátil

dividing breeching
conector^M de boca^F de riego^F

fire hydrant wrench
llave^F de boca^F de
riego^M

fire hose
manguera^F de
incendios^M

percussion bar
barra^F de percusión^F

ax
hacha^F

pike pole
pica^F

roof ladder
escalera^F de ganchos^M

SOCIETY

crime prevention

prevenciónᶠ **de la criminalidad**ᶠ

police station
estaciónᶠ **de policía**ᶠ

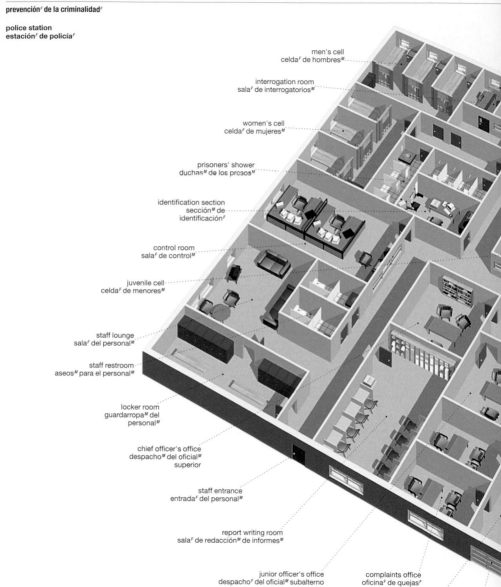

men's cell
celdaᶠ de hombresᴹ

interrogation room
salaᶠ de interrogatoriosᴹ

women's cell
celdaᶠ de mujeresᴹ

prisoners' shower
duchasᴹ de los presosᴹ

identification section
secciónᴹ de
identificaciónᶠ

control room
salaᶠ de controlᴹ

juvenile cell
celdaᶠ de menoresᴹ

staff lounge
salaᶠ del personalᴹ

staff restroom
aseosᴹ para el personalᴹ

locker room
guardarropaᴹ del
personalᴹ

chief officer's office
despachoᴹ del oficialᴹ
superior

staff entrance
entradaᶠ del personalᴹ

report writing room
salaᶠ de redacciónᴹ de informesᴹ

junior officer's office
despachoᶠ del oficialᴹ subalterno

complaints office
oficinaᶠ de quejasᶠ

waiting room
salaᶠ de esperaᶠ

main entrance
entradaᶠ principal

SOCIETY

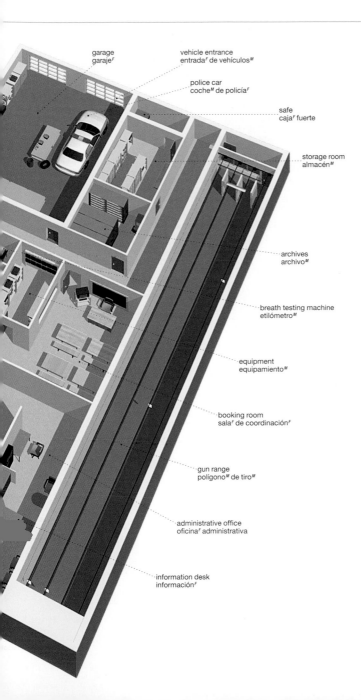

garage
garaje[F]

vehicle entrance
entrada[F] de vehículos[M]

police car
coche[M] de policía[F]

safe
caja[F] fuerte

storage room
almacén[M]

archives
archivo[M]

breath testing machine
etilómetro[M]

equipment
equipamiento[M]

booking room
sala[F] de coordinación[F]

gun range
polígono[M] de tiro[M]

administrative office
oficina[F] administrativa

information desk
información[F]

crime prevention

police officer
agente^M **de policía**^F

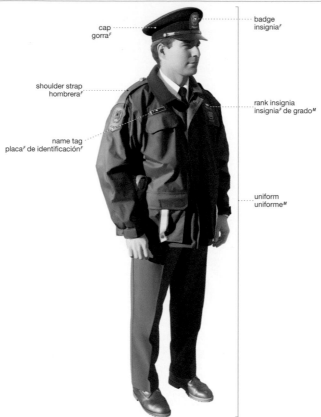

cap
gorra^F

badge
insignia^F

shoulder strap
hombrera^F

rank insignia
insignia^F de grado^M

name tag
placa^F de identificación^F

uniform
uniforme^M

duty belt
cinturón^M **de servicio**^M

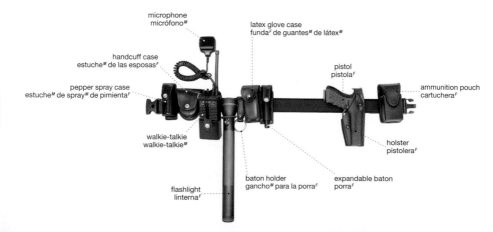

microphone
micrófono^M

latex glove case
funda^F de guantes^M de látex^M

handcuff case
estuche^M de las esposas^F

pistol
pistola^F

pepper spray case
estuche^M de spray^M de pimienta^F

ammunition pouch
cartuchera^F

walkie-talkie
walkie-talkie^M

holster
pistolera^F

flashlight
linterna^F

baton holder
gancho^M para la porra^F

expandable baton
porra^F

SOCIETY

crime prevention

**police car: dashboard
equipment
coche^M de policía^F :
equipamiento^M del
salpicadero^M**

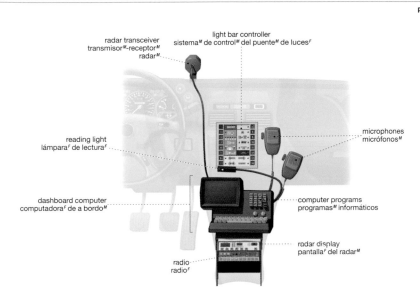

radar transceiver
transmisor^M-receptor^M
radar^M

light bar controller
sistema^M de control^M del puente^M de luces^F

microphones
micrófonos^M

reading light
lámpara^F de lectura^F

dashboard computer
computadora^F de a bordo^M

computer programs
programas^M informáticos

radar display
pantalla^F del radar^M

radio
radio^F

**police car
coche^M de policía^F**

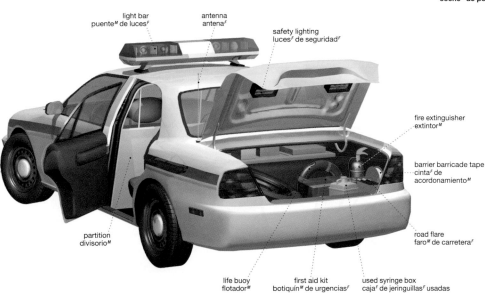

light bar
puente^M de luces^F

antenna
antena^F

safety lighting
luces^F de seguridad^F

fire extinguisher
extintor^M

barrier barricade tape
cinta^F de
acordonamiento^M

partition
divisorio^M

road flare
faro^M de carretera^F

life buoy
flotador^M

first aid kit
botiquín^M de urgencias^F

used syringe box
caja^F de jeringuillas^F usadas

SOCIETY

safety symbols

símbolos*M* de seguridad*F*

dangerous materials
materiales*M*
peligrosos

corrosive
corrosivo

high voltage
alta tensión*F*

explosive
explosivo

flammable
inflamable

radioactive
radioactivo

poison
veneno*M*

protection
protección*F*

eye protection
protección*F* para los ojos*M*

ear protection
protección*F* de los oídos*M*

head protection
protección*F* de la cabeza*F*

hand protection
protección*F* de las manos*F*

foot protection
protección*F* de los pies*M*

respiratory system protection
protección del sistema*M* respiratorio

ambulance

ambulancia^F

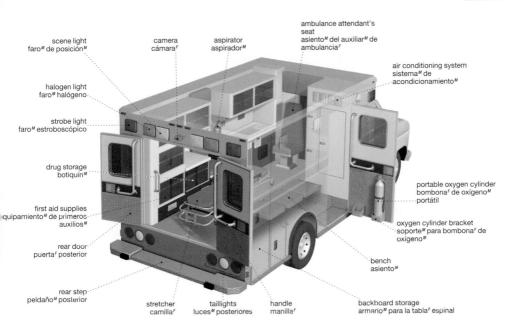

scene light
faro^M de posición^M

camera
cámara^F

aspirator
aspirador^M

ambulance attendant's seat
asiento^M del auxiliar^M de ambulancia^F

air conditioning system
sistema^M de acondicionamiento^M

halogen light
faro^M halógeno

strobe light
faro^M estroboscópico

drug storage
botiquín^M

portable oxygen cylinder
bombona^F de oxígeno^M portátil

first aid supplies
equipamiento^M de primeros auxilios^M

oxygen cylinder bracket
soporte^M para bombona^F de oxígeno^M

rear door
puerta^F posterior

bench
asiento^M

rear step
peldaño^M posterior

stretcher
camilla^F

taillights
luces^M posteriores

handle
manilla^F

backboard storage
armario^M para la tabla^F espinal

medical equipment

equipo^M médico

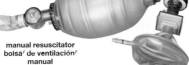

manual resuscitator
bolsa^F de ventilación^F manual

oxygen mask
máscara^F de oxígeno^M

oropharyngeal airway
cánula^F orofaríngea

cervical collar
collarín^M cervical

aspirator
aspirador^M

defibrillator
desfibrilador^M

SOCIETY

medical equipment

stethoscope
fonendoscopioM

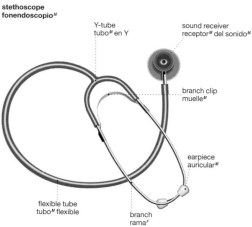

Y-tube
tubo M en Y

sound receiver
receptor M del sonido M

branch clip
muelle M

earpiece
auricular M

flexible tube
tubo M flexible

branch
rama F

hypodermic syringe
jeringuilla F

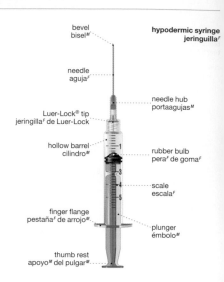

bevel
bisel M

needle
aguja F

needle hub
portaagujas M

Luer-Lock® tip
jeringilla F de Luer-Lock

hollow barrel
cilindro M

rubber bulb
pera F de goma F

scale
escala F

finger flange
pestaña F de arrojo M

plunger
émbolo M

thumb rest
apoyo M del pulgar M

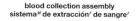

irrigation syringe
jeringuilla F **para irrigación** F

blood collection assembly
sistema M **de extracción** F **de sangre** F

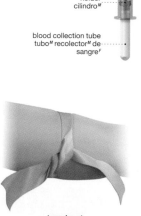

needle
aguja F

holder
cilindro M

blood collection tube
tubo M recolector M de
sangre F

lancing device
dispositivo M **de**
punción F

venom extractor
bomba F **antiveneno**

tourniquet
torniquete M

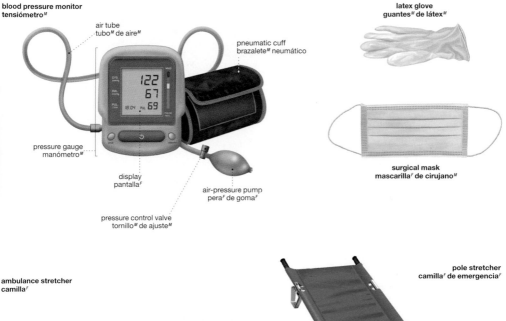

blood pressure monitor
tensiómetroᴹ

air tube
tubo ᴹ de aire ᴹ

pneumatic cuff
brazalete ᴹ neumático

SYS.

122

67

PUL.

69

pressure gauge
manómetro ᴹ

display
pantalla ᶠ

air-pressure pump
pera ᶠ de goma ᶠ

pressure control valve
tornillo ᴹ de ajuste ᴹ

latex glove
guantesᴹ **de látex**ᴹ

surgical mask
mascarillaᶠ **de cirujano**ᴹ

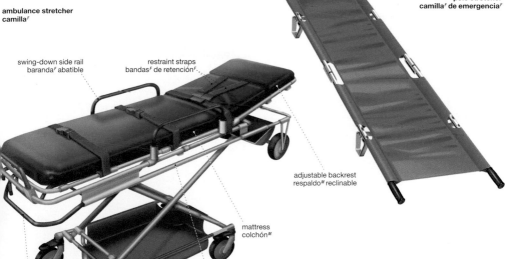

ambulance stretcher
camillaᶠ

pole stretcher
camillaᶠ **de emergencia**ᶠ

swing-down side rail
baranda ᶠ abatible

restraint straps
bandas ᶠ de retención ᶠ

adjustable backrest
respaldo ᴹ reclinable

mattress
colchón ᴹ

transport handle
sa ᶠ de transporte ᴹ

frame
chasis ᴹ

locking wheels
rueda ᶠ de freno ᴹ

SOCIETY

medical equipment

thermometers
termómetros^M

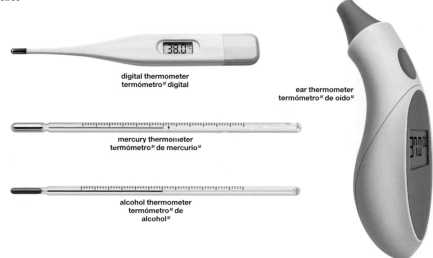

digital thermometer
termómetro^M digital

ear thermometer
termómetro^M de oído^M

mercury thermometer
termómetro^M de mercurio^M

alcohol thermometer
termómetro^M de
alcohol^M

forms of medications

formas^F **farmacéuticas de medicamentos**^M

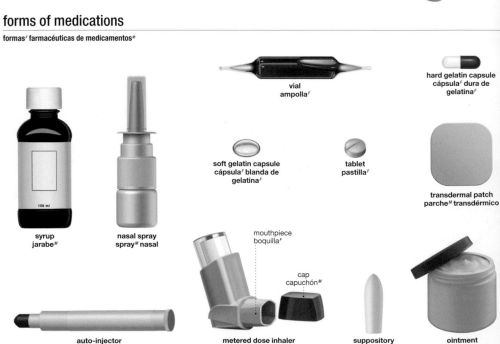

vial
ampolla^F

hard gelatin capsule
cápsula^F dura de
gelatina^F

soft gelatin capsule
cápsula^F blanda de
gelatina^F

tablet
pastilla^F

transdermal patch
parche^M transdérmico

syrup
jarabe^M

nasal spray
spray^M nasal

mouthpiece
boquilla^F

cap
capuchón^M

auto-injector
autoinyector^M

metered dose inhaler
inhalador^M-dosificador^M

suppository
supositorio^M

ointment
pomada^F

SOCIETY

100 ml

first aid kit

botiquín^M de primeros auxilios^M

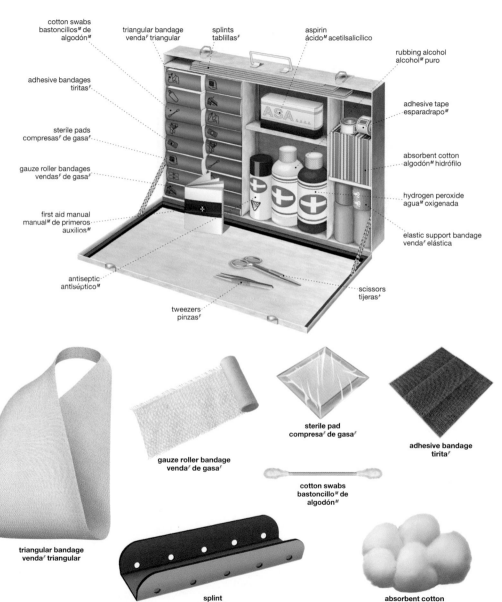

cotton swabs
bastoncillos^M de
algodón^M

triangular bandage
venda^F triangular

splints
tablillas^F

aspirin
ácido^M acetilsalicílico

rubbing alcohol
alcohol^M puro

adhesive bandages
tiritas^F

adhesive tape
esparadrapo^M

sterile pads
compresas^F de gasa^F

absorbent cotton
algodón^M hidrófilo

gauze roller bandages
vendas^F de gasa^F

hydrogen peroxide
agua^M oxigenada

first aid manual
manual^M de primeros
auxilios^M

elastic support bandage
venda^F elástica

antiseptic
antiséptico^M

scissors
tijeras^F

tweezers
pinzas^F

triangular bandage
venda^F triangular

gauze roller bandage
venda^F de gasa^F

sterile pad
compresa^F de gasa^F

adhesive bandage
tirita^F

cotton swabs
bastoncillo^M de
algodón^M

splint
férula^F

absorbent cotton
algodón^M

SOCIETY

walking aids

auxiliares^M ortopédicos para caminar

forearm crutch
muleta^F de antebrazo^M

underarm crutch
muleta^F de sobaco^M

forearm support
soporte^M para el
antebrazo^M

handgrip
empuñadura^F

adjuster
tubo^M ajustable

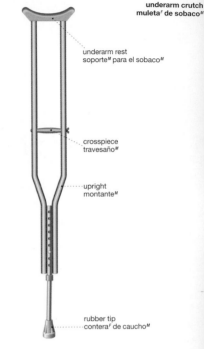

underarm rest
soporte^M para el sobaco^M

crosspiece
travesaño^M

upright
montante^M

rubber tip
contera^F de caucho^M

crook cane
bastón^M curvo

Fritz cane
bastón^M con
empuñadura^F en T^F

offset cane
bastón^M con empuñadura^F
ortopédica

quad cane
bastón^M cuadrangular

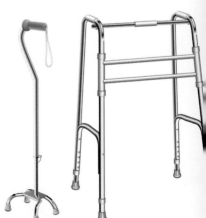

walker
andador^M

moving aids

ayudas^F para desplazarse

wheelchair
silla^F de ruedas^F

handle
agarrador^M

back
respaldo^M

armrest
reposabrazos^M

spacer
separador^M

arm
brazo^M

brake
freno^M

clothing guard
panel^M protector

hub
cubo^M

seat
asiento^M

push rim
rueda^F de empuje^M

hanger bracket
soporte^M colgante

large wheel
rueda^F

heel loop
talón^M

front wheel
rueda^F de la dirección^F

cross brace
travesaño^M

tipping lever
palanca^F estabilizadora

footrest
reposapiés^M

four-wheel scooter
scooter^M de cuatro
ruedas^F

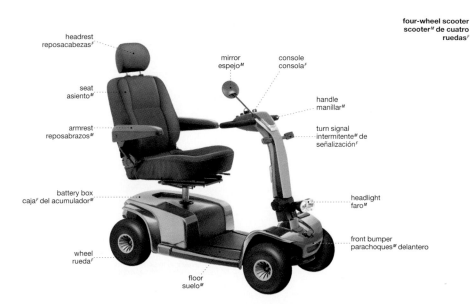

headrest
reposacabezas^F

mirror
espejo^M

console
consola^F

seat
asiento^M

handle
manillar^M

armrest
reposabrazos^M

turn signal
intermitente^M de
señalización^F

battery box
caja^F del acumulador^M

headlight
faro^M

front bumper
parachoques^M delantero

wheel
rueda^F

floor
suelo^M

SOCIETY

hospital

hospital^M

emergency department
urgencias^F

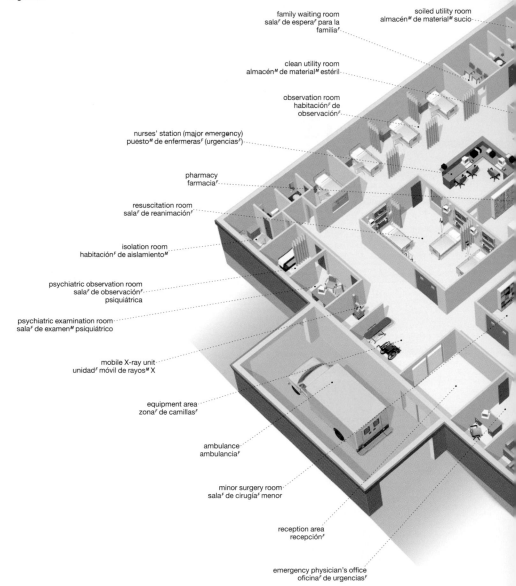

family waiting room
sala^F de espera^F para la
familia^F

soiled utility room
almacén^M de material^M sucio

clean utility room
almacén^M de material^M estéril

observation room
habitación^F de
observación^F

nurses' station (major emergency)
puesto^M de enfermeras^F (urgencias^F)

pharmacy
farmacia^F

resuscitation room
sala^F de reanimación^F

isolation room
habitación^F de aislamiento^M

psychiatric observation room
sala^F de observación^F
psiquiátrica

psychiatric examination room
sala^F de examen^M psiquiátrico

mobile X-ray unit
unidad^F móvil de rayos^M X

equipment area
zona^F de camillas^F

ambulance
ambulancia^F

minor surgery room
sala^F de cirugía^F menor

reception area
recepción^F

emergency physician's office
oficina^F de urgencias^F

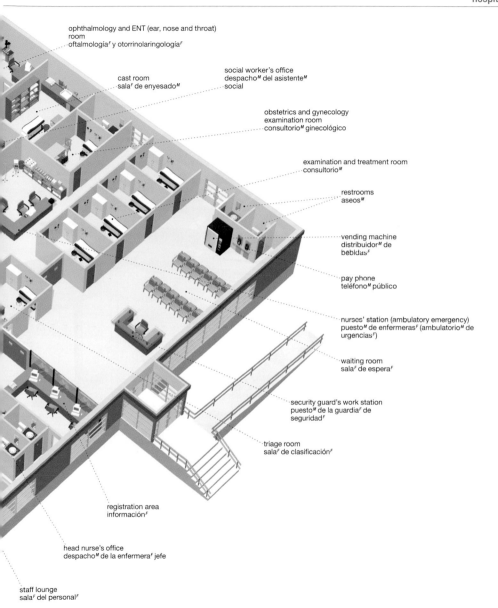

ophthalmology and ENT (ear, nose and throat) room
oftalmología^F y otorrinolaringología^F

cast room
sala^F de enyesado^M

social worker's office
despacho^M del asistente^M social

obstetrics and gynecology examination room
consultorio^M ginecológico

examination and treatment room
consultorio^M

restrooms
aseos^M

vending machine
distribuidor^M de bebidas^F

pay phone
teléfono^M público

nurses' station (ambulatory emergency)
puesto^M de enfermeras^F (ambulatorio^M de urgencias^F)

waiting room
sala^F de espera^F

security guard's work station
puesto^M de la guardia^F de seguridad^F

triage room
sala^F de clasificación^F

registration area
información^F

head nurse's office
despacho^M de la enfermera^F jefe

staff lounge
sala^F del personal^F

hospital

ambulatory care unit
ambulatorio^M

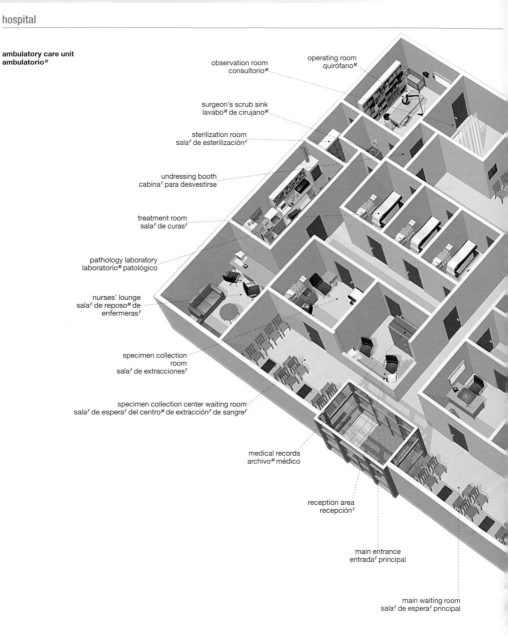

observation room
consultorio^M

operating room
quirófano^M

surgeon's scrub sink
lavabo^M de cirujano^M

sterilization room
sala^F de esterilización^F

undressing booth
cabina^F para desvestirse

treatment room
sala^F de curas^F

pathology laboratory
laboratorio^M patológico

nurses' lounge
sala^F de reposo^M de
enfermeras^F

specimen collection
room
sala^F de extracciones^F

specimen collection center waiting room
sala^F de espera^F del centro^M de extracción^F de sangre^F

medical records
archivo^M médico

reception area
recepción^F

main entrance
entrada^F principal

main waiting room
sala^F de espera^F principal

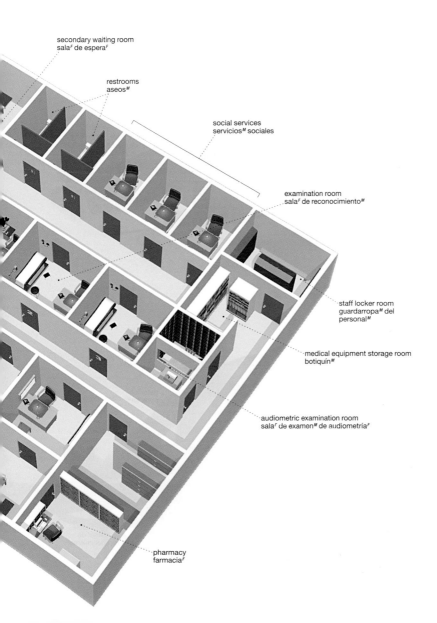

secondary waiting room
sala^F de espera^F

restrooms
aseos^M

social services
servicios^M sociales

examination room
sala^F de reconocimiento^M

staff locker room
guardarropa^M del
personal^M

medical equipment storage room
botiquín^M

audiometric examination room
sala^F de examen^M de audiometría^F

pharmacy
farmacia^F

medical examinations

endoscopy
endoscopia^F

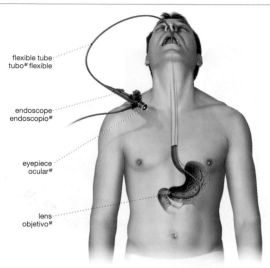

flexible tube
tubo^M flexible

endoscope
endoscopio^M

eyepiece
ocular^M

lens
objetivo^M

medical treatment

tratamiento^M **médico**

radiotherapy
radioterapia^F

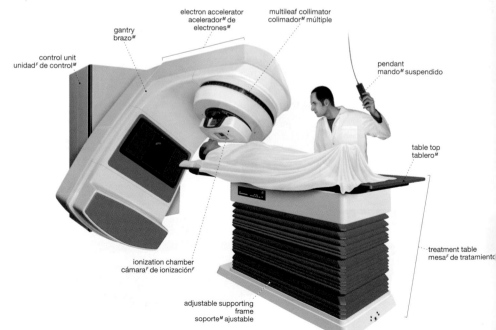

electron accelerator
acelerador^M de
electrones^M

multileaf collimator
colimador^M múltiple

gantry
brazo^M

control unit
unidad^F de control^M

pendant
mando^M suspendido

table top
tablero^M

treatment table
mesa^F de tratamiento

ionization chamber
cámara^F de ionización^F

adjustable supporting
frame
soporte^M ajustable

SOCIETY

pacemaker
marcapasos^M **artificial**

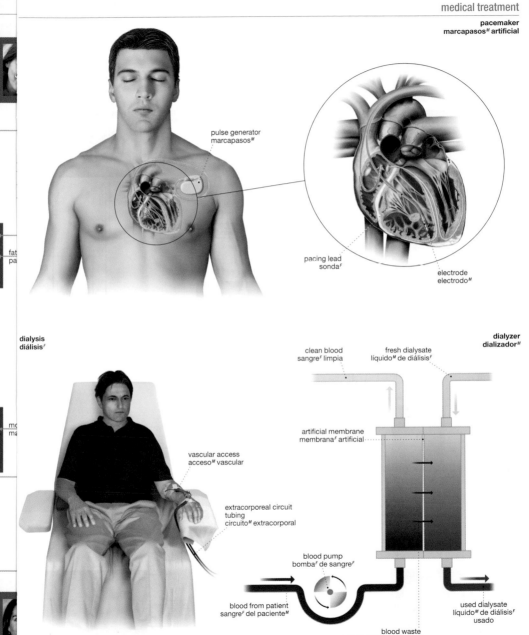

pulse generator
marcapasos^M

pacing lead
sonda^F

electrode
electrodo^M

brothers
hermanos^F

fat
pa

husband
marido^M

wife
mujer^M

m
ma

brother/sister
hermano^M/hermana^F

dialysis
diálisis^F

vascular access
acceso^M vascular

extracorporeal circuit
tubing
circuito^M extracorporal

dialyzer
dializador^M

clean blood
sangre^F limpia

fresh dialysate
líquido^M de diálisis^F

artificial membrane
membrana^F artificial

blood pump
bomba^F de sangre^F

blood from patient
sangre^F del paciente^M

blood waste
impurezas^F de la sangre^F

used dialysate
líquido^M de diálisis^F
usado

SOCIETY

family

vínculos^M fa|

grandson
nieto^M

grandfather
abuelo^M

SOCIETY

SPORTS FACILITIES 932

sports complex   932
scoreboard   933
competition   933

TRACK AND FIELD 934

track and field   934
jumping   936
throwing   937

BALL SPORTS 938

baseball   938
softball   941
cricket   942
field hockey   944
soccer   946
lacrosse   948
rugby   950
football   952
Canadian football   955
netball   955
basketball   956
volleyball   958
team handball   960

RACKET SPORTS 961

table tennis   961
badminton   962
racquetball   964
squash   965
tennis   966

GYMNASTICS 969

gymnastics   969
rhythmic gymnastics   972
trampoline   973

AQUATIC AND NAUTICAL SPORTS 974

water polo   974
swimming   975
diving   978
sailing   980
sailboard   983
rowing and sculling   984
canoe   986
canoe-kayak: flatwater racing   986
kayak   987
waterskiing   988
surfing   988
scuba diving   989

COMBAT SPORTS 990

boxing   990
wrestling   991
judo   992
karate   993
taekwondo   994
kendo   995
sumo   995
kung fu   996
jujitsu   996
aikido   996
fencing   997

STRENGTH SPORTS 999

weightlifting   999
fitness equipment   1000

EQUESTRIAN SPORTS 1002

show jumping   1002
riding   1004
dressage   1005
horse racing   1006
polo   1008

SPORTS AND GAMES

deportes y juegos

PRECISION AND ACCURACY SPORTS — 1009

archery	1009
shotgun shooting	1010
rifle shooting	1011
pistol shooting	1011
billiards	1012
lawn bowling	1014
pétanque	1014
bowling	1015
golf	1016

CYCLING — 1020

road racing	1020
mountain biking	1020
track cycling	1021
BMX	1021

MOTOR SPORTS — 1022

auto racing	1022
motorcycling	1024
personal watercraft	1026
snowmobile	1026

WINTER SPORTS — 1027

curling	1027
ice hockey	1028
figure skating	1031
speed skating	1032
bobsled	1034
luge	1034
skeleton	1035
sliding track	1035
ski resort	1036
snowboarding	1037
alpine skiing	1038
freestyle skiing	1040
ski jumping	1041
speed skiing	1041
cross-country skiing	1042
biathlon	1043
snowshoeing	1043

SPORTS ON WHEELS — 1044

skateboarding	1044
in-line skating	1045

AERIAL SPORTS — 1046

parachuting	1046
hang gliding	1047
glider	1048
ballooning	1049

MOUNTAIN SPORTS — 1050

mountaineering	1050

OUTDOOR LEISURE — 1052

camping	1052
knots	1058
fishing	1059

GAMES — 1062

dice and dominoes	1062
playing cards	1062
board games	1063
jigsaw puzzle	1066
mah-jongg	1066
video games	1067
roulette	1068
darts	1069
soccer table	1069
slot machine	1070
Ultimate	1070
pinball machine	1071
kite	1071

sports complex

polideportivoM

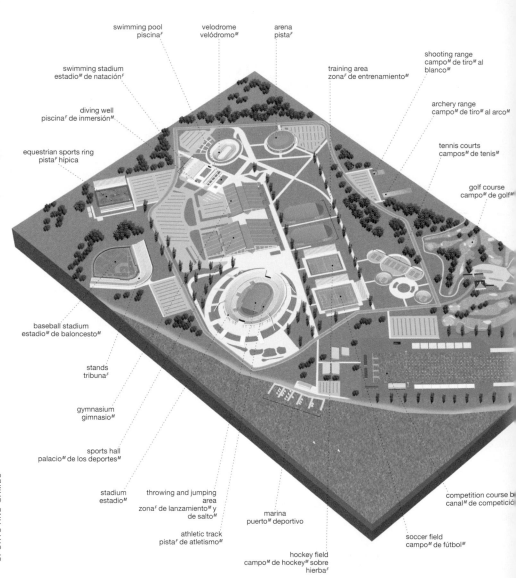

swimming pool
piscinaF

velodrome
velódromoM

arena
pistaF

shooting range
campoM de tiroM al
blancoM

swimming stadium
estadioM de nataciónF

training area
zonaF de entrenamientoM

archery range
campoM de tiroM al arcoM

diving well
piscinaF de inmersiónM

tennis courts
camposM de tenisM

equestrian sports ring
pistaF hípica

golf course
campoM de golfM

baseball stadium
estadioM de baloncestoM

stands
tribunaF

gymnasium
gimnasioM

sports hall
palacioM de los deportesM

competition course b
canalM de competició

stadium
estadioM

throwing and jumping
area
zonaF de lanzamientoM y
de saltoM

marina
puertoM deportivo

soccer field
campoM de fútbolM

athletic track
pistaF de atletismoM

hockey field
campoM de hockeyM sobre
hierbaF

scoreboard

marcador[M]

game clock
cronómetro[M]

period
tiempo[M]

video replay
reproductor de video[M]

score
tanteo[M]

fouls/penalties
faltas[F]/penalizaciones[F]

competition

competición[F]

**bracket
empate**[M]

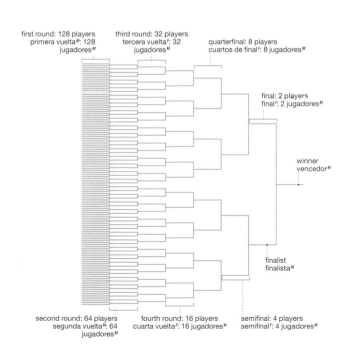

first round: 128 players
primera vuelta[M]: 128
jugadores[M]

third round: 32 players
tercera vuelta[F]: 32
jugadores[M]

quarterfinal: 8 players
cuartos de final[F]: 8 jugadores[M]

final: 2 players
final[F]: 2 jugadores[M]

winner
vencedor[M]

finalist
finalista[M]

second round: 64 players
segunda vuelta[M]: 64
jugadores[M]

fourth round: 16 players
cuarta vuelta[F]: 16 jugadores[M]

semifinal: 4 players
semifinal[F]: 4 jugadores[M]

SPORTS AND GAMES

track and field

pista^F y campo^M

200 m starting line
línea^F de salida^F de 200 m

5,000 m starting line
línea^F de salida^F de 5.000 m

long jump and triple jump
salto^M de longitud^F y triple
salto^M

shot put
lanzamiento^M de peso^M

landing area
área^F de caída^F

steeplechase hurdle jump
ría^F para la carrera^F de
obstáculos^M

lane
calle^F

exchange zone
zona^F de cambio^M

110 m hurdles starting line
línea^F de salida^F de 110 m
vallas^F

100 m and 100 m hurdles starting line
línea^F de salida^F de 100 m y 100 m vallas^F

throwing circle
círculo^M de lanzamiento^M

pole vault
salto^M de pértiga^F

track
pista^F

track equipment
equipo^M de pista^F

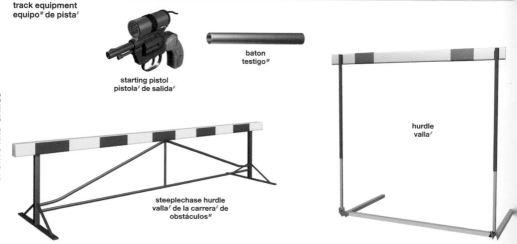

starting pistol
pistola^F de salida^F

baton
testigo^M

hurdle
valla^F

steeplechase hurdle
valla^F de la carrera^F de
obstáculos^M

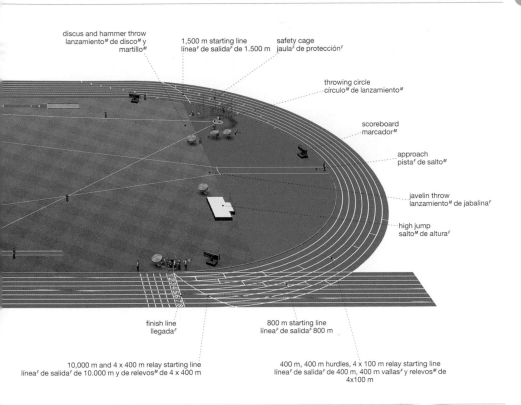

discus and hammer throw
lanzamiento^M de disco^M y martillo^M

1,500 m starting line
línea^F de salida^F de 1.500 m

safety cage
jaula^F de protección^F

throwing circle
círculo^M de lanzamiento^M

scoreboard
marcador^M

approach
pista^F de salto^M

javelin throw
lanzamiento^M de jabalina^F

high jump
salto^M de altura^F

finish line
llegada^F

800 m starting line
línea^F de salida^F 800 m

10,000 m and 4 x 400 m relay starting line
línea^F de salida^F de 10.000 m y de relevos^M de 4 x 400 m

400 m, 400 m hurdles, 4 x 100 m relay starting line
línea^F de salida^F de 400 m, 400 m vallas^F y relevos^M de 4x100 m

runner: starting block
corredora^F : taco^M de salida^F

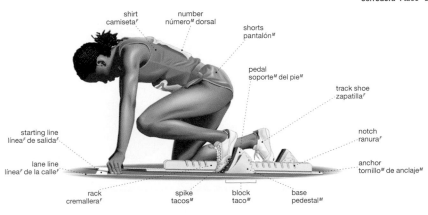

shirt
camiseta^F

number
número^M dorsal

shorts
pantalón^M

pedal
soporte^M del pie^M

track shoe
zapatilla^F

notch
ranura^F

anchor
tornillo^M de anclaje^M

starting line
línea^F de salida^F

lane line
línea^F de la calle^F

rack
cremallera^F

spike
tacos^M

block
taco^M

base
pedestal^M

SPORTS AND GAMES

jumping
saltos^M

high jump
salto^M de altura^F

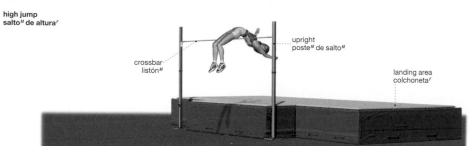

crossbar
listón^M

upright
poste^M de salto^M

landing area
colchoneta^F

pole vault
salto^M de pértiga^F

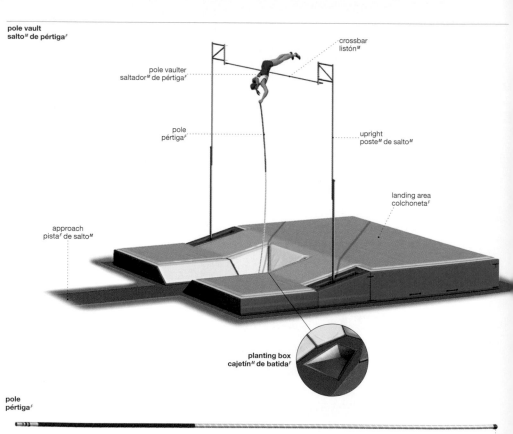

crossbar
listón^M

pole vaulter
saltador^M de pértiga^F

pole
pértiga^F

upright
poste^M de salto^M

landing area
colchoneta^F

approach
pista^F de salto^M

planting box
cajetín^M de batida^F

pole
pértiga^F

tip
punta^F

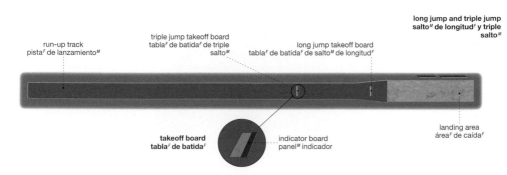

long jump and triple jump
salto^M de longitud^F y triple
salto^M

run-up track
pista^F de lanzamiento^M

triple jump takeoff board
tabla^F de batida^F de triple
salto^M

long jump takeoff board
tabla^F de batida^F de salto^M de longitud^F

landing area
área^F de caída^F

takeoff board
tabla^F de batida^F

indicator board
panel^M indicador

throwing

lanzamientos^M

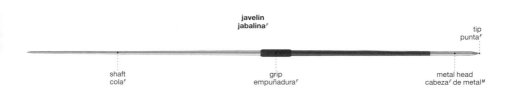

javelin
jabalina^F

tip
punta^F

shaft
cola^F

grip
empuñadura^F

metal head
cabeza^F de metal^M

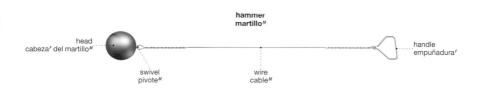

hammer
martillo^M

head
cabeza^F del martillo^M

handle
empuñadura^F

swivel
pivote^M

wire
cable^M

shot
peso^M

discus
disco^M

rim
canto^M

weight
peso^M

body
cuerpo^M

SPORTS AND GAMES

baseball

béisbol^M

player positions
posición^F de los
jugadores^M

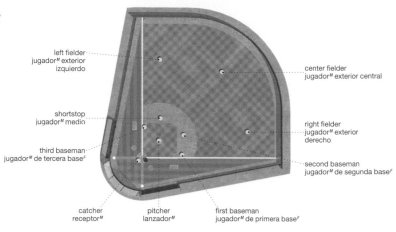

left fielder
jugador^M exterior
izquierdo

center fielder
jugador^M exterior central

shortstop
jugador^M medio

right fielder
jugador^M exterior
derecho

third baseman
jugador^M de tercera base^F

second baseman
jugador^M de segunda base^F

catcher
receptor^M

pitcher
lanzador^M

first baseman
jugador^M de primera base^F

baseball field
campo^M de béisbol^M

on-deck circle
círculo^M de espera^F

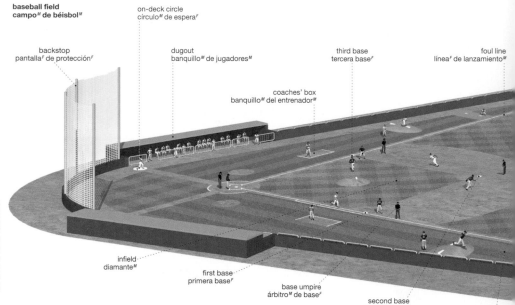

backstop
pantalla^F de protección^F

dugout
banquillo^M de jugadores^M

third base
tercera base^F

foul line
línea^F de lanzamiento^M

coaches' box
banquillo^M del entrenador^M

infield
diamante^M

first base
primera base^F

base umpire
árbitro^M de base^F

second base
segunda base^F

bullpen
zona^F de calentamiento^M

pitch
lanzamiento^M

home-plate umpire
árbitro^M de base^F meta

batter
bateador^M

pitcher
lanzador^M

catcher
receptor^M

home plate
base^F meta^F

pitcher's mound
base^F de lanzamiento^M

pitcher's rubber
plataforma^F de
lanzamiento^M

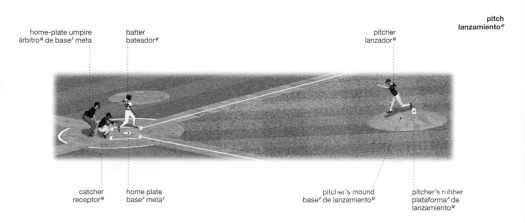

left field
exterior^M izquierdo

outfield fence
vallado^M del campo^M

center field
exterior^M

right field
exterior^M derecho

foul pole
poste^M de foul^M

warning track
zona^F de atención^F

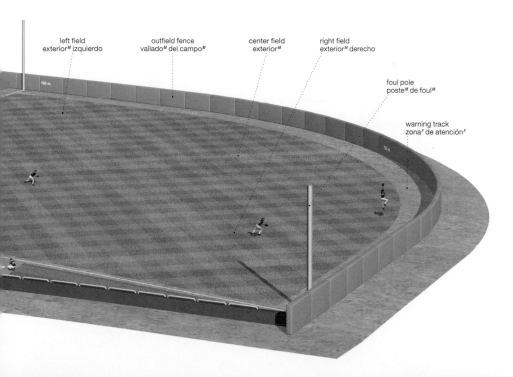

baseball

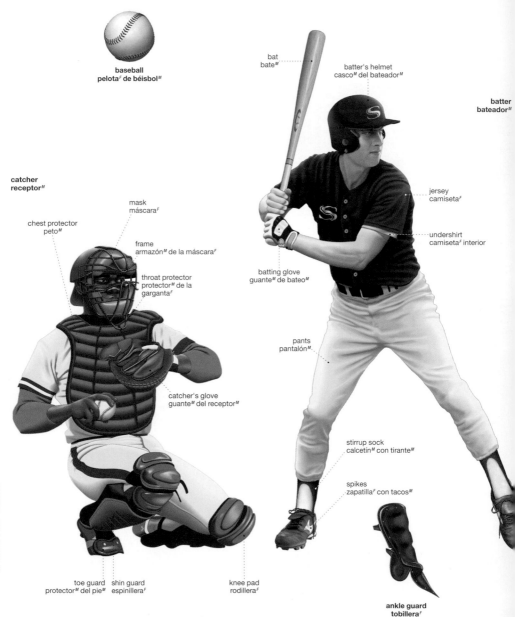

baseball
pelota^F de béisbol^M

bat
bate^M

batter's helmet
casco^M del bateador^M

batter
bateador^M

catcher
receptor^M

mask
máscara^F

chest protector
peto^M

frame
armazón^M de la máscara^F

throat protector
protector^M de la
garganta^F

jersey
camiseta^F

undershirt
camiseta^F interior

batting glove
guante^M de bateo^M

pants
pantalón^M

catcher's glove
guante^M del receptor^M

stirrup sock
calcetín^M con tirante^M

spikes
zapatilla^F con tacos^M

toe guard
protector^M del pie^M

shin guard
espinillera^F

knee pad
rodillera^F

ankle guard
tobillera^F

baseball

baseball bat
bate^M **de béisbol**

knob
puño^M

handle
empuñadura^F

crest
emblema^M

barrel
cuadro^M de bateo^M

section of a baseball
corte^M **de una pelota**^F **de**
béisbol^M

fielder's glove
guante^M **de recogida**^F

web
canasta^F

cork ball
bola^F de corcho^M

yarn ball
bola^F de hilo^M

strap
trabilla^F

thumb
pulgar^M

finger
dedo^M

palm
palma^F

heel
talón^M

lace
cordón^M

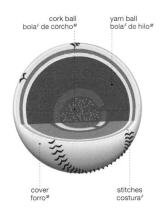

cover
forro^M

stitches
costura^F

softball

softball^M

softball glove
guante^M **de softball**^M

softball
pelota^F **de softball**^M

softball bat
bate^M **de softball**^M

SPORTS AND GAMES

cricket

cricket^M

batsman
bateador^M

helmet
casco^M

face mask
máscara^F

bat
pala^F

glove
guante^M

pad
protector^M

cricket shoe
zapatilla^F

stud
taco^M

cricket ball
pelota^F **de cricket**^M

leather skin
forro^M de cuero^M.

seam
costura^F

bat
bate^M

handle
mango^M

willow
pala^F

front view
vista^F **frontal**

side view
vista^F **lateral**

cricket

player positions
posición^F de los
jugadores^M

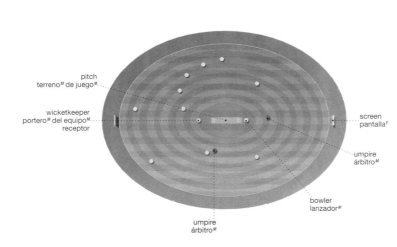

pitch
terreno^M de juego^M

wicketkeeper
portero^M del equipo^M
receptor

screen
pantalla^F

umpire
árbitro^M

bowler
lanzador^M

umpire
árbitro^M

wicket
puerta^F

bail
travesaño^M

stump
estaca^F

pitch
terreno^M de juego^M

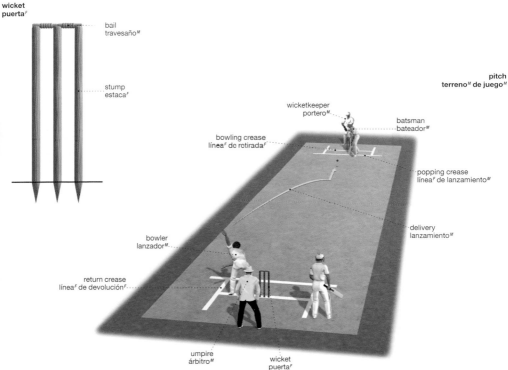

wicketkeeper
portero^M

batsman
bateador^M

bowling crease
línea^F de rotirada^F

popping crease
línea^F de lanzamiento^M

delivery
lanzamiento^M

bowler
lanzador^M

return crease
línea^F de devolución^F

umpire
árbitro^M

wicket
puerta^F

rugby
rugby^M

player positions
posición^F de los jugadores^M

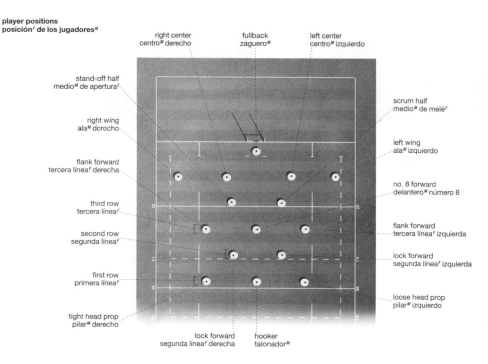

right center
centro^M derecho

fullback
zaguero^M

left center
centro^M izquierdo

stand-off half
medio^M de apertura^F

scrum half
medio^M de melé^F

right wing
ala^M derecho

left wing
ala^M izquierdo

flank forward
tercera línea^F derecha

no. 8 forward
delantero^M número 8

third row
tercera línea^F

flank forward
tercera línea^F izquierda

second row
segunda línea^F

lock forward
segunda línea^F izquierda

first row
primera línea^F

loose head prop
pilar^M izquierdo

tight head prop
pilar^M derecho

lock forward
segunda línea^F derecha

hooker
talonador^M

rugby field
campo^M de rugby^M

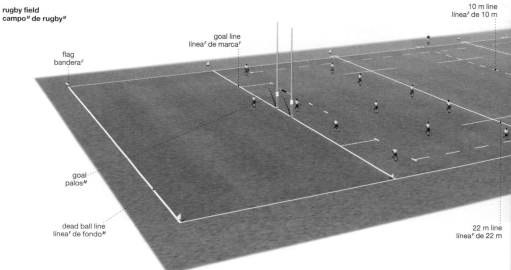

10 m line
línea^F de 10 m

goal line
línea^F de marca^F

flag
bandera^F

goal
palos^M

dead ball line
línea^F de fondo^M

22 m line
línea^F de 22 m

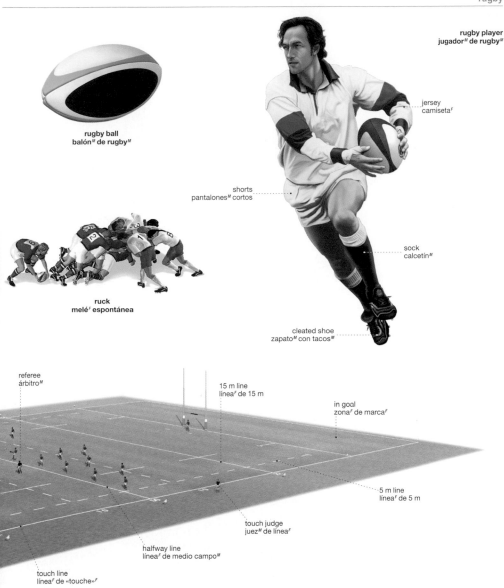

rugby player
jugador^M **de rugby**^{M}

jersey
camiseta^F

rugby ball
balón^M **de rugby**^{M}

shorts
pantalones^M cortos

sock
calcetín^M

ruck
melé^F **espontánea**

cleated shoe
zapato^M con tacos^M

referee
árbitro^M

15 m line
línea^F de 15 m

in goal
zona^F de marca^F

5 m line
línea^F de 5 m

touch judge
juez^M de línea^F

halfway line
línea^F de medio campo^M

touch line
línea^F de «touche»^{F}

football

fútbol^M americano

scrimmage: defense
melé^F: defensa^F

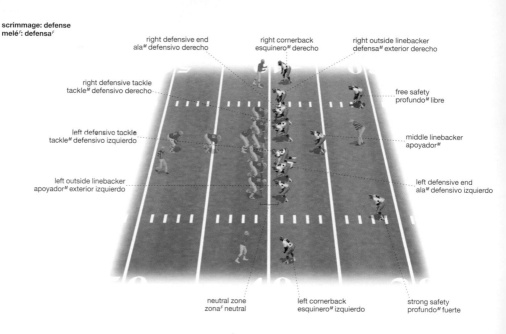

right defensive end
ala^M defensivo derecho

right cornerback
esquinero^M derecho

right outside linebacker
defensa^M exterior derecho

right defensive tackle
tackle^M defensivo derecho

free safety
profundo^M libre

left defensive tackle
tackle^M defensivo izquierdo

middle linebacker
apoyador^M

left outside linebacker
apoyador^M exterior izquierdo

left defensive end
ala^M defensivo izquierdo

neutral zone
zona^F neutral

left cornerback
esquinero^M izquierdo

strong safety
profundo^M fuerte

American football field
campo^M de fútbol^M americano

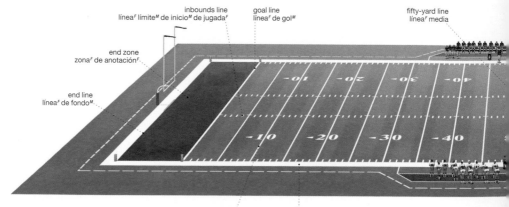

inbounds line
línea^F límite^M de inicio^M de jugada^F

goal line
línea^F de gol^M

fifty-yard line
línea^F media

end zone
zona^F de anotación^F

end line
línea^F de fondo^M

yard line
línea^F yardas^F

sideline
banda^F

SPORTS AND GAMES

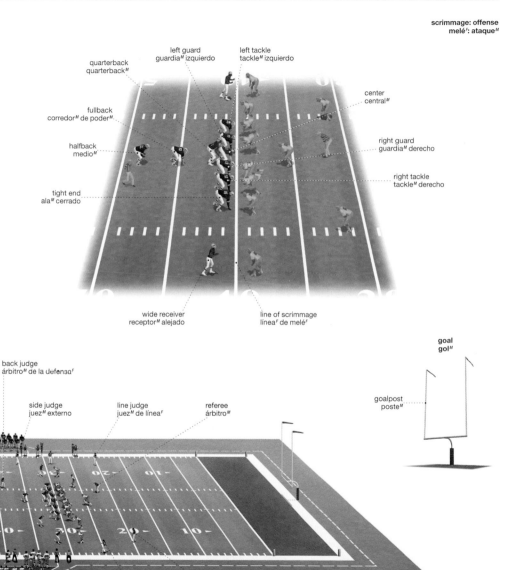

scrimmage: offense
melé^F: ataque^M

left guard
guardia^M izquierdo

left tackle
tackle^M izquierdo

quarterback
quarterback^M

center
central^M

fullback
corredor^M de poder^M

right guard
guardia^M derecho

halfback
medio^M

right tackle
tackle^M derecho

tight end
ala^M cerrado

wide receiver
receptor^M alejado

line of scrimmage
línea^F de melé^F

goal
gol^M

back judge
árbitro^M de la defensa^F

goalpost
poste^M

side judge
juez^M externo

line judge
juez^M de línea^F

referee
árbitro^M

players' bench
banquillo^M de jugadores^M

umpire
juez^M

head linesman
juez^M de línea^F

SPORTS AND GAMES

football

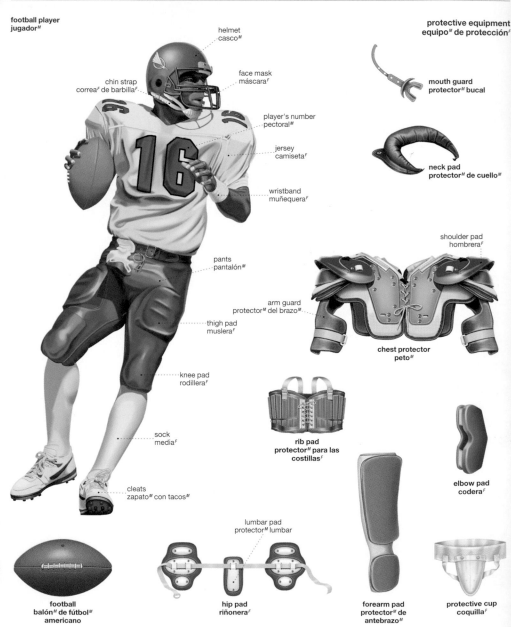

football player
jugador^M

protective equipment
equipo^M **de protección**^F

helmet
casco^M

chin strap
correa^F de barbilla^F

face mask
máscara^F

player's number
pectoral^M

jersey
camiseta^F

wristband
muñequera^F

pants
pantalón^M

arm guard
protector^M del brazo^M

thigh pad
muslera^F

knee pad
rodillera^F

sock
media^F

cleats
zapato^M con tacos^M

mouth guard
protector^M bucal

neck pad
protector^M de cuello^M

shoulder pad
hombrera^F

chest protector
peto^M

rib pad
protector^M **para las**
costillas^F

elbow pad
codera^F

lumbar pad
protector^M lumbar

football
balón^M **de fútbol**^M
americano

hip pad
riñonera^F

forearm pad
protector^M **de**
antebrazo^M

protective cup
coquilla^F

Canadian football
fútbol^M canadiense

**Canadian football field
campo^M de fútbol^M canadiense**

center line
línea^F de centro^M

goal line
línea de meta^F

players' bench
banquillo^M de los jugadores^M

end zone
zona^F de fondo^M

goal
gol^M

netball
netball^M

**netball court
campo^M de netball^M**

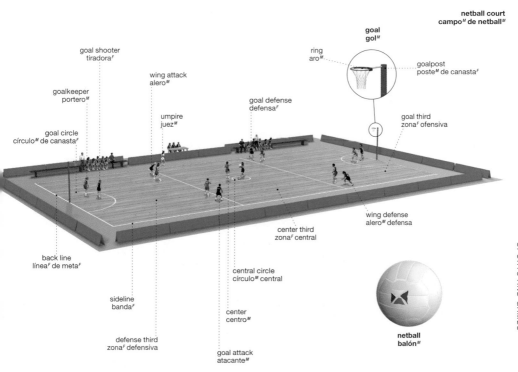

goal
gol^M

ring
aro^M

goalpost
poste^M de canasta^F

goal shooter
tiradora^F

wing attack
alero^M

goalkeeper
portero^M

umpire
juez^M

goal defense
defensa^F

goal circle
círculo^M de canasta^F

goal third
zona^F ofensiva

wing defense
alero^M defensa

center third
zona^F central

back line
línea^F de meta^F

central circle
círculo^M central

sideline
banda^F

center
centro^M

defense third
zona^F defensiva

goal attack
atacante^M

netball
balón^M

basketball

baloncesto^M

**basketball player
jugador**^M **de baloncesto**^M

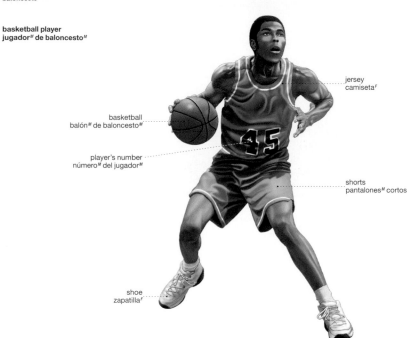

jersey
camiseta^F

basketball
balón^M de baloncesto^M

player's number
número^M del jugador^M

shorts
pantalones^M cortos

shoe
zapatilla^F

**basketball court
cancha**^F **de baloncesto**^M

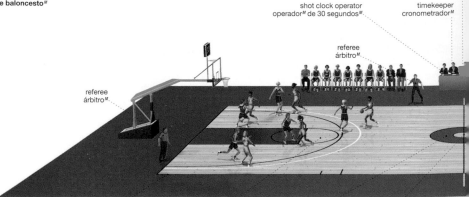

scorer
anotador^M

shot clock operator
operador^M de 30 segundos^M

timekeeper
cronometrador^M

referee
árbitro^M

referee
árbitro^M

sideline
banda^F

semicircle
semicírculo^M de la zona^F de tiro^M
libre

restraining circle
círculo^M central

midcourt line
línea^F de medio campo^M

center circle
círculo^M central

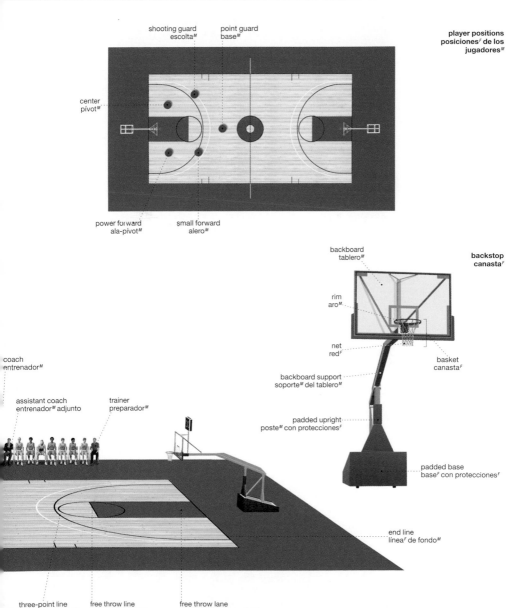

shooting guard
escolta^M

point guard
base^M

**player positions
posiciones^F de los
jugadores^M**

center
pívot^M

power forward
ala-pívot^M

small forward
alero^M

backboard
tablero^M

**backstop
canasta^F**

rim
aro^M

net
red^F

basket
canasta^F

backboard support
soporte^M del tablero^M

coach
entrenador^M

assistant coach
entrenador^M adjunto

trainer
preparador^M

padded upright
poste^M con protecciones^F

padded base
base^F con protecciones^F

end line
línea^F de fondo^M

three-point line
línea^F de tres puntos^M

free throw line
línea^F de tiro^M libre

free throw lane
zona^F de tres segundos^M

SPORTS AND GAMES

volleyball
voleibol^M

volleyball court
cancha^F de voleibol^M

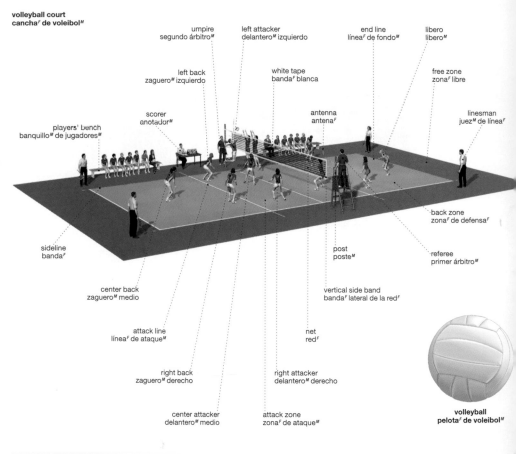

umpire
segundo árbitro^M

left attacker
delantero^M izquierdo

end line
línea^F de fondo^M

libero
libero^M

left back
zaguero^M izquierdo

white tape
banda^F blanca

free zone
zona^F libre

scorer
anotador^M

antenna
antena^F

linesman
juez^M de línea^F

players' bench
banquillo^M de jugadores^M

back zone
zona^F de defensa^F

sideline
banda^F

post
poste^M

referee
primer árbitro^M

center back
zaguero^M medio

vertical side band
banda^F lateral de la red^F

attack line
línea^F de ataque^M

net
red^F

right back
zaguero^M derecho

right attacker
delantero^M derecho

center attacker
delantero^M medio

attack zone
zona^F de ataque^M

volleyball
pelota^F de voleibol^M

techniques
técnicas^F

dig
plancha^F

bump
recepción^F

serve
saque^M

volleyball

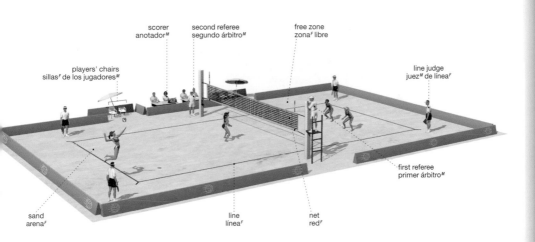

beach volleyball court
pista^F **voley**^M **playa**^M

scorer
anotador^M

second referee
segundo árbitro^M

free zone
zona^F libre

players' chairs
sillas^F de los jugadores^M

line judge
juez^M de línea^F

first referee
primer árbitro^M

sand
arena^F

line
línea^F

net
red^F

beach volleyball
voley^M **playa**^M

techniques

set
toque^M

spike
remate^M

block
tapón^M

team handball

balonmano^M^

player positions
posición^F^ **de los jugadores**^F^

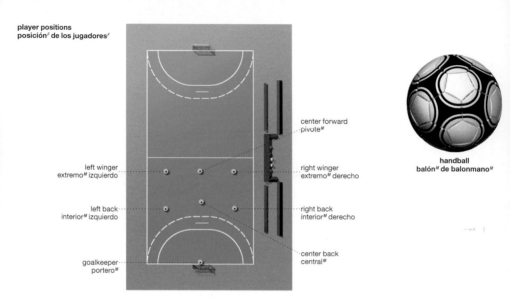

center forward
pivote^M^

left winger
extremo^M^ izquierdo

right winger
extremo^M^ derecho

left back
interior^M^ izquierdo

right back
interior^M^ derecho

center back
central^M^

goalkeeper
portero^M^

handball
balón^M^ **de balonmano**^M^

handball court
cancha^F^ **de balonmano**^M^

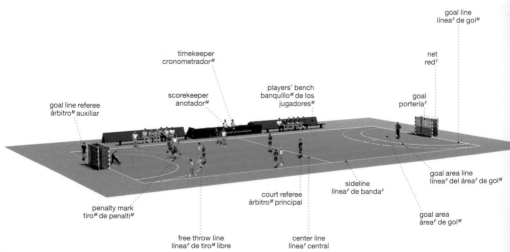

goal line
línea^F^ de gol^M^

timekeeper
cronometrador^M^

net
red^F^

scorekeeper
anotador^M^

players' bench
banquillo^M^ de los
jugadores^M^

goal
portería^F^

goal line referee
árbitro^M^ auxiliar

goal area line
línea^F^ del área^F^ de gol^M^

penalty mark
tiro^M^ de penalti^M^

court referee
árbitro^M^ principal

sideline
línea^F^ de banda^F^

goal area
área^F^ de gol^M^

free throw line
línea^F^ de tiro^M^ libre

center line
línea^F^ central

SPORTS AND GAMES

table tennis

tenis^M de mesa^F

tennis table
mesa^F de tenis^M

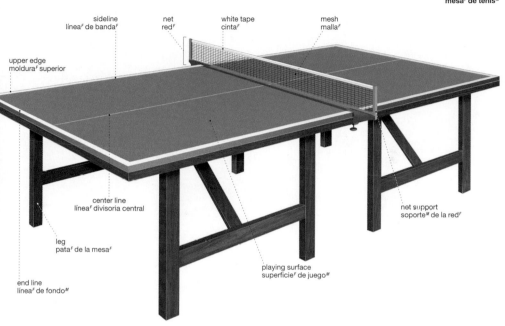

sideline
línea^F de banda^F

net
red^F

white tape
cinta^F

mesh
malla^F

upper edge
moldura^F superior

center line
línea^F divisoria central

net support
soporte^M de la red^F

leg
pata^F de la mesa^F

playing surface
superficie^F de juego^M

end line
línea^F de fondo^M

table tennis paddle
pala^F

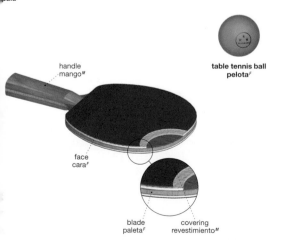

handle
mango^M

table tennis ball
pelota^F

face
cara^F

blade
paleta^F

covering
revestimiento^M

types of grip
formas^F de agarrar la
paleta^F

penholder grip
oriental

shake-hands grip
occidental

badminton

bádminton^M

badminton court
cancha^F de bádminton^M

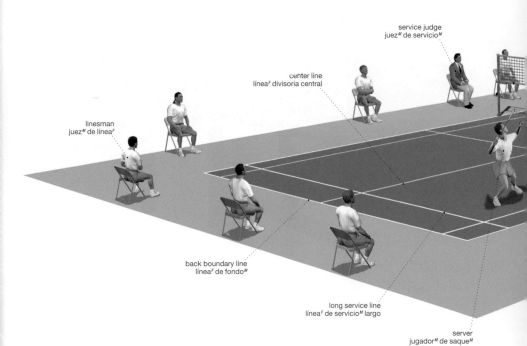

service judge
juez^M de servicio^M

center line
línea^F divisoria central

linesman
juez^M de línea^F

back boundary line
línea^F de fondo^M

long service line
línea^F de servicio^M largo

server
jugador^M de saque^M

badminton racket
raqueta^F de bádminton^M

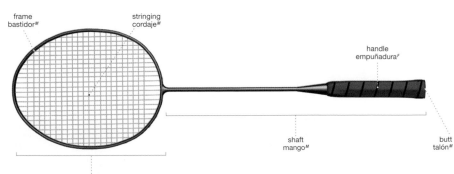

frame
bastidor^M

stringing
cordaje^M

handle
empuñadura^F

shaft
mango^M

butt
talón^M

head
cabeza^F

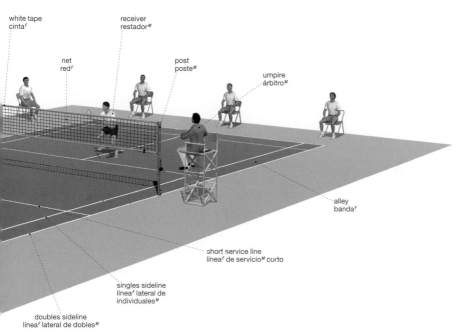

white tape
cinta^F

receiver
restador^M

net
red^F

post
poste^M

umpire
árbitro^M

alley
banda^F

short service line
línea^F de servicio^M corto

singles sideline
línea^F lateral de
individuales^M

doubles sideline
línea^F lateral de dobles^M

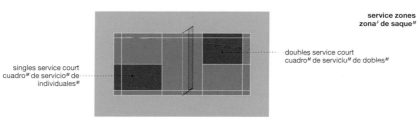

**service zones
zona^F de saque^M**

singles service court
cuadro^M de servicio^M de
individuales^M

doubles service court
cuadro^M de servicio^M de dobles^M

**synthetic shuttlecock
volante^M sintético**

**feathered shuttlecock
volante^M de plumas^F**

feather crown
penacho^M de plumas^F

cork tip
corcho^M

racquetball
raquetball^M

racquetball court
cancha^F de raquetball^M

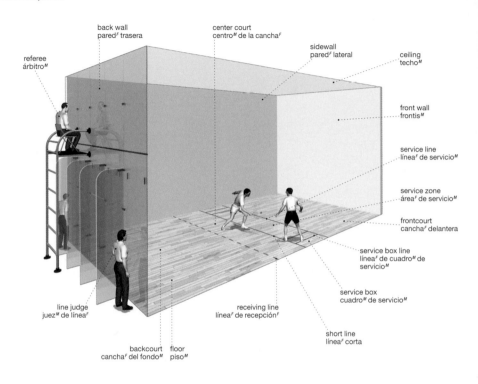

back wall
pared^F trasera

center court
centro^M de la cancha^F

sidewall
pared^F lateral

ceiling
techo^M

referee
árbitro^M

front wall
frontis^M

service line
línea^F de servicio^M

service zone
área^F de servicio^M

frontcourt
cancha^F delantera

service box line
línea^F de cuadro^M de
servicio^M

service box
cuadro^M de servicio^M

line judge
juez^M de línea^F

receiving line
línea^F de recepción^F

short line
línea^F corta

backcourt   floor
cancha^F del fondo^M   piso^M

racquetball racket
raqueta^F de raquetball^M

safety cord
correa^F de seguridad^F

bumper guard
marco^M

I.R.F

racquetball
pelota^F de raquetball^M

protective goggles
gafas^F de protección^F

squash
squash[M]

squash court
cancha[F] de squash[M]

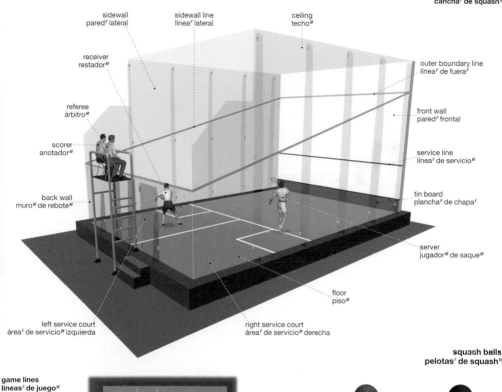

sidewall
pared[F] lateral

sidewall line
línea[F] lateral

ceiling
techo[M]

receiver
restador[M]

outer boundary line
línea[F] de fuera[F]

referee
árbitro[M]

front wall
pared[F] frontal

scorer
anotador[M]

service line
línea[F] de servicio[M]

back wall
muro[M] de rebote[M]

tin board
plancha[F] de chapa[F]

server
jugador[M] de saque[M]

floor
piso[M]

left service court
área[F] de servicio[M] izquierda

right service court
área[F] de servicio[M] derecha

squash balls
pelotas[F] de squash[M]

training ball
pelota[F] de
entrenamiento[M]

tournament ball
pelota[F] de torneo[M]

game lines
líneas[F] de juego[M]

half-court line
línea[F] de medio campo[M]

service box
cuadro[M] de servicio[M]

short line
línea[F] de servicio[M]

squash racket
raqueta[F] de squash[M]

protective goggles
gafas[F] protectoras

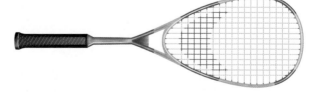

SPORTS AND GAMES

tennis

tenis^M

tennis court
cancha^F de tenis^M

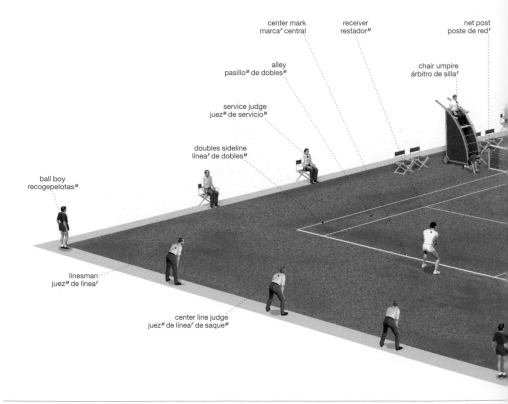

center mark
marca^F central

receiver
restador^M

net post
poste de red^F

alley
pasillo^M de dobles^M

chair umpire
árbitro de silla^F

service judge
juez^M de servicio^M

doubles sideline
línea^F de dobles^M

ball boy
recogepelotas^M

linesman
juez^M de línea^F

center line judge
juez^M de línea^F de saque^M

strokes
golpes^M

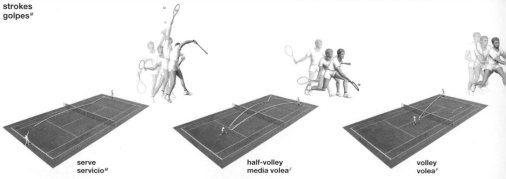

serve
servicio^M

half-volley
media volea^F

volley
volea^F

tennis

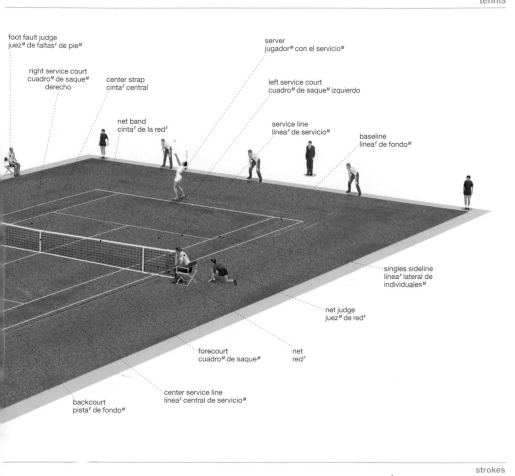

foot fault judge
juez^M de faltas^F de pie^M

server
jugador^M con el servicio^M

right service court
cuadro^M de saque^M
derecho

center strap
cinta^F central

left service court
cuadro^M de saque^M izquierdo

net band
cinta^F de la red^F

service line
línea^F de servicio^M

baseline
línea^F de fondo^M

singles sideline
línea^F lateral de
individuales^M

net judge
juez^M de red^F

forecourt
cuadro^M de saque^M

net
red^F

backcourt
pista^F de fondo^M

center service line
línea^F central de servicio^M

strokes

lob
globo^M

drop shot
dejada^F

smash
smash^M

SPORTS AND GAMES

tennis

tennis racket
raqueta^F **de tenis**^M

frame
bastidor^M

stringing
cordaje^M

head
cabeza^F

shoulder
hombro^M

throat
garganta^F

shaft
mango^M

handle
empuñadura^F

butt
puño^M

tennis ball
pelota^F **de tenis**^M

tennis player
tenista^{M/F}

polo shirt
polo^M

wristband
muñequera^F

skirt
falda^M

sock
calcetín^M

tennis shoe
zapatilla^F de tenis^M

scoreboard
marcador^M

previous sets
mangas^F anteriores

set
manga^F

GAMES   POINTS

points
puntos^M

game
juego^M

players
jugadores^M

playing surfaces
superficies^F **de juego**^M

grass
hierba^F

clay
tierra^F batida

hard surface
superficie^F dura

synthetic surface
superficie^F sintét...

gymnastics
gimnasia^F

pommel horse
caballo^M con aros^M

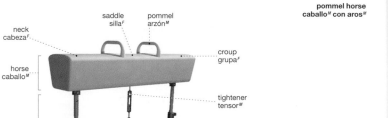

saddle
silla^F

pommel
arzón^M

neck
cabeza^F

croup
grupa^F

horse
caballo^M

tightener
tensor^M

height adjustment
regulador^M de altura^F

base
base^F

upright
soporte^M

chain
cadena^F

antislip shoe
zapata^F antideslizante

balance beam
barra^F de equilibrio^M

height adjustment
regulador^M de altura^F

beam
barra^F

upright
montante^M

vault
potro^M

springboard
plancha^F de muelles^M

SPORTS AND GAMES

gymnastics

event platform
área^F de competición^F

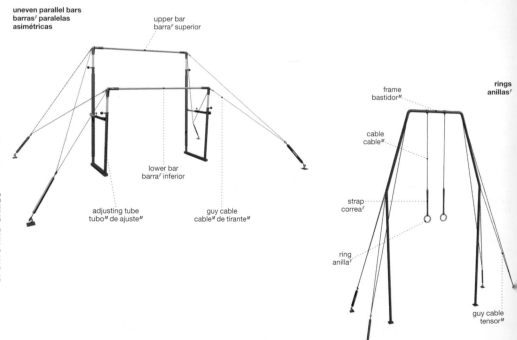

overall standings scoreboard
marcador^M de clasificación^F
general

balance beam
barra^F de equilibrio^M

floor exercise area
practicable^M para ejercicios
de suelo

uneven parallel bars
barras^F paralelas
asimétricas

pommel horse
caballo^M con arcos^M

line judge
juez^M de línea^F

judges
jueces^M

floor mats
colchoneta^F de
recepción^F

horizontal bar
barra^F fija

vault
potro^M

approach runs
pistas^F de carreras

uneven parallel bars
barras^F paralelas
asimétricas

upper bar
barra^F superior

rings
anillas^F

frame
bastidor^M

cable
cable^M

lower bar
barra^F inferior

strap
correa^F

adjusting tube
tubo^M de ajuste^M

guy cable
cable^M de tirante^M

ring
anilla^F

guy cable
tensor^M

scoreboard
marcador^M

gymnast's name
nombre^M del gimnasta^M

current event scoreboard
marcador^M del evento^M en
curso^M

nationality
nacionalidad^F

judges
jueces^M

vault
potro^M

rings
anillas^F

parallel bars
barras^F paralelas

score
nota^F

magnesium powder
polvo^M de magnesio^M

judges
jueces^M

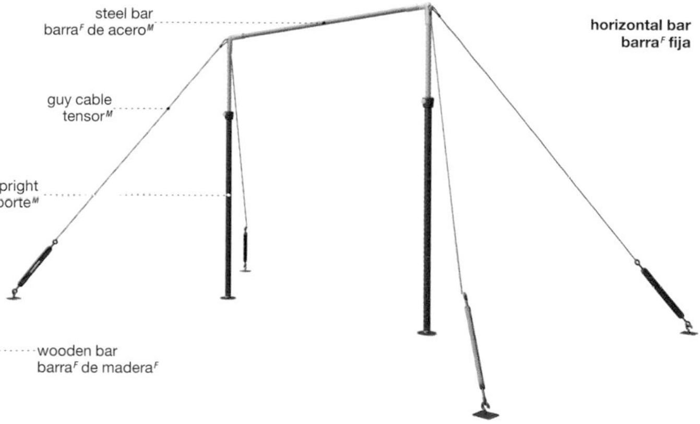

steel bar
barra^F de acero^M

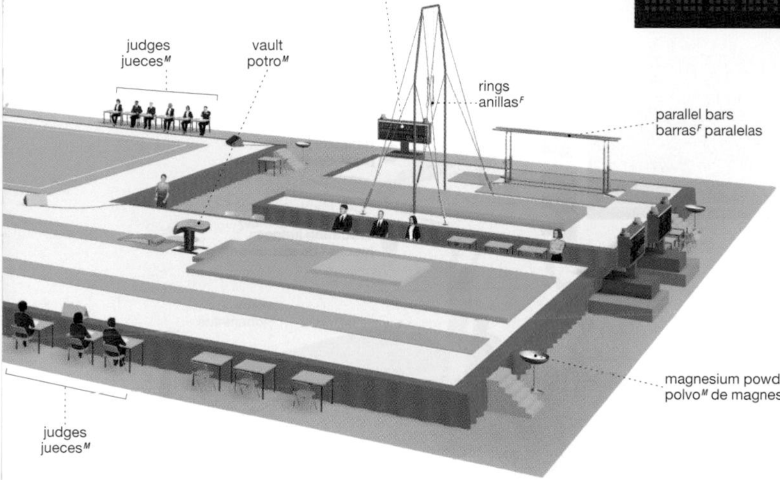

horizontal bar
barra^F fija

guy cable
tensor^M

upright
soporte^M

parallel bars
barras^F paralelas

wooden bar
barra^F de madera^F

adjusting tube
tubo^M de ajuste^M

base
base^F

SPORTS AND GAMES

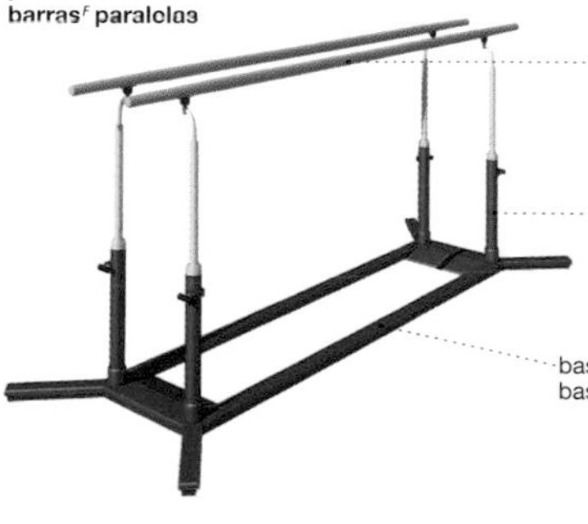

water polo

waterpolo^M

water polo player
jugador^M **de waterpolo**^M

water polo ball
balón^M

cap
gorro^M de baño^M

goal
portería^F

crossbar
larguero^M

net
red^F

floater
flotador^M de la portería^F

post
poste^M

water polo pool
piscina^F **de waterpolo**^M

timekeepers
cronometradores^M

secretaries
secretarios^M

team bench
banquillo^M del equipo^M

goal judge
juez^M de gol^M

goalkeeper
portero^M

coach
entrenador^M

goal line
línea^F de meta^F

2 m line
línea^F de 2 m

referee
árbitro^M principal

excluded players re-entry area
zona^F de entrada^F de los jugadores^M
expulsados

4 m line
línea^F de 4 m

half-distance line
línea^F del medio campo^M

7 m line
línea^F de 7 m

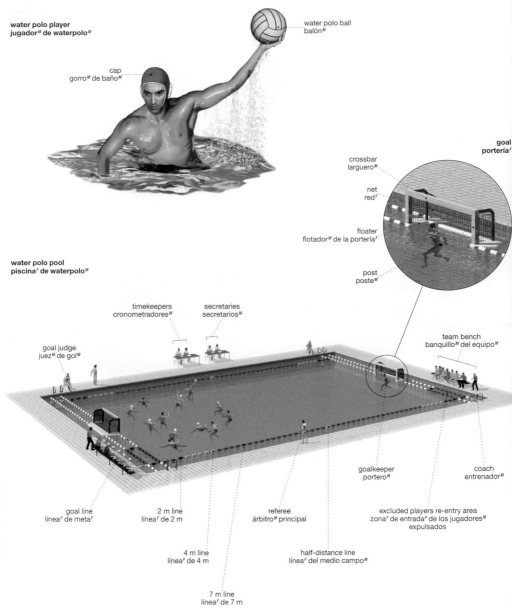

SPORTS AND GAMES

swimming
natación^F

types of strokes
estilos^M de natación^F

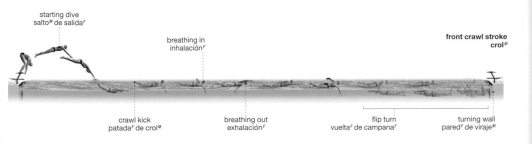

starting dive
salto^M de salida^F

breathing in
inhalación^F

front crawl stroke
crol^M

crawl kick
patada^F de crol^M

breathing out
exhalación^F

flip turn
vuelta^F de campana^F

turning wall
pared^F de viraje^M

breaststroke
braza^F

breaststroke kick
patada^F de rana^F

breaststroke turn
toque^M con dos manos^F

butterfly stroke
mariposa^F

butterfly kick
patada^F de mariposa^F

butterfly turn
viraje^M de mariposa^F

backstroke
espalda^F

backstroke start
posición^F de salida^F de
espalda^F

flip turn
vuelta^F de campana^F

SPORTS AND GAMES

swimming

starting block
plataforma^F de salida^F

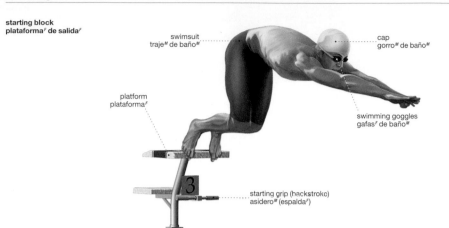

swimsuit
traje^M de baño^M

cap
gorro^M de baño^M

platform
plataforma^F

swimming goggles
gafas^F de baño^M

starting grip (backstroke)
asidero^M (espalda^F)

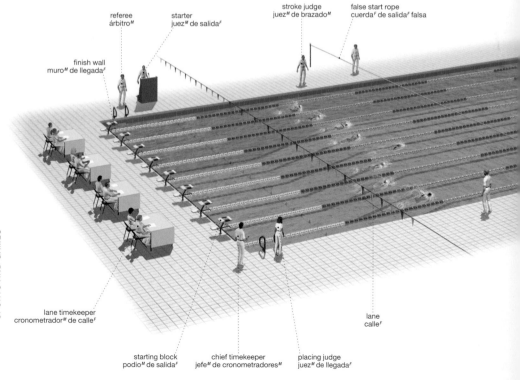

referee
árbitro^M

starter
juez^M de salida^F

stroke judge
juez^M de brazado^M

false start rope
cuerda^F de salida^F falsa

finish wall
muro^M de llegada^F

lane timekeeper
cronometrador^M de calle^F

lane
calle^F

starting block
podio^M de salida^F

chief timekeeper
jefe^M de cronometradores^M

placing judge
juez^M de llegada^F

swimming

scoreboard
marcador^M

event
prueba^F

WOMEN'S 400 IND FREE
0.00

LANE
1 IRL SMITH   8 4:21.00
2 CAN LIMPERT   4 4:14.65
3 CHN LI LIN   3 4:12.71
4 USA WAGNER   1 4:02.06
5 SUI FRISCHKN.   6 4:16.56
6 ALL HASE   7 4:17.20
7 HOL VLIEGHUIS   2 4:06.90
8 RUS PANKRATOV   5 4:14.77

EVENT 018   HEAT 19

lane
calle^F

timer
cronómetro^M

swimmer's country
país^M del nadador^M

swimmer's name
nombre^M del nadador^M

order of finish
orden^M de llegada^F

swim times
tiempos^M realizados

backstroke turn indicator
indicador^M para viraje^M en nado^M de
espalda^F

sidewall
pared^F lateral

turning wall
pared^F de viraje^M

turning judges
jueces^M de virajes^M

competitive course
piscina^F olímpica

lane rope
corchoras^F

bottom line
línea^F del fondo^M de la
piscina^F

automatic electronic timer
cronómetro^M electrónico
automático

diving
saltos^M

starting positions
posiciones^F de salida^F

reverse dive
salto^M inverso

inward dive
salto^M interior

backward dive
salto^M hacia atrás

forward dive
salto^M frontal

armstand dive
salto^M en equilibrio^M

flight positions
posiciones^F de salto^M

tuck position
posición^F C - cuerpo^M
encogido

straight position
posición^F A - en
plancha^F

pike position
posición^F B - hacer la
carpa^F

diving installations
torre^F de saltos^M

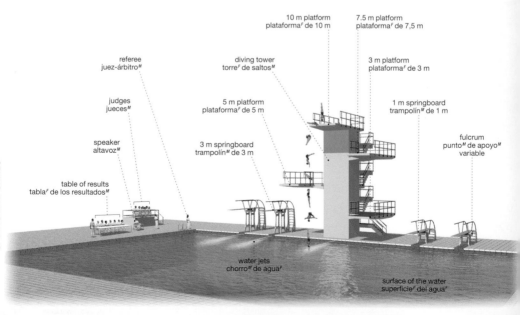

10 m platform
plataforma^F de 10 m

7.5 m platform
plataforma^F de 7,5 m

referee
juez-árbitro^M

diving tower
torre^F de saltos^M

3 m platform
plataforma^F de 3 m

judges
jueces^M

5 m platform
plataforma^F de 5 m

1 m springboard
trampolín^M de 1 m

speaker
altavoz^M

3 m springboard
trampolín^M de 3 m

fulcrum
punto^M de apoyo^M
variable

table of results
tabla^F de los resultados^M

water jets
chorro^M de agua^F

surface of the water
superficie^F del agua^F

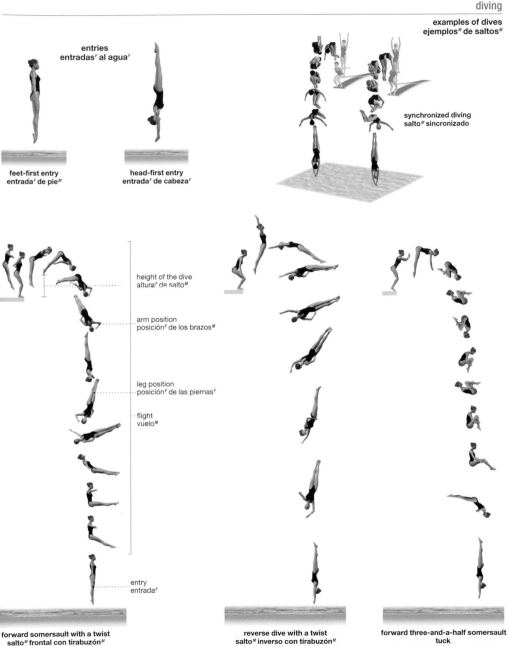

examples of dives
ejemplos^M de saltos^M

entries
entradas^F al agua^F

synchronized diving
salto^M sincronizado

feet-first entry
entrada^F de pie^M

head-first entry
entrada^F de cabeza^F

height of the dive
altura^F de salto^M

arm position
posición^F de los brazos^M

leg position
posición^F de las piernas^F

flight
vuelo^M

entry
entrada^F

forward somersault with a twist
salto^M frontal con tirabuzón^M

reverse dive with a twist
salto^M inverso con tirabuzón^M

forward three-and-a-half somersault
tuck
triple salto^M mortal y medio hacia
delante encogido

sailing
vela^F

sailboat
velero^M

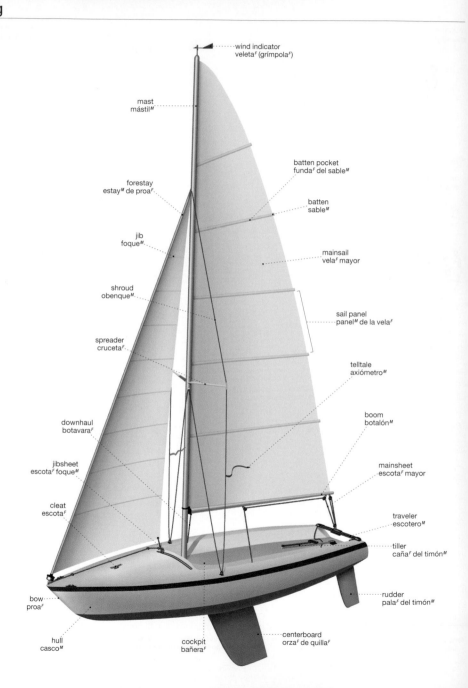

wind indicator
veleta^F (grímpola^F)

mast
mástil^M

batten pocket
funda^F del sable^M

forestay
estay^M de proa^F

batten
sable^M

jib
foque^M

mainsail
vela^F mayor

shroud
obenque^M

sail panel
panel^M de la vela^F

spreader
cruceta^F

telltale
axiómetro^M

downhaul
botavara^F

boom
botalón^M

jibsheet
escota^F foque^M

mainsheet
escota^F mayor

cleat
escota^F

traveler
escotero^M

tiller
caña^F del timón^M

bow
proa^F

rudder
pala^F del timón^M

hull
casco^M

cockpit
bañera^F

centerboard
orza^F de quilla^F

multihulls
multicasco^M

monohulls
monocascos^M

centerboard boat
deriva^F móvil

keel boat
quilla^F

catamaran
catamarán^M

trimaran
trimarán^M

upperworks
obra^F **muerta**

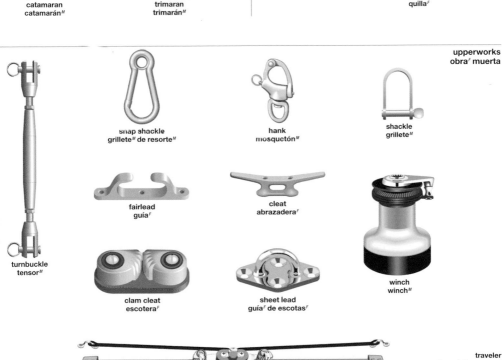

snap shackle
grillete^M de resorte^M

hank
mosquetón^M

shackle
grillete^M

fairlead
guía^F

cleat
abrazadera^F

turnbuckle
tensor^M

clam cleat
escotera^F

sheet lead
guía^F de escotas^F

winch
winch^M

traveler
barra^F de escotas^F

sliding rail
riel^M corredizo

car
carro^M

clam cleat
abrazadera^F

end stop
amarre^M

SPORTS AND GAMES

sailing

points of sailing
disposiciones^F de las velas^F

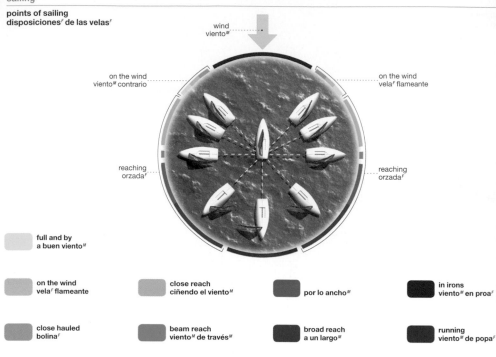

wind
viento^M

on the wind
viento^M contrario

on the wind
vela^F flameante

reaching
orzada^F

reaching
orzada^F

full and by
a buen viento^M

on the wind
vela^F flameante

close reach
ciñendo el viento^M

por lo ancho^M

in irons
viento^M en proa^F

close hauled
bolina^F

beam reach
viento^M de través^M

broad reach
a un largo^M

running
viento^M de popa^F

sailing course
regata^F

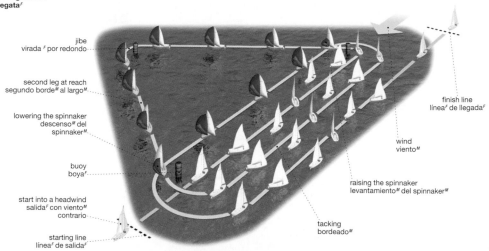

jibe
virada ^F por redondo

second leg at reach
segundo borde^M al largo^M

lowering the spinnaker
descenso^M del
spinnaker^M

buoy
boya^F

start into a headwind
salida^F con viento^M
contrario

starting line
línea^F de salida^F

finish line
línea^F de llegada^F

wind
viento^M

raising the spinnaker
levantamiento^M del spinnaker^M

tacking
bordeado^M

sailboard
windsurf^M

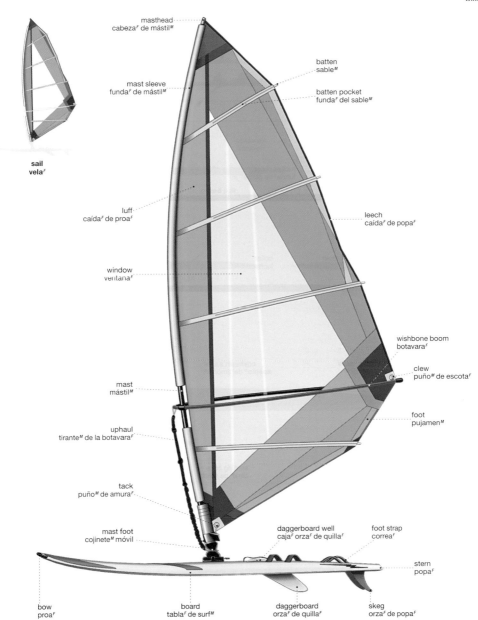

sail
vela^F

masthead
cabeza^F de mástil^M

batten
sable^M

batten pocket
funda^F del sable^M

mast sleeve
funda^F de mástil^M

luff
caída^F de proa^F

leech
caída^F de popa^F

window
ventana^F

wishbone boom
botavara^F

clew
puño^M de escota^F

mast
mástil^M

foot
pujamen^M

uphaul
tirante^M de la botavara^F

tack
puño^M de amura^F

mast foot
cojinete^M móvil

daggerboard well
caja^F orza^F de quilla^F

foot strap
correa^F

stern
popa^F

bow
proa^F

board
tabla^F de surf^M

daggerboard
orza^F de quilla^F

skeg
orza^F de popa^F

SPORTS AND GAMES

kung fu

kung fu*M*

kung fu practitioner
practicante*M*

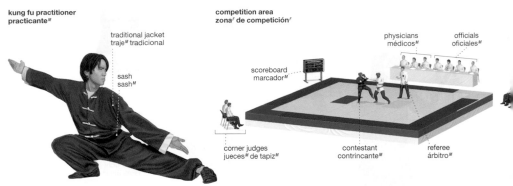

traditional jacket
traje*M* tradicional

sash
sash*M*

competition area
zona*F* de competición*F*

scoreboard
marcador*M*

physicians
médicos*M*

officials
oficiales*M*

corner judges
jueces*M* de tapiz*M*

contestant
contrincante*M*

referee
árbitro*M*

jujitsu

ju-jitsu*M*

competition area
zona*F* de competición*F*

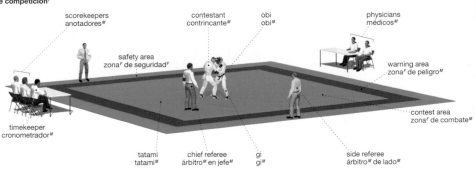

scorekeepers
anotadores*M*

contestant
contrincante*M*

obi
obi*M*

physicians
médicos*M*

safety area
zona*F* de seguridad*F*

warning area
zona*F* de peligro*M*

contest area
zona*F* de combate*M*

timekeeper
cronometrador*M*

tatami
tatami*M*

chief referee
árbitro*M* en jefe*M*

gi
gi*M*

side referee
árbitro*M* de lado*M*

aikido

aikido*M*

aikidoka
aikidoka*M*

aikidogi
aikidogi*M*

obi
obi*M*

hakama
hakama*M*

jo
bastón*M*

bokken
bokken*M*

sailboard

windsurf^M

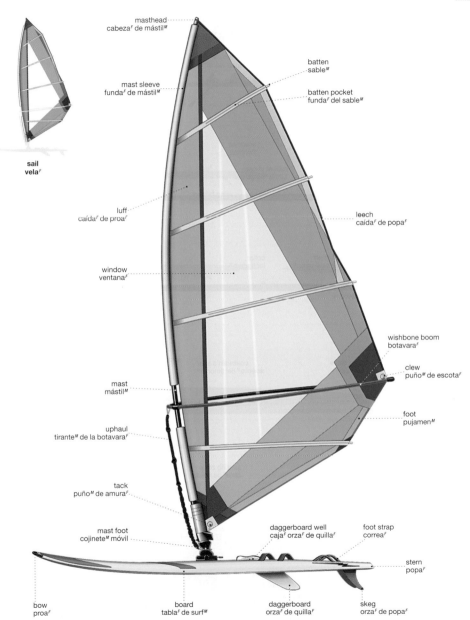

sail
vela^F

masthead
cabeza^F de mástil^M

batten
sable^M

mast sleeve
funda^F de mástil^M

batten pocket
funda^F del sable^M

luff
caída^F de proa^F

leech
caída^F de popa^F

window
ventana^F

wishbone boom
botavara^F

clew
puño^M de escota^F

mast
mástil^M

foot
pujamen^M

uphaul
tirante^M de la botavara^F

tack
puño^M de amura^F

mast foot
cojinete^M móvil

daggerboard well
caja^F orza^F de quilla^F

foot strap
correa^F

stern
popa^F

bow
proa^F

board
tabla^F de surf^M

daggerboard
orza^F de quilla^F

skeg
orza^F de popa^F

SPORTS AND GAMES

canoe

canoa^F

whitewater canoe
canoa^F de aguas^F bravas

recreational canoe
canoa^F recreativa

thwart
bancada^F

carrying yoke
yugo^M de transporte^M

seat
sillín^M

end deck
extremo^M de popa^F

gunwale
bordal^F

hull
casco^M

forestem
proa^F apuntada

single-bladed paddle
remo^M de una sola pala^F

canoe-kayak: flatwater racing

canoa^F-kayak^M: regata^F

C1 canoe
canoa^F C1

deck
cubierta^F

forestem
proa^F apuntada

kayak

kayak^M

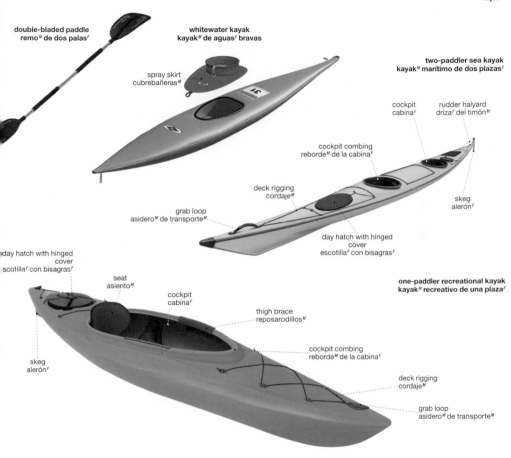

double-bladed paddle
remo^M de dos palas^F

whitewater kayak
kayak^M de aguas^F bravas

spray skirt
cubrebañeras^M

two-paddler sea kayak
kayak^M marítimo de dos plazas^F

cockpit
cabina^F

rudder halyard
driza^F del timón^M

cockpit combing
reborde^M de la cabina^F

deck rigging
cordaje^M

grab loop
asidero^M de transporte^M

skeg
alerón^F

day hatch with hinged
cover
escotilla^F con bisagras^F

day hatch with hinged
cover
scotilla^F con bisagras^F

seat
asiento^M

cockpit
cabina^F

thigh brace
reposarodillos^M

one-paddler recreational kayak
kayak^M recreativo de una plaza^F

cockpit combing
reborde^M de la cabina^F

skeg
alerón^F

deck rigging
cordaje^M

grab loop
asidero^M de transporte^M

canoe-kayak: flatwater racing

K1 kayak
kayak^M K1

seat
asiento^M

tapered end
proa^F afilada

rudder
timón^M

waterskiing

esquí^M acuático

examples of skis
ejemplos^M de esquís^M

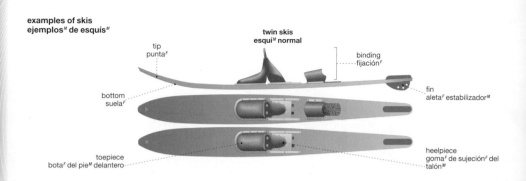

twin skis
esquí^M normal

tip
punta^F

binding
fijación^F

bottom
suela^F

fin
aleta^F estabilizador^M

toepiece
bota^F del pie^M delantero

heelpiece
goma^F de sujeción^F del talón^M

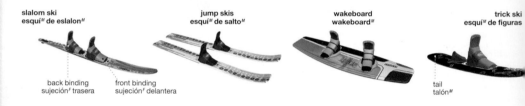

slalom ski
esquí^M de eslalon^M

jump skis
esquí^M de salto^M

wakeboard
wakeboard^M

trick ski
esquí^M de figuras

back binding
sujeción^F trasera

front binding
sujeción^F delantera

tail
talón^M

examples of handles
ejemplos^M de empuñaduras^F

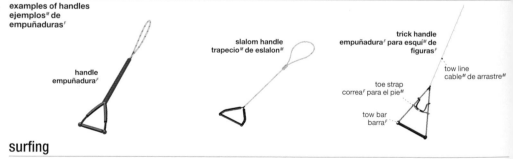

slalom handle
trapecio^M de eslalon^M

trick handle
empuñadura^F para esquí^M de figuras^F

tow line
cable^M de arrastre^M

toe strap
correa^F para el pie^M

handle
empuñadura^F

tow bar
barra^F

surfing

surf^M

surfer
surfista^M

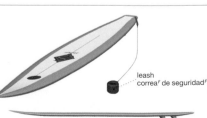

leash
correa^F de seguridad^F

boot
escarpín^M

surfboard
tabla^F de surf^M

skeg
alerón^M

scuba diving
buceo^M

scuba diver
buceador^M

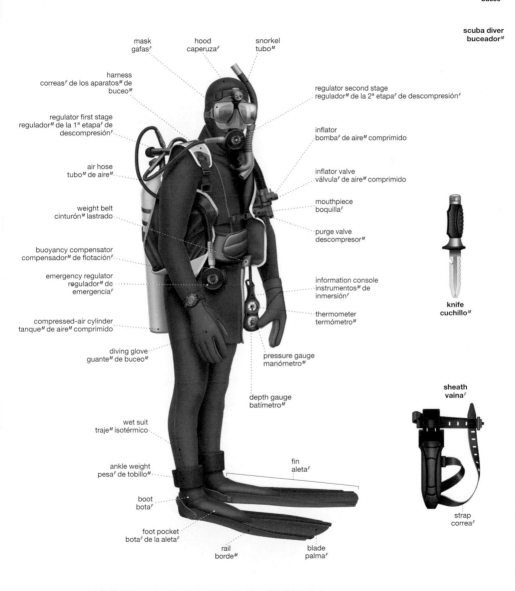

mask
gafas^F

hood
caperuza^F

snorkel
tubo^M

harness
correas^F de los aparatos^M de
buceo^M

regulator second stage
regulador^M de la 2ª etapa^F de descompresión^F

regulator first stage
regulador^M de la 1ª etapa^F de
descompresión^F

inflator
bomba^F de aire^M comprimido

air hose
tubo^M de aire^M

inflator valve
válvula^F de aire^M comprimido

weight belt
cinturón^M lastrado

mouthpiece
boquilla^F

buoyancy compensator
compensador^M de flotación^F

purge valve
descompresor^M

emergency regulator
regulador^M de
emergencia^F

information console
instrumentos^M de
inmersión^F

compressed-air cylinder
tanque^M de aire^M comprimido

thermometer
termómetro^M

knife
cuchillo^M

diving glove
guante^M de buceo^M

pressure gauge
manómetro^M

depth gauge
batímetro^M

wet suit
traje^M isotérmico

sheath
vaina^F

ankle weight
pesa^F de tobillo^M

fin
aleta^F

boot
bota^F

foot pocket
bota^F de la aleta^F

strap
correa^F

rail
borde^M

blade
palma^F

speargun
arpón^M submarino

SPORTS AND GAMES

boxing

boxeo^M

boxer
boxeador^M

headgear
casco^M

boxing glove
guante^M de boxeo^M

boxing trunks
pantalones^M de boxeo^M

punching bag
saco^M de arena^F

speed ball
pera^F de maíz^M

ring
cuadrilátero^M

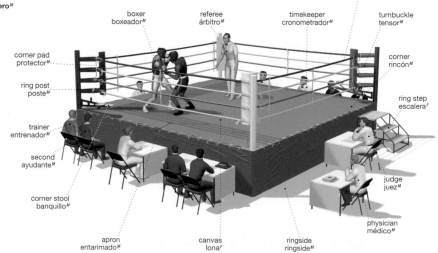

rope
cuerda^F

boxer
boxeador^M

referee
árbitro^M

timekeeper
cronometrador^M

turnbuckle
tensor^M

corner pad
protector^M

ring post
poste^M

trainer
entrenador^M

second
ayudante^M

corner stool
banquillo^M

corner
rincón^M

ring step
escalera^F

judge
juez^M

physician
médico^M

apron
entarimado^M

canvas
lona^F

ringside
ringside^M

boxing

boxing equipment
equipo^M de boxeo^M

lace
cordones^M

boxing gloves
guantes^M de boxeo^M

handwrap
vendaje^M

protective cup
coquilla^F

mouthpiece
protector^M bucal

wrestling

lucha^F

starting positions
posiciones^M iniciales

wrestler
luchador^M

singlet
camiseta^F

crouching position (freestyle wrestling)
posición[,] en guardia^F: (lucha^F libre)

standing position (Greco-Roman wrestling)
posición^F vertical: (lucha^F greco-romana)

wrestling shoe
botas^F de lucha^F

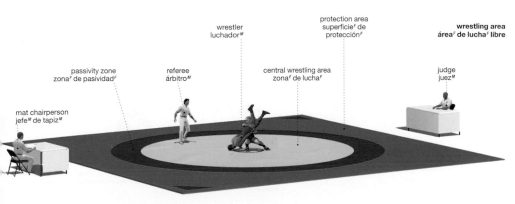

protection area
superficie^F de protección^F

wrestling area
área^F de lucha^F libre

wrestler
luchador^M

passivity zone
zona^F de pasividad^F

referee
árbitro^M

central wrestling area
zona^F de lucha^F

judge
juez^M

mat chairperson
jefe^M de tapiz^M

SPORTS AND GAMES

judo
judo^M

mat
tatami^M

scorers and timekeepers
anotadores^M y
cronometradores^M

scoreboard
marcador^M

medical team
equipo^M médico

contestant
uke (defensor^M)

safety area
zona^F de seguridad^F

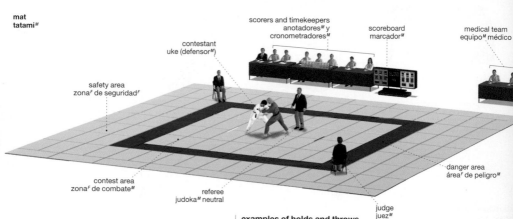

contest area
zona^F de combate^M

referee
judoka^M neutral

danger area
área^F de peligro^M

judge
juez^M

judogi
traje^M de judo^M: judoji^M

jacket
kimono^M

belt
cinturón^M

trousers
pantalón^M

examples of holds and throws
ejemplos^M de llaves^F

holding
inmovilización^F

stomach throw
proyección^F en círculo^M

sweeping hip throw
proyección^F primera de
cadera^F

major outer reaping throw
osoto-gari (gran siega^F) exterior

major inner reaping throw
gran siega^F interior

naked strangle
estrangulación^F

arm lock
inmovilización^F de
brazo^M

one-arm shoulder throw
proyección^F por encima del hombro^M con una mano^F

karate

karate^M

karateka
karateka^M

karate-gi
karategi^M

obi
obi^M

contest area
zona^F de combate^M

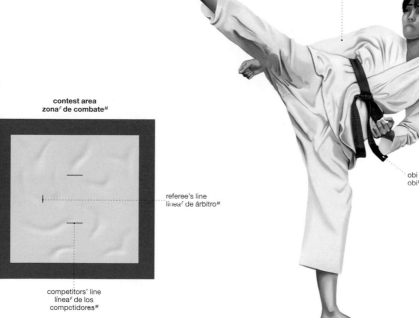

referee's line
línea^F de árbitro^M

competitors' line
línea^F de los
compotidores^M

competition area
zona^F de competición^F

arbitration committee
comité^M de arbitraje^M

corner judge
juez^M de ángulo^M

scorekeeper
anotador^M

timekeeper
cronometrador^M

referee
árbitro^M

karateka
karateka^M

taekwondo

taekwondo^M

competition area
zona^F de competición^F

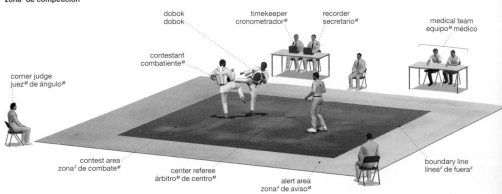

corner judge
juez^M de ángulo^M

dobok
dobok

contestant
combatiente^M

timekeeper
cronometrador^M

recorder
secretario^M

medical team
equipo^M médico

contest area
zona^F de combate^M

center referee
árbitro^M de centro^M

alert area
zona^F de aviso^M

boundary line
línea^F de fuera^F

taekwondo equipment
equipo^M de taekwondo^M

head guard
casco^M

forearm guard
protector^M para
antebrazo^M

male groin protector
coquilla^F

chest protector
peto^M

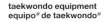

belt
cinturón^M

breast guard
protección^F para
pecho^M

shin guard
tobillera^F

female groin protector
coquilla^F femenina

techniques
técnicas^F

front kick
patada^F frontal

stance
guardia^F

extension
extensión^F

block
bloqueo^M

flying side kick
patada^F lateral con
salto^M

kendo
kendo^M

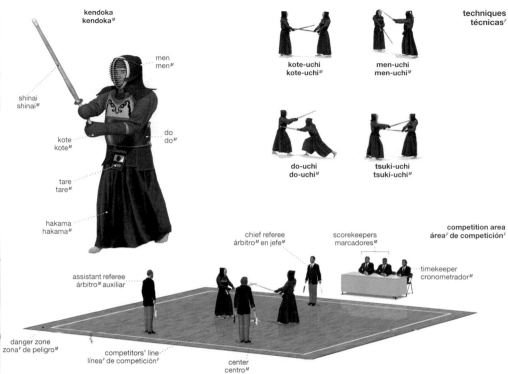

kendoka
kendoka^M

men
men^M

shinai
shinai^M

kote
kote^M

do
do^M

tare
tare^M

hakama
hakama^M

techniques
técnicas^F

kote-uchi
kote-uchi^M

men-uchi
men-uchi^M

do-uchi
do-uchi^M

tsuki-uchi
tsuki-uchi^M

competition area
área^F de competición^F

chief referee
árbitro^M en jefe^M

scorekeepers
marcadores^M

timekeeper
cronometrador^M

assistant referee
árbitro^M auxiliar

danger zone
zona^F de peligro^M

competitors' line
línea^F de competición^F

center
centro^M

tirad

sumo
sumo^M

dohyo
dohyo^M

mawashi
mawashi^M

gyoji
gyogi^M

sagari
sagari^M

salt
sal^M

step
peldaño^M

water
agua^M

mage
mage^M

sumotori
sumotori^M

línⅇ

SPORTS AND GAMES

fitness equipment

aparatos^M de ejercicios^M

dumbbell
pesas^F

bar
barra^F

weight
pesas^F

handgrips
empuñaderas^F

ankle/wrist weight
pesas^F para muñecas^F y
tobillos^M

jump rope
cuerda^F

chest expander
tensores^M pectorales

twist bar
barra^F de torsión^F

tension spring
resorte^M de tensión^F

grip
empuñadura^F

exercise ball
balón^M de ejercicios^M

exercise mat
esterilla^F

aerobics step
step^M de aeróbic^M

barbell
haltera^F

disk
disco^M

collar
collarín^M

sleeve
barra^F

bar
barra^F

SPORTS AND GAMES

fitness equipment

rowing machine
remo^M

treadmill
máquina^F **de correr**

display
pantalla^F

chain
cadena^F

display
pantalla^F

pulse monitor
pulsómetro^M

handle
barra^F

running surface
banda^F continua

sliding seat
asiento^M de corredera^F

resistance adjustment
ajuste^M de resistencia^F

footrest
reposapiés^M

stair climber
escalera^F

home gym
banco^M **de**
musculación^F

high pulley
polea^F alta

latissimus dorsi bar
barra^F de dorsales^F

stationary bicycle
bicicleta^F **estática**

low pulley
polea^F baja

pulse monitor
pulsómetro^M

electronic console
consola^F electrónica

backrest
respaldo^M

resistance adjustment
ajuste^M de resistencia^F

saddle
sillín^M

press arm
prensa^F de brazos^M

handlebar
manillar^M

bench
banco^M

wheel case
caja^F de la rueda^F

height adjustment
ajuste^M de altura^F

leg curl bar
barra^F de flexión^F de
piernas^F

footstrap
trabilla^F para el pie^M

leg extension bar
barra^F de extensión^F de
piernas^F

weights
pesas^F

pedal
pedal^M

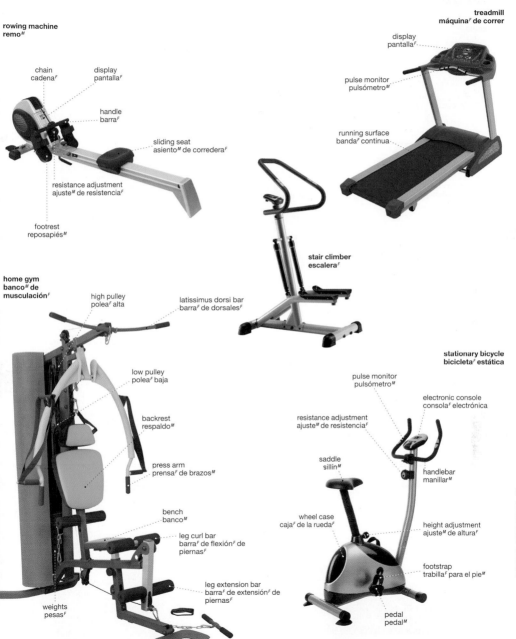

SPORTS AND GAMES

show jumping

salto^M de obstáculos^M

obstacles
obstáculos^M

gate
barrera^F

wall and rails
valla^F sobre muro^M

brush and rails
valla^F sobre seto^M

post and plank
palancas^F

triple bar
triple^M de barras^F

post and rail
vertical^M de barras^F

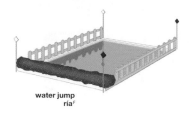

water jump
ría^F

wall
muro^M

oxer
óxer^M de barras^F

competition ring
pista^F para salto^M de
obstáculos^M

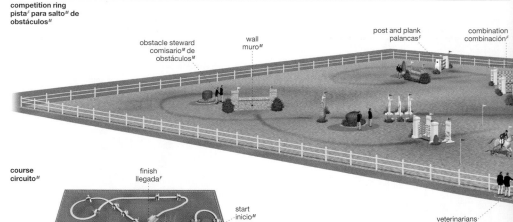

obstacle steward
comisario^M de
obstáculos^M

wall
muro^M

post and plank
palancas^F

combination
combinación^F

course
circuito^M

finish
llegada^F

start
inicio^M

veterinarians
veterinarios^M

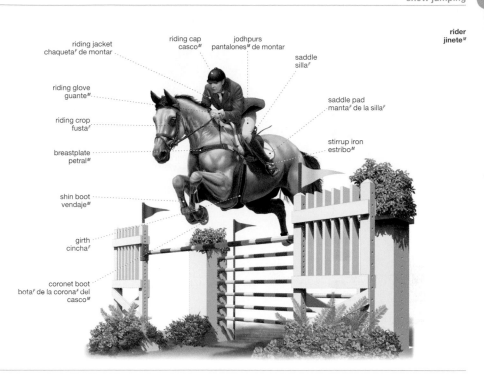

rider
jinete^M

riding jacket
chaqueta^F de montar

riding cap
casco^M

jodhpurs
pantalones^M de montar

saddle
silla^F

riding glove
guante^M

saddle pad
manta^F de la silla^F

riding crop
fusta^F

breastplate
petral^M

stirrup iron
estribo^M

shin boot
vendaje^M

girth
cincha^F

coronet boot
bota^F de la corona^F del
casco^M

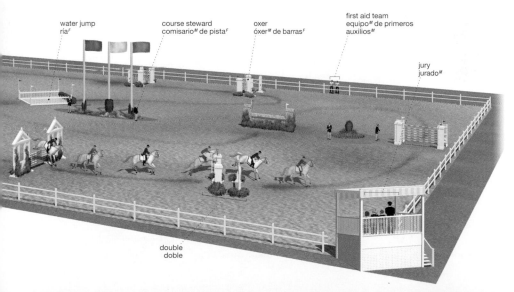

water jump
ría^F

course steward
comisario^M de pista^F

oxer
óxer^M de barras^F

first aid team
equipo^M de primeros
auxilios^M

jury
jurado^M

double
doble

SPORTS AND GAMES

riding

equitación^F

double bridle
brida^F

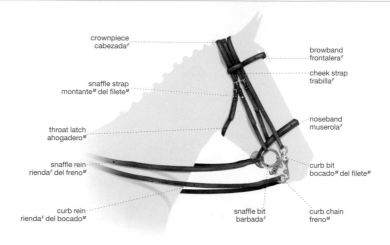

crownpiece
cabezada^F

browband
frontalera^F

cheek strap
trabilla^F

snaffle strap
montante^M del filete^M

noseband
muserola^F

throat latch
ahogadero^M

snaffle rein
rienda^F del freno^M

curb bit
bocado^M del filete^M

curb rein
rienda^F del bocado^M

snaffle bit
barbada^F

curb chain
freno^M

---

snaffle bits
bocados^M **de filete**^M

snaffle bit parts
partes^F **de un bocado**^M
de filete^M

jointed mouthpiece
filete^M articulado

rein ring
anillo^M de las riendas^F

full cheek snaffle bit with toggles
freno^M **de quijada**^F **acodado**

full cheek snaffle bit
filete^M **de quijada**^F
acodado

toggles
caireles^M

rubber snaffle bit
filete^M **acodado elástico**

egg butt snaffle bit
filete^M **ovoide acodado**

---

curb bits
bocados^M **con la**
barbada^F

curb bit parts
partes^F **de bocado**^M **con**
la barbada^F

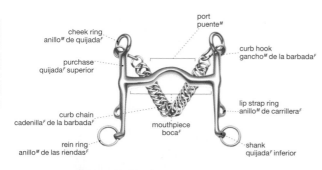

port
puente^M

cheek ring
anillo^M de quijada^F

curb hook
gancho^M de la barbada^F

purchase
quijada^F superior

lip strap ring
anillo^M de carrillera^F

curb chain
cadenilla^F de la barbada^F

mouthpiece
boca^F

rein ring
anillo^M de las riendas^F

shank
quijada^F inferior

sliding cheek bit
bocado^M **corredizo**

military bit
bocado^M **de codo**^M
militar

jointed mouth Pelham bit
bocado^M **articulado**

English saddle
silla^F de montar

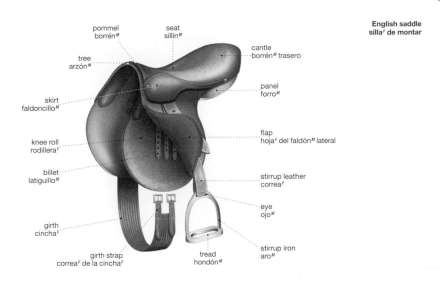

pommel
borrén^M

seat
sillín^M

tree
arzón^M

cantle
borrén^M trasero

skirt
faldoncillo^M

panel
forro^M

knee roll
rodillera^F

flap
hoja^F del faldón^M lateral

billet
latiguillo^M

stirrup leather
correa^F

eye
ojo^M

girth
cincha^F

stirrup iron
aro^M

girth strap
correa^F de la cincha^F

tread
hondón^M

dressage

doma^F

show ring
pista^F de competición^F

rider
jinete^M

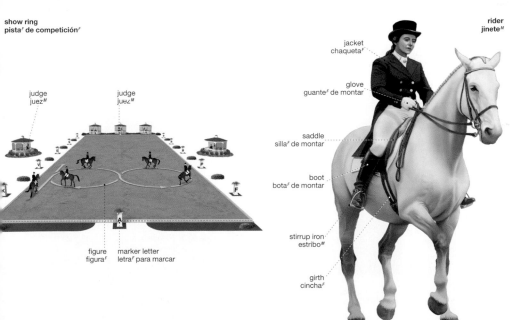

jacket
chaqueta^F

glove
guante^F de montar

judge
juez^M

judge
juez^M

saddle
silla^F de montar

boot
bota^F de montar

stirrup iron
estribo^M

figure
figura^F

marker letter
letra^F para marcar

girth
cincha^F

horse racing

carreraᶠ **de caballos**ᴹ

mounted racing
carreraᶠ **de caballos**ᴹ

riding cap
gorraᶠ

jockey
jockeyᴹ

saddle
sillaᶠ

shadow roll
muserolaᶠ

rein
riendaᶠ

saddlecloth
sudaderoᴹ

riding crop
fustaᶠ

girth
cinchaᶠ

racetrack
hipódromoᴹ

length post
posteᴹ indicador

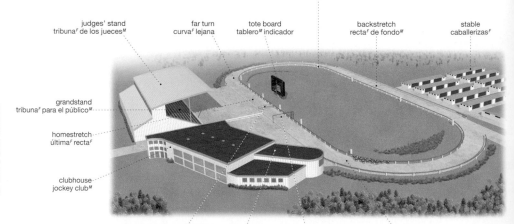

judges' stand
tribunaᶠ de los juecesᴹ

far turn
curvaᶠ lejana

tote board
tableroᴹ indicador

backstretch
rectaᶠ de fondoᴹ

stable
caballerizasᶠ

grandstand
tribunaᶠ para el públicoᴹ

homestretch
últimaᶠ rectaᶠ

clubhouse
jockey clubᴹ

starting gate
puertaᶠ de salidaᶠ

paddock
picaderoᴹ

finish line
líneaᶠ de llegadaᶠ

clubhouse turn
curvaᶠ del clubᴹ

SPORTS AND GAMES

harness racing: trotter
carreras^F con
arneses^M: trotón^M

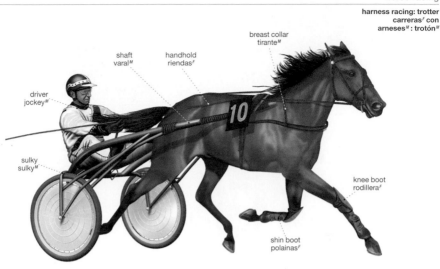

breast collar
tirante^M

shaft
varal^M

handhold
riendas^F

driver
jockey^M

sulky
sulky^M

knee boot
rodillera^F

shin boot
polainas^F

harness racing: pacer
carreras^F con
arneses^M: caballo^M de
paso^M

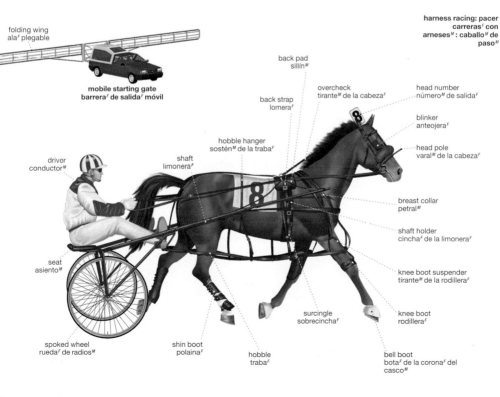

folding wing
ala^F plegable

mobile starting gate
barrera^F de salida^F móvil

back pad
sillín^M

overcheck
tirante^M de la cabeza^F

head number
número^M de salida^F

back strap
lomera^F

blinker
anteojera^F

hobble hanger
sostén^M de la traba^F

head pole
varal^M de la cabeza^F

driver
conductor^M

shaft
limonera^F

breast collar
petral^M

shaft holder
cincha^F de la limonera^F

seat
asiento^M

knee boot suspender
tirante^M de la rodillera^F

knee boot
rodillera^F

surcingle
sobrecincha^F

spoked wheel
rueda^F de radios^M

shin boot
polaina^F

hobble
traba^F

bell boot
bota^F de la corona^F del
casco^M

SPORTS AND GAMES

polo

polo^M

rider and horse
jinete^M y poni^M

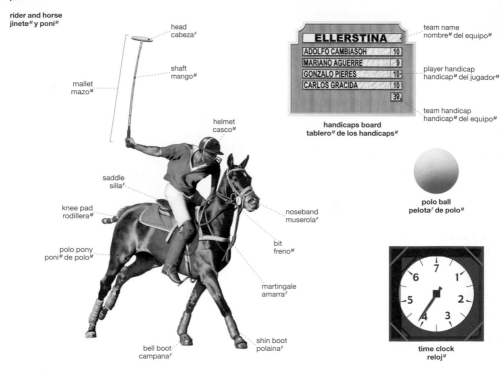

head
cabeza^F

shaft
mango^M

mallet
mazo^M

helmet
casco^M

saddle
silla^F

knee pad
rodillera^M

polo pony
poni^M de polo^M

noseband
muserola^F

bit
freno^M

martingale
amarra^F

bell boot
campana^F

shin boot
polaina^F

ELLERSTINA	
ADOLFO CAMBIASOH	10
MARIANO AGUERRE	9
GONZALO PIERES	10
CARLOS GRACIDA	10
	39

team name
nombre^M del equipo^M

player handicap
handicap^M del jugador^M

team handicap
handicap^M del equipo^M

handicaps board
tablero^M de los handicaps^M

polo ball
pelota^F de polo^M

time clock
reloj^M

polo field
campo^M de polo^M

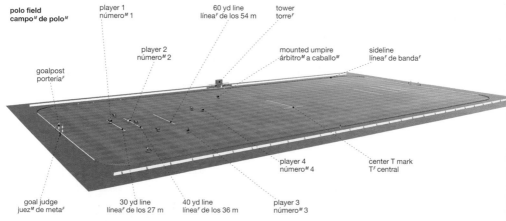

player 1
número^M 1

60 yd line
línea^F de los 54 m

tower
torre^F

player 2
número^M 2

mounted umpire
árbitro^M a caballo^M

sideline
línea^F de banda^F

goalpost
portería^F

player 4
número^M 4

center T mark
T^F central

goal judge
juez^M de meta^F

30 yd line
línea^F de los 27 m

40 yd line
línea^F de los 36 m

player 3
número^M 3

archery

tiro^M con arco^M

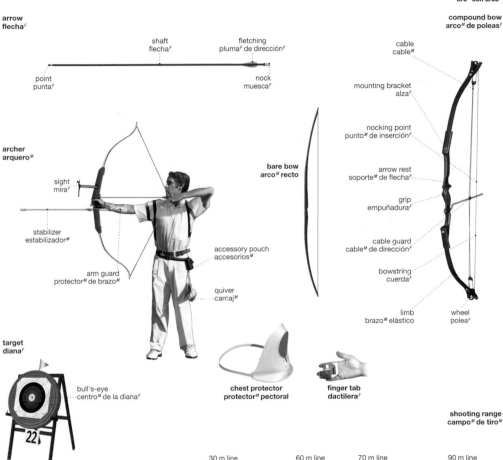

arrow
flecha^F

shaft
flecha^F

fletching
pluma^F de dirección^F

point
punta^F

nock
muesca^F

compound bow
arco^M de poleas^F

cable
cable^M

mounting bracket
alza^F

nocking point
punto^M de inserción^F

arrow rest
soporte^M de flecha^F

grip
empuñadura^F

cable guard
cable^M de dirección^F

bowstring
cuerda^F

limb
brazo^M elástico

wheel
polea^F

archer
arquero^M

sight
mira^F

stabilizer
estabilizador^M

arm guard
protector^M de brazo^M

bare bow
arco^M recto

accessory pouch
accesorios^M

quiver
carcaj^M

target
diana^F

bull's-eye
centro^M de la diana^F

chest protector
protector^M pectoral

finger tab
dactilera^F

22

shooting range
campo^M de tiro^M

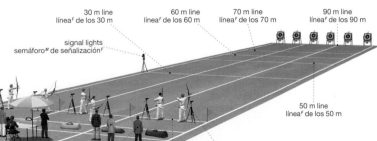

30 m line
línea^F de los 30 m

60 m line
línea^F de los 60 m

70 m line
línea^F de los 70 m

90 m line
línea^F de los 90 m

signal lights
semáforo^M de señalización^F

judge
juez^M

50 m line
línea^F de los 50 m

director of shooting
director^M de tiros^M

scorers
marcadores^M

shooting line
línea^F de tiro^M

telescope
telescopio^M

SPORTS AND GAMES

shotgun shooting

tiroᴹ al platoᴹ

shotgun
escopetaᶠ calibreᴹ 12

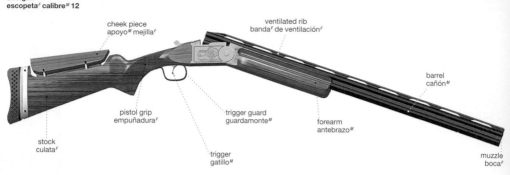

cheek piece
apoyoᴹ mejillaᶠ

ventilated rib
bandaᶠ de ventilaciónᶠ

barrel
cañónᴹ

pistol grip
empuñaduraᶠ

trigger guard
guardamonteᴹ

forearm
antebrazoᴹ

stock
culataᶠ

trigger
gatilloᴹ

muzzle
bocaᶠ

plastic case
cartuchoᴹ de plásticoᴹ

base
casquilloᴹ

cartridges
cartuchosᴹ

clay pigeon
platoᴹ

clay pigeon
platoᴹ

trap
lanzaplatosᴹ

shooting range
campoᴹ de tiroᴹ

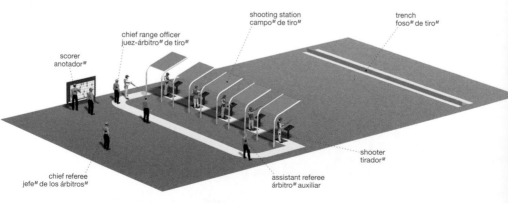

chief range officer
juez-árbitroᴹ de tiroᴹ

shooting station
campoᴹ de tiroᴹ

trench
fosoᴹ de tiroᴹ

scorer
anotadorᴹ

shooter
tiradorᴹ

chief referee
jefeᴹ de los árbitrosᴹ

assistant referee
árbitroᴹ auxiliar

SPORTS AND GAMES

rifle shooting

tiro^M al blanco^M

.22-caliber rifle
carabina^F 22

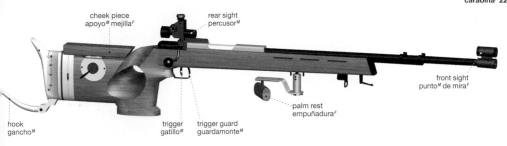

cheek piece
apoyo^M mejilla^F

rear sight
percusor^M

front sight
punto^M de mira^F

palm rest
empuñadura^F

hook
gancho^M

trigger
gatillo^M

trigger guard
guardamonte^M

shooting positions
posiciones^M de tiro^M

cartridges
cartuchos^M

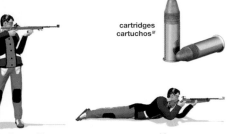

kneeling position
posición^F de rodillas^F

standing position
posición^F de pie^M

prone position
posición^F supina

target
blanco^M

pistol shooting

tiro^M de pistola^F

8 mm pistol
pistola^F de 8 mm

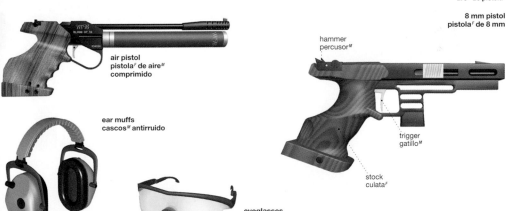

hammer
percusor^M

air pistol
pistola^F de aire^M
comprimido

trigger
gatillo^M

ear muffs
cascos^M antirruido

stock
culata^F

eyeglasses
gafas^F de protección^F

billiards
billar^M

carom billiards
billar^M francés

pool
pool^M

object balls
bolas^F numeradas

cue ball
bola^F blanca

red ball
bola^F roja

white object ball
bola^F pinta

pocket
tronera^F

cue ball
bola^F blanca

billiards table
mesa^F de billar^M

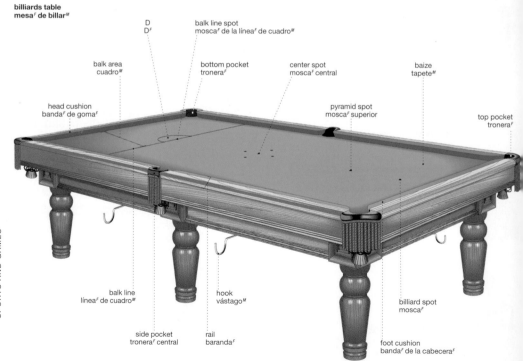

D
D^F

balk line spot
mosca^F de la línea^F de cuadro^M

balk area
cuadro^M

bottom pocket
tronera^F

center spot
mosca^F central

baize
tapete^M

head cushion
banda^F de goma^F

pyramid spot
mosca^F superior

top pocket
tronera^F

balk line
línea^F de cuadro^M

hook
vástago^M

billiard spot
mosca^F

side pocket
tronera^F central

rail
baranda^F

foot cushion
banda^F de la cabecera^F

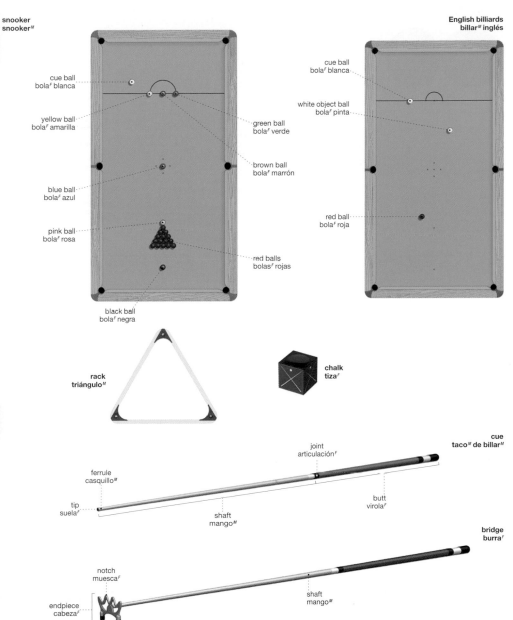

snooker
snooker^M

cue ball
bola^F blanca

yellow ball
bola^F amarilla

green ball
bola^F verde

brown ball
bola^F marrón

blue ball
bola^F azul

pink ball
bola^F rosa

red balls
bolas^F rojas

black ball
bola^F negra

English billiards
billar^M **inglés**

cue ball
bola^F blanca

white object ball
bola^F pinta

red ball
bola^F roja

rack
triángulo^M

chalk
tiza^F

cue
taco^M **de billar**^{M}

joint
articulación^F

ferrule
casquillo^M

tip
suela^F

shaft
mango^M

butt
virola^F

bridge
burra^F

notch
muesca^F

endpiece
cabeza^F

shaft
mango^M

SPORTS AND GAMES

lawn bowling

bolos^M sobre hierba^F

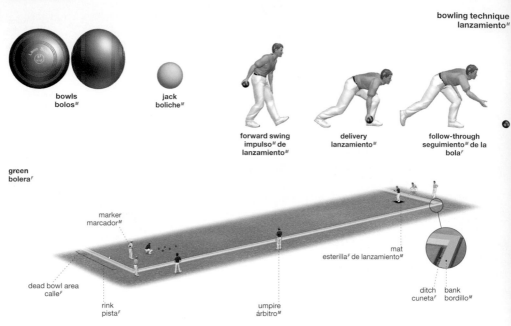

bowling technique
lanzamiento^M

bowls
bolos^M

jack
boliche^M

forward swing
impulso^M de
lanzamiento^M

delivery
lanzamiento^M

follow-through
seguimiento^M de la
bola^F

green
bolera^F

marker
marcador^M

mat
esterilla^F de lanzamiento^M

dead bowl area
calle^F

rink
pista^F

umpire
árbitro^M

ditch
cuneta^F

bank
bordillo^M

pétanque

petanca^F

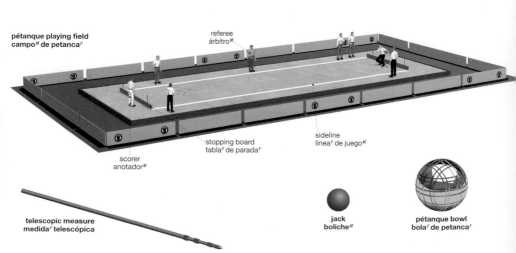

pétanque playing field
campo^M de petanca^F

referee
árbitro^M

stopping board
tabla^F de parada^F

sideline
línea^F de juego^M

scorer
anotador^M

telescopic measure
medida^F telescópica

jack
boliche^M

pétanque bowl
bola^F de petanca^F

bowling
juego^M de bolos^M

examples of pins
ejemplos^M de bolos^M

American duckpin
bolo^M chico

tenpin
bolo^M

candlepin
bolo^M cilíndrico

fivepin
bolo^M pequeño

Canadian duckpin
bolo^M chico

setup
disposición^F de los bolos^M

bowling shoe
zapatos^M para bolos^M

bowling ball
bola^F

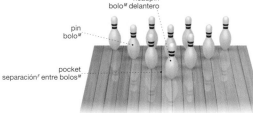

headpin
bolo^M delantero

pin
bolo^M

pocket
separación^F entre bolos^M

ball return
devolvedor^M

score console
marcador^M

ball
bola^F

bowler
jugadora^F de bolos^M

keyboard
teclado^M

ball stand
stand^M de bolos^M

setup
disposición^F de los bolos^M

bowling alley
pista^F de bolos^M

bowler
jugador^M de bolos^M

pit
foso^M de recepción^F

gutter
canal^M

approach
antepista^F

foul line
línea^F de lanzamiento^M

SPORTS AND GAMES

golf

golf[M]

golf course
campo[M] de golf[M]

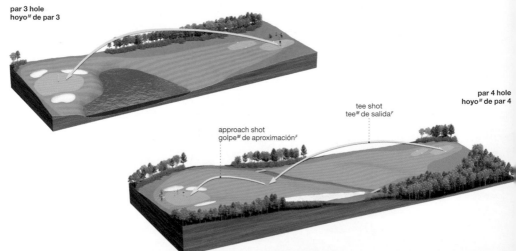

green
green[M]

hole
zona[F] del hoyo[M]

cart path
vereda[F]

clubhouse
casa[F] club[M]

fairway
pista[F]

practice green
green[M] de
entrenamiento[M]

pond
estanque[M]

sand bunker
foso[M] de arena[F]

trees
árboles[M]

rough
maleza[F]

teeing ground
punto[M] de salida[F]

water hazard
trampa[F] de agua[F]

holes
hoyos[M]

par 3 hole
hoyo[M] de par 3

par 4 hole
hoyo[M] de par 4

tee shot
tee[M] de salida[F]

approach shot
golpe[M] de aproximación[F]

golf

golf ball
pelota^F de golf^M

cover
revestimiento^M

dimple
hoyuelo^M

shaft
mango^M

tee
tee^M

types of golf clubs
palos^M

grip
empuñadura^F

head
cabeza^F

face
cara^F

wood
madera^F

hybrid
híbrido^M

iron
hierro^M

putter
putter^M

holes

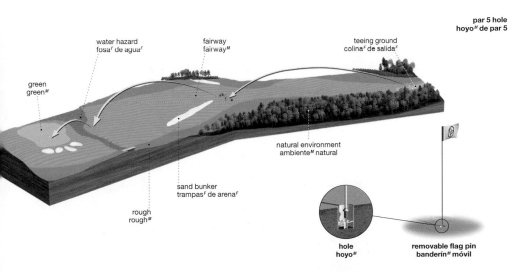

par 5 hole
hoyo^M de par 5

water hazard
fosa^F de agua^F

fairway
fairway^M

teeing ground
colina^F de salida^F

green
green^M

natural environment
ambiente^M natural

sand bunker
trampas^F de arena^F

rough
rough^M

hole
hoyo^M

removable flag pin
banderín^M móvil

golf

wood
palo^M

iron
hierro^M

toe
toe^M

neck
pescuezo^M

heel
talón^M

groove
surco^M

sole
zapata^F

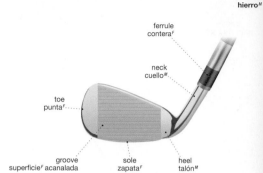

ferrule
contera^F

neck
cuello^M

toe
punta^F

groove
superficie^F acanalada

sole
zapata^F

heel
talón^M

driver
madera^M n° 1

3-wood
madera^F n° 3

5-wood
madera^F n° 5

putter
putter^M

3-iron
hierro^M n° 3

4-iron
hierro^M n° 4

5-iron
hierro^M n° 5

6-iron
hierro^M n° 6

7-iron
hierro^M n° 7

8-iron
hierro^M n° 8

9-iron
hierro^M n° 9

pitching wedge
wedge^M para rough^M

sand wedge
wedge^M para arena^F

lob wedge
lob wedge^M

SPORTS AND GAMES

golf

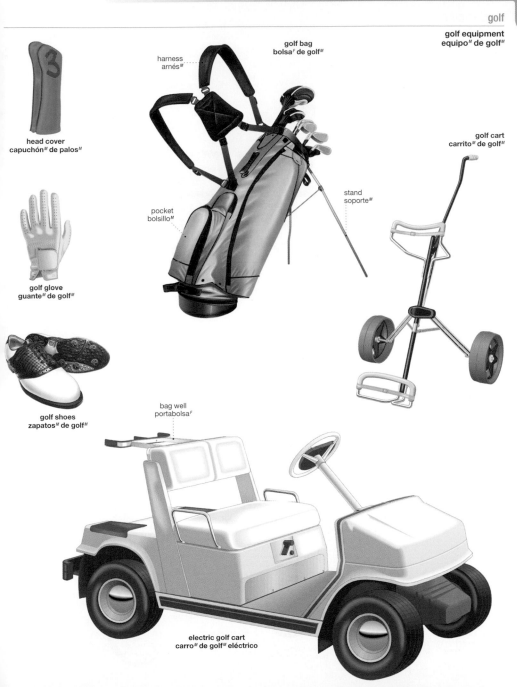

golf equipment
equipo^M **de golf**^{M}

head cover
capuchón^M de palos^M

golf glove
guante^M de golf^M

golf shoes
zapatos^M de golf^M

golf bag
bolsa^F **de golf**^{M}

harness
arnés^M

pocket
bolsillo^M

stand
soporte^M

golf cart
carrito^M **de golf**^{M}

bag well
portabolsa^F

electric golf cart
carro^M **de golf**^{M} **eléctrico**

road racing

ciclismo^M en carretera^F

**road-racing bicycle and cyclist
bicicleta^F de carreras^F y
ciclista^M**

helmet
casco^M

jersey
malla^F

shorts
pantalones^M elásticos

glove
guante^M

frame
bastidor^M

brake lever and shifter
palanca^F del freno^M y cambio^M de
velocidades^F

tire
neumático^M

brake
freno^M

derailleur
cambio^M de velocidades^F

fork
horquilla^F

wheel
rueda^F

shoe
zapato^M

pedal
pedal^M

chain wheel
cadena^F

**road-racing competition
competición^F de ciclismo^M en
carretera^F**

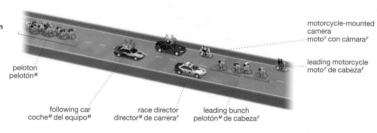

motorcycle-mounted
camera
moto^F con cámara^F

leading motorcycle
moto^F de cabeza^F

peloton
pelotón^M

following car
coche^M del equipo^M

race director
director^M de carrera^F

leading bunch
pelotón^M de cabeza^F

mountain biking

ciclismo^M de montaña^F

**cross-country bicycle and
cyclist
bicicleta^F de cross^M y ciclista^M**

**downhill bicycle and cyclist
bicicleta^F de descenso^M y
ciclista^F**

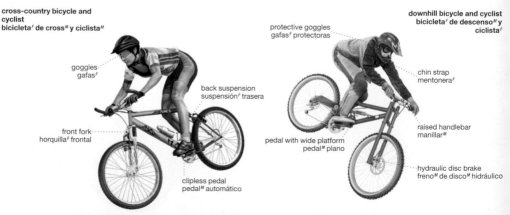

protective goggles
gafas^F protectoras

goggles
gafas^F

chin strap
mentonera^F

back suspension
suspensión^F trasera

front fork
horquilla^F frontal

raised handlebar
manillar^M

pedal with wide platform
pedal^M plano

hydraulic disc brake
freno^M de disco^M hidráulico

clipless pedal
pedal^M automático

track cycling
ciclismo^M **en pista**^F

pursuit bicycle and racer
bicicleta^F **de persecución**^F **y**
corredor^M

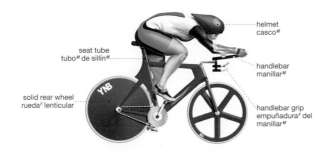

helmet
casco^M

seat tube
tubo^M de sillín^M

handlebar
manillar^M

solid rear wheel
rueda^F lenticular

handlebar grip
empuñadura^F del
manillar^M

velodrome
velódromo^M

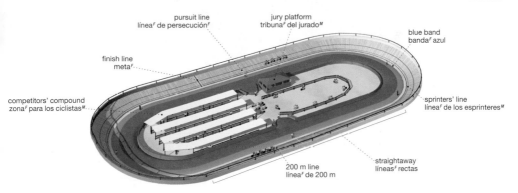

pursuit line
línea^F de persecución^F

jury platform
tribuna^F del jurado^M

blue band
banda^F azul

finish line
meta^F

competitors' compound
zona^F para los ciclistas^M

sprinters' line
línea^F de los esprinteres^M

200 m line
línea^F de 200 m

straightaway
líneas^F rectas

BMX
ciclocross^M

BMX bicycle and cyclist
bicicleta^F **BMX y**
ciclista^M

helmet
casco^M

half-pipe
half-pipe^M

glove
guante^M

handlebar
manillar^M

single chain wheel
rueda^F posterior lenticular

foot pegs
reposapiés^M

single sprocket
piñón^M simple

SPORTS AND GAMES

auto racing

carreras^F de coches^M

driver
piloto^M

balaclava
pasamontañas^M

earplugs/earbuds
tapones^M para los oídos^M

undergarment
ropa^F interior

head and neck support (HANS) system
sistema^M de sujeción^F de cabeza^F y cuello^M

wet-weather tire
neumático^M de lluvia^F

checkered flag
bandera^F de cuadros^M

gloves
guantes^M

dry-weather tire
neumático^M de seco^M

crash helmet
casco^M

flame-resistant driving suit
traje^M ignífugo

shoe
zapato^M

starting grid
parrilla^F de salida^F

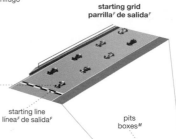

pole position
pole position^F

Formula 1 circuit
circuito^M de Fórmula 1^F

starting line
línea^F de salida^F

pits
boxes^M

track
pista^F

chicane
chicana^F

gravel bed
gravilla^F

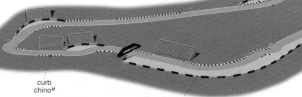

pit lane
entrada^F a boxes^M

curb
chino^M

tire barrier
barrera^F de contención^F

auto racing

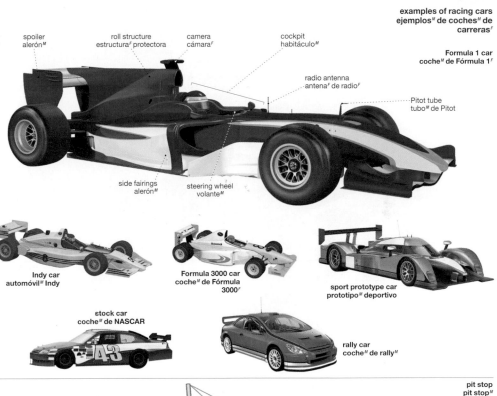

**examples of racing cars
ejemplos^M de coches^M de
carreras^F**

**Formula 1 car
coche^M de Fórmula 1^F**

spoiler
alerón^M

roll structure
estructura^F protectora

camera
cámara^F

cockpit
habitáculo^M

radio antenna
antena^F de radio^F

Pitot tube
tubo^M de Pitot

side fairings
alerón^M

steering wheel
volante^M

**Indy car
automóvil^M Indy**

**Formula 3000 car
coche^M de Fórmula
3000^F**

**sport prototype car
prototipo^M deportivo**

**stock car
coche^M de NASCAR**

**rally car
coche^M de rally^M**

**pit stop
pit stop^M**

starter mechanic
mecánico^M de arranque^M

compressed-air tank
bombona^F de aire^M
comprimido

chief mechanic
jefe^M de mecánicos^M

jack
gato^M

mechanic
mecánico^M

pneumatic drill
taladro^M neumático

motorcycling

motocicleta^F

Grand Prix motorcycle and rider
moto^F de carreras^F y
motociclista^M del Grand Prix^M

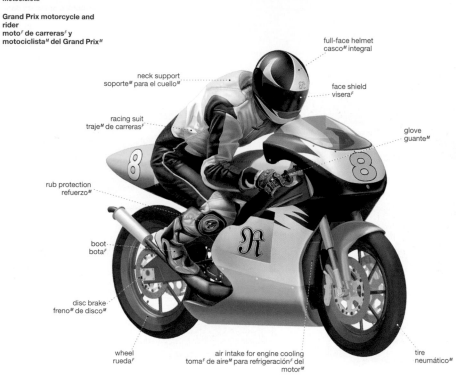

full-face helmet
casco^M integral

neck support
soporte^M para el cuello^M

face shield
visera^F

racing suit
traje^M de carreras^F

glove
guante^M

rub protection
refuerzo^M

boot
bota^F

disc brake
freno^M de disco^M

wheel
rueda^F

air intake for engine cooling
toma^F de aire^M para refrigeración^F del
motor^M

tire
neumático^M

Grand Prix circuit
circuito^M Grand Prix^M

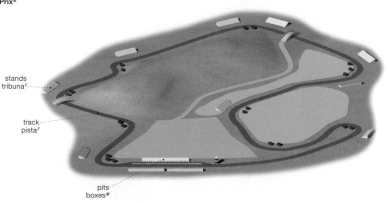

stands
tribuna^F

track
pista^F

pits
boxes^M

trial motorcycle
moto^F de trial^M

rally motorcycle
moto^M de rally^M

motocross and supercross motorcycle and
rider
moto^F de motocross^M y supercross^M y
motociclista^M

protective suit
traje^M de protección^F

helmet
casco^M

glove
guante^M

protective goggles
guantes^M protectores

pants
pantalones^M

hand protector
protector^M de mano^F

number plate
placa^F de número^M

fork
horquilla^F

nubby tire
neumático^M de tacos^M

boot
bota^F

protective plate
placa^F protectora

motocross circuit
circuito^M de
motocross^M

obstacles
obstáculos^M

triple jump
triple salto^M

bridge
puente^M

multiple jumps
saltos^M múltiples

bump
montículo^M

spine
colina^F

start area
parrilla^F de salida^F

marshall
comisario^M

markers
hitos^M

riders
corredores^M

straw bales
balas^F de paja^F

starting gate
zona^F de salida^F

personal watercraft

moto^F acuática

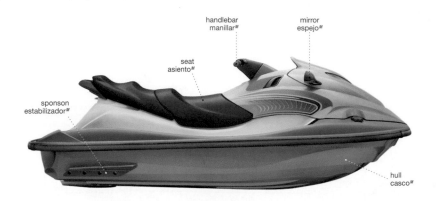

handlebar
manillar^M

mirror
espejo^M

seat
asiento^M

sponson
estabilizador^M

hull
casco^M

snowmobile

moto^F de nieve^F

seat
asiento^M

brake handle
palanca^F del freno^M

handlebar
manillar^M

windshield
parabrisas^M

backrest
respaldo^M

headlight
faro^M delantero

luggage rack
portaequipajes^M

cab
capó^M

rear bumper
parachoques^M

air scoop
entrada^F de aire^M

snow guard
guardanieve^M

sprocket
diente^M

track
rueda^F de cadena^F

footboard
estribo^M

reflector
reflector^M

body
carrocería^F

idler wheel
rueda^F de transmisión^F

shock absorber
amortiguador^M

ski
esquí^M

SPORTS AND GAMES

curling
curling^M

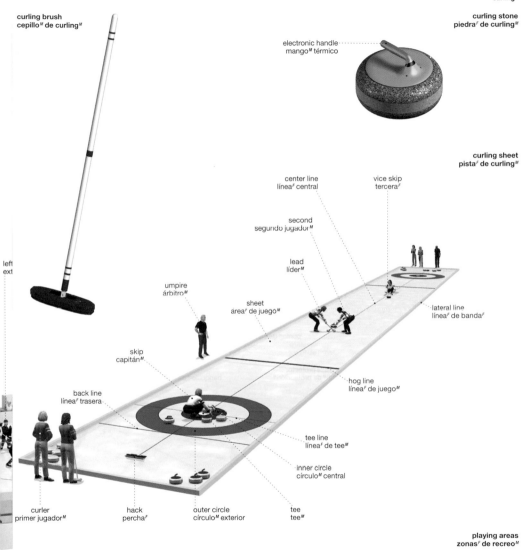

curling brush
cepillo^M de curling^M

curling stone
piedra^F de curling^M

electronic handle
mango^M térmico

curling sheet
pista^F de curling^M

center line
línea^F central

vice skip
tercera^F

second
segundo jugador^M

lead
líder^M

left
ext

umpire
árbitro^M

sheet
area^F de juego^M

lateral line
línea^F de banda^F

skip
capitán^M

back line
línea^F trasera

hog line
línea^F de juego^M

tee line
línea^F de tee^M

inner circle
círculo^M central

curler
primer jugador^M

hack
percha^F

outer circle
círculo^M exterior

tee
tee^M

playing areas
zonas^F de recreo^M

house
casa^F

free guard zone
zona^F de defensa^F protegida

SPORTS AND GAMES

bobsled

bobsleigh^M

four-person bobsled
bobsleigh^M a cuatro

brakeman
guardafrenos^M

captain
capitán^M

retractable handle
asa^M retráctil

shell
bob^M

rear runner
patín^M trasero

front runner
patín^M delantero

two-person bobsled
bobsleigh^M de dos

luge

luge^M

luge racer
corredor^M de luge^M

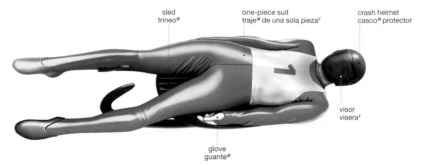

sled
trineo^M

one-piece suit
traje^M de una sola pieza^F

crash helmet
casco^M protector

visor
visera^F

glove
guante^M

singles luge
luge^M simple

doubles luge
luge^M doble

runner
patín^M

edge
canto^M

curling
curling^M

curling brush
cepillo^M de curling^M

curling stone
piedra^F de curling^M

electronic handle
mango^M térmico

curling sheet
pista^F de curling^M

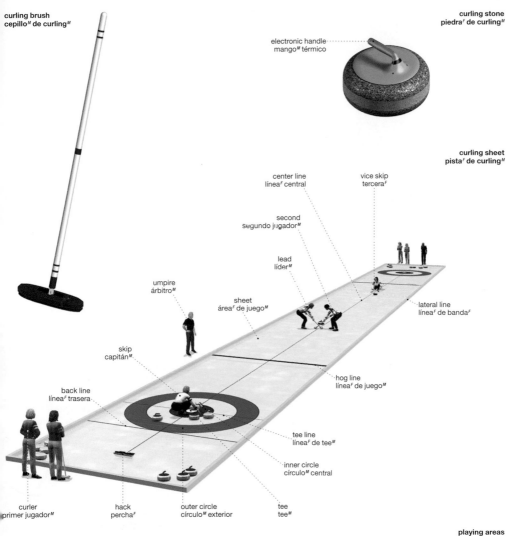

center line
línea^F central

vice skip
tercera^F

second
segundo jugador^M

lead
líder^M

umpire
árbitro^M

sheet
área^F de juego^M

lateral line
línea^F de banda^F

skip
capitán^M

back line
línea^F trasera

hog line
línea^F de juego^M

tee line
línea^F de tee^M

inner circle
círculo^M central

curler
primer jugador^M

hack
percha^F

outer circle
círculo^M exterior

tee
tee^M

playing areas
zonas^F de recreo^M

house
casa^F

free guard zone
zona^F de defensa^F protegida

SPORTS AND GAMES

ice hockey

hockey^M **sobre hielo**^M

ice hockey player
jugador^M

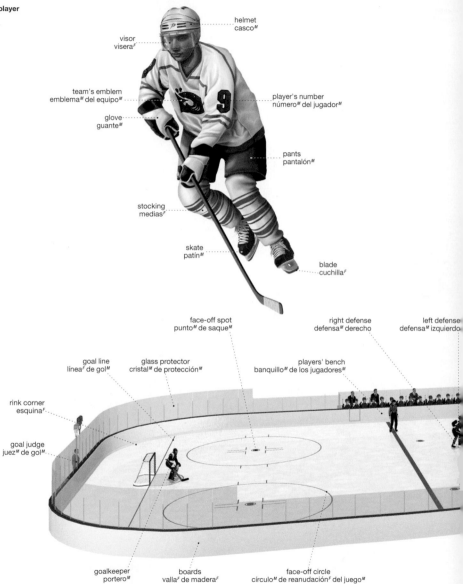

helmet
casco^M

visor
visera^F

team's emblem
emblema^M del equipo^M

player's number
número^M del jugador^M

glove
guante^M

pants
pantalón^M

stocking
medias^F

skate
patín^M

blade
cuchilla^F

rink
pista^F

face-off spot
punto^M de saque^M

right defense
defensa^M derecho

left defense
defensa^M izquierdo

goal line
línea^F de gol^M

glass protector
cristal^M de protección^M

players' bench
banquillo^M de los jugadores^M

rink corner
esquina^F

goal judge
juez^M de gol^M

goalkeeper
portero^M

boards
valla^F de madera^F

face-off circle
círculo^M de reanudación^F del juego^M

SPORTS AND GAMES

ice hockey

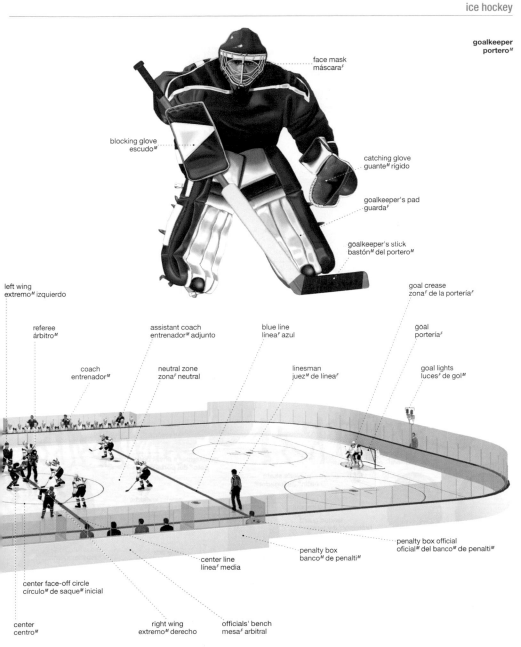

goalkeeper
portero^M

face mask
máscara^F

blocking glove
escudo^M

catching glove
guante^M rígido

goalkeeper's pad
guarda^F

goalkeeper's stick
bastón^M del portero^M

left wing
extremo^M izquierdo

goal crease
zona^F de la portería^F

referee
árbitro^M

assistant coach
entrenador^M adjunto

blue line
línea^F azul

goal
portería^F

coach
entrenador^M

neutral zone
zona^F neutral

linesman
juez^M de línea^F

goal lights
luces^F de gol^M

penalty box official
oficial^M del banco^M de penalti^M

penalty box
banco^M de penalti^M

center line
línea^F media

center face-off circle
círculo^M de saque^M inicial

center
centro^M

right wing
extremo^M derecho

officials' bench
mesa^F arbitral

SPORTS AND GAMES

bobsled

bobsleigh^M

four-person bobsled
bobsleigh^M a cuatro

brakeman
guardafrenos^M

captain
capitán^M

retractable handle
asa^M retráctil

shell
bob^M

rear runner
patín^M trasero

front runner
patín^M delantero

two-person bobsled
bobsleigh^M de dos

luge

luge^M

luge racer
corredor^M de luge^M

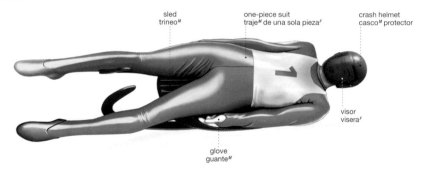

sled
trineo^M

one-piece suit
traje^M de una sola pieza^F

crash helmet
casco^M protector

visor
visera^F

glove
guante^M

singles luge
luge^M simple

doubles luge
luge^M doble

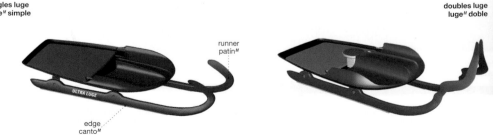

runner
patín^M

ULTRA LUGE

edge
canto^M

ice hockey

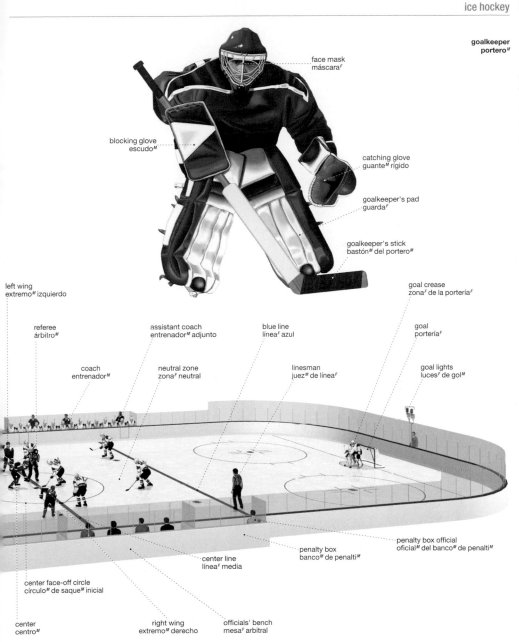

goalkeeper
portero^M

face mask
máscara^F

blocking glove
escudo^M

catching glove
guante^M rígido

goalkeeper's pad
guarda^F

goalkeeper's stick
bastón^M del portero^M

left wing
extremo^M izquierdo

goal crease
zona^F de la portería^F

referee
árbitro^M

assistant coach
entrenador^M adjunto

blue line
línea^F azul

goal
portería^F

coach
entrenador^M

neutral zone
zona^F neutral

linesman
juez^M de línea^F

goal lights
luces^F de gol^M

penalty box official
oficial^M del banco^M de penalti^M

penalty box
banco^M de penalti^M

center line
línea^F media

center face-off circle
círculo^M de saque^M inicial

center
centro^M

right wing
extremo^M derecho

officials' bench
mesa^F arbitral

SPORTS AND GAMES

ice hockey

**ice hockey equipment
equipo^M de hockey^M sobre hielo^M**

**player's stick
palo^M del jugador^M**

butt end
pomo^M

shaft
mango^M

heel
talón^M

blade
pala^F del stick^M

**neck guard
protector^M de cuello^M**

**elbow pads
codera^F**

cuff
muñequera^F

**goalkeeper's stick
palo^M del portero^M**

**throat protector
protector^M de cuello^M**

**shoulder pads
hombrera^F**

**protective cup
coquilla^F**

**puck
pastilla^F**

arm pad
protector^M del brazo^M

**goalkeeper's chest pad
peto^M del portero^M**

knee pad
rodillera^F

**player's skate
patín^M de jugador^M**

tendon guard
protector^M del tendón^M

toe box
puntera^F reforzada

boot
bota^F

**goalkeeper's skate
patín^M del portero^M**

**shin guards
tobillera^F**

blade
hoja^F de cuchilla^F

point
puntera^F

figure skating

patinaje^M artístico

figure skate
patín^M para figuras^F

dance blade
cuchilla^F de baile^M

lining
forro^M

hook
corchete^M

backstay
contrafuerte^M

boot
bota^F

heel
tacón^M

free skating blade
cuchilla^F de patinaje^M
artístico

stanchion
montante^M

edge
canto^M

tongue
lengüeta^F

lace
cordón^M

eyelet
ojal^M

sole
suela^F

toe pick
dientes^M

blade
hoja^F de cuchilla^F

examples of jumps
ejemplos^M de
piruetas^F

axel
axel^M

salchow
salchow^M

toe loop
loop^M de puntera^F

flip
flip^M

lutz
lutz^M

rink
pista^F de patinaje^M
sobre hielo^M

referee
presidente^M de jurado^M

assistant referee
asistente^M de presidente^M
del jurado^M

technical delegates
delegados^M técnicos

judges
jueces^M

timekeeper
cronometrador^M

technical specialist
especialista^M técnico

pair
pareja^F

technical controller
controlador^M técnico

coaches
entrenadores^M

SPORTS AND GAMES

speed skating

patinaje^M de velocidad^F

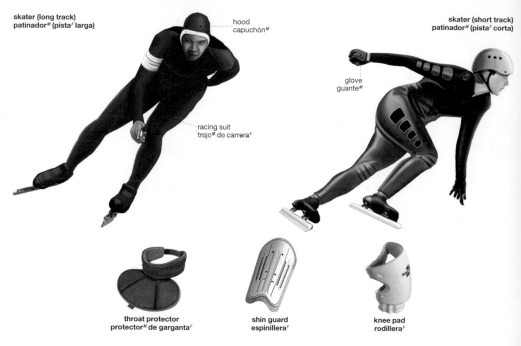

skater (long track)
patinador^M (pista^F larga)

hood
capuchón^M

skater (short track)
patinador^M (pista^F corta)

glove
guante^M

racing suit
traje^M de carrera^F

throat protector
protector^M de garganta^F

shin guard
espinillera^F

knee pad
rodillera^F

long track
pista^F larga

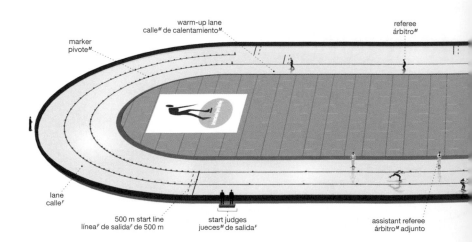

warm-up lane
calle^M de calentamiento^M

referee
árbitro^M

marker
pivote^M

lane
calle^F

500 m start line
línea^F de salida^F de 500 m

start judges
jueces^M de salida^F

assistant referee
árbitro^M adjunto

speed skates
patines de carreras**

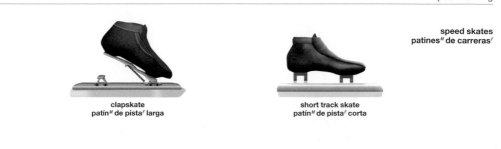

clapskate
patín** de pista** larga

short track skate
patín** de pista** corta

short track
pista corta**

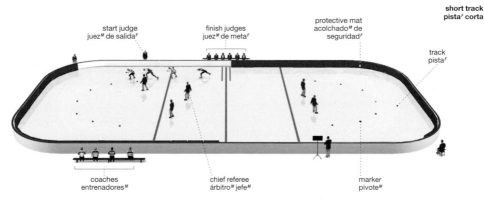

start judge
juez** de salida**

finish judges
juez** de meta**

protective mat
acolchado** de
seguridad**

track
pista**

coaches
entrenadores**

chief referee
árbitro** jefe**

marker
pivote**

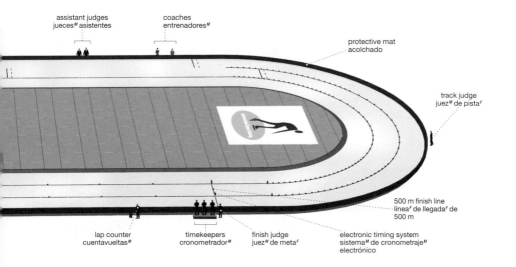

assistant judges
jueces** asistentes

coaches
entrenadores**

protective mat
acolchado

track judge
juez** de pista**

500 m finish line
línea** de llegada** de
500 m

lap counter
cuentavueltas**

timekeepers
cronometrador**

finish judge
juez** de meta**

electronic timing system
sistema** de cronometraje**
electrónico

SPORTS AND GAMES

bobsled

bobsleigh^M

four-person bobsled
bobsleigh^M a cuatro

brakeman
guardafrenos^M

captain
capitán^M

retractable handle
asa^M retráctil

shell
bob^M

rear runner
patín^M trasero

front runner
patín^M delantero

two-person bobsled
bobsleigh^M de dos

luge

luge^M

luge racer
corredor^M de luge^M

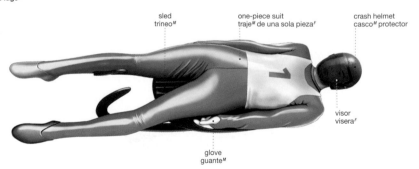

sled
trineo^M

one-piece suit
traje^M de una sola pieza^F

crash helmet
casco^M protector

visor
visera^F

glove
guante^M

singles luge
luge^M simple

doubles luge
luge^M doble

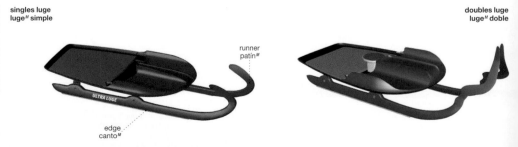

runner
patín^M

ULTRA LUGE

edge
canto^M

skeleton

skeleton^M

sledder
corredor^M

cleated shoes
botas^F con clavos^M

crash helmet
casco^M protector

skeleton
skeleton^M

chin guard
mentonera^F

skeleton
skeleton^M

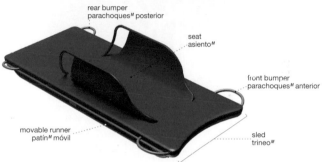

rear bumper
parachoques^M posterior

seat
asiento^M

front bumper
parachoques^M anterior

movable runner
patín^M móvil

sled
trineo^M

sliding track

recorrido^M deslizador^M

start (men's singles luge)
salida^F (luge^M simple masculino)

start (bobsled and skeleton)
salida^F (bobsleigh^M y skeleton^M)

start (women's and doubles luge)
salida^F (luge^M femenino y doble)

deceleration stretch
pista^F de deceleración^M

finish area
área^F de llegada^F

180-degree curve
curva^F de 180 grados^M

labyrinth
laberinto^M

SPORTS AND GAMES

ski resort

estación^F de esquí^M

general view
vista^F general

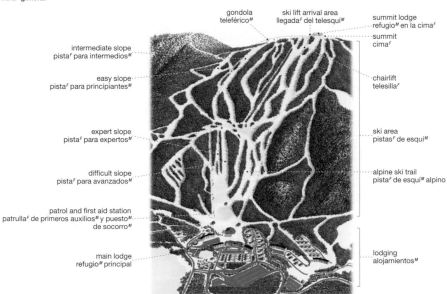

gondola
teleférico^M

ski lift arrival area
llegada^F del telesquí^M

summit lodge
refugio^M en la cima^F

summit
cima^F

intermediate slope
pista^F para intermedios^M

easy slope
pista^F para principiantes^M

chairlift
telesilla^F

expert slope
pista^F para expertos^M

ski area
pistas^F de esquí^M

difficult slope
pista^F para avanzados^M

alpine ski trail
pista^F de esquí^M alpino

patrol and first aid station
patrulla^F de primeros auxilios^M y puesto^M
de socorro^M

main lodge
refugio^M principal

lodging
alojamientos^M

view of the base of the mountain
vista^F de la base^F de la montaña^F

snow-grooming
machine
máquina^F pisanieve

skiers' lodge
hospedería^F para
esquiadores^M

chairlift departure area
embarque^M del telesilla^M

ski school
escuela^F de esquí^M

T-bar
telesquí^M

cross-country ski trail
pista^F de fondo^M

gondolas departure area
embarque^M teleférico^M

ice rink
pista^F de patinaje^M

condominium
bloque^M de
apartamentos^M

mountain lodge
refugio^M de montaña^F

hotel
hotel^M

information desk
punto^M de información^F

village
pueblo^M

parking
aparcamiento^M

SPORTS AND GAMES

snowboarding

snowboard^M

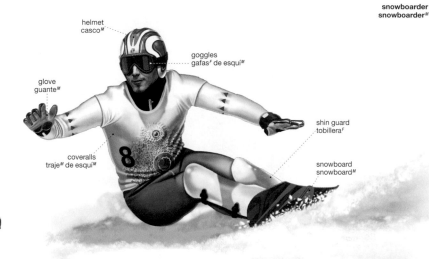

snowboarder
snowboarder^M

helmet
casco^M

goggles
gafas^F de esquí^M

glove
guante^M

hard boot
bota^F rígida

coveralls
traje^M de esquí^M

shin guard
tobillera^F

snowboard
snowboard^M

flexible boot
bota^F blanda

freestyle snowboard
tabla^F de freestyle^M

alpine snowboard
tabla^F alpina

plate binding
fijaciones^F

soft binding
fijaciones^M blandas

tail
cola^F

nose
cabeza^F

edge
borde^M

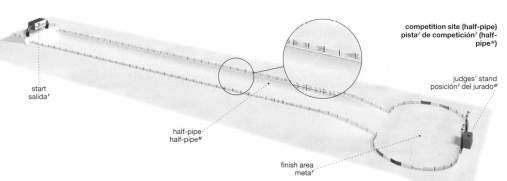

competition site (half-pipe)
**pista^F de competición^F (half-
pipe^M)**

judges' stand
posición^F del jurado^M

start
salida^F

half-pipe
half-pipe^M

finish area
meta^F

SPORTS AND GAMES

alpine skiing

esquí^M alpino

alpine skier
esquiador^M alpino

ski goggles
gafas^F de esquí^M

ski suit
traje^M de esquí^M

basket
arandela^F

helmet
casco^M

ski pole
bastón^M de esquí^M

ski glove
guante^M de esquí^M

wrist strap
correa^F para la mano^F

ski boot
bota^F

handle
empuñadura^F

groove
ranura^F guía^F

ski
esquí^M

alpine ski
esquí^M alpino

bottom
superficie^F de deslizamiento^M

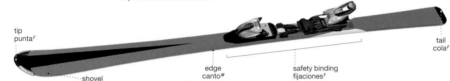

tip
punta^F

tail
cola^F

edge
canto^M

safety binding
fijaciones^F

shovel
pala^F

examples of skis
ejemplos^M de esquís^M

skiboard
skiboard^M

slalom ski
esquí^M de eslalon^M

giant slalom ski
esquí^M de eslalon^M
gigante

downhill and super-G ski
esquí^M de descenso^M/eslalon^M
supergigante

**technical events
pruebas^F**

**downhill
descenso^M**

**super giant (super-G) slalom
eslalon^M supergigante**

**giant slalom
eslalon^M gigante**

**special slalom
eslalon^M especial**

**ski boot
botas^F para esquiar**

inner boot
botín^M interior

upper cuff
guarnición^F

upper
alto^M de caña^F

tongue
lengüeta^F

upper shell
bota^F externa

upper strap
correa^F de ajuste^M

buckle
hebilla^F

adjustable catch
cierre^M de la bota^F

hinge
pivote^M

sole
suela^F rígida

lower shell
contrafuerte^M

**safety binding
fijación^F de seguridad^F del
esquí^M**

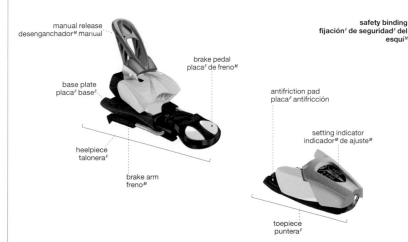

manual release
desenganchador^M manual

brake pedal
placa^F de freno^M

base plate
placa^F base^F

antifriction pad
placa^F antifricción

setting indicator
indicador^M de ajuste^M

heelpiece
talonera^F

brake arm
freno^M

toepiece
puntera^F

SPORTS AND GAMES

freestyle skiing

esquí^M artístico

moguls course
pista^F de obstáculos^M

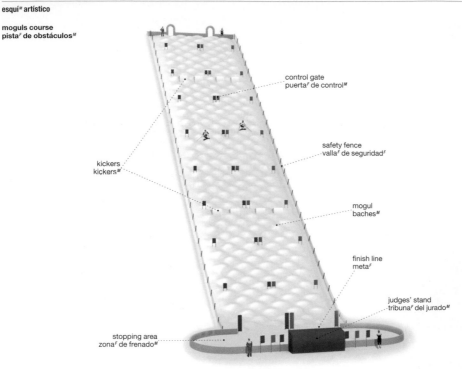

control gate
puerta^F de control^M

safety fence
valla^F de seguridad^F

kickers
kickers^M

mogul
baches^M

finish line
meta^F

judges' stand
tribuna^F del jurado^M

stopping area
zona^F de frenado^M

aerial skiing course
pista^F de salto^M de esquí^M

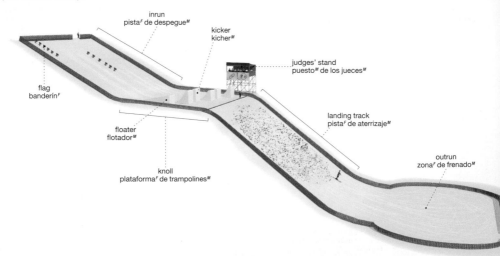

inrun
pista^F de despegue^M

kicker
kicher^M

judges' stand
puesto^M de los jueces^M

flag
banderín^F

floater
flotador^M

landing track
pista^F de aterrizaje^M

knoll
plataforma^F de trampolines^M

outrun
zona^F de frenado^M

ski jumping

salto^M de esquí^M

jumping technique
salto^M de esquí^M

ski jumper
saltador^M

ski jumping suit
traje^M de salto^M de esquí ^M

glove
guante^M

helmet
casco^M

ski jumping boot
bota^F de salto^M de esquí^M

jumping ski
esquí^M de salto^M

binding
fijación^F

inrun
lanzamiento^M

takeoff
despegue^M

flight
vuelo^M

landing
aterrizaje^M

ski jump
saltos^M de esquí^M

ski jumping track
pista^F de salto^M de esquí^M

start platform
plataforma^F de salida^F

takeoff table
punto^M de despegue^M

inrun
rampa^F de lanzamiento^M

landing slope
área^F de aterrizaje^M

coaches' stand
puesto^M de los
entrenadores^F

norm point
punto^M de norma^F

judges' stand
puesto^M del jurado^M

landing area
zona^F de aterrizaje^M

finish area
área^F de llegada^F

critical point
punto^M crítico

braking zone
zona^F de frenado^M

jury point
línea^F de jurado^M

outrun
zona^F de frenado^M

speed skiing

esquí^M de velocidad^F

speed skier
esquiador^M de
velocidad^F

speed track
pista^F de velocidad^F

speed skiing suit
traje^M de esquí^M de velocidad^F

fairing
alerón^M

helmet
casco^M

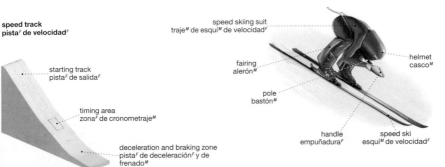

starting track
pista^F de salida^F

timing area
zona^F de cronometraje^M

pole
bastón^M

deceleration and braking zone
pista^F de deceleración^F y de
frenado^M

handle
empuñadura^F

speed ski
esquí^M de velocidad^F

SPORTS AND GAMES

cross-country skiing

esquí^M de fondo^M

cross-country skier
fondista^M

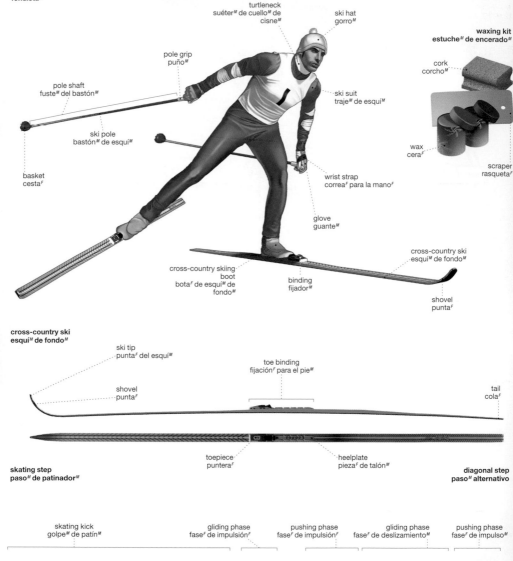

turtleneck
suéter^M de cuello^M de cisne^M

ski hat
gorro^M

waxing kit
estuche^M de encerado^M

pole grip
puño^M

cork
corcho^M

pole shaft
fuste^M del bastón^M

ski suit
traje^M de esquí^M

ski pole
bastón^M de esquí^M

wax
cera^F

scraper
rasqueta^F

basket
cesta^F

wrist strap
correa^F para la mano^F

glove
guante^M

cross-country ski
esquí^M de fondo^M

cross-country skiing
boot
bota^F de esquí^M de fondo^M

binding
fijador^M

shovel
punta^F

cross-country ski
esquí^M de fondo^M

ski tip
punta^F del esquí^M

toe binding
fijación^F para el pie^M

tail
cola^F

shovel
punta^F

toepiece
puntera^F

heelplate
pieza^F de talón^M

skating step
paso^M de patinador^M

diagonal step
paso^M alternativo

skating kick
golpe^M de patín^M

gliding phase
fase^F de impulsión^F

pushing phase
fase^F de impulsión^F

gliding phase
fase^F de deslizamiento^M

pushing phase
fase^F de impulso^M

biathlon

biathlon^M

biathlon rifle
rifle^M de biathlon^M

shooting positions
posiciones^M de tiro^M

rear sight
alza^F

magazine
cargador^M

front sight
punto^M de mira^F

prone position
posición^M supina

standing position
posición^F en pie^M

shooting slip
correa^F de tiro^M

shooting range
puesto^M de tiro^M

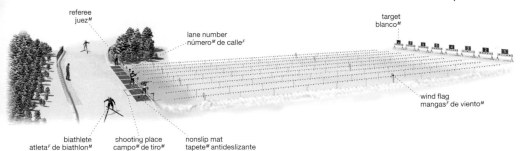

referee
juez^M

lane number
número^M de calle^F

target
blanco^M

wind flag
mangas^F de viento^M

biathlete
atleta^F de biathlon^M

shooting place
campo^M de tiro^M

nonslip mat
tapete^M antideslizante

snowshoeing

raquetas^F

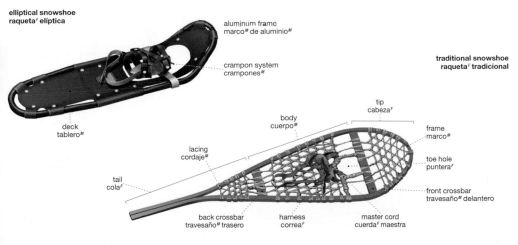

**elliptical snowshoe
raqueta^F elíptica**

aluminum frame
marco^M de aluminio^M

crampon system
crampones^M

**traditional snowshoe
raqueta^F tradicional**

deck
tablero^M

tip
cabeza^F

body
cuerpo^M

frame
marco^M

lacing
cordaje^M

toe hole
puntera^F

tail
cola^F

front crossbar
travesaño^M delantero

back crossbar
travesaño^M trasero

harness
correa^F

master cord
cuerda^F maestra

SPORTS AND GAMES

skateboarding

skateboard^M

inferior view
vista^F **inferior**

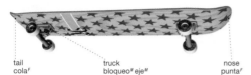

tail
cola^F

truck
bloqueo^M eje^M

nose
punta^F

superior view
vista^F **superior**

grip tape
banda^F antiadherente

wheel
rueda^F

skateboarder
monopatín^M

knee pad
rodillera^F

elbow pad
codera^F

helmet
casco^M

coping
coping^M

half-pipe
half-pipe^M

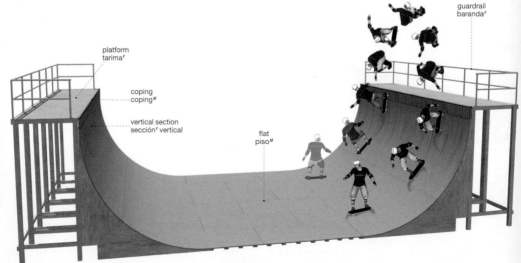

guardrail
baranda^F

platform
tarima^F

coping
coping^M

vertical section
sección^F vertical

flat
piso^M

SPORTS AND GAMES

in-line skating

patinaje^M en línea^F

acrobatic skate
patín^M acrobático

inner boot
botín^M interior

upper shell
bota^F externa

frame
bastidor^M

wheel
rueda^F

skater
patinadora^F

helmet
casco^M

elbow pad
codera^F

knee pad
rodillera^F

wrist guard
muñequera^F

in-line speed skate
patín^M en línea^F

in-line hockey skate
patín en línea^F de hockey^M

ROLLER

in-line skate
patín^M en línea^F

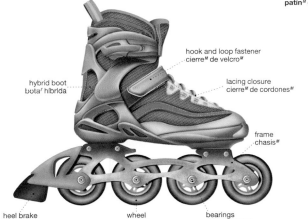

hook and loop fastener
cierre^M de velcro^M

lacing closure
cierre^M de cordones^M

hybrid boot
bota^F híbrida

frame
chasis^M

heel brake
freno^M trasero

wheel
rueda^F

bearings
rodamientos^M

SPORTS AND GAMES

camping

sleeping bags
sacos^M de dormir

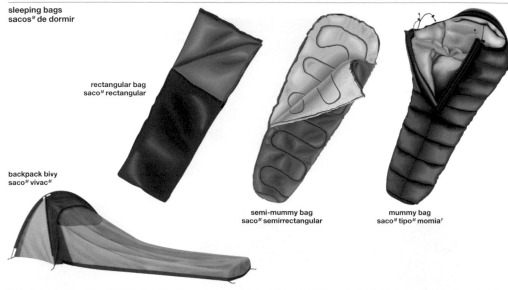

rectangular bag
saco^M rectangular

backpack bivy
saco^M vivac^M

semi-mummy bag
saco^M semirrectangular

mummy bag
saco^M tipo^M momia^F

bed and mattress
camas^F y
colchonetas^F

folding cot
catre^M desmontable

inflator-deflator
muelle^M para inflar y desinflar

inflator
inflador^M

air mattress
colchoneta^F de aire^M

self-inflating mattress
colchoneta^F aislante

foam pad
colchoneta^F de
espuma^F

SPORTS AND GAMES

in-line skating
patinaje^M en línea^F

acrobatic skate
patín ^M **acrobático**

inner boot
botín^M interior

upper shell
bota^F externa

frame
bastidor^M

wheel
rueda^F

skater
patinadora ^F

helmet
casco^M

elbow pad
codera^F

knee pad
rodillera^F

wrist guard
muñequera^F

in-line speed skate
patín ^M **en línea** ^F

in-line skate
patín ^M **en línea** ^F

in-line hockey skate
patín en línea ^F **de hockey** ^M

hook and loop fastener
cierre^M de velcro^M

hybrid boot
bota^F híbrida

lacing closure
cierre^M de cordones^M

frame
chasis^M

heel brake
freno^M trasero

wheel
rueda^F

bearings
rodamientos^M

SPORTS AND GAMES

parachuting

paracaidismo^M

sky diving
paracaidismo^M **en caída**^F **libre**

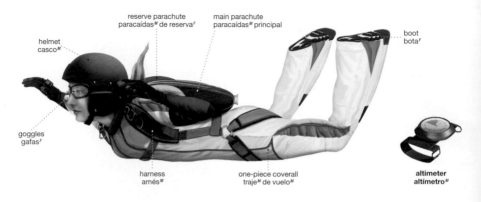

reserve parachute
paracaídas^M de reserva^F

main parachute
paracaídas^M principal

boot
bota^F

helmet
casco^M

goggles
gafas^F

harness
arnés^M

one-piece coverall
traje^M de vuelo^M

altimeter
altímetro^M

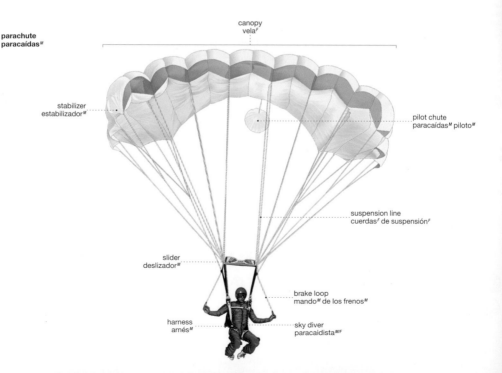

parachute
paracaídas^M

canopy
vela^F

stabilizer
estabilizador^M

pilot chute
paracaídas^M piloto^M

suspension line
cuerdas^F de suspensión^F

slider
deslizador^M

brake loop
mando^M de los frenos^M

harness
arnés^M

sky diver
paracaidista^{M/F}

hang gliding

vueloᴹ libre

paraglider
parapenteᴹ

canopy
velamenᴹ

half cell
célulaꟻ

trailing edge
bordeᴹ de salidaꟻ

paragliding pilot
parapentistaᴹ/ꟻ

leading edge
bordeᴹ de ataqueᴹ

riser
correaꟻ principal de
sustentaciónꟻ

helmet
cascoᴹ de saltoᴹ

brake loop
correaꟻ de
amortiguaciónꟻ

stabilizer
estabilizadorᴹ

harness
arnésᴹ

suspension line
cuerdasꟻ de suspensiónꟻ

saddle
sillaꟻ

hang glider
alaꟻ **delta**ᴹ

crossbar
barraꟻ transversal

sail
alaꟻ delta

leading edge tube
tuboᴹ del bordeᴹ de ataqueᴹ

hang gliding pilot
pilotoᴹ

batten
sableᴹ

king post
mástilᴹ

airframe
trapecioᴹ

keel
quillaꟻ

nose
proaꟻ

hang point
arzónᴹ de amarreᴹ

rigging wire
tiranteᴹ de fijaciónꟻ

flight bag
sacoᴹ de pilotajeᴹ

wing
alaꟻ

harness
arnésᴹ

trailing edge
caídaꟻ de popaꟻ

tip
puntaꟻ del alaꟻ

control bar
barraꟻ de direcciónꟻ

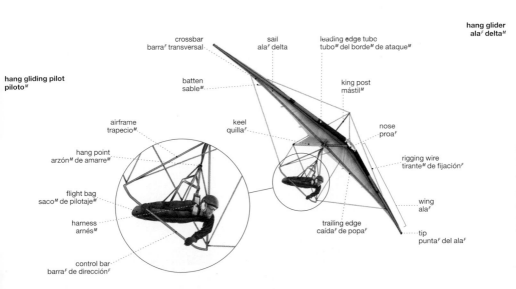

SPORTS AND GAMES

glider

planeador^M

general view
vista^F general

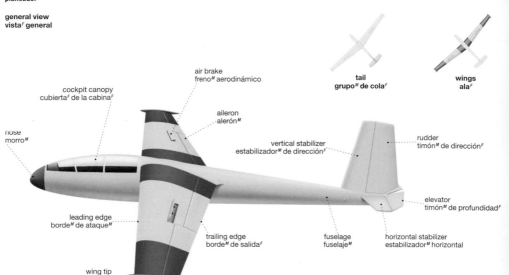

tail
grupo^M de cola^F

wings
ala^F

air brake
freno^M aerodinámico

cockpit canopy
cubierta^F de la cabina^F

aileron
alerón^M

nose
morro^M

vertical stabilizer
estabilizador^M de dirección^F

rudder
timón^M de dirección^F

leading edge
borde^M de ataque^M

trailing edge
borde^M de salida^F

fuselage
fuselaje^M

horizontal stabilizer
estabilizador^M horizontal

elevator
timón^M de profundidad^F

wing tip
borde^M marginal

cockpit
cabina^F del piloto^M

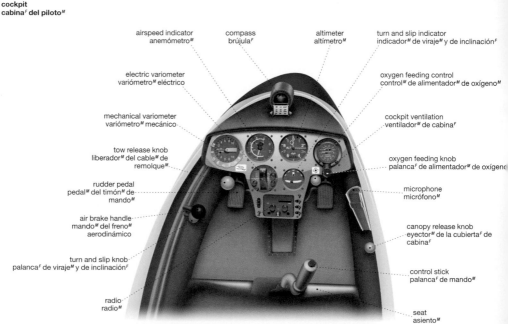

airspeed indicator
anemómetro^M

compass
brújula^F

altimeter
altímetro^M

turn and slip indicator
indicador^M de viraje^M y de inclinación^F

electric variometer
variómetro^M eléctrico

oxygen feeding control
control^M de alimentador^M de oxígeno^M

mechanical variometer
variómetro^M mecánico

cockpit ventilation
ventilador^M de cabina^F

tow release knob
liberador^M del cable^M de
remolque^M

oxygen feeding knob
palanca^F de alimentador^M de oxígeno

rudder pedal
pedal^M del timón^M de
mando^M

microphone
micrófono^M

air brake handle
mando^M del freno^M
aerodinámico

canopy release knob
eyector^M de la cubierta^F de
cabina^F

turn and slip knob
palanca^F de viraje^M y de inclinación^F

control stick
palanca^F de mando^M

radio
radio^M

seat
asiento^M

ballooning
vuelo^M en globo^M

general view
vista^F general

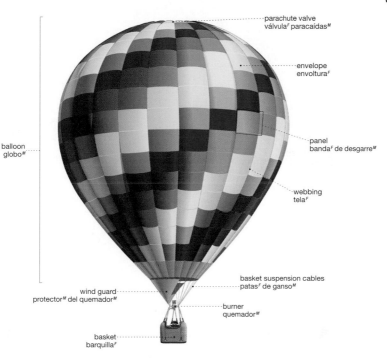

parachute valve
válvula^F paracaídas^M

envelope
envoltura^F

balloon
globo^M

panel
banda^F de desgarre^M

webbing
tela^F

basket suspension cables
patas^F de ganso^M

wind guard
protector^M del quemador^M

burner
quemador^M

basket
barquilla^F

basket
barquilla^F

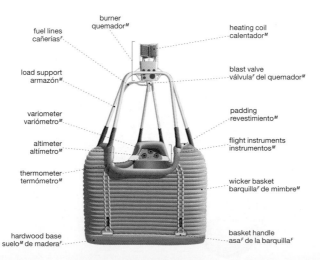

burner
quemador^M

fuel lines
cañerías^F

heating coil
calentador^M

load support
armazón^M

blast valve
válvula^F del quemador^M

padding
revestimiento^M

variometer
variómetro^M

flight instruments
instrumentos^M

altimeter
altímetro^M

thermometer
termómetro^M

wicker basket
barquilla^F de mimbre^M

hardwood base
suelo^M de madera^F

basket handle
asa^F de la barquilla^F

SPORTS AND GAMES

mountaineering

alpinismo^M

rock climber
escalador^M

rock
roca^F

qulckdraw
cinta^F exprés

belay rope
cuerda^F de amarre^M

climbing shoe
pies^M de gato^M

runner
cincha^F

seat harness
arnés^M

roped party
cordada^F

leader
cabeza^F de cordada^F

artificial climbing structure
rocódromo^M

belay beam
viga^F de sujección^F

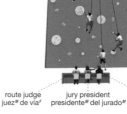

belayer
asegurador^M

route judge
juez^M de vía^F

jury president
presidente^M del jurado^M

timekeeper
cronometrador^M

---

mountaineering
equipment
equipamiento^M de
alpinismo^M

latch
traba^F

screwsleeve
cierre^M de rosca^F

gate
dedo^M

locking carabiner
mosquetón^M de
bloqueo^M

D carabiner
mosquetón^M curvo

rope
cuerda^F

expansion bolt
pitón^M de expansión^F

blade
pata^F

piton
pitón^M

eye
ojo^M

chock
cuña^F

wire sling
cable^M de acero^M

descender
descensor^M de ocho^M

seat harness
arnés^M

mountaineering

handholds
agarres con las manos**

foothold
agarres con los pies**

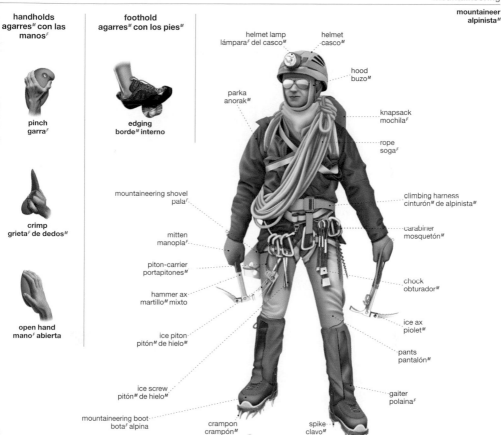

pinch
garra**

edging
borde** interno**

helmet lamp
lámpara** del casco**

helmet
casco**

hood
buzo**

parka
anorak**

knapsack
mochila**

rope
soga**

crimp
grieta** de dedos**

mountaineering shovel
pala**

mitten
manopla**

piton-carrier
portapitones**

hammer ax
martillo** mixto

open hand
mano** abierta

ice piton
pitón** de hielo**

ice screw
pitón** de hielo**

mountaineering boot
bota** alpina

crampon
crampón**

climbing harness
cinturón** de alpinista**

carabiner
mosquetón**

chock
obturador**

ice ax
piolet**

pants
pantalón**

gaiter
polaina**

spike
clavo**

mountaineering equipment

ice ax
piolet

hammer ax
martillo para hielo**

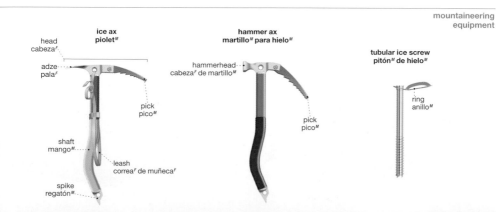

head
cabeza**

adze
pala**

pick
pico**

shaft
mango**

leash
correa** de muñeca**

spike
regatón**

hammerhead
cabeza** de martillo**

pick
pico**

tubular ice screw
pitón de hielo**

ring
anillo**

camping

acampada[F]

examples of tents
ejemplos[M] **de tiendas**[F] **de campaña**[F]

two-person tent
tienda[F] **para dos**

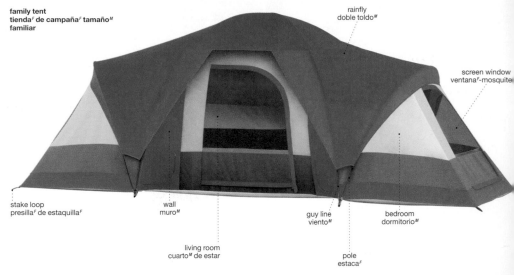

line tightener
tensor[M]

guy line
viento[M]

pole
estaca[F]

integrated groundsheet
suelo[M] aislante integrado

peg
piqueta[F]

rainfly
doble toldo[M]

family tent
tienda[F] **de campaña**[F] **tamaño**[M]
familiar

rainfly
doble toldo[M]

screen window
ventana[F]-mosquite

stake loop
presilla[F] de estaquilla[F]

wall
muro[M]

guy line
viento[M]

bedroom
dormitorio[M]

living room
cuarto[M] de estar

pole
estaca[F]

ridge tent
tienda[F] **tipo**[M] **vagón**[M]

wall ten
tienda[F] **rectangula**

roof
techo^M

eave
alero^M

pup tent
tienda^F de campaña^F
clásica

guy line
viento^M

integrated groundsheet
suelo^M aislante integrado

roof pole
palo^M de la tienda^F

peg
piqueta^F

one-person tent
tienda^F unipersonal

dome tent
tienda^F tipo^M domo^M

pop-up tent
tienda^F tipo^M iglú^M

propane or butane accessories
equipos^M de gas^M

lantern
linterna^F

globe
globo^M

burner frame
armazón^M del quemador^M

pressure regulator
regulador^M de presión^F

heater
calentador^M

pump
bomba^F

leakproof cap
tapón^M hermético

tank
tanque^M

double-burner camp stove
cocina^F de campo^M

single-burner camp stove
hornillo^M

burner
quemador^M

tank
bombona^F de gas^M

wire support
parrilla^F estabilizadora

control valve
válvula^F de control^M

SPORTS AND GAMES

camping

sleeping bags
sacos^M de dormir

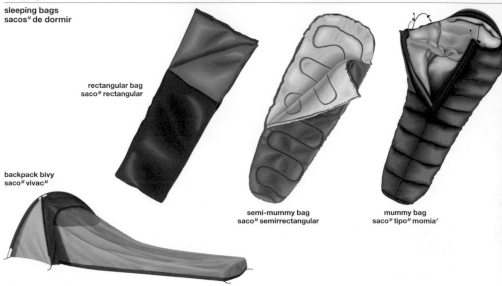

rectangular bag
saco^M rectangular

backpack bivy
saco^M vivac^M

semi-mummy bag
saco^M semirrectangular

mummy bag
saco^M tipo^M momia^F

bed and mattress
camas^F y
colchonetas^F

folding cot
catre^M desmontable

inflator-deflator
muelle^M para inflar y desinflar

inflator
inflador^M

air mattress
colchoneta^F de aire^M

self-inflating mattress
colchoneta^F aislante

foam pad
colchoneta^F de
espuma^F

cooking set
utensilios^M **de**
cocina^F

cutlery set
cubertería^F

sheath
funda^F

spoon
cuchara^F

belt loop
presilla^F

fork
tenedor^M

knife
cuchillo^M

coffee pot
cafetera^F

cup
taza^F

handle
mango^M

frying pan
sartén^F

saucepan
cazuela^F

plate
plato^M

camping equipment
equipamiento^M **para**
acampar

multipurpose knife
navaja^F **multiusos**

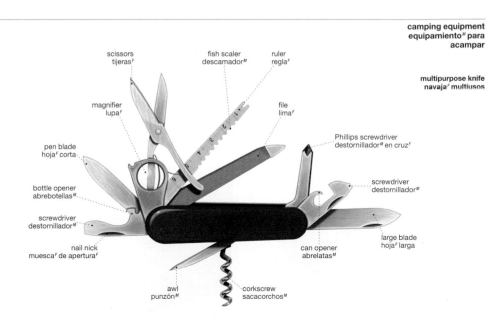

scissors
tijeras^F

magnifier
lupa^F

fish scaler
descamador^M

ruler
regla^F

file
lima^F

Phillips screwdriver
destornillador^M en cruz^F

pen blade
hoja^F corta

bottle opener
abrebotellas^M

screwdriver
destornillador^M

screwdriver
destornillador^M

large blade
hoja^F larga

nail nick
muesca^F de apertura^F

can opener
abrelatas^M

awl
punzón^M

corkscrew
sacacorchos^M

camping

camping equipment

backpack
mochila^F

top flap
solapa^F

shoulder strap
espaldera^F

tightening buckle
hebilla^F de regulación^F

side compression strap
correa^F de compresión^F

front compression strap
correa^F de cierre^M

strap loop
pasador^M

waist belt
cinturón^M

filter
filtro^M

water purifier
purificador^M **de agua**^F

sport bottle
botella^F **deportiva**

hurricane lamp
lámpara^F **de petróleo**^M

thermos bottle
termo^M

bottle
botella^F del termo^M

canteen
cantimplora^F

stopper
tapón^M

cup
taza^F

cooler
nevera^F

folding shovel
pala^F **plegable**

water carrier
termo^M **con llave**^F **de**
servicio^M

camping

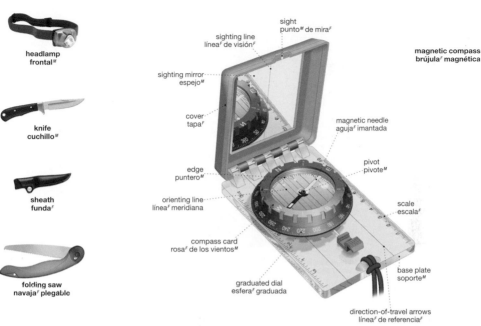

headlamp
frontal^M

knife
cuchillo^M

sheath
funda^F

folding saw
navaja^F plegable

sight
punto^M de mira^F

sighting line
línea^F de visión^F

sighting mirror
espejo^M

magnetic compass
brújula^F magnética

cover
tapa^F

magnetic needle
aguja^F imantada

edge
puntero^M

pivot
pivote^M

orienting line
línea^F meridiana

scale
escala^F

compass card
rosa^F de los vientos^M

base plate
soporte^M

graduated dial
esfera^F graduada

direction-of-travel arrows
línea^F de referencia^F

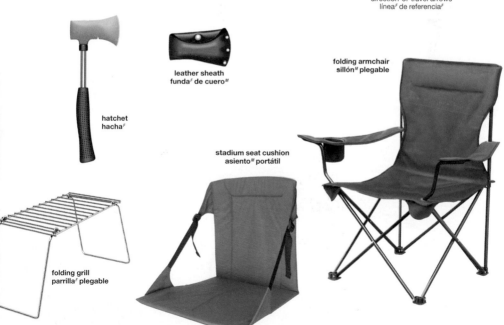

leather sheath
funda^F de cuero^M

folding armchair
sillón^M plegable

hatchet
hacha^F

stadium seat cushion
asiento^M portátil

folding grill
parrilla^F plegable

knots

nudos[M]

square knot
nudo[M] de rizo[M]

overhand knot
nudo[M] llano

running bowline
balso[M]

sheet bend
vuelta[F] de escota[F]

double sheet bend
vuelta[F] de escota[F]
doble

granny knot
nudo[M] de tejedor[M]

sheepshank
margarita[F]

cow hitch
vuelta[F] de cabo[M]

clove hitch
nudo[M] de dos cotes[M]

fisherman's knot
nudo[M] de pescador[M]

heaving line knot
nudo[M] de guía[F]

figure-eight knot
lasca[F] doble

common whipping
sobrenudo[M]

bowline
as[M] de guía[F]

bowline on a bight
as[M] de guía[F] de eslinga[F]
doble

short splice
empalmadura[F]

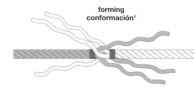

forming
conformación[F]

completion
acabado[M]

cable
cable[M]

twisted rope
cable[M] torcido

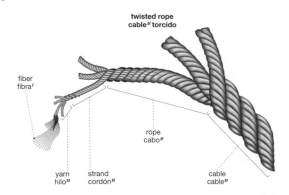

fiber
fibra[F]

rope
cabo[M]

yarn
hilo[M]

strand
cordón[M]

cable
cable[M]

braided rope
cable[M] trenzado

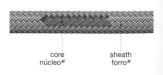

core
núcleo[M]

sheath
forro[M]

fishing
pesca^F

flyfishing
pesca^F con mosca^F

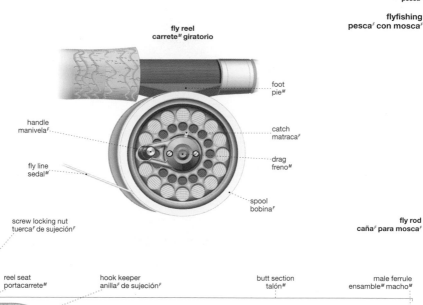

fly reel
carrete^M giratorio

foot
pie^M

catch
matraca^F

handle
manivela^F

drag
freno^M

fly line
sedal^M

spool
bobina^F

fly rod
caña^F para mosca^F

butt cap
contera^F

screw locking nut
tuerca^F de sujeción^F

reel seat
portacarrete^M

hook keeper
anilla^F de sujeción^F

butt section
talón^M

male ferrule
ensamble^M macho^M

female ferrule
ensamble^M hembra^F

handgrip
empuñadura^F

tip section
rabiza^F

guide
anilla^F guía^F

tip ring
guía^F de la punta^F

artificial fly
mosca^F artificial

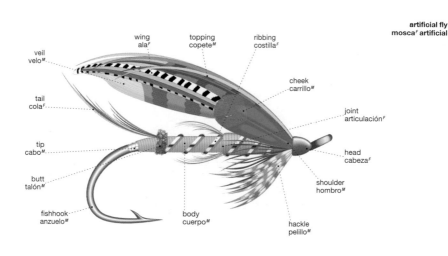

wing
ala^F

topping
copete^M

ribbing
costilla^F

veil
velo^M

cheek
carrillo^M

tail
cola^F

joint
articulación^F

tip
cabo^M

head
cabeza^F

butt
talón^M

shoulder
hombro^M

fishhook
anzuelo^M

body
cuerpo^M

hackle
pelillo^M

SPORTS AND GAMES

fishing

casting
pesca^F de lanzado^M

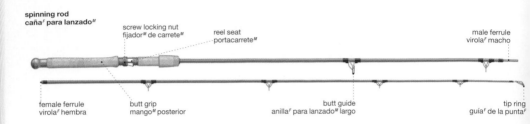

spinning rod
caña^F para lanzado^M

screw locking nut
fijador^M de carrete^M

reel seat
portacarrete^M

male ferrule
virola^F macho

female ferrule
virola^F hembra

butt grip
mango^M posterior

butt guide
anilla^F para lanzado^M largo

tip ring
guía^F de la punta^F

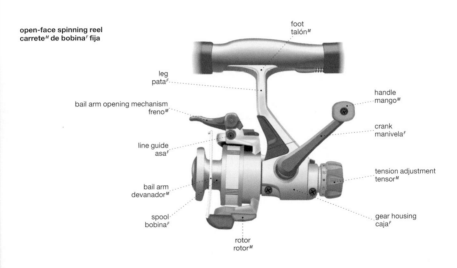

open-face spinning reel
carrete^M de bobina^F fija

foot
talón^M

leg
pata^F

bail arm opening mechanism
freno^M

line guide
asa^F

bail arm
devanador^M

spool
bobina^F

handle
mango^M

crank
manivela^F

tension adjustment
tensor^M

gear housing
caja^F

rotor
rotor^M

baitcasting reel
carrete^M de tambor^M

spool-release mechanism
disparador^M del tambor^M

spool
tambor^M

spool axle
eje^M del tambor^M

star drag wheel
estrella^F de frenado^M

crank
manivela^F

stand
pie^M

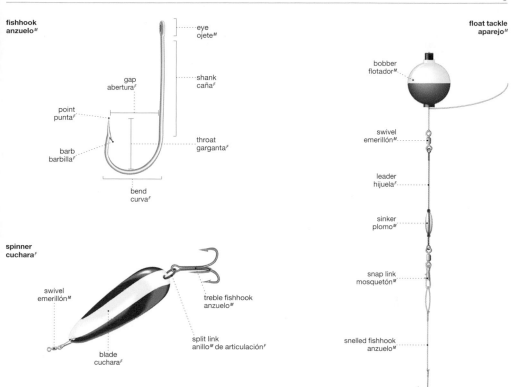

fishhook
anzueloᴹ

eye
ojeteᴹ

shank
cañaᶠ

gap
aberturaᶠ

point
puntaᶠ

throat
gargantaᶠ

barb
barbillaᶠ

bend
curvaᶠ

float tackle
aparejoᴹ

bobber
flotadorᴹ

swivel
emerillónᴹ

leader
hijuelaᶠ

sinker
plomoᴹ

snap link
mosquetónᴹ

snelled fishhook
anzueloᴹ

spinner
cucharaᶠ

swivel
emerillónᴹ

treble fishhook
anzueloᴹ

split link
anilloᴹ de articulaciónᶠ

blade
cucharaᶠ

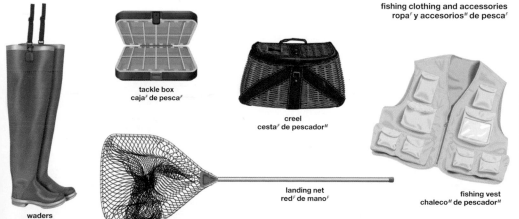

fishing clothing and accessories
ropaᶠ y accesoriosᴹ de pescaᶠ

tackle box
cajaᶠ de pescaᶠ

creel
cestaᶠ de pescadorᴹ

landing net
redᶠ de manoᶠ

fishing vest
chalecoᴹ de pescadorᴹ

waders
botasᶠ altas

SPORTS AND GAMES

dice and dominoes
dados[M] y dominós[M]

ordinary die
dado[M] común

poker die
dado[M] de póquer[M]

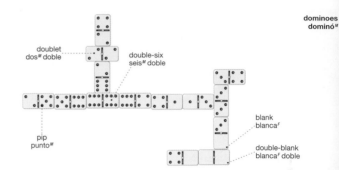

dominoes
dominó[M]

doublet
dos[M] doble

double-six
seis[M] doble

blank
blanca[F]

double-blank
blanca[F] doble

pip
punto[M]

playing cards
juego[M] de cartas[F]

suits
trajes[M]

hearts
corazones[M]

diamonds
diamantes[M]

clubs
tréboles[M]

spades
espadas[F]

court and special cards
figuras[F] y cartas[F]
especiales

joker
comodín[M]

ace
as[M]

king
rey[M]

queen
reina[F]

jack
sota[M]

standard poker hands
manos[F] de póquer[M]

high card
cartas[F] altas

one pair
pareja[F]

two pairs
dobles parejas[F]

three of a kind
trío[M]

straight
escalera[F]

flush
color[M]

full house
full[M]

four of a kind
póquer[M]

straight flush
escalera[F] de color[M]

royal flush
escalera[F] real

board games

juegos^M de mesa^F

backgammon
backgammon^M

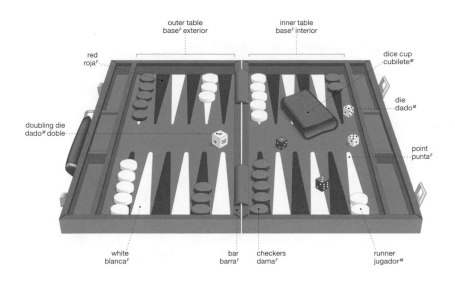

outer table
base^F exterior

inner table
base^F interior

red
roja^F

dice cup
cubilete^M

die
dado^M

doubling die
dado^M doble

point
punta^F

white
blanca^F

bar
barra^F

checkers
dama^F

runner
jugador^M

ludo
parchís^M

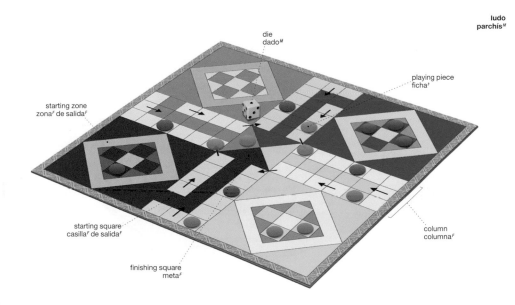

die
dado^M

playing piece
ficha^F

starting zone
zona^F de salida^F

starting square
casilla^F de salida^F

finishing square
meta^F

column
columna^F

board games

snakes and ladders
serpientes^F y escaleras^F

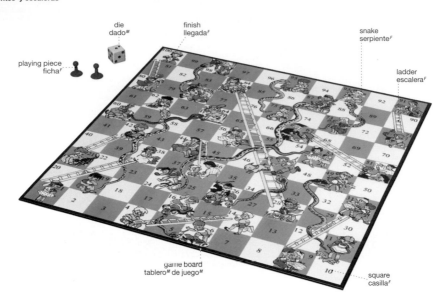

die
dado^M

finish
llegada^F

snake
serpiente^F

playing piece
ficha^F

ladder
escalera^F

game board
tablero^M de juego^M

square
casilla^F

game of the goose
juego^M de la oca^F

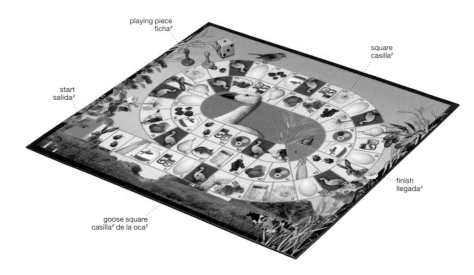

playing piece
ficha^F

square
casilla^F

start
salida^F

finish
llegada^F

goose square
casilla^F de la oca^F

chess
ajedrez^M

chess pieces
piezas^F de ajedrez^M

pawn
peón^M

rook
torre^F

bishop
alfil^M

knight
caballo^M

king
rey^M

queen
reina^F

queen's side
lado^M de la reina^F

king's side
lado^M del rey^M

chessboard
tablero^M de ajedrez^M

white square
escaque^M blanco

Black
negras^F

black square
escaque^M negro

White
blancas^F

chess notation
notación^F del ajedrez^M

types of movements
tipos^M de movimientos^M

diagonal movement
movimiento^M diagonal

vertical movement
movimiento^M vertical

L-shaped movement
movimiento^M en ángulo^M

horizontal movement
movimiento^M horizontal

major motions
principales
movimientos^M

connection
conexión^F

go
go (sun-tse)^M

board
tablero^M

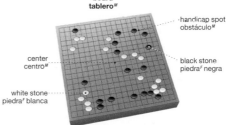

handicap spot
obstáculo^M

center
centro^M

black stone
piedra^F negra

contact
contacto^M

capture
captura^F

white stone
piedra^F blanca

checkers
damas^F

checkerboard
tablero^M de damas^F

checker
dama^F

jigsaw puzzle

puzle^M

piece
pieza^F

picture
imagen^F

board
tablero^M

mah-jongg

mah-jongg^M

square
muralla^F

East
Este^M

South
Sur^M

North
Norte^M

West
Oeste^M

wall
muro^M

breaking the wall
brecha^F del muro^M

suit tiles
fichas^F **ordinarias**

circles
círculos^M

characters
caracteres^M

bamboos
bambúes^M

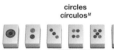

honor tiles
fichas^F **de honor**^M

winds
vientos^M

dragons
dragones^M

bonus tiles
fichas^F **de beneficio**^M

flower tiles
fichas^F de flores^F

season tiles
fichas^F de estaciones^F

video games

videojuegos^M

**video entertainment
system
videojuego^M**

display
pantalla^F

game console
consola^F de juego^M

eject button
botón^M de expulsión^F

cover
tapa^F

power/reset button
lector^M DVD^M

reset button
restablecimiento^M

directional buttons
botones^M de dirección^F

action buttons
botones^M de acción^F

joysticks
joysticks^M

controller
mando^M

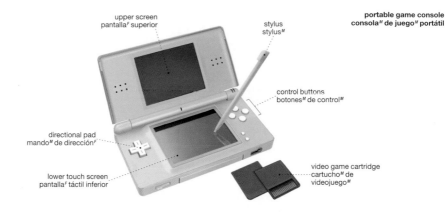

**portable game console
consola^M de juego^M portátil**

upper screen
pantalla^F superior

stylus
stylus^M

control buttons
botones^M de control^M

directional pad
mando^M de dirección^F

lower touch screen
pantalla^F táctil inferior

video game cartridge
cartucho^M de
videojuego^M

SPORTS AND GAMES

roulette

ruleta^F

roulette wheel
ruleta^F americana

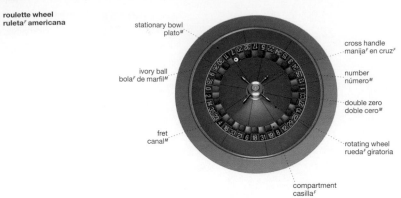

stationary bowl
plato^M

cross handle
manija^F en cruz^F

ivory ball
bola^F de marfil^M

number
número^M

double zero
doble cero^M

fret
canal^M

rotating wheel
rueda^F giratoria

compartment
casilla^F

American roulette table
tablero^M de ruleta^F
americana

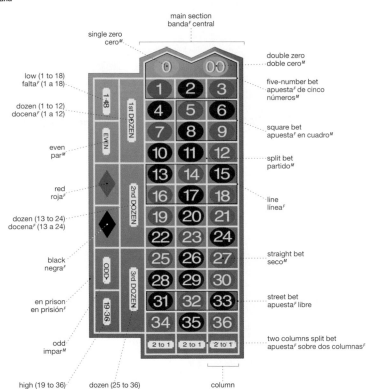

main section
banda^F central

single zero
cero^M

double zero
doble cero^M

low (1 to 18)
falta^F (1 a 18)

five-number bet
apuesta^F de cinco
números^M

dozen (1 to 12)
docena^F (1 a 12)

square bet
apuesta^F en cuadro^M

even
par^M

split bet
partido^M

red
roja^F

line
línea^F

dozen (13 to 24)
docena^F (13 a 24)

black
negra^F

straight bet
seco^M

en prison
en prisión^F

street bet
apuesta^F libre

odd
impar^M

two columns split bet
apuesta^F sobre dos columnas^F

high (19 to 36)
pasa^F (19 a 36)

dozen (25 to 36)
docena^F (25 a 36)

column
columna^F

1-18 | 1st DOZEN | EVEN | 2nd DOZEN | ODD | 3rd DOZEN | 19-36

2 to 1 | 2 to 1 | 2 to 1

French roulette wheel
ruleta^F francesa

French roulette table
tablero^M de ruleta^F
francesa

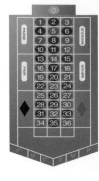

SPORTS AND GAMES

darts
juegoᴹ **de dardos**ᴹ

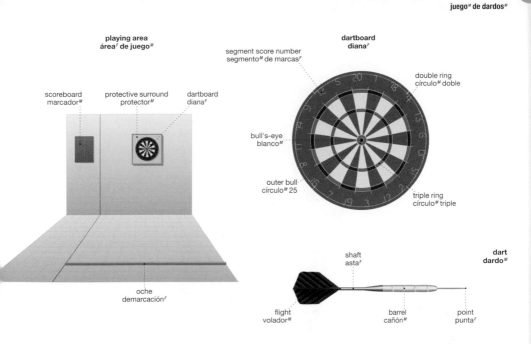

playing area
áreaᶠ **de juego**ᴹ

scoreboard
marcadorᴹ

protective surround
protectorᴹ

dartboard
dianaᶠ

oche
demarcaciónᶠ

dartboard
dianaᶠ

segment score number
segmentoᴹ de marcasᶠ

double ring
círculoᴹ doble

bull's-eye
blancoᴹ

outer bull
círculoᴹ 25

triple ring
círculoᴹ triple

dart
dardoᴹ

shaft
astaᶠ

flight
voladorᴹ

barrel
cañónᴹ

point
puntaᶠ

soccer table
futbolínᴹ

score counter
anotadorᴹ

rubber bumper
amortiguadorᴹ de cauchoᴹ

player
jugadorᴹ

goal
golᴹ

telescopic rod
barraᶠ telescópica

playing field
campoᴹ de juegoᴹ

ball
bolaᶠ

handle
empuñaduraᶠ

SPORTS AND GAMES

slot machine

máquina[F] **tragaperras**

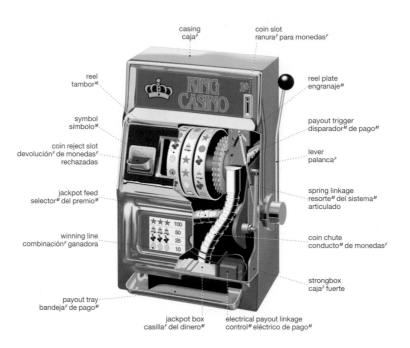

casing
caja[F]

coin slot
ranura[F] para monedas[F]

reel
tambor[M]

reel plate
engranaje[M]

symbol
símbolo[M]

payout trigger
disparador[M] de pago[M]

coin reject slot
devolución[F] de monedas[F]
rechazadas

lever
palanca[F]

jackpot feed
selector[M] del premio[M]

spring linkage
resorte[M] del sistema[M]
articulado

winning line
combinación[F] ganadora

coin chute
conducto[M] de monedas[F]

strongbox
caja[F] fuerte

payout tray
bandeja[F] de pago[M]

jackpot box
casilla[F] del dinero[M]

electrical payout linkage
control[M] eléctrico de pago[M]

Ultimate

disco[M] **volador**

disc
disco[M] volador

playing field proper
campo[M] de juego[M]

playing field
tablero[M] **de ultimate**[M]

end zone
zona[F] de fondo[M]

brick mark
marca[F] de ladrillo[M]

perimeter line
línea[F] de perímetro[M]

pinball machine

máquina^F de pinball

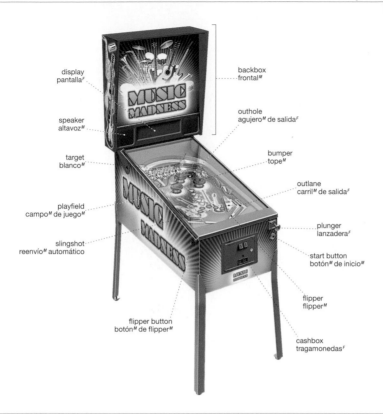

display
pantalla^F

speaker
altavoz^M

target
blanco^M

playfield
campo^M de juego^M

slingshot
reenvío^M automático

flipper button
botón^M de flipper^M

backbox
frontal^M

outhole
agujero^M de salida^F

bumper
tope^M

outlane
carril^M de salida^F

plunger
lanzadera^F

start button
botón^M de inicio^M

flipper
flipper^M

cashbox
tragamonedas^F

kite

cometa^F

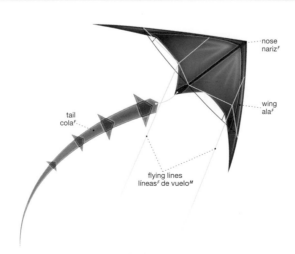

nose
nariz^F

wing
ala^F

tail
cola^F

flying lines
líneas^F de vuelo^M

SPORTS AND GAMES

INDEX

Índice

English Index

A

A 562
A, standard 564
abacus 500
abalone 265
abdomen 139, 140, 141, 142, 145, 192, 194
abdominal rectus 196
abdominal segment 141
aboriginal language 583
Abraham 870
abrasive belt 396
abrasive material 396
abruptly pinnate 111
ABS 679
absorbent cotton 915
absorbing plate 802
absorption by clouds 96
absorption by the Earth's surface 96
absorption of water and mineral salts 102
abstract art 530
abutment 506, 660, 661
Abyssinian 179
AC power inlet 614
acanthodian 129
acanthus leaf 501
acceleration lane 659
accelerator cable 419
accelerator control 417
accent mark 563
accept machine 798
access panel 338, 348
accessory 850, 851
accessory box 571
accessory gearbox 749
accessory shoe 592
accidental 563
accordion 560
account identification 859
accountant's office 644
accumulator 679
accuracy sports 1009
ace 1062
acetylene 407
acetylene valve 407
achene 114
Achilles tendon 197
achondrite 18
acid rain 97, 98
acid snow 98
acoustic meatus, external 205, 234, 235
acromion 201
acroterion 499, 500
acrylic fiber 424
actinides 814
actinium 814
action button 1067
actor 542
actors' seats 542
actress 543
actuator 894
actuator arm 638
actuator arm motor 638
acute accent 587
Adam's apple 192
adapter, plug 358
add/equals key 649
add to memory 649
addition 836
addition key 649
additional production personnel 605

adductor, long 196
adductor magnus 197
adhesive disk 153
adhesive tape 915
adjust button 629
adjustable catch 1039
adjustable channel 399
adjustable supporting frame 926
adjuster 916
adjusting band 618
adjusting lever 564
adjusting tube 971
adjustment pedal 526
adjustment slide 432
adjustment wheel 405
administration 522
administrative building 794
administrative office 852, 869, 900, 905
adrenal gland 229
Adriatic Sea 49
advertisement 590
advertising panel 714
advertising sign 716
adze 531, 1051
Aegean Sea 49
aerator 350
aerial skiing course 1040
aerial sports 1046
affluent 73
Afghanistan 58, 880
Africa 44, 60, 69, 879
African Plate 68
African Union 882
Afro pick 476
Afro-Asiatic languages 582
afterbay 785, 786, 791
afterfeather 158
aftershave 479
agar 244
agitator 378
agnathan 128
agricultural machinery 765
aiguillette 276
aikido 996
aikidogi 996
aikidoka 996
aileron 746, 1048
air bag 676
air bag, side curtain 676
air brake handle 1048
air bubble 651
air cap 408
air chamber 353
air cleaner 411
air compression unit 707
air compressor 408, 706
air conditioner 687
air conditioner, room 343
air conditioner, split system 343
air conditioning 342
air conditioning system 96, 911
air filter 417, 672, 706, 758
air flow 527
air hole 483, 585
air hose connection 408
air inlet 753
air inlet control 336
air intake 688, 727, 749, 1024
air leg 772
air mail 589
air mass 81
air navigation device 897
air pressure 85
air pump 668

air purifier 342
air relief valve 729
air return 338
air scoop 1026
air sealing gland 555
air shaft 498
air space 160
air start unit 744
air tank 408
air temperature 81
air transport 740
air tube 339
air valve 408
air vent 380
airbrush 527
air-conditioning equipment 730
aircraft, amphibious firefighting 750
aircraft, business 750
aircraft, cargo 589, 751
aircraft, combat 896
aircraft, light 750
aircraft, radar 751
aircraft, stealth 751
aircraft, vertical take-off and landing 750
aircraft carrier 897
airframe 1047
air-inlet grill 477
airliner 79
airlock 35, 796, 899
air-outlet grill 477
airplane 750
airplane, forces 752
airplane, movements 752
airplane route 64
airport 53, 740, 842, 857
airport ground equipment 744
airspeed indicator 748, 1048
air-supply tube 901
aisle 288, 507, 705
ajowan 261
ala 231
Alaska 46
Albania 57, 878
Albanian 583
albatross 161
albumen 160
alcohol, rubbing 915
alcohol bulb 827
alcohol column 827
alert area 994
Aleutian Islands 47
Aleutian Trench 69
alfalfa 252
alga 107
alga, brown 107
alga, green 107
alga, red 107
Algeria 60, 879
alidade 85, 833
alidade level 833
alighting board 144
aligner 984
alley 845, 963, 966
alligator 157
allspice 260
all-terrain vehicle 697
alluvial deposits 73
almond 255
alpine ski trail 1036
alpine skier 1038
alpine skiing 1038
alpine skiing, technical events 1039
Alps 49

altar 871
altar, high 871
altar cross 871
altar frontal 871
altarpiece 871
alteration line 569
alternate 632
alternating-current power cord 630
alternator 672, 682, 807, 819
alternator warning light 677
altimeter 748, 1046, 1048, 1049
altitude 45, 79
altitude clamp 24, 25
altitude fine adjustment 24, 25
altocumulus 82, 88
altostratus 82, 88
alula 158
aluminum 78, 812
aluminum foil 294
aluminum frame 536
aluminum layer 615
alveolus 215
amaranth 263
Amazon River 48
ambulance 911, 918
ambulance attendant's seat 911
ambulatory 507
ambulatory care unit 922
America 876
American football, protective equipment 954
American football field 952
American shorthair 179
americium 814
Amerindian languages 583
Amery Ice Shelf 46
amethyst 470
Amharic 582
ammunition pouch 906
ammunition stowage 895
amoeba 133
ampere 835
ampersand 587
amphibian 152, 153
amphitheater, Roman 503
amplifier 559
amplifier with tuner 614, 619
amplitude 821
ampli-tuner 614
ampulla 135
anaconda 156
anatomy 196
anchor 732, 935
anchor, mushroom 732
anchor, navy 732
anchor, plow 732
anchor, screw 732
anchor, sea 732
anchor, stocked 732
anchor, stockless 732
anchor pin 679
anchor point 145
anchor wire 777
anchorage block 660
anchor-windlass room 727, 731
anchovy 267
anconeus 197
Andes Cordillera 48
andiron 337
Andorra 56, 877
andouillette 277
Andromeda 22
anemometer 84, 85, 807
anesthesia room 921
angle 838

altar 871
angle, acute 836, 838
angle, measure 833
angle, obtuse 836, 838
angle, reentrant 838
angle, right 836, 838
anglerfish, deep sea 151
Anglicanism 870
Angola 61, 880
Anik 603
animal dung 98
animal fat 784
anise 262
ankle 192, 194
anklet 433, 446
annual ring 118
annulet 500
anode 820
anode rod 348
anorak 451
answer key 622
answering machine, digital 625
ant 146
Antarctic Circle 42, 46
Antarctic Peninsula 46
Antarctic Plate 68
Antarctica 44, 46
anteater 164
antefix 499
antelope 172
antenna 27, 32, 64, 86, 139, 140, 141, 142, 143, 602, 620, 621, 622, 623, 671, 697, 730, 731, 733, 746, 753, 895, 897, 899, 907, 958
antenna, dish 610
antenna, high-frequency 750
antenna, microwave 608
antenna, parabolic 602
antenna, radar 64, 896, 899
antenna, radio 726, 728, 730, 731, 899, 1023
antenna, telescoping 619
antenna, UHF 32, 86
antenna, VHF 898
antennae cleaner 142
antennule 139
anther 104, 112
anticline 776
antifriction pad 1039
Antigua and Barbuda 54, 876
antihelix 234
anti-leak guard 449
antilock braking system 679
antimissile self-defense 898
antimony 812
antireflection coating 802
antiseptic 915
antiskating device 617
antislip shoe 409
antitragus 234
Antlia 21
anus 135, 136, 137, 138, 139, 141, 145, 149, 155, 216, 226, 228
anvil 832
aorta 212
aorta, abdominal 210, 219
aorta, arch 210, 213
aorta, dorsal 143
aorta, thoracic 210
aorta, ventral 149
apartment building 845
aperture 136, 593, 597, 598
aperture changer 826
aperture door 27
apex 136, 137, 206, 233

Apollo 38
apostrophe 587
apothecium 106
Appalachian Mountains 47
apparatus room 900
apple 115, 255
apple corer 309
appliance, domestic 314, 850, 851
appliance, home 374
appliance, miscellaneous 318
applicator, sponge-tipped 473
appoggiatura 563
appointment book 650
approach 935, 936, 1015
approach run 970
apricot 254
apron 360, 361, 362, 697, 740, 990
apron, front 431
apron, rear 431
apse 507, 508
apsidiole 506, 507
Apus 20
aquamarine 470
aquarium 495
Aquarius 20
Aquastat 339
aquatic sports 974
aquifer, confined 770
Aquila 20, 22
Ara 20
Arabian Peninsula 51
Arabian Plate 68
Arabian Sea 51
Arabic 582
Arabic script 585
arachnid 140, 147
arachnoid 224
Aral Sea 51
Aramaic 582
arame 244
arbitration committee 993
arbor 410
arc 838
arc, graduated 734
arc welder 406
arcade 503, 506
arcature 508
arch 509, 514, 661
arch, basket handle 514
arch, blind 508
arch, dental 231
arch, equilateral 514
arch, fixed 661
arch, horseshoe 514
arch, lancet 514
arch, natural 70
arch, ogee 514
arch, open 508
arch, palatoglossal 231
arch, semicircular 514
arch, stilted 514
arch, three-hinged 661
arch, traverse 506
arch, trefoil 514
arch, trussed 661
arch, Tudor 514
arch, two-hinged 661
archaeognatha 129
archaeopteryx 130
archboard 653
archer 1009
archery 1009
archery range 932
archipelago 45

architectural style 500
architecture, ancient 498
architecture, Asian 513
architecture, elements 514
architecture, military 504
architecture, pre-Columbian 513
architecture, Western 506
architrave 499, 501, 509
archives 522, 905
Arctic 44, 46
Arctic Circle 42, 46, 47, 49, 51
arctic continental 81
arctic maritime 81
Arctic Ocean 44, 46
arena 503, 932
areola 227
argent 875
Argentina 55, 876
argon 814
Ariane IV 39
Ariane V 39
Ariel 15
Aries 22
ark 872
arm 135, 138, 185, 360, 372, 415, 555, 561, 566, 571, 732, 760, 025, 917
arm, hunting 887
arm, spiral 19
arm, upper 193, 195
arm elevator 617
arm lock 992
arm nut 571
arm rest 617
arm shoulder 275
arm slit 443
arm stump 360
armature 819
armature core 819
armature winding 819
armchair 331, 360, 868
armchair, folding 1057
armchair, swivel-tilter 646
Armenia 58, 880
Armenian 583
armhole 434
armoire 364
armor 884, 895
armored plate 895
armpit 192, 194
armrest 366, 674, 675, 917
arpeggio 563
arris 500
arrow 885, 1009
arrow key 342
arrow rest 885, 1009
arrowhead, flint 883
arsenic 812
art, fine 522
art, graphic 532
art, performing 540
art deco 511
art director 542
art room 868
artery 198, 209, 210, 212
artery, axillary 210
artery, brachial 210
artery, carotid 210
artery, dorsal 210
artery, dorsal abdominal 139
artery, femoral 210
artery, iliac 210, 219
artery, mesenteric 210, 219
artery, peroneal 210
artery, pulmonary 210, 212, 213
artery, radial 210

artery, renal 210, 219
artery, sternal 139
artery, subclavian 210
artery, tibial 210
artery, ulnar 210
artery, ventral abdominal 139
arthropleura 129
artichoke 251
article 590
articulation 677
arugula 247
asafetida 261
asbestos 78
Ascension setting scale 24, 25
ascot tie 431
ash 120, 483
ash layer 75
ashtray 483
Asia 44, 58, 69, 880
asparagus 250
asperity 615
asphalt 782
asphalt shingle 385
asphalt still 782
aspirator 911
aspirin 915
ass 172
assistant camera operator 542
assistant director 604, 605
assistant warden's office 864
astatine 813
asterisk 587
asteroid belt 15
asthenosphere 66
astigmatism 239
astragal 501, 890
astronautics 30
astronomical observation 20
astronomical observatory 28
astronomical unit 14, 15
at sign 587
Atacama Desert 48
athletic track 932
Atlantic Ocean 44, 46, 49, 50
atlas 153, 165, 170, 175, 204
atlas moth 147
Atlas Mountains 50
ATM 849, 858, 859
atmosphere 79, 94, 98
atoll 70
atom 810
atomic number 812
atrium 502, 508
atrium, left 212, 213
atrium, right 212, 213
attaché case 484
attack, goal 955
attack, wing 955
attack/defensive area 948
attack line 958
attack zone 958
attacker 958
attendant's desk 866
attic, finished 328, 331
attitude indicator 748
attraction 817
ATV 34
audio/video input 614
audio/video output 614
audio console 604, 605, 608
audio control technician 605, 608
audio in port 628
audio input 614
audio jack 629
audio library 867
audio out port 628

audio output 614
audio system 676
audioguide 522
audiometric examination
    room 923
audiovisual equipment 850
auditorium 20, 522, 844, 852, 866
auger 421, 763
auger control 421
auk 161
aunt 929
auricle 142
auriculars 158
Auriga 22
aurora 79
Australia 62, 69, 881
Australian-Indian Plate 68
Austria 56, 878
authorized landfill site 97
auto/manual range 404
auto racing 1022
autoclave 921
autofocus 593, 601
auto-injector 914
automated teller machine 849, 858, 859
Automated Transfer Vehicle 34
automatic dialer index 623
automatic sorting trays 647
automobile 669
automobile, electric 678
automobile, hybrid 678
automobile systems 672, 673
autopilot control 748
autotroph 94
autumn 80
avenue 52, 845
average button 597
avocado 248
awl 1055
awning channel 687
ax 165, 903
axe, polished stone 883
axel 1031
axis 165, 204
axle 706, 761
axle, planetary 763
axle shaft 673
axon 221
axon hillock 221
Aymara 583
Azerbaijan 58, 880
azimuth clamp 24, 25
azimuth fine adjustment 24, 25
azure 875

B

B 562
baboon 185
baby carrier, backpack 491
baby carrier, cloth 491
baby carrier, wrap 491
baby doll 447
baby grand 553
back 168, 174, 193, 195, 237, 298, 299, 300, 306, 361, 366, 386, 391, 430, 885, 917, 945, 947, 958, 960
back beam 572
back boundary line 962
back button 634
back check 553
back line 955, 1027

back rib 272
back zone 958
backboard 957
backboard storage 911
backboard support 957
backbone 641
backbox 1071
backcourt 964, 967
backdrop 540
backgammon 1063
background 495
backguard 378, 379
backhoe 759
backhoe control 759
backing 538
backing board 538
backing plate 679
backlighting button 613
backpack 489, 1056
backpack bivy 1054
backrest 675, 697, 1001, 1026
backrest, adjustable 913
backsaw 391
backspace 633
backstay 724, 1031
backstop 938, 957
backstretch 1006
backstroke 975
backstroke start 975
backstroke turn indicator 977
back-up light 674
backup storage unit 641
bacon 277
badge 906
badger 180
badminton 962
badminton court 962
Baffin Bay 46
Baffin Island 47
baffle 336
bag, accordion 487
bag, bicycle 700
bag, box 486
bag, camera 596
bag, carrier 486
bag, carry-on 488
bag, diaper 492
bag, drawstring 486
bag, duffel 487, 489
bag, freezer 295
bag, garment 488, 489
bag, golf 1019
bag, hobo 487
bag, men 487
bag, mesh 294
bag, messenger 486
bag, mummy 1054
bag, punching 990
bag, rectangular 1054
bag, sandwich 295
bag, satchel 486
bag, sea 486
bag, semi-mummy 1054
bag, shopping 487
bag, shoulder 487
bag, sleeping 1054
bag, snack 295
bag, tea 295
bag, tote 486, 488
bag, vegetable 295
bag compartment 375
bag well 1019
bagel 279
baggage check-in counter 742
baggage claim area 742

baggage compartment 688, 707, 753
baggage conveyor 745
baggage locker 704, 857
baggage room 704
bagger 289
bagpipes 560
baguette 279
Bahamas 54, 876
Bahrain 58, 880
bail 943
bail arm 1060
bail arm opening mechanism 1060
bailey 504
baize 1012
bakery 289
baking 310
balaclava 458, 1022
balalaika 561
balance, analytical 831
balance, beam 830
balance, Roberval's 830
balance, spring 831
balance, unequal-arm 830
balance rail 553
balancer 549
balcony 330, 510, 541, 872
balcony door 330
baler, hay 766
baling 99
balk area 1012
balk line 1012
Balkan Peninsula 49
ball 124, 567, 574, 889, 972, 1012, 1013, 1015, 1069
ball, bowling 1015
ball, cork 941
ball, cricket 942
ball, cue 1012, 1013
ball, exercise 1000
ball, golf 1017
ball, hockey 944
ball, ivory 1068
ball, lacrosse 949
ball, object 1012, 1013
ball, polo 1008
ball, rugby 951
ball, soccer 946
ball, speed 990
ball, squash 965
ball, table tennis 961
ball, tennis 968
ball, tournament 965
ball, training 965
ball, water polo 974
ball, yarn 941
ball assembly 350
ball bearing 584, 807
ball boy 966
ball mount 686
ball peen 388
ball return 1015
ball sports 938
ball stand 1015
ballast 713
ball-cock supply valve 347
ballet flat 461
balloon 1049
ballooning 1049
ballroom 731
Baltic Sea 49
baluster 335, 510
balustrade 510, 513, 518
Bambara 582
bamboo 1066

bamboo shoot 250
banana 258
band 617
band, net 967
band, suspension 908
band, vertical side 958
bandage, adhesive 915
bandage, elastic support 915
bandage, gauze roller 915
bandage, triangular 915
Bangladesh 58, 881
bangle 471
banister 329, 330, 335
banjo 560
bank 658, 794, 844, 849, 1014
bank branch 858
banknote 861
banner 522, 590
banquet hall 852
banquette 361
Bantu languages 582
baobab 120
baptismal font 871
bar 171, 290, 480, 541, 557, 816, 844, 848, 853, 865, 1000, 1063
bar, horizontal 970, 971
bar, latissimus dorsi 1001
bar, leg curl 1001
bar, leg extension 1001
bar, low 970
bar, lower 970
bar, push 515
bar, steel 971
bar, tow 988
bar, triple 1002
bar, twist 1000
bar, upper 970
bar, wooden 971
bar code reader 634
bar frame 373
bar line 562
bar nose 417
bar stool 290
barb 82, 158, 1061
Barbados 54, 877
barbell 999, 1000
barbican 504
baren 533
Barents Sea 46, 49
barge, self-propelled 729
barium 812
bark 118
barley 122, 263
barn 243
barograph 85
barometer 85
barometric pressure 81
barometric tendency 81
Baroque 510, 530
barrack buildings 505
barroom 290
bars, parallel 971
bars, uneven parallel 970
barstool 361
bartender 290
bartizan 504, 505
basal plate 105

basaltic layer 66
base 317, 318, 336, 355, 359, 372, 393, 395, 398, 478, 501, 512, 513, 538, 609, 617, 623, 634, 635, 651, 658, 713, 807, 815, 825, 830, 873, 874, 887, 903, 935, 938, 969, 971, 1010
base, bayonet 358
base, hardwood 1049
base, padded 957
base, screw 358
base of splat 360
base plate 84, 392, 617, 833, 892, 1039, 1057
base plug 893
base ring 890
base width 792
baseball 938, 940, 941
baseball, players 938
baseball field 938
baseboard 333, 335, 600
baseline 967
baseman 938
basement 328, 847
basic operation 649
basil 262
basilosaur 131
basin 794
basin, competition 932
basket 319, 377, 378, 491, 702, 957, 1038, 1042, 1049
basket, hanging 410
basket, wicker 1049
basketball 956
basketball, players 957
basketball court 956
basketball player 956
basmati rice 283
bass 269
bass clarinet 545
bass register 560
Bass Strait 52
bass tone control 549, 619
bass trap 605
bassinet 492
bassoon 545, 550
baster 309
bastion 505
bat 186, 187, 767, 940, 942
bat, baseball 941
bat, softball 941
bat, spear-nosed 187
bat, vampire 187
bath 855
bath, developer 600
bath, developing 600
bath, fixing 600
bath, stop 600
bath sheet 475
bathing wrap 448
bathrobe 447
bathroom 330, 346, 855, 920
bathroom articles 851
bathtub 330, 344, 346
baton 934
baton, expandable 906
baton holder 906
batsman 942, 943
batten 371, 540, 722, 980, 983, 1047
batten pocket 980, 983
batter 939, 940
batter head 556
battery 390, 595, 672, 678, 685, 702, 706, 803, 818, 894, 901
battery box 691, 917

battery case 685
battery charger 622
battery condition module 678
battery cover 685
battery level 593
battery modules 86
battery pack 389, 394, 595, 613
battery pilot light 634
battlement 504, 505
bay 17, 45
bay filler panel 629
Bay of Bengal 51
bayonet 886
bayonet mount 598
bazooka 893
beach 70
beach volleyball court 959
bead 684
bead wire 685
beak 138
beak, horny 155
beaker 815
beaker, measuring 308
beam 513, 765, 830, 969
beam, balance 969, 970
beam, belay 1050
beam, continuous 660
beam, electron 609
beam, high 674
beam, l-profiled 512
beam, laser 615
beam, low 674
beam, ridge 333
beam gantry 792
bean 253
bean, adzuki 253
bean, black 253
bean, broad 252
bean, dolicho 252
bean, green 253
bean, hyacinth 252
bean, Lima 253
bean, mung 253
bean, pinto 253
bean, red kidney 253
bean, roman 253
bean, scarlet runner 253
bean, wax 253
bean, yard-long 252
bean container 318
bean thread 283
beanbag chair 361
bear, black 94, 181
bear, polar 94, 181
bearer 555
bearing 1045
bearing pad 799
beater 314, 557, 572, 765
beater, egg 310
beater, four blade 314
beater, spiral 314
beater ejector 314
beater handtree 572
beater sley 572
Beaufort Sea 46, 49
beauty care 289
beaver 166, 884
becquerel 835
bed 363, 493, 538, 658, 973, 1054
bed, double 855
bed, hospital 920
bed, single 855
bed chamber 502
bedrock 76, 109
bedroom 330, 1052

beech 119
beechnut 255
beef 272
beer 288
beet 251
beetle, burying 146
beetle, furniture 146
beetle, scarab 146
begonia 113
Belarus 57, 878
belayer 1050
Belgium 56, 878
Belize 54, 876
bell 550, 551
bell, set 557
bell, sleigh 557
bell, tubular 557
bell bottoms 441
bell brace 550
bell tower 507, 871
bellkey 550
bellows 555, 560, 600
bellows strap 560
belly 158, 168, 198
below-stage 540
belt 387, 432, 435, 685, 733, 992, 994
belt, duty 906
belt, hip 489, 491
belt, money 487
belt, seat 675
belt, shoulder 675
belt, tool 387
belt, waist 1056
belt, weight 989
belt, weightlifting 999
belt clip 621
belt drive 727
belt loop 1055
beltway 53, 843
beluga whale 183
bench 361, 715, 771, 849, 911, 1001
bench, players' 945, 953, 955, 958, 960, 1028
bench, storage 361
bench, substitutes' 947
bench, team 974
bench height 771
bend 480, 664, 1061
bend, double 667
bend, sheet 1058
Bengal 179
Benin 60, 879
Berber 582
beret 458
bergamot 256
bergère 360
bergschrund 72
Bering Sea 44
Bering Strait 46, 47
berkelium 814
berm 790
Bermuda shorts 433, 441
berry 103, 254
berth 705
beryllium 812
bet, five-number 1068
bet, split 1068
bet, straight 1068
bet, street 1068
bevel 912
bevel square 387, 833
beverage can 295
beverage cooler 288
bezel 470

button, sew-through 567
button, shank 567
button loop 432
button placket 431
buttonhole 435
buttoning 435
buttress 506, 508, 510, 790
buttress, flying 506, 507
butt-strap 480
bypass duct 749
bypass feeder 647

C

C 562
cab 758, 759, 760, 761, 762, 763, 764, 767, 1026
cab, driver's 706, 707
cab, operator's 756
cab, pivot 760
cabbage, Chinese 246
cabbage, green 247
cabbage, red 247
cabbage, savoy 247
cabbage, white 247
cabin 730, 753
cabin, first-class 746
cabin, passenger 727, 730, 731, 747
cabinet 296, 377, 378, 379, 552, 609
cabinet, display 365, 645
cabinet, index card 653
cabinet, liquor 365
cabinet, stationery 645
cable 606, 620, 635, 686, 693, 885, 970, 1009, 1058
cable, arresting 897
cable, brake 699
cable, coaxial 631
cable, connecting 577, 618, 631
cable, control 700
cable, electrical 676, 678
cable, feeder 354
cable, fiber-optic 631
cable, guy 970, 971
cable, jumper 686
cable, lighting 687
cable, MIDI 559
cable, musical instrument digital interface 559
cable, patient 925
cable, power 354
cable, rudder 984
cable, suspension 660
cable, twisted-pair 631
cable, USB 631
cable distributor 602
cable guard 885, 1009
cable holder 375
cable line 642, 643
cable reels compartment 608
cable stay anchorage 660
caboose 710
cabriolet 360
cadmium 813
Caelum 21
cafeteria 869
caftan 429
cage 503
cage, animal 494
cage, safety 935
caiman 157
cajun spice 261
calamus 158
calcaneus 170, 201, 203
calcar 186, 187
calcium 812
calculating 649
calculator 484
calculator, graphing 649
calculator, pocket 649
calculator, printing 649
calculator dial 597
calendar, tear-off 650
calendar pad 650
calendering 125
calf 172, 193, 195
californium 814
caliper 535, 679
caliper, micrometer 832
caliper, vernier 832
call button 519, 621
call key 624
Callisto 14
calm 82
Calvinism 870
calyx 112, 114, 116
calyx, renal 219
cam ring 395
cambium 110, 118
Cambodia 59, 881
Cambrian 128
camcorder 612
camcorder, DVD 612
camcorder, hard disk drive 612
camcorder, miniDV 613
camcorder, shoulder mount 607
camel, Bactrian 173
camel, dromedary 173
Camelopardalis 22
Camembert 281
camera 32, 542, 606, 911, 1023
camera, compact 592
camera, digital 592, 599
camera, disposable 591
camera, film 591
camera, high definition 605, 606
camera, Polaroid® 591
camera, reflex 591, 592, 593
camera, ultracompact 592
camera, view 591
camera body 592
camera control unit 605, 608
camera group 542
camera key 622
camera lens 622
camera operator 542
camera pedestal 606
camera platform 596
camera platform lock 596
camera screw 596
camera viewfinder 606
camera with wide-angle lens 606
Cameroon 60, 879
camisole 440, 444
camp stove, double-burner 1053
camp stove, single-burner 1053
camper 687
camping 856, 1052
camping equipment 1055
camshaft 682
can 295
can opener 1055
Canada 46, 54, 876
Canadian football field 955
canal, Haversian 199
canal, radial 134, 135
canal, ring 134, 135
canal, root 206
canal, semicircular 235
canal, siphonal 136
canal bed 719
Cancer 23
candela 835
candle, Paschal 871
candlepin 1015
candy 851
cane, crook 916
cane, Fritz 916
cane, offset 916
cane, quad 916
Canes Venatici 23
canine 164, 206
Canis Major 21
Canis Minor 23
canister 294, 733
canned good 289
cannelloni 282
cannon 168, 889, 895
canoe 722, 986
canoe, C1 986
canoe, dugout 721
canoe, outrigger 721
canoe, recreational 986
canoe, whitewater 986
canoe-kayak 986
canopy 490, 515, 687, 733, 750, 761, 762, 896, 1046, 1047
canopy, cockpit 1048
canopy release knob 1048
cantaloupe 257
canteen 1056
canter 169
cantilever 791
cantle 1005
cantor's seat 872
canvas 529, 990
canyon, submarine 67
cap 108, 314, 335, 351, 358, 457, 458, 492, 527, 585, 600, 806, 820, 906, 914, 974, 976
cap, end 799
cap, garrison 457
cap, hunting 457
cap, leakproof 1053
cap, riding 1003, 1006
cap, safety 893
cap, screw 295
cap, stocking 458
cap, swimming 450
cap iron 397
capacitor 820
cape 45, 428, 443
Cape Horn 48
Cape of Good Hope 50
Cape Verde 60, 879
caper 286
capillary 212
capillary tube 827
capital 53, 501, 512, 586
capitals lock 632
capitate 202
capitulum 112
capon 271
caponiere 505
capped column 90
capped tee 337
capri pants 441
Capricornus 20
capsule 106, 116, 230
capsule, gelatin 914
captain 1034
captain's quarters 731
captain's seat 748
caption 590
capture 1065
capuchin 185
car 669, 981
car, automobile 711
car, coach 705
car, container 711
car, dining 705
car, following 1020
car, Formula 1 1023
car, Formula 3000 1023
car, freight 703, 709, 710
car, gondola 710, 711
car, hopper 710, 711
car, Indy 1023
car, intermodal 710
car, livestock 710
car, micro compact 669
car, motor 716
car, passenger 705, 707, 716
car, racing 1023
car, rally 1023
car, refrigerator 710
car, sleeping 705
car, sport prototype 1023
car, sports 669
car, stock 1023
car, tank 710
car, trailer 716
car, wood chip 711
car ceiling 519
car cleaning yard 708
car cover 686
car dealer 845
car floor 519
car rental 857
car safety 519
car seat, infant 491
car wash 668
carabiner 1051
carabiner, D 1050
carabiner, locking 1050
caraco jacket 427
carafe 319
carambola 259
carapace 139, 155
caravel 721
caraway 260
carbon 813
carbon cycle 95
carbon dioxide 95, 102, 800
carbon dioxide gas coolant 800
Carboniferous 129
carburetor 694
card, electronic 343
card, high 1062
card, playing 1062
card, special 1062
card number 861
card reader 624, 668
card reader slot 858, 859
card slot 613
card support 84
cardamom 260
cardboard 529
cardholder's name 861
cardholder's signature 861
cardigan 437, 442
cardinal 162
cardinal mark 738, 739
cardoon 250
cargo bay 36
cargo bay door 36
cargo hold 729
cargo pants 441
Caribbean Islands 876
Caribbean Plate 68
Caribbean Sea 44, 47
caribou 172
carina 148
Carina 21
carnation 113
carnivore 94
carnivorous mammal 174, 180
carp 269
Carpathian Mountains 49
carpentry 387
carpus 159, 165, 170, 175, 182, 184, 187, 188, 202
carriage 571, 754, 890, 892
carriage control dial 571
carriage handle 571
carriage return 648
carrier 367, 697, 698
carrier chassis 763
carrot 251
carrying yoke 986
cart, baggage 704
cart, golf 1019
cartilage 232
cartilage, articular 199, 207
cartilage, costal 165
cartography, physical 45
cartography, political 53
carton 124, 295
carton, brick 295
carton, egg 294
carton, small 295
cartoon 590
cartridge 350, 403, 584, 617, 887, 888, 909, 1010, 1011
cartridge stem 350
carving 531
carving, wood 531
carving accessory 531
carving tool 531
case 387, 463, 472, 564, 649, 827, 828, 832, 887, 1010
case, card 484
case, eyeglasses 480, 485
case, lens 481
case, passport 485
case, utility 488
case, waterproof 596
case, writing 485
casement 327
cash dispenser 858
cash register 289
cash supply 859
cashbox 1071
cashew 255
cashier 289
casing 327, 340, 343, 419, 1070
casing, head 325
casing, side 325
casing, steel 820
casing first string 780
Caspian Sea 44, 51
cassava 245
casserole 313
cassette 616
cassette, miniDV 612
cassette compartment 611
cassette holder 616
cassette tape deck 616
cassette tray 924
Cassini 31
Cassiopeia 22
cast room 919
castanet 545
caste 143
castenet 557
caster 366, 375, 556
casting 1060

castle 504
cat 178
cat, Norwegian forest 179
cat breeds 179
Catalan 583
catalog, online 867
catalyst 784
catalytic converter 673
catalytic reforming plant 782
catamaran 981
catapult 897
catch 1059
catcher 553, 938, 939, 940
category button 620
catenary 707, 717
catering vehicle 745
caterpillar 141
catfish 151
cathedral, Gothic 506, 507
cathode 820
cathode-ray tube television 609
Catholicism 870
catwalk 540
cauliflower 251
caulking gun 403
cave 67, 70
cavity, abdominal 226, 228
cavity, medullary 199
cavity, nasal 214
cavity, oral 214, 216
cavity, pleural 215
cayenne pepper 261
CB radio 621
C-clamp 401
CD/DVD-ROM drive 558, 628, 629, 630
CD/DVD-ROM eject button 629
cecum 135, 138, 145, 149, 159, 169, 217
cedar of Lebanon 121
cedilla 587
ceiling 337, 964, 965
ceiling, acoustic 541
ceiling fitting 372
ceiling projector 85
celeriac 251
celery 250
celestial body 14
celestial sphere 23
cell 140, 144, 503, 678, 818, 862, 865, 904
cell, alkaline-manganese-zinc 820
cell, animal 133
cell, carbon-zinc 820
cell, dry 820
cell, half 1047
cell, honey 144
cell, isolation 865
cell, plant 102
cell, pollen 144
cell, queen 144
cell, sealed 144
cell body 221
cell membrane 102
cell nucleus 133
cell wall 102
cella 499
cellar 365
cello 545, 547
cellulosic biomass 784
Celsius, degree 827, 835
Celsius scale 827
Celtic languages 583
celtuce 246
cement screed 334

cementum 206
cemetery 52, 845
cent 860
Centaurus 21
center 541, 838, 950, 953, 955, 957, 995, 1029, 1065
center base 874
center chief 874
center circle 947, 956
center court 964
center face-off circle 1029
center hole 617
center line 945, 955, 960, 961, 962, 997, 1027, 1029
center mark 966
center point 874
center service line 967
center spot 947
center T mark 1008
center third 955
centerboard 980
centering 648
centipede 135
Central African languages 582
Central African Republic 60, 879
Central America 44, 47, 54
central circle 955
central disk 135
central focusing wheel 824
central screw 538
centriole 133
cephalothorax 139, 145
Cepheus 22
ceramic pot, removable 317
cereal 263, 784
cereal, breakfast 123
cereal product 278
cerebellum 222, 223, 224
cerebrospinal fluid 224
cerebrum 222, 223, 224
Ceres 14
cerium 814
cervix 226, 227
cesium 812
Cetus 20, 22
Chac-Mool 513
Chad 60, 879
chaffinch 162
chain 698, 700, 829, 969, 1001
chain, lift 347
chain, mooring 737
chain brake 417
chain drive 765, 767
chain guide 700
chain mail 884
chain reaction 811
chain stay 698
chain wheel 1020, 1021
chainsaw 417
chainsaw chain 417
chair 293, 361, 868
chair, armless 868
chair, beanbag 361
chair, club 360
chair, director's 360
chair, folding 361
chair, high 366
chair, kneeling 646
chair, patient's 920
chair, player's 959
chair, rocking 360, 361
chair, side 361
chair, stacking 361
chair, tub 360
chair, typist 646
chair, Voltaire 360

chair, Wassily 360
chair, Windsor 361
chair bed 360
chairlift 1036
chairlift departure area 1036
chairperson, mat 991
chaise longue 361
chalaza 160
chalice 871
chalk 1013
chalk line 387
challah 279
Chamaeleon 21
chamber, anterior 238
chamber, king 498
chamber, posterior 238
chamber, queen 498
chamber, relieving 498
chamber, underground 498
chameleon 157
chamois leather 463, 472
chamomile 264
champagne flute 297
chandelier 373
change sign key 649
changing pad 492
changing pad, contour 366
changing room, miner's 773
changing table 366
channel 579, 739
channel, left 618
channel, right 618
channel scan button 611
channel select buttons 611
channel selection button 735
channel selector 621
channel selector controls 611
chanter 560
chanterelle 244
chapati 278
chapel 504
chapel, Lady 507
chapel, side 506
character 1066
character, position 586
character, shape 586
character correction 648
charcoal 524
charentais 257
charge 875, 887
charge air cooler 680
charge indicator 479
charger 394
charger base 482
charging light 479
charm 471
Charon 15
chart, line 838
chart room 726
chase 890
chat room 643
Chateaubriand 272
chayote 249
check 291, 860
check, traveler's 860
check nut 84
checkbook 484
checkbook case 485
checker 1063, 1065
checkerboard 1065
checkers 1065
check-in kiosk 742
checkout 289
checkout counter 293, 851
cheddar 281

cheek 168, 174, 194, 388, 890, 1059
cheek piece 1010, 1011
cheek ring 1004
cheek strap 1004
cheese 292
cheese, blue 281
cheese, cottage 280
cheese, cream 280
cheese, fresh 280
cheese, goat's-milk 280
cheese, pressed 281
cheese, soft 281
cheese, Swiss 281
cheese box 295
cheese counter 289
cheetah 181
chef 291
chemical bond 810
chemical element 812
chemical formula 834
chemical treatment 782
chemise 504
chemistry 810, 834
cherimoya 258
cherry 254
chervil 262
chess 1065
chess, movements 1065
chess notation 1065
chess pieces 1065
chessboard 1065
chest 168
chesterfield 360
chestnut 255
chevet 507
chevron 874
chicane 1022
chick 163
chicken 271
chickpea 252
chief 874
chief executive officer 644
chief's office 900
chiffonier 365
child 929
child care 491
child carrier 700
children's section 866
chile 261
Chile 55, 876
chile, bird's eye 261
chili powder 261
chili sauce 287
chimney 323, 337, 339
chimney cap 323
chimney connection 336
chimpanzee 185
chin 158, 194
chin bar 695
chin rest 547
China 59, 881
Chinese 582
Chinese character 585
chinois 308
chip 861
chip cover 393
chipmunk 166
chipolata 277
chisel 533
chisel, firmer 531
chiton 426
chive 245
chlamys 426
chlorine 813
chlorine bleach 425

chloroplast 102
chock 1050, 1051
chocolate 285
chocolate, dark 285
chocolate, milk 285
chocolate, white 285
choir 506, 507
choker 468
chondrite 18
chop 273, 274
chop, pork 275
chop, sirloin 274
chopper, ice 421
chopstick 303, 305
chopstick rest 305
chord 563
chord, lower 661
chord, tuning 561
chord, upper 661
chorizo 277
choroid 238
chow mein noodle 283
chowchow 176
Christianity 870
Christmas tree 777, 780
chroma-key curtain 606
chromium 78, 813
chromosphere 16
chronicler 604
chrysalis 141
chuck 272, 390, 394, 395, 398, 773
chuck key 394
Chukchi Sea 46
chukka 459
chunk 270
church 871
church, Baroque 510
Church, Orthodox 870
church, Romanesque 508
chute 421, 763, 774
chute directional control 421
chutney 287
cicada 147
cigar 483
cigar band 483
cigarette 483
ciliate 111
cilium 133
cine 597
cinnamon 260
Circinus 21
circle 838, 1066
circuit, 120-volt 354
circuit, 240-volt 354
circuit, electrical 818
circuit, integrated 820
circuit, packaged integrated 820
circuit, parallel 818
circuit, printed 820
circuit, series 818
circuit breaker 341
circular body 560
circular route 52
circular track 26
circulation, pulmonary 212
circulation, systemic 212
circulation desk 867
circumference 838
circumflex accent 587
cirque 17, 72
cirrocumulus 82, 88
cirrostratus 82, 88
cirrus 82, 88
citron 256
city 53, 842

hoisting rope 409, 756
hoisting system 757
holdback 368
holder 815, 912
holding 992
holding area marking 742
hole 535, 1016, 1017
hole, par 3 1016
hole, par 4 1016
hole, par 5 1017
hole, punch 450
hollow barrel 912
holmium 814
hologram foil strip 861
holster 906
holy water font 871
home 633
home button 639
home furnishings store 849
home gym 1001
home plate 939
home theater 612
home user 643
homestretch 1006
homing head, infrared 894
Homo sapiens 131
Honduras 54, 876
honey 285
honeybee 142, 143
honeycomb 144
hood 291, 336, 375, 420, 436,
    442, 448, 491, 670, 690, 989,
    1032, 1051
hood, drawstring 449
hood, range 292
hoof 168, 171
hook 327, 367, 387, 404, 413,
    566, 567, 570, 693, 733, 756,
    831, 1011, 1012, 1031
hook, boat 733
hook, dough 314
hook, lifting 776
hook, reed 573
hook keeper 1059
hooker 950
hoop 565, 972
hopper 762, 767
hopper, debris 763
horizontal motion lock 596
horizontal movement 1065
horizontal-circle image 833
horn 471, 676, 696, 706, 902
horn, air 690
horn, English 545, 550
horn, French 545, 551
hornet 146
Horologium 20
hors d'oeuvre 292
horse 168, 169, 170, 172, 969,
    1008
horse, pommel 969, 970
horsefly 146
horseradish 251
horseshoe 171, 471
horseshoe mount 28
hose 407, 445, 446, 903
hose, air 527, 772, 989
hose, drain 353, 378, 380
hose, emptying 378
hose, fire 903
hose, flexible 375, 773
hose, garden 414
hose, gasoline pump 668
hose, hydraulic 765, 766
hose, mud injection 776

hose, spray 346, 352
hose, sprinkler 414
hose, suction 902
hose, water 772
hose connection fitting 407
hose connector 415
hose dryer 900
hose holder 900
hose reel cart 414
hospital 845, 856, 918
host 604
host plant 103
host tree 103
hot food 292
hot plate 292
hot tub 324
hot-air outflow 338
hot-air outlet 336
hotel 844, 854, 1036
hotel reservation desk 742
hot-shoe contact 592
hot-water circuit 344
hot-water outlet 339, 348, 349
hot-water supply line 352, 353
houppelande 428
hour angle gear 28
hour hand 829
hourglass 85
house 320, 322, 325, 328, 541,
    1027
house, adobe 520
house, city 521
house, one-story 521
house, Roman 502
house, rooms 328
house, town 521
house, traditional 520
house, two-story 521
houseboat 729
household equipment 381
household linen 850
household products 288
housing 342, 394, 396, 406, 479,
    520, 604, 616, 736
hovercraft 727
howitzer, modern 892
hub 145, 640, 641, 654, 699,
    787, 807, 917
hub cover 787
Hubble Space Telescope 27, 79
Hubble's classification 19
hubcap 671
Hudson Bay 47
hull 116, 721, 980, 986, 1026
hull column 777
human body 192
humerus 153, 159, 164, 165,
    170, 175, 182, 184, 187, 188,
    200, 201, 207
humid continental climate 87
humid subtropical climate 87
humidifier 341
humidifier, portable 342
humidistat 342
humidity 85, 342
hummingbird 162
hummus 286
humor, aqueous 238
hump 708
hump lead 708
hump office 708
hundred, five 836
hundred, one 836
Hungarian 583
Hungary 56, 878
hunting 242

hunting arm 887
hurdle 934
hurdle, steeplechase 934
hurricane 83, 89
husband 929
husbandry, animal 242
husbandry, intensive 96, 97
husk 122
hut 520
hutch 329
Huygens 31
hybrid 1017
Hydra 21, 23
hydrant intake 902
hydraulic coupler 764
hydraulic system 754
hydroelectric complex 785
hydroelectricity 785
hydrofoil 731
hydrogen 812
hydrologic cycle 95
hydrolysis 784
hydrometer 685
hydrosphere 94
Hydrus 20
hyena 180
hygrograph 85
hygrometer 342, 495
hyperlink 642
hyperopia 239
hypha 108
hyphen 587
hypocotyl 105
hypothalamus 222, 229
hyracotherium 131
hyssop 262

I

Iapetus 15
Iberian Peninsula 49
ice 92, 95
ice ax 1051
ice cube dispenser 296
ice dispenser 668
ice hockey equipment 1030
ice machine 291
ice melter 421
ice screw, tubular 1051
iceberg lettuce 246
icebreaker 728
ice-cream maker 318
ice-cream scoop 309
Iceland 46, 49, 56, 878
Icelandic 583
ichthyosaur 130
ichthyostega 129
icon, application 622
ICS 35
ID window 484
identical 837
identification section 904
igloo 520
ignition box 749
ignition switch 676, 696
iguana 157
ileum 217
ilium 153, 159, 165, 200
image, virtual 823
image editor 599
image review 593
image sensor 594, 595
imager 86
image-recording quality 593

impactor 31
impluvium 502
impost 514
Impressionism 530
in goal 951
inbounds line 952
incineration 99
incised figure 532
incisor 164, 166, 167, 206
inclination 23
included 837
incus 235
indent 648
index 590, 734
index arm 734
index card 652
index finger 237
India 58, 881
Indian Ocean 44, 46, 50, 51, 52
indicator board 704, 937
indicator light 316, 317, 318,
    319, 374, 380, 478, 577, 629,
    633, 635, 903
indicator needle 597
indium 812
Indo-European languages 583
Indo-Iranian languages 583
Indonesia 51, 59, 881
Indonesian 583
indoor shutters 370
Indus 20
industrial area 843
industrial use 122
industry 643
Indy car 1023
inferior 586
infield 938
infiltration 95
infinity 837
infirmary 864
inflation system 733
inflator 989, 1054
inflator-deflator 1054
inflorescence 112
information 857
information booth 849
information console 989
information counter 742
information desk 853, 858, 867,
    905, 1036
information spreading 643
infrared port 630
infrared radiation 96
infrared sounder 86
infrared thermal mapper 32
infraspinatus 197
infusion 264
inhaled air 232
inhaler, metered dose 914
injection 681
ink 524, 533, 584
ink, color shifting 861
ink, screen printing 536
ink cartridge 637
ink sac 138
inked surface 532
inking slab 533
inlet 781
inlet valve 682
in-line skating 1045
inmates' admission office 864
inner circle 1027
inner core 66
inner edge 171
inner hearth 336

inorganic matter 94
input device 632
input device switching
    button 610
input jack 559
input paper tray 637
input receptacle 638
input select button 614
input selector 614
input terminal 404
input tray 637
inrun 1040, 1041
insect 103, 140, 146
insert 633
insertion 198
inside 299
inside-leg snap-fastening 448
insole 463
installation work 523
instant replay button 610
instep 192, 433
instrument panel 677
instrument platform 86
instrument shelter 84
instrumental group 546
instrumentation and propulsion
    module 38
insulating material 333, 334,
    380, 385
insulating sleeve 358
insulation 339, 348, 349, 385,
    802
insulator 683, 793
insulator, plastic 354
insurance service 858
intaglio printing, equipment 534
intake 680, 681
intake manifold 681, 682
intake port 681
intake valve 680
integral 837
Integrated Science Instrument
    Module 27
integrating sphere 597
Intelsat 603
intensive care unit 921
interactive terminal 523
interchange 658, 843
interchange, diamond 658
interchange, trumpet 658
intercom 604, 607
intercom microphone 607
interfacing 569
interlining 569
interlock 575
internal modem port 630
International Olympic
    Committee 882
international organization 882
international space station 34
International System of Units 835
Internet 641, 642, 643
Internet key 632
Internet service provider 642
Internet stick 631
Internet user 642
internode 109
Inter-Orbit Communication
    System 35
interpretation booth 852
interrogation room 904
interrupter 354
intersection 837
interval 562, 739
intervertebral disk 204, 208